PENGUIN CLASSICS

CONVERSATIONS WITH GOETHE

JOHANN PETER ECKERMANN was born in 1792. In 1823 he sent Goethe, his literary idol, a manuscript collection of essays, largely on Goethe's works, and he became Goethe's literary assistant till the latter's death in 1832. This long relationship led to the creation of Eckermann's best-remembered work *Conversations with Goethe*, first published in 1836. Eckermann died in 1854 in Weimar.

JOHANN PETER ECKERMANN

Conversations with Goethe
In the Last Years of his Life

Translated by ALLAN BLUNDEN
with an Introduction and Notes by
RITCHIE ROBERTSON

PENGUIN BOOKS

PENGUIN CLASSICS

UK | USA | Canada | Ireland | Australia
India | New Zealand | South Africa

Penguin Books is part of the Penguin Random House group of companies
whose addresses can be found at global.penguinrandomhouse.com

First published in Penguin Classics 2022

001

Translation copyright © Allan Blunden, 2022
Introduction copyright © Ritchie Robertson, 2022

The moral rights of the translator and introducer have been asserted

Set in 10.25/12.25 pt Sabon LT Std
Typeset by Jouve (UK), Milton Keynes
Printed and bound in Great Britain by Clays Ltd, Elcograf S.p.A.

The authorized representative in the EEA is Penguin Random House Ireland,
Morrison Chambers, 32 Nassau Street, Dublin D02 YH68

A CIP catalogue record for this book is available from the British Library

ISBN: 978-0-241-42167-3

The translation of this work was supported by a grant from the Goethe-Institut

www.greenpenguin.co.uk

Penguin Random House is committed to a
sustainable future for our business, our readers
and our planet. This book is made from Forest
Stewardship Council® certified paper.

Contents

List of Persons Mentioned	vii
List of Works by Goethe in	
Chronological Order	xxxi
Introduction by Ritchie Robertson	xxxv

CONVERSATIONS WITH GOETHE	1
Author's Preface	3

PART ONE

Introduction	9
1823	27
1824	66
1825	107
1826	139
1827	161

PART TWO

1828	227
1829	256
1830	321
1831	368
1832	427

PART THREE

Preface	433
1822	438
1823	442
1824	454

1825	468
1826	499
1827	502
1828	561
1830	592
1831	631
1832	642
Notes	649
Index	669

List of Persons Mentioned

Abeken, Bernhard Rudolf (1780–1866), literary historian.

Ampère, Jean-Jacques (1800–1864), literary critic and frequent contributor to *Le Globe*; son of the physicist André-Marie Ampère (1775–1836), who gave his name to a unit of electric current.

Angoulême, Louis Antoine, duc d' (1775–1844), elder son of Charles X of France; in 1823–4 commanded a French army sent into Spain to help the reactionary Ferdinand VII to gain absolute power by abolishing the constitution.

Ariosto, Ludovico (1474–1533), Italian epic poet; his main work is *Orlando Furioso* (1532).

Arnault, Lucien-Émile (1787–1863), dramatist whose works include *Gustave-Adolphe, ou La bataille de Lutzen* (1830).

Arndt, Ernst Moritz (1769–1860), German author of patriotic poetry.

Ballanche, Pierre-Simon (1776–1847), French philosopher.

Balzac, Honoré de (1799–1850), French novelist; his first major work, *Les Chouans*, appeared in 1829.

Basedow, Johann Bernhard (1724–90), educator, who founded a progressive school, the Philanthropinum, at Dessau; Goethe describes him in Book 14 of *Dichtung und Wahrheit*.

Beaumarchais, Pierre-Augustin Caron de (1732–99), French playwright, whose memoirs provided Goethe with material for his play *Clavigo*.

Bechtolsheim, Julie von (1751–1847), contributed the poem 'Elegie' to Ottilie von Goethe's journal *Chaos*.

Becker, Heinrich (1764–1822), actor.

viii LIST OF PERSONS MENTIONED

Behrisch, Ernst Wolfgang (1738–1809), tutor to young noble-men; close friend of the young Goethe, who met him in 1767 while studying in Leipzig. Goethe describes him in Book 7 of *Dichtung und Wahrheit*.

Bentham, Jeremy (1748–1832), English philosopher, spokesman for utilitarianism.

Béranger, Pierre-Jean de (1780–1857), French poet and song-writer, twice imprisoned in the 1820s for songs against the Bourbon monarchy; celebrated on his death as France's national poet.

Bernardin de Saint-Pierre, Jacques-Henri (1737–1814), French novelist, author of *Paul et Virginie* (1788) and *La Chaumière indienne* (*The Indian Cottage*, 1790).

Bethmann, Simon Moritz von (1768–1826), banker and diplo-mat, a leading citizen of Frankfurt; ennobled 1808 by the Emperor of Austria.

Beulwitz, Friedrich August von (1785–1871), army officer and chamberlain at Weimar.

Beuther, Friedrich (1777–1856), actor and stage designer.

Bignon, Louis Pierre Édouard, Baron (1771–1841), historian, author of *Histoire de France sous Napoléon* (10 vols, 1829–38).

Blumenbach, Johann Friedrich (1752–1840), naturalist and anthropologist in Göttingen.

Boisserée, Sulpiz (1783–1854), German art historian with a special interest in medieval art, a friend of Goethe from 1810 on.

Bonaparte, Lucien (1775–1840), younger brother of Napoleon; supported the French Revolution, and served as president of the Council of Five Hundred (the lower house of the revolu-tionary parliament) from 25 October 1795 till Napoleon overthrew the revolutionary constitution on 9 November 1799.

Bonstetten, Karl Viktor von (1745–1832), Swiss writer.

Böttiger, Karl August (1760–1835), classical scholar, whom Goethe and Schiller disliked for his malicious tale-bearing.

Bourrienne, Louis Antoine Fauvelet de (1769–1834), French diplomat who knew Napoleon well and was his private sec-retary from 1798 to 1802; author of *Mémoires sur Napoléon,*

LIST OF PERSONS MENTIONED

le directoire, le consulat, l'empire et la restauration (10 vols, 1828–30).

Bril, Paul (1554–1626), Dutch painter.

Bristol, Frederick Augustus Hervey, 4th Earl of (1730–1803), Lord Bishop of Derry (not Derby!) from 1768 to his death.

Buch, Leopold von (1774–1853), geologist in Berlin; he upheld the Vulcanist theory which Goethe rejected.

Bürger, Gottfried August (1747–94), poet, best known for his gothic ballad 'Lenore' (1774). His 'Frau Schnips' is a ribald colloquial poem about an old woman who goes to heaven and scolds various Old Testament characters for their bad behaviour.

Burns, Robert (1759–96), Scottish poet.

Bury, Friedrich (1763–1823), painter.

Byron, George Gordon, Lord (1788–1824), poet and celebrity, hugely popular across Europe for his poems, especially *Childe Harold's Pilgrimage* (Cantos 1 and 2 published 1812; the complete text 1818) and *Don Juan* (1819–24), and his plays, of which Goethe knew *Manfred* (1817), *Marino Faliero, The Two Foscari, Cain* and *Sardanapalus* (all 1821), and *The Deformed Transformed* (1824). Goethe also mentions Byron's early verse satire *English Bards and Scotch Reviewers* (1809). Byron died of fever at Missolonghi in Greece, where he had gone to support the Greek War of Independence (1821–30) against Turkish rule.

Cagliostro, Count, real name Giuseppe Balsamo (1743–95), notorious impostor and charlatan; Goethe, though sceptical, was intrigued by him, and in 1787 visited the Balsamo family in Palermo, pretending to be an Englishman who had known Cagliostro in London.

Calderón: Pedro Calderón de la Barca (1600–1681), dramatist of the Spanish Golden Age whom Goethe greatly admired, especially for *The Constant Prince* (1636).

Campe, Joachim Heinrich (1746–1818), educator.

Camper, Peter (correctly Pieter, 1722–89), Dutch anatomist.

Canning, George (1770–1827), British Foreign Secretary.

Carlyle, Thomas (1795–1881), Scottish translator, essayist and historian; his *Life of Schiller* appeared in 1825, and his translations, *German Romance*, in four volumes in 1827.

LIST OF PERSONS MENTIONED

Carracci, Lodovico (1555–1619), Agostino (1557–1602) and Annibale (1560–1609), family of Italian painters.

Carus, Carl Gustav (1789–1869), painter and writer on art; Goethe wrote an introduction to his *Briefe über Landschafts-malerei* (*Letters on Landscape Painting*, 1824).

Charles V (1500–1558), Holy Roman Emperor from 1519 till his abdication in 1556.

Chateaubriand, François-René, vicomte de (1768–1848), French Romantic writer; Goethe had read his treatise *Génie du christianisme* (1802).

Chodowiecki, Daniel Nikolaus (1726–1801), painter and prolific book illustrator.

Clauren, pseudonym of Karl Gottlob Samuel Heun (1771–1854), sentimental novelist.

Cooper, James Fenimore (1789–1851), American adventure novelist; his *The Red Rover* (1828) is mentioned on 27 December 1829.

Corneille, Pierre (1606–84), French dramatist.

Cornelius, Peter (1783–1867), painter, a member of the Nazarene school, which rejected classicism and drew inspiration from medieval and early Renaissance painting.

Correggio, Antonio da (1489–1534), Italian painter.

Cotta, Johann Friedrich von (1764–1832), publisher in Stuttgart, the sole publisher of Goethe's writings from 1809 on.

Coudray, Clemens Wenzeslaus (1775–1845), supervisor of building works in Weimar.

Courier, Paul Louis (1772–1825), classical scholar, who based his French edition of *Daphnis and Chloe* (1810) on a manuscript he had discovered in the Laurentian Library in Florence.

Cousin, Victor (1792–1867), French philosopher.

Cumberland, Duchess of: Friederike Karoline, born Princess of Mecklenburg-Strelitz (1778–1841), whose third marriage (1815) was to Ernst August, Duke of Cumberland. She and her sister Luise, later Queen of Prussia, had stayed with Goethe's mother in Frankfurt when attending the coronations of the Holy Roman Emperors Leopold II in 1790 and Franz II in 1792.

LIST OF PERSONS MENTIONED

Cumberland, Richard (1731–1811), playwright, author of the philosemitic comedy *The Jew* (1794).

Cuvier, Georges (1769–1832), French anatomist and zoologist, whose many works include *Le Règne animal* (*The Animal Kingdom*, 1817), of which the German translation appeared in two volumes in 1831–2.

Dalberg, Karl von (1744–1817), Prince-Archbishop of Regensburg and holder of many other dignities. After the dissolution of the Holy Roman Empire in 1806, Napoleon set up an association of sixteen German client states called the Confederation of the Rhine (*Rheinbund*) and appointed Dalberg its Prince Primate; it was in turn dissolved in 1813.

D'Alembert, Jean Le Rond (1717–83), mathematician, philosopher, and (till 1759) collaborator with Diderot on the *Encyclopédie*.

D'Alton, (Joseph Wilhelm) Eduard (1772–1840), osteologist.

David d'Angers, Pierre (1789–1856), French sculptor, who visited Weimar in 1829 and prepared the model for an outsize sculpture of Goethe's head.

Dawe, George (1781–1829), English painter, who painted Goethe in 1819.

de Candolle, Augustin Pyrame (1778–1841), botanist from Geneva.

Delacroix, Eugène (1798–1863), French painter.

Delavigne, Casimir (1793–1843), French poet and dramatist; Goethe reviewed his tragedy *Le Paria* (1821) in *Kunst und Altertum* (1824).

Delille, Jacques (1738–1813), French poet, author of the didactic poem *Les Jardins* (*Gardens*, 1782).

Deschamps, Émile (1791–1871), French poet.

Diderot, Denis (1713–84), major writer of the French Enlightenment, whose novel *Le Neveu de Rameau* (*Rameau's Nephew*) Goethe translated.

Dissen, Georg Ludolf (1784–1837), classical scholar at Göttingen.

Döbereiner, Johann Wolfgang (1780–1849), professor of chemistry at Jena.

Domenichino, correctly Domenico Zampieri (1581–1641), Italian painter.

xii LIST OF PERSONS MENTIONED

Doolan, Robert, English friend of Eckermann, probably one of the pupils to whom he taught German.

Dowager Grand Duchess: Luise (1757–1830), born Princess of Hessen-Darmstadt.

Du Châtelet, Émilie (1706–49), French writer and physicist, long-term companion of Voltaire.

Dumas, Alexandre, père (1802–70), French playwright, author of *Henri III* (1829).

Dumont, Pierre-Étienne-Louis (1759–1829), philosopher in Geneva, great-uncle of Frédéric Soret; his works included *Voyage à Paris* (1802) and *Souvenirs de Mirabeau* (1832), which Goethe read in manuscript.

Dupin, Charles (1784–1873), French economist.

Dupré, Guillaume (*c.*1576–1643), French artist and maker of medallions.

Duval, Marie, aunt of Goethe's Swiss friend Frédéric Soret.

Ebert, Karl Egon (1801–82), poet from Prague, author of *Wlasta* (1829), an epic poem about the Czech myth of ancient women warriors.

Eberwein, Franz Karl Adalbert (1786–1868), director of music at Weimar, who set many of Goethe's works to music.

Eberwein, Regina Henriette (1790–1849), singer.

Egloffstein, Karoline von (1789–1868), lady-in-waiting to Maria Pavlovna (wife of Karl Friedrich, who became Grand Duke of Weimar in 1828).

Enghien, Louis Antoine, duc d' (1772–1804), executed on the charge of plotting against Napoleon's rule in France.

Erasmus, Desiderius (1466–1536), Dutch humanist.

Eschwege, Wilhelm Ludwig von (1777–1855), army officer, director of mines in Brazil.

Fabvier, Charles-Nicolas, Baron (1782–1855), French general, who spent much of the 1820s in Greece supporting the War of Independence against the Ottoman Empire.

Facius, Friedrich Wilhelm (1764–1843), engraver in Weimar.

Fichte, Johann Gottlieb (1762–1814), philosopher, based at Jena 1794–9, but dismissed from his chair on the charge of atheism.

LIST OF PERSONS MENTIONED

Finckenstein, Countess Henriette von (1774–1847), Prussian noblewoman, who from 1819 till her death lived in a *ménage à trois* with Ludwig Tieck and his wife Amalia.

Fleming, Paul (1609–40), poet in German and Latin.

Fouqué, Friedrich Heinrich Karl, Freiherr de la Motte (1777–1843), prolific author of Romantic stories, including his masterpiece *Undine* (1811), and dramas (including *Der Sängerkrieg auf der Wartburg* (*The Singers' Contest at the Wartburg*), 1828).

Franke, Heinrich (1807–?), actor.

Franklin, Benjamin (1706–90), American scientist, journalist and diplomat, who in 1752 proved experimentally that lightning is a form of electricity.

Frommann, Carl Friedrich Ernst (1765–1837), bookseller and publisher in Jena.

Froriep, Emma von (1805–72), daughter of the Weimar surgeon and academic Ludwig Friedrich von Froriep.

Fürnstein, Anton (1783–1841), Bohemian poet; Goethe reviewed his poem on hop-growing in *Kunst und Altertum*, 1823.

Fuseli, correctly Füßli, Johann Heinrich (1741–1825), Swiss painter.

Gay, Delphine (1804–55), author of *Essais poétiques* (1824).

Genast, Eduard (1797–1866) and his wife Caroline (1800–1860), actors.

Genlis, Stéphanie Félicité de (1746–1830), French writer, who as a Catholic disapproved of Voltaire's anti-religious writings.

Geoffroy de Saint-Hilaire, Étienne (1772–1844), French naturalist.

Gérard, François (1770–1837), French painter.

Gerhard, Wilhelm (1780–1858), businessman from Weimar who translated Serbian poetry.

Goethe, Alma von (1827–44), daughter of August and Ottilie von Goethe.

Goethe, August von (1789–1830), Goethe's son.

Goethe, Katharina Elisabeth (1731–1808), Goethe's mother.

Goethe, Ottilie von, née Pogwisch (1796–1872), married August von Goethe on 17 June 1817; lived with him in the

xiv   LIST OF PERSONS MENTIONED

upper storey of his father's house, along with their three children, Walter, Wolfgang (see below) and Alma.

Goethe, Walter Wolfgang von (1818–85), elder son of August and Ottilie von Goethe.

Goethe, Wolfgang Maximilian von ('Wolf'), (1820–83), second son of August and Ottilie von Goethe.

Goldsmith, Oliver (1728–74), Irish writer, author of *The Vicar of Wakefield* (1766) and the poem *The Deserted Village* (1770).

Göttling, Karl Wilhelm (1793–1869), classical scholar in Jena.

Gozzi, Carlo (1720–1806), Italian dramatist, defender of the theatre of improvisation known as the *commedia dell'arte*.

Graff, Johann Jacob (1768–1848), actor.

Grillparzer, Franz (1791–1872), Austrian dramatist, who began his career with the fate-tragedy *Die Ahnfrau* (*The Ancestress*, 1817).

Grimm, Friedrich Melchior, Baron (1723–1807), German diplomat and leading figure of the French Enlightenment.

Grüner, Karl Franz (1780–1845), actor in Weimar 1803–4, later in Munich and elsewhere.

Guizot, François (1787–1874), French politician and historian; his *Histoire générale de la civilisation en Europe* (*General History of Civilization in Europe*) appeared in 1828.

Hackert, Jacob Philipp (1737–1807), landscape painter, with whom Goethe spent time during his stay in Italy.

Hafiz, real name Muhammad Shemseddin (1315–90), Persian poet; his sobriquet signifies that he knew the Qur'an by heart. Goethe read his work in German and English translations and paid homage to him in the *West-östlicher Divan* (1819).

Hagen, August (1797–1880), professor of literature and art history at Königsberg (now Kaliningrad), author of the narrative poem *Olfried und Lisena* (1820).

Hagn, Charlotte von (1809–91), actress in Munich.

Hamann, Johann Georg (1730–88), religious writer who cultivated an obscure and allusive style.

Haugwitz, Count Christian August Heinrich Kurt (1752–1832), accompanied Goethe and the Stolbergs to Switzerland in 1775.

LIST OF PERSONS MENTIONED

Heeren, Arnold Hermann Ludwig (1760–1842), professor of philosophy and later of history at Göttingen; author of the standard works *Handbuch der Geschichte der Staaten des Altertums* (*Historical Guide to the Ancient States*, 1799) and *Handbuch der Geschichte des Europäischen Staatensystems und seiner Colonien* (*Historical Guide to the European State System and its Colonies*, 1809).

Hegel, Georg Wilhelm Friedrich (1770–1831), philosopher in Berlin.

Herder, Johann Gottfried (1744–1803), philosopher, theologian and essayist, who became friendly with Goethe when the latter was studying at Strasbourg in the early 1770s. Goethe contributed an essay on Gothic architecture to Herder's collection *Von deutscher Art und Kunst* (*On German Character and Art*, 1773). Herder's major works include his collection of folk poetry, *Volkslieder* (1778–9), reissued as *Stimmen der Völker in Liedern* (*Voices of the Nations in Songs*, 1807), *Vom Geist der Ebräischen Poesie* (*On the Spirit of Hebrew Poetry*, 1782–3) and his great survey of history, *Ideen zur Philosophie der Geschichte der Menschheit* (*Ideas for the Philosophy of the History of Mankind*, 1784–91). In 1776, thanks to Goethe's influence, he was appointed superintendent of the Lutheran Church in Weimar, but in the 1790s his relations with Goethe and Karl August became strained.

Herschel, Sir William (1738–1822), astronomer and composer, born in Hanover (then in personal union with the British Crown), moved to Britain in 1757; discovered the planet Uranus, 1781.

Heygendorf, Karoline, née Jagemann (1777–1848), actress and singer in Weimar, mistress of Karl August, notorious as a theatrical *enfant terrible*; conflict with her induced Goethe to give up directing the Weimar Court Theatre in 1817.

Hinrichs, Hermann Friedrich Wilhelm (1794–1861), professor of philosophy in Halle, author of *Das Wesen der antiken Tragödie* (*The Nature of Ancient Tragedy*, 1827).

Hirt, Aloys (1759–1837), classical archaeologist.

xvi LIST OF PERSONS MENTIONED

Hoffmann, Ernst Theodor Amadeus (1776–1822), major Romantic author of tales and novels, including *Der goldne Topf* (*The Golden Pot*, 1814). Goethe disliked his work.

Holtei, Karl von (1798–1880), poet, dramatist and actor.

Horace: Quintus Horatius Flaccus (65–8 BCE), Roman poet.

Horn, Franz (1781–1837), Romantic novelist and literary historian.

Horn, Johann Adam (1749–1806), lawyer, one of Goethe's friends in Frankfurt in the 1760s.

Houwald, Christoph Ernst von (1778–1845), author of the popular fate-tragedies *Das Bild* (*The Picture*, 1821) and *Die Feinde* (*The Enemies*, 1825).

Hugo, Victor (1802–85), French poet, dramatist and novelist; Goethe read his *Odes et Ballades* (1826) and his novel *Notre-Dame de Paris* (1831).

Humboldt, Alexander von (1769–1859), traveller, geographer and scientist, who explored South America, Cuba and Mexico from 1798 to 1804 and wrote prolifically about his travels and discoveries. Goethe read his *Essai politique sur l'île de Cuba* (*Political History of the Island of Cuba*, 1826).

Humboldt, Wilhelm von (1767–1835), poet, linguistic theorist and leading civil servant, who initiated a reform of the Prussian educational system; elder brother of Alexander von Humboldt. His many writings included a long review of Goethe's *Hermann und Dorothea*.

Hummel, Johann Nepomuk (1778–1837), pianist and composer, pupil of Mozart; musical director at the Weimar court, 1819–22 and 1833–7.

Huschke, Wilhelm Ernst (1760–1828), physician to the Grand Ducal family in Weimar.

Iffland, August Wilhelm (1759–1814), noted actor and prolific and popular dramatist; *Die Hagestolzen* (*The Bachelors*, 1793) was among his most successful plays.

Immermann, Karl Leberecht (1796–1840), versatile writer who first made his reputation with comedies such as *Der Prinz von Syrakus* (*The Prince of Syracuse*, 1821); now remembered especially for his mock-epic *Tulifäntchen* (1832) and his

LIST OF PERSONS MENTIONED xvii

novels *Die Epigonen* (*The Latecomers*, 1836) and *Münchhausen* (1838–9).

Jacobi, Friedrich Heinrich (1743–1819), philosopher.

Janin, Jules (1804–74), French critic.

Jean Paul, pseudonym of Johann Paul Friedrich Richter (1763–1825), eccentric, popular and much-read novelist; Goethe thought poorly of him (30 March 1831).

Johnson, Samuel (1709–84), poet, essayist and lexicographer, author of the philosophical novel *The History of Rasselas, Prince of Abissinia* (1759).

Jung, Johann Heinrich (1740–1817), known as Jung-Stilling from the name he assumed in his autobiography, *Heinrich Stillings Jugend* (1777) and its sequels; religious author, economist and oculist, became friendly with Goethe when the latter was studying in Strasbourg 1770–72. Goethe describes in Book 16 of *Dichtung und Wahrheit* an occasion when Jung's skill in cutting cataracts failed him.

Kant, Immanuel (1724–1804), philosopher, whose major works include the *Kritik der reinen Vernunft* (*Critique of Pure Reason*, 1781) and *Kritik der Urteilskraft* (*Critique of Judgement*, 1790).

Kapo d'Istrias or Kapodistrias, Count Ioannis (1776–1831), first President of independent Greece.

Karl August, Grand Duke of Weimar (1757–1828).

Kauffmann, Angelika (1741–1807), painter; Goethe knew her in Italy and greatly admired her work.

Kestner, Charlotte, née Buff (1753–1828), the original of Lotte in Goethe's *Werther*.

Kind, Friedrich (1768–1843), poet, librettist of Weber's *Der Freischütz*.

Klettenberg, Susanne Katharina von (1723–74), a friend of Goethe's mother and a devout Protestant who influenced the young Goethe during his Christian phase around 1770.

Klopstock, Friedrich Gottlieb (1724–1803), poet who revitalized German poetry by his biblical epic *Der Messias* (*The Messiah*, 1748–73) and still more by his emotional odes, one of which, 'Die Frühlingsfeier' ('The Rite of Spring', 1759), Goethe alludes to in an important scene of *Werther*. In the conversation of 9 November 1824 Goethe mentions the ode 'Die beiden Musen' ('The Two Muses', 1752).

Knebel, Karl Ludwig (1744–1834), tutor to Prince Konstantin, brother of Duke Karl August; arranged Goethe's first meeting with Karl August in 1774; a close friend of Goethe till the latter's death.

Kniep, Christoph Heinrich (1755–1825), painter, who was with Goethe in Sicily in 1787.

Kolbe, Heinrich Christoph (1771–1836), painter responsible for several portraits of the elderly Goethe.

Körner, Theodor (1791–1813), patriotic poet who fell in the German War of Liberation against Napoleon's forces; author of the collection *Leyer und Schwerdt* (*Lyre and Sword*, 1814).

Kotzebue, August von (1761–1819), hugely popular dramatist; from 1813 he was employed in the Russian Foreign Service and was assassinated for his anti-liberal politics by the student Karl Sand (1795–1820) in 1819. His more than 230 plays include *Die beiden Klingsberg* (*The Two Klingsbergs*), *Verwandtschaften* (*Relationships*) and *Die Versöhnung* (*The Reconciliation*). His *Das Kind der Liebe* (1790), translated and adapted as *Lovers' Vows*, is performed in Jane Austen's *Mansfield Park*.

Krause, Gottlieb Friedrich (1805–60), Goethe's servant from 1824 on.

Kräuter, Friedrich Theodor (1790–1856), Goethe's secretary, responsible for his library.

Krüger, Wilhelm (1791–1841), actor.

La Roche, Carl August (1794–1884), actor.

Lagrange, Joseph-Louis (1736–1813), French mathematician.

Lamartine, Alphonse de (1790–1869), famous for *Méditations poétiques* (1820).

Lassen, Christian (1800–1876), Norwegian Orientalist, founder (along with A. W. Schlegel) of Sanskrit studies in Germany.

Lavater, Johann Caspar (1741–1801), Swiss clergyman and physiognomist; a friend of Goethe's from 1774 till 1786, when Goethe finally refused to be won over to Lavater's emotional brand of Christianity.

LIST OF PERSONS MENTIONED xix

Leibniz, Gottfried Wilhelm von (1646–1716), German philosopher and polymath.

Lenclos, Ninon de, properly Anne de L'Enclos (1620–1705), French author and lover of many notable men during the reign of Louis XIV.

Leo, Heinrich (1799–1878), Prussian historian.

Lessing, Gotthold Ephraim (1729–81), dramatist, critic and theologian; his best-known works include the comedy *Minna von Barnhelm* (1767), the tragedy *Emilia Galotti* (1772) and the drama supporting religious toleration, *Nathan der Weise* (*Nathan the Wise*, 1779). In his aesthetic treatise *Laokoon* (1766) he distinguished poetry and painting with reference to what each could represent.

Leuchtenberg, Eugène de Beauharnais, Duke of (1781–1824), adoptive son of Napoleon.

Lips, Johann Heinrich (1758–1817), painter and engraver.

Lockhart, John Gibson (1794–1854), son-in-law of Walter Scott; his *Life of Sir Walter Scott*, in seven volumes, appeared in 1837–8.

Lope de Vega (incorrectly called 'Lopez'), Spanish dramatist (1562–1635) who wrote over 800 comedies.

Lorrain, Claude (1600–82), real name Claude Gellée, French painter much admired by Goethe: see Franz Kempf, *Poetry, Painting, Park: Goethe and Claude Lorrain* (2020).

Lory, Gabriel (1784–1846), Swiss watercolour painter.

Lowe, Sir Hudson (1769–1844), Governor of St Helena during Napoleon's confinement there.

Luden, Heinrich (1778–1847), professor of history at Jena, who in 1825 published the first volume of *Geschichte des Teutschen Volkes* (*History of the Germans*; the twelfth and final volume appeared in 1837).

Malkolmi (or Malcolmi), Carl Friedrich (1745–1819), actor.

Manzoni, Alessandro (1785–1873), Italian poet and novelist, author of the historical novel *I promessi sposi* (*The Betrothed*, 1827).

Marmontel, Jean-François (1723–99), author and memoirist of the Paris Enlightenment.

Marot, Clément (1496–1544), poet of the French Renaissance.

xx LIST OF PERSONS MENTIONED

Martius, Karl Friedrich Philipp von (1794–1868), botanist.

Massot, Firmin (1766–1849), painter in Geneva.

Medem, Count Christoph Johann von (1763–1838), Prussian nobleman from Courland (now Latvia), married to Countess Mary Luise von der Pahlen (1778–1837).

Menander (*c*.342–*c*.292 BCE), Athenian comic dramatist.

Mengs, Anton (1728–79), known as 'Raphael', painter in neoclassical style.

Merck, Johann Heinrich (1741–91), poet and journalist, a friend of Goethe's from 1771 on.

Mérimée, Prosper (1803–70), French writer.

Metastasio, Pietro (1698–1782), Italian poet and librettist; his operas include *Issipile* (1732).

Meyer, Ernst (1791–1858), botanist.

Meyer, Friedrich Adolf Carl (1805–84), Westphalian poet.

Meyer, Johann Heinrich (1759–1832), Swiss painter and art historian and close friend of Goethe who advised him on artistic matters. His three-volume *Geschichte der bildenden Künste bei den Griechen* (*History of Greek Art*) appeared from 1824 to 1836.

Meyerbeer, Giacomo (1791–1864), operatic composer; Goethe knew his work only through his friend Zelter.

Milton, John (1608–74), English poet, author of the biblical drama *Samson Agonistes* (1671).

Mirabeau, Honoré Gabriel Riqueti, comte de (1749–91), a leading figure in the early stages of the French Revolution.

Molière: pseudonym of Jean-Baptiste Poquelin (1622–73), French dramatist, author of comedies, including *Tartuffe* (1664), *Le Misanthrope* (1666), *Le Médecin malgré lui* (*The Doctor in Spite of Himself*, 1666), *L'Avare* (*The Miser*, 1668) and *Le Malade imaginaire* (*The Imaginary Invalid*, 1673).

Moore, Thomas (1779–1852), Irish poet.

Mosheim, Johann Lorenz von (1694–1755), Church historian at Göttingen.

Mozart, Wolfgang Amadeus (1756–91), composer.

Müller, Friedrich von (1779–1849), Chancellor of Weimar from 1815; recorded many of Goethe's conversations.

LIST OF PERSONS MENTIONED xxi

Müllner, Adolf (1774–1829), dramatist, author of the popular fate-tragedy *Die Schuld* (*Guilt*, 1816).

Musäus, Johann Karl August (1735–87), compiler of *Volksmärchen der Deutschen* (*Folk Tales of the German People*, 1782–6).

Nees von Esenbeck, Christian Gottfried Daniel (1776–1858), physician and botanist in Bonn.

Neureuther, Eugen Napoleon (1806–82), draughtsman.

Niebuhr, Barthold Georg (1776–1831), historian of ancient Rome.

Ninon, see Lenclos.

Oels, Karl Ludwig (1771–1833), actor.

Oken, Lorenz (1779–1851), German naturalist.

Ostade, Adriaen van (1610–85), Dutch painter.

Ottilie, see Goethe, Ottilie von.

Paganini, Niccolò (1782–1840), violinist, who visited Weimar and met Goethe in 1829.

Panckoucke, Ernestine (1783–1860), wife of a Paris bookseller; she and Goethe exchanged letters.

Peel, Sir Robert (1788–1850), British politician.

Peter I, 'the Great' (1672–1725), Emperor of Russia.

Peucer, Heinrich Karl Friedrich (1779–1849), writer and administrator.

Platen, August, Count (1796–1835), poet and dramatist, best known for poetry in Oriental verse forms and for satirical plays such as *Der romantische Ödipus* (1829); lived in Italy from 1825 till his death.

Pogwisch, Henriette von (1776–1851), lady-in-waiting to the Grand Duchess Luise and mother of Ottilie von Goethe.

Pogwisch, Ulrike von (1798–1875), younger sister of Ottilie von Goethe. She had been living in Goethe's house since 1818.

Poussin, Nicolas (1594–1665), French painter.

Preller, Friedrich (1804–78), painter; his journey to Italy (see 5 June 1826) was financed by the Grand Duke Karl August.

Putyatin, Prince Nikolay Abramovich (1749–1830), who fell into disfavour at the Russian court and moved to Dresden; Goethe met him in Karlsbad in summer 1806.

xxii LIST OF PERSONS MENTIONED

Ramberg, Johann Heinrich (1763–1840), painter and engraver, who provided some illustrations for Goethe's *Ausgabe letzter Hand*, the last edition of Goethe's works that he authorized before his death.

Rapp, Count Jean (1771–1821), French officer, close associate of Napoleon.

Rauch, Christian Daniel (1777–1857), sculptor, who made several busts of Goethe in the 1820s.

Raupach, Ernst Benjamin Salomo (1784–1852), successful dramatist based in Berlin. His many plays included *Die Erdennacht* (*The Earthly Night, 1820*).

Reck (correctly Recke), Elise von der (1754–1833), writer, who had met Goethe in Karlsbad in 1820 and 1823.

Rehbein, Wilhelm (1776–1825), court doctor in Weimar and Goethe's personal physician.

Rehberg, August Wilhelm (1757–1836), political philosopher; the leading conservative critic of the French Revolution.

Reichardt, Johann Friedrich (1752–1814), composer.

Reinhard, Franz Volkmar (1753–1812), theologian and court preacher in Dresden, the capital of Saxony; Goethe met him in Karlsbad in 1807 and thought highly of him.

Reinhard, Karl Friedrich, Count (1761–1837), diplomat, since 1815 representing France at the German Federal Diet.

Reni, Guido (1575–1642), Italian painter. The 'pupil' mentioned on 13 April 1829 is Simone Cantarini (1612–48).

Reutern, Gerhardt Wilhelm von (1794–1865), army officer. Painting was originally his hobby; Goethe, who first met him in 1814, urged him to make it his profession. On resigning from the army in 1819, Reutern did so, with such success that in 1837 he was appointed court painter to the imperial Russian family.

Riemer, Friedrich Wilhelm (1774–1845), tutor to August von Goethe, then teacher at the Weimar grammar school; recorded many sayings by Goethe and helped Eckermann to edit his posthumous works.

Riepenhausen, Franz (1786–1831) and Johannes (1787–1860), artists and art historians.

LIST OF PERSONS MENTIONED xxiii

Röhr, Johann Friedrich (1777–1848), court preacher and chief superintendent of the Lutheran Church in Weimar; his book on the history and geography of Palestine in Jesus's time is mentioned on 13 February 1831.

Romano, Giulio (1492–1546), Italian painter.

Roos, Johann Heinrich (1631–85), Dutch artist who, despite Goethe's opinion, painted not only animals but also portraits and landscapes with great success.

Rossini, Gioachino (1792–1868), Italian composer; his operas include *Moses* (1818), of which Goethe attended a performance in Weimar in 1828, and *Il Conte Ory* (*Count Ory*, originally *Le comte Ory* with French libretto, 1828), which Eckermann saw in Milan (28 May 1830).

Rothschild, Amschel Mayer von (1773–1855), banker, eldest son of Mayer Amschel Rothschild (1744–1812), who founded the Rothschild banking house in Frankfurt; ennobled 1817, made a baron 1822; his four brothers established banking houses in Paris, London, Naples and Vienna.

Rubens, Peter Paul (1577–1640), Flemish painter.

Rückert, Friedrich (1788–1866), poet and professor of Oriental languages, whose collection *Östliche Rosen* (*Eastern Roses*, 1822) pays homage to Goethe's *West-östlicher Divan*.

Ruysdael, Jacob van (1628–82), Dutch painter, on whom Goethe wrote the essay 'Ruysdael the Poet' (1816); see *Goethe on Art*, ed. John Gage (1980).

Saint-Simon, Louis de Rouvroy, duc de (1675–1755), French diplomat whose *Mémoires*, first published in the 1820s, are an invaluable record of French court life in the reign of Louis XIV and the subsequent regency.

Sainte-Beuve, Charles-Augustin (1804–69), French literary critic.

Salvandy, Narcisse-Achille, comte de (1795–1856), French statesman.

Saussure, Horace-Bénédicte de (1740–99), Swiss natural scientist.

Savigny, Friedrich Karl von (1779–1861), legal historian who wrote especially about medieval German law.

Schellhorn, Franz Wilhelm (1750–1836), civil servant in Weimar, who had celebrated fifty years of service.

xxiv LIST OF PERSONS MENTIONED

Schelling, Friedrich Wilhelm Joseph von (1775–1854), Romantic philosopher who revised and developed Kantian idealism in *System des transzendentalen Idealismus* (*System of Transcendental Idealism*, 1800). He was professor of philosophy at Jena from 1798 to 1803; Goethe knew him and was particularly interested in his speculations about nature. His mythographic study *Über die Gottheiten von Samothrace* (*On the Divinities of Samothrace*, 1815) provided material for *Faust II*.

Schiller, Johann Christoph Friedrich (1759–1805). Educated at the military academy supervised by the Duke of Württemberg, and trained as a doctor. He had his first play, *Die Räuber* (*The Robbers*), performed at Mannheim in January 1782; forbidden by the Duke to write any more plays, he ran away from Württemberg and attempted a career in the theatre with *Don Carlos* (1787) and other plays. He became professor of history at Jena in 1789 and developed a close friendship with Goethe from 1794 on. For many years he abandoned theatre for history and philosophy, including the essay *Über naïve und sentimentalische Dichtung* (*On Naïve and Sentimental Poetry*, 1795), but returned to the stage with the dramatic trilogy *Wallenstein* (written 1797–9, first performed 1798–9 in Weimar); the first part is entitled *Wallensteins Lager* (*Wallenstein's Camp*), the second *Die Piccolomini*, the third *Wallensteins Tod* (*The Death of Wallenstein*). Almost his last completed play was *Wilhelm Tell* (1804).

Schinkel, Karl Friedrich (1781–1841), architect and painter in neoclassical style.

Schlegel, August Wilhelm (1767–1845), translator (of Shakespeare and much Romance literature), literary critic and pioneer of comparative literature and of Sanskrit studies.

Schlegel, Friedrich (1772–1829), brother of August Wilhelm, literary critic. Both Schlegels upheld Romanticism and often disagreed with Goethe, who nevertheless staged August Wilhelm's play *Ion* (1803) and Friedrich's tragedy *Alarcos* (1802) in Weimar. In 1808 Friedrich converted to Catholicism and became an Austrian civil servant with strongly conservative views.

LIST OF PERSONS MENTIONED

Schlosser, Friedrich Christoph (1776–1861), historian.

Schmidt, Christian Friedrich, lawyer in Weimar.

Schmidt, Maria (1808–75), singer.

Schöne (correctly Schön), Friedrich Gotthold (1806–57), classical scholar.

Schönemann, Anna Elisabeth, known as 'Lili' (1758–1817), daughter of a Frankfurt banker, briefly engaged to Goethe in 1775; married another banker, Bernhard von Türckheim, in 1778.

Schopenhauer, Johanna (1766–1838), novelist and travel writer, resident in Weimar with her daughter Adele after being widowed in 1804; mother of the philosopher Arthur Schopenhauer (1788–1860).

Schrön, Ludwig (1799–1875), astronomer in Jena.

Schubarth, Karl Ernst (1796–1861), philosopher, author of *Zur Beurteilung Goethes* (1818).

Schulenburg, Friedrich Albrecht, Count von der (1772–1853), diplomat.

Schultz, Christoph Ludwig Friedrich (1781–1834), Prussian administrator.

Schütze, Stephan (1771–1839), administrator and author in Weimar, author of *Heitere Stunden* (*Cheerful Hours*, 2 vols, 1821–5).

Schwabe, Johann Friedrich Heinrich (1779–1834), court preacher in Weimar from 1827.

Schweitzer, Christian Wilhelm (1781–1856), minister of state in Weimar.

Scott, Sir Walter (1771–1832), historical novelist, famous throughout Europe for *Waverley* (1814) and its many successors, including *Rob Roy* (1817), *Ivanhoe* (1819), *Kenilworth* (1821), *Peveril of the Peak* (1823) and *The Fair Maid of Perth* (1828). The first volume of his nine-volume *Life of Napoleon Bonaparte* appeared in 1827.

Seckendorff, Karl Sigmund von (1744–85), chamberlain in Weimar.

Ségur, Philippe-Paul, comte de (1780–1873), historian.

Seidel, Dorothea (1804–60), actress.

Seidel, Max Johann (1795–1855), Tyrolean actor.

Smollett, Tobias (1721–71), Scottish novelist whose works include *The Adventures of Roderick Random* (1748).

Solger, Karl Wilhelm Ferdinand (1780–1819), philosopher in Berlin, whose work on aesthetics Goethe valued highly.

Sömmerring, Samuel Thomas von (1755–1830), physician.

Sophocles (c.496–406 BCE), Athenian tragedian, whose surviving works include the *Oedipus* plays, *Antigone* and *Philoctetes*.

Soret, Frédéric Jakob (1795–1865), natural scientist from Geneva, tutor to young princes in Weimar from 1822 to 1836; translated Goethe's *Versuch, die Metamorphose der Pflanzen zu erklären* (*Attempt to Explain the Metamorphosis of Plants*, 1790) into French.

Spiegel, Karl Emil Freiherr von (1783–1849), Court Marshal at Weimar.

Spiegel, Wilhelmine Emilie von (1787–1870), wife of the Weimar Court Marshal.

Spinoza, Baruch (1632–77), Dutch-Jewish philosopher, much admired by Goethe.

Stadelmann, Karl Wilhelm (1782–1844), Goethe's servant from 1814 to 1815 and 1817 to 1824.

Staël, Germaine de (1766–1817), literary and political theorist, originally from Geneva; her antagonism to Napoleon obliged her to live in Switzerland for many years.

Stapfer, Frédéric-Albert-Alexandre (1802–92), generally known as 'Albert Stapfer', published in 1823 the first French translation of *Faust I*; it was reissued in 1828 with seventeen lithographic illustrations by Delacroix.

Stendhal: pseudonym of Marie-Henri Beyle (1783–1842), French novelist, author of *Le Rouge et le noir* (*The Red and the Black*, 1830).

Sterling, Charles (1804–80), son of the English consul in Genoa; visited Weimar in 1823.

Sternberg, Count Kaspar Maria von (1761–1838), statesman and author of a treatise on botany.

Sterne, Laurence (1713–68), British novelist, famous in Germany especially for *Tristram Shandy* (1759–67) and *A Sentimental Journey through France and Italy* (1768).

Stieler, Joseph Karl (1781–1858), Bavarian court painter.

LIST OF PERSONS MENTIONED

Stilling, see Jung.

Stolberg, Christian (1748–1821) and Friedrich Leopold (1750–1819), Counts, brothers with whom Goethe visited Switzerland from May to July 1775.

Stosch, Baron Philipp von (1691–1757), Prussian antiquarian who lived in Italy; his collection is illustrated in the catalogue *Description des pierres gravées du feu Baron de Stosch* (1760).

Streckfuss, Karl (1778–1844), administrator and author; his German translation of Dante's *Divine Comedy* appeared in 1824–6.

Svanevelt, Herman van (c.1600–1655), Dutch landscape painter.

Sylvestre, Espérance (1790–1842), from Geneva, spent 1823–8 as governess to the daughters of Karl Friedrich and Maria Pavlovna of Sachsen-Weimar.

Szymanowska, Maria (1789–1831), a pianist whom Goethe got to know in Marienbad in August 1823.

Talleyrand: Charles Maurice de Talleyrand-Périgord (1754–1838), French diplomat, notorious for his adroitness; Napoleon made him Foreign Minister, but he resigned in 1807, sided with Napoleon's enemies, and was chief French negotiator at the Congress of Vienna in 1814–15.

Tassi, Agostino (1566–1642), Italian painter.

Tasso, Torquato (1544–95), Italian poet, author of *La Gerusalemme liberata* (*Jerusalem Delivered*, 1581), and protagonist of Goethe's play *Torquato Tasso* (1790).

Tastu, Amable (1795–1885), French woman of letters; her early works include *Poésies* (1826).

Teniers, David, the Younger (1610–90), Flemish painter who painted many scenes of peasant life.

Thomson, James (1700–1748), Scottish poet, author of *The Seasons* (1730) and *Liberty* (1734).

Tieck, Ludwig (1773–1853), prolific author of Romantic stories, novels and dramas. His elder daughter Dorothea (1799–1841) completed the translation of Shakespeare begun by her father with August Wilhelm Schlegel. His younger daughter, Agnes (1802–80), married in 1843 and became Agnes Alberti.

LIST OF PERSONS MENTIONED

Tiedge, Christoph August (1752–1841), author of the long didactic poem *Urania* (1800).

Töpfer, Carl (1792–1871), theatre director.

Töpffer, Rudolf (or Rodolphe) (1799–1846), artist in Geneva.

Uhland, Ludwig (1787–1862), Romantic poet with a love of medieval German legend; a literary scholar, professor at Tübingen University (1829–32), and a liberal member of the Württemberg parliament (1819–39).

Ulrike, Fräulein, see Pogwisch, Ulrike von.

Unzelmann, Karl (1786–1843), actor, in Weimar from 1802 to 1821, then moved to Berlin.

Vernet, Horace (1789–1863), French painter living in Rome.

Vigny, Alfred de (1797–1863), French Romantic poet and novelist.

Villemain, Abel-François (1790–1870), French writer whose *Cours de la littérature française* appeared in 1828–9.

Vogel, Karl (1798–1864), Goethe's personal physician in succession to Rehbein.

Voigt, Friedrich Siegmund (1781–1850), zoologist in Jena.

Voltaire, pseudonym of François-Marie Arouet (1694–1778), leading figure of the Enlightenment as poet, dramatist, historian, philosopher, polemicist.

Voss, Johann Heinrich (1751–1826), poet, classical scholar and translator, famous for his version of Homer's *Odyssey* in German hexameters and for his mock-epic poem *Luise* (1795); headmaster of the school at Eutin in Holstein, 1782–1802, then lived at Jena, near Weimar, 1802–5; in 1777 married Ernestine Boie (1756–1834).

Waldner, Luise Adelaide von (1746–1830), lady-in-waiting to Duchess Luise.

Weber, Carl Maria von (1786–1826), composer of the Romantic operas *Der Freischütz* (*The Free Marksman*, 1821) and *Euryanthe* (1823).

Weissenthurn, Johanna Franul von (1772–1847), actress and dramatist from Vienna, whose works included many historical dramas.

Wellington, Arthur Wellesley, Duke of (1769–1852), who defeated Napoleon at Waterloo in 1815.

LIST OF PERSONS MENTIONED   xxix

Werner, Abraham Gottlob (1750–1817), geologist who put forward the 'Neptunist' theory that the earth's surface was formed by the gradual retreat of the primordial ocean; Goethe much preferred this theory to its rival, Vulcanism, upheld by Alexander von Humboldt, which attributed the formation of the earth's surface to volcanic upheavals.

Weygand, Christian Friedrich (1742–1807), publisher in Leipzig who published Goethe's *Werther* in 1774.

Wieland, Christoph Martin (1733–1813), a leading Enlightenment author, known especially for his Bildungsroman *Geschichte des Agathon* (*Story of Agathon*, 1766–7) and his humorous verse romance *Oberon* (1780). Wieland translated twenty-two of Shakespeare's plays into German and founded and edited the important periodical *Der teutsche Merkur* from 1773 to 1800. His political novel *Der goldene Spiegel* (*The Golden Mirror*, 1772) induced the Dowager Duchess Anna Amalia of Weimar to appoint him tutor to her son Karl August. From 1772 till his death Wieland lived at Ossmannstedt, a village near Weimar.

Willemer, Johann Jakob (1760–1838), banker; Goethe's affectionate relationship with his wife Marianne (née van Gangelt, 1784–1860) is reflected in the *West-östlicher Divan* (1819), to which Marianne contributed some poems.

Winckelmann, Johann Joachim (1717–68), art historian who rose from poverty to prominence; after publishing *Gedanken über die Nachahmung der griechischen Werke in der Malerei und Bildhauerkunst* (*Thoughts on the Imitation of Greek Works in Painting and Sculpture*, 1755) he moved to Rome and, as librarian to two cardinals in succession, extended his knowledge of classical art enough to write the epoch-making *Geschichte der Kunst des Altertums* (*History of Ancient Art*, 1764).

Winterberger, Georg (1804–60), actor.

Wolf, Friedrich August (1759–1824), classical scholar, professor at Berlin from 1810; argued in his *Prolegomena ad Homerum* (1795) that the Homeric epics were pieced together from many shorter heroic poems.

Wolff, Amalie (1780–1851), née Malcolmi, widow of Pius Alexander Wolff.

Wolff, Oskar Ludwig Bernhard (1799–1851), improviser; taught modern languages at Weimar from 1826 and in 1838 became professor of literature at Jena.

Wolff, Pius Alexander (1782–1828), actor in Weimar, and from 1816 in Berlin. The conversation about him on 11 October 1828 was prompted by his recent death.

Zahn, Wilhelm (1800–1871), archaeologist.

Zauper, Joseph Stanislaus (1784–1850), grammar-school teacher at Pilsen in Bohemia.

Zelter, Karl Friedrich (1758–1832), director of the Berlin Academy of Singing; had exchanged letters with Goethe since 1799.

List of Works by Goethe in Chronological Order

'Poetische Gedancken über die Höllenfahrt Jesu Christi' ('Poetic Thoughts on Jesus Christ's Descent into Hell'), poem written in 1764 or 1765.

'A Song over the Unconfidence towards my Self' (1766).

Reviews in *Frankfurter gelehrte Anzeigen* (1772–3).

'Brief des Pastors zu *** an den neuen Pastor zu ***' ('Letter from the Pastor at *** to the New Pastor at ***'), fictional letter advocating religious toleration (1773).

Götz von Berlichingen, historical prose drama, set in the sixteenth century and modelled on Shakespeare's dramatic form (1773).

Götter, Helden und Wieland (*Gods, Heroes and Wieland*), short satirical play (1773).

Hanswursts Hochzeit (*Hanswurst's Wedding*), ribald comedy, left unfinished (1773–5).

Die Leiden des jungen Werthers (*The Sorrows of Young Werther*, 1774), revised version *Die Leiden des jungen Werther* (1787).

Clavigo, tragedy (1774).

'An Schwager Kronos' ('To Coachman Kronos', 1774).

'Stirbt der Fuchs, so gilt der Balg', playful poem written around 1775.

Die Geschwister (*The Siblings*, 1776; published 1787).

'Jägers Abendlied' ('Huntsman's Serenade'), poem (1776).

'Der Fischer' ('The Fisherman'), ballad (probably 1778–9).

Die Fischerin (*The Fisherman's Wife*), *Singspiel* (musical drama), first performed at Tiefurt in 1781.

'Der Erlkönig' ('The Erl-King'), ballad (1782).

xxxii   LIST OF WORKS BY GOETHE IN CHRONOLOGICAL ORDER

'In this quiet place . . .', epigram written in 1782 for Frau von Stein; published under the title 'Erwählter Fels' ('Chosen Rock', 1789).

'Ilmenau', poem (1783).

Egmont, historical drama (begun in 1775, completed and published 1787).

Iphigenie auf Tauris, verse play (1787), modelled on *Iphigeneia among the Taurians* by Euripides but considerably modernized: the Furies, for example, no longer appear on stage, but are known only by their psychological effects on the matricide Orest (see 1 April 1827).

Claudine von Villa Bella, Singspiel (1788); revised version, referred to by Eckermann on 5 and 8 April 1829.

Das Römische Karneval (*The Roman Carnival*, 1789), later incorporated into the *Italienische Reise* (*Italian Journey*).

Torquato Tasso, drama (1790).

Versuch, die Metamorphose der Pflanzen zu erklären (*An Attempt to Explain the Metamorphosis of Plants*, 1790).

Faust, drama, first partially published as *Faust. Ein Fragment* (1790), expanded as *Faust. Der Tragödie erster Teil* (1808); Part Two as *Faust. Der Tragödie zweiter Teil* (1832).

Der Grosskophta, comedy satirizing Cagliostro and intrigues at the French court (1791).

Die Aufgeregten (*The Hotheads*), unfinished political drama (1791).

Der Bürgergeneral (*The Bourgeois General*), one-act comedy about a swindler posing as a revolutionary (1793).

Römische Elegien (*Roman Elegies*), cycle of poems in the classical metre called elegiac distichs, recounting a love affair in modern Rome (1795).

Wilhelm Meisters Lehrjahre (*Wilhelm Meister's Apprenticeship*), novel (1795–6).

'Alexis und Dora', narrative poem in elegiac distichs (1796).

Xenien, biting satirical epigrams composed jointly by Goethe and Schiller (1797).

'Der Gott und die Bajadere', Indian legend in verse (1797). A 'bayadere' is a temple prostitute.

LIST OF WORKS BY GOETHE IN CHRONOLOGICAL ORDER   xxxiii

'Die Braut von Korinth' ('The Bride of Corinth'), narrative poem (1797).

Hermann und Dorothea, humorous epic poem in nine cantos (1797).

'Legende vom Hufeisen' ('Legend of the Horseshoe'), ballad (1797).

Aus einer Reise in die Schweiz über Frankfurt, Heidelberg, Stuttgart und Tübingen im Jahre 1797 (Journey to Switzerland by way of Frankfurt, Heidelberg, Stuttgart and Tübingen), edited by Eckermann and published posthumously in *Goethes Werke. Vollständige Ausgabe letzter Hand*, vol. 43 (1833).

Achilleis, uncompleted epic poem (1799).

'Die Metamorphose der Pflanzen' ('The Metamorphosis of Plants'), poem – not the same work as the big botanical study mentioned *passim* (1799).

Die natürliche Tochter (The Natural Daughter), drama (1803).

Leben des Benvenuto Cellini (1803), Goethe's free translation of Cellini's autobiography *La Vita di Benvenuto Cellini* (written 1558–62).

'Die glücklichen Gatten' ('The Happy Couple'), poem (1804).

Rameaus Neffe (Rameau's Nephew, 1805), translation of Diderot's novel *Le Neveu de Rameau*.

Pandora, short verse drama (1807).

Die Wahlverwandtschaften (Elective Affinities), novel about marriage (1809).

Zur Farbenlehre (On the Doctrine of Colours, 1810).

Das Tagebuch (The Diary), narrative poem, written in 1810 but not published in Goethe's lifetime.

Aus meinem Leben. Dichtung und Wahrheit (From my Life: Poetry and Truth), autobiography in four parts, published respectively in 1811, 1812, 1814 and posthumously in 1833. Eckermann helped to edit the fourth part. Goethe worked on it in 1829 (see 20 February 1829).

'Kriegsglück' ('The Fortune of War'), poem written 1814, published 1815.

Sprichwörtliches (Proverbial Pieces, 1815).

Zahme Xenien, epigrams, published from 1815 onwards.

XXXIV   LIST OF WORKS BY GOETHE IN CHRONOLOGICAL ORDER

'Was wär ein Gott', untitled poem first published in 1815.
'Ruysdael the Poet' (1816).

Italienische Reise (*Italian Journey*, 1816–17). The section entitled 'Zweiter Römischer Aufenthalt' ('Second Sojourn in Rome') was written mainly in 1829 (see 10 April 1829).

Sankt-Rochus-Fest zu Bingen, autobiographical essay (1817).

'Um Mitternacht' ('At Midnight'), poem written on 13 February 1818.

West-östlicher Divan (*West-Eastern Divan*), collection of poetry modelled on translations from Arabic and Persian (1819). The text mentions 'Jussufs Reize möcht ich borgen' and 'Ach, um deine feuchten Schwingen'.

'Ballade' (1820).

'Metamorphose der Tiere' ('The Metamorphosis of Animals'), didactic poem (1820).

Über Kunst und Altertum, six volumes on art and antiquity edited and partly written by Goethe between 1816 and 1832.

Wilhelm Meisters Wanderjahre (*Wilhelm Meister's Journeyman Years*), continuation of the *Lehrjahre*, first published in 1821 and in enlarged form in 1829.

'An Werther' ('To Werther') and 'Marienbader Elegie' (1823), parts of *Trilogie der Leidenschaft* (*Trilogy of Passion*).

'Paria' ('The Pariah', i.e. an Indian Untouchable), poem (1824).

Helena. Klassisch-romantische Phantasmagorie. Zwischenspiel zu Faust (*Helen: Classical-romantic Phantasmagoria; Interlude to Faust*), the third Act of *Faust II*, published separately in 1827.

Novelle, short story (1828).

'Bei Betrachtung von Schillers Schädel' ('On Contemplating Schiller's Skull'), poem (1829).

'Vermächtnis' ('Legacy'), poem (1829).

Introduction by Ritchie Robertson

When the unknown Johann Peter Eckermann first wrote to him in 1821, Johann Wolfgang von Goethe was one of the most famous people in the world. Fifty years earlier he had become a celebrity as the author, first of the Shakespeare-inspired historical drama *Götz von Berlichingen* (1773), then of the epistolary novel *Die Leiden des jungen Werthers* (*The Sorrows of Young Werther*, 1774), which rapidly became a Europe-wide bestseller. In 1775 Karl August, the young Duke of Weimar, invited Goethe to his court. Thereafter most of Goethe's life, till his death in 1832, was spent in the small principality of Saxe-Weimar-Eisenach, covering about 700 square miles and with a population (in the 1770s) of about 106,000, of whom 6,000 lived in the main town, Weimar. Goethe took a prominent part in its government, till the burden of administrative duties, combined with emotional frustration, provoked in 1786 what he called, speaking to Eckermann, his 'flight to Italy' (10 February 1829). During his two years in Italy Goethe completed several masterpieces that he had begun in Weimar, notably the dramas *Egmont*, *Iphigenie auf Tauris* and *Torquato Tasso*. On his return to Weimar he met a young woman, Christiane Vulpius, and scandalized stuffy Weimar society by living with her without marrying her until 1806. Christiane bore five children, none of whom lived longer than seventeen days apart from August, who figures in Eckermann's recollections as 'young Goethe'. Goethe continued to produce a wealth of poetry, dramas and fiction, including the best-known work of German literature, *Faust*, of which Part One appeared in 1808.

However, Goethe's literary eminence was less secure than

present-day readers may imagine. Many of his later works were poorly received. Goethe increasingly favoured an indirect, ambiguous, even riddling and esoteric mode of expression, working through hints and suggestions rather than statements. For prudish readers, his works, as well as his life, were tainted with immorality. His novel *Die Wahlverwandtschaften* (*Elective Affinities*, 1809) seemed to treat the institution of marriage in a disturbingly sceptical way. He was known to be hostile to orthodox Christianity. Another group of readers condemned him for being the servant of a prince, deplored his steadfast hostility to the French Revolution, and took exception to the conservatism which was undoubtedly part of his outlook. To the new generation of Romantic writers, Goethe seemed something of a back number; his undeniable achievements lay in the past and would soon be overtaken. It was particularly frustrating for Goethe that his researches in natural science found so little agreement. The longest book he ever published, *Zur Farbenlehre* (*On the Doctrine of Colours*, 1810), setting out a theory of light and colour adamantly opposed to the theories put forward over a century earlier by Isaac Newton, met with almost universal disapproval. He responded to these disappointments by writing his autobiography, *Dichtung und Wahrheit* (*Poetry and Truth*), of which the first three parts were published in 1811–14. As the title intimates, however, this is not a no-holds-barred work of self-revelation such as Rousseau's *Confessions* (1782), but a carefully pondered work of art in which Goethe presents himself to the public as he wishes to be understood. Even this autobiographical masterpiece, however, did not restore his popularity.

Goethe's splendid isolation helps to explain why he was so responsive to Eckermann's approaches. Eckermann, born on 21 September 1792, had, as he recounts in the autobiographical sketch that precedes the *Conversations*, struggled up from poverty, was largely self-taught, and was animated by a deep enthusiasm for literature, especially for the works of Goethe. He himself had written a number of poems, and also a tragedy, *Graf Eduard*, which his friends advised him not to publish.

Eckermann's approach to the great man was carefully planned.

INTRODUCTION BY RITCHIE ROBERTSON xxxvii

It had to be, because Goethe was beleaguered not only by visitors (often from Britain) but by aspiring authors who wanted him to read and promote their works. Such correspondents received from Goethe's secretary a standard letter saying that Goethe was too busy to answer them individually, but that thoughts and feelings provoked by their work might find expression in *Über Kunst und Altertum* (*On Art and Antiquity*), a journal Goethe edited from 1816 till his death. So Eckermann first sent some of his poems to Goethe's friend Johannes Daniel Falk in August 1821, and received an encouraging reply. The following month, in which Goethe reached the age of seventy-two, he sent birthday congratulations with some poems and a sketch of his own life (as a kind of CV). In September Eckermann visited Weimar in person; Goethe was away in Bohemia, but he met Falk and Goethe's secretary Kräuter. In October he received the standard letter and was pleased with it. For the time being he had done all he could, without being intrusive, to make Goethe aware of his existence.

Two years later Eckermann made his decisive move. In May 1823 he sent Goethe the manuscript of his book *Beyträge zur Poesie mit besonderer Hinweisung auf Goethe* (*Essays on Poetry with Particular Reference to Goethe*). This is a collection of short essays, partly on works by Goethe, notably a substantial essay on *Die Wahlverwandtschaften*, partly on general literary questions, mostly illustrated from Goethe's works. It has often been observed that the style resembles Goethe's: concise, pithy, and clear. It could not be more different from the Hegelian jargon that Goethe, in conversation with Eckermann, later deplored in the critic Hinrichs (28 March 1827). The essays are sensitive, intelligent, and supported by close reference to the text. They also defend Goethe against his critics. The essay on *Die Wahlverwandtschaften* defends the novel against the frequent charge of immorality, maintaining that its central message is the sanctity of marriage. To present-day readers this will seem at best a one-dimensional reading, especially when Eckermann maintains that the novel's values are truly expressed by Mittler, the amateur marriage counsellor, himself unmarried, who constantly makes gaffes.[1] Discussing the tragedy *Egmont*,

Eckermann defends the softening of the tragic outcome by the dream-vision of Freedom that visits Egmont just before his death, and seeks thus to rebut Schiller's notorious criticism of it as a 'somersault into a world of opera'.[2]

Goethe was delighted by this book. Eckermann planned a visit in person, and announced his intention indirectly via Goethe's close friend Friedrich Wilhelm Riemer, with whom he had in the meantime also established contact. He walked from Hanover to Weimar (some 120 miles), and had his first meeting with Goethe on 10 June 1823, as he describes in the first of the recorded *Conversations*. Clearly, Goethe could not have been more genial. He recommended Eckermann's book to his publisher Cotta, with whom it appeared in 1824. He also proposed that Eckermann should settle in or near Weimar. Goethe had accumulated a huge mass of papers which needed to be put in order. He also needed someone to supervise the edition of his collected works which Cotta wanted to produce. His various secretaries were able to take dictation (though they were not wholly reliable even at that), but certainly not to undertake a task requiring literary knowledge and judgement. Eckermann was just the man.

From 1823 to 1832 Eckermann made himself altogether indispensable. His work on the edition began with a challenging task. In 1772–3 the young Goethe had contributed many book reviews to a journal published in his native Frankfurt, the *Frankfurter gelehrte Anzeigen*. The reviews were published anonymously, and Goethe, after the lapse of fifty years, could not remember which ones he had written, so Eckermann had to go through the journal's files and identify Goethe's reviews on stylistic grounds. When Eckermann had accomplished this, there followed years of intermittent work on the last edition of Goethe's works to have the author's imprimatur, known as the *Ausgabe letzter Hand*, which appeared in forty volumes between 1827 and 1830. After Goethe's death, Eckermann, with Riemer and several other collaborators, edited the posthumous and uncollected works, which appeared in twenty further volumes in 1832–42.

But Eckermann was far more than an editor. Some of

INTRODUCTION BY RITCHIE ROBERTSON

Goethe's later works would not have been completed without gentle pressure from Eckermann and frequent discussions with him. The third volume of *Dichtung und Wahrheit* (1814) had ended by recounting Goethe's first meeting with the future Duke of Weimar and the disagreement between Goethe and his father over the value and risks of getting involved with a princely court. The fourth volume was to recount Goethe's brief engagement to Lili Schönemann, a Frankfurt socialite, and his eventual departure for Weimar. Goethe showed Eckermann his plan, and Eckermann replied with a synopsis indicating what still had to be done; this, Eckermann tells us, was in order 'to instil a new passion and enthusiasm in Goethe for the work that was discontinued and laid aside for many years' (10 August 1824).

The completion of *Dichtung und Wahrheit* was hampered by the overriding project of Goethe's last decade: Part Two of *Faust*. Many conversations concern this work, and to follow them requires a first-hand knowledge of the text. In particular, the 'Classical Walpurgis Night' which forms Act II presented great challenges, since it draws on often recondite classical sources. Eckermann, despite lacking a classical education, did his best to enter into this imaginative world; for example, he read the mythographic book by the philosopher Schelling on ancient Greek mystery cults (17 February 1831).

Goethe undoubtedly set great store by Eckermann's practical and moral support. He acknowledged it in conversation with another Weimar friend, Chancellor von Müller: 'Eckermann knows best how to extort [*extorquieren*] literary productions from me, thanks to his intelligent appreciation of anything that I have already accomplished or begun. It is mainly because of him that I am continuing with *Faust* and that the first two Acts of Part Two are almost complete.'[3] He paid Eckermann another tribute when writing to his Scottish admirer Thomas Carlyle in 1831: 'His delicate yet also lively, I might say passionate feeling is of great value to me, since I tell him about much that remains unpublished and unused, and he has the delightful gift of appreciating what exists, as a satisfied reader, but can also state clearly what needs to be done in respect of feeling and taste.'[4]

What did Goethe give Eckermann in return for his invaluable

xl INTRODUCTION BY RITCHIE ROBERTSON

services? He never formally employed Eckermann and so never paid him a salary. Eckermann often dined at Goethe's table, and Goethe provided him with free tickets for the theatre, to which he was passionately devoted. Goethe also arranged for the University of Jena to confer a doctorate on Eckermann on the strength of the *Beyträge*; having a title was important in the hierarchical society of Weimar, where even a grammar-school teacher such as Riemer bore the title of Professor. Lacking a secure income, however, Eckermann lived for some time on the substantial *ex gratia* payment he had received from Cotta before the publication of the *Beyträge*. He then, thanks to Goethe's influence, became attached to an establishment kept by one Professor Melos to accommodate the many young Englishmen who visited Weimar, and where Eckermann was to teach them German. In return, Eckermann benefited from their company to improve his knowledge of English; Goethe had urged him to learn English so that he could read Byron in the original. This enabled Eckermann to live from hand to mouth. Since 1819, however, he had been engaged to Johanna (or Johanne) Bertram, who was waiting, not always patiently, in Hanover for the day when Eckermann could afford to marry her and set up house with her.

An opportunity seemed to offer itself later in 1824, when Eckermann was invited to work for an English journal, the *European Review* (edited by Alexander Walker), by supplying monthly reports on the latest German literature. The remuneration would have enabled Eckermann to marry. Moreover, the *European Review*, though it ran only from 1824 to 1826, was a highly regarded journal with distinguished contributors, and would have increased Eckermann's reputation. But Goethe, as we see from the conversation of 3 December 1824, firmly squashed the idea. It is one of the very few occasions when Eckermann describes Goethe as frowning. Goethe points out that the work would be extremely time-consuming, and advises him not to spread himself too thin. That was practical advice, especially since Eckermann was too conscientious just to skim-read books; on the other hand, he was spreading himself thin anyway by teaching, which he did not enjoy, and he would of

INTRODUCTION BY RITCHIE ROBERTSON xli

course have had considerably less time to assist Goethe. Goethe knew about Eckermann's marriage plans, and spoke of them with sympathy, to judge from a long verbatim report of Goethe's words in a letter Eckermann sent Johanna on 13 February 1825.[5] But he was in no hurry to advance them.

The project in which Eckermann invested his hopes was of course the *Conversations with Goethe*. Eckermann began writing up conversations as early as 1823, and showed samples to Goethe for the latter's approval in May or June 1825. It is not clear whether the possibility of publishing the *Conversations* was raised at this stage. But the idea was obvious. Goethe himself had read Thomas Medwin's *Conversations of Lord Byron* and Las Cases' recollections of Napoleon on St Helena. Such celebrity memoirs with a strong claim to authenticity were immensely popular. By 1826 Eckermann was not only thinking of publishing the *Conversations* but of having them translated into English by one of his pupils, Heavyside, who might further have helped to get them published by John Murray, famous as the publisher of Byron and Scott. Goethe, however, advised Eckermann to postpone any thoughts of publication until he had completed his job of editing the correspondence between Goethe and Schiller. When Eckermann returned to the idea in 1830, Goethe put his foot down, as Eckermann reports: 'Goethe had not given his approval for the early publication of my *Conversations*, which meant that I had to give up the idea of embarking successfully on a purely literary career' (see p. 364).

There is no doubt that Eckermann admired, revered, and even loved Goethe. But his relation to Goethe was also a kind of thralldom, and in 1830 he very briefly rebelled. In that year, Goethe's son August, whose physical and psychological health was poor, wanted to travel to Italy, and Goethe asked Eckermann to accompany him. While this was a great opportunity for Eckermann to see the country that Goethe had written about eloquently in his *Italienische Reise* (*Italian Journey*, 1816–17), August was not the ideal travelling companion; he and Eckermann did not get on, he was a heavy drinker and a philanderer, and Eckermann may well have been expected to keep him out of trouble. When the two arrived in Genoa,

Eckermann fell ill. This provided a reason (possibly a pretext) for returning to Weimar. Eckermann left August to continue his journey to Rome (where he died of a stroke, aged only forty, on 27 October), and went, not straight back to Weimar, but to Geneva, where the manuscript of the *Conversations* was in the keeping of his and Goethe's friend Frédéric Soret.

From Geneva, Eckermann wrote Goethe a long letter, of which a heavily edited version appears in the *Conversations* (12 September 1830). First Eckermann explains why he and August parted company: Eckermann fell ill, August advised him not to travel any further, and a letter opportunely arrived from Goethe, saying that Eckermann would be welcome to return. Eckermann also expresses anxiety about the manuscript of the *Conversations*, which needs much further polishing and is at present in Soret's hands. This both justifies Eckermann's visiting Geneva, and hints strongly at the importance of getting the *Conversations* published. He then tells how he heard that August had had an accident in Spezia and broken his collarbone, how he declared himself ready to rejoin August if asked, and how he stayed in Geneva for a fortnight until he heard that August had made a full recovery. All this serves to secure Eckermann against any reproaches for not coming straight back to Weimar or not returning to August. There follows a long account of his own situation, of which only scraps are included in the *Conversations*. Eckermann reiterates his desire to see the *Conversations* published. He then describes the drawbacks of his position in Weimar:

> My life in Weimar hitherto has of course been very precarious and anxious, since in any quarter [of the year] I never knew what I would be living on in the next, and giving lessons to young Englishmen, which I was obliged to do, was, with a few exceptions, extremely disagreeable, since such young gentlemen raised in the lap of luxury always feel how much better their situation is than their teacher's, and this feeling is clear, even unintentionally, and hurtful, even if no harm is meant. Moreover, in order to coexist with a pupil and have some influence on him, I had to adapt myself to his individuality, and, in doing so, to give up my own.

INTRODUCTION BY RITCHIE ROBERTSON   xliii

That often happens in life and does no damage. But when it continues for several hours a day over many years, it has a very damaging influence on the mind, character and aims of an adaptable and patient person, especially if that person is still resolved, when time at last allows, to act in a way that springs from his innermost nature. I put up with it in Weimar because there was no help for it, in view of higher purposes, and because I wanted to learn a language which I had no other way of acquiring. But to return to such destructive and degrading circumstances is something I would never do, and it would still be desirable for me to obtain in some other way a life free from worries.[6]

Thanks to Soret, Eckermann has been offered a post in charge of a library and reading room in Weimar, but he has no intention of accepting it. Instead, he would prefer to move to Berlin, a great capital city with its own Academy (the Prussian Academy of Sciences) and a busy intellectual life. But, he concludes, 'I can do nothing without you, without your blessing and approval.'

From this last sentence, one can see that it was really impossible for Eckermann to break away from Goethe. He returned to Weimar, where he found that, thanks to the influence of the ever-helpful Soret, he could have a regular salary for tutoring the Crown Prince, Karl Alexander. He accepted the offer and was at last able to marry, though marriage required sacrifices. Since 1828 he had had a romantic friendship with a young actress, Auguste Kladzig, though he had controlled himself enough to stop short of a full-blown love affair. He was not only an enthusiastic birdwatcher, but had a large collection of birds which were allowed to fly about freely in his house. A bachelor could indulge such passions, a married man could not: the birds had to go. His marriage anyway was short. After being engaged since 1819, Eckermann and Johanna were married in November 1831; Johanna died in spring 1834 giving birth to a boy, Karl (who survived, and proved a good son to his father).

The *Conversations* are Eckermann's lasting claim to fame and a major addition to German literature. Parts One and Two appeared with the publisher Brockhaus in 1836. Eckermann was disappointed by the sales and took the publisher to court, claiming that he had been denied the proceeds due to him, but lost his case. Part Three accordingly appeared with another publisher, Heinrichshofen, in 1848. This was unfortunate timing: in the Year of Revolutions, people had little attention to spare for books. Nevertheless, the *Conversations* have become a classic.

But a classic in which genre? Eckermann insisted that he was not a mere passive recorder of Goethe's sayings, but an artist in his own right. He explained his methods most fully in a letter of 5 March 1844 to the journalist and dramatist Heinrich Laube:

Many people have thought that my production is merely the work of a good memory, mechanically reflecting the impressions it receives. I can certainly boast of possessing this gift to my full satisfaction; but if I possessed it to the degree that people credit me with, and if this faculty alone had operated in the composition of my book, the result would have been something without any lofty effect, similar to the commonplace reality of photographs.

Instead, Eckermann practised selection:

I therefore took care not to write down my impressions as soon as I received them; rather, I waited for days and weeks so that the trivial should vanish and only the significant should remain. Indeed, the better parts were written down only after a year or so, and some passages even later. I wrote up the conversation of 11 March 1828 only in the year 1842, after fourteen years. My recollections of it, as you can imagine, were only vague. I went to my diary, but found only this note: 'Tuesday, 11 March, at Goethe's in the evening, interesting conversation, productivity, genius, Napoleon, Prussia.' That certainly wasn't much, and I felt almost like a sculptor who is presented only with a piece of the left hand and the right calf of an ancient statue, and is supposed to restore the entire statue from them. But the subject was still floating dimly before my mind, and after long contemplation the main parts became clear and arranged themselves in the proper order,

INTRODUCTION BY RITCHIE ROBERTSON xlv

according to the laws of intellectual crystallization. Of course it wasn't easy, and this one conversation took me four whole weeks.[7]

We should not, therefore, regard the *Conversations* as a strictly factual report, but rather as an imaginative recreation of Eckermann's meetings with Goethe. Continuing Eckermann's pictorial imagery, they are not like a photograph, but more like a painting by Joshua Reynolds or Goethe's admired contemporary Angelika Kauffmann. On the most trivial level, Eckermann sometimes gets dates wrong. Thus 10 November 1823 was not a Wednesday, as Eckermann says, but a Monday.[8] Eckermann's account of the composition of *Faust II* sometimes differs from other sources, notably Goethe's own diaries, and is internally inconsistent: thus Goethe is said to begin work on Act IV both on 30 November 1830 and on 11 February 1831.[9] Goethe cannot have mentioned his poem 'Vermächtnis' on 6 May 1827, since he wrote it in 1829 (see 12 February 1829).

Part Three of the *Conversations* raises particular doubts about authenticity. To supplement the unused material in his notes, Eckermann was allowed by Soret to use extensive records of meetings with Goethe that Soret himself had made. Eckermann marks the material obtained from Soret with an asterisk. Hence many statements that Goethe actually made to Soret now appear to have been made to Eckermann: for example, the well-known misunderstanding when Goethe is excited about events in France and turns out to be referring not to the July Revolution but to a scientific dispute (2 August 1830) actually occurred with Soret.[10] Eckermann doubtless felt that, since Goethe said this, it hardly mattered to whom he said it. Soret, a native speaker of French whose German was imperfect, made his notes in French and may not always have understood German conversation; so the Soret material Eckermann uses has been translated twice, first by Soret into French, and then by Eckermann back into German. Not all the Soret material is identified with an asterisk: for example, the conversation about French literature on 14 March 1830 comes largely from Soret, and deals in any case with a subject more congenial to Soret than to Eckermann.[11]

xlvi INTRODUCTION BY RITCHIE ROBERTSON

In Part Three Eckermann himself becomes more prominent. He gives long accounts of his dreams (12 March 1828; 21 December 1828). He also includes some famous set-pieces which seem to have been composed with unusual freedom and in which Eckermann, instead of deferring to Goethe, actually instructs him. There is the conversation about archery (1 May 1825), in which Eckermann explains the construction of an arrow and the two then go out shooting. Although Eckermann has been suspected of inventing this, it is confirmed by a letter in which he tells his fiancée how he and Goethe shot arrows in Goethe's garden.[12] Another set-piece, a favourite among readers, is the long conversation of 26 September 1827 in which the bird-watcher Eckermann for once turns out to know more about a subject than Goethe does, and delivers a lecture on ornithology. It is impossible to say how far this is based on a real event and how far Eckermann has allowed his enthusiasm to run away with him.

Since Eckermann did not aim at photographic accuracy, we must accept a large measure of artistic stylization. From other sources, especially the recollections by Chancellor von Müller, we know that Goethe did not always speak in the measured and dignified manner attributed to him here. Like most people, he was apt to say 'hm, hm' when searching for a word; his conversation included scraps of Italian and Latin, which Eckermann leaves out; and he could be colloquial, even vulgar. Talking to Müller in 1830 about what he considered the current crisis of religion, Goethe reportedly said: 'Since people have come to understand how much rubbish has been imposed on them, and since they started believing that the apostles and saints were no better fellows than lads like Klopstock, Lessing and other poor sods [*Hundsfötter*] like ourselves, their heads must be in an amazing muddle.'[13] Eckermann's Goethe says nothing like this. Nor was Goethe in the habit of delivering long monologues, such as Eckermann often puts into his mouth, clearly in order to combine a number of remembered remarks on the same subject.

Moreover, the Goethe of the *Conversations* is almost always serene. We only twice see him angry, once when Eckermann

INTRODUCTION BY RITCHIE ROBERTSON   xlvii

wants to write for the *European Review*, and again when Eckermann rashly criticizes the theory of colour (19 February 1829). When Eckermann borrows from Soret the account of Goethe receiving portraits of himself and of a beautiful actress (6 June 1828), he omits what followed. Müller, wishing to see both portraits, went into the next room, where that of Goethe was hanging, but did not come back. Goethe went in search of him and found that Müller had gone into a further room to see the portrait of the actress. Thereupon Goethe flew into a furious rage, shouting at Müller: 'Come out of there! One only has to leave you alone for a minute, and your curiosity leads you into an indiscretion!' After a further tirade, he went out, slamming the door, and left Müller and Soret dumbfounded. However, according to Soret, Goethe often treated Müller in this way, and the next day they would be good friends again.[14]

Eckermann had his own agenda. Naturally he wanted to express his own hero-worship. 'I had a hero to deal with', he told Laube in 1844.[15] He also wanted to defend Goethe against his many detractors. A writer's reputation often declines after his death, and this happened to Goethe too. The posthumous publication of *Faust II*, a great but perplexing work which few early readers could make any sense of, reinforced his reputation for wilful obscurity. For much of the nineteenth century Goethe was widely considered inferior to Schiller. Schiller's plays and poems were not only accessible but full of quotable sentiments; he had a blameless domestic life; and most of his plays were rousing defences of political liberty. By contrast, Goethe, even during his lifetime, was denounced as a 'Fürstenknecht' or servile vassal to a prince. The radical writers of the Young German movement especially pressed this charge. Heinrich Heine, who sympathized with the movement from a distance, observed in 1828, in a review of a book hostile to Goethe: 'The principle of the age of Goethe, the idea of art, is fading, a new age with a new principle is arising, and strange! as Menzel's book shows, it is beginning with an insurrection against Goethe.'[16] To the Young Germans, demanding the politicization of art, both Goethe's situation in Weimar, and the classical ideal of art that he upheld, were deeply reprehensible. The radical journalist

Ludwig Börne, an exile in Paris, went so far as to declare: 'Since I began to feel, I have hated Goethe; since I began to think, I have known why.'[17]

In response to such utterances, Eckermann presents Goethe's political views in a favourable and moderate light. Goethe may well have said everything that Eckermann attributes to him, yet the statement about freedom – 'If a man has just enough freedom to live a healthy life and carry on his trade, then he has sufficient – and that much anyone can easily have' (18 January 1827) – strongly resembles the statement by the hero of *Egmont*: 'A good citizen earning his living by honest work will always enjoy all the liberty he needs.'[18] It is hard to tell whether this resemblance shows the continuity of Goethe's thinking, or Eckermann's immersion in Goethe's works. Eckermann pointedly makes Goethe deplore the contamination of literature by 'party hatred' (2 May 1831). In the last conversation of the 1836 edition, Goethe again deplores the association between politics and poetry (March 1832); by placing these remarks at the end, Eckermann makes them appear like a kind of testament.

It would be too easy at this point to charge Eckermann with suppressing the real Goethe and creating the well-known image of Goethe the wise and serene Olympian. To return to Eckermann's pictorial image, however, this is not a photograph but a portrait, and if one is having one's portrait painted for posterity one may well pose in one's best clothes. The *Conversations* may be stylized and one-sided, and very different from the rounded presentation of Samuel Johnson which James Boswell undertook to provide in another classic work of biography (which Eckermann did not know).[19] But they are not a fabrication – in contrast, for example, to Gustav Janouch's *Conversations with Kafka*, which probably contain a few remarks Kafka made but are for the most part a shameless invention.[20] Some remarks attributed to Goethe can be checked against other sources. For example, his famous distinction between 'wholesome' Classicism and 'sickly' Romanticism corresponds to an aphorism found later among his papers, 'Classicism is health, Romanticism is sickness.'[21] Very little can be taken as an accurate record of what Goethe *did* say, but almost everything is what he *could*

INTRODUCTION BY RITCHIE ROBERTSON   xlix

have said and probably did say, albeit not quite in these words. Eckermann's stylization did not prevent the *Conversations*, on publication, from being praised as a truthful portrait by the people who had known Goethe best, including his friends Müller and Soret and his daughter-in-law Ottilie.

One can easily underestimate the art with which Eckermann has posed and portrayed his sitter. For example, Goethe's long speech about his career as theatre director (22 March 1825) is unlikely to have been made in that manner, or on that day, since Goethe spent the day working and saw no visitors except Müller and Riemer. More likely Eckermann has knitted together a number of observations about the theatre made by Goethe at different times and placed them at a thematically suitable point, just after the fire that destroyed the Weimar Court Theatre. Part II begins with a momentous event, the announcement of the Grand Duke's death, which occurred on 14 June 1828. Eckermann heightens the drama by telling how the news is initially kept from Goethe, who is puzzled by his guests' hasty departure, intended to leave young August alone to break the news to his father. On a smaller scale, Eckermann animates the conversations with little stage directions, e.g. 'We carried on sitting at the table, finishing our meal with several glasses of old Rhine wine to go with the good biscuits', and 'There was a brief lull in the conversation' (both 6 April 1829); 'Goethe rose to his feet and paced up and down the room, while I remained seated at the table [. . .] He paused for a moment at the stove' (29 January 1826); when he is annoyed, Goethe shows it by standing up and going over to the window (19 February 1829).

The setting for the conversations is usually Goethe's house in Weimar, a mansion overlooking the square called the Frauenplan. Anyone who has visited the house, now maintained as a museum by the Klassik Stiftung Weimar, will feel a thrill of recognition when Eckermann mentions the word 'SALVE' ('Welcome') inscribed on the threshold of Goethe's living quarters (10 June 1823).[22] The house was probably less tranquil than Eckermann's account suggests. The top floor, accessible by a spiral staircase, was occupied by Goethe's son August, his wife Ottilie (née von Pogwisch), their sons Walter (born 1818)

INTRODUCTION BY RITCHIE ROBERTSON

and Wolfgang (born 1820), and later their daughter Alma (born 1827). Another visitor, whose name is not recorded, recounts how he arrived unannounced and went into the courtyard, where he found the little boys running about and making a tremendous racket; whereupon Goethe, with blazing eyes, roared from an upper window: 'Will you brats shut up!', then slammed the window down.[23] Such incidents find no place in Eckermann's charming but idealized portrayal of family life, any more than the tensions between Ottilie and her scapegrace husband.

Occasionally Eckermann accompanies Goethe on excursions into the countryside, usually around Tiefurt, a park and country house just outside Weimar. Goethe goes a little further afield to Dornburg, some twenty miles away, which had three ducal hunting lodges; he spends two months there in the summer of 1828 to get over his grief at the death of the Grand Duke (see 15 June 1828). Goethe usually takes a summer holiday at one of the spas in Bohemia (now in the Czech Republic), either Karlsbad (Karlovy Vary) or Marienbad (Mariánské Lázně). It was in the latter resort that Goethe got to know Ulrike von Levetzow, fifty-five years his junior, and became so smitten with her that in 1823 he unsuccessfully proposed marriage; his grief at being rejected found expression in the great poem known as the 'Marienbader Elegie' ('Marienbad Elegy'; see 27 October 1823).

The ducal family of Weimar are often mentioned, but seldom appear. Karl August (1757–1828) succeeded to the Dukedom in 1758, but his mother the Duchess Anna Amalia (1739–1807) ruled as Regent till he came of age in 1775. At the Congress of Vienna in 1815, which settled the shape of post-Napoleonic Europe, his title was raised to that of Grand Duke as a reward for his steadfast resistance to the French. In 1775 he married Princess Luise of Hesse-Darmstadt (1757–1830), who after his death is referred to as the Dowager Grand Duchess; the marriage was based on dynastic politics rather than mutual attraction and was rendered unhappy by Karl August's numerous affairs. Their eldest son and heir, Karl Friedrich (1783–1853), a great admirer of Goethe, married the Russian Princess Maria Pavlovna, sister of the Tsar, in 1804. It was their son, Karl Alexander (1818–1901), who had Soret and later Eckermann as his tutors.

INTRODUCTION BY RITCHIE ROBERTSON   li

Karl August, who had invited Goethe to Weimar back in 1775, was one of the most important people in his life. It has therefore been found surprising that after the end of a mostly amicable, though sometimes tense relationship lasting over half a century, Goethe firmly refused to write an obituary.[24] The long tribute to Karl August which Eckermann reports on 23 October 1828, preceded by quotations from a eulogy by Alexander von Humboldt, looks like an attempt by Eckermann to fill this gap. In it, he steers clear of a delicate subject – the political differences between Goethe and his Duke, which could hardly have been avoided in an obituary. Goethe, an admirer of absolute rule by an enlightened prince, was not keen on the constitution which Karl August promulgated in 1816. Karl August had been prominent in the struggle against Napoleon, for whom Goethe retained an admiration. Goethe noted Napoleon's birthday in his diary.[25] In 1808 he had had an hour-long audience with Napoleon on 2 October, and another meeting four days later; Napoleon awarded him the Légion d'Honneur, which he proudly wore at every opportunity. On 11 March 1828 he described Napoleon to Eckermann as a superhuman figure: 'He lived life as a demigod who strode from battle to battle, and from victory to victory.' Since these were very unfashionable sentiments in post-Napoleonic Germany, there is every reason to think that Eckermann's report is substantially accurate, despite having been written down fourteen years later.

Among the many topics discussed in the *Conversations*, politics is far less conspicuous than literature. Thanks to Eckermann's encouragement, the last decade of Goethe's life was a very productive one; Eckermann made a particular contribution to the completion of *Dichtung und Wahrheit*. Accepting that his works would never have popular appeal (11 October 1828), Goethe indulged his taste for esoteric symbolism. An example is the short story, entitled simply *Novelle*, which occasioned Goethe's much-cited remark: 'what else is a novella if not an unheard-of event that has occurred?' (29 January 1827). Much attention is given to the revision of *Wilhelm Meisters Wanderjahre* (*Wilhelm Meister's Journeyman Years*), itself a sequel to the much earlier novel *Wilhelm Meisters Lehrjahre*

INTRODUCTION BY RITCHIE ROBERTSON

(*Wilhelm Meister's Apprenticeship*, 1795–6). The *Wanderjahre*, one of Goethe's most baffling works, found a hostile reception when first published in 1821, not least because at the same time a clergyman named Johann Pustkuchen brought out a hostile critique of Goethe in fictional form, purporting to be also a continuation of the *Lehrjahre*. The revised and expanded *Wanderjahre* appeared in 1829.

The most demanding preoccupation, and the greatest achievement, of these years was Part Two of *Faust*. *Faust I*, published in complete form in 1808, departed from the Faust tradition by centring on a love affair between the scholar Faust and a young woman called Margarete (Gretchen) which played no part in the sixteenth-century legend. The legendary Faust signs a pact with the Devil (as Goethe's does with Mephistopheles, a devil whose place in the infernal hierarchy is unclear), performs magical tricks at the Emperor's court, summons up and marries Helen of Troy, supposedly the most beautiful woman who ever lived, and is finally carried off to hell. Goethe's Faust goes to the Emperor's court (where Mephisto, to save the Empire from bankruptcy, invents paper money, thereby founding the modern credit-based economy) and summons up the semblance of Helen. To recover the real Helen, however, he magically returns to ancient Greece; the second Act of *Faust II* is the 'Classical Walpurgis Night', corresponding to the German Walpurgis Night (a festival of witches, rooted in folk belief) that forms a scene of Part One. Here Mephisto, to his discomfort, encounters all the strange monsters that figure in ancient Greek legend. In Act III, the marriage between Helen and Faust symbolizes the union of classical and modern art, and their son Euphorion, who tries to fly too high and plunges to earth, represents Byron, whom Goethe hugely admired (24 February 1825). In old age, Faust resolves to found a free society on land reclaimed from the sea; this recalls Goethe's interest in great engineering projects, like the canals which might be cut in the isthmus of Panama, in that of Suez, and between the Rhine and the Danube (21 February 1827). Finally, Goethe's Faust is not damned but translated to heaven amid entrancing and dubiously Christian symbolism, to which Goethe gives Eckermann important clues (6 June 1831).

We learn much also about Goethe's extensive and eclectic reading. He had a sound classical education and was familiar with Italian, French, and (to a somewhat lesser extent) English. He expresses enthusiasm for Shakespeare, Calderón, Molière and the ancient Greek dramatists. He reads Scott and Byron avidly, admiring especially Byron's plays (not much read nowadays), and praises (with reservations) Alessandro Manzoni's historical novel *I promessi sposi* (*The Betrothed*). He keeps up with modern literature, not only through reviews in *Le Globe*, the *Edinburgh Review* and elsewhere, but by voracious reading: the French Romantic poets, Victor Hugo's *Notre-Dame de Paris*, Stendhal's *Le Rouge et le noir* and early works by Balzac. He must have read very fast. He even reports on his reading of a Chinese novel (31 January 1827); there has been much dispute about which novel this was, but the strongest candidate appears to be a seventeenth-century verse romance whose title literally means *The Flowery Scroll*, but which had appeared in English in 1824 as *Chinese Courtship*.[26] This report leads on to Goethe's famous declaration that it is now time to turn from national literatures to world literature, appreciating the best that every literature has to offer. From this statement – which we have to hope that Eckermann recorded accurately – stems the enormous present-day interest in comparative literature and in the even more ambitious 'world literature'.[27]

Many conversations reflect Goethe's interest in the study of the natural world, to which he devoted much of his time from his early thirties onwards. Placed in charge of the project to reopen the silver mine at Ilmenau, and thereby, it was hoped, repair the Duchy's shaky economy, Goethe learned much about geology and mineralogy. He moved on to anatomy and the laws underlying the physical structure of animals and plants. He inquired into optics, and became convinced that Newton had misled the world with a false theory of light and colour. He attached immense value to the actual experience of nature, and was sceptical about mathematical models of the natural world. He disliked mechanical aids to observation such as the telescope and the microscope (though he did occasionally use both); this aversion is no doubt linked with his curious antipathy to spectacles and their wearers (5 April 1830).[28] Despite his commitment to empirical study and his dislike of abstraction, he felt that empiricism in itself could lead only to a mass of isolated and incoherent observations. Accordingly, he found in nature a number of 'primary phenomena' (*Urphänomene*) which could not be analysed any further. Granite, supposedly the oldest and most fundamental form of rock, was one; light was another; beauty (as he told Eckermann on 18 April 1827) was a third. These could not be analysed, but could be contemplated, in a form of intelligent absorption that Goethe called *Anschauung*.[29]

If light was a primary phenomenon, then Newton's attempt to analyse light into a mixture of rays, each made up of particles with different weights, was bound to antagonize Goethe. He would not accept Newton's explanation that rays passing through a prism bend at different angles, according to the weight of their component particles, and that these differences in refraction produce different colours. Having tried unsuccessfully to reproduce Newton's experiment with the prism, Goethe developed an alternative theory in which colours result from the intensification or combination of different degrees of light and its polar opposite, darkness. This illustrates how, in Goethe's view, empirical study needed to be interpreted by reference to underlying principles, of which polarity and intensification (*Steigerung*) were those he most often appealed to. Having devoted 'half a lifetime's work' to his colour theory (1 February 1827), Goethe is clearly obsessed with it. He suggests that he and Eckermann should read through Goethe's whole treatise on colours, and that Eckermann should write a synopsis of it (19 February 1829). When Eckermann ventures a mild criticism, Goethe is mightily offended, and draws a comparison with Christianity, in which 'faithful disciples' turn into 'heretics'. This comparison confirms that Goethe regarded his theory with quasi-religious devotion.[30]

Although Goethe was almost completely isolated in his opposition to Newton, he had more support in another scientific controversy, concerning the origins of the earth. There were two schools of thought, the Neptunist and the Vulcanist (or Plutonian). The Neptunian theory, put forward by the famous

INTRODUCTION BY RITCHIE ROBERTSON

lv

geologist Abraham Gottlob Werner, held that the earth had been formed by the gradual retreat of the primordial ocean; the Vulcanists, among them Goethe's friend Alexander von Humboldt, held that the earth's rugged surface was due to volcanic upheavals impelled by subterranean fires. Goethe, who hated revolution and preferred gradual change, not only in politics (see 27 April 1825) but everywhere else, detested this notion, and in Act IV of *Faust II* puts it into the mouth of the devil Mephisto. So when Georges Cuvier, who explained the existence of fossils by arguing that the earth's history consisted of a series of cataclysms that destroyed life-forms, was publicly opposed by the naturalist Étienne Geoffroy de Saint-Hilaire, Goethe was so excited at the latter's support for his pet theory that he completely ignored the simultaneous revolution in France and the expulsion of the French royal family. Here again Goethe was backing the wrong horse, but it should be remembered that for most of his lifetime even the boldest thinkers thought the earth could be no more than 100,000 years old at the very most, so that the primeval cataclysms had to be imagined not as gradual processes but as sudden and devastating outbursts.

The study of nature, for Goethe, was not in conflict with religion. He often affirmed his belief in a God who was immanent in nature and responsible for its dynamic energy and constant self-renewal (29 May 1831). This was not the God of the Churches nor of Christian theology. Goethe believed in personal immortality, but as early as 1773 he could see no point in imagining what a future existence might be like or in trying to prove it philosophically.[31] He later adopted the Aristotelian conception of the entelechy or dynamic core of a being which seeks to realize its potential (1 September 1829); this seems to be presupposed in the ascent of Faust's 'immortal part' to heaven at the end of *Faust II*.

These ideas differ considerably from those expressed in the long speech about religion which Eckermann makes Goethe deliver at the end of Part Three. This is clearly meant to be his religious testament, corresponding to the political testament which ends Part Two. According to this speech, religion is divinely revealed, and as only a few people can endure the light of revelation, the Church performs a valuable service in mediating between God and the laity. The Bible is for the most part 'truly excellent'. Even if a few parts of the Gospels are not factually authentic, they all genuinely reflect 'a glory that emanated from the person of Christ'. The Catholic Church is often corrupt, but Luther's Reformation has restored pure Christianity, and Protestantism is now the leading force for enlightenment. Yet Goethe, many years earlier, had declared himself 'a decided non-Christian';[32] he repeatedly satirized institutional Christianity, while advocating toleration and affirming a conception of God as immanent in the world, in which he was strengthened by reading Spinoza. On 22 March 1831 he wrote to his friend Sulpiz Boisserée that he felt religious sentiment, but 'from the creation of the world onwards, have never found a confession to which I could have fully committed myself'.[33] One can imagine him uttering a few of the sentences that Eckermann credits him with, but the whole speech could never have come from his lips. It is, however, well designed to round off the *Conversations* in an elevated tone and to reassure mid-century readers in Protestant Germany who were uneasy about Goethe's piety.

Despite Eckermann's efforts to present an acceptable image of Goethe, the *Conversations* were slow to attain classic status. Yet, as interest in Goethe revived, so did the reputation of his book. Friedrich Nietzsche, a discriminating judge, called it in 1880 'the best German book that there is'.[34] This is a tribute to the artistry of Eckermann's writing as well as to the intrinsic interest of his subject matter. On both counts – and so long as we are content to have a portrait rather than a photograph – the *Conversations* are of lasting value as an addition to the Goethe canon.

CONVERSATIONS
WITH GOETHE

AUTHOR'S PREFACE

This collection of conversations with Goethe is largely the result of my own natural inclination to take possession of any experience that strikes me as valuable or interesting by recording it in writing.

Furthermore, I always had so much to learn, both when I first met with that extraordinary man, and also later, when I had been with him for many years; and I liked to recall what he had said and to note it down, so that I would have it there for the rest of my life.

But when I reflect on the rich abundance of his observations, which gave me so much pleasure for nine whole years, and then see how little I managed to get down on paper, I feel like a child who tries to catch the refreshing spring rain in his cupped hands, only to find that most of it runs through his fingers.

But books have their own destinies, as the saying goes, and since this applies as much to their genesis as it does to their subsequent entry into the big wide world, it could be said of the present book, too. Whole months often went by when the stars were not favourable, and ill health, business affairs and the mundane demands of daily life prevented me from writing a single line. Then the stars would be aligned in my favour, and good health, leisure and the desire to write conspired to carry me a good step further forward. Then again, when you spend a lot of time with someone, familiarity can breed a kind of indifference – and who among us always values the present moment as it deserves?

I mention this mainly to explain and excuse the many significant gaps, which the reader will notice if he pays close attention to the dates of the entries. Many good things have been lost in these gaps, and in particular, many kind remarks that Goethe made about his extensive circle of friends, and about the works of this or that living German author, while similar comments made at other times have been duly noted. But as I say, books have their own destinies, even as they are being written.

I should also say that I owe my heartfelt thanks to a higher providence for what I have succeeded in making my own in these volumes, and which must surely be, in a manner of speaking, the crowning glory of my life; and I am reasonably certain, indeed, that the world will thank me for this publication.

I believe that these conversations not only offer many insights and invaluable lessons about life, art and science, but that these sketches drawn directly from life will also be especially helpful in rounding out the image of Goethe that people may already have formed from his many different works.

At the same time, I am not for a moment claiming that these sketches lay bare Goethe's soul in its entirety. One could liken this extraordinary mind, and this extraordinary human being, to a multifaceted diamond, which reflects a different colour in every direction. And as he was not the same Goethe in different situations and with different people, all I can say in my own case, and in all modesty, is that this is *my* Goethe.

And this applies not just to the way in which he presented himself to me, but also, and more especially, to my own ability to understand and represent him. There is a kind of two-way reflection that takes place in these situations, and as the image passes through another individual it is very seldom the case that nothing of the original gets lost, and nothing of that individual gets added. The physical representations of Goethe by Rauch, Dawe, Stieler and David are all very lifelike; and yet, to a greater or lesser extent, they all bear the stamp of the personality that created them. And if this is true for physical objects, how much more so for the fleeting, intangible things of the mind? Be that as it may in my own case, all those who are qualified to judge of these matters, by virtue of their intellectual prowess or their personal acquaintance with Goethe, will, I

AUTHOR'S PREFACE

hope, recognize that I have tried to portray him as accurately as possible.

Following the above comments, which relate largely to the way in which I approached my subject, it now remains for me to say a little about the actual contents of the book.

What people call the *truth*, even with respect to a single object, is not something small, narrow, or restricted; and while it may be simple, it is at the same time something very broad in its compass, which, like the myriad manifestations of a profound and far-reaching law of nature, is not easy to put into words. It defies definition, and no amount of talk or argument can do more than offer an approximation to the truth.

Just to cite one example of what I mean: Goethe's occasional remarks on poetry often appear one-sided, not to say flatly contradictory. Sometimes he places all the emphasis on the material, which comes from the outside world, at other times on the poet's own inner life; sometimes the secret of success is said to lie in the subject matter, at other times in the poet's treatment of it; sometimes it all comes down to perfection of form, and at other times to the creative vision that pays no heed to form.

But all of these comments and contradictions represent different aspects of the truth, and their cumulative effect is to tell us what the truth itself is like and bring us closer to it. In the present publication I have therefore taken good care, in these and similar instances, not to edit out apparent contradictions of this sort, as and when they have been elicited at random by events over the years. I rely on the discernment and detachment of the cultivated reader, who will not be misled by a single isolated example, but will instead keep the bigger picture in view and see things in their broader context.

Similarly, the reader may come across much that at first sight appears insignificant. But if he discovers, on closer inspection, that such insignificant occasions often lead on to something of importance, or pave the way for something else that happens later, or simply serve to supply some small additional detail of characterization, then they may perhaps be, if not vindicated, then at least excused as a kind of necessity.

And so, as this long-nurtured book enters the public domain, I bid it a fond farewell, with the fervent wish that it might find favour and be a force for good in the world.

Johann Peter Eckermann
Weimar, 31 October 1835

PART ONE

INTRODUCTION

The author gives an account of himself and his early life, and describes how he came to know Goethe.

I was born in the early 1790s in Winsen an der Luhe, a little town between Lüneburg and Hamburg, on the border of the marshland and heath. Our little house was not much more than a shack, with only one room that could be heated, and no staircase; you climbed straight up to the hayloft on a ladder that stood next to the front door.

As the youngest child of a second marriage, I really only knew my parents when they were quite elderly, and I was rather like an only child, growing up just with them. There were two sons from my father's first marriage, one of whom was a sailor; after various voyages, he was imprisoned in distant foreign parts and has not been heard of since. The other son, after several spells in Greenland hunting whales and seals, had returned to Hamburg, where he lived in modest circumstances. I had two older sisters from my father's second marriage, both of whom had already left home by the time I was twelve and were working in service in our own town and in Hamburg.

The principal means of support for our little family was a cow, which not only supplied us with milk for our daily needs, but also bore us a calf each year, which we could fatten up, while at certain times there was a surplus of milk that we could sell on for a few pennies. We also owned an acre of land, which supplied us with vegetables all year round. But we still had to buy corn for bread-making and flour for the kitchen.

My mother was a very skilled spinner of wool, and the local women also liked to come to her for the caps that she cut and sewed; so she was able to earn a little income from both these activities.

My father worked as an itinerant trader in small goods, the nature of which varied with the seasons; and he was frequently away from home, travelling around the local district on foot. In the summer, he could be seen going from village to village on the heath, with a light wooden box on his back, hawking ribbons, thread and silk. At the same time he was buying woollen stockings and *Beiderwand* (a double-woven cloth made from the brown wool of the moorland sheep and linen yarn), which he then sold in the *Vierlande* area on the other bank of the Elbe, where he also went to peddle his wares. In the winter, he traded in unfinished quill pens and unbleached linen, which he bought up in the villages of the marshland and heath and shipped to Hamburg on the next available boat. But his combined earnings must have been very small, because we always lived in some poverty.

Turning now to my own childhood activities, these also varied according to the seasons. At the start of spring, when the waters of the Elbe had receded after the usual flooding, I went out every day to gather the rushes that had been washed up on to the dykes and other high ground, piling them up at home as good bedding material for our cow. When the first green shoots appeared on the broad pastures, I would spend long days looking after the cows with other boys. During the summer I was busy tilling our own plot of land, and all year round I had to fetch dry wood from the woodland, a mile or so away, to feed the stove. At harvest time I was to be found in the fields for weeks on end, collecting the gleanings, and later on, when the autumn winds shook the trees, I gathered acorns and sold them by the bucket to wealthier locals to feed their geese. But as soon as I was old enough, I began to accompany my father on his travels from village to village and helped to carry one of the bales. This time is one of my happiest childhood memories.

Living under such conditions, and employed in such ways, while also attending school for periods of time and learning to read and write after a fashion, I reached the age of fourteen; and it has to be said that it was a big step, and an unlikely one, to go from this to a relationship of intimacy with Goethe. At

INTRODUCTION

the time, I didn't know that such things as poetry and the fine arts existed, so I was happily spared even a vague sense of longing and yearning for such things.

They say that animals learn through their organs, and it may be said of humans that they often learn about their own higher potential through something that they do quite by chance. Such a thing happened to me, and though it was of no significance in itself, it altered the whole course of my life, and is therefore indelibly imprinted on my memory.

One evening, I was sitting at the table with my parents by the light of a lamp. My father had just got back from Hamburg, and was telling us how his business there had gone. As he liked to smoke, he had come home with a pack of tobacco, which was lying on the table in front of me, with a picture of a horse as its emblem. I thought the horse was very well drawn, and as I had pen and ink and a sheet of paper to hand, I felt an irresistible urge to copy it. My father carried on talking about Hamburg while I, unnoticed by my parents, became completely engrossed in drawing the horse. When I had finished, I thought my copy looked exactly like the original, and I felt a delight I had not previously experienced. I showed my parents what I had done, and they were full of praise and admiration. I was awake half the night, too happy and excited to sleep; I kept on thinking about my drawing of the horse and couldn't wait for morning to come, so that I could look at it again and enjoy it all over again.

From that moment onwards, the urge to draw and copy things, once awakened, never left me. Since there was nobody else in our town who could help me with such matters, I was very glad when our neighbour, a potter, lent me some pattern books of his, which he used to copy from when painting his plates and dishes.

I copied these shapes with great care in pen and ink, and in due course I had two books of drawings, which were soon passed from hand to hand and eventually reached the chief administrator of our town, Councillor Meyer. He sent for me, gave me a present, and praised me in the most kindly way. He asked me if I wanted to become a painter; if so, then when I was confirmed, he would send me to a skilled master in

Hamburg. I said I would like that very much, and would talk it over with my parents.

But my parents, both coming from the peasant class and living in a community where virtually everyone worked in arable and livestock farming, thought that a painter was someone who painted doors and houses. They therefore advised me earnestly against it, pointing out that it was not only a very dirty trade, but also a very dangerous one, where one could break one's legs or neck, which happened a lot, especially in Hamburg, where the houses were seven storeys high. As I, too, had not realized that the term 'painter' was meant in the artistic sense, I lost my enthusiasm for this calling, and dismissed the good Councillor's offer from my mind.

But meanwhile I had attracted the attention of persons of importance, who took an interest in me and tried to help me on in various ways. I was allowed to take private lessons with the few children of upper-class families; I learned French, and some Latin and music; I was given better clothing, and the worthy church superintendent, Parisius, deigned to give me a seat at his own table.

From now on I loved going to school. I did my best to make my favourable situation last for as long as possible, and my parents happily consented to delay my confirmation until I was sixteen.

The question now arose as to what was to become of me. If I had had my way, I would have been sent to the grammar school to pursue academic studies; but this was out of the question. Not only could we not afford it, but the harsh reality of my circumstances required me to get myself quickly into a situation where I could not only provide for myself, but also help out my ageing and impoverished parents.

Such a situation presented itself immediately after my confirmation, when a local judicial officer offered to take me on as a clerk and general factotum – an offer I accepted with alacrity. During the last year and a half of my regular school attendance, I had not only learned to write neatly and clearly, but had also had a lot of practice in essay composition; so I had good reason to consider myself very well qualified for such a position. This

INTRODUCTION 13

employment, in the course of which I dealt with minor matters of law office business, and quite often found myself having to draft both the petition and the judgement in the proper legal form, lasted for two years, until 1810, when the Hanoverian administrative district of Winsen an der Luhe was dissolved and incorporated into the French Empire as part of the *département* of the Lower Elbe.[1]

I was then given a job in the head office of direct taxation in Lüneburg, and when this, too, was closed down the following year I was transferred to the office of the subprefecture in Uelzen. I worked here almost up until the end of 1812, when the prefect, Herr von Düring, promoted me to the position of town hall secretary in Bevensen. I held this post until the spring of 1813, when the approaching Cossacks gave us hope that we might soon be liberated from the French yoke.

I left my job, and returned home with no other thought in mind than to enrol as soon as possible in one of the patriotic militia units that were secretly being set up in various places. This I now proceeded to do: in the late summer, I joined the Kielmannsegg Rifle Corps as a volunteer, with rifle and holster, and served in the company commanded by Captain Knop during the winter campaign of 1813/14, fighting Marshal Davoust through Mecklenburg, Holstein and before the gates of Hamburg. We then crossed the Rhine and marched against General Maison, manoeuvring back and forth across the fertile plains of Flanders and Brabant throughout the summer.

Here I saw the great paintings by the Dutch school, and a new world opened up for me; I spent whole days in the churches and museums. These were really the first paintings I had seen in my life. I now understood what it meant to be a painter; I saw all the hard work of the pupils crowned with success, and I could have wept to think I had been denied the chance to pursue a similar path. So I came to a decision there and then; I made the acquaintance of a young artist in Tournay, got hold of some black crayon and the largest sheet of drawing paper I could find, and sat down straightaway in front of a picture to make a copy of it. What I lacked in practice and instruction I made up for in enthusiasm, and successfully reproduced the outlines of the figures. I had started shading in the whole design, working in from the left side, when my happy labours were interrupted by the arrival of marching orders. I quickly marked up the unfinished portions of the picture, using a system of single letters to indicate the required gradations of light and shade, in the hope that this would enable me to complete it later, when I had some leisure. I rolled up my picture and put it in a cylindrical case, which, slung over my back with my rifle, I carried with me on the long march from Tournay to Hameln.

Here the Rifle Corps was disbanded in the autumn of 1814. I returned home; my father was dead, my mother was still alive and living with my older sister, who had married in the meantime and taken over the parental home. I immediately took up my drawing again, and began by finishing the picture I had brought with me from Brabant. In the absence of any other suitable models, I then set about copying some small engravings by Ramberg, drawing them to larger scale in black crayon. But I very soon noticed my lack of knowledge and technique. I had very little idea about human or animal anatomy; I knew just as little about how to draw different kinds of trees and backgrounds; and so it was a huge effort, working in my own way, to produce something that looked vaguely like the original.

I very quickly realized, therefore, that if I wanted to become an artist I had to go about it in a rather different way, and that trying to teach myself by trial and error was a complete waste of time. So I planned to seek out an experienced master and start all over again from the beginning.

The master I had in mind was none other than Ramberg, in Hanover. I thought it would be easy enough to find accommodation in this city, because a dear friend from my youth was already living there in comfortable circumstances. I felt sure that I could rely on his friendship and hospitality – he was always inviting me to come and stay.

So without further ado I tied up my bundle, and in the middle of the winter of 1815 I set off alone, in the deep snow, to walk the distance of nearly forty leagues across the desolate heath. I reached Hanover safely a few days later.

I made it my business to call on Ramberg straightaway and

INTRODUCTION

tell him what I wanted to do. When I showed him some samples of my work, he seemed not to doubt my talent, but pointed out that it is hard to make a living from art, that mastering technique takes a very long time, and that the prospect of supporting oneself by art alone is a very remote one. That said, he was quite willing to give me whatever help he could; he promptly went through his drawings, picked out a few that showed parts of the human body, and gave them to me to copy.

So I lodged with my friend, and practised copying Ramberg originals. And I was making progress, because the drawings he gave me were more and more demanding. I went through the entire anatomy of the human body, and never tired of drawing hands and feet, which were particularly difficult. Several happy months went by in this fashion. Then May came round, and I began to feel unwell; June was approaching, and my hands were shaking so badly that I could no longer hold the pencil.

We consulted a reputable doctor. He found my condition alarming. He concluded that, as a result of the campaign, I was no longer able to perspire through my skin, that a consuming heat had attacked my internal organs, and that if I had carried on like this for another two weeks I would most certainly have died. He immediately prescribed hot baths and similar remedies to restore my natural skin function; welcome signs of recovery were quickly observed, but there was no question of continuing with my artistic studies.

The friend I was living with had been attending me and taking care of me with the utmost kindness, and there was no thought or hint on his part that I was a burden to him, or might become so as time went on. But the thought had occurred to me; I had secretly been worried on this score for some time, which had no doubt helped to bring on my dormant illness, and now that I could see my recovery would entail significant expense, I became acutely anxious.

At this time of great physical and mental stress, the prospect opened up of an appointment on a commission working for the war office, which was responsible for the clothing of the Hanoverian army. Not surprisingly, therefore, I yielded to the pressure of circumstances, abandoned my artistic career, applied for the job, and was delighted to get it.

My health was quickly restored, and I felt better, and lighter in spirit, than I had for a long time. I was now in a position to reimburse my friend in part for all his past generosity towards me. The need to learn the ropes at my new place of work kept my mind occupied. My superiors seemed to be very decent and high-minded men, and I very quickly found myself on an intimate footing with my colleagues, some of whom had served with me in the same corps during the campaign.

Only now, when my situation was secure, did I feel free to look around the city, where there was much of interest to see; and in my leisure hours I never tired of exploring and revisiting its delightful environs. I had become close friends with a promising young artist, a pupil of Ramberg's, and he was my constant companion on these outings. And since I was forced to discontinue my own artistic training because of my health and other circumstances, it was a great consolation to me that I could at least talk about our mutual mistress every day. I took an interest in his compositions, which he often showed to me in sketch form, and which we would then discuss. He introduced me to many instructive writings. I read Winckelmann, I read Mengs; but since I was not able to see the things these men were talking about, all I could take from their work were broad generalities, which weren't really much use to me.

Born and bred in that city, my friend was ahead of me on every count in cultural sophistication; he also had a good knowledge of literature, which I lacked entirely. At that time, Theodor Körner was hailed as the man of the moment; my friend brought me Körner's volume of poems entitled *Lyre and Sword*, which made a profound impression on me, as it had on others, and filled me with the same intense admiration.

People talk a lot about the *artistic* effect of a poem and consider it very important. But it seems to me that most of its effect comes from the *subject matter*, so that everything depends on that. Though I didn't realize it at the time, this is the lesson that the little *Lyre and Sword* anthology taught me. Because what made these poems resonate so powerfully with me was the fact that I, like Körner, nurtured hatred in my heart for those who had oppressed us for so many years; that I, like him, had fought in the War of Liberation, and, like him, had experienced every situation from forced marches and overnight bivouacs to picket duties and skirmishes, and had had similar thoughts and feelings about them.

Whenever I was exposed to something impressive, I was nearly always profoundly stimulated and inspired to produce something of my own; and so it was with these poems by Theodor Körner. I recalled that in my childhood and adolescent years I had written little poems myself on occasion, but had given them no further thought, because at the time I attached no great value to things that were so easily produced, and because a certain intellectual maturity is required to appreciate poetic talent. In Theodor Körner's case, it seemed to me that this gift was a thoroughly laudable and enviable thing, and I felt a powerful urge to try and see if I could emulate him somehow.

The return of our patriotic fighters from France gave me the opportunity I was looking for. As I still had vivid memories of the unspeakable hardships that soldiers have to endure in the field, while civilians living an easy life at home often want for nothing, I thought it might be a good idea to write a poem that drew attention to this contrast, and, by influencing the popular mood in this way, help to prepare a warmer welcome for the returning troops.

I had several hundred copies of the poem printed at my own expense, and distributed them throughout the city. The response was far better than I had expected. All kinds of nice people now got in touch with me, who shared the feelings and opinions I had expressed; they encouraged me to write more in similar vein, and there was general agreement that I had demonstrated a talent worth cultivating. The poem was published in journals, reprinted and sold separately in various places, and to crown it all I had the pleasure of seeing it set to music by a very popular composer of the day[2] – though it did not really suit the singing voice, on account of its length and its highly rhetorical style.

Not a week went by now when I was not inspired to write another poem of some sort. I was now in my twenty-fourth year, full of emotions and longings and goodwill, yet completely lacking in education and intellectual culture. I was advised to study our great writers, Schiller and Klopstock being particularly recommended. I got hold of their works, read them, admired them, but found they didn't help me very much. Although I didn't know it at the time, the paths pursued by these two geniuses were too far removed from my own natural tendency.

It was at this time that I first heard the name 'Goethe' and acquired a book of his poems. I read his ballads, over and over again, and felt a joy that words cannot describe. It was as if I were only now starting to wake up and become fully conscious; it felt as if my innermost self, previously unknown to me, were being reflected back at me in these poems. I didn't come across anything alien or abstruse, which would have been beyond the grasp of a mere mortal such as myself, nor did I encounter the names of outlandish or antiquated deities which meant nothing to me. Instead, I found the human heart, in all its yearnings, joys and sorrows, and I found a German nature as clear as day – pure reality, in the soft glow of a transfiguring light.

I immersed myself in these ballads for weeks and months on end. Then I managed to get hold of *Wilhelm Meister*, then his autobiography, and then his dramatic works. *Faust* I read on all of the holidays; initially recoiling from the dark abysses of human nature and depravity that it revealed, I was drawn back again and again by its highly enigmatic character. My admiration and affection grew by the day; these works took over my life, and I thought and talked of nothing but Goethe.

The benefit we derive from studying the works of a great writer can take many different forms. But one of the main advantages is probably that we become more aware, not just of our own thoughts and feelings, but of the rich diversity of the world around us, too. This was the effect that Goethe's works had on me. They also made me pay more attention to physical objects and characters; little by little, I came to understand the unity, or inward harmony, of the individual with itself, and so the secret of the great diversity of natural and artistic phenomena was gradually revealed to me.

After I had acquired a working knowledge of Goethe's writings and tried my hand at various forms of poetry myself, I turned my attention to some of the greatest authors from other countries and other times; and I read not only Shakespeare's major plays, but also Sophocles and Homer, in the best translations available.

However, I very soon realized that what I was getting from these sublime works was just a general sense of their humanity, and that any understanding of specifics, whether linguistic or historical, presupposed the kind of specialized knowledge and education that is normally acquired only in schools and universities.

Many people also pointed out to me that I would get nowhere by myself, and that without a so-called classical education a poet will never be able to write elegantly and expressively in his own language, or indeed produce work noted for the quality of its content and conception.

I was also reading many biographies of famous men at the time, to see what kind of educational path they had followed in order to make something of themselves; and I noted that they all went through school and university. So I decided to follow their example, despite being a late starter and living in challenging circumstances.

I applied straightaway to an eminent literary scholar who taught at the grammar school in Hanover, and took private lessons with him, not only in Latin, but also in Greek; and all the spare time left to me by my office job, which took up at least six hours each day, was devoted to these studies.

I kept this up for a year and made good progress. But I had such an overwhelming desire to get on that I felt things were moving too slowly, and that I needed to try something else. It seemed to me that if I could somehow contrive to attend the grammar school for four or five hours each day, and thus immerse myself totally in a learning environment, I would make much greater progress and achieve my aim far sooner.

Having been confirmed in this view by the advice I received from various knowledgeable persons, I resolved to act on my plan. I had no problem obtaining the consent of my superiors, as the school hours largely coincided with that part of the day when I was not at work.

I duly applied for admission to the grammar school, and one Sunday morning I went along, accompanied by my teacher, to see the worthy headmaster and take the necessary examination. He examined me in the most kindly way, but I had not been coached in the usual test questions asked on these occasions, and for all my hard work I lacked the necessary discipline. So I did not do as well as I really should have done. But after my teacher had assured him that I knew more than this examination might suggest, and in consideration of all the hard work I had put in, the headmaster gave me a place in the second form.

I need hardly say that as a grown man of nearly twenty-five, already working in the King's service, I cut a very odd figure among these youngsters, most of them still mere boys, and I myself found my new situation somewhat uncomfortable and strange at first; but my great thirst for knowledge enabled me to grin and bear it. And on the whole, I had nothing to complain about. The teachers respected me, the older and brighter pupils in the class were most friendly towards me, and even the troublemakers had enough consideration not to play any nasty tricks on me.

Now that I was where I wanted to be, I was very happy on the whole, and embraced my new schedule with enthusiasm. I woke at five in the morning, and soon afterwards was busy preparing for my lessons. I went to school shortly before eight and stayed until ten. From there, I hurried off to my office to attend to my business, which required my presence until shortly before one. I then raced home, bolted down a bit of lunch, and was back in school again just after one. Lessons went on until four, after which I was busy in my office again until gone seven, and then spent the rest of the evening on school homework and private lessons.

I kept up this busy life for several months; but my strength was not up to the strain, and the old adage was once again proved right: no man can serve two masters. The lack of fresh air and exercise, along with too little time for eating, drinking and sleeping, were gradually taking their toll on my health; I felt physically and mentally depleted, and in the end I realized that I must, as a matter of urgent necessity, give up either the school or my job. As I depended on the latter for my living, I had no other choice, and I duly left the school again in early spring 1817. It seemed to be my lot in life to try out all kinds of different things, and so I had no regrets at all about having tried a grammar school for a while.

In the meantime I had made good progress, and since I still had my heart set on going to university, there was nothing for it but to carry on with the private lessons, which I did with great relish.

Having got through the stresses and strains of the winter, I felt the joys of spring and summer all the more keenly. I spent a lot of time out in the countryside, which this year spoke to my heart with a special intimacy; and I wrote many poems, inspired particularly by the lofty example of Goethe's youthful ballads.

With the onset of winter, I began to think seriously about how I might gain entry to the university some time within the next year. I had made sufficient progress in Latin to be able to make verse translations of some pieces that particularly spoke to me from the *Odes* of Horace, the *Eclogues* of Virgil and the *Metamorphoses* of Ovid. I was also able to read the speeches of Cicero and the *Commentaries* of Julius Caesar with reasonable fluency. Even so, I could hardly consider myself properly prepared for academic studies; but I expected to be much further on in a year's time, and would be able to make good any deficiencies once I was at the university.

I had secured quite a few patrons among the leading figures of the city, who promised me their support – albeit on condition that I chose a course of study that would qualify me for paid employment. But as this was not my natural inclination, and as it was my firm belief that a person should only cultivate those things to which he feels irresistibly drawn, I stuck to my resolve, with the result that those acquaintances refused to help me, offering me nothing more than a free lunch.

So now I had to rely on my own resources to carry my plan through, and I prepared myself to embark upon a literary work of some significance.

Müllner's *Schuld* and Grillparzer's *Ahnfrau* were all the rage at the time, but these artificial works offended against my natural feeling;[3] I was even less enamoured of their ideas about fate, which I thought would have an adverse effect on public morality. So I decided to challenge them, and to show that fate lies in the characters. But I wanted to fight with deeds rather than words: I would write a play of my own, which would illustrate the truth that we all sow seeds in the present that germinate in the future, and bring forth fruit, good or bad, depending on what we have sown. Unschooled as I was in world history, I had no choice but to invent my own characters and plot. I was probably thinking about it for a year, and worked out the individual scenes and acts in great detail in my head before finally putting pen to paper in the winter of 1820 and writing it in the morning hours over several weeks. It was immensely gratifying to see how everything came together so easily and naturally. However, unlike the two writers mentioned above, I was too focused on real life, and never thought about the theatre stage. So it was more a leisurely sequence of vignettes than a dramatic action that moves swiftly forward, and it was poetic and rhythmical only where characters and situations demanded it. Minor characters were given too much space, and the whole play became too sprawling.

I showed it to my closest friends and acquaintances, but the reaction was not what I had hoped for. I was told that some of the scenes belonged in a comedy, and that I hadn't read enough. Having expected a better reception, I felt quietly offended at first; but I gradually came to the conclusion that my friends were not entirely wrong, and that even though my characters were correctly drawn, and the whole thing was well thought through and executed with a degree of care and facility, so that it came out much as I had intended, my play was far too crude a portrayal of human life to be fit for public performance.

And this was hardly surprising, considering my background and my lack of formal education. I resolved to rework the play and adapt it for the stage; but before that, I needed to continue my education, so that I would be capable of producing work of a higher calibre. The desire to go to the university, where I hoped to obtain everything that I now lacked, and through which I expected to improve my situation in life, became a consuming passion. I decided to publish my poems, as a way of perhaps achieving my aim. As I did not have an established reputation, and therefore could not expect a substantial fee from a publisher, I chose to publish by subscription instead, which better suited my situation.

My friends got the ball rolling, and the whole thing turned out very well. I now approached my superiors again about my plans for Göttingen and asked to be released from service; and when it became clear to them that I was in deadly earnest, and that I would not change my mind, they agreed to my request. My boss, Colonel von Berger, put in a request to the war office, and I was granted a leave of absence; they also approved an annual grant of 150 thalers to subsidize my studies, to be paid from my salary for a period of two years.

I felt happy that the plans I had nurtured for years were now coming to fruition. I had my poems printed and distributed as soon as possible, and after deducting all my expenses, I was left with a clear profit of 150 thalers. In May 1821 I travelled to Göttingen, leaving behind a girl whom I dearly loved.[4]

My first attempt to get to the university had failed because I was dead set against undertaking a course of study simply for the purpose of getting a paid job. But now, made wiser by experience, and only too aware of the terrible struggles I had had to endure at the time, both with my own circle of friends and with well-placed persons of influence, I was politic enough to yield to the weight of opinion, and to declare at once that I would choose a course of study that led to a proper job, and devote myself to jurisprudence.

My powerful patrons, and everyone else who cared about my worldly fortunes but had no idea how all-consuming my intellectual needs were, found this course of action eminently sensible. All objections were promptly dropped; everyone was suddenly friendly and accommodating, and quite ready to assist my endeavours. At the same time, people took care to encourage me in my good intentions by pointing out that the study of law was intellectually rewarding in its own right. I was told that it would give me a special insight into civil and social relations, which I could not get in any other way. Nor would this course of study take up so much of my time that it would prevent me pursuing all kinds of so-called 'higher' interests on the side. Various famous men were mentioned, all of whom had studied law, but who had then become leading experts in other fields.

However, what my friends and I both failed to consider was that these men had not only gone to university with an excellent school education behind them, but were also able to devote far more time to their studies than I could, given the harsh realities of my own particular circumstances.

In short, as I had deceived others, so I gradually deceived myself, and in the end I really imagined in all seriousness that I could study law and at the same time achieve my own personal goals.

Under this delusion – of seeking something I did not wish to have or put to use hereafter – I began my legal studies as soon as I arrived at the university. I did not find the subject repellent; indeed, if my head had not been so full of other plans and projects, I could quite happily have devoted myself to it. As it was, I was like a girl who comes up with all kinds of objections to a proposed marriage match, only because her heart unfortunately belongs to a secret lover of her own.

Sitting in the lectures on the fundamentals of Roman law, I often became absorbed in constructing dramatic scenes and acts in my head. I tried very hard to concentrate on what the lecturer was saying, but my mind kept wandering off. All I could think about was poetry and art, and the cultivation of my higher human faculties – which, of course, was the reason I had been dying to get to the university for years.

The man who did most to help me attain my immediate goals during that first year was Heeren. His work in ethnography and history gave me an excellent foundation for further studies of this sort, while the clarity and precision of his presentation taught me a great deal in other respects, too. I loved going to his lectures, and I never came away without feeling greater respect and affection for this brilliant man.

At the start of my second academic year, I decided that it

INTRODUCTION 25

made sense to give up law altogether. It was far too big a subject for me to pick it up on the side, and if I took it as my main course of study, it would prevent me from pursuing my own interests. So I took classes in philology instead. And just as Heeren had been my inspiration during the first year, so Dissen became my guiding light now. It was not just that his lectures gave my studies the nourishment I really wanted and needed, that I found myself making progress and learning more every day, and that his suggestions set me on the right path for my own future writings: I also had the pleasure of getting to know the great man personally and of being guided and encouraged by him in my studies.

Furthermore, daily association with the best minds among the students and endless conversations about deep matters on our walks together, and often late into the night, were invaluable to me, and had the most favourable influence on my own intellectual development.

I had reached the point where my financial support would soon be coming to an end. On the other hand, I had been acquiring new knowledge on a daily basis for a year and a half; just to go on adding to it, without putting it to practical use, did not accord with my natural disposition or my way of life. So I now felt a passionate desire to set myself free again and whet my appetite for further study by writing something of my own.

I had two projects in mind, to be undertaken in succession. I planned to complete my drama, in which I had not lost interest as far as the subject matter was concerned, but which needed to be refined in form and content; and I wanted to formulate some ideas on the principles of poetry, which had taken shape primarily in opposition to views that were prevalent at the time.

I therefore left the university in the autumn of 1822 and moved into lodgings in the countryside close to Hanover. I began by writing those essays on literary theory which I hoped would help young writers in particular not only to produce their own work, but also to judge existing poetic works. I gave them the collective title *Beiträge zur Poesie*.

I finished this work in May 1823. In my situation, I was keen not only to find a good publisher, but also to secure a substantial fee; and so I quickly made up my mind, and sent the manuscript to Goethe, asking him if he would put in a good word for me with Herr von Cotta.

Goethe was still the one writer to whom I looked up constantly as my infallible guiding star, whose pronouncements chimed with my own way of thinking and led me to see things from an ever higher point of view; whose supreme artistry in the treatment of all manner of different subjects I strove constantly to study and emulate; and for whom I felt a love and a veneration that were almost passionate in their intensity.

Soon after my arrival in Göttingen, I had sent him a copy of my poems, together with a brief résumé of my life and education; and I was delighted not only to receive a brief written acknowledgement from him, but also to hear from some travellers that he had formed a good opinion of me and intended to mention my name in the pages of *Kunst und Altertum*.

Knowing this meant a great deal to me in my situation at the time, and it gave me the confidence now to send him the manuscript I had just completed.

All I wanted to do now was to meet him briefly in person, and with that in mind I set off on foot, towards the end of May, and walked, via Göttingen and the valley of the Werra, to Weimar.

As I wended my way, often finding it hard going because of the extreme heat, I took comfort in my mind from the recurrent impression that I was under the especial guidance of benign powers, and that this journey might well have important consequences for the rest of my life.

1823

Weimar, Tuesday 10 June 1823

I arrived here a few days ago, and went to see Goethe for the first time today. I was received very warmly by him, and the impression made on me by his person was such that I count this day among the happiest of my life.

When I enquired yesterday, I was told that he would be pleased to see me at twelve o'clock today. So I called at the appointed hour and found the manservant waiting for me, ready to take me upstairs.

The interior of the house made a very agreeable impression on me; everything was very simple and elegant, without being showy, while a series of casts of antique statues lining the stairs testified to Goethe's particular fondness for sculpture and Greek antiquity. I saw various women bustling about downstairs, as well as one of Ottilie's bonny little boys, who came up to me with childlike trust and gazed at me with big eyes.[5]

After I had looked around a little, I went upstairs to the first floor with the very talkative manservant. He opened a door that had the word 'SALVE' inscribed on the threshold, intimating to the visitor that a friendly welcome awaited him inside. The manservant led me across this room and opened the door to a second, more spacious apartment, where he asked me to wait while he went to inform his master of my arrival. The air in here was very cool and refreshing; a carpet was spread out on the floor, and the furniture – a red sofa and chairs of the same colour – made the room look bright and cheerful. On one side stood a piano, and the walls were hung with various drawings and paintings of different sizes. Through an open door on the far wall one could see into another room, likewise lined with paintings, through which the servant had passed to announce me.

It was not long before Goethe appeared, wearing a blue frock coat and shoes: an august figure indeed! I was caught a little off guard, but his very friendly welcome immediately dispelled any embarrassment. We sat down on the sofa. The sight of him sitting so close made me feel both happy and flustered, and I could think of little or nothing to say.

He began straightaway to talk about my manuscript. 'I have just come from you,' he said; 'I have spent the whole morning reading your text. It needs no recommendation from me: it is its own recommendation.' He went on to praise the clarity of the style and the logical flow of the argument, and said that it all rested on solid foundations and was well thought through. 'I shall forward it without delay,' he added; 'I shall write to Cotta today by the mail rider, and tomorrow I shall send the package on with the mail coach.' I thanked him in words, and by the expression on my face.

We then spoke about my present travel plans. I told him that my ultimate destination was the Rhineland, where I was thinking to find a suitable place to stay and do some more writing. But from here I would go direct to Jena first, where I would await Herr von Cotta's response.

Goethe asked me whether I knew anyone in Jena. I said that I hoped to make contact with Herr von Knebel, whereupon he promised to give me a letter of introduction that would assure me of a very favourable reception.

'So,' he went on, 'if you are in Jena, we shall be close neighbours, and we can see each other and write to one another as and when there is something to report.'

We sat together for a long time, and it all felt very relaxed and affectionate. I brushed against his knee, and could not speak for looking at him; I could not take my eyes off him. His face is so strong-featured and tanned and full of creases, and every crease so expressive. There is such an integrity and strength about him, such composure and greatness! When he spoke, his delivery was calm and unhurried, rather as you might imagine an aged monarch to speak. You could tell by looking at him that he is a man at peace with himself, elevated above praise and blame. I felt indescribably comforted by his presence; I had a sense of calm reassurance, like someone who, after many toils and protracted hopes, finally sees his dearest wishes gratified.

He then spoke of my letter and said that I was right – that if a man is able to write about *one* thing with clarity, he is fitted for much else besides.

'One can never tell where these things will lead,' he said. 'I have many good friends in Berlin, and have recently mentioned your name in that quarter.'

He smiled benignly to himself as he said this. He then listed all the things that I really ought to see in Weimar in the next few days, and said that he would ask his secretary Kräuter to show me around. Above all, I must be sure to visit the theatre. He then enquired where I was staying, and said that he would like to see me again and would send for me at a suitable time.

We parted fondly, and with a sense of elation on my part: his every word bespoke goodwill, and I felt that he had my best interests at heart.

Wednesday 11 June 1823

This morning I received another invitation to call on Goethe, in the form of a card written in his own hand. So I went, and stayed about an hour. Today he seemed quite different from yesterday; he was like some youth, brisk and decisive in everything he did.

He was carrying two thick tomes when he entered the room. 'It would be a shame,' he said, 'for you to leave so soon – and much better for us to get to know each other. I should like to see more of you and to talk with you. But rather than lose ourselves in generalities, I have thought of something specific that will serve as common ground and give us something to talk about. In these two volumes you'll find all the numbers of the *Frankfurter gelehrte Anzeigen* for the years 1772 and 1773, and these contain nearly all my brief reviews from that period.

They are not marked, but since you are familiar with my style and way of thinking, you won't have any trouble finding them. Now I would like you to take a closer look at these youthful pieces and tell me what you think of them. I would like to know if they are worth including in a future edition of my works. I myself am so far removed from these things now that I cannot judge them. It's for you younger people to say whether they are of any use to you, and how far they are relevant in today's literary climate. I have already had copies made, which you shall have later, so that you can compare them with the originals. And after that, with careful editing, we could decide whether we should leave the odd thing out here and there, or clarify the odd point, without spoiling the overall effect.'

I replied that I would gladly see what I could do with these pieces, and that all I wanted was to try and edit them exactly as he himself would wish.

'Once you get into them,' he said, 'you'll find that you can do the job perfectly well. It will come quite naturally to you.'

He then told me that he planned to leave for Marienbad in a week or so, and that he would be very glad if I could remain in Weimar until then, so that we could see each other from time to time and talk and get to know each other better.

'I should also like it,' he added, 'if you could stay in Jena, not just for a few days or weeks, but set yourself up there for the whole summer, until I get back from Marienbad, towards the autumn. I wrote yesterday to arrange lodgings and some other things, to make life easier for you.

'You will find all kinds of resources and aids to further study there, not to mention a very cultivated circle of people. And besides, there is so much to see in the vicinity that you could probably take fifty different walks, all of them pleasant, and nearly all of them conducive to quiet reflection. While you are there you will have plenty of leisure and opportunity to write new things for yourself, and will also find time to help me out as well.'

I could find no fault with these excellent suggestions, and gladly consented to everything. As I was leaving, he was especially affectionate, and named a time the day after tomorrow for a further meeting.

Monday 16 June 1823

I have been to see Goethe several times in the last few days. Today we talked mainly about business matters. I also shared my thoughts about his Frankfurt reviews, which I described as 'echoes of his academic years' – a turn of phrase that seemed to appeal to him, because it summed up the standpoint from which those youthful works should be viewed.

He then gave me the first eleven issues of *Kunst und Altertum*, so that I could take them with me to Jena and work on them alongside the Frankfurt reviews.

'I would like you to make a careful study of these journals, and as well as drawing up a general list of contents I should like you to make a note of any subjects that are still open to discussion, so that it becomes obvious which threads I need to take up again and develop further. This will be a great help to me; and you yourself will also benefit, in that this practical exercise will force you to study and analyse the individual essays in much greater detail than if you were simply reading them for pleasure.'

I thought this all made perfect sense, and said that I would be happy to undertake this additional work.

Thursday 19 June 1823

I had really planned to be in Jena by today, but yesterday Goethe urged me to stay on until Sunday and then go by the mail coach. He also gave me the letters of recommendation yesterday, including one for the Frommann family. 'You will enjoy their company,' he said. 'I have spent some delightful evenings with them. Jean Paul, Tieck, the Schlegels and all the other leading names in Germany have been there and become regular guests, and their house is still a meeting place for many scholars and artists and other persons of note. You must write to me in Marienbad in a few weeks, and let me know how you are getting on and how you find Jena. I have also asked my son to come and visit you there while I am away.'

I greatly appreciated all the trouble Goethe had gone to on

my account, and it was heart-warming to see from all this that he regards me almost as one of the family and wishes me to be treated as such.

On Saturday 21 June I duly took my leave of Goethe and went to Jena the next day, where I took up residence in a garden apartment at the home of some very good, respectable people. On the strength of Goethe's recommendation, I was warmly welcomed into the families of Herr von Knebel and Herr Frommann, where I found the company most instructive. I made excellent progress with the work I had brought with me, and very shortly had the pleasure of receiving a letter from Herr von Cotta, in which he not only undertook to publish the manuscript that had been forwarded to him, but also promised me a handsome fee and arranged for the printing to be carried out under my supervision in Jena.

So now my livelihood was secured for another year, at least, and I felt an insistent urge to write something new during that time, and thus to establish my future fortunes as an author. I hoped that the essays in my *Beiträge zur Poesie* would be my final word on literary theory and criticism; in them I had sought to gain a clearer understanding of the principal laws, and now my whole being was telling me to put that knowledge to practical use. I had all kinds of plans for poems on an epic or intimate scale, as well as dramatic works of various kinds, and in my mind it was now just a matter of deciding where to begin, in order to produce a steady succession of works, one after another, at my own pace.

As time went by I soon tired of Jena; it was too quiet and dull for me. What I needed was a big city, one that had not only an excellent theatre, but also a vibrant, bustling street life, so that I could assimilate important aspects of life and very quickly cultivate my mind to a higher degree. I hoped to be able to live quite anonymously in such a city, free to isolate myself at any time in order to write without interruption.

In the meantime, I had drafted the list of contents for the first four volumes of *Kunst und Altertum*, as Goethe had requested, and sent it off to Marienbad with a covering letter, in which I

1823

talked openly about my wishes and plans. I received the following reply by return:

> The list of contents arrived at just the right time and is
> exactly what I wanted. If I can have the Frankfurt reviews
> edited in similar fashion and waiting for me on my return,
> I shall owe you a debt of gratitude – which I am already
> quietly repaying in advance by reflecting on your views,
> circumstances, wishes, aims and plans as I go about my
> daily business, so that when I get back we can have a
> proper discussion about your future. That's all I shall say
> for now. My departure from Marienbad is giving me
> much to think about and do, while it is painful to feel
> that my stay with these excellent people has been all too
> short.
>
> I hope I may find you quietly absorbed in your work – the
> surest and shortest route to worldly wisdom and experience.
> Farewell for now – I look forward to a long and close
> collaboration.
>
> Marienbad, 14 August 1823
> Goethe

These lines from Goethe, which I was delighted to receive, put
my mind at rest again for the time being. I was persuaded not
to act on my own initiative, but to be guided entirely by his
advice and wishes. In the meantime, I wrote a few short poems,
completed my editing of the Frankfurt reviews, and expressed
my opinion of them in a brief essay intended for Goethe. I
looked forward eagerly to his return from Marienbad; the
printers had nearly finished with my *Beiträge zur Poesie*, and I
was determined, come what may, to take a short break this
autumn and spend a few weeks by the Rhine.

Jena, Monday 15 September 1823

Goethe has returned safely from Marienbad, but will only be
staying here for a few days, as his garden house here lacks the

necessary amenities. He is fit and well, and quite able to walk for several miles at a stretch; it is a real delight to see him.

After a joyful exchange of greetings, Goethe embarked immediately on the subject of my situation. 'I must say at once,' he began, 'that I would like you to remain with me in Weimar for the winter.' These were his opening words, on which he then proceeded to elaborate:

'In poetry and criticism, you are very well placed. You have a natural grounding in these things; they are your calling, which you should stick to, and they will very soon earn you a decent living. But there are many things not strictly pertaining to the subject which you should nonetheless know. It's important not to spend too much time on this, but to get it behind you quickly. That you will do over the winter here in Weimar, and you'll be amazed how much progress you have made by Easter. You shall have the best of everything, because the best resources are in my hands. Then you will have a firm foundation for life; you will find contentment and have the confidence to hold your own in any company.'

I welcomed these suggestions, and said I would be guided entirely by his views and wishes.

'I shall find somewhere for you to live nearby,' Goethe went on, 'and not a moment of your time shall be wasted this winter. There are a lot of good things in Weimar, and in our higher circles you will gradually discover a society that is the equal of the best that any great city can offer. I also have personal connections to many eminent men, whom you will meet in due course; time spent in their company will be highly instructive and useful to you.'

Goethe then mentioned the names of various notable men and briefly outlined their particular accomplishments.

'Where else,' he continued, 'would you find so many good things in one small place? We also have a fine library, and a theatre which, in every important respect, is as good as the best that other German cities have to offer. So I say again: stay here with us, and not just for the winter; make Weimar your home. The roads from the gates lead to the four corners of the earth. In the summer you can travel, and gradually get to see whatever sights you wish. I have lived there for fifty years, and travelled far and wide in that time. But I was always glad to get back to Weimar.'

I was thrilled to be with Goethe again and to hear him talk, and I felt devoted to him heart and soul. As long as I have *you*, I thought, and while I *can* have you, I shan't care about anything else. I assured him again, therefore, that I was ready to do whatever he thought best with regard to my particular situation.

Jena, Thursday 18 September 1823

Yesterday morning, before Goethe left for Weimar, I was fortunate enough to spend an hour with him again. What he had to say was most remarkable, quite invaluable for me, and food for thought to last a lifetime. All Germany's young poets should hear this – it could be very helpful.

He began by asking me whether I had written any poems this summer. I said that I had written a few, but on the whole had not felt in the right frame of mind for poetry. To which he replied: 'Beware of embarking on a great work. This is the mistake that our best minds make, the very people with the most talent and the fiercest ambition. I made the same mistake myself, and I know what it cost me. There was so much that came to nothing! If I had written everything that I perfectly well could have, it would have filled more than a hundred volumes.

'The present demands its due; the thoughts and feelings that crowd in upon the poet every day need to be put into words, and so they should be. But if your mind is taken up with some great work, nothing else can get a look-in; all other thoughts are pushed aside, and you cannot even enjoy the ordinary pleasures of life. It requires a vast amount of exertion and mental effort just to shape and organize a great whole, and a vast amount of energy, plus a period of uninterrupted peace and quiet in one's life, to get it all down on paper in one continuous draft. But if you have picked the wrong subject to start with, then all your efforts are wasted; and if, furthermore, having undertaken something so large, you are not fully in command of your material in some of its parts, the whole thing will be unsatisfactory in places, and the critics will take you to task. So what the poet gets for so much effort and sacrifice is not reward and pleasure, but only stress and the undermining of his confidence. But if, on the other hand, the poet attends to the present moment each day, and writes with freshness and spontaneity about whatever comes his way, he is sure to produce something of value; and if, once in a while, something doesn't work out, then nothing is lost.

'August Hagen in Königsberg, for example, is a splendidly talented writer. Have you read his *Olfried und Lisena*? There are passages in there that cannot be improved upon: the evocation of life on the Baltic coast, and anything relating to the local setting, are all masterly. But these are only beautiful passages: the work as a whole fails to satisfy. And yet to think what labour and effort he lavished upon it – the man almost worked himself to exhaustion! And now he has written a tragedy.'

Goethe paused a moment and smiled. I spoke up to say that, unless I was very much mistaken, he had advised Hagen in *Kunst und Altertum* to tackle only *small* subjects.

'I certainly did,' replied Goethe, 'but do people take any notice of what we old-timers say? Everyone thinks he knows best, with the result that many young writers lose their way, and many stay lost for a long time. But people should not be getting lost now; that's what our generation was about – seeking and going astray; and what was the point of it all, if you young people are just going to go down the same paths that we did? We'd never get anywhere like that! Our generation's errors were not held against us, because we found no beaten paths to tread; but we must expect more of those who come after us. Instead of seeking and going astray all over again, they should be heeding the advice of us old folk and following the right path from the beginning. It is not enough to take steps that will one day lead you to your destination; each step should be both a destination in itself, and a step along the way.

'Keep in mind what I have said and see how much of it works for you. I am actually not worried about you, but with my encouragement, perhaps, you will quickly get through a phase

1823   37

that does not suit your present situation. For now, as I say, you
should stick to small subjects and keep it spontaneous, just the
things that present themselves each day – and generally speaking, you will always produce something good, and each day
will bring you joy. Start by sending your work to the pocket-
books and periodicals; but never submit to the demands of
others. Always follow your own instincts.

'The world is so vast and rich, and life so full of variety, that
you will never be short of inspiration for poems. But they must
always be "occasional poems", in the sense that real life must
present both the occasion and the material. A particular
instance becomes universal and poetic by virtue of the fact that
the *poet* writes about it. All my poems are "occasional", being
inspired by real life and firmly grounded in it. I have no time for
poems that are plucked out of thin air.

'Don't let anyone tell you that real life is lacking in poetic
interest. This is exactly what the poet is for: he has the mind and
the imagination to find something of interest in everyday things.
Real life supplies the motifs, the points that need to be said – the
actual heart of the matter; but it is the poet's job to fashion it all
into a beautiful, animated whole. You are familiar with Fürnstein, the so-called "nature poet"? He has written a poem about
hop-growing, and you couldn't imagine anything nicer. I have
now asked him to write some poems celebrating the work of
skilled artisans, in particular weavers, and I am quite sure he
will succeed; he has lived among such people from an early age,
he knows the subject inside out, and will be in full command of
his material. That is the advantage of small works: you need
only choose subjects that you know and have at your command.
With a longer poetic work, however, this is not possible. There
is no way around it: all the different threads that tie the whole
thing together, and are woven into the design, have to be shown
in accurate detail. Young people only have a one-sided view
of things, whereas a longer work requires a multiplicity of
viewpoints – and that's where they come unstuck.'

I told Goethe that I was planning to write a longer poem
about the seasons, into which I would weave the occupations
and amusements of all the different classes. 'This is exactly

what I am talking about,' said Goethe. 'You may succeed in large parts of the poem, but in others you will fail, because you have not studied the subject properly and lack the necessary knowledge. So you might get the fisherman right – but not the hunter. But if you get anything at all wrong, then the whole thing is compromised, however good it might be in parts; and you have failed to produce something perfect. If, on the other hand, you take only those parts that are within your capabilities, and make them into separate works, then you are sure to produce something good.

'I must warn you especially against grand subjects of your own invention. That involves giving a particular view of things – and young people are seldom mature enough for that. Furthermore, the poet's stock is depleted by the characters and viewpoints he creates; so he lacks the resources for further productions. And finally, think how much time it takes to dream up the material, then structure it and tie it all together – time that nobody thanks us for, even supposing we manage to complete the work in the first place.

'With *given* material, on the other hand, it's all different, and so much easier. The situations and characters are already supplied, and all the poet has to do is bring them to life. He keeps his own stock intact, not needing to bring much of himself to the task; and the expenditure of time and energy is far less, because all he has to worry about is the execution. I would go so far as to advise choosing subjects that have already been done. Iphigenia, for example, has been done so many times, yet each version is different, because each writer sees things differently and presents them in his own way.[6]

'But for now, you should put aside any grand schemes. You have pushed yourself hard for long enough; it is time for you to start enjoying life, and the best way to do that is to tackle small subjects.'

During this conversation we had been pacing up and down the room. I found myself agreeing with everything he said, as every word rang true in my innermost being. I felt lighter and happier with every step, for I have to confess that various larger projects of mine, which I had not yet been able to sort out in my mind, had been weighing quite heavily upon me. I have now put them to one side, where I will leave them until such time as I can come back to them with a light heart and work up one subject and one scene after another, as I gradually, through study of the world, become master of each part of my material.

I feel that I am several years further on and several years the wiser as a result of Goethe's words, and deep within my heart I know the special joy of understanding what it means to meet with a true master. The rewards are incalculable.

I shall learn so much from him this winter, and I shall gain so much just by spending time in his company – even when he is not saying anything of particular moment. It seems to me that his person, his mere physical presence, have a civilizing and formative effect, even if he says nothing at all.

Weimar, Thursday 2 October 1823

I came over from Jena yesterday, blessed by very fine weather. I had no sooner arrived than Goethe sent me a season ticket to the theatre, by way of welcoming me back to Weimar. I spent yesterday sorting out my domestic arrangements; they were very busy at Goethe's house anyway, as the French ambassador from Frankfurt, Count Reinhard, and the Prussian State Councillor Schultz from Berlin had come to visit him.

But I did go to see Goethe this morning. He was pleased to see me back and was all charm and kindness. As I made to leave, he said that he would like to introduce me first to State Councillor Schultz. He led me into the next room, where I found the gentleman in question studying some works of art. Goethe introduced me, then left us alone to talk.

'I am delighted to hear,' said Schultz, 'that you are staying on in Weimar to assist Goethe with the editing of his unpublished works. He has told me how helpful your involvement will be for him, and that he is hoping to finish off some new things as well.'

I replied that I had no other object in life but to serve the cause of German literature, and that I was happy to shelve my own literary ambitions for the present in the hope of being useful here. I added that working with Goethe would be hugely beneficial for my own apprenticeship as a writer; I am hoping that in a few years I will have attained a certain maturity as a result, which will enable me to accomplish far better things than I would be capable of now.

'Certainly,' said Schultz, 'the personal influence of such an extraordinary man and mentor as Goethe is absolutely priceless. I myself have come over to refresh my spirits by contact with this great mind.'

He then enquired about the printing of my book, which Goethe had mentioned in a letter to him the previous summer. I told him that I was hoping to receive the first copies from Jena in a few days and would be sure to present him with one, and would send it on to Berlin, should he no longer be here.

We then parted with a hearty handshake.

Tuesday 14 October 1823

This evening I attended my first big tea party at Goethe's house. I was the first to arrive, and thought how splendid the brightly lit rooms looked, with their interconnecting doors thrown open. In one of the rooms at the back I found Goethe, who came up to me in very cheerful mood. He was dressed in black and wearing his star, which suited him so well.[7] We were alone for a while, and stepped into the so-called Ceiling Room, where I was particularly struck by the painting of the Aldobrandini Wedding, on the wall behind a red sofa.[8] With the green curtains drawn back, the painting was very well lit, and I was glad of the chance to study it at my leisure.

'Yes, indeed,' said Goethe, 'the ancients not only had big ideas, they also came up with the goods. We moderns may have big ideas, too, but we are rarely capable of producing anything as fresh and vigorous as the thing we imagined.'

At this point Riemer and Meyer arrived, as well as Chancellor von Müller and several other distinguished gentlemen and ladies of the court. Goethe's son came in, and Frau von Goethe, whom I now met for the first time.[9] The rooms gradually filled

1823

with guests, and with the sound of lively conversation and laughter. A few handsome young foreigners were also present, with whom Goethe spoke French.

The company was very agreeable, the mood very free and informal; people stood or sat, joking, laughing, talking to all and sundry, just as the fancy took them. I had a very lively conversation with Goethe's son about Houwald's *Das Bild*, which had been performed a few days earlier. We were in agreement about the play, and I was gratified to hear young Goethe talk about the characters and situations with such wit and passion.

Goethe himself was a most gracious presence at the party, circulating constantly; he seemed to prefer listening, and letting his guests talk, rather than saying much himself. Frau von Goethe would often come and snuggle up to him and give him a kiss. I had recently told him that I was enjoying the theatre greatly, and that it really lifted my spirits just to let the plays speak to me directly, without trying to analyse them. He seemed to think this was the right approach in my present circumstances.

He approached me with Frau von Goethe. 'This is my daughter-in-law,' he said. 'Have you met?' We told him that we had just become acquainted. 'He is a great theatre-lover like yourself, Ottilie,' he said, and we were both pleased to discover our shared enthusiasm. 'My daughter,' he added, 'never misses an evening.' 'That's all right,' I said, 'as long as they are doing good, light-hearted pieces. But not if the plays are bad; then it's a real test of your endurance.'

'It's no bad thing,' said Goethe, 'that you cannot just leave, and are forced to hear and see the bad stuff, too. It makes you really detest bad theatre – and that in turn gives you a better appreciation of the good. It's different when you read a play. If you don't like it, you can just toss the book aside; but in the theatre you have to stick it out to the end.' I agreed with him and thought to myself: the old man always knows just the right thing to say.

We then separated and mingled with the other guests, who were talking loudly and merrily all around us, in this room and the next. Goethe went to join the ladies; I joined Riemer and Meyer, who talked a lot about Italy.

Later on, Councillor Schmidt sat down at the piano and played some Beethoven pieces, which seemed to be received with rapt attention by those present.[10] A witty lady then told us lots of interesting things about Beethoven's personality.[11] Time moved on, ten o'clock came around, and I had spent a highly enjoyable evening.

Sunday 19 October 1823

Today I dined with Goethe for the first time. Apart from him, only Frau von Goethe, Fräulein Ulrike and little Walter were present, so it was just us by ourselves. Goethe was quite the *paterfamilias*, serving all the dishes, carving the roast fowl with great skill and topping up our glasses as necessary. The rest of us chatted away merrily about the theatre, young Englishmen, and other events of the day; Fräulein Ulrike was in particularly good form, and very entertaining. Goethe was generally quiet, only occasionally coming out with some choice remark in passing. He glanced at the newspapers from time to time and read out the odd passage, especially about the advances made by the Greeks.[12]

There was then talk of the need for me to learn English, which Goethe strongly advised me to do, especially on account of Lord Byron – a figure of such eminence that his like had not been seen before, and very probably would not be seen again.[13] They went through the list of local teachers, but concluded that none of them had really good pronunciation. So it would be better, they thought, to stick to young Englishmen.

After dinner, Goethe showed me a few experiments relating to his theory of colour. The subject was entirely new to me; I didn't understand the phenomenon itself, or anything he said about it. But I hoped that in time I would have leisure and opportunity to acquaint myself rather better with this science.

Tuesday 21 October 1823

I spent the evening with Goethe. We talked about his *Pandora*. I asked him whether the work should be regarded as complete in itself, or whether there was any more of it. He said there was nothing else written; he did not go on with it, because the first part had grown so much in size that he was unable, when it came to it, to write a second. And anyway, the piece as it stood worked well as a whole, so he was happy to leave it at that.

I told him that I had only gradually come to understand this difficult work, having read it so often that I almost knew it by heart now. Goethe smiled at this. 'I can well imagine,' he said. 'It's as if the whole thing is made up of interlocking parts, so to speak.'

I then said that I could not entirely agree with Schubarth's view of the work, when he argues that it is an amalgam of everything that has been said separately in *Werther*, *Wilhelm Meister*, *Faust* and *Wahlverwandtschaften*, making it very difficult and hard to grasp.

'Schubarth often overanalyses things,' said Goethe. 'But he is very bright, and always worth listening to.'

We talked about Uhland. 'There is no smoke without fire,' said Goethe, 'and when someone is as popular as Uhland, there must be something special about him. That said, I haven't really formed a proper opinion of his work. I picked up his book with the best of intentions, but straightaway came across so many feeble and dreary poems that it put me off reading any more. I then tried his ballads, saw that they were the work of a very fine talent, and could quite see why he is so famous.'

I then asked Goethe about his views regarding verse forms in German tragedy. 'We are unlikely to reach any agreement on this in Germany,' he replied. 'Everyone does what he likes, and what seems most suitable for the subject in hand. The iambic hexameter would be the most dignified metre, of course, but it is too long for us Germans; because we use fewer epithets, five feet are generally enough for us. The English, with all their monosyllables, manage with even less.'

Goethe then showed me some copperplate engravings and talked about medieval German architecture, saying that in time he would show me more of the same sort. 'In the works of medieval German architecture,' he said, 'we see the flowering of a remarkable age. Anyone who is simply confronted by the fully formed flower can only marvel at the sight; but someone who sees into the secret inner life of the plant, into the stirring of its life-forces, and observes how the flower gradually takes shape and unfolds – he sees the thing with very different eyes, and understands what he is looking at.

'I shall see to it, over the winter, that you gain some insight into this important subject, so that when you visit the Rhine next summer you will have a better appreciation of the Strasbourg Minster and Cologne Cathedral.'

I looked forward to this, and felt greatly indebted to him.

Saturday 25 October 1823

I spent half an hour with Goethe as dusk was falling. He was sitting by his desk in a wooden armchair. I found him in a wonderfully mellow mood, like someone filled with a sense of heavenly peace, or someone who is remembering a time of sweet bliss that he has enjoyed, and which now comes back to him again in every detail. Stadelmann was asked to pull up a chair for me.

We talked about the theatre, which has become one of my main interests this winter. The last play I had seen was Raupach's *Erdennacht*. I gave my opinion of the piece – that what we saw on the stage did not truly reflect what was in the poet's mind, and that the *idea* was pushed at the expense of real life; that it was lyrical rather than dramatic; and that what was spun out over five acts would have been much better condensed into two or three. Goethe added that the whole play was built around the idea of aristocracy and democracy, which was not something of general human interest.

On the other hand, I was full of praise for what I had seen by Kotzebue, namely his *Verwandtschaften* and *Die Versöhnung*. I praised his fresh look at real life, his happy knack for capturing its interesting side, and his truthful, not to say down-to-earth on occasion, portrayal of things. Goethe agreed. 'If a piece of work has lasted for twenty years,' he said, 'and people still like it, there must be something to it. As long as he stuck to what he knew, and didn't try to exceed his capabilities, Kotzebue generally produced something good. He was like Chodowiecki in that respect; Chodowiecki was brilliant at doing scenes of ordinary, middle-class life, but when he tried drawing Roman or Greek heroes, it just didn't work.'

Goethe mentioned some other good plays by Kotzebue, in particular *Die beiden Klingsberg*. 'There is no denying,' he added, 'that he saw a good deal of life and went around with his eyes open.'

He went on: 'Our modern tragic writers are not without intellect, or a certain feeling for poetry, but most of them are incapable of bringing things to life with a light, easy touch. Instead, they strive for something that is beyond their powers, which is why I would call them *forced* talents.'

'I doubt,' I said, 'whether these people could write a play in prose, and that, to my mind, would be the true touchstone of their talent.' Goethe agreed, and added that the verse form intensified the poetic meaning, or even brought it out in the first place.

We then talked a little about various work projects. Mention was made of his 'Reise über Frankfurt und Stuttgart nach der Schweiz', which exists in draft form in three notebooks; he wants to send it to me, so that I can read the individual entries and make suggestions as to how they can be worked up into a complete whole. 'As you will see,' said Goethe, 'I just wrote things down on the spur of the moment, with no overall plan, and no attempt to give the thing artistic shape; it just came out, like pouring water from a bucket.'

I was struck by this image, which seemed to me a very good way to describe something that happens without a plan.

Monday 27 October 1823

This morning I was invited to a tea party and concert at Goethe's house this evening. The manservant showed me the guest list, and I could see that the company would be very large and distinguished. He told me that a young Polish lady had arrived, who would be playing the piano.[14] I accepted the invitation with pleasure.

Later on, the playbill was brought, and I saw that *Die Schachmaschine* was to be performed.[15] I did not know the play at all, but my landlady praised it so highly that I felt a strong desire to see it. Besides, I had been feeling rather out of sorts all day, and the conviction grew upon me that an entertaining comedy would do me more good than an evening in company, however distinguished.

In the early evening, an hour before the theatre, I went to see Goethe. The house was already bustling with activity; I heard the piano being tuned in the larger room as I went past, in preparation for the musical entertainment.

I found Goethe alone in his room. He was already dressed for the evening, and it seemed that my arrival was opportune. 'Stay here for a while,' he said, 'and we'll talk until the others arrive.' I thought to myself: 'You'll never get away – you'll be stuck here for the duration. It's all right now, being here with Goethe on his own; but when all the other guests turn up, ladies and gentlemen you don't know, you'll feel like a fish out of water.'

I walked up and down the room with Goethe. We soon got on to the subject of the theatre, and I had an opportunity to say again that it was a source of constant delight to me, especially as I had seen next to nothing in my earlier years, and now came fresh to virtually every play I saw. 'The fact is,' I added, 'I am in such a bad way that it has put me in a bit of a quandary today, even though a splendid evening's entertainment awaits me here with you.'

'You know what?' said Goethe, stopping short and looking straight at me with a kindly expression, 'you should go. Don't give it a second thought. If you feel that tonight's comedy will suit you better in your present mood, then just go! You'll miss the recital here, but there will be plenty of other opportunities.' 'Well then,' I said, 'in that case, I'll go. I expect it will do me good to laugh.' 'So now you can stay with me until just before six,' said Goethe, 'and we'll talk a little more.'

Stadelmann brought in a couple of candles and put them on Goethe's desk. Goethe invited me to take a seat by the candles; he wanted to give me something to read. And what should he give me, but his latest and most precious poem, his 'Elegie' from Marienbad![16]

Regarding the subject matter of this poem, I need to go back a little to explain. Goethe had only just returned from his most recent visit to Marienbad, when rumours began to circulate here about a young lady whom he had apparently met there; equally charming in body and mind, she became the object of his passion. It was said that whenever he heard her voice in the Brunnenallee, he grabbed his hat and hurried down to see her. He never missed a chance to spend time with her, and passed happy days in her company. Consequently, parting from her had been very difficult, and in this highly emotional state of mind he had written an exquisite poem, which (so it was said) he treasured and kept hidden away, like some holy relic.

I believed this story, because it was entirely consistent not only with his robust physical constitution, but also with the productive power of his mind and the youthful vigour of his heart. I had long desired to see the poem, but hesitated – and rightly so – to ask Goethe. So I gave thanks for this chance opportunity which had now placed it before me.

He had written the lines in his own hand, in Roman script on stout vellum paper, and placed the pages between covers of red morocco leather, tied with a silk cord; so one could tell, even from the outside, that he prized this manuscript above all the others.

I read the poem with great delight, and found confirmation in every line that the rumours were true. Yet the opening lines indicated that they were not meeting here for the first time, but renewing an existing acquaintance. The poem revolved about its own axis, and seemed always to return to the place it had started from. The ending, so wonderfully abrupt, was very unusual, I thought, and deeply moving.

When I had finished reading, Goethe came up to me again. 'It's good, isn't it? But you can give me your considered opinion in a few days' time.' I was very glad to hear that he did not want me to pass judgement there and then; my impressions were too fresh, anyway, and too fleeting, for me to be able to say anything useful.

Goethe promised to show it to me again in a quiet moment. By now it was time for me to leave for the theatre, and we parted with a hearty handshake.

Die Schachmaschine may well be a very good play, and it may have been very well performed; but my mind was elsewhere, thinking about Goethe.

After the theatre I walked past his house; it was all brightly lit inside, I could hear music playing, and I regretted that I hadn't chosen to stay.

The next day I heard that the young Polish lady, Madame Szymanowska, in whose honour the party had been given, had played the piano quite brilliantly, to the delight of the assembled company. I also gathered that Goethe had met her this summer in Marienbad, and that she had now come to visit him.

Around midday, Goethe sent me a short manuscript, *Studien* by Zauper, which contained some very astute observations. In return, I sent him some poems I had written this summer in Jena, which I had already mentioned to him.

Wednesday 29 October 1823

This evening I went to see Goethe just as the lights were being lit. I found him in very sprightly mood; his eyes sparkled in the candlelight, and his whole expression was one of gaiety, vitality and youth.

Pacing up and down the room with me, he started talking immediately about the poems I sent him yesterday.

'I understand now,' he began, 'why you said in Jena that you wanted to write a poem about the seasons. I think you should do it – and start with winter. You seem to have a special eye and feeling for the things of nature.

'I'd just say a couple of things to you about the poems. You are now at the point where you need to break through to the higher and more difficult realm of art – a grasp of the individual. You need to force the issue, in order to free yourself from the *idea*; you have the talent, you have made great strides – so now is the time. You went to Tiefurt recently, so I'm going to start by making a little exercise out of that.[17] You may need to go back three or four times, perhaps, and look at Tiefurt in detail, until you discover its defining aspect and gather together all the different motifs; but spare no effort, study everything well, and then write it up – the subject is worth the trouble. I would have done it myself a long time ago, but I can't; I was there myself, in its heyday, so it is all too close to home, and the memories come crowding in on me – it's just too much. But you come to it as an outsider; the castellan can tell you the past history, and you will see only what is present, notable and significant.'

I promised to try, although I couldn't deny that it was an exercise that did not come at all naturally or easily to me.

'I know it is difficult,' said Goethe, 'but seeing what is special, and representing it, is the heart and soul of art. To put it another way: if you never get beyond generalities, anyone else can do what you do; but nobody can copy what is individual to you. And why is that? Because the others have not experienced what you have.

'Nor need you fear that the individual will not strike a chord with your readers. Every character, however singular, and every object you seek to portray, from a stone all the way up to a human being, partakes of the general; for everything in nature repeats itself, and there is nothing in the entire world that is truly one of a kind.

'At this stage of individual representation,' Goethe went on, 'begins what we call "composition".'

I didn't quite understand this, but I refrained from asking questions. Perhaps, I thought to myself, he means the artistic fusion of the ideal with the real, the coalescence of what exists outside of us with what is innate within us. But perhaps he means something else. Goethe went on:

'And make sure you always put the date under each poem as you write it.' I looked at him quizzically, wondering why this was so important. 'Because then,' he explained, 'the poems will serve as a diary of your state of mind. And that is no small thing. I've been doing it for years, and I can see how useful it is.'

It was now time for the theatre and I took my leave. He

called after me in jest: 'So you're off to Finland now!' (That evening they were doing *Johann von Finnland*, by Frau von Weissenthurn.)

The play had some good scenes, but the pathos was laid on so thick, and the author's intentions were so clearly signposted, that the overall effect was disappointing. But I enjoyed the last act very much – which rather made up for the rest.

Seeing this play led me to make the following observation. Characters who are indifferently written by the dramatist will gain from theatrical performance, because the actors, being living persons, will make them come alive on the stage and invest them with a certain individuality. On the other hand, characters who are brought to life on the page by a great dramatist, and who all have their own very distinctive individuality, are bound to lose by live performance, because the actors, generally speaking, are not an exact fit with the character, and very few actors are capable of suppressing their own individuality. If the actor is not the exact embodiment of the character, or if he lacks the gift of being able to set aside his own personality completely, the result is a mishmash and the character loses his clear definition. This is why a play by a really great dramatist only ever comes across in the theatre as the author intended in the performances of a few cast members.

Monday 3 November 1823

I went to see Goethe shortly before five. As I went upstairs I heard the loud sound of lively conversation and laughter coming from the large salon. The manservant told me the young Polish lady had come to dinner, and the party had not yet broken up. I was about to leave again, but he told me he had instructions to announce me, adding that his master would probably be glad to see me, as it was now getting late. So I let him carry on and waited a while, until Goethe emerged in very cheerful mood and led me into his room opposite. He seemed pleased to see me. He had a bottle of wine brought in straightaway, poured me a glass, and occasionally topped up his own.

'Before I forget,' he said, searching for something on his desk, 'let me give you this concert ticket. Madame Szymanowska is giving a public concert tomorrow evening in the main room of the public hall, and you must on no account miss it.' I told him that I would not make the same mistake twice. 'I hear she played very well,' I added. 'Sublimely!' said Goethe. 'As good as Hummel?' I asked. 'You have to remember,' said Goethe, 'that she is not only a great virtuoso, but also a beautiful woman; and that lends a special charm to everything she does. She is wonderfully accomplished – quite astonishing!' 'But does she play with power as well?' I asked. 'She does indeed,' said Goethe, 'and that is perhaps the most remarkable thing about her. You don't usually find that with women.' I said that I was really looking forward to hearing her play.

Secretary Kräuter now came in to report on library matters. When he had left, Goethe was full of praise for his efficiency and reliability in business affairs.

I then turned the conversation to the journey he made to Switzerland by way of Frankfurt and Stuttgart in 1797, the manuscript account of which he had recently given to me in three notebooks, and which I had already studied closely. I remarked on how much thought he and Meyer had given at the time to the *subject matter* of the fine arts.

'Indeed,' said Goethe. 'What could be more important than the subject matter? All the art theory in the world is nothing without that. No amount of talent will help you if the subject is no good. This is the problem with all modern art: today's artists don't have any worthy subjects. We're all affected by this; I myself can't escape my own modernity.

'Very few artists,' he continued, 'understand this point and know what will work for them. For example: they try to do a painting of my poem "Der Fischer", not thinking that it can't be painted. This is a ballad all about the *feeling* of water, the seductive appeal that lures us in to bathe in the summer. That's all there is to it – and how are you going to paint that?'

I then said how I liked the way he took an interest in every single thing on that journey, and had taken it all in: the shape and lie of the mountains and their geology; soils, rivers, clouds, air, wind and weather; then towns and cities, their origins and development; architecture, painting, theatre; civic institutions and administration; trade and commerce, economy, road-building; humankind, ways of life, local peculiarities – as well as politics, warfare and a hundred other things besides.

Goethe replied: 'But you won't find a single word about music, for the simple reason that it was not within my sphere of competence. Everyone has to decide for himself what to look for on his travels, and what his particular thing is.'

At this point the Chancellor came in. He spoke briefly with Goethe, then turned to me and talked very graciously and perceptively about a little essay he had recently read. Then he went back to the ladies, where I could hear someone playing the piano.

After he had gone, Goethe spoke very highly of him and said: 'All these excellent men, with whom you are now on familiar terms – they are like a home, to which one is always glad to return.'

I replied that I was already starting to feel the beneficial effects of living here, and was gradually putting my old idealistic and theoretical tendencies behind me as I learned to appreciate the value of the present moment.

'Well, it would be a sorry state of affairs if you weren't,' said Goethe. 'Now you must just keep going and hold fast to the present. Every situation in life, indeed every moment, is of infinite value, because it represents an entire eternity.'

There was a brief pause, and then I brought up the matter of Tiefurt again and how to present it. 'It is a complex subject,' I said, 'and it will be difficult to give it a consistent form throughout. I would be happiest writing about it in prose.'

'The subject is not sufficiently weighty for that,' said Goethe. 'The so-called didactic-descriptive form would be the one to choose, on the whole; but even that is not appropriate throughout. The best thing would be to write ten or twelve separate little poems about the subject, in rhyme, but using a variety of verse forms, as the different aspects and views dictate; by doing that, you will have described the whole thing in the round and illuminated it from every side.' I took this practical advice to heart. 'And indeed, what is stopping you from taking a dramatic approach at some point – imagining a conversation with the gardener, say? By breaking down the whole into smaller parts like this, you'll make life easier for yourself, and can better bring out the characteristic features of the different aspects of the subject. But any large, all-embracing whole is always difficult, and the results are rarely satisfactory.'

Wednesday 10 November 1823

Goethe has been under the weather for the past few days, struggling with a heavy cold, it seems. He is coughing a lot, albeit loudly and lustily; but it must be painful, because he tends to clutch his left side when he coughs.

I spent half an hour with him this evening before the theatre. He was sitting in an armchair, with his back supported by a cushion; talking seemed to be an effort for him.

When we had exchanged a few words, he asked me to read a poem that he planned to use as the opening item in a new issue of *Kunst und Altertum*, which he was now working on. He remained sitting in his chair and showed me where to find the manuscript. I took a light and sat down at his desk, at a little distance from him, and started to read.

The poem had a magical quality, and although I didn't fully understand it on the first reading I found it strangely moving and affecting.[18] Conceived as a trilogy, its subject was the glorification of the pariah. The prevailing tone was like something from another world, and the style of writing made it very difficult for me to get inside the subject matter. Goethe's presence was also rather distracting; I could hear him coughing and sighing from time to time, and so my attention was divided – part of me was reading, the other part was aware all the time of his presence. So I had to keep on rereading the poem, just to make any kind of sense of it. The more I got into it, however, the more significant it seemed, and the more sophisticated as a work of art.

I then discussed both the subject matter and its treatment with Goethe, and some of his comments helped me to see things more clearly.

'It's certainly true,' he observed, 'that the treatment is very concise, and you have to get well into it if you really want to grasp it. I think of it myself as being like a Damascene blade, forged from steel wire. But then I've been thinking about the subject matter for forty years, so it's had plenty of time for any impurities to be refined out.'

'It will make quite an impact,' I said, 'when the public gets to read it.'

'Ah yes – the public!' said Goethe, with a sigh.

'Would it not be a good idea,' I said, 'to help the reader understand better by doing what they do with paintings, when they bring the scene before us to life by showing us what happened in the preceding moments?'

'I don't think so,' said Goethe. 'It's different with paintings. A poem is made up of words, and one word follows on from another.'

It seems to me that Goethe has correctly identified the trap into which literary critics so often fall. But I do wonder if it might not be possible to avoid that trap, and to provide a helpful commentary in words, without at all damaging the poem's delicate inner life.

As I was leaving, he asked me to take the pages for *Kunst und Altertum* home with me, so that I could study the poem at my leisure. Likewise the *Östliche Rosen* by Rückert, a poet he seems to esteem highly, and of whom he has great expectations.

Wednesday 12 November 1823

I went to see Goethe towards evening, but while I was still downstairs I heard that the Prussian Minister of State, von Humboldt, was with him. I was pleased for his sake, and felt sure that a visit from an old friend was just the thing to cheer him up.

I then went to the theatre, where they gave a wonderful performance of *Die Schwestern von Prag*, with an outstanding cast.[19] They had us laughing from start to finish.

Thursday 13 November 1823

A few days ago, as I was walking along the road to Erfurt one fine afternoon, I was joined by an elderly gentleman, whom I judged from his appearance to be a well-to-do citizen.[20] We had not been talking for long before the conversation turned to Goethe. I asked him if he knew Goethe personally. 'Know him personally?' he replied fondly. 'I was his valet for close on twenty years!' He then launched into the praises of his former master. I asked him to tell me a little about Goethe's earlier years, and he happily obliged.

'When I entered his service,' he said, 'he must have been about twenty-seven years old. He was very lean, nimble and dainty. I could easily have picked him up and carried him.'

I asked him if Goethe had been a fun-loving sort of person during their early time together. 'He certainly was,' he replied. 'When there was merrymaking, he kept up with the best of them, but he never took it too far; when things got out of hand, he generally became serious. Always working and studying, with his mind on art and science – that was generally the way with my master. The Duke often came to see him in the evening, and they would talk into the small hours about learned matters, so that I often had to hang around waiting, wondering if the Duke was ever going to leave. And even back then, the study of nature was his special thing.

'One time he rang for me in the middle of the night, and when I entered his room, he had rolled his iron bedstead from one end of the room to the other, right up to the window, and was lying there, gazing at the sky. "Did you see anything in the sky?" he asked, and when I said "No", he told me to run down to the guardhouse and ask the sentry if he had seen anything. I went and asked, but the sentry hadn't seen anything, so I reported back to my master, who was still lying in the same position, gazing up at the sky. "Listen," he said to me then, "we are at a critical moment: either there's an earthquake happening right now, or there's one about to happen." He made me sit down on the bed next to him and showed me by what signs and portents he knew this.'

I asked the good old man what the weather had been like.

'It was completely overcast,' he said, 'and not a breath of air, very still and sultry.'

I then asked if he believed what Goethe said was true.

'Yes,' he said, 'I believed every word, because his predictions always came true. Next day,' he went on, 'my master related his observations at court, and a lady whispered in her neighbour's ear: "Did you hear that? Goethe's lost the plot!" But the Duke and the other gentlemen present all believed Goethe, and it soon turned out that he had been right; news came a few weeks later that part of Messina had been destroyed by an earthquake that very night.'

Friday 14 November 1823

Towards evening Goethe sent me an invitation to call upon him. Humboldt was at court, he informed me, and so my visit would be all the more welcome. I found him sitting in his armchair again, just like a few days before. He stretched out a friendly hand and spoke a few words to me in that wondrously gentle way of his. Beside him stood a large firescreen, which also shaded him from the lights that were still burning on the table. The Chancellor now came in and joined us. We sat down near Goethe and talked of inconsequential matters, so that all he had to do was listen. Soon after that the doctor arrived, Councillor Rehbein. He checked Goethe's pulse and found it, as he put it, 'very sprightly and carefree'. We took this to be a good sign, while Goethe joked about it. 'If only I could get rid of the pain in my left side!' he complained. Rehbein suggested applying a plaster; we talked about the benefits of such a remedy, and Goethe agreed to try it. Rehbein brought the conversation round to Marienbad, which seemed to evoke pleasant memories for Goethe. Plans were made to return there next summer, and it was observed that the Grand Duke would be going along too – prospects that put Goethe in the brightest of moods. We also talked about Madame Szymanowska, and recalled the days when she was here, and all the men were competing for her favour.

When Rehbein had gone, the Chancellor read the Indian poems.[21] Meanwhile, Goethe talked to me about his Marienbad 'Elegie'.

The Chancellor left at eight o'clock, and I made to go too.

But Goethe asked me to stay a while longer, so I sat down again. The talk turned to the theatre, and to tomorrow's performance of *Wallenstein*. This got us on to the subject of Schiller.

'It's a funny thing about Schiller,' I said. 'Some scenes in his great plays I read with genuine love and admiration, but then I come across things that go against the truth of nature, and I cannot get any further. It's the same with *Wallenstein*. I can't help thinking that Schiller's philosophizing got in the way of his poetry; it led him to value the idea over nature, even to the point of negating nature completely. If he could think of it, then it had to happen – whether it was in accordance with nature or not.'

'It is sad,' said Goethe, 'to see how such an extraordinarily gifted man could struggle with philosophical ways of thinking that were of no help to him at all. Humboldt showed me letters that Schiller wrote to him during that unfortunate period of speculation. They show how he turned himself inside out, trying to separate sentimental poetry altogether from naïve poetry. The trouble with this was that he could not find anywhere to ground the former, and this caused him endless difficulties. As if,' Goethe added with a smile, 'sentimental poetry could possibly exist on its own without the naïve soil from which it has sprung, so to speak.

'It was not Schiller's style,' Goethe went on, 'to go about things in an unthinking and, as it were, instinctive way. Instead, he had to reflect on everything he did. This is why he could not help talking endlessly about his poetic intentions; he discussed all his later plays with me, scene by scene.

'With me it was different. It was entirely against my nature to discuss any poetic plans of mine with anyone – not even Schiller. I kept everything to myself, and, generally speaking, nobody knew anything about it until I had finished. When I presented Schiller with the final draft of my *Hermann und Dorothea* he was astonished, because I had never even mentioned that I was planning to write such a thing.

'But I can't wait to hear what you have to say about *Wallenstein* tomorrow! You are about to see some mighty figures on the stage, and the play will make an impression on you that will probably surprise you.'

Saturday 15 November 1823

This evening I went to the theatre, where I saw *Wallenstein* for the first time. Goethe had not exaggerated; it made a big impression, which stirred my innermost being. The actors, most of whom went back to the time when Schiller and Goethe directed them in person, brought to life a cast of memorable characters, who had not appeared to my imagination as distinctive individuals when I read the play. Seeing it on the stage was an extraordinarily powerful experience, and I could not get it out of my head the whole night.

Sunday 16 November 1823

Went to see Goethe this evening. He was still sitting in his armchair and seemed rather frail. He immediately asked about *Wallenstein*. I described the great impression the play had made on me in live performance, and he was visibly gratified to hear this.

M. Soret arrived, led in by Frau von Goethe, and stayed an hour or so. He brought some gold medals from the Grand Duke, and proceeded to show them around and talk about them, which seemed to afford Goethe a pleasant diversion.

Frau von Goethe and M. Soret then left for court, leaving me alone with Goethe once more.

Remembering his promise to show me his Marienbad 'Elegie' again when the time was right, Goethe stood up, placed a light on his desk and handed me the poem. I was thrilled to have it in my hands again. Goethe settled back into his seat and left me to read undisturbed.

After I had been reading for a while, I turned to make some comment, but he seemed to be sleeping. So I took advantage of the moment to read the poem through several times, which afforded me a rare delight. The fiery passion of young love, tempered by a refined moral sensibility – this, it seemed to me, was the driving force behind the whole poem. I also had the impression that the emotions expressed here were more intense than what we are used to from Goethe's other poems, and I concluded that this was due to Byron's influence – which Goethe did not deny.

'What you see there is the product of a highly impassioned state of mind,' he said, 'and while I was in it I would not, for the world, have been without it. Now I would do anything not to get into such a state again.

'I wrote the poem straight after leaving Marienbad, while the feeling of all I had experienced there was still fresh in my mind. I wrote the first stanza at eight in the morning, when we stopped at the first stage, and then carried on composing in the carriage, writing down at each stage what I had worked out in my head en route. So by the evening I had the whole thing down on paper. For this reason it has a certain immediacy, and feels like a seamless whole – and is probably all the better for it.'

'At the same time,' I said, 'the whole style is very distinctive, and doesn't remind one of any of your other poems.'

'That may be,' said Goethe, 'because I staked everything on the present, like a man who puts all his money on one card. I wanted to intensify that sense of the present as much as possible – but without overdoing it.'

I thought this was a very significant observation. It casts light on Goethe's method of working, and helps to explain the much-admired diversity of his output.

It was now coming up to nine o'clock, and Goethe asked me to call his manservant Stadelmann, which I duly did.

He then got Stadelmann to put the prescribed plaster on the left side of his chest. I went and stood by the window while this was done. I heard Goethe talking to Stadelmann behind me, complaining that his illness was not getting any better and was becoming a permanent condition. When the procedure was finished, I went and sat next to him for a little longer. Now it was my turn, and he complained to me that he had not slept at all for several nights and had no appetite. 'The winter is passing,' he said, 'and I can't do anything. I can't put anything together, I've got no mental energy at all.' I tried to reassure him by telling him not to think about his work so much, and that this present phase would soon pass, hopefully. 'It's not that I'm impatient,' he said. 'I've been through too many times like this before, and I have learned to suffer and endure.' He was sitting in his white flannel dressing gown, with a woollen blanket wrapped around his knees and feet. 'I shan't go to bed at all,' he said. 'I'll stay here in my chair tonight, because I won't be able to sleep properly anyway.'

It was now time for me to go. He gave me his dear hand, and I left.

When I entered the servants' room downstairs to get my coat, I found Stadelmann in great distress. He said he was alarmed by his master's condition; if *he* was complaining, then things must be bad. And his feet, which had previously been a little swollen, had suddenly become quite skinny. Stadelmann said he would go and see the doctor first thing next morning and tell him about these worrying signs. I tried to reassure him, but he would not be talked out of his fears.

Monday 17 November 1823

When I went to the theatre this evening, many people came up to me and enquired anxiously about Goethe's health. News of his condition must have spread rapidly through the town, perhaps making things sound worse than they really were. Some told me he had dropsy of the chest. I was in sombre mood all evening.

Wednesday 19 November 1823

Yesterday I went around feeling worried all day. Nobody apart from family members was allowed in to see him.

Towards evening I went to his house, and was received. I found him still sitting in his armchair. He looked just the same as when I left him on Sunday, but his mood now was much brighter.

We talked mainly about Zauper, and about the very different effects that can result from studying the literature of the ancients.

1823 61

Friday 21 November 1823

Goethe sent for me. To my great delight I found him up and about, moving around his room. He handed me a little book, *Ghaselen*, by Count Platen.[22] 'I had intended,' he said, 'to write something about this in *Kunst und Altertum*, because the poems are worth reviewing. But I just can't manage it in my present condition. Have a look, and see if you can make sense of the poems and get something out of them.'

I promised to see what I could do.

'The thing about ghazals,' Goethe went on, 'is that they call for an abundance of content; because the same rhyme is constantly recurring, it needs to be sustained by a steady supply of similar thoughts. This is why not everyone can do them. But you'll like these.' The doctor then came in, and I left.

Monday 24 November 1823

On Saturday and Sunday I studied the poems. This morning I put down my thoughts on paper and sent them to Goethe, having learned that he had not been receiving visitors for several days; the doctor had forbidden him to talk.

Despite this, he sent for me today towards evening. When I entered, I saw an empty chair waiting for me next to him. He extended his hand to me and was kindness itself. He began by talking about my little review. 'I liked it very much,' he said. 'You have a fine talent. And there's something I want to tell you,' he went on. 'If you are offered literary commissions from other quarters, I would like you to turn them down – or at least consult me first; now that you are working with me, I would not like it if you had similar arrangements with others.'

I replied that I wished to stick with him alone, and that I had no thought for now of entering into other relationships.

He was pleased to hear it, and said that we would be doing a lot of good work together this winter.

We then got to talking about the *Ghaselen* themselves. Goethe took great pleasure in the perfection of these poems, and in the fact that contemporary German writers are producing a lot of good work.

'In fact,' he went on, 'I'd like to commend our emerging literary talents to your special attention and study. It would be good if you could follow the German literary scene and let me know about any new publications of note, so that we can review them in the latest numbers of *Kunst und Altertum*, and single out the best and finest work for special mention. With the best will in the world I cannot, at my age and with all my other obligations, keep up with it all without outside help.'

I promised to do as he asked, and was pleased to note that Goethe cared a lot more about our new writers and poets than I had imagined.

Over the next few days Goethe sent me the latest literary journals for the purpose we had discussed. For several days I didn't go and see him and was not summoned. I heard that his friend Zelter had come to visit him.

Monday 1 December 1823

Today I was invited to dine with Goethe. I found Zelter sitting with him when I entered. They both stepped forward and shook my hand. 'This is my friend Zelter,' said Goethe. 'You'll find he is a good man to know! I will be sending you off to Berlin some time soon, and he will take excellent care of you.' 'I imagine Berlin is a good place to be,' I remarked. 'Oh yes,' said Zelter with a laugh. 'There's a lot to be learned and unlearned there.'

We sat down and talked about all manner of things. I asked after Schubarth. 'He visits me at least once a week,' said Zelter. 'He's married now, but he has no position, having fallen out with the literary scholars in Berlin.'

Zelter then asked me if I knew Immermann. 'I have often heard his name mentioned,' I replied, 'but I know nothing about his writings.' 'I met him in Münster,' said Zelter. 'He's a very promising young man, and it's a shame that his job leaves him so little time for his art.' Goethe also praised his talent: 'We shall have to see how he develops. It depends whether he is

1823 63

prepared to refine his taste and be guided, in matters of form, by the example of those who are acknowledged as the best models. His pursuit of originality has its good side, but it is all too easy to lose one's way.'

Young Walter now came bounding into the room, with lots of questions for Zelter and his grandfather. 'When you turn up, restless spirit,' said Goethe, 'all conversation comes to an end!' But he loves the boy dearly and was tireless in his efforts to please him.

Frau von Goethe and Fräulein Ulrike now came in, together with young Goethe, dressed for court in full uniform and sword. We sat down at the table. Fräulein Ulrike and Zelter were on very good form, teasing each other in the most delightful way throughout dinner. Zelter's person and presence made me feel good. He was such a happy and wholesome man, who always lived entirely in the moment and was never lost for words. Good-natured and easy-going, he spoke his mind freely, and could be downright earthy on occasion. He was a free spirit – and it was infectious; when you were with him, you very quickly shed any polite inhibitions. Privately, I wished that I could live with him for a while, and am certain that it would do me good.

Soon after dinner, Zelter left us. He had been invited to spend the evening with the Grand Duchess.

Thursday 4 December 1823

This morning Secretary Kräuter brought me an invitation to dine with Goethe. He also passed on a suggestion from Goethe that I might present a copy of my *Beiträge zur Poesie* to Zelter. I did as he suggested, taking the book to the inn where Zelter was staying. In return, Zelter gave me Immermann's *Gedichte*. 'I would happily give it to you as a present,' he said, 'but as you see, the author has dedicated this copy to me. So it is a precious memento, which I must therefore keep.'

Before dinner, I took a walk with Zelter through the park, towards Upper Weimar. Several places along the way put him in mind of earlier times, and he told me stories about Schiller, Wieland and Herder, who had been good friends of his – which he regarded as one of the great blessings of his life.

He then talked a great deal about musical composition, and recited several songs by Goethe. 'When I want to put a poem to music,' he said, 'I start by trying to understand the full meaning of the words and imagining myself in the situation described. I then read it aloud until I know it by heart, and eventually, as I keep on reciting it to myself, the melody just comes to me.'

Wind and rain forced us to return earlier than we really wanted to. I accompanied him as far as Goethe's house, where he went upstairs to Frau von Goethe in order to sing through a few things with her before dinner.

I returned at two o'clock for dinner. I found Zelter already sitting with Goethe, looking at some engravings of Italian landscapes. Frau von Goethe came in, and we sat down to dinner. Fräulein Ulrike was not with us today, likewise young Goethe, who just looked in to say hello, and then went off to court again.

The conversation at table today ranged far and wide. There were lots of amusing anecdotes from Zelter and Goethe, all of them highlighting various characteristics of their mutual friend in Berlin, Friedrich August Wolf. This led on to a discussion of the *Nibelungen*, followed by talk of Lord Byron and hopes of a possible visit to Weimar – a prospect that seemed to interest Frau von Goethe greatly.[23] The festival of St Roch at Bingen was another topic that gave rise to some mirth, with Zelter recalling a pair of beautiful girls whose charms had evidently made a deep impression on him, since he still remembered them so fondly today.[24] Goethe's jolly ballad 'Kriegsglück' was then discussed with great merriment. Zelter had an inexhaustible supply of anecdotes about wounded soldiers and beautiful women, all of which served to show how true to life the poem was. Goethe himself said that he had not needed to go very far to find such realities; he had seen it all himself in Weimar. Frau von Goethe put up a light-hearted fight, refusing to allow that women were like the ones portrayed in that 'beastly' poem.

And so we spent some very pleasant hours around the table again today.

Later on, when I was alone with Goethe, he asked me about Zelter. 'Well now,' he said, 'what do you make of him?' I said that he was the sort of person you just couldn't help liking. 'He can seem pretty rough and ready on first acquaintance,' Goethe added, 'perhaps even a touch crude sometimes. But that's just on the outside. I know of hardly anyone who is as *tender* as Zelter. And don't forget: this is a man who has lived in *Berlin* for more than fifty years. The sort of people you find there – or so everything tells me – are a pretty tough bunch, and fine feelings don't get you very far with them. You need to have a sharp tongue in your head and cut up a bit rough sometimes, just to keep your head above water.'

1824

Tuesday 27 January 1824

Goethe spoke to me about the continuation of his memoirs, which he is currently working on.[25] He remarked that he would not be covering this later period of his life in the same detail as the period of his youth, as related in *Dichtung und Wahrheit*.

'I must treat these later years,' said Goethe, 'more as a chronicle of events. It is less about my life, and more about what I have been doing. The most important time in anyone's life is the period of their development, which in my case was covered in detail in the various volumes of *Dichtung und Wahrheit*. Later on, we begin to find ourselves at odds with the world, and that is only interesting if something worthwhile comes out of it.

'And anyway, what does it amount to, the life of a German scholar? In my case, whatever may be good about it cannot be shared with others, and what *can* be shared is not worth the effort. And besides, where are the listeners one would be comfortable telling these things to?

'When I look back at my earlier life and middle years and reflect now, in my old age, how few of my contemporaries are still left, I always think it's like staying in a spa town for the summer. When you arrive, you make friends with people who have already been there a while, and who will be leaving in the coming weeks. It hurts to see them go. Then you embrace the second generation, and you live with them for a good while and become very attached to them. But eventually they go as well, and you are left alone with the third – people who arrive shortly before you are due to leave, and with whom you have no connection at all.

'People have always regarded me as someone specially favoured by fortune. And I can't complain, or regret the course my life has taken. But if I'm honest, it has been nothing but work and toil, and it is fair to say that I have not known four weeks of pure contentment in all my seventy-five years. It's been like rolling a heavy stone the whole time, lifting it, turning it over, and then having to do it all over again. My memoirs will spell it out very clearly. There were just too many claims on my time and energy, both from others and from myself.

'My true happiness has come from my poetic musings and writings. But when I think how these have been interrupted, curtailed, and held back by the demands of my official position! Had I been able to distance myself more from public life and business affairs and live a more solitary life, I would have been a happier man and would have accomplished far more as a poet. But as it was, not long after I wrote my *Götz* and *Werther* I became living proof of what some wise man once said: if you do something to please the public, the public will make darn sure you don't do it again.

'A celebrated name and a prominent position in life are all very fine. But see where my celebrity and standing have got me; now I have to keep quiet about the opinions of others, in case I give offence. This would be no fun at all, except that I have the advantage of knowing what others think, while they don't know what I think.'

Sunday 15 February 1824

Today Goethe had invited me to take a drive with him before dinner. I found him breakfasting when I entered the room; he seemed in a very jolly mood.

'I have had a pleasant visit,' was his cheery greeting to me. 'A most promising young man from Westphalia, by the name of Meyer, came to see me earlier. He has written poems that lead one to expect great things. He is only eighteen, but incredibly far on already.

'I wouldn't want to be eighteen now,' said Goethe with a laugh. 'When I was eighteen, so was Germany – and you could still make your mark. But now the pressures are unbelievable, and every avenue is barred.

'Germany itself is now so advanced in every field that we can scarcely grasp the full extent of it. And now we are supposed to be Greek and Latin scholars too, not to mention au fait with all things English and French. As if that's not enough, the latest craze would have us look to the East as well. It's no wonder the young are confused.

'By way of reassurance, I showed him my colossal Juno, as a token that he was better off sticking to the Greeks, and finding peace of mind there.[26] He really is a very fine young man. As long as he doesn't go off in too many different directions, he should make something of himself.

'But as I say, I thank heaven that I am no longer young today, in these times when everything has already been done. I wouldn't be able to stay here. But even if I were to escape to America, I should arrive too late; there would be too much light over there as well.'

Sunday 22 February 1824

Dined with Goethe and his son. The latter told us a few funny stories from his student days, when he was studying in Heidelberg. During the vacations he had made several excursions with friends along the Rhine, and cherished special memories of one landlord with whom he had once stayed overnight with ten other students, and who had served them with wine free of charge, just so that he could have the pleasure of hosting a student drinking party.

After dinner, Goethe showed us some watercolour drawings of Italian landscapes, particularly in northern Italy, with the mountains of neighbouring Switzerland and Lago Maggiore. The Borromean Islands were reflected in the water, and along the shore one could see boats and fishing gear, which prompted Goethe to observe that this was the lake featured in his *Wanderjahre*. To the north-west, in the direction of Monte Rosa, lay the foothills bordering the lake, forming a dark, inky-blue mass, as they appear shortly after sunset.

I remarked that there was something sinister for me, as someone born in the flat country, about the gloomy grandeur of these towering masses, and that I had no desire at all to explore those wild recesses.

'This is a natural feeling,' said Goethe. 'At bottom, people are only comfortable with the condition in which, and for which, they were born. Unless some great enterprise takes you abroad, you are much better off staying at home. Switzerland made such a deep impression on me at first that I was left feeling confused and unsettled. It was only in later years, after going back there many times, when I was seeing the mountains through the eyes of a mineralogist, that I could take a calm and detached view of them.'

We then looked through a large set of engravings after paintings by contemporary artists from a French gallery. Nearly all the pictures showed a woeful lack of imagination, and out of forty we were hard put to find four or five good ones. These were: a girl dictating a love letter; a woman in a house up for sale, but with no buyers; a fishing scene; and musicians before an image of the Madonna. A landscape in the style of Poussin was also not bad, prompting the following remark from Goethe: 'Artists like these have picked up the general idea of Poussin's landscapes, and then keep on reworking it. You can't say their pictures are good or bad. They are not bad, because you catch glimpses everywhere of the excellent model that inspired them. But you can't call them good, either, because most artists don't have Poussin's strength of character. It's exactly the same with poets, and there are plenty who would cut a sorry figure if they tried to write in the grand manner of Shakespeare, for example.'

Finally, we spent a long time studying and discussing Rauch's model for the statue of Goethe commissioned by the Frankfurt city fathers.[27]

Tuesday 24 February 1824

Called on Goethe at one o'clock. He showed me various manuscripts that he had dictated for the first number of the fifth volume of *Kunst und Altertum*. I discovered an appendix he had written to my review of the German *Paria*,[28] in which he refers both to the French tragedy and to his own lyrical trilogy – in a sense, therefore, bringing the discussion of this topic to a close.

'It's good,' said Goethe, 'that you used your review as an opportunity to acquaint yourself with Indian life and culture. In the end, all that we remember from our studies are the things that we put to practical use.'

I agreed, and said that I learned this lesson myself when I was a student: all I remembered from my teachers' lectures were the things I was disposed by nature to apply in my own life; everything else, which I never subsequently made use of, was completely forgotten. 'I went to Heeren's lectures on ancient and modern history, but I don't remember a single word. But if I were to study some historical event now, with a view to dramatizing it, say, then that knowledge would surely stay with me for ever.'

'The fact is,' said Goethe, 'they teach far too many things in universities, and far too much that is useless. And the individual lecturers try to cover too much ground, way beyond what the students need. In the past, chemistry and botany were only taught as adjuncts to pharmacology, and that was sufficient for medical students. But now, chemistry and botany have become separate sciences in their own right, each so vast that it requires a lifetime's study; but medical students are now expected to fit them in as well! No good can come of it; if you try to pack too much in, something has to give. Anyone with any sense will therefore ignore all such distractions, and will focus instead on *one* subject and master it fully.'

Goethe then showed me a brief review of Byron's *Cain* that he had written, which I read with great interest.

'You can see,' he said, 'how a free spirit like Byron really struggled with the limitations of Church dogma, and how writing a piece like this was his way of trying to free himself from a doctrine that had been forced upon him. The English clergy will not thank him for it; but I shall be surprised if he doesn't go on to write about similar biblical themes. I can't see him passing up a subject like the destruction of Sodom and Gomorrah.'

1824 71

After these literary reflections, Goethe directed my attention to the visual arts, showing me an antique engraved gemstone that he had spoken of with admiration the day before. I was enchanted by the naïveté of the image. It showed a man who had lifted a heavy vessel from his shoulder so that a boy could drink from it. But he is not holding it quite right for the boy to drink from it easily, and the liquid is not coming out. The boy is grasping the vessel with both his little hands, and gazing up at the man as if to ask him to tip it a little more.

'Well, what do you think of that?' said Goethe. 'We moderns,' he went on, 'can appreciate the beauty of such a purely natural, purely naïve motif, and we also have the technical knowledge to understand how such a thing is done. But we cannot do it ourselves; our rational nature gets in the way, and the delightful charm of these things invariably eludes us.'

We then looked at a medal by Brandt in Berlin, showing the young Theseus taking the weapons of his father from under the stone. There was much to commend in the way the figure is posed, but we thought the limbs did not look as if they are straining under the heavy weight of the stone. It also seemed a bad idea to show the youth holding the weapons in one hand while still lifting the stone with the other. The natural thing would be for him to push the heavy stone to one side and then pick up the weapons. 'By way of contrast,' said Goethe, 'I'll show you a gemstone from classical times, where the same subject has been treated by an ancient.'

Stadelmann was asked to fetch a box containing several hundred impressions taken from antique gemstones, which Goethe had brought back from Rome at the time of his travels in Italy. I now saw the same subject treated by an ancient Greek – and what a difference! The youth is bracing himself against the stone with all his might, and his strength is equal to the task; we can see he has overcome the weight and lifted the stone to the point where it can now be heaved to one side. The young hero is bringing all his physical strength to bear on the heavy mass; only his gaze is directed downwards, at the weapons lying on the ground before him.

We both applauded the realism of this scene.

'Meyer always says,' observed Goethe with a laugh, '"if only thinking were not such hard work!" But the worst part,' he continued cheerfully, 'is that all the thinking in the world doesn't make thinking any easier. We have to be right by nature, so that good ideas just come to us, like free children of God, shouting "Here we are!".'

Wednesday 25 February 1824

Today Goethe showed me two very remarkable poems, both highly moral in their tendency, but at the same time so unashamedly natural and true in their individual motifs that the world generally adjudges such things 'immoral'.[29] This is why he has kept them secret, with no intention of publishing them.

'If intellect and cultural refinement were the common property of all,' he said, 'the poet would have an easy time of it; he could always speak the unvarnished truth and need not worry about saying the best that came to mind. But as things are, he is always obliged to maintain a certain decorum; he has to remember that his works will fall into the hands of a mixed public, and must therefore take care not to offend the majority of good people by being too explicit. Time is a strange thing, too. Time is a tyrant, which has its whims, and looks differently upon our words and actions from one century to the next. What the ancient Greeks were permitted to say is somehow not appropriate for *us* to say; and what was entirely acceptable to Shakespeare's down-to-earth contemporaries is too much for an Englishman of 1820, which is why there was such a ready market for the recent *Family Shakespeare*.'[30]

'The form also makes a great deal of difference,' I added. 'One of the two poems, written in the style and metre of the ancients, is far less likely to give offence than the other. Some motifs are repugnant in themselves, certainly, but the treatment imbues the whole with so much grandeur and dignity that we feel we are listening to some red-blooded ancient and have been transported back to the age of Greek heroes. The other poem, by contrast, written in the style and metre of Master Ariosto, is a lot trickier. It recounts a present-day adventure in the language of today, and because it seems part of our own here and now, not cloaked in the trappings of the past, the more daring passages appear far more risqué.'

'You are quite right,' said Goethe. 'The effects produced by the different poetic forms are mysterious and powerful. If one were to rewrite my *Römische Elegien* in the style and metre of Byron's *Don Juan*, it would come across as thoroughly immoral.'

The French newspapers were then brought in. The end of the French campaign in Spain under the Duke of Angoulême was of great interest to Goethe.[31] 'I applaud the Bourbons for this action,' he said, 'because they need to secure the army in order to secure the throne. And this they have now done. The soldier returns home loyal to his king, having learned from his own victories, and from the defeats of the Spanish under a succession of generals, what a difference there is between obeying one and obeying many. The army has lived up to its past glory and shown that it is still a brave fighting force in its own right, capable of winning victories even without Napoleon.'

Goethe then turned his thoughts to earlier history, and spoke at length about the Prussian army in the Seven Years' War; accustomed to constant victories under Frederick the Great, and growing complacent as a result, it lost many battles in later years from overconfidence. He knew it all in minute detail, and I could only admire his excellent memory.

'I have the great advantage,' he went on, 'that I was born at a time when the most momentous world events were taking place, and these have continued throughout my long lifetime. I was a living witness to the Seven Years' War, then the separation of America from Britain, then the French Revolution, and finally the whole Napoleonic era, until the downfall of that heroic figure and the events that followed. Consequently I have arrived at very different conclusions and insights to those available to anyone born now, who will have to learn about those great events from books that he doesn't understand.

'What the next few years will bring is impossible to say; but I fear that things will not settle down any time soon. It is not the way of the world to be content with what we have; not the way of the great to renounce the abuse of power; and not the way of the masses to accept their mediocre lot in the hope that things will gradually improve. If we could perfect *human nature*, then a perfect state of affairs might be conceivable. But as it is, the pendulum will continue to swing back and forth; some will suffer while others prosper, selfishness and envy will always be about their work, like evil demons; and party strife will never cease.

'The most sensible thing, always, is for everyone to keep to his own trade, the one he was born to and the one he has learned, and not to interfere with others in the pursuit of theirs. The cobbler should stick to his last, the farmer should follow the plough, and the prince should concentrate on the business of government. Because it *is* a business, which has to be learned, and those who don't understand it should not presume to meddle with it.'

Returning to the French newspapers, Goethe then said: 'It's fine for the liberals to have their say, when they are talking sense, because we like to listen to them. But the royalists, in whose hands the executive power rests, should leave the talking to others; they need to act. Let them march their troops, guillotine and hang – this is in order; but attacking the views of others in print and justifying their measures – this does not become them. It would be a different matter if the public were made up of kings; then they could talk.

'As for myself,' Goethe went on, 'I have always been a royalist. I have let others prattle on, while I just did as I saw fit. I knew what I was doing, and where I wanted to go. If I made a mistake, acting by myself, I was able to put it right again; but had I slipped up along with three or four others, it would have been impossible to make things good, because there are always differences of opinion within a group.'

At table, Goethe was in ebullient mood. He showed me Frau von Spiegel's album, in which he had written some very beautiful verses. For two years she had left a blank space for him to write in, and he was pleased that he was now finally able to fulfil an old promise. After reading his poem to Frau von Spiegel, I leafed through the rest of the album, and came across many a well-known name. On the very next page was a poem

1824 75

by Tiedge, written in the style and spirit of his *Urania*. 'In a moment of recklessness,' said Goethe, 'I was about to write some verses of my own below his. But I'm glad I didn't, because it would not have been the first time that I have offended good people by unguarded comments, and spoiled the effect of my best works.

'Mind you,' Goethe went on, 'I have had to endure quite a lot of Tiedge's *Urania*. There was a time when this *Urania* of his was the only thing you heard sung and declaimed. Wherever you went, there was a copy of *Urania* on the table. Every conversation was about *Urania* and immortality. Now I would not wish to forfeit the joy of believing in the afterlife – not at all; indeed, I would echo Lorenzo de' Medici when he says that those who do not have hopes of another life are dead to this one. But such imponderables are too far beyond our grasp to be the subject of daily reflection and mind-numbing speculation. Furthermore: those who believe in immortality are welcome to their happiness in private, but there's no reason to be smug about it. When Tiedge's *Urania* was all the rage, I made the observation that pious folk constitute a kind of aristocracy, just like the nobility. I met stupid women who were proud of the fact that they shared Tiedge's belief in immortality, and I had to endure some of them quizzing me on this point in the most condescending way imaginable. But I annoyed them by saying I should be quite happy to be blessed with an afterlife when the present one is ended, as long as I don't have to meet anyone in that life who believed in it in this one. Because then my torment would begin in earnest! The pious would crowd around me and say: "We told you so, didn't we? We said how it would be. Has it not turned out exactly like we said?" So there would be no escape, even in the next world, from the endless tedium.

'This preoccupation with immortality,' Goethe went on, 'is for people of rank, and especially for women who have nothing to do. But an industrious man, who intends to make something of himself in this life, and therefore has to strive and struggle and be about his business every day, leaves the next world to take care of itself, and is active and useful in this one. Furthermore, thoughts about immortality are for those who have not done all that well for themselves in this life, and I'd be prepared to wager that if good old Tiedge had enjoyed better fortunes, he would also have had better thoughts.'

Thursday 26 February 1824

Dined with Goethe. When we had finished and the table had been cleared, he asked Stadelmann to bring in some large portfolios of engravings. The covers were rather dusty, and as we couldn't find a cloth to wipe the dust off, Goethe became quite irritated and reprimanded his manservant. 'I shall not tell you again,' he said. 'If you do not go this very day and buy those cloths I have asked you for so often, I'll go and get them myself tomorrow – and I mean it.' Stadelmann departed.

'I once had a similar situation with the actor Becker,' said Goethe brightly, turning to me. 'He was refusing to play a trooper in *Wallenstein*. I let him know that if he would not play the part, I would play it myself. That had the desired effect. They knew me well at the theatre, and they knew that in such matters I was not to be trifled with, and was crazy enough to keep my word and do the daftest thing.'

'And would you really have played the part?' I asked.

'Certainly I would,' said Goethe, 'and I would have acted Herr Becker off the stage, because I knew the part better than he did.'

We now opened the portfolios and began to study the engravings and drawings. Goethe proceeds very carefully with me in such matters, and I sense that he wants to take me to a higher level of discernment in the study of art. He shows me only works that are perfect examples of their kind, and explains the artist's intentions and merits to me, so that I might learn to think the thoughts of the best of them and to feel as they do. 'This is the way to cultivate what we call taste,' he said today. 'Taste is not to be cultivated by studying works of middling quality, but only through exposure to true excellence. This is why I am showing you only the best works; once you are well grounded in these, you will have a yardstick for judging all the rest, which you will not then overrate, but value at their true worth. I also want to show you the best work in each genre, so that you see that no genre as such is to be despised; they all give pleasure when an artist of real talent brings them to the peak of perfection. This picture by a French artist, for example, is *galant* like no other, and that makes it a classic of its kind.'[32]

Goethe handed me the engraving, and I found it most pleasing. We see a group of charming figures sitting in a delightful room in a summer residence, with a view of the garden through the open doors and windows. An attractive woman of about thirty is sitting holding a music book, from which she has apparently just been singing. Sitting beside her, a little further back, a young girl of about fifteen is leaning over. At the back, standing by an open window, is another young lady; she is holding a lute, which she appears still to be playing. A young gentleman has just entered the room, and all the women are looking at him; he seems to have interrupted their musical entertainment, and as he stands before them, bowing slightly, he looks as if he is making an apology – which evidently pleases the women.

'Now that, I would have thought,' said Goethe, 'is every bit as *galant* as any of Calderón's plays, and you have now seen the finest example of its kind. But what do you make of these?'

And with that, he handed me some etchings by the celebrated animal painter Roos; they were all of sheep, depicted in every variety of pose. Their blank expressions and scruffy, shaggy fleeces were all captured with the utmost fidelity to nature.

'I always feel slightly anxious when I look at these animals,' said Goethe. 'The dull, narrow life they lead, nothing to do but daydream and gawp, makes me empathize with them; I worry that I might become one of them, and it's almost as if the artist were a sheep himself. Anyway, it is quite astonishing how he was able to think and feel his way into the souls of these creatures, so that their true internal character shows through the external physical shell. It just goes to show what a man of superior talent can achieve if he sticks to subjects for which he has a natural affinity.'

'I wonder,' I said, 'if this artist also depicted dogs, cats and beasts of prey with similar truthfulness? And since he had this great gift for feeling his way into the mind and soul of another being, surely he must have portrayed human characters with the same fidelity?'

'No,' Goethe replied, 'all that lay outside his ambit. But the gentle herbivores, such as sheep, goats, cows and the like – he never tired of drawing them, over and over again. This was home territory for his particular talent, and he never strayed beyond it all his life. A wise decision! He had a natural empathy for these animals, an innate understanding of their psychology, and that's why he had such a good eye for their physical attributes as well. It may be, however, that other creatures were not so transparent to him, and so he did not feel called or driven to portray them.'

This remark of Goethe's reminded me of other, similar things he had said, all of which now came flooding back to me. A little while ago, for example, he had said that the true poet is born with an understanding of the world, and that he does not need a lot of experience or empirical knowledge to write about it. 'I wrote my *Götz von Berlichingen* as a young man of twenty-two,' he said, 'and ten years later I was amazed to see how true to life my portrayal had been. Obviously I had not personally experienced or seen anything like that, so I must have had an instinctive fore-knowledge of the human condition in its various manifestations.

'The fact is, until I got to know the world at large I was only interested in portraying my own inner world. When I subsequently discovered that the real world was just as I had imagined it to be, I found it tedious and had no more interest in depicting it. I'd go so far as to say that if I had held off writing about the real world until I had got to know it, I would have ended up satirizing it.'

On another occasion he said: 'There is a certain law of character, a sort of inbuilt imperative, whereby this or that basic character trait is always accompanied by certain secondary traits. We learn this soon enough from practical experience, but some people are born knowing this. Now whether innate knowledge and acquired experience are combined in my case, is not for me to judge; but this much I do know: if I have spoken to somebody for a quarter of an hour, I will happily let him talk on for two hours.'

Similarly, Goethe had said of Lord Byron that the world was transparent to him, and that he was able to portray it by intuitive foreknowledge. I had my doubts about this, and wondered whether, for example, Byron would be capable of depicting a lower animal nature, since his personality seemed to me too overpowering for him to devote himself wholeheartedly to such subjects. Goethe conceded the point, and replied that such foreknowledge only goes so far, depending on the degree of natural affinity the talent in question has for the subject matter. We agreed that the artistic talent itself will be adjudged greater or smaller, depending on how limited or extensive that foreknowledge is.

'If Your Excellency is claiming,' I then said, 'that the world is innate in the poet, I take it you mean the internal world only, and not the empirical world of outward appearance and social convention; so if the poet is to portray the latter faithfully, then surely he will need to study the real things of life?'

'Indeed,' replied Goethe, 'so he will. The domain of love, hate, hope, despair, and all the other emotional conditions and passions, is innate in the poet, and writing about it presents no difficulties for him. But we are not born knowing how a law court functions, how a parliament conducts its business, or what takes place at an imperial coronation; and in order to get his facts right in such matters, the poet must acquaint himself with the facts at first hand, or by referring to others. In *Faust*, for example, it was well within my power to invoke the hero's dark, world-weary mood, and Gretchen's feelings of love, through the power of imaginative intuition. But in order to write lines such as:

> How sorrowfully does the part-formed disc
> Of the tardy moon with humid glow arise —[33]

some observation of nature was required.'

'And yet,' I said, 'there is not a single line in the whole of *Faust* that does not bear the unmistakable hallmark of a careful study of the world and of life; and nobody would suppose for a moment that it all came to you just like that, without your having a wealth of experience to draw on.'

'Perhaps so,' replied Goethe. 'But if I did not already have within me some foreknowledge of the world at large, I would have remained blind with sighted eyes, and no amount of study and experience would have made the slightest difference. The light is there, and we are surrounded by colours; but if we didn't have the light, and the colours, in our own eyes we would not be able to see them in the outside world.'

Saturday 28 February 1824

'There are,' said Goethe, 'excellent people who are unable to do anything impromptu or superficially, but whose nature compels them to study the subject in hand at their leisure and at length. Minds of this sort often make us impatient, because they rarely give us what we want right now; but the end result is work of the highest quality.'

I mentioned Ramberg's name. 'Now he is a very different type of artist,' said Goethe, 'a most delightful talent, with a unique gift for improvisation. He asked me once in Dresden to give him a subject. I suggested Agamemnon, at the moment when he returns home from Troy, alighting from his chariot, and pausing at the threshold of his house, as if unsure whether to enter. As subjects go, this was a huge challenge, as I'm sure you'll agree, and any other artist would have needed to reflect long and hard. But the words were hardly out of my mouth before Ramberg started to draw, and I had to admire the way he immediately got the measure of the subject. I won't deny that I should dearly like to own some drawings by Ramberg.'

We then talked about other artists who are not serious about their work, and who eventually degenerate into mannerism.

'Mannerism,' said Goethe, 'can't wait to be finished, and takes no pleasure in the work itself. But an artist of real talent finds his greatest enjoyment in the execution. Roos is a tireless draughtsman, busily drawing the hair and wool of his goats and sheep; you can see from the endless detail that he was blissfully happy in his work, and didn't care about finishing.

'Art for its own sake is not enough for lesser talents; as they work on something, they are thinking only of the profit they

1824

hope to make from the finished piece. But nothing great can ever come from such worldly aims and ambitions.'

Sunday 29 February 1824

At noon I called on Goethe, who had invited me to take a drive with him before dinner. I found him breakfasting when I entered the room, so I sat down opposite him and brought up the subject of the work we are doing together for the new edition of his works. I encouraged him to include both his *Götter, Helden und Wieland* and his 'Brief des Pastors' in this new edition.

'From where I stand now,' said Goethe, 'I don't really have an opinion on those products of my youth. I leave it to you younger people to decide. But I'm not disparaging those humble beginnings. I was still feeling my way, it is true, and pressing ahead without really knowing what I was doing; but I had an instinct for what was right, a divining rod that showed where gold was to be found.'

I pointed out that this must be the case with any great talent, which otherwise, on awakening in this confusing world of ours, would not choose the right path and avoid the wrong one.

By now the horses had been hitched up, and we set off along the road towards Jena. We talked about this and that, and Goethe mentioned the most recent French newspapers.

'The constitution of France,' he said, 'in a nation that contains so many corrupt elements, rests on very different foundations from that of Britain. In France you can achieve anything by bribery; the entire French Revolution ran on bribery.'

Goethe then told me about the death of Eugène Napoleon, Duke of Leuchtenberg, the news of which had arrived this morning. He seemed deeply saddened by it. 'He was one of those great figures,' said Goethe, 'who are becoming increasingly rare, and the world is the poorer for the loss of yet another eminent man. I knew him personally; I saw him in Marienbad only last summer. He was a handsome man of forty-two or so, but he looked older – which is not surprising, when you consider everything he went through, and how his whole life was just one campaign and one great exploit after another. In Marienbad he told me about a plan he had, and discussed the details of its execution at length with me. He wanted to construct a canal linking the Rhine to the Danube – a massive undertaking when you consider the difficulties of the terrain! But to a man who served under Napoleon and turned the world upside down with him, nothing seems impossible. Charlemagne had the same plan, and even made a start on the work; but the project soon ground to a halt: the sand would not hold, and the walls of the trench were constantly collapsing.'

Monday 22 March 1824

Drove out with Goethe to his garden before dinner.

The situation of this garden, on the other side of the Ilm, near the park, and on the western slopes of a line of hills, is most inviting. Shielded from the north and east winds, it is exposed to the warming and invigorating influences of the southern and western skies, which make it a very agreeable place to be, especially in the autumn and spring.

The town lies to the north-west, so close that you can be there within minutes, and yet, when you look around you, you cannot see a single building or spire to remind you of the town's presence; the view from the park in that direction is blocked by dense woodland. The line of trees marches away to the left, towards the north – they call this section the 'Star' – extending right up to the road that runs directly past the garden.

Towards the west and south-west you have an open view across a spacious meadow, through which, a good arrow-shot away, the Ilm quietly winds its way. Beyond the river the bank rises up to form a hill, on whose slopes and crest, resplendent in the many-hued foliage of tall alders, ash trees, poplars and birches, the verdant park stretches away, bounding the view to the south and west at an agreeable distance.

This view of the park across the meadow gives you the impression, especially in summer, that you are on the edge of a forest that stretches for miles. Any minute now, you think, a deer is going to leap out on to the meadow. You feel transported to some peaceful, secluded spot in the depths of the countryside;

for the profound silence is often broken only by the solitary notes of the blackbird, or the intermittent, ever-changing song of the wood thrush.

But we are roused from such dreams of utter solitude by the occasional striking of the church clock, the cry of the peacocks from the high ground, or the sound of drums and horns coming from the military barracks. And it is not unpleasant; these sounds are an agreeable reminder that we are not far from the town we call home, even though we fancied ourselves miles away.

At certain times of day and certain times of the year these meadows are far from deserted. Sometimes you see country folk going to market in Weimar, or heading off to work in the town and returning home again; at other times you see all sorts of people out walking, following the meandering course of the Ilm, and often in the direction of Upper Weimar, which on certain days is a very popular destination. Then there is the haymaking season, when the whole place is a bustle of activity. In the background, flocks of sheep can be seen grazing, and often enough the fine Swiss cows from the nearby farm.

But today there was no trace yet of such summer sights to quicken the senses. The meadows showed only isolated patches of green growth, and the trees of the park were still bare, just brown twigs and buds; but the trill of finches and the occasional burst of song from the blackbird and thrush announced the approach of spring.

The air felt pleasantly summery; a balmy wind was blowing from the south-west. Small, isolated thunderclouds were moving across the clear sky; high above these, you could see wisps of cirrus clouds dissolving into the air. We studied the clouds closely, and saw that the thicker cloud masses moving across the lower regions of the sky were also breaking up, which led Goethe to conclude that the barometer must be rising.

Goethe then talked at length about the rise and fall of the barometer, which he referred to as the 'water affirmation' and the 'water negation'. He spoke of the earth breathing in and out, in accordance with eternal laws, and of a possible deluge if the 'water affirmation' continues. Furthermore, he stated that although every location has its own atmosphere, barometer readings across Europe are very similar. Nature, he said, is unfathomable, and with all her irregularities it is very hard to discern a pattern.

While he thus instructed me in loftier matters, we paced up and down the broad, sandy path of the garden. We approached the garden house, which he told his servant to open up, so that he could then show me round inside. The whitewashed outside walls were completely planted all around with rose bushes, which, supported by trellises, had grown all the way up to the roof. I went round the house and was particularly interested to see, sitting up against the walls in the branches of the rose bushes, a large number and variety of birds' nests left over from the previous summer, which were fully exposed to view now that the leaves were gone; many of the nests belonged to linnets and various species of warbler, constructed higher or lower, as the habits of these birds dictated.

Goethe then took me inside the house, which I had not seen when I was here last summer. Downstairs there was just one habitable room, which had a few maps and engravings hanging on the walls, as well as a life-size portrait of Goethe, painted by Meyer soon after the two friends returned from Italy.[34] Goethe appears here in the prime of his middle age, very suntanned and somewhat portly. His impassive face looks very serious; here is a man, one feels, whose mind is burdened by thoughts of work still to be done.

We went upstairs to the rooms on the first floor; I found three of them, plus a tiny closet, but all very small and not very inviting. Goethe said that in former years he had lived here very happily for an extended period, and had found it a good place to work undisturbed.

These rooms felt a little chilly, and we sought the warmth of the mild air outside again. As we walked up and down the main path in the midday sun, we talked about contemporary literature, Schelling, and some new plays by Count Platen.

But the natural world about us soon reclaimed our attention. The crown imperials and lilies were now growing fast, and the green shoots of the mallows were visible on both sides of the path.

1824 85

The upper section of the garden, on the slopes of the hill, consists of a grassy meadow dotted with fruit trees. Paths wind their way up the hill, along the crest and down again, and I felt drawn to walk to the top and have a look round. Goethe strode on up ahead of me, following these paths, and it was good to see him looking so sprightly.

At the top, by the hedge, we came upon a peahen, which had apparently made its way across from the royal park. Goethe told me that on summer days he liked to lure the peacocks across with their favourite food and make them feel at home.

Coming down the winding path on the other side of the hill, I found a stone surrounded by shrubs, on which had been chiselled this line from the well-known poem:

In this quiet place did the lover think upon his beloved –[35]

and I felt as if I was standing on classical ground.

A little further on we came to a thicket of young oaks, firs, birches and beech trees. Beneath the firs I found a pellet from some bird of prey; I showed it to Goethe, who told me that he often finds such things at this spot. I concluded from this that these fir trees are a favourite resting place for owls, which are a common sight in this area.

We skirted around this thicket and found ourselves back on the main path, close to the house. The mixed plantation of oaks, firs, birches and beeches we had just walked around form a semicircle here, their overarching branches turning the enclosed space into a sort of grotto, where we now sat down on little chairs ranged around a circular table. The sun was so strong that even the modicum of shade afforded by these leafless trees was very welcome. 'In the heat of the summer,' said Goethe, 'I find this the best place to escape to. I planted all the trees myself, forty years ago; I've had the pleasure of watching them grow on, and have enjoyed their refreshing shade for many years now. The leaves of these oaks and beeches keep the fiercest sun out; I like to sit out here after dinner on hot summer days, when there is often such a stillness in these meadows and in the whole park all around that the ancients would say "Pan is sleeping".'

Then we heard the clock in the town strike two, and we drove back.

Tuesday 30 March 1824

Spent the evening with Goethe. I was alone with him, and we talked of many things and drank a bottle of wine. We discussed the differences between the French theatre and the German.

'It will be difficult,' said Goethe, 'for German audiences to form some kind of clear judgement, as they do, say, in Italy and France. The biggest problem for us is that in our theatres they put everything on in any old order. On the same stage where we saw *Hamlet* yesterday, we get to see *Staberle* today;[36] and where *Die Zauberflöte* entrances us tomorrow, we are expected to laugh at the jokes in *Das neue Sonntagskind* the day after.[37] This just confuses the public's judgement, so that they get the different genres mixed up, and never quite learn how to appreciate and understand them. The other thing is that everyone has his own individual needs and preferences, and tends to go back to the place where he satisfied them before. If he picked figs from this tree today, he wants to pick them from the same tree tomorrow; and if it turned out that sloes had grown there overnight, he would be extremely put out. Those who want sloes should go and find a blackthorn bush.

'Schiller had the bright idea of building a separate theatre for tragedies, and of staging one production a week exclusively for men. But this presupposed a very large local population, and in our little community such a thing could never work.'

We talked about the plays of Iffland and Kotzebue, which Goethe rated highly as fine examples of their kind. 'For the very reason we were just talking about,' he said, 'namely, that nobody can distinguish properly between the different genres, the plays of these two men have often been very unfairly criticized. But we'll be waiting a long time before two such popular talents come along again.'

I praised Iffland's *Die Hagestolzen*, which I had enjoyed very much when I saw it on stage. 'It is unquestionably Iffland's best work,' said Goethe, 'and the only one where he goes from prose to the ideal.'

He then told me about a play that he and Schiller had planned as a continuation of *Hagestolzen*; they had not actually written it, just talked it through. Goethe went through the plot for me, scene by scene; it was very amusing and nicely done, and I liked it very much.

Goethe then talked about some new plays by Count Platen. 'You can see Calderón's influence in these plays. They are full of wit, and complete in their way, but they lack density, a certain gravity of content. They are not the sort of thing to spark a deep and abiding interest in the mind of the reader; they merely graze the strings of our soul in passing. They are like cork, which floats lightly on the surface of the water and makes no impression upon it.

'We Germans expect a certain seriousness, a certain breadth of vision, a certain depth of feeling – which is why Schiller is so universally admired. I don't doubt for a moment that Platen is a man of many talents, but that doesn't come across here, probably because he has a different view of art. He displays a cultivated mind, intelligence, a keen wit, and great artistic refinement; but somehow that is not enough, especially for us Germans.

'The fact is, it is the personality of a writer that makes him important in the eyes of the public, not his talents as an artist. Napoleon said of Corneille: "S'il vivait, je le ferais Prince!"; but he never read him. Racine he did read, but he did not say the same thing about him. This is why La Fontaine is so highly regarded by the French – not because of his poetic merits, but because of his noble character, which comes out in his writings.'

We then started talking about *Die Wahlverwandtschaften*, and Goethe told me about an Englishman who passed through on his travels and announced that he planned to get a divorce when he got back to England. Goethe laughed at such folly, and mentioned several more examples of people who had got divorced and then could not leave each other alone.

'The late Reinhard in Dresden,' he said, 'was often surprised that I have such strict principles with regard to marriage, when I am so easy-going about everything else.'[38]

I was struck by this remark of Goethe's, because it clearly showed what he had in mind when he wrote that much-misunderstood novel.

We then talked about Tieck, and his personal attitude to Goethe.

'I am very fond of Tieck,' he said, 'and on the whole he is well disposed towards me. But there is something not quite right in his relationship to me. It's not my fault, and nor is it his; the reasons lie elsewhere.

'When the Schlegels were first coming to prominence, I was too powerful for them, and to counterbalance me they looked around for a man of talent they could put up against me. They found such a man in Tieck, and in order for him to appear a worthy rival to me in the eyes of the public they had to make more of him than he really was. This damaged our relationship, because it put Tieck in a false position vis-à-vis me, without him really being aware of it.

'Tieck is a very significant talent, and nobody appreciates his remarkable achievements better than me. But when they try to make him more than he is, and put him on a par with me, they are making a mistake. I can say this quite openly, because it makes no difference to me; I didn't make myself. It would be like me comparing myself to Shakespeare, who didn't make himself either; but he is nonetheless a being of a higher order, to whom I look up, and whom it is right for me to venerate.'

This evening Goethe was particularly lively, full of energy and good cheer. He went to fetch a manuscript of unpublished poems, from which he read aloud to me. It was a special delight to listen to him; as well as being very excited by the original force and freshness of the poems themselves, I saw a revealing new side to Goethe when he read aloud. His voice was so expressive and powerful! His broad, wrinkled face was so mobile and animated! And those eyes!

Wednesday 14 April 1824

Went for a drive with Goethe at one o'clock. We discussed the styles of various writers.

'On the whole,' said Goethe, 'philosophical speculation is bad for the Germans, because it often makes them write in a style that is abstract, difficult, vague and obscure. The more they subscribe to certain schools of philosophy, the worse their writing becomes. Germans who have a business life and a social life, and who therefore concern themselves only with practical matters, are the ones that write best. Schiller's style, for example, is at its most brilliant and effective when he is not philosophizing, as I saw today in his wonderful letters, which I happen to be rereading.

'There are likewise some very clever German women who have an excellent writing style – better, in fact, than many of our highly regarded male writers.

'The English all write well on the whole, being born orators and practical people who concern themselves with the real world.

'The French are true to type even in their writing style. They are sociable people, and as such they never forget the public they are speaking to; they endeavour to write clearly, in order to persuade their readers; and elegantly, in order to please them.

'In general, a writer's style is a true reflection of his mind. So someone who aspires to write in a clear style must be clear-headed in his thinking, and someone who would write in a grandiloquent style must be larger than life in his character.'

Goethe then spoke about his enemies and detractors, saying they would never die out as a breed. 'Their number is legion,' he said, 'but it is not impossible to classify them, after a fashion.

'I call the first group my stupid enemies. These are people who didn't understand me, and found fault with me without knowing anything about me. There are many of them, and they have given me a tedious time over the years; but they shall be forgiven, for they knew not what they did.

'The second large group consists of those who envy me. These people begrudge me my good fortune and the honourable status I have earned through my talent. They pick away at my reputation and would like to destroy me. If I were unhappy and wretched, they would leave me alone.

'Then there are all those who have taken against me because of their own lack of success. There are some really talented men among them, but they can't forgive me for putting them in the shade.

'Fourthly, there are the ones who criticize me for a reason. As I am only human, and therefore have human weaknesses and failings, my writings are bound to have them too. But as I was serious about cultivating my mind, and worked ceaselessly to improve myself, I was always making progress and moving on; and it often turned out that they were taking me to task for some fault I had long since put behind me. These good folk have done me the least damage; they shot at me when I was already miles away. The fact is, once I had finished a work, I rather lost interest in it; I didn't think about it any more, and moved swiftly on to something new.

'Another large group of persons oppose me because they have a different way of thinking and different views. We are told that no two leaves on a tree are exactly the same; and it will be hard to find two people out of a thousand who think in exactly the same way and share the exact same views. That being so, I ought really to be less surprised that the number of my enemies is so large, and more surprised that I still have so many friends and followers. My contemporaries parted company with me, being entirely caught up in their pursuit of subjectivity, while my own objective tendency left me quite isolated and at a disadvantage.

'In this respect, Schiller had great advantages over me. A well-meaning general once told me in no uncertain terms that I should be writing like Schiller. Whereupon I elaborated at length on Schiller's merits and accomplishments, which I knew rather better than he did. I carried on in my own sweet way, not caring if I was a "success" or not, and taking as little notice as possible of all my detractors.'

We drove back, and were in very good spirits at dinner. Frau von Goethe had much to tell us about Berlin, having only just returned from there. She spoke with particular affection about the Duchess of Cumberland, who had been most kind to her. Goethe had especially fond memories of this lady, who had lived with his mother for a while when she was a very young princess.

In the evening I had a special musical treat at Goethe's house: a group of excellent singers had assembled there, under the direction of Eberwein, to perform extracts from Handel's *Messiah*. The Countess Karoline von Egloffstein, Fräulein von Froriep, together with Frau von Pogwisch and Frau von Goethe, had joined the other lady singers, very kindly doing their part to fulfil a long-cherished wish of Goethe's.

Goethe sat and listened at a little distance, completely absorbed, and enjoyed a happy evening, filled with admiration for that magnificent choral work.

Monday 19 April 1824

The greatest literary scholar of our time, Friedrich August Wolf from Berlin, is here, passing through on his way to the south of France. Today Goethe gave a dinner in his honour, attended by Weimar friends General Superintendent Röhr, Chancellor von Müller, Chief Planning Officer Coudray, Professor Riemer and Councillor Rehbein, in addition to myself. The conversation at dinner was very lively; Wolf came out with all kinds of witty quips, and Goethe, in the best of moods, always took the opposite tack. 'The only way Wolf and I can get along,' Goethe told me later, 'is if I play Mephistopheles to him. It's the only way I can get him to open up properly.'

The witty repartee at dinner was too quick, and too much a product of the passing moment, for me to remember anything specific. Wolf was very good at this sort of banter, yet it seemed to me that Goethe somehow had the edge on him.

The hours around the table positively flew by, and it was six o'clock before we knew it. I went off to the theatre with young Goethe, to see *Die Zauberflöte*. Later on I saw Wolf up in the box with the Grand Duke Karl August.

Wolf stayed in Weimar until the 25th, when he set off for the south of France. The state of his health was such that Goethe was plainly very worried about him.

Sunday 2 May 1824

Goethe took me to task for not having visited a particular family of some standing in the town. 'You could have spent many an enjoyable evening with them over the winter,' he said, 'and would have met quite a few interesting strangers there; but now you've missed out on all that – heaven knows why.'

'With my excitable temperament,' I replied, 'and my natural inclination to take an interest in many things and put myself in other people's shoes, exposing myself to too many new impressions would have been the worst possible thing for me. I was not brought up to mix in society, and do not come from that sort of background. The circumstances of my early life were such that I feel as if I have only started to live in the short time I have been here with you. So now everything is new to me. Every evening at the theatre, every conversation with you, is a landmark event for me. Things that are taken for granted by persons of different education and upbringing make a deep impression on me; and as my desire for self-improvement is so great, my mind seizes eagerly upon every new thing, and sucks as much nourishment from it as possible. Being that way inclined, I had everything I needed last winter from the theatre and the time I spent with you, and I could not have devoted myself to new acquaintances and different company without going out of my mind.'

'You *are* a strange fellow,' said Goethe with a laugh. 'You must do as you please, and I won't stand in your way.'

'And then,' I went on, 'I tend to take my personal likes and dislikes with me into society, along with a certain need to love and be loved. I seek out someone who I feel is a kindred spirit, and am happy to give my time to that person and ignore everyone else.'

'This natural tendency of yours,' replied Goethe, 'is not going to do much for your social skills. What is the point of culture, if we are not prepared to try and subdue our natural tendencies? It is very foolish to expect other people to be like us. I have never done it. I have always looked upon each person as a completely separate individual, whom I tried to sound out and get to know in all his peculiarities, but with whom I never

1824   93

expected to sympathize or identify. The result is that I can now hold a conversation with anybody, and that is the only way to learn about all different types of people and acquire the necessary social skills. Especially when dealing with people who are awkward or contrary, you have to make a real effort to get along with them, which in turn stimulates all the different sides of our character and helps to form and develop them; and before long you feel yourself a match for anyone. You should do the same. You have more natural aptitude for it than you think. And anyway, that's just the way it is: you have to go out into the big wide world, whether you want to or not.'

I took note of this good advice and resolved to follow it to the best of my ability.

Goethe had invited me to go for a drive with him towards evening. Our route took us through Upper Weimar and over the hills, where one has a view of the park to the west. The trees were in blossom, the birches were out in leaf, and the meadows were one continuous carpet of green, lit up by the glancing rays of the setting sun. We scanned the landscape with eager eyes, looking for picturesque compositions. We decided that trees with white blossom are best not painted, because they don't make much of a picture, and that birch trees coming into leaf should not be placed in the foreground of a picture, because the pale leaves cannot compete with the white trunk; the leaves don't form discrete masses, which could be dramatized and given depth by the use of light and shade. 'This is why Ruysdael,' said Goethe, 'never put birch trees in leaf in the foreground, but only broken-off birch trunks, which have no leaves. Those bare trunks look perfect in the foreground, where their pale forms stand out to very dramatic effect.'

After touching briefly on other subjects, we then talked about the misguided thinking of those artists who try to turn religion into art, when art should be their religion. 'Religion,' said Goethe, 'has the same relationship to art as any other topic of serious interest in life. It should be viewed simply as subject matter, with the same claims as all the other subjects that life throws up. Belief and unbelief are not at all the right organs for apprehending a work of art; that requires very different human powers and abilities. Art should address itself to those organs with which we apprehend it; if it fails to do so, it defeats its purpose and has no real effect on us. A religious subject can also make good material for art, but only if it is of general human interest. That's why a Virgin and Child is an excellent subject, which has been done a hundred times, and yet we never tire of it.'

By now we had circled round the wood known as the Webicht, and just before Tiefurt we turned on to the road that leads back to Weimar, where we had a prospect of the setting sun. For a while Goethe was lost in thought, and then he quoted the words of an ancient Greek poet to me: 'The sun that sets is still the sun that always was.'[39]

'At the age of seventy-five,' he went on in a jaunty tone, 'it's impossible not to think about death sometimes. But the thought of it doesn't trouble me at all, because I am firmly convinced that our spirit is an indestructible entity, which lives on from age to age. It's like the sun, which only appears to set to our earthly eyes; in fact, it never sets, but shines on ceaselessly.'

Meanwhile the sun had set behind the Ettersberg, and we felt the chill of the evening air in the wood. So we drove back quickly into Weimar and stopped outside Goethe's house. He asked me to come upstairs and stay a while, which I did. He was in particularly mellow and amiable mood. He talked a great deal about his theory of colour, about his entrenched opponents, and said that he felt he had made a real contribution to this science.

'It's a well-known fact,' he said, 'that if you want to make your mark in this world, two things are necessary: you need a good head on your shoulders, and you need to come into a great inheritance. Napoleon inherited the French Revolution; Frederick the Great, the Silesian War; Luther, the benighted ignorance of priests; and my portion is the error of the Newtonian theory. The present generation has no idea what I have achieved in this area; but posterity will grant that my particular inheritance was not at all bad.'

This morning Goethe had sent me a bundle of papers pertaining to the theatre. Among them I found scattered observations on the rules and exercises he had been through with Wolff and Grüner in order to refine their acting skills. I thought these detailed points were of great interest, and highly instructive for young actors; and so I decided that I would put them all together and make a sort of theatre handbook out of them. Goethe approved the idea, and we discussed the matter further. This prompted us to recall a number of distinguished actors who had emerged from his school, and one of those I took the opportunity to ask about was Frau von Heygendorf. 'I may have had some influence on her,' said Goethe, 'but she is not really a pupil of mine. She was a born actress, who knew exactly what she was doing; she took to it like a duck to water. She needed no instruction from me; she did the right thing instinctively, perhaps without knowing it herself.'

We then talked about his many years as a theatre manager, and about the endless hours that were thus lost for his writing work. 'It's true,' said Goethe, 'that I could have written some good plays in that time. But when I think about it, I'm not sorry. I have always regarded all my work and achievements as purely symbolic, and it never really mattered to me whether I was turning out pots or bowls.'

Thursday 6 May 1824

When I came to Weimar last summer it was not my intention, as I said before, to remain here. I just wanted to make Goethe's personal acquaintance and then travel on to the Rhine, where I planned to find a suitable place and settle there for a while.

However, I felt tied to Weimar by Goethe's great kindness towards me, and my relationship to him increasingly became a practical one, as he asked me to do more and more things for him – including important editing tasks, in preparation for a complete edition of his works.

So this winter, for example, I compiled several sections of *Zahme Xenien* from bundles of completely disorganized papers, and edited a volume of new poems, the aforementioned theatre handbook and the draft of an essay on dilettantism in the various arts.[40]

Meanwhile, I had not forgotten my plan of seeing the Rhine; and so that I wouldn't carry on feeling the itch of an unsatisfied desire, Goethe himself encouraged me to spend a few months of the summer visiting that region.

But he very much wanted me to return to Weimar afterwards. He argued that it was not good to break ties that had scarcely been formed, and that every enterprise in life has to be seen through if it is to prosper. He made it clear that he had chosen me, along with Riemer, not only to provide every practical assistance with the preparation of the new edition of his works, but also to take sole charge of the project, with the aforementioned friend, in the event that he should pass away at his advanced age.

This morning he showed me large bundles of his correspondence, which had been laid out in the room known as the Room of Busts.[41] 'These are all letters,' he said, 'that I have received from the most eminent men of our nation since 1780; they are a veritable treasure trove of ideas, and it will be your job to make them public at some future date. I am having a cabinet made, where these letters and the rest of my literary estate will be stored. I would like you to sort them out and put them in proper order before you go on your travels, so that my mind is at rest and I have one less thing to worry about.'

He then told me that he was thinking of visiting Marienbad again this summer, but he could not go before the end of July – the various reasons for which he confided to me. He expressed the wish that I should be back before his departure, so that he could speak to me first.

A few weeks after this I visited my loved ones in Hanover, and then spent June and July exploring the Rhine, where I made many valuable acquaintances among Goethe's friends, particularly in Frankfurt, Heidelberg and Bonn.

Tuesday 10 August 1824

I returned from my travels on the Rhine about a week ago. Goethe greeted me with great joy on my arrival, and I was equally happy to be back with him again. He had a great deal to tell me, which meant that I hardly left his side for the first few days. He has abandoned his earlier plan of going to Marienbad, and does not intend to go away anywhere this summer. 'Now that you are back again,' he said yesterday, 'August could turn out very well for me.'

A few days ago he showed me the beginnings of a continuation of *Dichtung und Wahrheit*: a booklet of quarto sheets, barely the thickness of a finger. Some of it has been written up, but most of it is there only in outline. However, it has already been divided into five books, and the pages of the outline draft have been so arranged that it is possible, with a little study, to get a good sense of the whole work.

The parts that have been written up seem to me so good, and the material contained in the outline draft of such importance, that I am sorry to see the work come to a standstill, when it promises to be so instructive and enjoyable; and I shall now do whatever I can to encourage Goethe to carry on and finish it.

The whole thing is structured very much like a novel. A tender, charming, passionate love affair – all sunshine and joy at the beginning, idyllic while it lasts, ending tragically in an unspoken but mutual renunciation – weaves its way through four books and ties them together to form a well-ordered whole. The seductive appeal of Lili's character, described here in detail, is sure to captivate the reader, just as it held the lover himself in its thrall – to the point where he could only save himself by repeatedly running away.[42]

The time of life portrayed here is likewise highly romantic – or at least, it is here, as experienced through the main character. What makes it so very important and significant, however, is that it is the precursor to the Weimar years, and therefore shapes the entire course of his life. If any period in Goethe's life is going to interest us and make us wish for a detailed account, it is this one.

To instil a new passion and enthusiasm in Goethe for the work that was discontinued and laid aside for many years, I not only discussed the matter with him in person at the time, but also sent him the following notes today, so that he can see for himself what has already been completed and what still needs to be written up and rearranged.

First Book

This book, which on the basis of the original plan may be regarded as finished, serves as a kind of exposition, in so far as the author tells us here that he wants to become involved in the affairs of the world – a wish that finds fulfilment at the end of this whole period when he is invited to Weimar. To tie it in more closely with the rest of the narrative, however, I suggest that the relationship with Lili, which runs through the next four books, should begin in this first book, and then be continued as far as the excursion to Offenbach. This would make the first book longer and more meaningful, while ensuring that the second book doesn't become disproportionately large.

Second Book

The second book would then open with the idyllic life in Offenbach and continue with the happy love affair, until it eventually starts to take a darker, more serious, not to say tragic, turn. This is probably the right place to reflect on serious matters, as the outline promises with reference to Stilling; and from the brief indications given there we can doubtless expect to learn much that is instructive and of great import.

Third Book

The third book, containing the plan for a continuation of *Faust*, etc., should be regarded as an episode, which is also connected to the other books by the attempted break with Lili, which has yet to be written up.[43]

Whether this plan for *Faust* should be included or held back is an open question, which can only be resolved after we have looked at the already finished fragments and decided whether or not we must give up any hope of a continuation of *Faust*.

Fourth Book

The third book would end with the attempt to break with Lili. This fourth book then begins very aptly with the arrival of the Stolbergs and von Haugwitz, which leads on to the journey to Switzerland and thus the first attempt to escape from Lili. The detailed notes that we have for this book promise a most interesting account, and make us eager to see the full story told in as much detail as possible. The passion for Lili, which is constantly being rekindled and cannot be suppressed, infuses this book, too, with the warm glow of young love, and casts a very special and magical light on the traveller's state of mind.

Fifth Book

This wonderful book is likewise almost finished. The main narrative and ending, at least, which touch upon the unfathomable nature of fate, and indeed address it openly, can be considered quite complete, and only a little work is needed to finish the introduction, for which we already have a very clear outline. However, it is really important and desirable that this should be written up properly, because it contains the first mention of the Weimar situation, and thus excites our interest in Weimar for the first time.

Monday 16 August 1824

My conversations with Goethe these last few days have covered a lot of ground, but I have been so busy with other things that I have not been able to write down anything of particular importance.

I did note down the odd remark of his in my diary, but I have forgotten the context and the occasion that prompted them:

'People are floating pots, which bump up against each other.'

'We think most clearly in the morning, but that's also when we worry most – worry being itself a form of clear thinking, albeit only a passive one. The stupid have no worries.'

'There's no need to perpetuate the errors of one's youth into old age; old age comes with enough failings of its own.'

'Life at court is like a piece of music, where everybody has to keep time and pause in all the right places.'

'Courtiers would die of boredom if they could not fill their time with ceremonial.'

'Advising a prince not to interfere, even in the most trifling matter, is not a smart move.'

'Training actors takes infinite patience.'

Tuesday 9 November 1824

At Goethe's house this evening. We talked about Klopstock and Herder, and it was a joy to listen to him, as he explained to me what these men had achieved.

'Our literature,' he said, 'would not be what it is today without these great pioneers. When they came on the scene they were ahead of their times, and had to drag their times along behind them, so to speak. But now the times have overtaken *them*, and they who were once so necessary and important are no longer agents of change. A young man today who took Klopstock and Herder as his cultural mentors would be left far behind.'

We talked about Klopstock's *Messias* and his *Oden*, and reflected on their merits and faults. We agreed that Klopstock had no natural talent or aptitude for observing and apprehending the physical world and portraying characters, so that he lacked the basic qualities needed for an epic or a dramatic poet – or for any kind of poet, come to that.

'It puts me in mind of that ode he wrote,' said Goethe, 'about a race between the German muse and the British one. And it's true: when you stop and think what that would actually look like, with the two girls running against each other and kicking up their legs and throwing up the dust with their feet, you can only assume that dear old Klopstock didn't have the scene in his mind's eye when he wrote it, and didn't picture the physical reality to himself – otherwise he would not have got it so wrong.'

I asked Goethe what he had thought of Klopstock in his youth, and how he had rated him back then.

'I revered him,' said Goethe, 'with every bone in my body. He was like an uncle to me. I was in awe of what he was doing, and it never occurred to me to analyse it, or find fault with it in any way. I took the best things from it – and then went my own way.'

We returned to Herder, and I asked Goethe which of his works he thought the best. 'His *Ideen zur Geschichte der Menschheit*,' replied Goethe, 'is unquestionably his finest work. Later on his thinking took a negative turn, and it was not a pleasure to read him.'

'Considering what an important figure Herder was,' I volunteered, 'I simply cannot understand his seeming lack of judgement in certain matters. For example, I cannot forgive him – especially given the state of German literature at the time – for sending back the manuscript of *Götz von Berlichingen* with marginal comments making fun of the text, and no acknowledgement of the play's merits. He must have been completely insensitive to certain things.'

'Herder was difficult like that,' replied Goethe. 'Indeed,' he added briskly, 'if he were here with us now in spirit, he would not understand us.'

'On the other hand,' I said, 'I have to give credit to Merck, for encouraging you to have *Götz* printed.'

'Yes, he was quite a character,' said Goethe. '"Print the damn thing," he said to me. "It's no good, but just get it printed!" He didn't believe in reworking things, and he was right; it would have come out differently, but not better.'

Wednesday 24 November 1824

I went to see Goethe this evening before the theatre and found him in fine form. He asked after the young Englishmen who are here, and I told him I was planning to read a German translation of Plutarch with Mr Doolan. This got us on to the subject of Roman and Greek history, which prompted the following observations from Goethe:

'Roman history,' he said, 'has really had its day, as far as we're concerned. We have become too civilized not to be repelled by the triumphs of Caesar. And Greek history does not have a lot to offer, either. When the Greeks were facing a foreign enemy, they were great and glorious, certainly – which makes the fragmentation of the city states and the endless internal wars, with Greeks taking up arms against other Greeks, all the harder to stomach. Apart from which, the history of our own times has plenty of drama to offer; the Battles of Leipzig and Waterloo were such huge events that they put the Battle of Marathon, and others like it, in the shade. Nor are our own heroic figures in any way inferior; the French marshals and Blücher and Wellington can stand comparison with any heroes of antiquity.'

The conversation then turned to recent French literature, and the growing interest of the French in German literary works.

'The French have done the right thing,' said Goethe, 'by starting to study and translate our authors; limited as they are in both form and motifs, they have no choice but to look elsewhere. We Germans may be accused of a certain formlessness, but we are ahead of them when it comes to subject matter. The plays of Kotzebue and Iffland contain such a wealth of motifs that they can go on picking from them for a very long time before they are all used up. But our philosophical idealism holds a special appeal for them, given that idealism of any kind serves the cause of revolution.

'The French,' Goethe went on, 'have understanding and wit, but no solid foundation and no respect. Whatever serves their immediate purpose, whatever might help their party, is fine by them. So when they praise us, it is not from a desire to acknowledge our merits, but only because they can use our views to strengthen their own party.'

We then talked about our own literature, and what was holding back some of our newest young writers.

'The only problem with most of our young poets,' said Goethe, 'is that their subjectivity doesn't amount to much, and they don't know how to find suitable material in the objective world. The best they can do is to find a subject that is like themselves, that speaks to them personally; but as for writing about a subject for its own sake, because it is poetic, even if they find it personally repugnant – not a chance!

'But as I said, if it were only important personages who were formed by great studies and situations in life, all might still be well, at least as far as our young lyric poets are concerned.'

Friday 3 December 1824

A few days ago I received an invitation to write for an English journal on very favourable terms, contributing monthly reports on the latest products of German literature. I was very tempted to accept, but thought it might be a good idea to discuss the matter with Goethe first.

So I went to see him this evening just as the lights were being lit. The window blinds were down, and he was sitting at a large table where dinner had been eaten, and where a pair of candles were now burning, illuminating both his face and a colossal bust that sat on the table in front of him, which he was studying closely. 'Now then,' said Goethe, pointing to the bust after greeting me cordially, 'who's this?' 'He looks like a poet,' I said, 'an Italian poet.' 'It's Dante,' said Goethe. 'He's been done well, and it's a fine head; but still, he's not altogether pleasing. He looks old, bowed down, morose; the features are slack and drooping, as if he had just come from hell. I have a medal that was made during his lifetime, and there he looks much better.' Goethe got up and went to fetch the medal. 'See here, how powerful the nose is, and the fullness of the upper lip, and the thrusting chin, which merges so beautifully with the cheekbones. The area around the eyes, and the forehead, are virtually unchanged in this colossal bust, but all the rest looks weaker and older. But that's not to criticize the new work, which has many merits and deserves our praise.'

Goethe then enquired how I had been lately, and what I had been thinking and doing. I told him that I had been asked to write for an English journal, on very favourable terms, contributing monthly reports on the latest products of German *belles-lettres*, and that I was very much minded to accept.

At these words the friendly look on Goethe's face gave way to a frown, and it was plain to see that he disapproved.

'I wish,' he said, 'that your friends had left you in peace. Why would you want to concern yourself with things that are not for you, which indeed are quite contrary to your natural bent? We have gold, silver, and paper money, and each has its own value and worth; but to appreciate each one you must know its true value. It's no different with literature. You know what the coins are worth, but not the paper money. You don't have the right experience, so your criticisms will be unfair and you will tear everything to shreds. If you wish to be fair, however, and give everything its proper due, you will first have to come to terms with our middling literature, which is going to require a fair amount of study. You will need to go back and see what the Schlegels set out to do and what they achieved, and then you'll have to read all our modern authors – Franz Horn, Hoffmann, Clauren and the rest. And that's not all. You'll have to take all the journals, from the *Morgenblatt* to the *Abendzeitung*, so that you know about all the latest things as soon as they appear – and that will take up hours and days of your time that could be much better spent.[44] And what about all the new books that you'd want to review in some depth? It won't be enough just to leaf through them: you'll have to read them properly. Is that what you want? And in the end, if the work you are reviewing is bad, you won't be able to say so – not unless you want to risk falling out with everybody.

'No: as I said, you should turn the offer down. It's not for you. In fact, you should take care generally not to spread yourself too thin and to conserve your energies. If only I had known that thirty years ago, I would have done things very differently. When I think of all the time Schiller and I wasted on his *Horen* and *Musenalmanach*![45] Rereading our correspondence recently has brought it all back to me, and I can't help feeling annoyed when I think back to those ventures, which earned us a lot of abuse and otherwise did absolutely nothing for us. Talent thinks it can do whatever it sees other people doing, but this is not the case; and it will live to regret its wasted effort. What is the point of putting your hair in curlers for one night? You've got paper in your hair, that's all; and the next night your hair is straight again.

'What really matters,' Goethe went on, 'is that you build up a stock of capital that will never be exhausted. And you'll get that

1824 105

from your present study of the English language and literature. Keep at it, and take every opportunity to practise while these young Englishmen are here. You largely missed out on the ancient languages in your youth, which is why you should try and get a grounding now in the literature of so able a nation as the English. And besides, our own literature is largely derived from theirs. Our novels, our tragedies – where do they come from, if not from Goldsmith, Fielding and Shakespeare? Even in our own day, where in Germany are you going to find three literary giants to set beside Lord Byron, Moore and Walter Scott? So I say again: concentrate on improving your English, save your energies for something worthwhile and let go of everything that doesn't get you anywhere and isn't right for you.'

I was pleased that I had got Goethe to speak his mind, felt thoroughly reassured, and resolved to follow his advice in every particular.

Chancellor von Müller was announced, and he sat down with us. And so the conversation turned again to the bust of Dante in front of us, and his life and works – more specifically, the obscurity of those works, how his own countrymen never understood him, and how impossible it must therefore be for a foreigner to penetrate such mysteries. Goethe turned to me and said with a friendly smile: 'So your father confessor absolutely forbids you to study this poet.'

Goethe went on to observe that one of the main reasons why he is so hard to understand is the difficult rhyme. For the rest, Goethe spoke of Dante with great reverence, and I noticed that he referred to him as a 'force of nature' rather than a mere 'talent', by which he seemingly meant something altogether more all-encompassing and intuitive, more far-sighted and profound.[46]

Thursday 9 December 1824

I went to see Goethe towards evening. He extended a friendly hand and greeted me with words of praise for my poem in honour of Schellhorn's many years of service. I responded by telling him I had written to refuse the offer from England.

'Thank heavens,' he said, 'that you are free again, and your time is your own. Now here's another thing you need to watch out for. Composers will come knocking on your door to commission an opera; but you must stand firm again and refuse them, because that is something else that leads nowhere and just wastes your time.'

Goethe then told me that he had sent a theatre programme, via Nees von Esenbeck, to the author of *Der Paria* in Bonn, so that the playwright could see that his work had been performed here. 'Life is short,' he added, 'and we must try to do each other a good turn whenever we can.'

He had the Berlin newspapers in front of him and told me about the floods in St Petersburg. He gave me the paper to read. He talked about the exposed location of St Petersburg and chuckled with approval as he quoted a remark of Rousseau's, to the effect that you cannot prevent an earthquake by building a city next to a volcano.[47] 'Nature goes her own way,' he said, 'and what looks like an exception to us is normal for nature.'

We then talked about the great storms that had been raging on every coast, and about the other violent natural events reported in the newspapers; and I asked Goethe if it was known how such things might be connected. 'Nobody knows,' replied Goethe. 'We scarcely know ourselves what to think of such mysteries, let alone put it into words.'

Chief Planning Officer Coudray was announced, together with Professor Riemer. Both joined us, and we talked about the floods in St Petersburg again. Coudray drew a map of the city to show us the general lie of the land and the flood risk posed by the Neva.

1825

Monday 10 January 1825

Very interested as he is in the English nation, Goethe had asked me to introduce to him at some point the young Englishmen who are currently here. So today at five o'clock he was expecting me, together with the English engineering officer, Mr H., of whom he had already had many good reports from me.[48] We arrived at the appointed hour and were shown by the manservant into a comfortably heated room, where Goethe likes to spend his afternoons and evenings. Three lights were burning on the table, but Goethe was not there; we could hear him talking in the neighbouring room.

Mr H. had a look around while we waited, and noticed, apart from the paintings and a large mountain map on the walls, a filing cabinet with many portfolios. I told him that these contained many drawings by celebrated masters and engravings after the best paintings of all schools, which Goethe had been gradually collecting over the years, and which he often liked to look at.

After we had been waiting a few minutes, Goethe came in and welcomed us warmly. 'I presume I may speak to you in German,' he said to Mr H., 'since I hear your German is very good.' Mr H. replied with a few polite words, and Goethe invited us to take a seat.

Mr H.'s character and demeanour must have made a favourable impression on Goethe, because his great charm and gentle, genial manner were seen at their beautiful best today in his encounter with this stranger. 'You were right to come over here to learn German,' he said. 'Not only will you learn the language quickly and easily here, but you will also take back with you to England a knowledge of the things it is based on – our soil, climate, way of life, customs, social relations, constitution and the like.'

'There is a lot of interest in the German language in England now,' replied Mr H., 'and it is growing by the day. Now there are hardly any young Englishmen of good family who are not learning German.'

'We Germans,' replied Goethe genially, 'are half a century ahead of your nation in this respect. I have been studying the English language and literature for fifty years, and so am very familiar with your writers and your country's way of life and way of doing things. If I were to come across to England I would feel quite at home there.

'But as I say, your young people do well to come to us now and learn our language. It's not just that our literature deserves your attention in its own right; it is also the case that if you know German, you can dispense with many other languages. I'm not talking about French; French is the language of conversation, and indispensable for travellers because everyone understands it, and you can get by with it in every country without having to engage a good interpreter. But as for Greek, Latin, Italian and Spanish, we can read the best works of these nations in such excellent German translations that we have no need to spend a lot of time and effort learning these languages, unless it is for some special reason of our own. It is part of the German character to appreciate everything foreign for what it is, and to adjust to foreign peculiarities. This, and the great flexibility of our language, are what makes German translations so faithful and accomplished.

'And there is no denying that you can get very far with a good translation, generally speaking. Frederick the Great had no Latin, but he read Cicero in the French translation just as well as the rest of us who read him in the original.'

Turning the conversation to the theatre, Goethe then asked Mr H. whether he went very often. 'I go to the theatre every evening,' he replied, 'and I find it very helpful for my understanding of the language.' 'It is curious,' said Goethe, 'how the ear, and the ability to understand the language, always outstrip the ability to speak, so that we can quite quickly understand everything we hear, but not express everything we want to say.' 'I find that to be very true every day,' replied Mr H. 'I have no trouble understanding everything that is said, and everything I read – in fact, I even notice if someone expresses himself incorrectly in German. But when I speak, it doesn't flow freely and I don't know how to say the things I want to say. I can pass the time of day at court, banter with the ladies, manage some small talk at a ball or some other social occasion; but if I want to express my views in German on some serious matter, if I want to say something original and witty, I get stuck, and can't go on.' 'I shouldn't worry about that,' said Goethe. 'It's hard enough to say that kind of thing in one's own language.'

Goethe then asked Mr H. what he had read in the way of German literature. 'I've read *Egmont*,' he replied, 'and enjoyed it so much that I've now gone back to it three times. *Torquato Tasso* has also given me a lot of pleasure. Now I'm reading *Faust*, but am finding it rather difficult.' Goethe laughed at these last words. 'I won't deny,' he said, 'that I would not have advised you to tackle *Faust* just yet. It is crazy stuff, and goes beyond all normal feelings. But since you chose to do it without asking me, you'll just have to see how you get on. Faust is such a strange individual that very few people are able to empathize with his state of mind. And the character of Mephistopheles is also very difficult because of his irony, and because he is the living result of extensive observation of the world. But you'll just have to see what sense you can make of it. *Tasso*, on the other hand, is much closer to normal human experience, and its formal explicitness makes it easier to understand.' 'All the same,' replied Mr H., '*Tasso* is considered difficult in Germany, and people were surprised when I said I was reading it.' 'The main thing about reading *Tasso*,' said Goethe, 'is that you need to be a grown-up with some experience of polite society. A young man of good family, with reasonable intelligence and delicacy of feeling, who has acquired sufficient social graces by consorting with polished persons from the upper classes, will not find *Tasso* difficult.'

The conversation turned to *Egmont*, and Goethe made the following observation: 'I wrote *Egmont* in 1775, fifty years ago. I kept close to the historical facts and tried to be as truthful as possible. Ten years later, when I was in Rome, I read in the newspapers that the revolutionary scenes in the Netherlands shown in the play had literally just repeated themselves. This taught me that the world always stays the same, and that my portrayal must have been quite true to life.'

As we talked of these and similar matters, the time came to leave for the theatre. We rose from our seats, and Goethe bade us a friendly goodbye.

As we were going home, I asked Mr H. what he made of Goethe. 'I have never seen anyone,' he replied, 'who combines such a gentle, charming manner with so much natural dignity. However much he pretends otherwise and stoops to your level, he is always the great man.'

Tuesday 18 January 1825

I went to see Goethe today at five o'clock, not having seen him for several days, and spent a delightful evening with him. I found him in his study, sitting in the twilight, talking to his son and Councillor Rehbein, his doctor. I sat down at the table with them. We chatted for a while in the failing light; then candles were brought in, and it was wonderful to see Goethe sitting there in front of me, looking so fresh and bright.

As usual, he wanted to know what I had been doing in recent days, and I told him that I had met a lady poet.[49] I praised her uncommon talent, and Goethe, who also knew some of her work, agreed with me. 'One of her poems,' he said, 'in which she describes an area near her home, is very curious indeed. She writes well about physical objects, and is not lacking in mental and emotional strength. One could find fault with her work, certainly, but I think we should let her go her own way and not interfere, wherever her talent might take her.'

The conversation now moved on to female poets in general, and Councillor Rehbein observed that the poetic talent of women often struck him as a kind of intellectual sex drive.

'Listen to him,' said Goethe, laughing as he looked across at me, '*intellectual sex drive* indeed! What these doctors come out with!' 'I don't know if I have expressed myself correctly,' Rehbein went on, 'but it's something like that. Generally speaking, these women have not known the joys of love, and so they seek compensation in intellectual pursuits. If they had got married at the right time and had children, they would never have thought of writing poetry.'

'It's not for me to say,' said Goethe, 'whether you are right in this case. But women who are talented in other ways, so I have always found, give it up when they get married. I have known girls who could draw brilliantly, but as soon as they became wives and mothers, that was that; they had enough to do looking after their children, and never picked up a pencil again.'

Warming to his theme, he then went on: 'I'd be perfectly happy for our female poets to scribble away to their hearts' content, if only our men didn't write like women! That's what I don't like. You only have to look at our periodicals and pocket-books to see how feeble it all is – and it's getting worse all the time! Imagine if they were to print a chapter from *Cellini* in the *Morgenblatt* now: what would that look like!'[50]

'But we'll leave it at that for now,' he continued cheerfully, 'and be glad of our feisty girl in Halle, who has manfully taken us into the Serbian world.[51] The poems are first-rate. Some of them are good enough to set beside the Song of Solomon – and that's saying something. I have finished my essay on these poems, and it is already published.' With these words he handed me the first four advance sheets of a new issue of *Kunst und Altertum*, where I found this essay. 'I have summarized the main theme of each poem in a few words, and you will be much taken by the delightful motifs. Rehbein here knows a bit about poetry, too, at least as far as theme and content are concerned, and he might like to hear you read this passage aloud to us.'

I read out the summarized themes of each poem, slowly. The situations suggested by the summary were so expressive and graphic that a complete poem took shape, one word at a time, before my eyes. I thought the following were especially charming:

1. Modesty of a Serbian girl, who never raises her beautiful eyelashes.
2. Mental anguish of a lover who, as bridesman, has to escort his beloved to another man.
3. Worried about her lover, the girl is reluctant to sing, for fear of seeming happy.
4. The poet deplores the perversion of morals, with youths wooing widows and old men virgins.
5. A boy complains that his mother gives her daughter too much free rein.
6. The girl's intimate/joyful conversation with the horse, which tells her of its master's affections and intentions.
7. Girl doesn't want the man she doesn't love.
8. The pretty barmaid: her lover is not there with the other customers.
9. Finding the beloved and gently rousing her from sleep.
10. What will be my husband's trade?
11. The joys of love forgone in idle chatter.
12. The lover returns from abroad, spies on her by day, surprises her at night.

I remarked that these motifs by themselves excited such vivid impressions in my mind that I felt as if I were reading the actual poems, and therefore had no desire to see the finished article.

'I quite agree,' said Goethe. 'But you can see from this how important motifs are – which nobody seems to understand. Our women writers don't have the faintest idea. "This poem is beautiful," they say, thinking only of the feelings, the words, the verse. People don't realize that the true power and impact of a poem lies in the situation, in the motifs. This is why we have thousands of poems with no motif worth speaking of, which just rely on feelings and fine-sounding verse to create some semblance of life. Dilettantes, and women in particular, have a very poor notion of what poetry is. They generally think it's just a matter of technique, and that once they have mastered that they have got it made. But they are very much mistaken.'

Professor Riemer was announced, and Councillor Rehbein took his leave. Riemer sat down with us. We carried on discussing the motifs in the Serbian love poems. Riemer knew what we were talking about, and observed that not only was it possible to write poems based on the aforementioned summary of contents, but that those same motifs had already been developed and used by German writers, without any knowledge of this Serbian connection. He recalled a few poems of his own as examples, and I myself, while reading out the list, had been reminded of some of Goethe's poems, which I now mentioned.

'The world always stays the same,' said Goethe. 'The same conditions are repeated, one nation lives, loves and feels much like another, so why should one poet not write much like another? The situations in life are the same, so why should the situations in poems not be the same?'

'And it's because we share the same life and feelings,' said Riemer, 'that we are able to understand the poetry of other nations. If this were not the case we would never know what foreign poems are talking about.'

'Which is why,' I then said, 'I've always thought it very strange how scholars seem to think poetry comes, not from life, but from books. They are always saying: "He got this from here, and that from there!" So if they find passages in Shakespeare, say, which also occur in the ancients, they claim that he, too, must have got them from the ancients! There is a scene in Shakespeare, for example, where someone sees a beautiful girl and says how happy are the parents who call her daughter, and how happy will be the young man who makes her his bride.[52] And just because the same scene occurs in Homer, they argue that Shakespeare must have got it from Homer! How bizarre is that? As if one needed to go looking for such things – as if we didn't see them, feel them and talk about them every day of the week!'

'Indeed,' said Goethe, 'it is utterly ludicrous.'

'And even Lord Byron,' I continued, 'is no better, when he takes your *Faust* to pieces, and claims that you took this bit from here and that bit from there.'[53]

Goethe replied: 'I have not even read most of those splendid works cited by Lord Byron, far less had them in mind while I was working on *Faust*. But Lord Byron is only great when he's being a poet; when he stops to think, he's a child. So he has no idea how to defend himself against ignorant attacks of a similar kind made on him by his own countrymen; he should have spoken out more vigorously against them. "What you see is my own," he should have said, "and whether I got it from life or from a book is neither here nor there; all that matters is that I put it to good use." Walter Scott used a scene from my *Egmont*, and he was entitled to do so; and because he made a good job of it he deserves our praise. He also has a character in one of his novels who is modelled on my Mignon; though whether that was so well advised is another question.[54] Lord Byron's transformed devil is my Mephistopheles taken one stage further – which is fine by me.[55] Had he insisted on being original and doing something different, he would have made a worse job of it. Similarly, my Mephistopheles sings a song from Shakespeare; and why not, indeed? Why should I go to the trouble of making up one of my own, when the one from Shakespeare was just the thing and said exactly what I wanted? And if the prologue to my *Faust* is somewhat similar to the beginning of the Book of Job, then that's fine too, and a reason to praise me rather than take me to task.'

Goethe was in the best of moods. He sent for a bottle of wine, and poured a glass for Riemer and me, while he himself drank Marienbad mineral water. It appeared that he had made arrangements with Riemer to go through the manuscript of the continuation of his autobiography this evening, perhaps with a view to improving the style here and there.[56] 'I expect Eckermann will stay and listen in,' said Goethe, which I was very pleased to hear. Whereupon he put the manuscript in front of Riemer, who began to read, starting in 1795.

Over the summer I had had the pleasure of reading and rereading the as yet unpublished notes on all these years, right up to the most recent time. But to hear them now, read aloud in Goethe's presence, afforded me a whole new kind of enjoyment. Riemer paid special attention to the style, and it was an opportunity for me to marvel at his great skill, and his vast store of words and phrases. Goethe, meanwhile, was reliving in his mind the period of his life described in the manuscript; the memories came flooding back, and when particular persons and events were mentioned he reminisced about them in more detail, telling us things that were not in the written account. It was a delightful evening. Repeated mention was made of his most distinguished contemporaries, but the conversation kept on coming back to Schiller, the figure most closely associated with this period between 1795 and 1800. They had both been very much involved with the theatre, and Goethe's finest works came out of those years. *Wilhelm Meister* was finished then, *Hermann und Dorothea* was planned and written next; *Cellini* was translated for *Die Horen*, and the *Xenien* were written in collaboration for Schiller's *Musenalmanach*. The two men were in constant daily contact. All of this came up in the conversation this evening, prompting Goethe to make all kinds of interesting observations.

'*Hermann und Dorothea*,' he said at one point, 'is almost the only one of my longer poems that still gives me pleasure; every time I read it, I get drawn right in again. I particularly enjoy it in the Latin translation; that makes it sound more dignified somehow, as if it had gone back to its formal origins.'

There was also much mention of *Wilhelm Meister*. 'Schiller,' he said, 'objected to the introduction of the tragic element, saying it didn't belong in the novel. But he was wrong, as we all know. His letters to me contain many fascinating thoughts and observations on *Wilhelm Meister*. It is, by the way, one of my most unaccountable works, to which I scarcely have the key myself. People try to find a centre to it, but that is difficult, and not necessarily a good thing. I rather think that a rich and varied life, unfolding before our eyes, is something worthwhile in itself, without trying to argue some sort of point, which only speaks to the intellect, after all. But if that's what people want, then I suggest they look at what Friedrich says to our hero at the end: "You remind me of Saul, the son of Kish, who went forth to seek his father's asses, and found a kingdom." People should hold on to that. Because basically, what the whole thing seems to be saying is simply that man, for all his follies and errors, is guided by a higher hand, and finds happiness in the end.'

We then talked about the cultural sophistication of the

middle classes, which has spread throughout Germany in the last fifty years, and Goethe said the credit for this should go not to Lessing, but to Herder and Wieland. 'Lessing,' he said, 'was a man of great intellect, and only someone of equal stature could truly learn from him. To someone of middling talents, he was dangerous.' He mentioned a journalist who had modelled himself on Lessing and played a role at the end of the previous century, albeit not a distinguished one, as he was far inferior to his great predecessor.[57]

'The whole of Upper Germany,' said Goethe, 'owes its style to Wieland. It has learned a great deal from him, not least the ability to express itself properly.'

At the mention of the *Xenien*, Goethe particularly commended the ones by Schiller, which he called cutting and hard-hitting, whereas his own he regarded as harmless and slight. 'The *Tierkreis* [*Zodiac*] is one of Schiller's,' he said, 'and I always admire it when I read it. The beneficial impact the *Xenien* had on German literature at the time is incalculable.' Many of the people at whom they were aimed were mentioned in the course of the conversation, but I don't remember their names.

When the manuscript up to the end of 1800 had been read aloud and discussed, interspersed with these and a hundred other comments and asides from Goethe, he put the papers to one side and ordered on a light supper, which was laid out at one end of the table where we were sitting. We tucked in, although Goethe himself didn't eat a thing; in fact, I've never seen him eat in the evening. But he sat with us, topped up our glasses, trimmed the candle wicks and regaled us with the most wonderful talk. The memory of Schiller was so alive in him that the conversation during the latter half of the evening was devoted entirely to him.

Riemer remembered what Schiller was like in person. 'His physique, the way he walked down the street, every one of his movements,' he said, 'were all proud; only his eyes were gentle.' 'Yes,' said Goethe, 'everything else about him was proud and magnificent, but his eyes were gentle. And his talent was built like his body. He grabbed hold of some big theme and turned it this way and that, looked at it every which way, tried all the angles, tried different approaches. But he looked at his subject only from the outside, as it were; quietly developing it from within was not his thing. His talent was more erratic. That's why he was never decisive and could never stop tinkering. He would often change a part just before a rehearsal.

'And just as his approach to everything was big and bold, he didn't bother much with motivation, either. I remember all the trouble I had with him over *Tell*, when he wanted to have Gessler just pick an apple off the tree and get Tell to shoot it off the boy's head.[58] That went against all my natural instincts, and I persuaded him to at least motivate this act of cruelty by getting Tell's son to boast to Gessler about his father's skill, saying he could shoot an apple off a tree from a hundred paces. Schiller was dead set against it at first, but in the end he gave in to my protestations and pleas and followed my advice.

'I myself, on the other hand, often placed too much emphasis on motivation, and that has kept my plays out of the theatre. My *Eugenie* is just a sequence of motives, and that is never going to work well on the stage.[59]

'Schiller's talent was made for the theatre. With every play he got better and grew more accomplished. But it was strange how a certain fascination with cruelty, which started with *Die Räuber*, never really left him, even in his prime.[60] I remember very clearly how, in the dungeon scene in *Egmont*, where the sentence is being read out, Schiller wanted to have Alba appear at the back of the stage, masked and wrapped in a cloak, to enjoy the effect that the death sentence would have on Egmont. This was supposed to show Alba's insatiable appetite for revenge and his delight in the suffering of others. But I protested, and Schiller dropped the idea. He was a strange man, but a great one.

'He changed and grew more accomplished with each passing week; every time I saw him I felt he was further on in his reading, learning and judgement. His letters are the finest mementoes of him that I have, and they are among the very best things he wrote. I keep his last letter with my other treasures, as a sacred relic.' Goethe stood up and went to fetch it. 'Here you are – read it,' he said, handing it to me.

It was a wonderful letter, written in a bold hand. It contained

Schiller's thoughts on Goethe's notes for *Rameau's Nephew*, which paint a picture of French literature at the time, and which he had sent to Schiller in manuscript form for him to have a look at.[61] I read the letter aloud to Riemer. 'As you can see,' said Goethe, 'his judgement is as sound and acute as ever, and his handwriting gives no hint of any failing. He was a brilliant man, and he left us at the peak of his powers. This letter is dated 24 April 1805. Schiller died on 9 May.'

We took turns studying the letter and commented on the clarity of the style and the elegance of the handwriting. Goethe had many more words of affectionate remembrance for his friend before the evening was out, and it was nearly eleven o'clock when we left.

Thursday 24 February 1825

'If I were still interested in running the theatre,' said Goethe this evening, 'I would put Byron's *Doge of Venice* on the stage.[62] The play is too long, of course, and would need shortening; but the way to do that is not to make cuts as such, but rather to condense the content of each scene, and just say the same thing in fewer words. The whole play would end up shorter, without being adversely affected by the changes; and it would have a greater impact, without losing anything of its essential beauty.'

This remark of Goethe's gave me a new insight into how one might adapt for the theatre in a hundred similar cases, and I thought the principle an excellent one; though it presupposes a very good mind – a poet, in fact – who knows what he is doing.

We carried on talking about Lord Byron, and I mentioned how he had said, in his conversations with Medwin, that writing for the theatre was an extremely difficult and thankless task. 'It all depends,' said Goethe, 'on whether the writer can see where the public's taste and interest are going. If the writer's instincts are attuned to what the public wants, then he is on to a winner. Houwald was on the right track with his *Bild* – hence all the plaudits it received. Lord Byron would not have been so fortunate, perhaps, in so far as he and the public were moving in different directions. This has nothing to do with how great the poet is; indeed, a writer who does not particularly stand out from the crowd often finds the most favour with the public for that very reason.'

We continued our conversation about Lord Byron, and Goethe spoke admiringly of his extraordinary talent. 'In all the world,' he said, 'I have never seen anyone who had a greater gift for what I call "invention" than he did. The way he resolves a dramatic entanglement always comes as a surprise, and is always better than one was expecting.' 'I find the same thing with Shakespeare,' I replied, 'especially when Falstaff has tied himself up in knots with his lies, and I wonder what *I* would now make him do to get out of it – when of course Shakespeare has come up with something I would never have thought of.[63] But for you to say the same thing about Lord Byron is probably the highest compliment one could pay him. All the same,' I added, 'the poet who can clearly see how his work begins and ends has a big advantage over the uninformed reader.'

Goethe agreed with me, and then laughed to think that Lord Byron, who flouted convention all his life and had no time for conformity, should in the end submit to the most idiotic convention of all – the law of the three unities. 'He no more understood the point of this law,' he said, 'than anyone else. The point is to be *intelligible*, and the three unities are only use-ful in so far as they help you achieve that. If they get in the way of intelligibility, however, then it is just stupid to take them as gospel and insist on observing them. Even the Greeks, who invented this rule, didn't always follow it. In the *Phaethon* of Euripides and in other plays, we have a change of place, which shows that telling the story well was more important to them than blind adherence to a law that never signified much in itself. Shakespeare's plays ignore the unities of time and place completely, yet they are intelligible – none more so – and there-fore even the Greeks would find them perfectly acceptable. French writers have sought to observe the law of the three unities more strictly than anyone else, but in trying to respect the dramatic unities through reliance on narrative exposition rather than dramatic action, they end up making themselves *less* intelligible.'

This put me in mind of Houwald's *Die Feinde*, a play in which we are all too aware of the dramatist's presence; in order to preserve the unity of place he made the first act harder to follow, and very possibly diminished the overall impact of his play for the sake of a whim that nobody cares about. By way of contrast, I also thought of *Götz von Berlichingen*, a play that is as far removed from the unities of time and place as it is possible to be; but because the action unfolds in the present, right before our eyes, it is as genuinely dramatic and intelligible as any play ever written. It also occurred to me that the unities of time and place would be preserved naturally, in the way the Greeks intended, if the action in question were on a small enough scale to unfold in full before our eyes in real time; whereas, in the case of some sweeping, large-scale action that moves from one place to another, there is no reason why it should be confined to *one* place, especially as our modern theatre stages can cope with any number of scene changes.

Goethe continued on the subject of Lord Byron. 'Still, given his natural disposition to push the boundaries at all times, the constraint he imposed on himself by observing the three unities does him credit. If only he had exercised similar self-control in moral matters! The fact that he couldn't was his undoing, and it is fair to say that his dissolute ways were the ruin of him.

'He did not know himself sufficiently. He always lived passionately, in the moment, and neither knew nor reflected upon what he did. Permitting himself everything, and condoning nothing in others, he was bound to fall out with himself and set the whole world against him. Right from the outset, he offended the chief men of letters with his *English Bards and Scotch Reviewers*. After that, he had to back off a little just to make a living. In the works that followed he continued to pursue the path of opposition and censure; State and Church did not escape unscathed. This reckless behaviour drove him out of England, and in time would have driven him out of Europe, too. Everywhere was too confining for him, and for all his unbounded personal freedom he felt anxious and oppressed; the world was a prison to him. Going to Greece was not a voluntary decision; at odds with the world, he was forced to go.

'Not only did breaking with tradition and the mother country bring personal ruin on a fine man; his revolutionary sympathies, and the constant mental agitation that went with them, stunted the development of his talent. Furthermore, his endless opposition and fault-finding detract enormously from his brilliant works as they stand. Not only does the poet's own discontent infect the reader, but all opposition ends in negativity; and negativity is nothing. If I say that something bad is bad, it's just not very helpful. But if I say that something good is bad, I do a lot of harm. If we want to achieve something worthwhile, we must never denigrate, or waste time on what has been badly done; we must focus only on doing good work. The point is not to tear things down, but to build something up – something that gives people pure joy.'

I drank in these wise words and was much taken with this wonderful maxim.

'We have to view Lord Byron,' Goethe went on, 'as a man, an Englishman, and a formidable talent. His good qualities are largely attributable to Byron the man; his bad ones to the fact that he is an Englishman and a peer of the realm; and as for his talent, it is beyond measure.

'All Englishmen as such lack any real capacity for reflection; distractions and factionalism do not allow them to cultivate their minds in quiet contemplation. But they really excel in all practical matters.

'Hence the fact that Lord Byron was never able to reflect upon himself – which is why his maxims in general never quite work, as demonstrated by his creed: "A lot of money and no authority!" Because excess of money does indeed paralyse authority.

'But all his creative writings have turned out well, and with him, it is true to say, inspiration takes the place of introspection. He was born to write; and so everything that came from the man, and especially from the heart, was first-rate. He produced his works the way women produce beautiful children: they do it without thinking, and have no idea how it was done.

'He is a great talent, a *born* talent, and I know of nobody whose poetic powers as such are greater. In his grasp of externals and his clear insight into the past he is as great as Shakespeare.

But as a pure individual, Shakespeare is superior. Byron was well aware of this, which is why he doesn't say much about Shakespeare, even though he knows whole passages by heart. He would gladly have disowned him altogether, for Shakespeare's jollity is a thorn in his side; he knows he can't compete. Pope he doesn't disown, because he had no reason to fear him. Indeed, he mentions him and acknowledges him at every turn, knowing full well that Pope is just a backdrop to himself.'

Goethe seemed inexhaustible on the subject of Byron, and I never tired of listening to him. After a few brief digressions, he returned to his theme:

'Byron's lofty status as an English peer was very damaging to him. Every talent struggles with the outside world – and it is harder still for someone of high birth and great wealth. A middling sort of condition is far more congenial to talent – which is why all our great artists and poets come from the middle classes. Byron's fondness for excess would have been far less dangerous to him if he had been of lower birth and humbler means. As it was, he had it in his power to fulfil his every whim, and that landed him in endless trouble. And besides, how could he, coming from the upper class himself, be impressed or inhibited by social rank of any kind? He said whatever was on his mind, and that brought him into ceaseless conflict with the world.

'It is astonishing,' Goethe went on, 'how much of a wealthy English aristocrat's life is taken up with duels and elopements. Lord Byron tells us himself that his father ran off with three women. How could any son of his turn out sane and sensible after that!

'The fact is, Byron lived his whole life in a state of nature, and being the way he was, he must have thought constantly about the need to defend himself. Hence his obsessive pistol practice. He had to reckon on being challenged to a duel at any time.

'He was incapable of living alone. This is why, for all his eccentricities, he was always very forgiving towards those he associated with. One evening, he recited the splendid poem on the death of General Moore, and his aristocratic friends didn't know what to make of it.[64] This didn't upset him and he just put it away again. As a poet, he really was as meek as a lamb. Anyone else would have told them to go to hell!'

Wednesday 20 April 1825

This evening Goethe showed me a letter from a young student, who writes to ask him for the plan for the second part of *Faust*, which he intends to complete himself.[65] Earnest, good-natured and ingenuous, he just comes straight out with his hopes and ambitions, and ends by announcing quite openly that all other recent literary endeavours amount to nothing, but that a new literature is destined to blossom afresh in him.

Were I to meet a young man in life who was getting ready to continue Napoleon's campaigns of world conquest, or a young dabbler in architecture who was shaping up to finish Cologne Cathedral, they would not surprise me any more, or seem any crazier or more ridiculous, than this young lover of literature, who is deluded enough to think that he can write the second part of *Faust* just because he feels like it.[66]

In fact, I think it might be easier to finish Cologne Cathedral than to continue Goethe's *Faust* in the way the author intended. With the former, you could at least come at it with the help of mathematics; the building is standing there, after all, where you can see it and touch it. But what chalk lines and yardsticks could possibly help us get to grips with an invisible work of the mind, which relies entirely on the subjective point of view, where everything depends on the creative idea, which requires a lifetime of first-hand experience to furnish the material and, for its execution, a technique practised over many years and honed to perfection?

Anyone who thinks such an undertaking easy, or even possible at all, plainly has very little talent, precisely because anything exacting or difficult is quite beyond his ken; and it would be fair to say that if Goethe were to finish his *Faust* himself, leaving just a few lines to be added, a young man such as this would be incapable of supplying even these few missing lines satisfactorily.

I couldn't possibly say where the youth of today gets the

strange idea that it is somehow born with accomplishments that have hitherto taken years of study and personal experience to acquire. But what I can say is this: the view we hear so often expressed in Germany now – that one can happily skip the whole business of gradual self-development – inspires little hope of future masterpieces.

'The trouble with the state,' said Goethe, 'is that nobody is content just to sit back and enjoy life – everyone wants to be in charge; and the trouble with art is that nobody is content just to enjoy what others have produced – now everyone wants to be an artist himself.

'And nobody turns to a work of poetry for encouragement to help him on his way; now everyone immediately wants to do the same thing himself.

'Furthermore, there is no sense of dedication to a greater good, no desire to do something for the sake of the generality; people are only interested in getting themselves noticed and cutting a figure in the eyes of the world. We see these misguided souls all around us, and people are taking their cue from the new generation of virtuosi, who choose their programme pieces not because they will afford the audience maximum musical pleasure, but because they give the player an opportunity to show off his skills. It's the same everywhere; the individual wants to be the centre of attention, and you never see the kind of honest endeavour that subordinates the self to the generality and the common good.

'And then there's the way people acquire the habit of producing bad poetry without even realizing it. They make up verses as children; time goes by, and then they think, in their youth, that they are pretty good, until eventually, as grown men, they learn to appreciate true excellence – and realize with horror how many years they have wasted on their misguided and utterly futile efforts.

'Many of them never come to know what perfection is and how inadequate their own efforts are, and so they go on producing half-baked stuff to the end of their days.

'What is certain is that if everyone could be made aware at a young age that the world is full of brilliant work, and what it takes to produce something of comparable quality, barely one in a hundred of today's young writers would feel they had the determination, the talent and the courage to stay the course and attain a similar mastery.

'Many young painters would never have picked up a paintbrush if they had known and understood early enough what a master like Raphael had actually accomplished.'

The conversation turned to misguided tendencies in general, and Goethe went on:

'My own practical tendency towards painting was misguided, in fact, because I had no natural aptitude for it, and so nothing could possibly come of it. I had a certain sensitivity to my natural surroundings, so my first attempts were quite promising. My journey to Italy shattered these cosy illusions; I tried my hand at distant prospects, but my sensitivity deserted me. As I was never going to develop any artistic talent, either technically or aesthetically, my efforts came to nothing.

'It is rightly said,' Goethe went on, 'that the communal cultivation of human powers is desirable, and the finest thing of all. But we are not born to that; each of us must cultivate himself as a separate being, while seeking to gain an understanding of what constitutes humankind.'

This put me in mind of *Wilhelm Meister*, where it is also said that humanity must be made up of *all* men, and that we are only deserving of respect in so far as we know how to value others.[67]

I also thought of the *Wanderjahre*, where Montan's advice to everyone is to learn one trade only, saying that this is now the age of specialization; and happy is the man who understands this and labours for himself and others in that spirit.[68]

The question is, however, what kind of trade should a person pursue, so that he doesn't overstep the limits, or indeed do too little?

Someone whose job it will be to oversee, pass judgement, and provide leadership in many different fields should try to get as much insight as possible into many different subjects. So the education of a prince, or a future statesman, can never be too broad and well rounded, given that there are so many different sides to his job.

Similarly, the poet should seek to know as much as possible;

for his subject matter is the world and everything in it, which he must learn to process and express.

But the poet should not try to be a painter; he should be content instead to render the world through words, just as he leaves it to the actor to show us the world through personal performance.

There is a difference between understanding a thing and making it your life's business, and we should bear in mind that all art, when it comes down to the practice of it, is something very difficult and challenging, which it takes a whole lifetime to master.

Goethe sought to gain understanding in as many different areas of life as possible. But in his life's business he confined himself to one thing. He has practised only one art, and he has done so in masterly fashion: the art of writing German. The fact that the content of his writings is very varied is another matter.

In the same way, we need to make a distinction between our education and our life's business.

Part of a poet's education is that his eye should get as much practice as possible in the apprehension of external objects. And when Goethe calls his practical tendency towards painting 'misguided', in so far as he had planned to make it his life's business, it was nevertheless very helpful for his education as a poet.

'I owe the concrete character of my poetry,' said Goethe, 'to the fact that I paid close attention to what I saw, and trained my eye; and the knowledge that I gained as a result has been of great value to me.'

But we should beware of letting our education become too broad.

'Natural scientists,' said Goethe, 'are most at risk here, because the observation of nature really does call for a very balanced, general education.'

Then again, when it comes to the specialized knowledge that all of us must have in our own field, we need to guard against tunnel vision and one-sidedness.

A poet who wants to write for the theatre needs to have a knowledge of stagecraft, so that he can reflect on the resources at his disposal and understand what he can and can't do.

Likewise, the composer of operas needs to have an understanding of poetry, so that he can distinguish the bad from the good and not squander his talent on something second-rate.

'Carl Maria von Weber,' said Goethe, 'would have done better not to compose *Euryanthe*; he should have seen straightaway that this was poor material, and that nothing could be done with it. We have a right to expect that much understanding from any composer: it's part of his job as an artist.'

In the same way, the painter should know how to distinguish between different subjects; for knowing what to paint, and what not to paint, is part of his job, too.

'But in the end,' said Goethe, 'the greatest art of all is to know how to limit and isolate oneself.'

Ever since I have been with him, therefore, he has always tried to shield me from distractions of any kind and to keep me focused on one specific subject. If I showed an inclination to dabble in the natural sciences, for instance, he always advised me to leave well alone and to stick to poetry for now. If I wanted to read a book that he knew would not help me with what I am doing now, he always advised against it, saying it was of no practical use to me.

'I have spent far too much time on things,' he said to me one day, 'that were not really my department. When I think how much Lope de Vega achieved, my own body of poetic work seems very slight by comparison. I should have stuck more to my own trade.'

Another time he said: 'If I had not been so taken up with stones, and had used my time for something better, I might have had the finest diamond jewels.'

For the same reasons, he respects and admires his friend Meyer for having devoted his entire life to the study of art, as a result of which he is now an acknowledged expert on the subject.

'I was similarly inclined myself when I was growing up,' said Goethe, 'and have also spent nearly half a lifetime in the contemplation and study of works of art; but all the same, I am no match for Meyer in certain respects. So I am careful not to show a new painting to this particular friend straightaway; instead, I see what I can make of it myself first. When I think I've got a clear idea of its good and bad points, I show it to Meyer, who of course is a far more acute observer, and sees all kinds of things that I haven't. And so I am reminded every time what it means, and what it takes, to master *one* subject completely. Meyer is a walking encyclopaedia of art history down the millennia.'

Now it might be asked why Goethe himself, he of all people, insistent as he is that a man should focus on one thing only, has spent his life pursuing so many different interests.

My answer to that would be this: if Goethe were to come into the world now and find the poetic and scientific endeavours of his nation in their present advanced stage of development – largely as a result of his efforts, incidentally – he would surely have no reason to pursue such a diverse range of interests, but would instead confine himself to one particular area.

As it was, however, it was not only in his nature to inquire deeply into everything and to seek to understand all earthly things, but it was also a need of the times to put into words what he saw.

When he came on to the scene he inherited two major legacies, *error* and *deficiency*, and it fell to him to sweep these away – a task that called for a lifetime of effort on many different fronts.

If Goethe had not viewed the Newtonian theory as a grave and pernicious error, do we seriously think it would ever have occurred to him to write his own *Farbenlehre*, and to devote so many years of effort to such a secondary interest? Surely not. It was his feeling for the truth, in conflict with error, that prompted him to shine his pure light into these dark regions as well.

The same could be said of his theory of metamorphosis, in which he has given us a model of scientific study and analysis; but it would certainly never have occurred to Goethe to write such a book if he had seen his contemporaries already working towards that goal.

Indeed, the same might well apply to his very diverse poetic output. For it is open to question whether Goethe would ever have written a novel, if a work such as *Wilhelm Meister* had already been produced by his countrymen. And open to question whether, had that been the case, he might not perhaps have devoted himself exclusively to dramatic poetry.

What he would have produced and achieved, had he confined himself to just the one literary genre, it is quite impossible to say. This much is certain, however, that if we take his writings as a whole, no sensible man will wish that Goethe had not produced all those things towards which it has pleased his Creator to direct him.

Thursday 12 May 1825

Goethe spoke with great enthusiasm of Menander. 'Apart from Sophocles, I know of nobody I love so much. He is altogether pure, noble, great and serene, and a writer of supreme grace and charm. It is a pity we possess so little of him, but even the little we have is of inestimable value, and highly instructive for people of talent.

'The great thing to remember,' said Goethe, 'is that the person we wish to learn from should be compatible with our own nature. Calderón, for example, as great as he is and as much as I admire him, has not influenced me at all, either for good or for ill. But he would have been dangerous for Schiller, who would have been led astray by him; so it is fortunate that Calderón did not become widely known in Germany until after Schiller's death. Calderón is supremely accomplished in all things technical and theatrical; Schiller, on the other hand, is far more sound, earnest and intense, and it would have been a pity, therefore, if he had sacrificed something of these virtues, perhaps, while falling short of Calderón's greatness in other respects.'

We turned to the subject of Molière. 'Molière,' said Goethe, 'is so great that one is astonished anew every time one reads him. He is one of a kind: his plays verge on the tragic, they are unsettling, and nobody dares to try and imitate him. His *L'Avare*, where vice destroys all family feeling between father and son, is especially great, and in the true sense tragic. But when a German adaptation replaces the son with a family relative, the piece loses its impact and doesn't have very much to say to us. They were afraid to show vice in its true colours, but what are we left with then? And what can ever be tragic, except what is unbearable?

'I reread several of Molière's plays every year, just as I go back from time to time to my engravings after the great Italian masters. We little men are not capable of retaining the greatness of such things in our minds, and so we must revisit them from time to time in order to refresh our impressions.

'People are always talking about "originality", but what does that mean? From the moment we are born, the world begins to influence us, and that continues right up to the end. And anyway, what can any of us call our own, except our energy, our strength and our force of will? If I could list everything I owe to great predecessors and contemporaries, there would not be much left.

'However, it makes a difference at what point in our lives we are exposed to the influence of a significant figure. The fact that Lessing, Winckelmann and Kant were all older than me, and that the first two influenced me in my youth, and Kant in my later years, was very important for me. Likewise the fact that Schiller was so much younger than me, and only just embarking on his career as I began to tire of the world; and that the von Humboldt and Schlegel brothers were starting to become known on my watch – all this was of the utmost importance. And the advantages I derived from this are incalculable.'

Following these observations on other great men who had influenced him, the conversation turned to the influence he had had on others; I mentioned Bürger, and said the trouble with him was that he was a wholly natural talent, whose work shows no trace of any influence by Goethe.

'Bürger,' said Goethe, 'undoubtedly had an affinity to me as a talent, but the tree of his moral culture was rooted in very different soil and leaned in a very different direction. And all of us continue as we first began, following the natural growth curve of our education. But a man who could write a poem like "Frau Schnips" at the age of thirty was clearly treading a path that deviated somewhat from mine. His considerable talents had also won him an audience that he satisfied completely, and so he had no reason to look around and see what he might borrow from a fellow writer who was of no concern to him.

'It's always the case,' Goethe went on, 'that we learn only from those we love. Some of the young talents now emerging are well disposed towards me, I think, but I was hard put to find such an attitude among my contemporaries. Indeed, I could scarcely name one man of any stature who entirely approved of me. Right away, with my *Werther*, people found so much to criticize that if I had erased every passage they objected to, there would hardly be a single line of the book left. Still, all that negative criticism did me no harm, because the subjective judgements of a few individuals, however eminent, were outweighed by the approval of the masses. But anyone who does not expect to get a million readers should not write a single line.

'The public has been arguing for twenty years now about who is the greater – Schiller or me. They should be glad that they've got the two of us to argue about in the first place.'

Saturday 11 June 1825

At dinner today Goethe spoke at length about Major Parry's book on Byron.[69] He had nothing but praise for it, and remarked that Lord Byron comes across as a far more rounded character in this account, with much clearer ideas about himself and his intentions, than in anything previously written about him.

'Major Parry,' Goethe went on, 'must also be a very remarkable, and indeed superior, man, to be able to understand his friend so clearly and portray him so perfectly. I particularly like one observation in his book, which is worthy of an ancient Greek, or indeed of Plutarch himself. "The noble lord," says Parry, "lacked all those virtues that are the adornment of the middle classes, and which he was prevented from acquiring by birth, education and way of life. But those who judge unfavourably of him are all from the middle classes, who of course regret and bemoan the lack in him of those virtues that they have reason to prize in themselves. These good people fail to consider that he, in his elevated station, possessed merits of which they have no conception." What do you think of that?' said Goethe. 'Not the kind of thing you hear every day, is it?'

'I am delighted,' I replied, 'to hear someone publicly express a view whereby all those petty critics and detractors who attack anyone of higher status than themselves are trounced and silenced once and for all.'

We then talked about world history as a suitable subject for poetry, and specifically how far the history of one nation can be more fruitful for the poet than that of another.

'The poet,' said Goethe, 'should seize on the particular, and as long as it is something wholesome, he will end up saying something of general significance. English history is ideal for poetic representation, because it is something sound, wholesome and therefore general, which repeats itself. French history, on the other hand, is ill suited to poetry, because it represents an era that will not come again. The literature of the French, in so far as it is rooted in that era, is something of an oddity, which will become outdated over time.

'As for the present period of French literature,' said Goethe, 'it is too early to say. The German influence has caused a great ferment there, and it will take twenty years to see exactly what the outcome is.'

We then talked about literary critics, who struggle to encapsulate the essence of poetry and the poet in abstract definitions, without arriving at any clear conclusions.

'What is there to define?' said Goethe. 'The capacity to feel and empathize with situations, and the ability to express those feelings – that's what makes a poet.'

Wednesday 15 October 1825

I found Goethe in a particularly elated mood this evening, and once again had the pleasure of hearing many wise observations from his lips. We talked about the state of contemporary literature, and Goethe expressed the following views:

'Lack of character in individual scholars and writers,' he said, 'is the root cause of everything that's wrong with our modern literature.

'This deficiency shows itself to particularly damaging effect in critical writings, where either falsehood is peddled as truth, or else some paltry truth deprives us of something important that would be better for us.

'Hitherto, the world believed in the heroism of a Lucretia, a Mucius Scaevola, and was heartened and inspired by that belief.[70] But now we are told by a historian that those persons never lived, and are to be viewed as fictions and fables, invented by the great Roman mind. What are we supposed to do with a paltry truth like that? If the Romans were great enough to invent such stories, we should at least be big enough to believe them.

'I had always relished a great episode from the thirteenth century, when the Emperor Frederick the Second was at odds with the Pope, and northern Germany was exposed to attack from all sides. Asiatic hordes did actually invade and got as far as Silesia; but the Duke of Liegnitz struck terror into their hearts by inflicting a great defeat on them. Then they turned towards Moravia, but were defeated here by Count Sternberg. So I have always thought of these valiant warriors as the great saviours of the German nation. But now some historian has claimed that these heroes sacrificed themselves to no purpose, since the Asiatic army had already been recalled and would have gone home anyway. So now a great episode from our country's past has been blighted and destroyed, and I think it's absolutely terrible.'

Having shared his views on historians, Goethe now turned to scholars and writers in other fields.

'I would never have learned so much about the pitiful nature of men, and how little they care about the pursuit of truly noble aims,' he said, 'if I had not put them to the test through my scientific work. I saw then that science, for most of them, is just a means of earning a living, and that they will glorify error itself if it pays their wages.

'And things are no better in the world of literature. Here, too, it is very rare to find noble aims and a genuine feeling for the true and the good, and a desire to propagate them. One person nurtures and supports another, because he in turn is nurtured and supported by him; true greatness is hateful to them, and they would dearly like to get rid of it altogether, so that they alone might be considered important. That's how the masses think – and prominent individuals are not much better.

'With his great talent and prodigious learning, *** [Böttiger] could have been a great asset to the nation. But as it was, his lack of character deprived the nation of extraordinary benefits and cost him the nation's respect.

'What we need is a man like Lessing. For what is it that makes him great, if not his strength of character and unwavering conviction? There are plenty of other men equally clever and cultured, but who among them possesses such character?

'Many are witty enough and full of knowledge, but they are also full of vanity; and in their desire to be admired as wits by the blinkered masses they are without shame or scruple, and to them nothing is sacred.

'Madame de Genlis was quite right, therefore, when she took exception to Voltaire's liberties and insults. Because in the end, the world is not well served by all that superficial brilliance; it is not a foundation you can build on. Indeed, it could even be extremely harmful, in that it just confuses people and robs them of their certainties.

'And anyway, what do we know, and where does all our clever wit get us? Man is not born to solve the world's problems; his job is to try and discover where the problem begins, and then to keep within the bounds of what is comprehensible. He does not have the capacity to measure the operations of the universe, and any attempt to understand the cosmos by the application of human reason, given our own tiny vantage point, is doomed to failure. Human reason and divine reason are two very different things.

'Once we grant that man has free will, we can say goodbye to the idea of an omniscient God; for if the Deity knows what I am going to do, I am forced to act in accordance with that divine knowledge. I mention this just to show how little we know, and that it is not good to meddle with divine mysteries.

'And furthermore, we should only express high-minded principles where they can benefit the world. Otherwise we should keep them to ourselves; but we may be sure that they will shed their light on all that we do, like the soft radiance of a hidden sun.'

Sunday 25 December 1825

I called on Goethe at six this evening, found him alone, and spent several delightful hours in his company.

'I have had a lot on my mind lately,' he said. 'I have been shown so much kindness from every quarter that I have spent all my time thanking people, instead of getting on with my life. One by one, agreements to protect the publication of my works have been coming in from the various courts, and because the circumstances were different in each case, each one required a separate reply. Then I've had offers from countless booksellers, which had to be considered, attended to and answered. Then there's my Jubilee, which has brought me so many kind attentions that I am still writing thank-you letters.[71] And I like to write something that has personal relevance to the recipient, rather than fobbing people off with bland generalities. But now I am gradually finding that I have more time, and I feel in the mood for conversation again.

'I recently made an observation that I will share with you. Everything we do has consequences. But doing the wise thing and the right thing does not always end well, and doing the opposite does not always end badly. It often works the other way round, in fact.

'Some time ago I made a mistake in one of those negotiations with booksellers, and I regretted my error. But in the meantime, circumstances have changed in such a way that it would have been a bigger mistake not to have made the mistake that I did. That kind of thing happens a lot in life, and that's why we see men of the world – who know this – going about their business with great self-assurance and audacity.'

I made a mental note of this observation, which was new to me. I then brought the conversation round to some of his works, including his elegy 'Alexis und Dora'.

'People complained about this poem's highly emotional ending,' said Goethe, 'and told me I should have ended the elegy on a quiet and gentle note, without that outburst of jealousy. But I was not convinced that those people were right. The potential for jealousy here is so great that the poem would be seriously lacking something if I had left it out. I once knew a young man who, in his passionate love for a girl who was easily wooed, cried out: "But won't she do the same with another as she's done with me?".'

I agreed wholeheartedly with Goethe, and then mentioned the very particular setting of this elegy, where, in such a small compass and with so few strokes, everything is so well drawn that we have a vivid sense of the domestic circumstances and the entire lives of the characters. 'The picture you paint,' I said, 'seems so true to life that one would think the poem was based on personal experience.'

'I am pleased if that's how it strikes you,' said Goethe. 'There are few people who have the imagination to see the truth of real life. Instead, they go on about exotic lands and situations, of which they know nothing at all, and which their imagination doubtless pictures in very curious ways.

'And then there are others who can't see beyond real life, and because they lack any sense of poetry they take a very literal-minded view of things. In the case of this elegy, for example, some said that I should have given Alexis a servant to carry his bundle – not realizing that this would have ruined everything that was poetic or idyllic about the situation.'

From 'Alexis und Dora' the conversation now turned to *Wilhelm Meister*.

'There are some very strange critics out there,' Goethe went on. 'In the case of this novel, they complained that the hero spends too much time in bad company. But by treating this so-called bad company as a vessel into which I could put everything I had to say about polite society, I found a way to give concrete poetic expression to all kinds of things. Had I, on the other hand, chosen to portray polite society by showing so-called polite society, nobody would have bothered to read the book.

'There is always a higher meaning behind the seeming trivialities of *Wilhelm Meister*, and it is just a matter of having the eyes, the knowledge of the world and the breadth of vision to discern the greater meaning in small things. For others, the scenes of life portrayed may well be sufficient in themselves.'

1825   137

Goethe then showed me a very remarkable English work, which illustrated all of Shakespeare's plays in a sequence of copperplate engravings. On each page there were six small pictures depicting key scenes from one particular play, with a few lines of quoted text underneath, so that one had a summary of the main theme and the most important plot points. All the immortal tragedies and comedies were thus paraded before the mind's eye, as if in a carnival procession.

'It is frightening,' said Goethe, 'to look through these little pictures. That's when you realize how infinitely prolific and great Shakespeare is. There is no aspect of human life that he does not bring before us in actions and words. And it's all done with such facility and freedom!

'It's impossible to talk about Shakespeare; words are inadequate. I made a stab at it in my *Wilhelm Meister*, but there's not much to show for it. He is not a dramatist in the conventional sense; he never thought about the stage, which was far too confining for his great mind. Indeed, the entire visible world was too small for him.

'He is just too bountiful and too overwhelming. Anyone who writes should not read more than one of his plays a year, otherwise Shakespeare will be his undoing. I did well to get him off my back by writing *Götz von Berlichingen* and *Egmont*, and Byron did very well not to have too much respect for him and to go his own way. So many gifted Germans have been undone by him, by him and Calderón!

'Shakespeare,' Goethe went on, 'gives us golden apples in silver bowls. We get the silver bowl by studying his plays; but the trouble is, we only have potatoes to put in it.'[72]

I laughed, and enjoyed this splendid image.

Goethe then read me a letter from Zelter about a performance of *Macbeth* in Berlin, where the musical accompaniment had struggled to keep up with the great spirit and character of the play – as Zelter intimates in a series of asides. The letter came vividly to life again in Goethe's reading, and he paused frequently so that we could both enjoy the writer's happy choice of words at certain points.

'*Macbeth*,' said Goethe at this point, 'is Shakespeare's best stage play, I think, where he shows the greatest grasp of stage-craft. But if you want to see his mind ranging freely you should read *Troilus and Cressida*, where he reworks the subject matter of the *Iliad* in his own way.'

The conversation turned to Byron, and specifically how he suffers by comparison with Shakespeare's innocent jollity, and how the negativity of much of his own work attracted so much hostile criticism – not unfairly, for the most part. 'If Byron had had the opportunity,' said Goethe, 'to get all this confront-ational stuff out of his system by speaking his mind bluntly from time to time in parliament, he would have made a purer poet. But as it was, he hardly ever spoke in parliament, and so all the resentment he felt towards his nation stayed bottled up inside him; and the only outlet he had for it was to turn it into poetry and give voice to it that way. So a large part of Byron's negative writings are what I would call "sublimated parliamentary speeches" – which I think says it rather well.'

Mention was then made of one of our most recent German writers, who had quickly made a name for himself, but whose negative tendencies were similarly frowned upon.[73] 'There's no denying,' said Goethe, 'that he possesses many brilliant qual-ities; but what he lacks is love. He loves his readers and his fellow poets as little as he loves himself, and the words of the apostle seem particularly appropriate in his case: "Though I speak with the tongues of men and angels, and have not love, I am become as sounding brass and a tinkling cymbal." I have read some poems by *** [Platen] just recently, and there is no mistaking his abundant talent. But as I said, he lacks love, and that will always prevent him from gaining the following he might have had. People will fear him, and he will be the idol of those who would like to be as negative as him, but don't have his talent.'

1826

Sunday evening, 29 January 1826

The foremost German improviser, Dr Wolff from Hamburg, has been here for several days and has already given public demonstrations of his rare talent.[74] On Friday evening he gave a brilliant performance before a numerous audience and in the presence of the Weimar court. That same evening he received an invitation from Goethe to call on him the following day at noon.

I spoke to Dr Wolff yesterday evening, after he had improvised for Goethe at lunchtime. He was elated, and said that their meeting would be a turning point in his life; in just a few words Goethe had steered him in an entirely new direction, and in what he had said by way of criticism he had hit the nail on the head.

So this evening, when I was with Goethe, the conversation turned immediately to Wolff. 'Dr Wolff is very pleased,' I said, 'that Your Excellency has given him the benefit of your advice.' 'I was perfectly frank with him,' said Goethe, 'and if my words have made an impression on him and given him encouragement, that's a very good sign. He is a man of considerable talent, no question, but he suffers from the general malaise of our times, namely subjectivity; and I'd like to cure him of that if I can. I set him a challenge, to see what he could do. "Describe to me," I said, "your return to Hamburg." He accepted the challenge straightaway, and off he went, speaking in well-turned verse. I had to admire him; but I could not praise him. What he described to me was not his return to Hamburg, but simply the emotions that a son feels on returning to his parents, relations and friends; and his poem could just as well have been about a return to Merseburg or Jena as about a return to Hamburg. Yet Hamburg is such a magnificent and singular city, offering such a wealth of specific features for him to describe – if only he had known how to tackle the subject properly, and been bold enough to take it on.'

I remarked that the blame for this subjective tendency lies with the public, which likes nothing better than sentimentality.

'That may be so,' said Goethe, 'but if you give the public something better, it likes that even more. I am quite sure that if a talented improviser like Wolff could describe the life of great cities like Rome, Naples, Vienna, Hamburg and London exactly as it is, and so vividly that people feel they are seeing it with their own eyes, they would be thrilled and delighted. If he can only make the breakthrough to the objective, he will be home and dry; he has it in him, for he is not without imagination. But he needs to make up his mind quickly and seize the initiative now.'

'I fear,' I said, 'that this is harder than one thinks, because it calls for a complete change of thinking. If he succeeds, then at the very least there will be a momentary pause in his production, and it will take a lot of practice before he feels comfortable with the objective and it becomes second nature to him.'

'It is a very big transition, I grant you,' replied Goethe. 'But he just needs to be bold and make up his mind quickly. It's like being scared of going into the water; you just have to jump right in, and then you're in your element.

'When someone is learning how to sing,' Goethe went on, 'all the notes that lie within his normal range come naturally and easily to him; but the other ones, the notes outside his normal range, are extremely hard for him at first. But in order to be a singer he has to master them, because he needs to have them *all* at his command. It's just the same with a poet. You can't call him a poet as long as he is merely giving voice to his own subjective feelings; but once he knows how to appropriate and articulate the outside world, *then* he is a poet. And then he is inexhaustible, and can always be new and fresh, whereas a subjective character soon exhausts his own limited resources and succumbs in the end to mannerism.

'People are always saying we should study the ancients. But what does that mean, if not that we should focus our attention on the real world, and try to express that? Because that's what the ancients did in their day.'

Goethe rose to his feet and paced up and down the room, while I remained seated at the table, as he likes me to do. He paused for a moment at the stove, and then, like someone who has thought something through, he came up to me, laid a finger on his lips, and spoke as follows:

'Now I want to tell you something which you'll often find to be true in your life. All historical epochs that are in a state of retrogression and decline are subjective, while all progressive epochs are objective in tendency. Our entire present age is retrogressive, because it is subjective. You see this not only in poetry, but also in painting and many other things. By contrast, all serious and worthwhile endeavours are directed from the inside to the outside world, as you see with all great epochs, which have really been times of striving and progress, and all of them objective in character.'

These words led on to a most stimulating conversation, in which the great period of the fifteenth and sixteenth centuries figured prominently.

The conversation then turned to the theatre, and to the feeble, sentimental and dismal character of recent efforts. 'I am currently drawing strength and consolation from Molière,' I said. 'I have translated his *L'Avare*, and am now working on *Le Médecin malgré lui*. What a great and upright man Molière is!'

'Yes,' said Goethe, '"upright" sums him up exactly. There's nothing twisted or corrupt about him. And as for his greatness! He ruled the morals of his day, whereas our own Iffland and Kotzebue allowed themselves to be ruled by the morals of their times, and were thus confined and constrained by them. Molière chastised men by showing them as they truly are.'

'I would pay good money,' I said, 'to see the plays of Molière performed on the stage as they were originally intended. But if I know theatre audiences, they would find that kind of thing much too earthy and realistic. I wonder if this over-refinement doesn't stem from the so-called ideal literature produced by certain authors?'

'No,' said Goethe, 'it comes from society itself. And anyway, what are our young girls doing in the theatre? They don't belong there – they belong in a convent, and the theatre is for grown men and women who have some experience of life. When Molière wrote his plays, girls were in the convent, and he didn't have to take account of them at all. But as it will be difficult to get our young girls out of the theatre now, and people won't stop putting on plays that are feeble, and therefore just right for girls, the sensible thing is to do what I do and stay away.

'My interest in the theatre really only lasted as long as I was directly involved in it myself. My pleasure lay in raising the standard of our theatre establishment, and during performances I was less interested in the plays themselves and more concerned to see whether the actors were doing their job properly or not. If I didn't like something, I made a note on a piece of paper and sent it along to the director next morning; and I could guarantee that the mistake would not be repeated at the next performance. But now that I no longer have any say in what happens in the theatre, I have no special urge to go there. I would have to endure inferior productions without being able to correct the mistakes – and that's not for me.

'It's the same with the reading of plays. Young German writers are constantly sending me their tragedies; but what am I supposed to do with them? I have only ever read German plays in order to see whether I could put them on the stage; apart from that, they were of no interest to me. So what am I supposed to do with the plays of these young people now, in my present situation? I get nothing out of it myself, reading how it should *not* be done; and I can't help these young writers with something they've already finished. If they were to send me their outline for a play, instead of the final printed text, then at least I could say: "do it", or "don't do it", or "do it this way", or "do it differently", and then there would be some point to it.

'The trouble is, poetic culture is now so widespread in

1826   143

Germany that nobody writes a bad verse any more. The young
writers who send me their work are no less accomplished than
their predecessors; and because they see those men so highly
praised, they cannot understand why they themselves are not
getting any praise. And yet we dare not encourage them, precisely because such talents are ten a penny now, and we should
not be helping to create something we don't need when there
is still so much useful work to be done. If there were one
who stood head and shoulders above the rest, that would
be a different matter; for the world can only be served by the
exceptional.'

Thursday 16 February 1826

I went to see Goethe at seven o'clock this evening and found
him alone in his room. I sat down at the table with him and
told him my news: yesterday, at the inn, I had seen the Duke of
Wellington, passing through on his way to St Petersburg.[75]

'So what was he like?' asked Goethe with eager interest. 'Tell
me all about him. Does he look like his portrait?'

'Yes,' I said, 'but better, more distinctive. Once you have
looked into his face, all his portraits count for nothing. And to
see him once is never to forget him – so strong is the impression
he makes. His eyes are brown, bright and shining, and you feel
the power of his gaze. His mouth speaks to us, even when it is
closed. He looks like a man who has thought a great deal and
lived through momentous events, and who now views the
world with great serenity and calm, and whom nothing more
can dismay. To me he seemed as hard and tough as a Damascene blade.

'To look at him, I'd say he was in his upper fifties, upright in
bearing, slim, not very tall, and lean rather than stout. I saw
him as he was about to get into his carriage and drive off. There
was something extraordinarily gracious about the way he
acknowledged the crowd as he passed through it, bowing
almost imperceptibly and touching his finger to the brim of his
hat.'

Goethe listened to my account with evident fascination.

'Well, that's one more hero you have seen,' he said, 'and that's always quite something.'

We got on to the subject of Napoleon, and I said I was sorry not to have seen *him*. 'Yes, indeed,' said Goethe, 'that was also well worth the effort. What a compendium of the world he was!' 'Did he look special somehow?' I asked. 'He *was* special,' replied Goethe, 'and you could tell he was special just by looking at him – it was as simple as that.'

I had brought along a very curious poem for Goethe to look at, having mentioned it to him a few evenings previously. It was an old poem of his own, which he couldn't remember any more because it was so long ago.[76] Printed at the beginning of 1766 in *Die Sichtbaren*, a periodical published at the time in Frankfurt, it had been brought to Weimar by an old servant of Goethe's, and had come into my hands by way of his descendants.[77] Undoubtedly the earliest known poem of Goethe's, it was about the descent of Christ into hell, and I was struck by how familiar this very young writer was with religious thought and imagery. The content and spirit of the poem were reminiscent of Klopstock, but the execution was quite different; it was stronger, freer, with a lighter touch and greater energy, a better flow. Its extraordinary ardour was suggestive of a wild and boisterous youth. It went round in circles for lack of subject matter, and ended up being too long.

I showed Goethe the yellowed page from the periodical, now almost falling apart; and as soon as he saw it he remembered the poem again. 'It's possible,' he said, 'that Fräulein von Klettenberg asked me to write it; it says in the heading "written at the request of a friend", and I can't think of any other friends who would have requested such a subject. I was short of subject matter at the time, and I was glad to have something, anything, that I could write about. Just recently I came across a poem from that time that I'd written in English, in which I complain about the lack of poetic subjects.[78] We Germans are at a real disadvantage here: our earliest history is hidden in the mists of time, and later history is of no general national interest because we don't have one ruling dynasty. Klopstock tried to do something on Arminius, but the subject is too far removed from us; nobody can relate to it, nobody knows what to make of it, and so his efforts failed to make an impact or achieve popularity.[79] I made a wise choice with my *Götz von Berlichingen*; that was bone of my bones and flesh of my flesh, and I could do something with it.

'With *Werther* and *Faust*, however, I had to dig deep into my own bosom, because the material I inherited was not up to much. All that business with devils and witches, I did it just the once; glad to have devoured my Nordic inheritance, I went and supped with the Greeks. But had I known then, as clearly as I know now, how much excellent work has been produced over hundreds and thousands of years, I would not have written a single line, but would have done something else instead.'

Easter Day, 26 March 1826

At dinner today Goethe was in the sunniest and most genial of moods. He had just received a document today that he treasured greatly, namely Lord Byron's handwritten dedication to his *Sardanapalus*.[80] He showed it to us over dessert, teasing his daughter the while to give him back Byron's letter from Genoa. 'The thing is, my dear child,' he said, 'now that this remarkable document has miraculously come into my hands today, everything relating to my connection with Byron is now gathered together in one place – all except for that one letter.'

But our charming admirer of Byron was not minded to give up the letter. 'You gave it to me as a present, dear father,' she said, 'and I'm not giving it back. If you are so keen to keep like with like, then I suggest you give me today's precious document as well, and I'll keep them all together myself.' Goethe liked that idea even less, and their playful dispute went on for some time, until it merged into a general lively conversation.

When we had risen from table and the ladies had gone upstairs, I was left alone with Goethe. He fetched a red portfolio from his study, took it over to the window with me and opened it up. 'See here,' he said, 'this is where I keep all the papers relating to my connection with Lord Byron. Here is his letter from Livorno; this is a copy of his dedication; this is my poem; and this here is what I wrote about Medwin's *Conversations*. The only thing that's missing is his letter from Genoa, but she won't give it to me.'

Goethe then told me about a friendly request regarding Lord Byron that he had received from England today, which had given him great pleasure.[81] So his mind was filled with thoughts of Byron at this juncture, and he had countless interesting things to say about the man, his works and his talent.

'The English,' he said at one point, 'can think what they like of Byron, but one thing is certain: they have no other poet to compare with him. He is different from all the rest, and for the most part, greater.'

Monday 15 May 1826

I talked to Goethe about Stephan Schütze, of whom he spoke very warmly.

'A week or so ago, when I was feeling unwell for a few days,' he said, 'I read his *Heitere Stunden*. I enjoyed the book greatly. If Schütze had lived in England, he would have been a publishing sensation; with his gift for observation and description, all that he needed was the spectacle of life lived on a larger stage.'

Thursday 1 June 1826

Goethe talked about *Le Globe*.[82] 'The contributors,' he said, 'are men of the world, debonair, clear-sighted and utterly audacious. When they find fault they do so with finesse and grace, whereas our German academics always think they have to hate anyone who thinks differently from them. I regard the *Globe* as one of the most interesting periodicals, and I could not do without it.'

Wednesday 26 July 1826

This evening I had the good fortune to hear Goethe talk at length about the theatre.

I told him that one of my friends was planning to put Byron's *Two Foscari* on the stage. Goethe doubted whether it would be a success.

'It's very tempting, I know,' he said. 'When we read a play and it makes a great impression on us, we think it is bound to be just as effective on the stage, and we tell ourselves it would be easy enough to put it on successfully. But it's a funny thing. A play that was not originally written for stage performance and consciously crafted by the dramatist with that in mind will simply not work on the stage; and whatever you do to it, there will always be something not quite right about it. I took so much trouble with my *Götz von Berlichingen*, and yet it won't quite work as a piece for the theatre. It's just too long, and I had to break it down into two parts, the second of which is effective as drama, whereas the first is really only exposition. One solution might be to put on the first part just the once, to set up the dramatic situation, and then to keep on staging the second part on its own. That might work. It's a bit like that with *Wallenstein*; you don't see the *Piccolomini* performed very often, whereas *Wallensteins Tod* is always popular with theatregoers.'

I asked how a play had to be constructed in order to work well on the stage.

'It has to be symbolic,' replied Goethe. 'That is to say, every action must be significant in itself, while also leading up to something even more important. Molière's *Tartuffe* is a classic example of this. Think of the opening scene, what a brilliant piece of exposition that is! From the very beginning, everything is highly significant and leads us to expect something even more important to come. The exposition of Lessing's *Minna von Barnhelm* is also excellent, but the one in *Tartuffe* is simply the best there is.'

We then moved on to the plays of Calderón.

'In Calderón,' said Goethe, 'you find the same consummate stagecraft. His plays are made for the theatre, and everything about them is calculated to produce the desired effect. Calderón was a genius, but he also understood his craft better than anyone else.'

'It is strange,' I said, 'how Shakespeare's plays are not really stage plays, since he wrote them all for his theatre.'

'Shakespeare,' replied Goethe, 'wrote those plays from the heart; the age in which he lived and the set-up of the theatre back then placed no constraints on him, and people accepted what Shakespeare gave them. But if he had been writing for the court in Madrid, or for the theatre of Louis XIV, he probably would have adopted a stricter theatrical form. But we shouldn't complain: what Shakespeare has lost for us as a writer for the stage he has gained as a poet in the broader sense. Shakespeare is a great psychologist, and his plays teach us what goes on in people's minds.'

We talked about the difficulties of managing a theatre successfully.

'The difficult part,' said Goethe, 'is how to deal with contingencies without deviating from one's general management policy. That policy is about developing a core repertoire of good tragedies, operas and comedies, and then sticking to it. What I mean by "contingencies" is a new play that audiences are keen to see, a special appearance by some famous performer, and other things of that kind. We must not allow ourselves to be distracted by such things, but always go back to the repertoire. We have such an abundance of really good plays these days that it is very easy for a connoisseur to put together a good repertoire. But keeping to it – that's the really difficult part.

'When I ran the theatre together with Schiller, we had the advantage of playing a summer season in Lauchstädt.[83] There we had a very select audience, who only wanted to see the best. So we always came back to Weimar with the best plays already well rehearsed, and could repeat all our summer performances here throughout the winter. And besides, Weimar audiences had confidence in our management, and even in the case of things that left them rather baffled, they never doubted that we made our choices for very good reasons.

'By the nineties,' Goethe went on, 'the period of my real interest in the theatre was already past, and I wrote nothing more for the stage; I wanted to devote myself entirely to the epic form. It was Schiller who reawakened my interest, and I got involved in the theatre again for his sake and the sake of his works. At the time I wrote my *Clavigo* I could easily have written a dozen plays; there was no shortage of material, and the writing of them came easily to me. I could have turned out a new play every week, and it still vexes me that I didn't do it.'

Wednesday 8 November 1826

Goethe spoke admiringly of Lord Byron again today. 'I've just reread his *Deformed Transformed*,' he said, 'and I must say that his talent impresses me more and more. His devil is derived from my Mephistopheles, but it is no imitation; it's all thoroughly original and new – concise, clever and witty. There's not a weak passage in it, nowhere you could stick the head of a pin and not find inventiveness and wit. If it were not for his hypochondria and negativity, he would be as great as Shakespeare and the ancients.' I expressed surprise. 'Oh yes,' said Goethe, 'you can take it from me; I have been studying him again, and I find he just gets better and better.'

In an earlier conversation Goethe had said that Lord Byron was too 'empirical'. I didn't really understand what he meant, but I refrained from asking him, and thought about it afterwards by myself. But I couldn't work it out, and so could only wait until my advancing education, or some chance circumstance, should solve the mystery for me. And sure enough, my chance came one day when, having seen an excellent performance of *Macbeth* in the theatre the night before, I picked up the works of Lord Byron to read his *Beppo*. I found myself not enjoying Byron's poem after the *Macbeth*, and the more I read, the more I began to understand what Goethe might have meant by his remark.

Watching *Macbeth*, I felt the force of a spirit so great, powerful and sublime that it could only have emanated from Shakespeare himself. It was the innate power of a nature more highly and deeply gifted, which set its owner apart from all other men and thus made him the great poet that he was. Whatever this play owed to worldly knowledge and experience was subordinated to the poetic spirit, and served only to make that spirit speak and take command. The great poet reigned supreme, and we were raised up beside him to see things from his loftier perspective.

When reading *Beppo*, on the other hand, the main impression was of a dissolute empirical world, with which the mind that brings it before us has in a certain sense identified itself. What I found here was no longer the inherently greater and purer mind of a highly gifted poet; instead, the writer's way of thinking seemed to have been formed by frequent association with the world of men. He seemed to be on the same level as all the witty, upper-class men of the world, the only difference being his great talent for literary representation, so that in effect he could be regarded as their mouthpiece.

And so my reading of *Beppo* led me to conclude that Lord Byron was indeed too 'empirical' – not because he showed us too much of real life, but because his higher poetic nature seemed to be silenced, or even supplanted altogether by an empirical way of thinking.

Wednesday 29 November 1826

By now I had read Lord Byron's *Deformed Transformed* myself, and I discussed it with Goethe after dinner.

'You see what I mean?' he said. 'The opening scenes are great – and great in the poetic sense. The rest, where it opens out and moves on to the siege of Rome, is not what I would call poetic, but you must admit that it is clever stuff.'

'Absolutely,' I said, 'but it is not difficult to be clever if you don't respect anything.'

Goethe laughed. 'You're not entirely wrong there,' he said, 'and it's true that the poet says more than one would like. He speaks the truth, but it makes us feel uncomfortable; and we would prefer him to keep his mouth shut. There are things in the world that the poet does better to cover up than to reveal; but that's just the way Byron is, and if you wanted him any different, he wouldn't be Byron any more.'

'Yes,' I said, 'he is very clever indeed, no question. This passage, for example, is superb:

> The Devil speaks truth much oftener than he's deemed,
> He hath an ignorant audience.'

1826 151

'That's certainly as good and as free as anything my Mephistopheles said. And while we are on the subject of Mephistopheles,' Goethe went on, 'let me show you something that Coudray has brought back from Paris. What do you think of that?'

He produced a lithograph showing the scene where Faust and Mephistopheles, on their way to free Gretchen from the dungeon, are galloping past a gallows at night on two horses.[84] Faust is riding a black horse that is straining forward at full gallop, seemingly afraid, like its rider, of the spectres beneath the gallows. They are riding so fast that Faust can barely hold on; the strong rush of air has blown his cap off his head, and it is trailing far behind him, held only by the straps around his neck. His fearful, enquiring face is turned towards Mephistopheles, listening to his words. Mephistopheles is sitting calm and unconcerned, like some superior being. He is not riding a living horse, for he dislikes anything living. Nor does he need to; he can move as fast as he wishes by willpower alone. He only has a horse because he needs to look as if he is riding; he is quite content with some half-starved bag of bones, picked up from the nearest knacker's yard. The horse is pale in colour and appears to glow in the dark. It is neither bridled nor saddled, having no need of such things. The unearthly rider sits with an easy insouciance, turned towards Faust as he speaks; the rush of air does not exist for him, he and his horse feel nothing, and not a hair stirs on either of them.

We both admired the brilliance of the composition. 'I must confess,' said Goethe, 'that I myself did not imagine the scene so perfectly. Here is another one – what do you make of that?'

This one showed the rowdy drinking scene in Auerbach's Cellar, the whole episode captured here at the critical moment when the spilled wine bursts into flames, and the coarse brutality of the drinkers finds expression in various ways. The whole scene is alive with passion and movement, and only Mephistopheles maintains his usual calm composure. He pays no heed to all the furious cursing and shouting and the drawn dagger of the man standing next to him. He is perched on the corner of a table, dangling his legs; his raised finger is enough to subdue the flames and the passions.

The more we looked at this wonderful picture, the more we could see the artist's great mind at work; no two figures were alike, and each one represented a different stage of the action.

'M. Delacroix,' said Goethe, 'is a highly talented artist, who found in *Faust* the right material to feed his talent. The French criticize him for his wild streak, but here it serves him very well. I hope he will do the whole of *Faust*, and I look forward especially to his witches' kitchen and the scenes on the Brocken. You can tell that he has lived life to the full – something for which a city like Paris has given him every opportunity.'

I pointed out that such images do a great deal to help us understand the poem better. 'No question about it,' said Goethe. 'The more sophisticated imagination of such an artist compels us to picture the various situations as vividly as he has. And if *I* have to confess that M. Delacroix has done a better job than me of visualizing scenes that I myself wrote, how much more will readers find it all brought to life in a way that surpasses their imagination.'

Monday 11 December 1826

I found Goethe in a very cheery and animated mood. 'Alexander von Humboldt was here for a few hours this morning,' he said excitedly. 'What an amazing man! I've known him for so long, and yet I still find him full of surprises. I don't think anyone can equal him for knowledge and practical wisdom. And he is interested in so many different things – again, unlike anyone else I've met. Whatever subject you care to mention, he knows his way around it and showers you with intellectual gems. He's like a fountain with many different spouts; you only need to hold a jar underneath and out it flows, refreshing and inexhaustible. He's staying for a few days, and I have the feeling it will be as if I have lived several years of my life.'

Wednesday 13 December 1826

Over dinner, the ladies were full of praise for a portrait by a young painter. 'And the most admirable thing about him,' they added, 'is that he is entirely self-taught.' This was particularly obvious from the hands, which were not drawn correctly in the way that artists are taught.

'You can see,' said Goethe, 'that the young man has talent. But the fact that he is self-taught is cause for rebuke rather than praise. A man of talent is not born to be left to his own devices, but to apply himself to art and learn from good masters who can make something of him. I recently read a letter of Mozart's, in reply to some baron who had sent him his compositions, and it goes something like this: "The trouble with you dilettanti is that one of two things normally happens: either you have no ideas of your own and you steal other people's; or, if you do have ideas of your own, you don't know what to do with them." Isn't that wonderful? And doesn't Mozart's great dictum about music apply to all the other arts as well?'[85]

Goethe went on: 'Leonardo da Vinci says: "If your son doesn't think to give depth and body to what he draws by the use of bold shading, so that we want to reach out and touch it, he has no talent." And then Leonardo says: "When your son has fully mastered perspective and anatomy, send him to a good master."[86]

'And now,' said Goethe, 'our young artists barely understand either one when they leave their masters. That's how much times have changed.

'Our young painters,' Goethe went on, 'are lacking in soul and spirit. They fabricate images that say nothing and do nothing for us; they paint swords that don't cut and arrows that don't hit the mark; and I often get the feeling that there is no spirit left in the world.'

'And yet,' I replied, 'one would have thought that the great military events of recent years would have stirred the spirit.'

'They have stirred the will,' said Goethe, 'rather than the spirit, and roused the political spirit rather than the artistic one; and all naïveté and sensuality have been completely lost. But without these two great qualities, how can a painter produce anything that gives pleasure?'

I said that I had just been reading in his *Italienische Reise* about a painting by Correggio which shows the weaning of the baby Jesus; the child is sitting on Mary's lap, uncertain which to choose between his mother's breast and a proffered pear.

'Yes,' said Goethe, 'that's a wonderful little picture! There you have spirit, naïveté and sensuality all combined. And the sacred subject matter is invested with universal human significance, and symbolizes a stage in life that we all have to go through. An image like that is eternal, because it reaches back to the earliest times of humanity, and forward to its most distant future. But if you were to paint Christ when He suffers the little children to come unto Him, it would be a picture that had nothing at all to say, or at least nothing of significance.

'I have been observing German painting,' Goethe went on, 'for more than fifty years, and not only observing, but also trying to exert some influence over it myself. And I can only say, with the way things are now, that we shouldn't expect much. A man of great talent needs to come along, who will quickly acquire all that is best in our contemporary artists and thus surpass them all. The means are there, the way has been marked out and made straight. We now have the works of Phidias to look at, after all, which was unthinkable in our youth.[87] All that's missing, as I say, is a man of great talent, and I hope such a one will come along; he may be lying in his cradle right now, and you may live to see his glory.'

Wednesday 20 December 1826

After dinner, I told Goethe that I had made a discovery that gave me great delight. Observing a burning wax candle, I had noticed that the transparent lower portion of the flame exhibits the same phenomenon as the one whereby the sky appears blue, in that we are looking at the darkness through a cloudy medium suffused with light.

I asked Goethe whether he had come across this phenomenon with the candle and discussed it in his *Farbenlehre*. 'Most certainly,' he said. He took down a copy of the *Farbenlehre* and read me the paragraphs where he describes everything I had seen. 'I'm very pleased,' he said, 'that you have observed this phenomenon yourself without having read about it first in my

1826 155

Farbenlehre; because now you have understood it and made it your own. And that has given you a vantage point from which you will be able to move on to the other phenomena. I can show you another one right now.'

It was around four o'clock; the sky was overcast, and the light was beginning to fail. Goethe lit a candle and took it over to a table by the window. He placed the candle on a sheet of white paper and stood a small stick on the paper, so that the light from the candle caused the stick to cast a shadow towards the daylight. 'Now,' said Goethe, 'what can you tell me about this shadow?' 'The shadow is blue,' I replied. 'So there's your blue again,' said Goethe. 'But here, on the other side of the stick, towards the candle: what do you see there?' 'Another shadow.' 'But what colour?' 'That shadow is a reddish yellow,' I replied, 'but how does this double phenomenon come about?' 'That's for you to find out,' said Goethe. 'See if you can work it out. There is an explanation, but it is difficult. Don't look it up in my *Farbenlehre* until you have given up hope of working it out for yourself.' I consented with alacrity.

'The phenomenon with the lower part of the candle,' Goethe went on, 'whereby a transparent flame produces a blue colour when placed against a dark background – I'm now going to show it to you on a larger scale.' He took a spoon, poured some alcohol into it and set it alight. This produced a transparent flame again, which made the darkness appear blue. If I held the burning alcohol against the darkness of the night sky, the blue increased in intensity; if I held it against the light, the blue became fainter or disappeared altogether.

I was fascinated by this phenomenon. 'Yes,' said Goethe, 'that's the great thing about the natural world: it's so simple, and its greatest manifestations are always repeated on a smaller scale. The same law that makes the sky appear blue is also at work in the lower part of a burning candle, in the burning alcohol, and in the illuminated smoke that rises from a village seen against a backdrop of dark mountains.'

'But how do Newton's disciples explain this very simple phenomenon?' I asked.

'You don't need to know,' replied Goethe. 'It's too stupid for words, and you wouldn't believe the harm it does to a good brain to dwell on something stupid. Don't worry about the Newtonians; just be content with the pure doctrine, and you won't go far wrong.'

'Thinking about something completely wrong-headed,' I said, 'is perhaps as unpleasant and damaging in this case as if one were to study a bad tragedy in order to illuminate all its aspects and expose all its weaknesses.'

'It's exactly the same,' said Goethe, 'and one should not meddle with such things unless one has to. I respect mathematics as the most sublime and useful science, as long as it is applied where it belongs. But I don't approve of its misuse in matters that lie entirely outside its sphere, which simply make a mockery of the noble science. As if things could only exist if they can be mathematically proven! It would be absurd for a man not to believe in his girlfriend's love just because she can't prove it to him mathematically. She can prove her dowry to him with mathematics – but not her love. It wasn't the mathematicians, after all, who discovered the metamorphosis of plants. I did that all by myself, without the aid of mathematics, and the mathematicians had to accept it. All you need in order to understand the phenomena of the colour theory is a good eye and a sound mind – although both are less common than you might think.'

'So where do the present-day French and English stand on the colour theory?' I asked.

'Both nations,' replied Goethe, 'have their advantages and their disadvantages. The good thing about the English is their practical approach to everything; but they are pedants. The French have a good head on their shoulders, but with them everything has to be positive – and if it isn't, they make it so. But they are on the right track when it comes to colour theory, and one of their best thinkers is getting close.[88] He says that colour is an inherent property of things; just as there is an acidifying principle in nature, so there is a colouring principle too. This doesn't explain the phenomena, of course; but at least he is looking at the subject in the context of the natural world, and freeing it from the confines of mathematics.'

The Berlin newspapers were brought in, and Goethe sat down

to read them. He handed one to me, and in the theatre news section I discovered that they put on plays at the Berlin Opera House and Theatre Royal that were just as bad as the ones here.

'How could it be otherwise?' said Goethe. 'There's no doubt that one could, with the aid of good English, French and Spanish plays, put together a decent enough repertoire to stage a good play every night. But where is the appetite in our nation to see good plays all the time? Times were very different when Aeschylus, Sophocles and Euripides were writing; the life of the mind was valued then, and people wanted only the greatest and the best. But in our paltry age, where is the appetite for the best? And where are the organs to appreciate it anyway?

'The other thing,' Goethe went on, 'is this obsession with novelty! In Berlin, Paris, wherever – audiences are all the same. In Paris they write and perform countless new plays every week, and you have to sit through five or six dreadful ones before you find a good one to make up for them.

'The only way to keep a German theatre afloat these days is to book star performers for special appearances. If I was still running the theatre, I would pack the winter schedule with guest appearances by the best actors. Not only would all the good plays get performed on a regular basis, but people would focus more on the acting than on the plays themselves; it would be an opportunity to compare and contrast, audiences would gain a greater insight, and our own actors would be kept on their toes and spurred on to emulate the performances of distinguished visiting stars. As I said: keep up a steady stream of star bookings, and you'll be amazed at how much the theatre and audiences will benefit.

'I foresee the time when a clever man who is up to the job will take on *four* theatres at once, moving his star performers around from one to the other. And I think he will do a better job of managing all *four* than if he had only the one.'

Wednesday 27 December 1826

Back at home, I had been thinking long and hard about the phenomenon of the blue and yellow shadows, and although it remained a mystery to me for a long time, the answer finally dawned on me after lengthy contemplation, and I gradually became convinced that I had understood the phenomenon.

Today at dinner I told Goethe that I had solved the riddle. 'That would be quite something,' said Goethe. 'You can show me after dinner.' 'I would rather write it down,' I said, 'because I'm not sure I can find the right words to explain it here.' 'You can write it down later, if you like,' said Goethe, 'but today you shall show me what you have found and talk me through it, so that I can see whether or not you are on the right track.'

After dinner, when it was still bright daylight, Goethe asked: 'Can you do the experiment now?' 'No,' I said. 'Why not?' asked Goethe. 'It's still too light,' I replied. 'We need to wait until the light is starting to fade, so that the candlelight casts an obvious shadow; but it needs to be light enough still for the daylight to fall on the shadow.' 'Hm,' said Goethe, 'I take your point.'

At last dusk began to fall, and I said to Goethe that the time had come. He lit a wax candle and gave me a sheet of white paper and a small stick. 'Now, do your experiment and explain it to me!' he said.

I placed the candle on the table near the window and laid the sheet of paper near the candle; when I then placed the stick in the middle of the paper, between the daylight and the candlelight, the phenomenon could be seen in all its beauty. The shadow cast towards the candle was definitely yellow, while the one cast towards the window was a perfect shade of blue.

'Well now,' said Goethe, 'the blue shadow first: how is that produced?' 'Before I explain,' I said, 'let me state the fundamental law which I believe accounts for both phenomena.

'Light and darkness,' I said, 'are not colours, but two extremes between which the colours lie, the colours themselves being produced by modifications of the two. The two colours produced closest to the extremes of light and darkness are yellow and blue. The yellow nearest to light is produced when I view the light through a dimmed transparency, and the blue nearest to darkness is produced when I view the darkness through an illuminated transparency.

'Moving on now,' I continued, 'to our phenomenon, we can see that the stick casts an obvious shadow, due to the strength of the candlelight. This shadow would appear as black darkness if I were to close the shutters and shut out the daylight. But as it is, the daylight enters freely by the window, and so acts as an illuminated medium through which I view the darkness of the shadow – which then appears blue, in accordance with the law.' Goethe laughed. 'So that's the blue,' he said, 'but how do you explain the yellow shadow?'

'By the law of the dimmed light,' I replied. 'The burning candle sheds a light on to the white paper that already has a slight yellowish tinge. But the daylight from the window is strong enough for the stick to cast a faint shadow back towards the candle, which dims the light within its compass and thus, in accordance with the law, produces the yellow colour. If I lessen the dimness by bringing the shadow as close as possible to the candle, we get a pure, bright yellow; if I increase the dimness by moving the shadow as far away as possible from the candle, the yellow takes on a deeper, reddish tinge, or even turns red.'

Goethe laughed again, and assumed an air of mystery. 'Well,' I said, 'am I right?' 'You have observed the phenomenon very well, and described it very neatly,' replied Goethe, 'but you haven't explained it. Your explanation is clever – ingenious even – but it is not the right one.'

'Then help me out here,' I said, 'and solve the riddle for me, because I am dying to hear it.' 'And so you shall,' said Goethe, 'but not today, and not in this way. I will show you another phenomenon shortly, which will make the law plain to see. You are very close, and have pursued this line as far as you can. But once you have grasped the new law you will be in a different place altogether and will have made great strides. Come an hour before dinner one day, when the sky is clear, and I'll show you a more obvious phenomenon, where you'll have no difficulty understanding the law – the same law that explains this one.

'I am delighted,' he continued, 'that you take such an interest in colour. It is something that will give you endless pleasure.'

When I left Goethe that evening, I could not stop thinking about the phenomenon, and even found myself dreaming about

160 CONVERSATIONS WITH GOETHE

it. But none of this made things any clearer, and I was no closer to solving the mystery.

Some time ago Goethe said: 'I am carrying on, slowly, with my papers on natural science. Not because I think I can materially contribute to the advancement of science, but because it keeps me in touch with many congenial colleagues. The study of nature is the most innocent of pursuits. I am not interested in having any contact or correspondence relating to aesthetic matters. Now they want to know which town on the Rhine I had in mind when I wrote *Hermann und Dorothea*! As if it mattered – they'd do better just to pick any one at random! People want truth, they want reality – and that ruins the poetry.'

1827

Wednesday 3 January 1827

At dinner today we talked about Canning's brilliant speech in support of Portugal.[89]

'Some people,' said Goethe, 'have called this speech coarse, but these people don't know what they want. They have a morbid desire to carp at anything great. It is not a reasoned opposition, just a desire to find fault at any price. They have to have something great that they can hate. When Napoleon was alive they hated him, and he was a good lightning rod for all their prejudices. When he was no longer around, they turned their guns on the Holy Alliance; yet nothing greater or more beneficial for mankind has ever been devised. Now it is Canning's turn. His speech in support of Portugal is the product of a great consciousness. He is well aware of the power he wields, and of the eminence of his position, and he is right to speak as he feels. But these sans-culottes cannot comprehend that, and what seems great to the rest of us seems coarse to them. Greatness makes them uncomfortable, they don't have it in them to respect it, and they cannot abide it.'

Thursday evening, 4 January 1827

Goethe was full of praise for the poems of Victor Hugo. 'He is a very talented writer,' he said, 'who was influenced by German literature. Unfortunately his poetic youth was blighted by the pedantry of the classical school; but now he has *Le Globe* on his side, so he is sitting pretty. I would compare him to Manzoni. He writes very objectively, and seems to me just as important as Messieurs de Lamartine and Delavigne. On closer examination, I can see where he and other young talents like him come from. They all come from Chateaubriand, who is a very notable rhetorical-poetic talent. If you want to see how Victor Hugo writes, just read this poem about Napoleon, "Les deux îles".'

Goethe placed the book in front of me and went over to the stove. I read the poem. 'Hasn't he got some fine images,' said Goethe, 'and hasn't he handled his subject matter with great freedom?' He came over to me again. 'Just look at this passage, it is so beautifully done!' He read the passage about the storm cloud, from which the lightning bolt strikes up at the hero from below. 'That is beautiful! The picture he paints is true, as you will find in the mountains, where you often have the storm beneath you and the lightning strikes upwards from below.'

'What I like about the French,' I said, 'is that their poetry is always firmly grounded in reality. You can translate their poems into prose, and the essence remains intact.'

'That's because,' said Goethe, 'the French poets are men of knowledge. Our own German fools, on the other hand, think they would lose their talent if they bothered with knowledge, even though all talent must be nourished by knowledge, and only then can it make proper use of its powers. But let's leave them to it – they are beyond help anyway, and true talent will always find a way. The many young poets who are currently plying their trade have no real talent; they are just incompetents, deluded into thinking they should write something just because German literature is riding so high at present.

'It's not surprising,' Goethe went on, 'that the French have moved on from pedantry to a freer style in their poetry. Diderot and other kindred spirits were pioneers in this regard, even before the revolution. Then the revolution itself, and the reign of Napoleon, helped to advance the cause. For even if the years of war were not conducive to an interest in poetry as such, and were for the moment unfavourable to the muses, they were formative years for a large number of freethinkers, who are now collecting their thoughts in time of peace and emerging as significant talents.'

1827   163

I asked Goethe if the classical school had been opposed to the splendid Béranger. 'The genre in which Béranger writes,' said Goethe, 'is an older, traditional one, and people were used to it. But he too was in many respects freer than his predecessors, and has been duly attacked for it by the pedantic party.'

The conversation turned to painting and to the harm done by the antiquarian school. 'You claim not to be a connoisseur,' said Goethe, 'and yet I will show you a painting, done by one of our best living German artists, in which you will immediately notice glaring violations of the first laws of art. You will see that the details are done well enough, but that the picture as a whole doesn't quite work – and you won't know what to make of it. And this is not because the artist in question is lacking in talent, but because his mind, which should be directing his talent, is just as benighted as the brains of all the other antiquarian painters; so he ignores the masters who perfected their art and goes back instead to their imperfect predecessors, modelling himself on them.

'Raphael and his contemporaries made the breakthrough from a narrow mannerism to nature and freedom. But today's artists, instead of thanking God and using these advantages and continuing to follow the progressive path, are turning back again to a narrow-minded past. It's too bad, and you really wonder what is going on in their benighted brains. And because art itself does not support them in their chosen path, they use religion and faction as a crutch; without them, they would be too weak to carry on.'

Goethe went on: 'There is a line of provenance running through the whole of art. When you see a great master, you will always find that he used what was good in his predecessors, and that it was this that made him great. Men like Raphael don't just spring from nowhere. They were grounded in antiquity, and in the best that had been done before them. Had they not used the advantages of their time, there would be little to say about them.'

Our talk then turned to old German poetry, and I mentioned Fleming. 'Fleming,' said Goethe, 'is a decent enough talent, a little prosaic and conventional; he can't do much for us now.

It's strange,' he went on. 'I've written quite a lot, and yet not one of my poems would be considered suitable for the Lutheran hymn book.' I laughed, and agreed with him, while thinking to myself that there was more to this curious remark than meets the eye.

Sunday evening, 12 January 1827

I found that Goethe was having a musical evening, courtesy of the Eberwein family and a few members of the orchestra. The small audience included General Superintendent Röhr, Councillor Vogel and a few ladies. Goethe had expressed a wish to hear a quartet by a famous young composer, and this was the first item on the programme.[90] The twelve-year-old Karl Eberwein played the piano to Goethe's great satisfaction – and he did play very well – so that the quartet was well performed all round.

'It is curious to see,' said Goethe, 'where all these sophisticated technical and mechanical advances are taking our new composers. Their works are not music any more; they go beyond the level of human emotions, and it's impossible to relate to such things from one's own heart and mind. What about you? I hear it in my ears, but that's as far as it goes.' I said that I fared no better in this instance. 'Still, the allegro was quite impressive,' Goethe went on. 'All that whirling and spinning put me in mind of the witches' dances on the Blocksberg – so in the end I did find an image that I could associate with this strange music.'

After a break, during which people chatted and took some light refreshments, Goethe asked Madame Eberwein if she would give us a brief song recital. She began by singing the lovely song 'Um Mitternacht', set to music by Zelter, which made a profound impression on us all. 'It's always a lovely song,' said Goethe, 'no matter how often you hear it. There's something eternal and enduring about the melody.' This was followed by a number of songs from *Die Fischerin*, set to music by Max Eberwein. 'Der Erlkönig' was loudly applauded; then the aria 'Ich hab's gesagt der guten Mutter' prompted the general observation that the words and music went together so well that it was hard to imagine the piece any other way. Goethe himself was delighted with it.

To conclude a pleasant evening's entertainment, Madame Eberwein, at Goethe's request, sang some songs from his *Divan*, in the well-known settings composed by her husband. The passage 'Jussufs Reize möcht ich borgen' pleased Goethe especially. 'Eberwein,' he said to me, 'surpasses himself on occasion.' He then requested the song 'Ach, um deine feuchten Schwingen', which likewise was calculated to excite the deepest emotions.[91]

When the guests had gone, I was left alone with Goethe for a few moments. 'I noticed this evening,' he said, 'that these songs from the *Divan* feel quite disconnected from me. The Oriental and passionate aspects of them feel like something from another lifetime; I've left them behind, like a cast-off snakeskin lying beside the path. But I still feel very connected to the song "Um Mitternacht"; it is still a living part of me, and continues to resonate with me.

'And I often find, with my things, that I no longer recognize them immediately as my own. I recently read something in French, and as I was reading it I thought to myself: "This man makes a lot of sense. It's just what you would have said yourself." And when I looked more closely I found it was a passage from my own writings that had been translated into French.'

Monday evening, 15 January 1827

Last summer, after finishing his *Helena*,[92] Goethe had turned his attention to the continuation of the *Wanderjahre*.[93] He often told me how the work was progressing. 'In order to make better use of the available material,' he said to me one day, 'I have taken the first part to pieces, and I plan to make it into two parts by combining the old with the new. I am having the printed text copied out complete; the places where I need to add new material have been marked up, and when the copyist comes to one of these marks, I shall then dictate the additional material. This will force me to keep the work going and not let things slide.'

Another time he said to me: 'The printed text of the *Wander-jahre* has all been copied out now. The places where I want to add new material have been marked with slips of blue paper, so that I can see exactly what I still have to do. At my present rate of progress the blue slips are disappearing fast – which is very pleasing to see.'

Several weeks ago, I heard from his secretary that he is now working on a new novella.[94] I therefore refrained from calling on him in the evenings, and contented myself with seeing him once a week at dinner.

This novella had now been finished for some time, and this evening he showed me the first few pages. I was very excited, and read as far as the key passage where they are all standing around the dead tiger, and the warden arrives with the message that the lion is sunning itself up by the castle ruin.

As I was reading, I couldn't help admiring the extraordinary clarity with which everything was invoked, down to the smallest detail of the setting. The departure of the hunting party, the descriptions of the castle ruin, the fair, the track leading to the castle – all of it was so sharply delineated that you found yourself seeing it exactly as the poet had intended. At the same time it was all written with such assurance, deliberation and mastery that you could not tell what was to come and could not see beyond the line that you were reading.

'Your Excellency,' I said, 'must have worked to a very specific plan.'

'Yes, I did,' replied Goethe. 'I planned to write about the subject thirty years ago, and it's been on my mind ever since. But in the end it didn't turn out quite as I expected. At the time, just after I had finished *Hermann und Dorothea*, I planned to write it in epic form and in hexameters, and had prepared a detailed outline to that end. Then, when I decided recently to go back to my notes and finally write the thing, I couldn't find that old outline, so I was forced to draw up a new one – one that reflected the different form that I now envisaged. Now that I've finished writing it, the original outline has turned up again, and I am now very pleased that it didn't come to hand any earlier, because it would only have confused me. The plot and the development of the action were unchanged, but the detailed execution was completely different; everything had been conceived for epic treatment, in hexameters, so it would have been no use at all for this prose version.'

We then turned to the content of the work. 'I love the scene,' I said, 'where Honorio is facing the princess over the outstretched body of the dead tiger, the weeping and wailing woman has turned up with the boy, and the prince, with his hunting party, is just hurrying to join the strange group. It would make a marvellous picture, and I'd love to see it painted.'

'Yes,' said Goethe, 'it would certainly make a fine picture. Although,' he went on after some reflection, 'there is almost too much to show, and too many figures, so that the artist would have a lot of problems with the composition and the distribution of light and shade. But the earlier moment, when Honorio is kneeling on the tiger and the princess is facing him on horseback, would make a good picture, I thought, and it could be done.' I felt that Goethe was right, and added that this particular moment was of course the crux of the whole situation, on which everything else turned.

The other comment I had to make was that this novella is very different in character from all the others in the *Wanderjahre*, in that the world it portrays is the outward world of physical reality. 'You're right,' said Goethe. 'You'll find hardly any reference to thoughts and feelings in what you've read, whereas there's almost too much of that in my other things.'

'I'm curious to know,' I said, 'how the lion is going to be subdued; I get the feeling this is going to happen in a very different way, but I've no idea how.' 'I wouldn't want you to guess it,' said Goethe, 'and I'm not going to tell you today. I'll show you the ending on Thursday evening; till then the lion can lie in the sun.'

I brought the conversation round to the second part of *Faust*, and in particular the 'Classical Walpurgis Night', which as yet existed only in sketch form.[95] Goethe had told me some time ago that he intended to publish it in this form. I had been meaning to advise Goethe not to do so, because I feared that once the sketch was in print he would never get round to finishing the thing properly. Goethe must have thought about this himself in the meantime, because he now set my mind at rest by saying that he had decided not to publish the sketch after all. 'I'm very pleased to hear it,' I said, 'because now I have reason to hope that you will finish it.'

'I could get it done in three months,' he said, 'but where am I going to find the time? Everyday life makes too many demands on me, and it's difficult to cut myself off and be alone. This morning the hereditary Grand Duke was here, and the Grand Duchess is coming tomorrow at noon.[96] I'm very honoured by such visits, of course, and they enrich my life; but they do occupy all my attention, as I have to stop and think of something new that I can show to these important personages, and how I can suitably entertain them.'

'And yet,' I said, 'you completed *Helena* last winter, and you had just as many distractions then as you do now.' 'That's true,' said Goethe. 'I'll manage it somehow – I'll have to manage. But it's hard.' 'It's a good thing you have such a detailed outline,' I said. 'The outline is there,' said Goethe, 'but I've still got the most difficult part to do; and when you are writing something up, everything depends so much on luck. The "Classical Walpurgis Night" has to be written in rhyme, yet the whole thing has to have an antique flavour. Finding the right verse form is not easy. And then there's the dialogue!' 'Isn't that already in the outline?' I asked. 'The "what", yes,' replied Goethe, 'but not the "how". And you have to remember how much is said in the course of that one madcap night! Faust's speech to Proserpine, to persuade her to give up Helen – what a speech that has to be, given that Proserpine herself is moved to tears by it![97] None of this is easy, and it depends very much on luck – almost entirely on the mood of the moment, in fact, and how strong I am feeling.'

Wednesday 17 January 1827

In recent weeks, when Goethe was not feeling all that well on occasion, we had dined in his study, which looks out on the garden. Today the table was laid in the so-called Urbino Room again, which I took to be a good sign.[98] When I entered, I found Goethe and his son; both welcomed me warmly with their usual spontaneous affection. Goethe himself seemed in the best of spirits, as his very animated face indicated. Through the open door I could see into the adjacent Ceiling Room, as they call it, where Chancellor von Müller was bending over a large engraving. He soon joined us, and I was happy to greet him as a congenial table companion. We were expecting Frau von Goethe, but sat down at the table while we waited. The engraving was spoken of in admiring terms, and Goethe told me it was by the famous Gérard in Paris, who had recently sent it to him as a present. 'Go and have a quick look now,' he added, 'before the soup arrives.'

I was curious anyway, and did as he asked; I was delighted by the sight of this admirable work, and no less so by the artist's inscription, dedicating it to Goethe as a mark of his respect. I could not look at it for long, however, as Frau von Goethe now came in, and I hurried back to my seat. 'Isn't that something special?' said Goethe. 'You can study it for days and weeks before you discover all the ideas in there, and all the perfect little touches,' he said. 'But that's something for another day.'

We were a merry party at table. The Chancellor shared with us a letter he had received from an eminent man in Paris, who had held a difficult post here as ambassador at the time of the French occupation and had remained in friendly contact with Weimar ever since. He mentioned the Grand Duke and Goethe in his letter, and said that Weimar was fortunate indeed that genius could enjoy such an intimate relationship with royalty here.

Frau von Goethe brought her own special charm to the conversation. There was talk of certain purchases, which she teased young Goethe about, and which the latter would not agree to. 'We must not overindulge the fair ladies,' said Goethe, 'because things very quickly get out of hand. Even when he was on Elba, Napoleon received bills from milliners that he was expected to pay. But in such matters he would as soon do too little as too much. On an earlier occasion in the Tuileries, a fashion merchant was showing his wife a selection of expensive things in his presence. When Napoleon made no move to buy anything, the man gave him to understand that he was rather neglecting his wife in this regard. Napoleon said nothing, but gave the man such a look that he immediately packed up his things and never showed his face again.' 'Was that when he was Consul?' asked Frau von Goethe. 'He was probably Emperor by then,' replied Goethe, 'otherwise that look of his would not have been so fearsome. But I can't help laughing at the man, and the fright he got when he saw that look; he probably expected to be guillotined or shot out of hand.'

The mood around the table was very merry, and we talked more of Napoleon. Young Goethe said: 'I should like to have good paintings or engravings recording all his great deeds, and I would hang them all in one large room.' 'It would have to be a very large room,' said Goethe, 'and it would still not be big enough to hold all the pictures, so great are his deeds.'

The Chancellor mentioned Luden's *History of the Germans*, and I had to admire the skilful and forceful way young Goethe defended the book against the attacks of critics in the press, arguing that the faults they found were all attributable to the time when the book was written, and to the national sentiments and sympathies with which the author identified. It was noted that the wars of Napoleon showed us Caesar's campaigns in a whole new light. 'Before that,' said Goethe, 'Caesar's account was not much more than a textbook for learning Latin in school.'

The conversation moved on from medieval German times to the Gothic period. There was mention of a bookcase that was designed in the Gothic style; this in turn brought us on to the latest craze for having entire rooms decorated in the medieval German and Gothic manner and living surrounded by the trappings of a bygone age.

'That might work,' said Goethe, 'in a house with so many rooms that you can leave some of them standing empty, and only go into them three or four times a year. You could have a Gothic room, I suppose, in the same way that Madame Panckoucke in Paris has a Chinese room – which I think is quite nice. But I don't approve of fitting out one's normal living room with alien and old-fashioned objects of that sort. It's always a kind of charade, which can't be good for us in the long run, and can only have a bad effect on the person who goes in for such things. There's a contradiction between that sort of thing and the life we actually live now; it is the product of an empty and hollow mentality, and will only encourage people to think like that. It's all well and good for someone to go to a masquerade on a winter's evening dressed as a Turk for a bit of fun, but what if he went around dressed like that all the time? We would think he was crazy – or well on the way to becoming so.'

We found Goethe's observations on such a matter of every-day interest eminently sensible, and as nobody in the room had reason to think that Goethe's disapproval was aimed at him personally, we felt the truth of what he said and were much amused.

The conversation turned to the theatre, and Goethe teased me about having given up the theatre for him last Monday evening. 'He's been here three years,' he said, turning to the others, 'and this was the first evening that he gave the theatre a miss on my account. I'm very impressed. I had invited him, and he had promised to come; but I still doubted whether he would keep his word, especially when it got to half past six and he still wasn't here. I would actually have been pleased if he hadn't come, because then I could have said: "Here is a man who is so crazy that he loves the theatre more than his dearest friends, and will not allow anything to divert him from his obsession." But I made it up to you, didn't I? Did I not show you something good?' Goethe was referring here to his new novella.

We then talked about Schiller's *Fiesko*, which had been per-formed the previous Saturday.[99] 'It was the first time I'd seen the play,' I said, 'and I've been wondering ever since if the very rough scenes could not be toned down a little. But I think there's not much you could do without damaging the character of the whole.'

'You're absolutely right,' replied Goethe, 'it wouldn't work. Schiller and I often talked about this, because he himself couldn't stand his early plays, and would never allow them to be performed while we were running the theatre. We were short of plays, and it would have been good to have those three tempestuous early pieces in the repertoire. But it just didn't work; everything was so tightly interwoven that Schiller himself gave up in despair, and was forced to abandon the idea and leave the plays as they were.'

'That's such a pity,' I said, 'because for all their rough edges I still find them infinitely preferable to the feeble, limp, contrived and unnatural offerings of some of our current tragic poets. With Schiller, you always hear the voice of a great mind and a powerful personality.'

'You're right there,' said Goethe. 'Try as he might, Schiller was incapable of producing anything that was not far greater than the best efforts of these newcomers. Even when he was cutting his nails, Schiller stood head and shoulders above these gentlemen.'

We laughed, and savoured this striking image.

'But I have known people who could never accept Schiller's early plays. One summer I was in a spa town, walking through a very narrow alleyway leading to a mill. There I met Prince *** [Putyatin], and as a train of mules laden with sacks of flour was just then coming the other way, we had to duck into a small house to avoid them. Inside, in a tiny parlour, we immediately got into a deep conversation about matters divine and human, as was the way with the Prince. One of the things we talked about was Schiller's *Räuber*, and the Prince said to me: "If I had been God, on the point of creating the world, and I had foreseen in that moment that Schiller's *Räuber* would be written in it, I would not have created the world."' We had to laugh. 'What do you say to *that*?' said Goethe. 'As dislikes go, that one went a bit far; where did *that* come from, I wonder.'

'And yet there is no trace of that dislike in our young people,' I observed, 'especially our students. When the finest and most mature works by Schiller and others are performed, you see few, if any, young persons or students in the audience; but if Schiller's *Räuber* or *Fiesko* are on the programme, you get a full house made up almost entirely of students.'

'It was the same fifty years ago as it is now,' said Goethe, 'and it will probably be just the same fifty years from now. Something that's been written by a young person will be best enjoyed by young persons. And don't think for a moment that the world has made such progress in culture and good taste that even the young have moved beyond such coarser times. Even if the world in general is progressing, young people will always have to start from the beginning again and make their individual journeys through the different epochs in world culture. It doesn't bother me any more; I wrote a verse about it a long time ago, which goes like this:

> Let none from bonfire fun be kept,
> Nor joy be ever stinted!
> Brooms wear out from being swept,
> As boys are born new-minted.[100]

'I need only look out of the window to see, in the brooms sweeping the street and the children running around, the ever-present symbols of a world that is forever wearing out and renewing itself. So children's games and the amusements of youth go on from century to century; as silly as these things might appear when we are older and wiser, children are always children, and they are much the same in every age. That's why we should let them have their bonfires, and not spoil the fun for the little dears.'

The hours at table passed very quickly in entertaining talk of this and other matters. We younger members of the party then went on up to the upstairs rooms, while the Chancellor stayed behind with Goethe.

Thursday evening, 18 January 1827

Goethe had promised to show me the ending of his novella this evening. I called on him at half past six and found him alone in his cosy study. I sat down at the table with him, and after we had talked over the events of the day Goethe stood up and handed me the last few sheets I had come to see. 'Here you are – read the ending,' he said. I began to read while Goethe paced up and down the room, occasionally pausing to stand by the stove. I read quietly to myself, in my usual fashion.

The sheets from the earlier evening had ended with the lion

lying in the sun, at the foot of a century-old beech tree, outside the outer walls of the old ruin, while preparations are being made to subdue him. The prince is all for sending huntsmen out after him, but the stranger begs him to spare his lion, saying he is sure that he can get the beast back into its iron cage by gentler means. 'This child,' he says, 'will coax him in with mellifluous songs and the sweet strains of his flute.' The prince agrees to his request, and after giving instructions for appropriate precautions to be taken, he rides back into town with his entourage. Honorio and a number of huntsmen take up their positions in the defile; if the lion comes down this way, they will light a fire to drive him back. Mother and child, led by the castle warden, climb up the ruined keep, on the far side of which the lion is lying under the outer wall.

The plan is to entice the mighty beast into the spacious castle courtyard. Mother and warden hide themselves in the crumbling knights' hall, while the child walks on alone, through the dark opening in the wall of the courtyard, and out to the lion. An expectant pause ensues; nobody knows what has become of the child, no sound is heard from his flute. The warden blames himself for not going with the boy; the mother is quite composed.

At last the strains of the flute are heard again, coming closer all the time; the child walks back through the opening into the castle courtyard, the lion following tamely on behind with slow and ponderous tread. They do a circuit of the courtyard, then the child sits down in a sunny spot, the lion lies down meekly beside him and places a heavy paw in the child's lap. A thorn has lodged in it; the boy pulls it out, takes his silk kerchief from his neck and uses it to bind up the paw.

Mother and warden, who have witnessed the whole scene from above, looking down from the knights' hall, are delighted. The lion is now secure and tamed, and as the child has calmed the beast by singing sweet, pious songs in between playing on his flute, so he now concludes the novella by singing the following lines:

> The blessed angel, kind of heart,
> Communes with children well-behaved,

1827

To help them choose the better part,
And turn away from acts depraved.
Thus is the beast from forest wild
By godly thoughts and melody
Captivated and beguiled
To lay its head at infant's knee.

I had not been able to read the ending without emotion. And yet I didn't know what to say. I was taken by surprise, but not satisfied. I felt that the ending was too solitary, too ideal, too lyrical, and that some, at least, of the other characters should have reappeared to round the whole thing off and give the ending more breadth.

Goethe could see that I had a doubt in my mind, and he sought to put me straight. 'If I had introduced some of the other characters again at the end,' he said, 'the ending would have been prosaic. And what was there for them to do or say, when everything was already settled? The prince and his entourage have ridden back into town, where his help will be needed; Honorio will follow on with the huntsmen as soon as he hears that the lion has been secured up at the castle; and the man from the town will be there very soon with the iron cage to take the lion back. These are all things that we can foresee, and therefore they don't need to be said or shown. Had I done so, the effect would have been prosaic.

'What was needed was an ideal, not to say lyrical, ending, and so it had to be. Following on from the stirring speech of the man, which is already poetic prose, a further heightening of the language was needed, so I had to go for lyrical poetry, and indeed song, pure and simple.

'If you want an image for the way this novella develops,' Goethe went on, 'then think of it as a green plant sprouting from the root, which for a while puts forth vigorous green side shoots from its sturdy stem and finally terminates in a flower. The flower is unexpected, surprising; but it had to come. In fact, the green foliage only existed to produce that flower, and would have been a waste of time without it.'

When I heard this, I felt a sense of relief; the scales fell from my eyes, and a faint notion of just how good this marvellous composition was began to stir within me.

Goethe continued: 'The purpose of this novella was to show how something wild and untameable can often be more effectively subdued by love and piety than by force; and this beautiful moral, embodied here in the child and the lion, was what drew me to write it. This is the ideal – the flower. And the green foliage of the altogether real exposition is only there for the sake of the flower, and only worth anything because of it. What is the point of the real as such? It gives us pleasure if it is portrayed with accuracy, and it can even give us a clearer knowledge of certain things; but the true gain for our higher nature lies solely in the ideal, which proceeds from the heart of the poet.'

I felt keenly how right Goethe was; the ending of his novella was still going through my mind, having evoked in me a mood of piety more intense than any I had felt for a long time. How pure and heartfelt, I thought to myself, must the feelings of the poet still be at his advanced age, for him to be able to produce something so beautiful! I couldn't help saying as much to Goethe, and expressing my delight that this unique work now existed.

'I am glad that you like it,' said Goethe, 'and I myself am pleased to be finally rid of a subject that I've been carrying around in my head for thirty years. I told Schiller and Humboldt about my plans at the time, and they both advised me not to go ahead, because they couldn't see the potential, and because only the writer knows what he can do with his subject matter. This is why you should never ask anyone else when you want to write something. If Schiller had asked me, *before* he wrote *Wallenstein*, whether he should do it, I would have advised him against it, for sure, because I could never have imagined that such a splendid play could be made out of material like that. Schiller was opposed to the idea of tackling the subject in hexameters, which is what I wanted to do at the time, immediately after *Hermann und Dorothea*; he advised *ottava rima* instead. But as you see, prose turned out to be the right way forward for me. A lot depended on the precise depiction of the locale, which would have been awkward to do in rhyming verse. And besides, the wholly real character of the novella at the beginning, and its wholly ideal character at the end, are best conveyed in prose, which also makes the little songs stand out very nicely – which would not have been the case, of course, if I had used hexameters or *ottava rima*.'

We then talked about the other tales and novellas in the *Wanderjahre*, and noted that each one differs from the others in character and tone. 'I'll tell you why that is,' said Goethe. 'I went about it rather like a painter, who with certain subjects avoids certain colours and allows others to predominate. If he is painting a morning landscape, for example, he will put a lot of blue on his palette, but not much yellow. But if he is painting an evening scene, he will use a lot of yellow and hardly touch the blue at all. I have adopted much the same approach to my various literary projects, and if people see each of them as different in character, that is probably the reason.'

I thought to myself that this was a very sound principle, and was glad that Goethe had shared it with me.

I then said, particularly apropos of this last novella, how much I admired the detailed descriptions, especially of the landscape.

'I have never studied nature for purely poetic purposes,' said Goethe. 'But because my early landscape drawing, and then my later scientific studies, led me to observe the natural world closely at all times, I have gradually got to know nature intimately, down to the very last detail – so much so, that when I need something as a poet I have it ready to hand and am not likely to get it wrong. Schiller wasn't one to observe nature like that. What local colour there is in his *Tell* is based on what I told him; but he had such a brilliant mind that he could take something he heard about at second hand and make it seem real.'

The conversation now focused entirely on Schiller, and Goethe went on: 'Schiller's real talent lay in the ideal, and it is fair to say that he has no equal in German literature, or indeed in any other. He has most of Lord Byron's qualities, except that the latter knew more of the world than he did. I really wish Schiller had lived long enough to read Lord Byron; I wonder what he would have said about such a kindred spirit. Did Byron actually publish anything during Schiller's lifetime?'

I thought probably not, but couldn't say for certain. Goethe took down the encyclopaedia and read out the article on Byron, adding his own asides in passing. It turned out that Lord Byron had not published anything before 1807, so Schiller had not seen anything of his.

'The idea of freedom,' Goethe went on, 'runs through all of Schiller's work, and this idea assumed a different form as Schiller progressed in his cultural development and became a different person himself. In his youth it was physical freedom that exercised him and informed his works; in his later life it was ideal freedom.

'It's an odd thing about freedom: it's easy enough to have a sufficiency, if only we can learn to be content and accept what we have. What is the point of having too much freedom if it is no use to us? Look at this room and the one next to it, where you can see my bed through the open door. Neither of them is big, and a lot of space is taken up anyway with all the things I need – books, manuscripts and *objets d'art*. But they are enough for me. I've lived in them all winter and hardly set foot in the rooms at the front. What is the good of having a large house and the freedom to go from one room to another if I have no need to use them?

'If a man has just enough freedom to live a healthy life and carry on his trade, then he has sufficient – and that much anyone can easily have. Then again, all of us are only free subject to certain conditions that we have to fulfil. The bourgeois is as free as the aristocrat, as long as he stays within the limits that God assigned to him by virtue of the social class he was born into. The aristocrat is as free as the prince; as long as he observes the modicum of ceremonial required at court, he may feel himself the prince's equal. What makes us free is not our refusal to acknowledge anything higher than ourselves, but the very fact that we do respect something higher than ourselves. For by respecting it we lift ourselves up to it, and show by our acknowledgement of it that we too bear something higher within us, and are worthy to be placed on the same level. On my travels I have often met merchants from northern Germany who thought that by plonking themselves down next to me at table they became my equals. That didn't make them so; but had they known how to treat me with proper respect, then they would have been.

'The fact that Schiller was so exercised in his youth by this business of physical freedom was partly due to his particular mentality, but it had a lot more to do with the stress he had suffered at the military academy. In his more mature years, when he had all the physical freedom he needed, he turned his attention to the ideal kind, and I would almost go so far as to say that this idea killed him – because it led him to make demands on his physical constitution that were simply too much for him.

'The Grand Duke awarded Schiller an annual salary of a thousand thalers when he came here, and undertook to double it if he were ever prevented from working by illness. Schiller declined this last offer and never took advantage of it. "I have the talent," he said, "and should be able to manage by myself." But the thing is, when his family got larger in those last few years he had to write two plays a year just to earn a decent living, and in order to do that he forced himself to work during the days and weeks when he was unwell. He expected his talent to be at his beck and call at all times.

'Schiller never drank much – he was very moderate in that regard. But if he was feeling under the weather, he would seek to revive his strength with a little liqueur or some other strong alcohol. But it undermined his health, and it wasn't good for his work, either.

'Personally, I think this explains the faults that some clever people find with his work. All the passages that they claim are not quite right are what I would call pathological passages – by which I mean that he wrote them on days when he lacked the strength to come up with the right motifs. I have every respect for the categorical imperative, and I know how much good can come of it; but one mustn't take these things too far, otherwise this idea of ideal freedom is sure to lead to no good.'

With these interesting remarks and similar conversations about Lord Byron and famous German men of letters, of whom Schiller had said that he liked Kotzebue best because he actually produced something, the evening hours were swiftly whiled away, and Goethe gave me the novella to take home and read again at my leisure.

Sunday evening, 21 January 1827

I called on Goethe at half past seven this evening and stayed an hour or so. He showed me a book of new French poems by Mlle Gay, and praised them highly. 'The French,' he said, 'are really coming to the fore, and they are well worth keeping an eye on. I am making a big effort to get an idea of the present state of French literature, and if I can I am hoping to write something about it. It is fascinating to see how those elements that were accepted here a long time ago are just now starting to come through there. Mediocre talents are always prisoners of their own times, of course, and have to feed on the elements that the times bring with them. But everything – apart from the revivalist piety – is the same with them as it is here, just that it takes a slightly more *galant* and witty form with them.'

'What does Your Excellency make of Béranger and the author of the *Théâtre de Clara Gazul*?'[101]

'They are the exception,' said Goethe. 'They are highly talented writers, who are firmly grounded within themselves and stand apart from the prevailing mentality of their day.' 'I am very pleased to hear you say that,' I said, 'because I felt much the same about these two myself.'

The conversation then turned from French literature to German. 'Let me show you something,' said Goethe, 'that will interest you. Hand me one of the two volumes in front of you, if you would. Solger is a name you know?' 'Certainly,' I said, 'and he's someone I like. I have his translation of Sophocles, and have always rated him very highly, both for that and for the foreword he wrote to it.' 'You know that he died several years ago,' said Goethe, 'and now they have brought out a collection of his unpublished writings and letters. His philosophical inquiries, which he casts in the form of Platonic dialogues, are not altogether successful, but his letters are wonderful. In one of them he writes to Tieck about *Die Wahlverwandtschaften*, and

I'll have to read it to you, because I don't think anything better has ever been said about that novel.'

Goethe read Solger's excellent little essay to me and we discussed it point by point, admiring both his opinions, which spoke volumes for the man's character, and the rigorous logic of his reasoning and conclusions. Although Solger conceded that the events in *Die Wahlverwandtschaften* derive naturally from the personalities of the characters, he took exception to the character of Eduard.

'I can't blame him,' said Goethe, 'for not liking Eduard; I don't like him myself. But I had to make him like that in order to drive the action. And he's quite true to life; you can find plenty of people in the upper classes just like him, in whom obstinacy takes the place of character.'

Solger placed the architect highest in his estimation, arguing that while all the other characters in the novel show themselves to be loving and weak, he is the only one who remains strong and free. And the beautiful thing about his personality, says Solger, is not so much that he doesn't fall into the errors of the other characters, but that the poet has made him so noble that he is quite incapable of doing so.

We both liked this very much. 'That really is very good,' said Goethe. 'I myself,' I said, 'have always found the character of the architect very significant and likeable, but it has never occurred to me that the reason why he is so special is that his nature will not *allow* him to get caught up in the entanglements of love.' 'Don't be surprised by that,' said Goethe, 'considering that it never occurred to me either, when I created the character. But Solger is right: such is the nature of the man.

'This essay,' Goethe went on, 'was written in 1809, and it might have cheered me to hear such a positive reaction to *Die Wahlverwandtschaften* back then, when people at the time, and later on, did not have many good things to say about the book.

'As I can see from these letters, Solger was very attached to me. In one of them, he complains that I didn't even reply when he sent me a copy of his Sophocles translation. Dear heavens – but that's just how it is with me! And it's not surprising. I have known eminent men who had lots of things sent to them. They had certain formulas and stock phrases which they used to acknowledge these gifts, and so they wrote hundreds of letters that were all the same – just a bunch of platitudes. I could never do that. Unless I could write somebody a proper, personal letter I preferred not to write at all. I considered it insulting to fob people off with banalities, and for that reason I have disappointed quite a few deserving souls to whom I would gladly have written. You have seen for yourself how it is with me, how I get things sent to me every day from all over the place; and you can't deny that it would take more than a lifetime to reply to every one, however briefly. But I feel bad about Solger; he was such a fine man, and he more than many others deserved a friendly reply.'

I then brought the conversation round to the new novella, which I had now reread several times and thought about at home. 'The whole first section,' I said, 'is pure exposition, but nothing is introduced there that is not necessary, and it is all presented with such charm that the reader never thinks it is there for some other reason, but takes it at face value, as something that is there for its own sake.'

'I am glad that you think so,' said Goethe. 'But there's one thing I still need to do. According to the laws of a good exposition, I should introduce the owners of the animals at the beginning. When the princess and her uncle are riding past the fairground booth, the people need to come out and invite the princess to honour their booth with a visit.' 'Yes, you are right,' I said. 'Since everything else is prefigured in the exposition, these people must be brought in here too; and since they would normally be outside taking the money, it is perfectly natural that they would not just let the princess ride past without accosting her.' 'As you can see,' said Goethe, 'there's quite a bit of tinkering still to be done with a work of this kind, even when it is basically finished.'

Goethe then told me about a foreigner who had recently visited him on a number of occasions and talked about translating one or two of his works.[102] 'He is a decent enough fellow,' said Goethe, 'but in literary matters he shows himself to be a true dilettante. He has no German, and yet he is talking about doing

1827 183

translations and prefacing them with portraits. But that's the thing about dilettantes; they have no idea of the difficulties involved in any undertaking, and they always want to tackle something for which they have no aptitude at all.'

Thursday evening, 29 January 1827

I called on Goethe shortly before seven, bringing with me the manuscript of the novella and the Béranger edition. I found him and M. Soret in conversation about contemporary French literature. I listened with interest, and it was remarked that the latest poets to emerge had learned a great deal from Delille in matters of versification. Since M. Soret, a native of Geneva, was not altogether fluent in German, while Goethe speaks French tolerably well, the conversation was conducted mainly in French, switching to German only when I wanted to join in. I took my Béranger out of my pocket and handed it to Goethe, who wanted to read these wonderful songs again. M. Soret thought the portrait at the front of the book was not a good likeness. Goethe was pleased to get his hands on this neat little edition. 'These songs,' he said, 'are pure perfection, and the best of their kind – especially when you think of them being sung with the lusty refrain; otherwise they would almost be too serious, too clever, too epigrammatic for songs. Béranger always reminds me of Horace and Hafiz, both of whom also stood aloof from their times and wrote about the corruption of morals in a satirical and playful way.[103] Béranger takes a similar view of his own world. But because he has risen from the lower classes he has no horror of the licentious and the vulgar, and in fact writes about such things with a certain relish.'

We talked back and forth in similar vein about Béranger and other contemporary French writers, until M. Soret left to go to court and I remained alone with Goethe.

A sealed package lay on the table. Goethe placed his hand on it. 'What's that?' I asked. 'It's my *Helena*, which is going off to Cotta to be printed.' What I felt when I heard these words was more than I could say; I knew this was a very significant moment. As when a newly built ship puts to sea for the first time, headed for an unknown future, so it is with the intellectual creation of a great master when it goes out into the world for the first time, destined to exert an influence for generations to come, change men's fortunes, and undergo its own vicissitudes.

'Up until now,' said Goethe, 'I have always found little things to tinker with and improve. But at some point you have to call a halt, and now I'm glad that it is going off with the post and I can turn my hand to something else with a lighter heart. It must take its chances in the world! I am consoled by the fact that the level of culture in Germany is now incredibly high; so I need not fear that such a work will languish in obscurity because nobody understands it.'

'There is an entire antiquity in it,' I observed. 'Indeed,' said Goethe, 'the literary scholars will have their work cut out.' 'I have no worries about the ancient part,' I said, 'because the writing is very specific and detailed, individual motifs are fully developed, and everything says exactly what it is supposed to say. But the modern, romantic part is very difficult; half the history of the world has gone into it, and with such a broad, sweeping canvas the treatment can only be suggestive, which makes great demands on the reader.' 'But there is a physicality to it all,' said Goethe, 'and in a stage performance it will be obvious what is going on. And that's all I ask for. As long as the general public enjoys the *spectacle*, the higher meaning will not be lost on the initiated, any more than it is with *Die Zauberflöte* and other things.'

'It will make for an unusual stage event,' I said, 'to have a piece start as a tragedy and end as an opera. But it will be quite a challenge to portray the majesty of these figures, and to deliver the sublime lines and speak the verse.' 'The first part,' said Goethe, 'calls for first-rate tragedians, just as the later, operatic section needs to be cast with the finest singers. The role of Helen cannot be played by a single great artiste; it has to be played by two. It's very rare to find an opera singer who is also an accomplished tragic actress.'

'The whole production,' I said, 'will be an opportunity to go to town on the scenery and costumes, and I can't deny that I am looking forward to seeing it on the stage. If only you could find

1827 185

a really good composer to take it on.' 'It would have to be someone,' said Goethe, 'who has lived in Italy for a long time, like Meyerbeer, so that he combines his German temperament with Italian flair. But we'll find someone, I'm sure; I'm just glad to be rid of it. I am really rather pleased with my idea not to have the chorus descend to the underworld again, but to cast itself to the elements on the bright face of the earth.' 'It's a new kind of immortality,' I said.

'So,' Goethe went on, 'how did you get on with the novella?'

'I've brought it with me,' I said. 'Having read it again, I think Your Excellency should not make the intended change. It is very effective to have the people turn up for the first time by the dead tiger as strange, new beings, with their exotic dress and manners, and announce themselves as the owners of the animals. If you had introduced them earlier, as part of the exposition, the effect here would be diminished or completely lost.'

'You're right,' said Goethe, 'I should leave it as it is. No, you're absolutely right. It must have been my original intention, when I drafted the thing, not to introduce the people earlier – that's why I left them out. The intended change was dictated by reason, and that almost led me to make a mistake. But it's a strange aesthetic predicament, when you have to disobey a rule in order not to make a mistake.'

We then discussed what the title of the novella should be, and came up with various suggestions, some of them appropriate for the beginning, others for the end; but we could think of none that were right for the whole story. 'You know what?' said Goethe, 'we'll just call it "Novelle"; for what else is a novella if not an unheard-of event that has occurred? That's the proper meaning of the term, and a lot of what goes by that name in Germany is not a novella at all, but just a short story, or whatever else you want to call it. The "Novelle" in *Die Wahlverwandtschaften* is a novella in the true sense of an unheard-of event.'

'When you think about it,' I said, 'every poem gets written without a title, and it is what it is, even without a title. Which rather suggests that the title is not actually relevant.' 'It isn't relevant,' said Goethe, 'and ancient poems didn't have titles;

this is a practice of modern writers, who gave titles to the poems of the ancients in retrospect. This practice derives from the need to name things and differentiate them from each other when the volume of writings has become so large.

'Here's something new,' said Goethe, 'have a look at this.' With these words he handed me a translation by Herr Gerhard of a Serbian poem. I read it with great pleasure, for the poem was very beautiful, and the translation so simple and clear that it never came between the reader and the subject matter. The poem was entitled 'The Key to the Dungeon'. I will say nothing here about the course of the action, but the ending struck me as too abrupt and rather unsatisfying.

'But that's the beauty of it,' said Goethe. 'This way, it leaves a barb behind in the heart, and stimulates the reader's imagination to picture all the possibilities that could now ensue. The ending leaves enough material for an entire tragedy hanging in the air, but of a kind that has often been done before. The real novelty and beauty of the poem lie in the picture that the poet paints for us here, and he very wisely confined himself to this and left the rest to the reader. I would gladly publish the poem in *Kunst und Altertum*, but it is too long; so I asked Gerhard if I could have these three pieces in rhyming verse instead, which I shall print in the next issue. What do you think of these? Listen.'

Goethe began by reading the song of the old man who loves the young maiden, then the women's drinking song, and finally the spirited 'Dance for us, Theodor!'. He read them all beautifully, varying his tone and pace for each one; it was as fine a rendition as one could wish for.

We both admired the way Herr Gerhard had chosen the most appropriate verse forms and refrains for each poem and executed everything with a light and perfectly judged touch, so that it was hard to see how he could possibly have done it better. 'There you see,' said Goethe, 'what all that technical practice does for a talent such as Gerhard's. He has also been helped by the fact that he is not an academic or scholar, but has a job that keeps him in contact with practical, everyday life. He has also travelled extensively in England and other countries, and this, together with his natural feeling for the real, gives him a significant advantage over our own scholarly young writers. As long as he sticks to good source material and only works on this, he is not likely to go far wrong. Original compositions, on the other hand, demand a great deal and are difficult to pull off.'

This led on to various reflections on the work of our most recent young writers, and it was noted that hardly any of them are capable of writing decent prose.

'It's very simple,' said Goethe. 'In order to write prose, one must have something to say; but those who have nothing to say can still make up verses and rhymes, where one word suggests another, and something comes out at the end which in fact is nothing, but looks as if it were something.'

Wednesday 31 January 1827

Dined with Goethe. 'These last few days, since I last saw you,' he said, 'I have been reading all kinds of different things, including a Chinese novel, which I haven't finished yet, and which seems to me highly remarkable.'[104] 'A Chinese novel?' I said. 'That must be a very strange beast.' 'Not as strange as you would think,' said Goethe. 'The characters think, act, and feel almost the same as us, and you very soon feel at home with them, except that everything is clearer, purer and more decorous with them. They live orderly, respectable lives, with no great passions or poetic flights, and in that respect their world is a lot like my *Hermann und Dorothea*, or the English novels of Richardson. But what is different again is the constant presence of the natural world alongside the human characters. You always hear the goldfish splashing in the ponds, the birds are constantly singing in the branches, the days are always bright and sunny, the nights always clear. The moon is mentioned a lot, but it doesn't alter the look of the landscape; in their minds, the light of the moon is as bright as the day itself. And the interior of their houses is as neat and graceful as their pictures. For example: "I heard the sweet girls laughing, and when I saw them they were sitting on delicate cane chairs." Right there you have the most delightful situation, because we always picture cane chairs as being extremely light and graceful. Then there are the countless legends that run alongside the main narrative, which function rather like proverbs. For example, there's the legend about a girl who was so light and dainty on her feet that she could balance on a flower without snapping the stem. And the one about the young man who was so virtuous and moral that in his thirtieth year he was granted the honour of an audience with the Emperor. And another one, about pairs of lovers who behaved with such restraint during their long relationship that when forced on one occasion to spend the night together in the same room, they passed the time in conversation, with no physical contact at all. There are any number of these legends, all of them lessons in morality and decorum. But then it is precisely because of this strict moderation in all things that the Chinese Empire has kept going for thousands of years and will live on into the future.

'There is a most remarkable contrast between this Chinese novel,' said Goethe, 'and the songs of Béranger, which are nearly all based on some immoral, licentious subject matter, and which I would find quite repugnant if they had not been written by such a supremely talented man as Béranger, who knows how to make the material acceptable and even charming. But tell me, don't you find it remarkable yourself that the subjects dealt with by the Chinese poet are so thoroughly moral, while those of France's foremost contemporary poet are the exact opposite?'

'A man with Béranger's particular gifts,' I said, 'wouldn't know what to do with a moral subject.' 'You're right,' said Goethe, 'the follies of our times are the very thing that has brought out and nurtured Béranger's better nature.' 'But perhaps,' I said, 'this Chinese novel is one of their best?' 'Not at all,' said Goethe. 'The Chinese have thousands of them, and they had them back when our ancestors were still living in the forests.

'I see more and more,' he went on, 'that poetry is the common property of all mankind, and that it manifests itself at all times and in all places in hundreds and hundreds of people. Some are a little better at it than others and ride the crest of the wave a little longer than the others, but that's all. So Herr von

1827 189

Matthisson need not think that he is special, any more than I should think that I am special; we should all be telling ourselves that the gift of poetry is not all that unusual, and that nobody has any reason to have a high opinion of himself just because he has written a decent poem. But that's what happens when we Germans don't look beyond our own little world: we all too easily fall prey to this pedantic conceit. This is why I like to have a look at what other nations are doing – and I advise everyone to do the same. National literature has more or less had its day, now that the age of world literature is at hand; and everyone should now do what they can to hasten its arrival. But while it is good to appreciate foreign literature, we should not get hung up on one particular thing and try to turn it into the ultimate ideal. We must not think that Chinese literature is everything, or Serbian literature, or Calderón, or the *Nibelungen*; if we are looking for the ultimate ideal, then we need to go back every time to the ancient Greeks, in whose works the finest human qualities are always represented. We must regard all the rest as just the product of its times, and take from it such good things as we can find.'

It was a joy to hear Goethe talking at length like this on such an important subject. The jingle of sleigh bells drew us to the window, in the expectation of seeing the procession of sledges that had gone past this morning returning from Belvedere. Meanwhile Goethe continued with his fascinating observations. We talked about Alexander Manzoni, and he told me that Count Reinhard had recently seen Manzoni in Paris, where he had been well received in society as a young author of repute, and that he was now living happily back on his estate near Milan with a young family and his mother.

'The only trouble with Manzoni,' Goethe went on, 'is that he doesn't realize what a good poet he is, and what liberties he is entitled to as such. He has too much respect for history, and for this reason he always likes to append notes to his plays, in which he shows how faithfully he has kept to the facts of history. Now his facts may be historically accurate, but his characters are not – any more than my Thoas or my Iphigenie are. No writer has ever known the historical characters he portrays;

had he known them, he would have struggled to make use of them as they were. The writer needs to be clear about the effects he wants to produce, and then he has to fashion his characters accordingly. If I had wanted to make Egmont as history presents him to us, the father of a dozen children, his reckless behaviour would have seemed utterly improbable. So I needed to have a different Egmont, one who was more in tune with his own actions and my poetic intentions; the result is "my" Egmont, as Klärchen puts it.

'And what would be the use of poets anyway, if they only repeated the accounts of historians? The poet must go further, and if possible give us something better and more edifying. The characters of Sophocles all have something of that great poet's lofty mind and spirit, just as Shakespeare's characters possess something of his. And rightly so: this is how it should be. In fact, Shakespeare goes even further and makes his Romans into Englishmen; and rightly so again, since otherwise his countrymen would not have understood him.'

Goethe continued: 'This was another of the Greeks' great strengths, that they were less interested in historical accuracy than in the way the poet treated history. Fortunately, we have an excellent example in the story of Philoctetes, a subject treated by all three of the great Greek tragedians – the play by Sophocles being the last and best. As luck would have it, this poet's splendid text has come down to us intact, whereas only fragments of the *Philoctetes* of Aeschylus and Euripides have been found; but these are enough to tell us how they treated their subject. If time permitted, I would restore these plays, just as I did with the *Phaethon* of Euripides. I should rather enjoy it – and it would be time well spent.

'In the case of this subject, the problem was very simple: it was a matter of fetching Philoctetes and his bow from the island of Lemnos. But how this was to be done – that was for the poet to decide, and this was an opportunity for each of them to demonstrate his powers of invention, and for one of them to outdo his rivals. Odysseus is meant to fetch him; but should he be recognized by Philoctetes or not? And if not, how should he be disguised? Should Odysseus go alone, or should he have companions? And if so, who? In Aeschylus, the companion is unknown; in Euripides it is Diomedes, and in Sophocles it is the son of Achilles. Next: in what circumstances should Philoctetes be found? Should the island be inhabited or not, and if inhabited, should some compassionate soul have taken pity on him – or not? And so on, with a hundred other things that these writers had to decide for themselves; and it was by his choices, for or against, that one of them could demonstrate his superiority in wisdom over the others. This is the point; and our present-day poets should do likewise, and not be forever asking whether a subject has already been done or not, while they hunt high and low for unheard-of events, which are often outlandish enough, and strike the reader as just that – chance events, and nothing more. But of course, to make something of a simple subject by a masterly treatment requires intellect and great talent – and these are in short supply.'

The sound of passing sledges drew us to the window again, but again it was not the expected party from Belvedere. We talked and joked for a while about insignificant matters. Then I asked Goethe how he was getting on with his 'Novelle'.

'I haven't touched it for a few days now,' he said, 'but there's one thing I need to do in the exposition. The lion needs to roar when the princess rides past the booth; then I can give the characters some good lines about how frightful the mighty beast is.'

'That's a very good idea,' I said. 'It not only serves a useful and necessary purpose as a piece of exposition in its own right, but also enhances the effect of everything that follows. Up until now the lion has seemed almost too tame, showing no sign of ferocity. But by roaring he at least lets us know what a formidable beast he is; and when, later on, he meekly follows the sound of the child's flute, the effect will be all the more powerful.'

'Making changes and improvements like this,' said Goethe, 'is the right way to go about it – taking something that's not yet perfect, coming up with new ideas, and working at it until it is perfected. But to take something that's finished and then keep on reworking it and taking it further, as Walter Scott, for instance, has done with my Mignon by making her deaf and dumb as well as everything else – those sorts of changes I do *not* approve of.'

Thursday evening, 1 February 1827

Goethe told me about a visit from the Crown Prince of Prussia, accompanied by the Grand Duke. 'The Princes Karl and Wilhelm of Prussia,' he said, 'were also here this morning. The Crown Prince and the Grand Duke stayed for nearly three hours, and we talked about all kinds of things. I came away with a high opinion of the intellect, taste, knowledge and mentality of this young prince.'

Goethe had a copy of the *Farbenlehre* in front of him. 'I still owe you an answer,' he said, 'regarding the phenomenon of the coloured shadows. But as this assumes a lot of prior knowledge, and is bound up with many other things besides, I won't be giving you an explanation today, either – not when you don't have any background or context. Instead, I thought it would be good if we could read the whole of the *Farbenlehre* together on the evenings when we meet. That will give us something specific to discuss, and you'll find that you have absorbed the entire theory before you know it. Things you have learned at second hand will start to make real sense and get you thinking for yourself, and I predict that you will master this science very quickly. Now you can read the first section.'

And with that, Goethe placed the open book before me. I felt privileged to think that he took such an interest in me. I read the first paragraphs, about physiological colours.

'You see,' said Goethe, 'there is nothing outside us that is not also within us, and just as the external world has its colours, so too does the eye. As this science is all about distinguishing clearly between what is objective and what is subjective, I have made a start with the colours belonging to the eye, so that in all our observations we may be able to tell whether the colour really exists outside of us, or whether it is only an appearance of colour produced by the eye itself. So I do think I have gone about presenting this science in the right way by first explaining the operation of the organ through which all our perceptions and observations must pass.'

I read on as far as the interesting paragraphs about the 'required colours', where we are told that the eye needs change; it never likes to linger on the same colour, but immediately requires a different one – and so urgently that it will produce its own colours if it does not find them out there in the real world.

This got us talking about a great law that runs right through nature, and on which all life, and all our joy in life, are founded. 'The same law,' said Goethe, 'governs not only all our other senses, but also our higher spiritual being; but because the eye is so pre-eminent among the senses, the way we see colour is a particularly clear example of this law of required change at work, and this is where we are made most aware of it. We have dances that delight the ear because the music shifts between major and minor, whereas dances that are all major or all minor soon become wearisome.'

'The same law,' I said, 'might explain good writing style, where we like to avoid repetition of the same sound. And properly applied, the law could be very helpful when it comes to drama. There is something tedious and wearisome about plays, especially tragedies, where the same unchanging tone is sustained throughout; and when the orchestra plays mournful, depressing music between the acts of a tragedy the effect on us is unbearable, and we just want to escape.'

'It may be,' said Goethe, 'that the scenes of light relief interwoven into Shakespeare's tragedies are also dictated by this law of required change; but it seems not to apply to the higher tragedy of the Greeks, where there's a sort of constant undertone running through the whole play.'

'Then again,' I observed, 'a Greek tragedy is not so long that the same tone sustained throughout would become tiresome. You also have the alternation of choruses and dialogue, and the sublime import is such that it cannot become tedious, because it is always underpinned by a certain honest reality that is never drab or dull.'

'You may well be right,' said Goethe, 'and it would probably be worth investigating to what extent Greek tragedy, too, is subject to the general law of required change. But you see how everything is interconnected, and how a law derived from colour theory can lead on to an investigation of Greek tragedy. But we must be careful not to take things too far by trying to make such a law the foundation for all kinds of other things. We do better just to apply it by way of analogy or example.'

We then talked about Goethe's presentation of his theory of colour, the way he traces everything back to fundamental laws of nature and always explains individual phenomena by reference to those laws – which is why the resulting work is so accessible and intellectually rewarding.

'That may be so,' said Goethe, 'and I believe I do deserve credit for that. But this method calls for students who are not easily distracted and are capable of getting to the heart of the matter. Some very able men have studied my theory of colour, but unfortunately they have wandered from the straight and narrow, and before you know it they have gone off in pursuit of some idea of their own, instead of focusing properly on the matter in hand. But someone with a good mind who cares about the truth could still accomplish a great deal.'

We spoke about university professors who are still lecturing on Newton's theory, even after a better alternative has been found. 'It's not surprising,' said Goethe; 'such people continue in error because they make their living from it. They would have to relearn their trade, and that would be very inconvenient for them.' 'But how can their experiments prove the truth,' I said, 'if their teaching is based on false premises?' 'They don't prove the truth,' said Goethe, 'and that isn't their intention; they are only interested in proving their opinions. They keep quiet about any experiments that might reveal the truth and show their own theory to be untenable.

'And as for the students, what do they care about the truth? They are human beings like everybody else, and perfectly happy if they can put in their empirical twopenny worth on the subject. And that's about the size of it. People are an odd bunch: as soon as a lake freezes over, they turn up in their hundreds to play around on the smooth surface; but who ever thinks to ask how deep the lake is, and what kind of fish are swimming

1827   195

around under the ice? Niebuhr has just discovered a trade treaty between Rome and Carthage dating from very early times, which shows that Livy's entire account of the early life of the Romans is pure fiction; the treaty makes it clear that the civilization of Rome in very early times was far more advanced than Livy would have us believe. But if you think that the discovery of this treaty will completely transform the way Roman history is taught, then think again. Remember the frozen lake: that's how people are, as I have learned, and they are not going to change.'

'But you surely don't regret writing the *Farbenlehre*,' I said. 'Not only have you laid a firm foundation for this important science, but you have also given us a textbook example of the scientific method, which others can follow in their investigations of similar subjects.'

'I don't regret it in the least,' said Goethe, 'even though I've put half a lifetime's work into it. I could have written half a dozen more tragedies, perhaps, but that's all. And there'll be plenty of people after me who can do that.

'But you are right, and I think the way I have gone about it is good; there is certainly method in it. I have also written a theory of music, adopting the same approach. And my *Metamorphose der Pflanzen* is based on the same principles of observation and deduction.

'It was a strange thing with my *Metamorphose der Pflanzen*; I came to it in the same way that Herschel arrived at his discoveries. Herschel was so poor, you see, that he could not afford a telescope, so he was forced to build his own. But this turned out to be his good fortune, because his home-made telescope was better than all the others – and he used it to make his great discoveries. I came to botany by the empirical route. I remember clearly that the theory relating to the formation of the species went into so much detail that I gave up trying to understand it. That prompted me to pursue the subject in my own way, and to find out what it is that all plants, without distinction, have in common; and that's how I discovered the law of metamorphosis.

'I have no intention of doing further research on specific

aspects of botany. I'll leave that to others, who are far better qualified than I am. I was only interested in finding a universal law that would explain the individual phenomena. Similarly, mineralogy interested me for two reasons only: first, because of its great practical value, and secondly, following up on Werner's theory, in the hope of discovering in it a record of how the primeval world was formed. But now that that brilliant man's death has left the science in a state of total disarray, I am not officially pursuing the subject any further, and I shall keep my private convictions to myself.

'In colour theory I still have to tackle the subject of rainbows, and how they are formed. That's my next job. And an extremely difficult problem, which I am hoping to solve nonetheless. This is why I want to go through the *Farbenlehre* again with you now; everything will then be fresh in my mind again, especially as you take such an interest in the subject yourself.

'I have ventured into nearly every area of the natural sciences,' Goethe went on. 'But I was only ever interested in the things of this earth, which could be directly apprehended by the senses. This is why I have never bothered with astronomy, because there the senses are not sufficient; you have to resort to instruments, calculations and mechanics, which require a lifetime's study, and they were not my thing.

'But if I have achieved anything in those areas that did interest me, I was helped by the fact that I was living in an age that has witnessed more scientific discoveries than any other. When I was still a child, I encountered Franklin's theory of electricity, the law of which he had just discovered. And throughout my lifetime, right up until the present day, I have seen one great discovery after another. So not only was my attention drawn to the natural world at an early age, but my interest in it has been kept constantly stimulated ever since.

'Advances such as I could never have imagined are now being made, some of them in areas that I myself pioneered, and I feel like someone who is walking towards the dawn, only to be astonished by the brightness of the sun when it rises.'

Among the Germans whose names Goethe mentioned here with admiration were Carus, D'Alton, and Meyer in Königsberg.

1827   197

'If only,' Goethe went on, 'people didn't pervert and obscure the truth once it had been found, I should be content; for mankind needs something positive that can be handed down from generation to generation, and it would be good if that something positive were also right and true. In that sense, I should be very pleased if they could sort things out in the natural sciences and then stick to what they know, instead of engaging in more wild speculation once they've exhausted what is humanly comprehensible. But people just can't leave things alone, and before you know it, confusion reigns again.

'Now they are having a go at the Pentateuch, and if negative criticism has a damaging effect anywhere, it is in matters of religion; because here everything depends on faith, and once that is lost, you can never get it back again.

'In literature, negative criticism is not so damaging. Wolf demolished Homer, but it didn't do the poem any harm; this poem possesses the same magic powers as the heroes of Valhalla, who hack each other to pieces in the morning, and sit down to lunch with whole limbs again.'

Goethe was in fine form, and it was a delight to hear him holding forth again on such important matters. 'The best thing is for us to quietly keep going on the right path,' he said, 'and leave the others to go their own sweet way.'

Wednesday 7 February 1827

Today Goethe complained about certain critics who were unhappy with Lessing and had unreasonable expectations of him. 'When people compare Lessing's plays with those of the ancients,' he said, 'and find them paltry and pathetic, what can one say? We should pity that extraordinary man, rather, that he had to live in such wretched times, which afforded him no better subjects than the ones he wrote about in his plays. And pity him that in his *Minna von Barnhelm* he had to deal with the quarrels between the Saxons and the Prussians, because he couldn't find anything better. The impoverishment of the age he was living in made him the polemicist he always was. In *Emilia Galotti* princely rulers were his target; in *Nathan* it was priests.'

Friday 16 February 1827

I told Goethe that I had recently been reading Winckelmann's essay *On the Imitation of Greek Works of Art*, and I confessed that I often had the impression that Winckelmann was not entirely on top of his subject at the time.

'You're quite right,' said Goethe. 'There are times when he seems to be feeling his way rather. But the great thing about him is that he is always feeling his way towards *something*; he's like Columbus, when he had not yet discovered the New World but somehow knew deep down in his mind that it was there. You don't *learn* anything when you read him – but it changes you.

'Meyer went further, and took our knowledge of art to new heights. His *History of Art* is a timeless work; but he would not be the man he is if he had not learned from Winckelmann in his youth and pursued the path that Winckelmann had trod before him. You see once again what a difference a great predecessor makes, and what it means to make proper use of him.'

Wednesday 11 April 1827

I went to Goethe's house around one o'clock today, having been invited to take a drive with him before dinner. We headed out on the Erfurt road. The weather was very fine, and the vivid green of the cornfields on either side of the road was a joy to behold. Goethe seemed to be feeling as bright and young as the early spring, but his talk was full of the wisdom of old age.

'I always say, and I'll say it again now,' he began, 'the world could not exist if it were not so simple. This poor soil has been cultivated for a thousand years, and yet it remains as fertile as ever. A little rain, a little sun, and each spring it turns green again, year in, year out.' I could think of nothing to say or add to this. Goethe let his gaze wander over the greening fields, and then, turning back to me, resumed the conversation on other subjects:

'I've just been reading something very curious, namely, the correspondence of Jacobi and his friends. This is a remarkable book, and you must read it – not because you will learn anything

1827   199

from it, but because it gives you an insight into the state of
culture and literature in those days, which people now know
nothing about. We see a series of individuals, all fairly eminent
in their way, but with no sign of any common purpose or interest, each one in a world of his own, going his own sweet way,
completely unaware of what anyone else is doing. They
reminded me of billiard balls, shooting about all over the place
on the green baize, not knowing that the others are there; and
if they do happen to touch, they career off in different directions, further apart than ever.'

I laughed at this striking image. I asked about the writers of
these letters, and Goethe went through the names, telling me a
little about each one of them.

'Jacobi was really a born diplomat, a handsome man of slim
build and refined and noble demeanour, who would have been
in his element as an ambassador. As a poet and a philosopher,
however, he didn't quite have what it takes.

'We had a curious relationship. He liked me personally, but
did not take any interest in my endeavours, or even approve of
them. So the bond between us was purely one of friendship.
What made my relationship with Schiller so unique, on the
other hand, was the wonderful bond we formed through our
common endeavours, so that we had no need of any so-called
special friendship.'

I asked about Lessing, and whether he is also mentioned in
the letters. 'No,' said Goethe, 'but Herder and Wieland are.
Herder was not comfortable with these connections; he was
too superior not to be bored in the long run by this empty chatter. Hamann, too, treated these people with condescension.

'Wieland, as always, comes across in these letters as a man of
sunny disposition, at ease with the world. Not wedded to any
particular opinion, he was adroit enough to go along with
everything. He was like a reed, tossed this way and that by the
wind of opinion, but always firmly attached to its little root.

'My personal relationship with Wieland was always very
good, especially in the early days, when he belonged to me
alone. His little tales were written at my suggestion. But when
Herder came to Weimar, Wieland deserted me. Herder took

him away from me; the man's personal magnetism was very powerful.'

The carriage turned to go back. Towards the east we saw a mass of rain clouds bunched together. 'Those clouds,' I said, 'look as if they could come down as rain any minute. Is it possible they might break up again, if the barometer were to rise?' 'Yes,' said Goethe, 'those clouds would immediately collapse in on themselves from the top and be spun up like a distaff. So strong is my faith in the barometer. I always say that if the barometer had risen on the night of the great St Petersburg flood, the storm surge would not have been able to reach the city.

'My son believes the weather is influenced by the moon, and perhaps you think so, too; I don't blame you, because the moon seems too important a celestial body for us not to suppose that it influences our planet directly. But changes in the weather and the rise and fall of the barometer have nothing to do with the phases of the moon; the causes are purely terrestrial.

'I think of the earth and its atmosphere as being like a great living organism, perpetually inhaling and exhaling. When the earth inhales, it draws the atmosphere downwards, so that it approaches the earth's surface, condenses, and forms clouds and rainfall. This is the state I call "water affirmation"; if it were to persist for an inordinate length of time, the earth would be drowned. But this the earth does not allow; it exhales again and lets the water vapours escape upwards, where they are dissipated throughout the upper atmosphere and become so rarefied that not only does the sun shine through in all its brightness, but the eternal darkness of outer space appears to us as a vivid blue.

'This latter atmospheric state I call "water negation". In the other, contrary state, not only does water fall frequently from above, but the moisture on the earth cannot evaporate and dry out. In this state, however, not only is there no water coming from above, but the moisture on the earth escapes upwards and evaporates; which means that if *this* condition were to persist for an inordinate length of time the earth, even in the absence of sunshine, would be in danger of drying up and withering.'

I listened attentively as Goethe held forth on this important subject. 'The matter is very simple,' he went on, 'and I stick to what is simple and broadly applicable, ignoring any occasional aberrations. A high barometer means dry weather and an east wind, a low barometer means wet weather and a west wind: that's the general principle I follow. If a damp mist sometimes blows in when the barometer is high and the wind is in the east, or if we have blue sky when the wind is coming from the west, it doesn't bother me or shake my faith in the general principle; it simply tells me that there are other influences at work here that we do not yet understand.

'I will tell you something that you can rely on as you go through life. There are accessible things in nature, and there are inaccessible things. It's important to keep this in mind and distinguish between the two, and to respect the distinction. It helps to know this as a general principle, although it is always very difficult to tell where the one ends and the other begins. Those who don't know this may spend their entire lives wrestling with the inaccessible, without ever getting close to the truth. Those who do know, if they are wise, will stick to what is accessible; and by exploring this realm in every direction and building up their knowledge they may even be able to make some sense of the inaccessible – although in the end they will have to admit that many things can only be grasped up to a point, and that there is always a problematic dimension to nature which the mind of man is incapable of fathoming.'

By this point, we were back in the town again. The conversation turned to more mundane matters, which left my mind free to dwell a little longer on Goethe's lofty thoughts.

We had returned too early to go straight to the dinner table, so Goethe used the time to show me a landscape by Rubens – a summer evening scene.[105] On the left, in the foreground, you saw farm labourers returning home from the fields; in the centre of the picture a flock of sheep were following their shepherd towards the village; on the right, further back in the picture, stood a hay wagon, surrounded by labourers who were busy loading it, while unharnessed draught horses grazed close by; in the distance several mares were grazing with their foals on pastures dotted with thickets, and you could tell that they would be spending the night outdoors. A few villages and a town were visible on the bright horizon of the picture, in which the cycle of work and rest was most charmingly represented.

The whole scene seemed to me so entirely credible as a true representation of reality, and each separate detail was so faithfully rendered, that I ventured the opinion that Rubens must have copied his picture direct from nature.

'Not at all,' said Goethe. 'Such a perfect picture has never been seen in nature; we owe this composition to the painter's own poetic spirit. But the great Rubens possessed such an extraordinary memory that he had the whole of nature in his head, and could summon up the smallest detail at any time. This is why his paintings seem so realistic, both in their entirety and in their details, so that we think he must have copied them straight from nature. Nobody paints a landscape like this any more. That way of feeling, and of seeing nature, has disappeared entirely; our modern painters have no poetry in them.

'The other thing is that our young artists are left to themselves; there are no living masters to initiate them into the mysteries of art. There is something to be learned from the dead, of course. But this, it seems, is more a matter of copying details than of learning to understand a master's thoughts and methods at a deeper level.'

Goethe's son and daughter-in-law came in and we sat down to dinner. The conversation ranged back and forth over various lighter topics of the day, touching on the theatre, balls, and the court. But we soon got back to more serious matters, and found ourselves deeply immersed in a conversation about religious doctrines in England.

'To understand all the ins and outs of it,' said Goethe, 'you would need to study Church history for fifty years, as I have. But it is very interesting to see what Muslims are taught at the start of their education. As the basis of their religion, their young people are taught to believe that nothing can happen to a man that was not decreed long ago by an all-seeing divinity; this equips them for the rest of their lives and sets their minds at rest, and they hardly need anything else.

'It's not for me to say whether this doctrine is true or false, helpful or harmful, but at bottom there is something of this belief in all of us, even though we have not been taught it. As the soldier going into battle says: "The bullet that hasn't got my name on it can't hit me." And without that conviction, where would he find the courage to keep his spirits up in the face of mortal danger? The teaching of the Christian faith – "Not a single sparrow can fall to the ground without your Father's leave" – comes from the same source, and points to a providence that watches over the smallest thing, and without whose will and leave nothing can happen.

'After that, the Muslims begin their instruction in philosophy with the doctrine that nothing exists of which the contrary cannot be stated. Thus they train the minds of their young people by setting them the task of finding and formulating the opposite of every proposition – an exercise calculated to foster mental dexterity and verbal fluency.

'Once the contrary of any given proposition has been stated, *doubt* arises as to which of the two is true. But we cannot live in a permanent state of doubt; instead, the mind is compelled to inquire more closely and *test* the two opposing propositions, from which process, if it is properly done, *certainty* emerges. And therein lies the peace of mind that all men seek.

'As you can see, this doctrine tells us everything we need to know, and we, with all our systems, are no further on; indeed, that's as far as anyone can go.'

'This reminds me,' I said, 'of the Greeks, whose method of philosophical instruction must have been similar, as we can tell from their tragedy, which relies entirely on contradiction to drive it forward; none of the characters can say anything without the other person arguing just as eloquently for the exact opposite.'

'You are absolutely right,' said Goethe, 'and the doubt is there, too, awakened in the mind of the spectator or reader. And we arrive at certainty in the end through the intervention of fate, which allies itself with moral virtue and espouses its cause.'

We rose from the table, and Goethe took me down into the garden to continue our conversation. 'The curious thing about Lessing,' I said, 'is that in his theoretical writings – *Laokoon*, for example – he never goes straight for results, but always leads us down that circuitous philosophical path via opinion, counter-opinion and doubt, before finally allowing us to arrive at a kind of certainty. We are observing the processes of thinking and seeking at work, rather than gaining any great insights or learning any great truths that might stimulate our own thinking and make us productive in our own right.'

'I dare say you are right,' said Goethe. 'Lessing himself apparently said once that if God wanted to give him truth, he would decline the gift, and would rather make the effort to seek it out for himself.[106]

'The philosophical system of the Muslims is a handy yardstick that we can apply to ourselves and others to find out how far we have actually progressed in mental virtue.

'In keeping with his polemical bent, Lessing is most at home in the realm of contradiction and doubt; drawing distinctions is his thing, and in that he was greatly aided by his powerful intellect. You will find me quite different. I have never gone in for contradictions; I tried to settle any doubts in my mind, and have only ever formulated my final conclusions.'

I asked Goethe which of today's philosophers he regards as the best.

'Kant,' he replied, 'is the best, beyond a doubt. He is also the one whose influence has lasted, and whose teachings have had the greatest impact on our German culture. He has influenced you, too, even though you have not read him. Now you no longer need him, because what he had to give you is already yours. If you ever want to read something of his later on, I would recommend his *Critique of Judgement*, in which he is brilliant on the subject of rhetoric, passable on poetry, but disappointing on the fine arts.'

'Has Your Excellency ever had any personal connection with Kant?' I asked.

'No,' said Goethe, 'Kant never took any notice of me, even though I pursued a similar path to him quite independently. I wrote my *Metamorphose der Pflanzen* before I knew anything about Kant; and yet it is entirely in the spirit of his teachings. The differentiation of the subject from the object, and the view that every creature exists in its own right, and that cork trees, for instance, do not grow simply to provide us with stoppers for our bottles – all this Kant and I had in common, and I was pleased to discover such a meeting of minds. Later on I wrote a paper on the theory of experimentation, which is effectively a critique of subject and object and the interactive relationship between the two.

'Schiller always advised me against studying Kant's philosophy. He used to say that Kant had nothing to offer me. But he studied Kant intensively himself, and I have studied him too – and not without profit.'

We walked up and down the garden as we talked. In the meantime the clouds had gathered and it began to spit with rain, so that we were obliged to go back indoors, where we continued our conversation for a while.

Wednesday 20 June 1827

The family table was laid for five; the rooms were empty and cool, which was very pleasant in the heat of the day. I entered the spacious room next to the dining room, the one with the woven carpet on the floor and the colossal bust of Juno. I had not been pacing up and down on my own for long before Goethe came in from his study and greeted me in his usual warm and affectionate way. He sat down on a chair by the window. 'Pull up a chair yourself,' he said, 'and come and sit with me; we'll talk for a bit before the others arrive. I'm glad you were able to meet Count Sternberg here; he has left now, so I am back to my usual round of work and rest.'

'I was most impressed by the person of the Count,' I said, 'and also by the great extent of his knowledge. Wherever the conversation went he was always at home with it, and he talked about everything in such a perceptive and thoughtful way, yet with such a light touch.'

'Yes,' said Goethe, 'he is a most remarkable man, and his influence and connections in Germany are very extensive. As a botanist he is known throughout Europe for his *Flora Subterranea*, and he is also a very considerable mineralogist. Do you know his story?' 'No,' I said, 'but I should very much like to know more about him. I saw him as an aristocrat and a man of the world, but also as a scholar and a polymath. I find him something of a paradox, so I wonder what the explanation is.' Goethe then proceeded to tell me how the Count, destined for the priesthood in his youth, had begun his studies in Rome, but later moved to Naples, after Austria had withdrawn certain benefits. Goethe went on to give a detailed and interesting account of a remarkable life, which would not have been out of place in his *Wanderjahre*, but which I do not feel I want to repeat here. It was a joy to listen to him, and I thanked him from the depths of my heart. The conversation now turned to the Bohemian schools and their great advantages, especially the high quality of their aesthetic education.

By now Goethe's son and daughter-in-law had come in, together with Fräulein Ulrike, and we all sat down to dinner. The conversation was lively and wide-ranging, but the subject of religious zealotry in some north German cities came up more than once. It was noted that these pietistic sects had been the cause of family rifts and break-ups. I was able to report a similar case, where I had almost lost a good friend because he could not convert me to his way of thinking. 'He believed fervently,' I said, 'that all our merits and good works count for nothing, and that men can only be in a right relationship with God through the grace of Christ.' 'A friend of mine,' said Frau von Goethe, 'said something similar to me, but I still don't know what these good works and this grace are all about.'

'It's like everything else that people talk about in the world today,' said Goethe; 'it's just a hotchpotch of ideas, and I dare say none of you knows where it all comes from. So I'll tell you. The doctrine of good works, whereby man can work off a sin and rise in God's favour by good deeds, legacies and charitable donations, is a Catholic thing. But the Protestant reformers, being opposed to Catholicism, rejected this doctrine and replaced it with the idea that men must seek only to discern the merits of Christ and become partakers of His grace – from which good works then follow, of course. Those are the facts; but nowadays it all gets thrown together and mixed up, and nobody knows where these things come from any more.'

I thought to myself, though I didn't say as much, that differences of opinion in religious matters had always caused people to fall out and become enemies, and that the first murder, in fact, was the result of people worshipping God in different ways. I said that I had just been reading Byron's *Cain*, and had particularly admired the third act and the motivation of the murder.

'Isn't it good?' said Goethe. 'The motivation is brilliant. The whole thing is so beautifully done – there's nothing like it in the whole of literature.'

'Yet *Cain*,' I said, 'was originally banned in England, but now everyone reads it, and most young Englishmen take a complete set of Byron with them on their travels.'

'It's all foolishness,' said Goethe, 'because in essence there is nothing in *Cain* that the English bishops themselves do not teach.'

The Chancellor was announced. He came in and sat down at the table with us. Goethe's grandchildren, Walter and Wolfgang, also came bounding in, one after the other. Wolf snuggled in to the Chancellor. 'Go and get your album,' said Goethe, 'and show the Chancellor your princess, and what Count Sternberg wrote in it for you.' Wolf jumped up and quickly returned with the book. The Chancellor looked at the portrait of the princess, with some lines written by Goethe. He leafed through the album and came across Zelter's inscription, which he read aloud: 'Learn to obey!'

'That's the only sensible thing in the entire book,' said Goethe with a laugh. 'Zelter always does things in style! Riemer and I are going through his letters at the moment, and there are some priceless things in there. The letters he wrote to me on his travels are especially fine; as an accomplished architect and musician, he has the advantage of never lacking interesting subjects to write about. As soon as he enters a city, the buildings are there in front of him, telling him their good points and bad. And then the music societies are quick to welcome him in their midst and reveal themselves to the maestro in all their strengths and weaknesses. If only his conversations with his music pupils had been recorded by a shorthand writer, we would possess something quite unique. For in such matters Zelter is quite brilliant, and always hits the nail on the head.'

Thursday 5 July 1827

I met Goethe in the park towards evening today, as he was returning from a drive. He waved at me as he went past, indicating that I should come and see him. So I turned round at once and went to his house, where I found Chief Planning Officer Coudray. Goethe got out of his carriage and we all went upstairs together. We sat down at a round table in the so-called Juno Room. We had not been talking for long when the Chancellor came in and joined us. The conversation turned on political matters: Wellington's mission to St Petersburg and its probable consequences, Kapo d'Istrias, the delayed liberation of Greece, the confinement of the Turks to Constantinople, and other things of that sort. The earlier years under Napoleon were also discussed, and especially the duc d'Enghien and his ill-advised revolutionary conduct.

We then turned to more peaceful matters, and there was much talk of Wieland's grave at Ossmannstedt. Coudray told us that he was planning to put some iron railings around the grave. He gave us a clear idea of what he had in mind, making a sketch of the ironwork on a piece of paper while we looked on.

When the Chancellor and Coudray left, Goethe asked me to stay with him a little while longer. 'As someone who sees the bigger historical picture,' he said, 'I always find it strange when people talk about statues and monuments. I can never think of a statue erected in honour of some distinguished man without picturing it being pulled down and smashed by a future generation of warriors. I can already see Coudray's iron bars around Wieland's grave forged into horseshoes, winking in the sunlight under the hooves of some future cavalry troop. I saw something similar in Frankfurt once. And anyway, Wieland was buried much too close to the Ilm; the river is eroding the bank on that sharp bend, and in less than a hundred years it will have reached the grave.'

We engaged in some good-humoured banter about the shocking inconstancy of earthly things, and then, taking up Coudray's drawing again, admired the delicate and forceful strokes of the English pencil, which had been so obedient to the draughtsman's will that his thoughts were transferred directly to the paper, with nothing lost in the process.

This got us on to the subject of drawings in general, and Goethe showed me a wonderful example by an Italian master depicting the boy Jesus in the temple among the scribes. He then showed me an engraving after the finished picture and we compared the two, which prompted many observations – all of them favouring the drawing.

'I recently had the good fortune,' said Goethe, 'to buy many fine drawings by famous masters at a very good price. Such drawings are invaluable, not only because they convey a very clear idea of the artist's original vision, but also because they make us privy to the artist's state of mind at the moment of creation. Every line in this drawing of the boy Jesus in the temple bespeaks a great clarity and a quiet, serene resolve in the mind of the artist; and this beneficent mood is communicated to us when we look at the picture. Moreover, paintings and sculptures have the great advantage that they are purely objective things, and they compel our attention without unduly exciting our emotions. Such works either speak to us very directly or they don't speak to us at all. A poem, on the other hand, has a much more indefinite effect; it excites an emotional response, yes, but one that differs from one person to the next, depending on the listener's character and abilities.'

'I've just been reading the excellent English novel *Roderick Random* by Smollett,' I said, 'and this almost had the feeling of a good freehand drawing. A very direct portrayal, without a hint of sentimentality; what we have before us is real life, just as it is, often hideous and repellent enough, but the overall effect is always uplifting, on account of its unabashed realism.'

'I've heard a lot of good things about *Roderick Random*,' said Goethe, 'and I believe what you tell me about it; but I have never read it. Do you know Johnson's *Rasselas*? Do read it some time and tell me what you think of it.' I promised to do so.

'In Lord Byron, too,' I said, 'I often find descriptions that are so direct and immediate that they simply show us the thing itself, without exciting our emotions, just as a drawing by a good painter does. *Don Juan* in particular has many such passages.'

'Yes,' said Goethe, 'Lord Byron is very good at that; his descriptions have a kind of casual, throwaway realism, as if they had been improvised. I am not very familiar with *Don Juan*, but I do recall such passages from his other poems, especially poems about the sea, where every now and then a sail peeps out, and it's so brilliant – as if you can actually feel the sea breeze.'

'What I particularly admired in his *Don Juan*,' I said, 'is his portrayal of London, which his light verses seem to bring to life before our eyes. And he doesn't much care whether a subject is poetic or not; he just grabs hold of whatever comes his way and uses it, down to the curled periwigs in the barber's window and the men who keep the street lamps topped up with oil.'

'Our German literary critics,' said Goethe, 'talk a great deal about poetic and unpoetic subject matter, and in some ways they may not be altogether wrong; but ultimately, no subject taken from the real world is unpoetic, provided the poet knows how to make proper use of it.'

'Very true,' I said, 'and I wish that view were accepted as a general principle.' We then talked about *The Two Foscari*, and I remarked that Byron wrote women very well indeed.

'His women,' said Goethe, 'are good. But then, women are the only vessel we moderns have left into which we can pour our notions of the ideal. There's nothing to be done with the men. Homer said it all with his Achilles and Odysseus – the bravest of the brave and the wisest of the wise.'

'Incidentally,' I continued, 'there is something unsettling about *The Two Foscari* because of the recurring torture scenes, and one wonders how Byron could live with this distressing subject matter for long enough to write the play.'

'That kind of thing was Byron's natural element,' said Goethe. 'He was forever tormenting himself, so subjects like this were meat and drink to him – as you can see from the rest of his works, where there is scarcely a cheerful subject to be found.

1827

But you've got to admire the way he presents it, don't you think, even in the *Foscari*?'

'It's excellent,' I said, 'every word is powerful, significant and to the point; in fact, I have yet to come across a weak line in Byron. I always picture him emerging from the waves, fresh and full of creative vigour.' 'You're quite right,' said Goethe, 'that's it exactly.' 'And the more I read him,' I went on, 'the more I admire the greatness of his talent, and you were quite right to establish that immortal monument of love to him in *Helena*.'[107]

'As he was without question the greatest talent of our century,' said Goethe, 'there is no one else I could have used to represent the modern poetic age. The thing is, Byron is neither classical nor romantic, but as contemporary as today. That's the kind of man I had to have. And he also fitted the bill perfectly because of his restless, dissatisfied nature and his warlike tendency, which led him to his death at Missolonghi. It is not convenient or advisable to write a treatise on Byron, but I shall continue to pay tribute to him and make reference to him as the occasion arises.'

Since the subject of *Helena* had been brought up, Goethe continued on this theme. 'I'd previously had a very different ending in mind,' he said. 'I had thought of various ways it could go, and one of them was pretty good – though I won't tell you what it was. Then this one with Lord Byron and Missolonghi came to me in the course of events, and I gladly let go of all the rest. Have you noticed how the chorus acts out of character for the elegy? Hitherto it has been consistently classical, or at least it has never denied its girlish nature; but here, all of a sudden, it becomes serious and deeply reflective, and says things it has never thought about and never could have.'

'I did notice that,' I said, 'but having seen the Rubens landscape with the double shadow,* and been introduced to the idea of fictions, I am not bothered by that kind of thing. Such minor inconsistencies are of no consequence if they help the artist to attain a higher beauty. The elegy had to be sung

---

* See below, p. 521.

somehow, and since there was no other chorus to hand, the girls had to sing it.'

'I do wonder,' said Goethe with a laugh, 'what the German critics will make of it – whether they will be sufficiently open-minded and bold to get past it. *La raison* will be a stumbling block for the French, and they'll forget that the imagination has its own laws, which cannot, and should not, be amenable to human reason. If imagination did not create things that remain eternally problematic for the rational mind, imagination would not amount to much. This is what distinguishes poetry from prose, where the rational mind is always at home, as it rightly should be.'

I was very taken with this important observation and made a mental note of it. I then made to leave, for it was getting on for ten o'clock. We had been sitting without candles, the brightness of the summer evening lighting up the sky from the north, above the Ettersberg.

Monday evening, 9 July 1827

I found Goethe alone, studying the plaster casts taken from the Stosch collection. 'My friends in Berlin,' he said, 'have been kind enough to send me this entire collection to look at. I am already familiar with most of these fine pieces, but seeing them now in sequence, following Winckelmann's arrangement, is most helpful; I'm also referring to his description and consulting his opinion in cases where I myself am not sure.'

We had not been talking for long before the Chancellor came in and sat down with us. He shared with us some things he had read in the newspapers, including a report about a menagerie keeper who had a craving for lion meat, killed a lion, and cooked himself a generous portion. 'I'm surprised he didn't go for a monkey instead,' opined Goethe; 'monkey is said to be a very tasty delicacy.' We talked about how ugly these beasts are, and agreed that the more they resemble humans, the more unpleasant they are. 'I cannot understand,' said the Chancellor, 'how princes can tolerate such animals near them, and even take pleasure in them.' 'Princes,' observed Goethe, 'are plagued so much by obnoxious men that they regard these even more

1827

obnoxious creatures as a kind of antidote to the disagreeable impression left by the humans. The rest of us understandably find monkeys and screeching parrots obnoxious, because we encounter them here outside their natural habitat. If we had occasion to ride on elephants under palm trees, we would probably find monkeys and parrots quite acceptable, and maybe even delightful, in such surroundings. But as I say, princes are right to try and dispel something obnoxious with something even more obnoxious.' 'Talking of which,' I said, 'I've just remembered some lines that you yourself may have forgotten:

> When humans are minded to monkey about,
> Bring monkeys indoors, to sort them all out;
> Our bad behaviour will quickly be mended,
> Given that we are from Adam descended.'[108]

Goethe laughed. 'Yes,' he said, 'how very true that is! The only way to deter brutish behaviour is to behave even more brutishly. I recall an incident from my earlier years, when you occasionally came across an aristocrat who was a really nasty piece of work. We were at table, in very distinguished company and in the presence of ladies, when a rich nobleman used very coarse language, to the discomfort and annoyance of all who had to listen to him. Words of reproof would have been wasted on him. So a determined worthy sitting opposite him, taking the view that actions speak louder than words, promptly – and very loudly – committed an act of gross impropriety which shocked everybody, including the boorish aristocrat, with the result that he felt chastened and didn't open his mouth again. From then onwards the conversation took a much lighter and more amusing turn, to the relief of all those present; and everyone was grateful to that determined gentleman for his outrageous audacity, given the excellent effect it had.'

We were all highly amused by this anecdote. The Chancellor then brought the conversation round to the latest clash between the opposition party and ministerial party in Paris, quoting, virtually verbatim, a powerful speech attacking the ministers which had been delivered by a very audacious democrat speaking in his own defence in court. We had occasion once again to admire the Chancellor's formidable memory. There was much back and forth between Goethe and the Chancellor on this matter, and on the press censorship law in particular; it was a fertile topic of conversation, in which Goethe took his usual liberal-aristocratic line while his friend seemed to side, as ever, with the common people.

'I have no fears for the French,' said Goethe. 'They now have such a well-developed understanding of world history that there is no possibility at all of suppressing freedom of thought. The censorship law can only do good, especially as the restrictions on the press do not affect matters of real substance, but are only aimed at specific individuals. An opposition without constraints becomes inert. Restrictions force them to think and be inventive, and this is a very great advantage. Speaking one's mind with brutal frankness is only excusable and in order if one is totally in the right. But a political party is never totally in the right – that's why it is called a "party" – and therefore it does well to adopt an indirect approach, of which the French have always been the great masters. I can command my servant: "Hans, take my boots off!" and he understands. But if I am with a friend and wish him to perform this service, I cannot express myself so bluntly; instead, I have to speak to him in an agreeable and friendly way in order to get him to do me this favour. Constraint stimulates the mind, and for that reason, as I say, I actually welcome some restriction of press freedom. Hitherto the French have always enjoyed the reputation of being the most ingenious of nations, and they deserve to remain so. We Germans like to come straight out with our opinions, and we have not made much progress in the art of the indirect.

'The parties in Paris,' Goethe went on, 'could be greater than they are if they were more liberal and free, and made more concessions to each other than they do now. They have a more sophisticated understanding of world history than the English, whose parliament is made up of powerful opposing forces that create a deadlock, and where one man's visionary ideas struggle to get a hearing – witness Canning, and all the carping criticism directed against that great statesman.'

We stood up to leave. But Goethe was in such lively form that we carried on talking for a while as we stood there. He finally bade us an affectionate farewell, and I accompanied the Chancellor as far as his house. It was a fine evening, and we talked a great deal about Goethe as we walked. We were especially struck by his observation that an opposition without constraints becomes inert.

Sunday 15 July 1827

I called on Goethe this evening after eight, finding him just returned from his garden. 'See what I've got here?' he said. 'A novel in three volumes. And who do you think it's by? Manzoni!' I examined the books, which were very handsomely bound and contained an inscription to Goethe. 'Manzoni has been busy,' I said. 'Yes, he gets on with it,' said Goethe. 'I don't know anything of Manzoni's,' I said, 'apart from his ode to Napoleon, which I read again only recently, in your translation, and admired enormously. Every stanza is a picture in itself.' 'You're right,' said Goethe, 'the ode is superb. But does anybody talk about it in Germany, do you think? It might as well not exist, and yet it is the best poem that's been written on the subject.'

Goethe carried on reading the English newspapers, which I had found him poring over when I came in. I picked up a copy of Carlyle's *German Romance*, his translations of German novels – the volume containing Musäus and Fouqué. The Englishman, who is intimately acquainted with our literature, had prefaced each translated work with a brief biography and critical appraisal of the author.[109] I read the introduction to Fouqué and noted with pleasure that the biographical part was written with wit and great attention to detail, while the critical standpoint from which this popular author was viewed had been set out with great intelligence and much quiet, gentle insight into his poetic merits. At one point the Englishman cleverly compares our Fouqué to the voice of a singer who has no great range and only a few notes, but who knows how to make those few notes sound wonderful. Elsewhere he uses an ecclesiastical analogy to make the same point, remarking that Fouqué's position in the poetic Church might not be that of a bishop or other high-ranking cleric, but, contenting himself with the functions of a chaplain, he acquits himself admirably in this middling office.

While I was reading this, Goethe had withdrawn into his back room. He sent his manservant in to invite me to join him for a while, which I did. 'Sit down with me for a bit,' he said, 'and we'll talk a little more. A new translation of Sophocles has also arrived. It reads well and seems to be very competently done. I shall compare it with Solger. So – what do you think of Carlyle?' I told him what I had read about Fouqué. 'Isn't it good?' said Goethe. 'There are clever people across the sea, too, who know us, and know how to appreciate us.

'Mind you,' Goethe went on, 'we Germans also have some clever people in other disciplines, too. I've just been reading a very fine review of Schlosser by a historian writing in the *Berliner Jahrbücher*. It is signed "Heinrich Leo", a name I haven't come across – we must look into him. He is better than the French, which is saying something for a historian. The French are too wedded to the real and cannot get their heads around the ideal – while our German is completely at home with it. He has some wonderful things to say about the Indian caste system. There is a lot of talk about aristocracy and democracy, but the matter is very simple, really. In our youth, when we own nothing, or attach no value to steady ownership, we are democrats. But if, in the course of a long life, we come into property, we not only want it to be secure, we also want our children and grandchildren to carry on enjoying it in peace. Which is why we are all, without exception, aristocrats in our old age, whatever we may have thought in our youth. Leo writes very perceptively on this point.

'Aesthetics is where we are weakest, and we will be waiting a long time before a man like Carlyle comes along again. But it is very nice to think, now that there is so much contact between the French, the English and the Germans, that we shall be in a position to correct each other. That is the great advantage of a world literature, as will become increasingly apparent over time. Carlyle has written a critical biography of Schiller that it is hard to imagine any German author writing. We, on the other hand, have a very clear idea of Shakespeare and Byron, and are perhaps better able to appreciate their merits than the English themselves.'

Wednesday 18 July 1827

'I have to tell you,' was Goethe's opening remark at dinner, 'that Manzoni's novel surpasses anything else we have seen in this genre.[110] Suffice it to say that the inner world of the book, everything that comes from the heart of the writer, is perfectly realized, and that his treatment of the outer world – the descriptions of locale and that kind of thing – is every bit as good. Now that's saying something!' I was both surprised and excited to hear this. 'The effect on the reader,' Goethe went on, 'is such that you go constantly from being moved to being filled with admiration, and then from admiration you go back to feeling moved again; you alternate between these two sensations the whole time. This, I rather think, is about as good as it gets. In this novel we really see what Manzoni is made of. Here his consummate mind and character are revealed, which he had no opportunity to display in his theatrical works. I am now planning to go straight on to the best of Walter Scott's novels, perhaps *Waverley*, which I have not yet read; and I shall be interested to see how Manzoni compares with this great English writer. Manzoni's sensibility appears so refined here that it is hard to imagine anything comparable; it satisfies us like a perfectly ripe fruit. And there is a clarity in the treatment and the rendering of details that is like the Italian sky itself.' 'Is he at all sentimental?' I asked. 'Absolutely not,' replied Goethe. 'He has sentiment, but not a hint of sentimentality; his feeling for every situation is manly and sincere. I won't say any more today, I'm still reading the first volume. But I'll have more to tell you soon.'

Saturday 21 July 1827

When I entered Goethe's room this evening I found him reading Manzoni's novel. 'I'm on the third volume already,' he said, as he put the book down, 'and all kinds of new thoughts are occurring to me. As you know, Aristotle says of tragedy that it must excite *fear* if it is to be any good. This applies not only to tragedy, but to many other types of literature as well. You find it in my "Gott und die Bajadere"; you find it in every good comedy, in the entanglements of the characters; and you even find it in our *Sieben Mädchen in Uniform*, in the sense that we can never know how the affair is going to turn out for the dear things.[111] There are two kinds of fear here: it can take the form of fright, or it can take the form of trepidation. The latter emotion is aroused in us when we see the characters in the story threatened and engulfed by some moral evil, as for example in *Die Wahlverwandtschaften*. Fright, on the other hand, is felt by the reader or spectator when the characters are threatened by some physical danger – as in the *Galeerensklaven*,[112] for example, or in *Der Freischütz*.[113] In fact, the scene in the Wolf's Glen is more than frightening; everyone who watches it feels a sense of utter annihilation.

'It's this feeling of fright that Manzoni uses to such wonderful effect by dissolving it into stirring emotion and leading us via this sensation to a state of admiration. The feeling of fright is a physical reaction, and every reader will feel it; admiration, on the other hand, comes from a recognition of the author's skilful handling of every situation, and only the connoisseur will be fortunate enough to experience this sensation. What do you reckon to my new aesthetic? If I were younger, I would write something based on this theory, although it wouldn't be on the same scale as Manzoni's work.

'I am really curious to know what the gentlemen at the *Globe* will make of this novel. They are clever enough to recognize its fine qualities, and the whole tendency of the work is grist to the mill of these liberals, even though Manzoni has taken a very moderate line. But the French rarely welcome a work with open arms the way we do; they are not happy just to go along with the author's point of view, but always find something, even in the best work, which is not to their way of thinking and which the author should have done differently.'

Goethe then went through some passages from the novel, to

give me an idea of the quality of the writing. 'Manzoni has *four* big advantages,' he then went on, 'which have contributed to the excellence of his book. First, he is an outstanding historian, which has given his literary work a dignity and validity that raise it far above what we normally expect a novel to be. Secondly, Catholicism has been a help to him, since it gives rise to many situations of a poetic nature which he would not have encountered as a Protestant. Thirdly, his work has benefited from the fact that its author has suffered a great deal in revolutionary struggles, which, though he was not involved in them personally, have affected his friends and ruined some of them. Fourthly and lastly, it helps this novel that the action takes place in the delightful area around Lake Como, whose sights and sounds the writer has absorbed since his early youth, so that he knows the area inside out. From this the book derives one of its main strengths, namely the clear and admirably detailed descriptions of the locale.'

Monday 23 July 1827

When I called at Goethe's house shortly before eight this evening and asked after him, I was told that he had not yet returned from the garden. I therefore went to meet him and found him in the park, sitting on a bench in the cool shade of some lime trees, his grandson Wolfgang by his side.

Goethe seemed pleased when he saw me coming, and motioned me to sit down next to him. We had scarcely exchanged the usual pleasantries by way of greeting when the conversation turned to Manzoni again.

'I said to you the other day,' began Goethe, 'that the historian was a great help to the poet in this novel. But now, in the third volume, I find that the historian has played a mean trick on the poet: all of a sudden, Signor Manzoni casts aside the mantle of the poet and stands before us, for quite some time, as the naked historian. This happens when he is describing war, famine and pestilence – things which are repellent anyway, but when chronicled in long-winded detail in this dry account they become quite unbearable. The German translator must try to avoid this mistake; he needs to cut the description of war and famine substantially, while the account of the plague needs to be cut by two-thirds, leaving only as much as is necessary to explain what happens to the characters. If Manzoni had had a friend at his side to advise him, he could easily have avoided this mistake. But as a historian, he had too much respect for the facts. This creates problems for him in his dramatic works, too, but there he gets out of it by incorporating the extraneous historical material in the form of notes. In this case, though, he could not find a way to offload his historical baggage and just let go of it. This is very curious. However, as soon as the novel's characters reappear, the poet stands before us again in all his glory, and compels us to admire him again in the same old way.'

We stood up and headed back towards the house. 'It is very hard to understand,' said Goethe, 'how a writer like Manzoni, who is able to produce such an admirable piece of work, could have offended against poetry even for a moment. But the explanation is simple, and it's this: Manzoni is a born poet, just as Schiller was, but ours is such a wretched age that in the human life all around him the poet can find no nature fit for his use. For his own edification Schiller took up two great subjects of study, namely philosophy and history, while Manzoni had recourse to history alone. Schiller's *Wallenstein* is so great that there is nothing else of its kind that comes close; but you'll find that these two powerful aids, history and philosophy, get in the way of the work at certain points and detract from its purely poetic impact. Likewise Manzoni, who suffers from an excessive weight of history.'

'Your Excellency,' I said, 'speaks things of great import, and it is a joy to listen to you.' 'Well,' said Goethe, 'Manzoni inspires great thoughts.' He was about to continue his observations when the Chancellor met us at the gate to Goethe's private garden and our conversation was interrupted. We were glad to see him, and we both accompanied Goethe up the back stairs, through the Room of Busts and into the long room where the blinds had already been lowered and two candles were burning on the table by the window. We sat down around the table, where Goethe and the Chancellor then proceeded to discuss other matters.

1827   221

Monday 24 September 1827

I went with Goethe to Berka. We set off soon after eight – it was
a beautiful morning. The road climbs to begin with, and as the
scenery was nothing much to look at, Goethe talked of literary
matters. A well-known German poet had passed through Weimar in recent days and had given Goethe his album.[114]

'You wouldn't believe the feeble stuff that's in there,' said
Goethe. 'The poets all write as if they were ill, and the world
one big sickbay. They all go on about the sorrows and woes of
this life and the joys of the hereafter, and even though they are
all unhappy to start with, they vie with each other to see who
can make the others even more miserable. It's a downright
abuse of poetry, which is basically given to us to compensate
for life's little tribulations and make us content with the world
and our situation. But the present generation is afraid of any
genuine strength, and only feels comfortable, and poetic, in the
presence of weakness.

'I've thought of a good name,' Goethe went on, 'to annoy
these fellows. I am going to call their poetry "sickbay poetry";
the other sort I shall call "Tyrtaean", not because it is about
songs of war necessarily, but because it also gives men the courage to cope with life's battles.'

I agreed completely with every word Goethe had said.

Lying at our feet in the carriage was a basket woven from
rushes, with two handles, which caught my attention. 'I brought
it back from Marienbad,' said Goethe, 'where they have these
baskets in all sizes, and I've grown so attached to it that I can't
travel anywhere without it. When it is empty, you see, it folds
up and occupies very little space; when it is full it opens right
out and holds more than you would think. It is soft and flexible, and yet so tough and strong that you can carry the heaviest
things in it.'

'It looks very picturesque,' I said, 'almost classical.'

'You're right,' said Goethe, 'there is something quite classical
about it. As well as being the most sensible and practical thing
possible, it also has the simplest and most pleasing form, so
that you could say it has attained the peak of perfection. I've

found it particularly useful on my mineralogical excursions into the Bohemian mountains. For now it is our breakfast hamper. If I had a hammer with me, I dare say there would be opportunities today to break off little pieces and bring the basket back full of rock samples.'

We had reached the highest point in the road, and had an uninterrupted view of the hills behind which Berka lies. Off to the left we looked down into the valley that leads to Hetschburg, and where, on the far side of the Ilm, there is a hill whose side facing us lay in shadow; and because of the mists in the Ilm valley it appeared blue to my eyes. I trained my glass on one spot, and as I gazed at it the blue became noticeably less intense. I remarked on this to Goethe. 'You can see,' I said, 'what a difference the subject makes, even with purely objective colours. A weak eye augments the cloudiness, whereas an acute eye dispels it, or at least diminishes it.'

'Your observation is entirely correct,' said Goethe. 'With a good telescope you can even make the blue of the farthest mountains disappear. The subject plays a more important part in all natural phenomena than one would imagine. Wieland, in his day, understood this very well. As he liked to say: "It would be easy enough to amuse people if only they were amusable."' We both laughed at Wieland's good-humoured quip.

By now we had descended into the little valley, where the road passes across a covered wooden bridge beneath which the rainwater run-off flowing down towards Hetschburg has carved out a channel for itself, which for now was dry. A gang of road workers was busy building up the sides of the bridge with blocks of masonry cut from red sandstone, which caught Goethe's attention. A stone's throw beyond the bridge, where the road gradually climbs up the side of the hill that separates the traveller from Berka, Goethe asked the coachman to stop. 'We'll get out here for a while,' he said, 'and see if a little breakfast in the open air doesn't go down well.' We got out and took in our surroundings. The servant spread a napkin over a square pile of stones of the kind you often see by the roadside, and fetched the woven rush basket from the carriage, from which he now produced fresh bread rolls, some roast partridges and

1827   223

pickled gherkins. Goethe cut a partridge in half and gave me my half. I ate it standing, as I wandered around our picnic spot; Goethe had seated himself on the corner of a pile of stones. Sitting on the cold stones, with the dew from the night before still lying on them, can't possibly be good for him, I thought, and voiced my concern. But Goethe assured me that he would come to no harm, which put my mind at rest, and I saw it as a new sign of how strong he must feel in himself. Meanwhile the servant had fetched a bottle of wine from the carriage and poured us a glass each. 'Our friend Schütze,' said Goethe, 'knows what he is doing when he takes a drive out to the country every week; we'll follow his example, and as long as the weather holds, this won't have been our last jaunt.' I was very pleased to hear it.

I then spent a most remarkable day with Goethe, partly in Berka, partly in Tonndorf. He talked constantly in the most brilliant way about all manner of things, and also shared many of his thoughts about the second part of *Faust*, which he was then just starting to work on in earnest. I regret all the more, therefore, that I did not note down anything in my diary beyond this brief introduction.

PART TWO

1828

Sunday 15 June 1828

We had not long been sitting at table when Herr Seidel and his Tyrolese singers were announced. The singers were placed in the garden room, where they could be seen easily through the open doors and their singing heard clearly from this distance. Herr Seidel sat down with us at the table. The singing and yodelling of the jolly Tyrolese really appealed to us young people; Fräulein Ulrike and I particularly liked 'Der Strauss' and 'Du, du liegst mir im Herzen', and we asked for a copy of the words. Goethe seemed a lot less enthralled than the rest of us. Or as he put it: 'The taste of cherries and berries, I've heard, is best described by a boy or a bird.' In between the songs, the Tyrolese played all manner of national dances on zithers laid flat across their laps, accompanied by a high-pitched flute.

Goethe's son was called outside and returned shortly afterwards. He went up to the Tyrolese and sent them away. He sat back down at the table with us. We talked about *Oberon*, and how so many people had come from far and wide to see this opera that the tickets were sold out by lunchtime.[1] Goethe's son rose to his feet. 'Dear father,' he said, 'I think we might leave the table now? The ladies and gentlemen may wish to get to the theatre a little earlier this evening.' Goethe found this haste rather odd, as it was scarcely four o'clock yet, but he went along with it and rose from the table, and we dispersed to different rooms. Herr Seidel came up to me and a few others, looking very sombre, and said in a quiet voice: 'There's no point looking forward to the theatre – the performance is cancelled. The Grand Duke is dead! He died on the way here from Berlin.'

We all felt a deep sense of shock. Goethe came in, and we acted as though nothing had happened and talked of mundane matters. Goethe led me across to the window and talked about the Tyrolese and the theatre. 'You can have my box this evening,' he said. 'That gives you time until six; let the others go on, and stay with me so we can chat a little longer.' Goethe's son was trying to get the other guests to leave, so he could break the news to his father before the return of the Chancellor, who had delivered the message earlier. Goethe could not understand why his son was in such a hurry to break up the party, and he seemed quite put out. 'Won't you stay for coffee, at least? It's hardly four o'clock yet!' The others now left, and I too picked up my hat. 'Are you leaving as well?' said Goethe, looking at me in astonishment. 'Yes,' said young Goethe, 'Eckermann has things to do before the theatre.' 'Yes,' I said, 'there's something I wanted to do.' 'Well, you'd better go, then,' said Goethe, shaking his head dubiously, 'but I don't understand what's got into you all.'

We went upstairs with Fräulein Ulrike, while Goethe's son stayed down with his father and broke the terrible news to him.

I saw Goethe later that same evening. I could hear him sighing and talking aloud to himself even before I entered the room. He seemed to feel that a void had opened up in his life that could never be filled. He was inconsolable, and would not let himself be comforted. 'I thought,' he said, 'that I would have gone before him; but God disposes as He thinks best, and all we poor mortals can do is to endure and keep going as best we can and for as long as we can.'

The Dowager Grand Duchess received the news of the Grand Duke's death at Wilhelmsthal, her summer residence, while the young royals were in Russia when they heard. Goethe soon took himself off to Dornburg, to get away from the sadness he saw around him every day and to restore his spirits through fresh activity in new surroundings. Encouraged by an important new French publication in his area of research, he was drawn back to his theory of plants again, and his present rural retreat, where he was surrounded at every step by the lush vegetation of climbing vines and budding blooms, proved most conducive to his studies.

I visited him there a few times, accompanied by his daughter-in-law and grandchildren. He seemed to be very happy and kept on saying how fortunate he was, and how splendidly situated the castle and gardens were. And indeed, from that high elevation one had a magnificent view from the windows. Below lay the valley, full of interesting sights and sounds, with the Saale meandering through the meadows. Over to the east lay a line of wooded hills, above which the gaze wandered off into the far distance; so that this felt like an excellent vantage point from which to watch the passing rain showers disappearing into the distance during the day, and observe the host of stars in the eastern sky at night, followed by the sunrise.

'The days and nights are equally good here,' said Goethe. 'I'm often awake before dawn, and I lie by the open window to revel in the splendour of the three planets now in conjunction, and drink in the growing brightness of the dawn sky. Then I'm outside practically all day, communing spiritually with the tendrils of the vines, which speak good thoughts to me, and of which I could tell you wondrous things. I'm also writing poems again, which are not bad, and all I want, in short, is to be allowed to carry on living like this.'

Thursday 11 September 1828

Goethe returned from Dornburg at two o'clock today, accompanied by glorious weather. He looked fit and very suntanned. We soon sat down to dinner, in the room that gives directly on to the garden, the doors of which had been opened up. He told us about the various visitors he had had and the presents he had received, and seemed to enjoy punctuating his account with little jokes and asides. But underneath it all you could sense that he was feeling a certain anxiety, as people do when returning to their former way of life, defined as it is by all kinds of relationships, expectations and demands.

We were still on the first course when a message came from the Dowager Grand Duchess, conveying her delight at Goethe's return and announcing that she would have the pleasure of calling on him next Tuesday.

Since the death of the Grand Duke, Goethe had not seen anyone from the royal family. He had been in constant contact with the Dowager Grand Duchess by letter, so they must have said what they had to say about their common loss already. But now he had to face seeing her again in person, which was bound to be a little upsetting for both of them, and so he was no doubt feeling a little apprehensive. Nor had Goethe seen the young royals yet, to pay his respects to them as the new rulers of the land. All this now had to be faced, and even though it would not bother him in the least as a distinguished man of the world, it was unsettling for him as a man of talent, who always liked to follow his natural inclinations and throw himself into his work.

He also had to contend with an influx of visitors from every quarter. The meeting of famous natural scientists in Berlin had attracted many distinguished men whose travels took them through Weimar; some of them had written to announce their arrival and were expected any day. Weeks of interruptions, taking away his concentration and disrupting his normal routine, and all the other inconveniences associated with visitors who in themselves were all very worthy – Goethe must have had an eerie premonition of all this as soon as he set foot on the threshold again and walked through his rooms.

What made the prospect of all this even more tiresome was a circumstance that I feel I must mention. The fifth batch of his collected works, which was supposed to include the *Wanderjahre*, has to be delivered to the printer by Christmas. This novel was originally published as a single volume, but Goethe has set about revising it completely, incorporating so much new material with the old that it is now going to come out in three volumes in the new edition. A lot of the work has already been done, but there is still much left to do. The manuscript pages are peppered with gaps waiting to be filled in: here, something is missing from the exposition; here, a neat transition is needed, so that the reader is less aware of the text as a work of compilation; and here, we have very significant fragments, some of which lack a beginning, others an ending. In short, much work still needs to be done on all three volumes in order to make this important book both accessible and appealing.

Goethe gave me the manuscript to look over last spring, and we discussed this major undertaking in some detail at the time, both face to face and in writing. I advised him to devote the entire summer to the completion of this book, and to lay aside all other work in the meantime; he could see the necessity for this and had every intention of doing as I suggested. But then the Grand Duke died; Goethe felt as if his life had been torn apart, and he had to give up all thought of pursuing a literary project that requires peace of mind and a cheerful spirit; it was all he could do to keep on going and try to recover from the blow.

But now, returning from Dornburg in the early autumn and entering the rooms of his Weimar home again, the thought of completing his *Wanderjahre*, for which he only had a few months left, was bound to be uppermost in his mind – and the prospect of all these interruptions, preventing him from quietly getting on with his work, was the last thing he needed.

Given all this, it is not hard to understand why I say that for all Goethe's light-hearted banter at dinner, one could sense an underlying anxiety in him.

There is another reason why I mention these circumstances, and it has to do with a remark of Goethe's that struck me as very curious. It revealed much about his state of mind and his personal character – as I shall now relate.

Professor Abeken in Osnabrück had written to me in the days preceding 28 August, enclosing a birthday present which he asked me to give to Goethe at a suitable moment. He said it was a memento of Schiller that was sure to give pleasure.

When Goethe was telling us at dinner today about all the different birthday presents he had received in Dornburg, I asked him what had been in the package from Abeken.

'It was a curious gift,' said Goethe, 'which gave me much pleasure. A charming lady with whom Schiller took tea had the nice notion of writing down his remarks. She took it all in and recorded it accurately, and after all this time it reads very well, instantly transporting you back to a situation in life that is past and gone, like a thousand other significant moments, but which in this case has fortunately been captured on paper in all its immediacy.

'Schiller appears here, as always, in full possession of his sublime nature; he is as great a man at the tea-table as he would have been in the council of state. Nothing unsettles him, nothing constrains him, nothing can arrest the flight of his thoughts; he speaks his great mind freely, without favour or compunction. He was a remarkable human being – and an example to us all. The rest of us live contingent lives; we are influenced by the people and objects around us; a gold teaspoon troubles us because we think it should be made of silver, and so, paralysed by a thousand minor considerations, we are not able to express freely whatever great things may lie in our nature. We are the slaves of the objects around us, and appear insignificant or important, depending on whether they stunt us or give us space to expand freely.'

Goethe said no more, and the conversation moved on to other topics. But I pondered these curious words in my heart, for they touched upon and articulated my own innermost thoughts and feelings.

Wednesday 1 October 1828

Dining with Goethe today was Herr Hönninghausen from Krefeld, head of a great trading house and an amateur natural scientist with a particular love of mineralogy, who was well informed on many subjects as a result of his extensive travels and studies. He was on his way back from the meeting of natural scientists in Berlin, so there was much talk of matters relating to that, and of mineralogy in particular.

There was also some discussion of the Vulcanists, and the ways in which people form their views and hypotheses about the natural world. Some of the great natural scientists were mentioned in this connection, as was Aristotle, of whom

1828 233

Goethe had this to say: 'Aristotle saw nature more clearly than any of our moderns, but he was too hasty with his opinions. You have to be slow and gentle with nature if you want to get something out of her.

'When I formed an opinion after researching some subject in natural science, I didn't expect nature to prove me right straight-away; instead I sought to learn her ways through observation and experiment, and was content if she was kind enough to confirm my opinion on occasion. If she did not, then at least she prompted me to try a different tack – which I did, in the hope that she might be more willing to vindicate me this time.'

Friday 3 October 1828

At dinner today Goethe and I talked about Fouqué's *Sänger-krieg auf der Wartburg*, which I read at his suggestion. We both agreed that this writer had devoted a lifetime to medieval German studies without deriving any cultural benefit from it in the end.

'Those German dark ages,' said Goethe, 'have as little to offer us as the Serbian songs and other primitive folk poetry. We read these things and take an interest in them for a while, but then we put them aside and move on. Our lives are sufficiently clouded by our own passions and misfortunes, without needing to seek out the darkness of some barbarous antiquity. We need to be enlightened and cheered up, so we should be turning to periods of art and literature that produced brilliant and supremely cultivated men who felt at ease with themselves and so are able to share the blessings of their culture with others.

'But if you want to think well of Fouqué you should read his *Undine*, which is really delightful. He had good material to work with as a writer, of course, and I wouldn't even say that he made the most of what he had. But even so, *Undine* is good and you will enjoy it.'

'I'm not getting on very well with recent German literature,' I said. 'I came to the poems of Egon Ebert from Voltaire, whom I had just read for the first time – those little poems of his addressed to particular individuals, which must be some of the best things he ever wrote. Now I've got the same problem with Fouqué. Immersed in Walter Scott's *Fair Maid of Perth*, likewise the first thing I have read by this great writer, I now find I have to put this to one side and get into the *Sängerkrieg auf der Wartburg*.'

'Well, of course,' said Goethe, 'our modern German writers cannot compete with such great foreigners. But it's good that you are gradually getting to know the literature here and in other countries, so that you can see where writers are going to find the more sophisticated, cosmopolitan culture they need.'

Frau von Goethe now came in and joined us at the table.

'Ah yes,' Goethe went on cheerily, 'Walter Scott's *Fair Maid of Perth* is good, isn't it? Now that is a piece of work! That is the hand of a master! The whole structure of the book is handled with such assurance, and there is nothing on the page that does not carry the plot forward. And what an abundance of detail, both in the dialogue and in the descriptions, both of which are equally superb. His scenes and situations are like paintings by Teniers; in their overall composition they attain the highest level of art, the individual figures are strikingly true to life, and everything down to the smallest detail is executed with loving artistry, so that not a single stroke is wasted. How far have you read?'

'I've got to the place,' I said, 'where Henry Smith takes the pretty minstrel girl home through the streets and back alleys, and where he is met, to his great annoyance, by the bonnet-maker Proudfute and the apothecary Dwining.'

'Yes,' said Goethe, 'that's a good scene. The way the honest, obstinate armourer is driven to the point where he even takes the little dog along in the end, as well as the less than respectable girl, is one of the best things you'll find in any novel. It shows an understanding of human nature that sees right to the heart of the deepest mysteries.'

'I'm also full of admiration,' I said, 'for the way Walter Scott hit on the idea of making the father of the heroine a glovemaker, who through the trade in skins and hides has long had dealings with the Highlanders and continues to do so.'

'Yes,' said Goethe, 'that was a masterstroke. And that in turn

1828

gives rise to all kinds of circumstances and situations that help to move the story along, and, being based on that practical reality, they seem utterly convincing. You'll find that everything in Walter Scott is portrayed with great assurance and attention to detail – and that comes from his extensive knowledge of the real world, which he has acquired through a lifetime of study and observation, and daily discussion of the most important matters. Add to that his great natural talent and the vast range of his interests! You will recall the English critic who compared poets with human singing voices, where some can manage only a few good notes, while others can command the full musical range, from the very lowest notes to the highest. Well, Walter Scott is in the second category. You won't find a single weak passage in the *Fair Maid of Perth*, nowhere that would suggest his knowledge and talent were not up to the task. He is equal to his material in every respect. The King, the King's brother, the Crown Prince, the head of the clergy, the nobles, the Provost, the citizens and artisans, the Highlanders – they are all drawn with the same assured hand and captured to perfection.'

'The English,' said Frau von Goethe, 'are particularly fond of the character of Henry Smith, and Walter Scott does seem to have made him the hero of the book. But he's not my own favourite; I rather fancy the Prince.'

'The Prince,' I said, 'is likeable enough, for all his wild ways, and he is every bit as well drawn as any of the characters.'

'The scene where he is on horseback,' said Goethe, 'and gets the pretty minstrel girl to place her foot on his, so that he can pull her up for a kiss, is a very bold touch and typically English. But you ladies are wrong to take sides like that all the time. You generally read a book to find nourishment for the heart, a hero whom you could love. But that's not really the way to read; the point is not whether you like this or that character, but whether you like the book as a whole.'

'That's just how we women are made, father dear,' said Frau von Goethe, leaning over the table to squeeze his hand. 'Then we must let you charming creatures have your way,' replied Goethe.

Lying next to him was the latest issue of *Le Globe*, which he now picked up. Meanwhile I chatted to Frau von Goethe about some young Englishmen whom I had met at the theatre.

'We really have no idea,' began Goethe again, with considerable feeling, 'what sort of men these fellows at the *Globe* are, how they grow greater and more impressive by the day, as if all imbued with the same sense of purpose. In Germany such a journal would simply be impossible. We are all individualists here, and there's no question of any common accord; everyone's opinions are those of his province, his town, or else they are his own personal opinions, and we'll be waiting a long time before we arrive at any sort of common culture.'

Tuesday 7 October 1828

At dinner today we were a very lively gathering. Besides the Weimar friends, there were also several natural scientists on their way back from Berlin, including Herr Martius from Munich, whom I knew, who sat next to Goethe. We talked and joked back and forth on all manner of topics. Goethe was in particularly good humour, and very communicative. The subject of the theatre came up, and the last opera to be shown, Rossini's *Moses*, was discussed at length. The subject matter was criticized, the music was praised – and criticized. Goethe then gave us his views.

'I do not understand, my friends,' he said, 'how you can separate the subject matter from the music and enjoy each by itself. You say the subject matter is no good, but you ignored it and enjoyed the wonderful music. I really admire the way your bodies work, how your ears are able to listen to delightful sounds while your eyes, the most powerful of the senses, are assaulted by the most absurd spectacles.

'And you can't deny that your *Moses* really is too absurd for words. When the curtain rises, you see people standing there and praying. This is entirely unsuitable. When you pray, so it is written, you should "go into your room and shut the door". The theatre stage is not the place for praying.

'I would have done *Moses* very differently, with a very different beginning. I would have started by showing you how the children of Israel are suffering, put to hard labour by their tyrannical Egyptian overlords, so that the merits of Moses in freeing his people from such shameful oppression become all the more apparent.'

Goethe went on to lay out the entire opera step by step, merrily breezing through every scene and act; it was brilliantly done, and brought the historical subject matter vividly to life, to the delight and amazement of the entire company, who marvelled at the unstoppable flow of his ideas and his sparkling inventiveness. It all went past too quickly for me to take it in, but I do remember the dance of the Egyptians, which Goethe introduced after they had endured the plague of darkness, to express their joy at the return of the light.

From Moses the conversation moved on to the biblical flood, and soon took a scientific turn, encouraged by our bright natural scientist.

'They claim,' said Herr von Martius, 'to have found a petrified piece of Noah's ark on Mount Ararat, and it wouldn't surprise me if they also found the petrified skulls of the first humans.'

This remark gave rise to others in similar vein, and so the conversation turned to the various races of men – black, brown, yellow and white – that inhabit the different countries of the earth. Which then brought us to the question of whether we could really suppose that all humans were descended from the one couple, Adam and Eve.

Herr von Martius favoured the biblical account, which, as a natural scientist, he sought to corroborate by invoking the principle that nature produces her works as economically as possible.

'I have to disagree,' said Goethe. 'I maintain that nature is always lavish, not to say profligate, and that it would therefore make much more sense to suppose that she produced, not just one paltry couple, but human beings by the dozen or hundred.

'When the earth had reached a certain point in its maturity, and the waters had receded and plant life became sufficiently established on the dry land, the epoch of human creation began, and men were brought forth by the power of almighty God wherever the soil permitted – and very possibly on the high ground to begin with. I think it reasonable to suppose that this happened; but I think it a waste of time to speculate on *how* it happened. We will leave that to those who like to busy themselves with unsolvable problems, having nothing better to do.'

'Much as I would like, as a natural scientist, to be persuaded by Your Excellency's views,' said Herr von Martius roguishly, 'as a good Christian I find myself in some difficulty about embracing a view that is not entirely consistent with the biblical account.'

'Holy Scripture,' rejoined Goethe, 'does indeed only talk about one human couple, whom God created on the sixth day. But the gifted men who wrote down the Word of God, as handed down to us in the Bible, were thinking in the first instance about their own chosen people; so if that nation claims the honour to be descended from Adam, we will not argue otherwise. The rest of us, however, as well as the negroes and Laplanders and slender men who are better looking than any of us, surely had different ancestors; and the present worthy company will surely admit that we differ in all kinds of ways from the true descendants of Adam, and that they are way ahead of us, especially where money is concerned.'

We laughed, and the conversation became more general. Provoked to argument by Herr von Martius, Goethe came out with many striking observations which, under the guise of light-hearted banter, nevertheless concealed something more profound.

After dinner the Prussian Minister, Herr von Jordan, was announced, and we withdrew into the next room.

Wednesday 8 October 1828

Tieck was expected for dinner at Goethe's today, returning from his travels to the Rhine with his wife and daughters and Countess Finckenstein. I met them in the anteroom. Tieck was looking very well; the Rhine waters seemed to have done him good. I told him I had read my first Walter Scott novel in the meantime, and how much I had enjoyed this remarkable talent. 'I doubt,' said Tieck, 'if this latest novel, which I haven't read yet, is the best thing Walter Scott has written; but he is such an impressive writer that the first thing of his that one reads always astonishes, no matter how one came to discover him.'

Professor Göttling came in, having just returned from his travels in Italy. I was really pleased to see him again, and ushered him over to a window to hear what he had to say. 'Rome is the place,' he said, 'you *have* to visit Rome if you want to make something of yourself! Now *that* is a city! Buzzing with life, a whole new world! Here in Germany, we cannot excise the petty side of our nature. But the moment we enter Rome a transformation takes place within us, and we feel ourselves to be bigger, like our surroundings.' 'So why didn't you stay longer?' I asked. 'I ran out of money, and my time was up,' he replied. 'But it felt very strange to be crossing the Alps again, leaving the lovely sights of Italy behind me.'

Goethe came in and greeted his guests. He talked about various things with Tieck and his family, and then offered the Countess his arm to escort her in to dinner. The rest of us followed on behind and took our seats, the men and the ladies alternating around the table. The conversation was lively and flowed easily; but I remember very little of what was actually said.

After dinner the Princes von Oldenburg were announced. We all went up to Frau von Goethe's apartment, where Fräulein Agnes Tieck sat down at the piano and sang the lovely song 'Im Felde schleich ich still und wild' in her fine alto voice, conveying the spirit of the situation so perfectly that it made an unforgettable impression on us all.[2]

Thursday 9 October 1828

I dined with Goethe and Frau von Goethe today, just the three of us. As so often happens, a conversation begun on previous days was taken up again and continued. We talked about Rossini's *Moses* again, and fondly recalled Goethe's spirited reimagining of the day before yesterday.

'I don't remember now,' said Goethe, 'what I may have said about *Moses* in jest and good humour. That kind of thing happens quite unconsciously. But this much is certain: I can only enjoy an opera if the story is as good as the music, so that the two move forward in parallel. If you ask me to name a good opera, I would say *Le Porteur d'eau*; the storyline is so perfect that you could perform it without music, as a play, and people would flock to see it.[3] Either composers don't understand the importance of a good libretto, or they can't find competent writers to supply them with good material. If *Der Freischütz* were not such a good story, the music would have struggled to attract the kind of crowds that the opera now gets; so Herr Kind deserves his share of the credit here.'

We talked some more on this subject before turning our attention to Professor Göttling and his travels in Italy.

'I can't blame the dear man,' said Goethe, 'for speaking so warmly of Italy. I remember how it affected me at the time. It's fair to say that it was only in Rome that I felt what it means to be human. I have never again reached such heights or experienced such elation; compared with my state of mind in Rome, I have not known true gladness ever since.

'But let's not dwell on these melancholy thoughts,' Goethe continued after a brief pause. 'How are you getting on with your *Fair Maid of Perth*? How's it going? How far have you got? Tell me what you think.'

'I'm a slow reader,' I said, 'but I've got as far as the scene where Proudfute is struck down while wearing the armour of Henry Smith and imitating his gait and way of whistling, and is found next morning in the streets of Perth by the local citizens, who mistake him for Henry Smith and raise the alarm throughout the city.'

'Yes,' said Goethe, 'that's a very impressive scene, one of the best in the book.'

'What I especially admired,' I went on, 'is Walter Scott's great talent for explaining complicated situations very clearly, so that everything is resolved into a series of separate, distinct tableaux, which leave such a profound impression in our minds that it's as if we are looking down from above, like omniscient beings, able to take in at a single glance things that are happening at the same time in different places.'

1828

'Walter Scott's understanding of art,' said Goethe, 'is altogether remarkable. Which is why people like us, who always want to know *how* a thing is done, are doubly interested in his work and find it wonderfully rewarding. I don't want to spoil the surprise, but you'll find that he does something really clever in the third part. You've already read about the Prince making the shrewd proposal in council that the rebellious Highlanders should be left to kill each other, and also that Palm Sunday is the appointed day when the two warring clans of Highlanders are to come down to Perth and fight each other to the death – thirty men against thirty. Now just you wait and see how Walter Scott arranges things so that one side is a man short on the day of the combat, and how artfully he contrives a long chain of events to get his hero, Henry Smith, to take the place of the missing man on the day. It's a masterstroke, and you'll enjoy it when you get there.

'But when you've finished the *Fair Maid of Perth* you must go straight on to *Waverley*, which is written from a very different perspective, and unquestionably ranks among the best works of world literature. You can tell that it was written by the same man who wrote the *Fair Maid of Perth*, but at a time when he had yet to win the hearts of the public; and so he gives it everything he's got and doesn't put a foot wrong anywhere. The *Fair Maid of Perth*, on the other hand, is written in broader strokes, by an author who is sure of his public and can afford to let himself go a bit. When you've read *Waverley*, you'll understand why Walter Scott still styles himself as the author of that book. For there he showed us what he can do, and he has never written anything better, or indeed anything to equal that first published novel.'

Thursday 9 October 1828

This evening a most entertaining tea party in honour of Tieck was given in Frau von Goethe's apartment. I was introduced to the Count and Countess Medem; the latter told me that she had seen Goethe during the day and could not get over the joy of meeting him. The Count was particularly interested in *Faust* and its continuation, and we carried on an animated conversation about this for a while.

Our hopes had been raised that Tieck might give us a reading, and so it turned out. The company soon retired to a more secluded room, and after we had all made ourselves comfortable on chairs and sofas drawn up in a wide circle, Tieck read us *Clavigo*.

I had read the play many times myself and felt its power, but now it seemed entirely fresh, and it affected me in a way that it hardly ever had before. It was as if I was hearing it acted on the stage, but better than that; the individual characters and situations were more fully inhabited, and the whole thing felt like a performance in which every part was brilliantly played.

It is hard to say which parts of the play Tieck read better: those in which the male characters are roused to passion and anger, or the scenes of calm, rational discussion, or the moments of tormented love. His delivery was particularly well suited to scenes of this last type. The scene between Clavigo and Marie is still ringing in my ears; the oppressed bosom, the faltering and trembling of the voice, words and sounds broken off or half stifled, the panting and sighing of hot breath accompanied by tears – I can still hear it all quite clearly, and will never forget it. Everyone was listening with rapt attention, completely enthralled; the candles were guttering, but nobody thought or dared to trim the wicks, for fear of breaking the spell. The tears that welled up constantly in the eyes of the ladies were testimony to the profound effect of the play – and surely the most heartfelt tribute that could be paid to the reader and the poet.

Tieck had finished. He rose to his feet, wiping the sweat from his brow, but his listeners stayed in their seats as if transfixed; everyone seemed too deeply affected, still, by what they had just experienced to find suitable words of thanks for the man who had produced such a wondrous effect on us all.

But we gradually came to ourselves again. People stood up, chatted and mingled freely. Then we took ourselves off to the adjoining rooms, where a supper had been laid out on little tables.

Goethe himself was not present this evening, but we all felt he was there with us in mind and spirit. He sent his apologies to Tieck, and to Tieck's daughters, Agnes and Dorothea, he sent two shawl pins with a little portrait of himself and red ribbons, which Frau von Goethe presented to them and pinned on their frocks like little medals.

Friday 10 October 1828

This morning I received a package from Mr William Fraser in London, editor of the *Foreign Review*, containing two copies of the third number of that periodical, one of which I gave to Goethe when we dined today.

Once again I found a lively company assembled round the table, invited in honour of Tieck and the Countess, who had agreed to stay on an extra day at the request of Goethe and their other friends, while the rest of the family had left this morning for Dresden.

Much of the talk at table was about English literature, and in particular Walter Scott. This prompted Tieck to point out that it was he who had brought the first copy of *Waverley* to Germany ten years previously.

Saturday 11 October 1828

Among the many important and interesting articles in the aforementioned number of Mr Fraser's *Foreign Review* was a very fine piece on Goethe by Carlyle,[4] which I read closely this morning. I went a little earlier to Goethe's for dinner, so that I would have a chance to discuss the article with him before the other guests arrived.

I found him, as I had hoped, on his own, awaiting his guests. He was wearing his black frock coat and star, which I always like to see him in. He seemed especially youthful and cheery today, and we got talking straightaway about the subject that interested us both. Goethe told me that he, too, had read Carlyle's essay this morning, and so we were able to share our appreciation of the work being done by foreign critics.

'It's a joy to see,' said Goethe, 'how the former pedantry of the Scots has been transformed into seriousness and attention to detail. When I think how the Edinburgh critics treated my work not that many years ago, and when I now see everything that Carlyle is doing for German literature, it is quite evident that things have taken a significant turn for the better.'

'What I particularly admire about Carlyle,' I said, 'is the quality of mind and character that underlies all his work. What matters most to him is the culture of his nation, and so when he finds foreign literary works that he wishes to acquaint his countrymen with, he is less interested in the finer points of artistic technique than he is in the degree of moral edification to be derived from such works.'

'Yes,' said Goethe, 'his actions are always driven by the noblest of sentiments. And he is so earnest – and has studied us Germans so well! He knows our literature almost better than we do ourselves. At any rate, we are no match for him when it comes to our knowledge of English literature.'

'His essay,' I said, 'is written with so much passion and feeling that you can tell there are still many prejudices and objections to contend with in England. *Wilhelm Meister*, in particular, seems to have been placed in an unfavourable light by malicious critics and bad translations. Carlyle, on the other hand, behaves very well. He blithely counters the stupid and defamatory claim that no true noblewoman should read *Wilhelm Meister* by citing the example of the late Queen of Prussia, who had read the book and is rightly regarded as one of the foremost women of her time.'

Some of the dinner guests now came in, and Goethe greeted them. He then turned his attention back to me and I carried on. 'Of course,' I said, 'Carlyle has studied *Wilhelm Meister*, and is so persuaded of the book's merits that he would like it to become more widely known; he would like every educated man to read it with the same profit and enjoyment.'

Before replying to this, Goethe drew me across to the window. 'My dear fellow,' he said, 'I'm going to let you into a secret that will help you on now and stand you in good stead throughout your life: my works will never have popular appeal. Anyone who thinks otherwise and seeks to popularize them is making a mistake. They are not written for the masses, but only for individuals who want and look for this kind of thing, and who are engaged in similar sorts of endeavours themselves.'

He would have said more, but he was interrupted by a young lady who came up to us and drew him into conversation. I turned and talked briefly to the other guests before we then sat down to dinner.

I have no recollection of what was said around the table. My mind was full of Goethe's words, and I could think of nothing else. Of course (I thought to myself), a writer such as he, a man of such towering intellect, a personality of such infinite range – how could he ever become popular? Barely anything of his could ever become popular. The odd song at most, sung by drinking companions and lovesick girls, but meaning nothing to anyone else.

And when you think about it, is it not the same with everything extraordinary? Is Mozart popular? Is Raphael? And don't people go to these great sources of rich intellectual life just for an occasional taste, content to be sustained for a while by something more wholesome?

Goethe is quite right, I thought to myself. A man of his range can never become popular, and his works are only for select individuals who are looking for this kind of thing and are engaged in similar sorts of endeavours.

In general, they are for contemplative types, who wish to explore the depths of the world and mankind and follow in his footsteps. More specifically, they are for those who live life to the full, who seek the heart's joys and woes in the poet. They are for young poets who wish to learn how to express themselves, and how to turn a subject into art. They are for critics, who find in them a template for the principles of literary judgement and how to make a book review interesting and engaging, so that people read it with pleasure. His works are for the artist, because they enlighten his mind in general, and because they teach him, more specifically, which subjects have artistic potential and what, therefore, he should paint and what he should avoid. They are for the natural scientist, not only because they talk about important laws of nature that Goethe has discovered, but more especially because they demonstrate the *method* whereby a man of science must approach nature so that she yields up her secrets.

And so all those with scientific or artistic ambitions dine at the richly furnished board of his works; and whatever they accomplish thereafter bears witness to the universal source of a great light and life on which they have all drawn.

These and similar thoughts were going through my head at table. I called to mind specific individuals, fine German artists, natural scientists, writers and critics, who owe much of their culture to Goethe. I thought of brilliant Italians, Frenchmen and Englishmen who look to him and seek to follow his example.

All around me, meanwhile, my table companions had been engaged in lively conversation and banter while enjoying the good fare. I had spoken the odd word, but was not really concentrating on what was being said. A lady had addressed a question to me which I must have answered the wrong way, because now everyone was teasing me.

'Leave poor Eckermann alone,' said Goethe, 'he's always distracted, except when he's at the theatre.'

Everyone laughed at my expense, but I was not in the least offended. I was in a particularly happy frame of mind today. I blessed my good fortune, which, after many strange twists of fate, had led me here, to join the select few who enjoy the company and the confidence of a man whose greatness had been so vividly borne in upon me only moments before, and whom I now saw before me, in person, in all his charm and amiability.

Sweet pastries and luscious grapes were served for dessert. The latter had been sent from distant parts, and Goethe was secretive about their provenance. He handed them round and reached across the table to give me a very ripe bunch. 'Here you are, my friend,' he said, 'try some of these – and enjoy.' I ate the grapes from Goethe's hand with special relish, and felt with heart and soul just how close we were.

We talked about the theatre, and about Wolff's achievements, and how much good that excellent artist had done.

'I know very well,' said Goethe, 'that our older actors here have learned a good deal from me, but Wolff is the only one I can truly call my pupil. I'll tell you a story which I'm fond of repeating, which shows you how thoroughly he had understood my principles and come round to my way of thinking.

'I was really angry with Wolff on one occasion, for various reasons. He was due to perform that evening and I was sitting in my box. I thought to myself: "You must keep a close eye on him tonight, because you're in no mood to let him get away with anything." Wolff came on stage, and I followed his every move with a keen eye. And what a performance he gave! He did not put a single foot wrong. Try as I might, I couldn't catch him out doing anything that even looked as if it went against the rules I had taught him. So there was nothing for it: I had to be friends with him again.'

Monday 20 October 1828

Senior Mining Engineer Noeggerath from Bonn, on his way home from the meeting of natural scientists in Berlin, was a very welcome guest at Goethe's table today. There was much discussion of mineralogy, and our esteemed visitor talked very knowledgeably about the mineralogical deposits and conditions in the Bonn area.

After dinner we went into the room where the colossal bust of Juno is kept. Goethe showed his guests a long strip of paper with outlines of the frieze of the temple at Phigalia.[5] We looked closely at these drawings, and someone observed that when the Greeks portrayed animals they did not really copy from nature, but rather followed certain conventions. Their portrayals of animals, it was argued, are not true to life, and their rams, oxen and horses, as they appear in bas-reliefs, are often very stiff, misshapen and imperfect creatures.

'I won't argue with that,' said Goethe, 'but it is important to distinguish between works from different periods and different artists. Because it is possible to find plenty of examples where Greek artists have not only equalled nature in their depiction of animals, but far surpassed her. The English, who know more about horses than anyone else, have now acknowledged that two heads of horses from the ancient world are more perfect in their form than any breed to be found on earth today. These heads date from the classical Greek period; and if such works astonish us now, the inference is not that those artists had a more perfect nature to work from than the one we have now, but rather that they themselves had become more accomplished as art developed over time, so that they brought their own greatness to the task of portraying nature.'

While this was being said, I was standing by a table off to one side, in the company of a lady, looking at an engraving. So I could only lend half an ear to Goethe's words. But they made a profound impression on my mind.

The guests had gradually departed and I was left alone with Goethe, who went and stood by the stove. I joined him. 'Your Excellency said something very shrewd earlier,' I said, 'when you talked about the Greeks bringing their own greatness to the task of portraying nature, and I don't think it is possible to overstate the importance of that idea.'

'Yes, my friend,' said Goethe, 'this is the crux of the matter. One has to *be* something in order to *do* something. Dante appears great to us, but he had centuries of civilization behind him. The house of Rothschild is wealthy, but it has taken more than a lifetime to amass such a fortune. These things run deeper than we think. Those artists of ours who paint in the German Renaissance style know nothing of this; lacking strength of character and artistic ability, they set out to imitate nature and think they've done a good job. They stand *below* nature. But in order to accomplish something great, an artist first needs to cultivate himself to the point where he is able, like the ancient Greeks, to elevate the meaner realities of nature to the level of his own mind, and to make real that which, in natural phenomena, has remained mere intention, thwarted by internal weakness or external obstacles.'

Wednesday 22 October 1828

Today the subject of women came up at the dinner table, and Goethe said something very nice. 'Women,' he observed, 'are silver dishes into which we put golden apples. My idea of women does not derive from what I see in real life, but is either inborn or has developed within me – heaven knows how. So all my female characters have turned out well; in fact, they are better than any you'd find in real life.'

Tuesday 18 November 1828

Goethe talked about a new issue of the *Edinburgh Review*. 'It's a pleasure to see,' he said, 'the heights of excellence to which the English critics have now risen. There's no trace of their former pedantry, and instead we see only their great qualities. In the last issue, in an article on German literature, someone writes: "There are some poets who always like to write about the things that others would rather forget."[6] Now what do you say to that? We know straightaway where we are, and into which category we should place a large number of our modern literati.'

Tuesday 16 December 1828

I dined alone with Goethe in his study today, and we talked of various literary matters.

'The Germans,' he said, 'just can't help themselves; once a pedant, always a pedant. Now they are arguing and squabbling about various couplets published in Schiller's works and in mine, and they think it a matter of great importance to establish which were really written by Schiller and which by me.[7] As if it mattered one way or the other, as if knowing the answer made any difference, and as if it weren't enough that the things exist in the first place!

'Friends like Schiller and me, close to each other for years, sharing the same interests, in daily contact and conversation with each other – we lived so much in each other's pockets that it was impossible to say if this or that idea came from him or me. We often worked together on these couplets; sometimes it was me who came up with the idea, and Schiller wrote the lines, sometimes it was the other way round, and sometimes Schiller wrote one line and I wrote the other. So who is to say what is 'mine' and what is 'yours'? Only a small-minded pedant could possibly think it mattered in the slightest.'

'We see this sort of thing quite often in the literary world,' I said, 'when, for example, people question the originality of this or that famous man and try to discover where he got his culture from.'

'That's ridiculous,' said Goethe. 'You might as well ask a well-nourished man which bullocks, sheep and pigs he has eaten to make him strong. We are born with certain abilities, no doubt, but we owe our development to a thousand different influences out there in the wider world, from which we take what we can and what suits us best. I owe a great deal to the Greeks and the French, and I am infinitely indebted to Shakespeare, Sterne and Goldsmith. But that doesn't tell you the full story of where my culture comes from; that would be an endless task, and an unnecessary one. The main thing is to have a soul that loves truth and embraces it wherever it is found.

'Anyway,' Goethe went on, 'the world is now so old, and so many eminent men have lived and thought for thousands of years, that there is nothing much new to be discovered or said. Even my theory of colour is not entirely new. Plato, Leonardo da Vinci, and many other excellent men before me have discovered some of the same things and talked about them; but the fact that I discovered them too, and said them again, and that I have sought to reinstate the truth in a confused world – the credit for *that* is mine alone.

'And we must go on repeating the truth, because error is being preached around us all the time – not just by individuals, but by the masses. In newspapers and encyclopaedias, in schools and universities, error reigns supreme, comfortable in the knowledge that it has the majority on its side.

'Truth and error are frequently taught in the same breath, and people cling to the latter. A few days ago, for example, I read an article in an English encyclopaedia about how the colour blue is produced. It started by citing the correct view of Leonardo da Vinci, but then went on, as calmly as you please, to peddle Newton's error, advising its readers to go with that because it is the generally accepted view.'

I laughed in amazement when I heard this. 'Every time I see a wax candle,' I said, 'or the smoke from a kitchen fire catching the light against a dark background, or a light morning mist seen against a patch of shadow, it tells me how the colour blue is produced and why the sky is blue. But what the Newtonians think when they see such things – that the air possesses the property of absorbing all the other colours and reflecting only the blue – I find utterly incomprehensible, and I cannot see what benefit or pleasure they derive from a doctrine where they suspend the use of their brains and their eyes.'

'My dear fellow,' said Goethe, 'these people are not interested in using their brains or their eyes. They are quite happy as long as they have words which they can bandy about – something my Mephistopheles understood, and put rather well:

> Stick to words, that's what I say!
> Then you'll tread the hallowed way
> To the shrine of certain knowledge.
> Mind gone blank? Don't have a clue?
> Then count on words to see you through.'[8]

Goethe recited the passage with a laugh and seemed in general to be in the best of moods. 'I'm just glad,' he said, 'that it's all in print already – and I intend to carry on publishing my views on false doctrines and the people who spread them.'

After a pause he continued: 'There are some very good men coming to the fore in the natural sciences now, and I am delighted to see them. Others make a good start, but they can't keep it up; their subjectivity gets in the way and leads them astray. Others set too much store by facts and collect vast quantities of them – which end up proving nothing. What we lack is the kind of theoretical thinking that is able to infer the existence of primary phenomena and then make sense of their scattered manifestations.'

Our conversation was briefly interrupted by a visitor. When we were alone again the talk turned to poetry, and I told Goethe that I had recently been rereading his shorter poems and had lingered over two of them in particular: the ballad about the children and the old man, and 'Die glücklichen Gatten'.[9]

'I'm quite fond of those two poems myself,' said Goethe, 'even though the German public has not made much of them so far.'

'In the ballad,' I said, 'you have managed to compress a very complex subject into a very small space by using all sorts of poetic forms and devices; I especially like the way the children's past history is narrated by the old man up until the point when it merges with the present, after which the rest of the story unfolds before our eyes.'

'I was thinking about the ballad for a long time,' said Goethe, 'before I wrote it down. Years of reflection have gone into it, and I had three or four attempts at it before it finally worked out in its present form.'

'The other poem, about the happy couple,' I went on, 'likewise has an abundance of motifs; in it we see whole landscapes and human lives, warmed by the sunshine of a lovely spring sky stretching out overhead.'

'I've always liked the poem,' said Goethe, 'and I'm glad that it's caught your attention. And the way it ends, with a double christening, is a nice touch, I like to think.'

We then got on to the subject of his *Bürgergeneral*, and I explained that I had recently been reading this amusing piece with an Englishman, and that we were both very keen to see it performed on stage. 'In terms of the spirit of the piece, nothing about it has aged,' I said, 'and every aspect of its dramatic development has been designed with the stage in mind.'

'It was a very good play in its day,' said Goethe, 'and we had many an entertaining evening with it. Of course, it had an excellent cast, and was so well rehearsed that the dialogue went back and forth very snappily. Malkolmi played Märten, and you never saw anything more perfect.'

'The part of Schnaps,' I said, 'seems to me equally felicitous; I fancy there are not many better or more rewarding ones in the entire repertoire. There is a directness and a presence about this character, and about the whole play, which are just made for the theatre. The scene where he arrives with his knapsack and produces all the contents one after another, where he sticks the moustache on Märten and dons the liberty cap, uniform and sword – that's one of the best.'

'That scene,' said Goethe, 'always went down very well in our theatre back then. The other interesting thing about it was that the knapsack and its contents had a real history. I found it myself during the time of the Revolution, when I was travelling near the French border; the émigrés had passed through that area, and it had probably been lost or abandoned by one of them. All the items that are produced from it in the play were already inside when I found it. So I wrote the whole scene around that, and thereafter the knapsack and all its contents came out whenever the play was performed, to the great amusement of our actors.'

We talked for a while about whether present-day audiences would still find things of interest and value in *Der Bürgergeneral.*

Goethe then asked how I was getting on with my study of French literature, and I told him that I was still reading Voltaire in between times, and that this man's great talent gave me enormous pleasure. 'I still know very little of his work,' I said, 'and for now I am sticking to his short poems addressed to specific individuals, which I continue to read and reread. I find I can't put them down.'

'The fact is,' said Goethe, 'everything that a great talent like Voltaire writes is good, even though his lack of respect is sometimes too much for me. But you are not wrong to give so much time to those little personal poems of his; they are definitely some of the most delightful things he wrote. There's not a line in them that isn't full of wit, clarity, gaiety and charm.'

'And we can see from them how he was connected to all the great and powerful persons of this world,' I said, 'and we note with pleasure what a distinguished figure Voltaire himself cuts; he always seems to think himself the equal of any man, however highly placed, and there is never any suggestion that any royal ever succeeded in discomfiting his free spirit.'

'Indeed so,' said Goethe. 'Distinguished he certainly was. And for all his liberties and audacities, he was always careful not to overstep the mark. Which is perhaps even more remarkable. I can quote the Empress of Austria as an authority in such matters; she often said to me that there was nothing in Voltaire's poems addressed to princely personages that ever crossed the line into impropriety.'

'Does Your Excellency recall the little poem,' I said, 'where he makes a charming declaration of love to the Princess of Prussia, who later became Queen of Sweden, telling her that he had dreamed about being elevated to the ranks of the royals?'

'That's one of his best,' said Goethe, and recited these lines:

> Je vous aimais, princesse, et j'osais vous le dire.
> Les Dieux à mon réveil ne m'ont pas tout ôté,
> Je n'ai perdu que mon empire.[10]

'That is delightful! And what's more,' Goethe went on, 'there has probably never been a poet who could command his talent so readily as Voltaire. There is one story I remember, when he had been visiting a lady friend of his, Du Châtelet, and was about to leave, with his carriage already waiting at the door, when he was handed a note from a large number of young girls in a neighbouring convent, who were planning to mark the birthday of their abbess with a performance of *La Mort de César* and wanted him to write a prologue. Voltaire found the challenge too delightful to refuse; he quickly called for pen and paper, and wrote what they wanted standing up, using a mantelpiece as a desk. It's a poem of about twenty lines, beautifully composed and constructed, and perfectly suited to the occasion – in short, the very best of its kind.'

'I can't wait to read it,' I said. 'I doubt,' said Goethe, 'if it is in your edition, as it has only recently come to light. He wrote hundreds of these poems, and I dare say many of them are hidden away in private ownership.'

'I recently came across a passage in Lord Byron,' I said, 'from which I was glad to see that Byron, too, held Voltaire in very high esteem. And I think we can tell from his works that he read and studied Voltaire a lot and made good use of him.'

'Byron,' said Goethe, 'knew exactly where there was something worthwhile to be had, and he was too clever not to draw from this universal source of light like everyone else.'

The conversation now focused entirely on Byron and on specific works of his, and Goethe had frequent occasion to repeat many of his earlier admiring observations on that great talent.

'I agree wholeheartedly with everything Your Excellency says about Byron,' I replied. 'But however important and impressive he may be as a poet in his own right, I very much doubt whether his works have a great deal to offer for the cultivation of mankind as such.'

'I have to disagree there,' said Goethe. 'Byron's boldness, audacity and splendour: surely we can learn from these? We must take care that we don't look only to what is pure and moral for cultural inspiration. Whatever is *great*, once we are aware of it, serves to cultivate the mind.'

1829

Wednesday 4 February 1829

'I've been continuing my reading of Schubarth,' said Goethe. 'He is a remarkable man, and he has some very interesting things to say, once you translate them into your own language. The main thesis of his book is that there is a point of view outside of philosophy, namely that of plain common sense, and that art and science have always flourished best independently of philosophy, through the free operation of natural human powers. This is very much grist to our mill. I have always steered clear of philosophy; the common-sense point of view has always been my own, and so Schubarth confirms what I have been saying and doing all my life.

'The one thing about him that I do not altogether approve of is that he knows more about some things than he says, so that he is not always entirely honest in his approach. Like Hegel, he drags the Christian religion into philosophy, where it doesn't belong. The Christian religion is a powerful institution in its own right, by means of which fallen, suffering humanity has from time to time hauled itself up from the depths; and if we allow that it has that kind of power, then it stands higher than any philosophy and needs no support from that quarter. And nor does the philosopher need the prestige of religion to prove certain doctrines, such as that of eternal existence. Man should believe in immortality; he has a right to do so, it accords with his nature, and he may trust in the promises of religion. But for the *philosopher* to seek proof of the immortality of our soul in some myth is very feeble and unconvincing. For me, the belief in our eternal existence comes from the idea of activity; for if I carry on working tirelessly until the end of my life, then nature is obliged to give me another form of existence when my spirit has outlived the present one.'

My heart swelled with love and admiration at these words. Never, I thought, has anyone ever stated a doctrine more calculated to inspire us to noble deeds than this one. For who among us would not wish to carry on working and doing to the end of his days, if he finds in this the assurance of eternal life?

Goethe called for a portfolio of drawings and engravings to be brought in. After silently studying some of the sheets and turning them over, he handed me a fine engraving after a painting by Ostade. 'Here,' he said, 'you have the scene with our "Good man and good wife".'[11] I studied the sheet with great pleasure. I saw the interior of a peasant's cottage, where kitchen, parlour and bedroom were all together in one room. Husband and wife were sitting close together and facing each other, the wife spinning, the husband winding yarn; a small child played at their feet. In the background you could see a bed and only the simplest, most basic household utensils; the door opened straight to the outside. The picture perfectly conveyed the idea of simple marital joy; the faces of husband and wife, as they gazed at each other, expressed contentment, ease and a kind of revelling in loving marital feelings. 'The longer one looks at this picture,' I said, 'the better one feels; it has a very special kind of charm.' 'It is the charm of sensuality,' said Goethe, 'which no art can do without, and which pervades subjects of this kind in ample measure. In works of a higher sort, however, where the artist tends towards the ideal, it is difficult to incorporate the sensual element that stops him becoming dry and cold. Now youth or old age may be a help or a hindrance here, and the artist must consider his age and choose his subjects accordingly. My *Iphigenie* and *Tasso* were successful because I was young enough to be able to suffuse and animate the idealism of the material with my own sensuality. Now, at my age, subjects of this ideal nature would no longer suit me, and I am better off choosing ones that already have an element of sensuality within them. If the Genasts remain here I shall write two plays, both in one act and in prose. One will be thoroughly amusing, ending with a wedding; the other will be gruesome and shocking, with two corpses left on stage at the end. The second one dates from the time of Schiller, who wrote one of the scenes at my request. I have given a great deal of thought to both these subjects, and am so familiar with the material that I could dictate either one of them in a week, just as I did with my *Bürgergeneral*.'

'Do it,' I said. 'You should definitely write both plays; it will be light relief after the *Wanderjahre*, like going on a little holiday. And just think how thrilled everyone would be if you wrote something for the stage again – which nobody is expecting.'

'As I say,' Goethe went on, 'if the Genasts decide to stay, I'm not at all sure that I won't oblige you. But without this prospect there would be little incentive, since a play on paper is nothing at all. The poet needs to know what resources he has to work with, and he must write his parts for the actors who are going to play them. So if I can count on Genast and his wife, and if I also include La Roche, Herr Winterberger and Madame Seidel, I know what I have to do, and can rely on them to carry out my intentions.

'Writing for the stage,' he continued, 'is an odd business, and unless you know it inside out you're better off leaving it alone. Everyone thinks that an interesting occurrence must make for interesting theatre. But it isn't so. There are things that are interesting to read about and think about, but if they are acted out on stage they come across very differently; and what enchanted us on the printed page may leave us cold in the theatre auditorium. People think, when they read my *Hermann und Dorothea*, that it would work quite well on the stage. Töpfer rashly chose to try and stage it; but is it worth doing, especially if the performances are not first-rate? And who can say if it makes for a good play in every respect? Writing for the stage is a trade that you have to learn; and it requires a talent that you've either got or you haven't. The two things are rarely found together, and unless they are, nothing good is likely to come of it.'

Monday 9 February 1829

Goethe talked a great deal about *Die Wahlverwandtschaften*, telling me that someone he had never known or seen before thought that the figure of Mittler had been based on him. 'So there must be some truth to the character,' he said, 'and more than one of them in the real world. There's not a single line in *Die Wahlverwandtschaften* that doesn't come from my own experience, and there is more in there than anyone could possibly take in on first reading.'

Tuesday 10 February 1829

I found Goethe surrounded by maps and plans relating to the construction of the harbour at Bremen, a large-scale project in which he took a particular interest.

We then talked at length about Merck, and Goethe read me a poetic epistle that Merck had sent to Wieland in 1776, written in very witty but somewhat earthy doggerel. The piece is a very amusing attack on Jacobi, whom Wieland seems to have overrated in an excessively favourable review in the *Merkur* – for which Merck cannot forgive him.

We also talked about the state of literary culture back then, and how hard it was to move on from the so-called *Sturm und Drang* period to a more refined culture. And about his early years in Weimar, his poetic talent in conflict with the reality that he was forced to embrace, to his own greater advantage, through his position at court and his various administrative responsibilities. Hence the fact that he produced no poetic work of significance during his first decade here. He read several fragments to me. Clouded by love affairs. His father never had any time for court life.

Advantages: that he stayed in the same place, and didn't have to learn the same lessons twice.

The flight to Italy, to restore himself and rediscover his poetic powers. His superstitious belief that he would never get there if anyone knew about it. So all done in complete secrecy. Wrote to the Duke from Rome. Returned from Rome determined to do great things.

The Duchess Amalie. The perfect royal, blessed with the common touch and a liking for the pleasures of life. She was very fond of Goethe's mother and wanted her to come and live in Weimar. He opposed the idea.

Then about the genesis of *Faust*. 'I was working on *Faust* at the same time as my *Werther*. I brought it with me to Weimar in 1775. I had written it on letter paper, with no corrections; for I took good care not to write down a single line that was not good enough to be worth keeping.'

Wednesday 11 February 1829

Dined at Goethe's with Chief Planning Officer Coudray. Coudray talked at length about the vocational school for poor young women and the orphans' institute, describing them as the best institutions of their kind in the region – the former founded by the present Grand Duchess, the latter by the Grand Duke Karl August. Then we talked about theatre scenery and road-building. Coudray showed Goethe the sketch for a royal chapel. He explained where the sovereign's chair was to be placed; Goethe had some alternative suggestions, which Coudray accepted. Soret arrived after dinner. Goethe again showed us the watercolours by Herr von Reutern.

Thursday 12 February 1829

Goethe read me the splendid poem he had just written, beginning 'No being can decay to nothing ...' etc.[12] 'I wrote this poem,' he said, 'as the antithesis of the lines "For all things must decay to nothing, if they would remain in being ..." etc., which are stupid, and which my Berlin friends, to my annoyance, saw fit to display in gold letters at their recent meeting of natural scientists.'

The conversation moved on to the great mathematician Lagrange, whose admirable character Goethe particularly emphasized: 'He was a *good* man,' he said, 'and that's why he

1829 261

was also great. When a good man is blessed with talent, he is always a moral force for good in the world, whether as an artist, natural scientist, poet or whatever.

'I am glad you were able to get to know Coudray better yesterday,' Goethe went on. 'He is not a great talker at social gatherings, but you saw, when it was just us together, what a fine mind and character the man has. He encountered a lot of opposition to begin with, but he has battled on through it and now enjoys the complete confidence and favour of the court. Coudray is one of the most accomplished architects of our time. He has stood by me, and I have stood by him – and we have both gained by it. If only I had known him fifty years ago!'

We then talked about Goethe's own knowledge of architecture. I observed that he must have learned a great deal in Italy. 'It gave me a sense of the sublime and the great,' he replied, 'but no practical skills. The building of the palace here in Weimar taught me more than anything else. I had to get directly involved in the work, and even found myself doing drawings of mouldings. In a way, I did a better job than the professionals, because I had a clearer idea of what was needed.'

Then we talked about Zelter. 'I've just had a letter from him,' said Goethe, 'in which he says that the performance of the *Messiah* was spoiled by one of his female pupils, whose rendition of a particular aria was too soft, too feeble and too sentimental. This feebleness is a characteristic of our age. My own theory is that here in Germany it is the result of trying to get rid of the French. Painters, natural scientists, sculptors, musicians, poets – they are all feeble, with one or two exceptions, and it's no better with the general populace.'

'All the same,' I said, 'I am still hopeful that somebody might compose some suitable music for *Faust*.'

'There's no possibility of that,' said Goethe. 'It would have to contain passages that are repellent, hideous and frightful, and that goes against contemporary taste. The music would have to be similar in mood to *Don Giovanni*; Mozart should have written the music for *Faust*. Meyerbeer could do it, perhaps, but he won't take on something like that; he is too involved with Italian theatres.'

Afterwards – and I don't remember in what connection or context – Goethe made this important observation: 'Whatever is great or wise, exists in the minority. There have been ministers who had the people and the king against them, and they carried out their grand schemes alone. There can never be any question of reason becoming popular. Passions and feelings may become popular, but reason will always be the sole preserve of a few outstanding individuals.'

Friday 13 February 1829

Dined alone with Goethe. 'When I have finished the *Wanderjahre*,' he said, 'I shall go back to botany again, to continue the translation with Soret. I'm just afraid that I shall be taking on too much again, and that it will turn into another nightmare. Great secrets are yet to be discovered; there is much that I already know, and much that I surmise. I'm going to tell you something that will sound a little peculiar.

'The plant grows from node to node and terminates in the flower and the seed. It is no different in the animal world. The caterpillar, the tapeworm, grow from node to node and finally form a head; in the case of the higher animals and humans it is the vertebrae that grow one upon the other, until they terminate in the head, where the powers are concentrated.

'The same pattern that we see in individuals is repeated in collectives. The bees, similarly a series of individuals that come together, produce something as a totality that also completes the series, and is in effect the head of the whole: the queen bee. How this happens is a mystery, hard to put into words; but I may say that I have my thoughts on the subject.

'So it is that a nation brings forth its heroes, who stand at its head like demigods, to protect and save; and so it is that the poetic powers of the French are concentrated in Voltaire. Such heads of a nation are great in their own generation; some endure beyond their time, but most of them are replaced by others and then forgotten by posterity.'

I listened with fascination to these thought-provoking reflections. Goethe went on to talk about natural scientists who are mainly concerned only with proving that their opinions are right. 'Herr von Buch,' he said, 'has published a new work whose very title contains a hypothesis. His paper is apparently about the granite boulders that lie dotted around here and there, and nobody knows how they got there or where they came from. But since Herr von Buch has a theory to promote, which claims that these boulders were spewed forth and scattered about in some sort of violent eruption, he signals this straightaway in his title, which talks about "dispersed" granite boulders; so it's a short step from this to taking the theory as proven – and the unsuspecting reader is ensnared in error before he knows it.

'It takes a lifetime to see the bigger picture, and you need sufficient money to pay the price of experience. Every *bon mot* I utter costs me a purseful of money; half a million of my own private fortune has passed through my hands so that I could learn what I know today; not just my father's entire fortune, but also my own salary and my substantial literary earnings over more than fifty years. I have also seen a million and a half spent on grand projects by royal personages with whom I was closely associated, and whose initiatives, successes and failures were a matter of personal interest to me.

'It is not enough to have talent; it takes more than that to know the way of the world. One needs to live among the great and the good, and have an opportunity to see the cards held by the leading players of the time and to play the game oneself, win or lose.

'Without my work in the natural sciences I would never have got to know people as they really are. No other discipline teaches you so much about pure contemplation and thought, about the errors of the senses and the intellect, or about the weaknesses and strengths of character; in other fields, nothing is really fixed or permanent, and everything is more or less negotiable. But *nature* won't be trifled with; she is always true, always in earnest, always rigorous. And she is always right; the errors and mistakes are always made by man. She has no time for fools; she will only give herself up to someone who is competent, true and pure, and only reveal her secrets to him.

'She is too high for human understanding; a man must be capable of ascending to the highest plane of reason in order to touch the divinity that manifests itself in primary phenomena, both physical and moral, behind which she dwells, and which emanate from her.

'The divinity is at work in the living, but not in the dead; she is found in what is coming into being and passing from one form to another – not in what has already become, whose form is fixed. Hence the fact that reason, which aspires to the divine, only deals with the living and with what is coming into being, while the understanding deals with what has already become and taken shape, so that it might make use of it.

'So mineralogy is a science for the understanding, for practical life, since it deals with things that are dead and no longer coming into being, so that there is no place here for synthesis. Meteorology deals with living things, which we see working and creating every day, and they cry out for synthesis; but there are so many other factors involved that such a synthesis is beyond the ability of any man, and we weary ourselves to no purpose with our observations and studies. We set out in search of hypotheses, imaginary islands; but the synthesis itself will probably remain an undiscovered land beyond the sea. And I am not surprised, when I think how hard it was, even with such simple things as plants and colours, to arrive at some sort of synthesis.'

Sunday 15 February 1829

Goethe greeted me with fulsome praise for my editing work on the natural-history aphorisms for the *Wanderjahre*. 'Throw yourself into the study of nature,' he said, 'you are born for the work. Begin by writing a synopsis of the *Farbenlehre*.' We discussed this project at some length.

A crate arrived from the Lower Rhine containing excavated antique vessels, minerals, miniature altarpieces and carnival poems, all of which were unpacked after dinner.

1829

Tuesday 17 February 1829

We had a long discussion about *Der Grosskophta*. 'Lavater,' said Goethe, 'believed in Cagliostro and his magic tricks. When he had been unmasked as a fraud, Lavater claimed that this was a different Cagliostro; the Cagliostro who worked wonders, he said, was a holy man.

'Lavater was a thoroughly decent man, but seriously delusional. The truth – the whole truth and nothing but – was not his thing, and he lied to himself and to others. So he and I parted company in the end. The last time I saw him was in Zurich, though he didn't see me. I was walking down an avenue in disguise and saw him coming towards me; I turned away to the side, he walked right past me and didn't recognize me. He walked like a crane, which is why he appears as a crane on the Blocksberg.'

I asked Goethe if Lavater had an interest in nature, as his *Physiognomische Fragmente* might lead one to suppose. 'Not at all,' Goethe replied. 'His interests were confined to the moral and the religious. What he says about animal skulls in the *Fragmente* he got from me.'

The conversation turned to the French, to the lectures of Guizot, Villemain and Cousin, and Goethe spoke with great respect of the approach adopted by these men, how they took a fresh and untrammelled view of everything and always went straight to the point. 'It is as if,' said Goethe, 'we had previously entered a garden by all sorts of detours and winding paths; but these men are bold and free-spirited enough to tear down the wall and put in a door at the point where one can go straight through on to the main garden walk.'

From Cousin we got on to the subject of Indian philosophy. 'This philosophy,' said Goethe, 'is not at all alien to us, if what the Englishman says is true.[13] On the contrary: we see repeated in it the various stages that we all go through in life. We are sensualists in our childhood; idealists when we are in love and attribute to the object of our love qualities that she does not actually possess. Love wavers, we doubt her fidelity, and before we know it we are sceptics. The rest of our life is of no account; we let it run its course as it will. And we end with quietism – just like the Indian philosophers.

'In German philosophy there are two important tasks still to be done. Kant wrote the *Critique of Pure Reason*, which has moved things on no end, but the circle is not yet closed. Now we need an eminent and highly able man to write the critique of the *senses*, and of human understanding; and if he were to make as good a job of that, then we could not wish for much more in German philosophy.

'Hegel,' Goethe went on, 'has written a review about Hamann in the *Berliner Jahrbücher* which I've just been reading – and rereading. I think it's very good. Hegel's opinions as a critic have always been sound.

'Villemain is also a very fine critic. The French will never see another talent to compare with Voltaire; but the thing about Villemain is that his intellectual standpoint places him above Voltaire, whose virtues and failings he is therefore able to judge.'

Wednesday 18 February 1829

We talked about the *Farbenlehre*, including the glass tumblers where the obscure figures appear yellow against the light and blue against a dark background, thus allowing us to observe a primary phenomenon.

'The highest state of mind we can attain to,' observed Goethe at this point, 'is wonderment, and if the primary phenomenon excites wonderment we must be content with that. It cannot give us anything more, and we should not look beyond it for anything more; this is where the line is drawn. But the sight of a primary phenomenon is generally not enough for people. They think there must be more to see, and they are like children who look in a mirror and then turn it round to see what's on the back.'

The conversation turned to Merck, and I asked if Merck had also had an interest in studying nature. 'Definitely,' said Goethe; 'in fact, he had some important natural history collections of his own. Merck was a man of many interests. He also loved art – so much so that when he saw a fine piece of work in the hands of a philistine, who he thought was not able to appreciate it properly, he went to great lengths to secure it for his own collection. In such matters he was quite ruthless, and would use any means to get what he wanted; indeed, he was not averse to a bit of elaborate deception, if that's what it took.' Goethe related some very interesting examples of this practice.

'A man like Merck,' he went on, 'will not come again, and if he did, the world would take him in a different direction. It was a good time to be alive, when Merck and I were young. German literature was still a clean slate, on which one looked forward to drawing all kinds of good things. Now the slate is so defaced and congested with scribblings that there is no pleasure in looking at it, and a thinking man doesn't know where to inscribe anything of his own.'

Thursday 19 February 1829

Dined alone with Goethe in his study. He was in very good spirits and told me that he had had a good day, including the successful completion of a piece of business involving Artaria and the court.[14]

We then talked at length about *Egmont*, which had been performed the evening before in Schiller's adaptation. We discussed the various ways in which the play had suffered as a result of Schiller's changes.

'For many reasons,' I said, 'it was not a good idea to cut the part of the Regent; she is integral to the play. Not only does her royal presence raise the tone of the whole play, but her dialogues with Machiavelli give us a much clearer picture of the political situation, especially with regard to the Spanish court.'[15]

'You are quite right,' said Goethe. 'And the stature of Egmont himself is enhanced by the lustre that the affection of this princess casts on him, just as Klärchen also appears a more exalted figure when we see her vanquishing even royal rivals to become the sole object of Egmont's love. These are all very subtle effects, which cannot be tampered with without compromising the whole play.'

'It also seems to me,' I said, 'that with so many strong male characters a single female figure like Klärchen seems somewhat overpowered and weak. The presence of the Regent makes the whole story more balanced. The fact that she is talked about in the play is not enough; she needs to appear in person in order to make a lasting impression.'

'You understand very well how these things work,' said Goethe. 'When I wrote the play I gave everything a great deal of thought, as you can imagine, and so it is not surprising if the play as a whole is seriously compromised by the removal of a principal character who was part of my thinking from the beginning and integral to the whole composition. But there was something violent in Schiller's nature; he often acted on a preconceived idea, without paying sufficient regard to the subject matter he had to work with.'

'Some might say that you were remiss in letting it happen,' I observed, 'and that you allowed him too much freedom in a matter of such importance.'

'One is often more casual about these things than one should be,' replied Goethe. 'And besides, I was very busy with other things at the time. I had no particular interest in *Egmont* or the theatre in general. So I let him do as he pleased. Now, at least, it's a consolation to know that the play is out there in print, and that there are theatres with the good sense to stage it as I wrote it, true to the text and without cuts.'

Goethe then enquired about the *Farbenlehre* and whether I had given any more thought to his suggestion that I write a synopsis. I told him how things stood, and that led on to an unexpected difference of opinion, which I will explain, given the importance of the subject.

As those who have observed it will recall, shadows falling on the snow on a bright, sunny winter's day frequently appear blue. In his *Farbenlehre* Goethe classes this as a subjective phenomenon, based on the assumption that the colour of the sunlight when it reaches us – since we do not live on high mountain peaks – is not pure white but yellowish, owing to the fact that it has to pass through a more or less misty atmosphere; so that the snow, when the sunlight falls upon it, does not appear pure white, but has a yellowish tinge to it. That stimulates the eye to produce the opposite colour, which in this case is blue. So the blue shadow seen on the snow is a so-called 'required' colour, and Goethe accordingly discusses the phenomenon under this heading, and comes up with a logical explanation for the observations made by Saussure on Mont Blanc.

As I was rereading the first chapters of the *Farbenlehre* over the last few days, to see whether I was up to the task of writing the synopsis that Goethe had kindly invited me to produce, the weather conditions were such – snow and sunshine – that I found myself revisiting and re-examining the phenomenon of the blue shadow described above. I was rather surprised to find that Goethe's explanation was founded on an error. I will now relate how I arrived at this insight.

From the windows of my living room I look due south, out on to a garden, which is bounded by a building that in the winter, when the sun is low, casts such a long shadow in my direction that it covers half the garden. A few days ago, when the sky was perfectly blue and the sun was shining, I observed this shaded area on the snow and was surprised to see that it was completely blue. This cannot be a 'required' colour, I said to myself, because my eye is not in contact with any sunlit patch of snow that could produce that kind of contrast; all I see is that mass of blue shadow. But in order to be sure, and to prevent the dazzling glare off the neighbouring roofs from affecting my eye, I rolled up a sheet of paper to make a tube and looked through that at the shaded area, which still appeared blue as before.

So now I was in no doubt that this blue shadow could not be a subjective phenomenon. There the colour was, outside of me, existing in its own right; my subjective self had no influence upon it. But what was it? And since it was there, how did it come to be there?

I looked again, surveyed the scene, and all at once the explanation dawned on me. What can it be, I said to myself, but the reflection of the blue sky, which has been drawn down by the shade and looks to dwell within that shade? For it is written: colour is akin to shade, readily combines with it, and readily appears to us in and through it, whenever the occasion presents itself.

The next few days gave me an opportunity to confirm my theory. I went out into the fields; there was no blue sky, the sun shone through mist, like a heat haze, and shed an unmistakably yellow light on the snow. The sunlight was bright enough to cast strong shadows, and under these conditions, according to Goethe's theory, should have produced a vibrant blue. But there was no blue to be seen; the shadows remained grey.

The next morning the sky was cloudy, and the sun peeped through from time to time and cast strong shadows on the snow. But again they were not blue, but grey. In both cases there was no reflection from a blue sky to give the shadow its colour.

So I was now sufficiently persuaded that Goethe's explanation for the phenomenon in question was not borne out by the natural world, and that the paragraphs discussing this subject in his *Farbenlehre* were in urgent need of revision.

I had a similar experience with the coloured double shadow, which can be seen especially clearly, with the aid of a burning candle, at daybreak, in the early evening at the onset of dusk, and under bright moonlight. Goethe has not expressly stated that one of the shadows involved – the yellow one illuminated by the candlelight – is an objective phenomenon that forms part of the theory of the cloudy media; but such is the case. The other shadow, which appears bluish or a bluish green in poor daylight or under moonlight, he declares to be subjective, a 'required colour', which is produced in the eye by the yellow light of the candle falling on the white paper.

Having observed the phenomenon minutely, I now concluded that this theory likewise was not entirely borne out by the evidence. It seemed to me, rather, that the poor daylight or moonlight entering from outside brings with it a bluish tone, which is then intensified both by the shadow and by the yellow light of the candle 'requiring' the blue; so that here too the observed phenomenon rests on an objective factual foundation.

It is common knowledge that the dawning day and the moon cast a pale light. We know from experience that a face seen at daybreak or in moonlight appears pallid. Shakespeare appears to have known this too; the curious scene where Romeo leaves his beloved at dawn, and each suddenly appears so pallid to the other when they go outside, is surely based on this experience. The fact that such a light makes all things appear pale seems to suggest that it must be suffused with a greenish or bluish tinge, since such a light has the same effect as a mirror made of bluish or greenish glass. The following observations may serve as further confirmation.

The light we see in our mind's eye is likely to be pure white in colour; but empirical light, as perceived by the physical eye, is seldom seen in such pure form. Instead, modified by mists or some other factor, it inclines either to the plus or the minus side, appearing with a yellowish or bluish tinge accordingly. Direct sunlight inclines very definitely to the plus side and appears yellowish, as does candlelight; but moonlight, as well as the daylight we see at dawn and dusk – both of which are not direct but reflected light, which is further modified by twilight and night – incline to the passive, or minus, side and appear bluish to the eye.

Suppose it is dusk, or the moon is shining, and we place a sheet of white paper in such a way that one half is illuminated by the moonlight or daylight, and the other half by the light from a candle. One half will have a bluish, the other half a yellowish tinge, so the two colours will be seen to lie on the passive and active side respectively, with no shadows or subjective heightening involved.

The result of my observations therefore indicated that Goethe's theory of the coloured double shadow is likewise not entirely correct; that there is a larger objective element at work in this phenomenon than he has observed; and that the law of subjective 'requirement' plays only a secondary role here.

If indeed the human eye were so sensitive and susceptible that at the slightest contact with any given colour it was immediately stimulated to generate the opposite, the eye would be constantly transposing one colour into another, which would produce the most disagreeable mélange.

Fortunately, however, this is not the case. Instead, a healthy eye is so organized that it either does not notice the 'required' colours at all, or, if made aware of them, strains to produce them; indeed, this operation requires some practice and skill to succeed, even under favourable conditions.

The defining feature of such subjective phenomena, namely that the eye, in effect, requires a powerful stimulus to produce them, and that, once produced, they are unstable, fleeting and evanescent, has been somewhat overlooked by Goethe, both in the case of the blue shadows falling on snow and in the case of the coloured double shadows. For in both instances we are talking about a barely perceptible tingeing of the surface, and in both instances the 'required' colour is immediately apparent at first glance.

But, having discovered a scientific law, Goethe did what he always does: he supposed it to be at work even in cases where there was no outward evidence for this, thereby exposing himself to the risk of pushing a synthesis too far, and discerning the operation of a cherished law in situations where in fact a very different one applied.

When he brought up the subject of his *Farbenlehre* today and enquired how I was getting on with the synopsis we had discussed, I would have preferred not to mention the points I have just argued, because I could see it would be difficult to tell him the truth without offending him.

But as I was really serious about writing the synopsis, it was necessary, before I could proceed with confidence, to dispel any fallacies first and to discuss and clear up any misunderstandings.

So there was nothing for it but to go forth in faith and confess to him that, after careful observation, I found myself compelled to differ from him on some points, having found that neither his explanation of the blue shadows on the snow nor his theory of the coloured double shadows is entirely borne out by the facts.

I told him about my observations and thoughts on these points; but as I have no gift for developing a detailed and coherent argument in a face-to-face exchange, I confined myself to a brief account of my findings without going into particulars, which I offered to do later in writing.

1829 273

But I had scarcely opened my mouth when Goethe's august and serene countenance darkened, and I saw only too clearly that he did not like my objections.

'Of course,' I said, 'any man who would prove Your Excellency wrong needs to get up very early in the morning. But it is possible for the wise man to miss something in his haste and for the fool to find it.'

'As if you had found it!' scoffed Goethe. 'You belong in the fourteenth century with your idea of coloured light, besides which you're engaging in pure sophistry. Your only redeeming feature is that you are at least honest enough to come out and say what you think.

'What I've found with my *Farbenlehre*,' he went on, in a rather more conciliatory tone, 'is exactly like what happened with the Christian religion. For a while you think you have faithful disciples; but before you know it they go off on their own and form a sect. You are a heretic like the rest – you are certainly not the first one to turn away from me. I have fallen out with some very eminent men over contested points in the *Farbenlehre*. With *** about . . ., and with *** about . . .'. Here he mentioned some very well-known names.

We had finished dinner by now, and the conversation flagged. Goethe stood up and went over to the window. I went up to him and squeezed his hand; I loved him, despite the dressing-down, and felt moreover that I was in the right and that he was the afflicted party.

Before long we were talking and joking again about mundane matters. But as I was leaving, having told him that I would send him my objections in writing so that he could study them more closely, and that it was only my own inability to explain things clearly face to face that prevented him from agreeing with me, he could not resist sending me on my way at the door with some further reference to heretics and heresy, half in jest, half in mocking reproof.

While it may seem paradoxical that Goethe did not take kindly to being contradicted in his *Farbenlehre*, whereas he was always very easy-going about his poetic works and grateful for any informed criticism, we may perhaps solve the riddle by recalling that his work as a poet met with universal approval, while for his *Farbenlehre*, the greatest and most difficult of his works, he received nothing but hostile criticism and rejection. For half a lifetime he had had to listen to the most ignorant objections from every quarter, so it was natural enough that he should find himself on a kind of constant war footing, ready to go on the attack at the drop of a hat.

When it came to his *Farbenlehre* he was like a fond mother, who loves a gifted child all the more, the less he or she is esteemed by others.

He often used to say: 'I don't flatter myself that my achievements as a poet are anything special. There have been excellent writers among my contemporaries, there were even better ones before me, and there will be others after me. But I *am* rather proud of the fact that, in the difficult science of colour, I am the only one in my century who has got it right; and that gives me a sense of superiority over many others.'

Friday 20 February 1829

Dined with Goethe. He is pleased to have finished the *Wanderjahre*, which he will be sending off tomorrow. In the *Farbenlehre* he is coming round somewhat to my view regarding the blue shadows on the snow. He talked about his *Italienische Reise*, which he has just taken up again. 'We're just like the women,' he said. 'When they give birth, they swear they will never sleep with their husband again. And before you know it, they are pregnant again.'

He then talked about the fourth volume of his autobiography, explaining how he plans to approach it, and said that the notes I made in 1824, about what he had already written up and what existed only in outline form, were proving very helpful.

He read to me from Göttling's diary, where he writes with great affection about former fencing masters at Jena. Goethe speaks very highly of Göttling.

1829

Monday 23 March 1829

'I've found a page among my papers,' said Goethe, 'where I describe architecture as "frozen music". And there's something in that, you know; the state of mind produced by architecture is similar to the effect of music.

'Magnificent buildings and rooms are for princes and wealthy men. Those who live in them feel contented and satisfied, and want nothing more.

'Such things are repugnant to my nature. Living in a sumptuous apartment, like the one I had in Karlsbad, immediately makes me lazy and indolent. A modest dwelling, on the other hand, such as the plain room we are in now, tidy in a slightly untidy sort of way, a bit bohemian – that suits me perfectly; it gives my inner self complete freedom to be creative, and to produce something from within myself.'

We talked about Schiller's letters, and the life they had lived together, and how they had constantly encouraged and spurred each other on in their work. 'Schiller seems to have taken a great interest in *Faust*, too,' I said. 'It's very endearing, the way he keeps on at you to write, and then gets fixated on the idea of continuing the story of *Faust* himself. From what I have seen, there was something impetuous in his nature.'

'You're right,' said Goethe, 'he was like all the rest who set too much store by the idea. He was also very restless, and could never leave things alone, as you can see from the letters about *Wilhelm Meister*, where he's forever changing his mind about how I should approach it. I had my work cut out just to stand my ground and make sure that his stuff and mine were not affected by that kind of thing.'

'I read his "Nadowessische Totenklage" this morning,' I said, 'and thought it was a wonderful piece of work.'[16]

'You can see,' replied Goethe, 'what a great artist Schiller was, and how he was able to capture objective reality as well, when he came across some ancient tradition. The "Nadowessische Totenklage" is certainly one of his very best poems, and I only wish he had written a dozen like it. But can you imagine: his closest friends criticized him for this poem because they thought it was not sufficiently idealistic for him! In my experience, my dear fellow, one's friends can be a pain in the neck! Humboldt, for example, said that my Dorothea would never have taken up arms and fought back when she was attacked by the soldiers. But if she hadn't, the entire character of this extraordinary girl, so right for her times and circumstances, would have been lost; she would have been just an ordinary nobody. But as you go through life you will discover more and more that few people are capable of appreciating what has to be, instead of only praising and acknowledging what happens to suit them. And I'm talking about the leading men of the age here; so you can imagine what the general populace thought of me, and how, essentially, I was always on my own.

'Had I not had a solid foundation in the visual arts and the natural sciences, I would have struggled to keep going through those difficult times and the constant stresses and strains they put on me; but that was my salvation, and it also enabled me to support Schiller.'

Tuesday 24 March 1829

'The more highly refined a man is,' said Goethe, 'the more he is subject to the influence of daemons, and he needs to be very careful that his guiding will doesn't lose its way.[17]

'There was definitely something daemonic about my relationship with Schiller. We might have met sooner, we might have met later; but the fact that we met at the very time when my Italian journey was behind me, and Schiller was starting to tire of philosophical speculation, had important and hugely positive consequences for both of us.'

Thursday 2 April 1829

'I will tell you a political secret,' said Goethe at dinner today, 'that will become public knowledge sooner or later. Kapo d'Istrias cannot stay at the head of Greek affairs indefinitely, because he lacks one quality that is essential for someone in his position: he is no soldier. No civilian government minister has ever succeeded in organizing a revolutionary state and bringing the military and army generals under his control. Brandishing a sabre at the head of an army, a man may command and lay down the law, in the certainty of being obeyed; but without that, he's in trouble. If Napoleon had not been a soldier, he would never have been able to rise to supreme power, and by the same token Kapo d'Istrias will not remain the leader for very long; he will quickly be relegated to a secondary role. This is my prediction, and you will see it come true; it's in the nature of things, and the only possible outcome.'

Goethe then talked a great deal about the French, in particular Cousin, Villemain and Guizot. 'These men,' he said, 'see things in the round, and see through to the heart of the matter; they combine an encyclopaedic knowledge of the past with the spirit of the nineteenth century, to wondrous effect.'

From them we moved on to the subject of the latest French writers, and the meaning of the terms 'classical' and 'romantic'. 'I've thought of two new words,' said Goethe, 'that sum up the differences quite well. I call the classical "wholesome" and the romantic "sickly". Which makes the *Nibelungenlied* as classical as Homer, because both are wholesome and sound. Most modern stuff is not "romantic" because it is modern, but because it is feeble, sickly and diseased; and the old stuff is not classical because it is old, but because it is strong, fresh, joyous and wholesome. If we distinguish between the classical and the romantic in these terms, we shall not go far wrong.'

The conversation turned to Béranger's imprisonment. 'It serves him right,' said Goethe. 'His most recent poems have really overstepped the mark, and he has incurred his punishment by his attacks on King and State and peaceful law and order. His earlier poems, on the other hand, are light-hearted and innocuous, and calculated to make people happy – which is probably the best thing that can be said of *chansons*.'

'I am sure,' I replied, 'that the company he kept had an adverse effect on him, and that in order to please his revolutionary friends he said many things that he would not otherwise have said. Your Excellency ought to complete the outline you prepared and write that essay on influences; the more you think about it, the bigger and more important the subject seems.'

'It is altogether *too* big,' said Goethe, 'because in the end everything counts as influence, apart from ourselves.'

'The only thing,' I said, 'is to be clear whether an influence is a hindrance or a help, whether it suits and favours our nature or is contrary to it.'

'That's the main thing, certainly,' said Goethe, 'but that is also the hard part, when our better nature has to battle on through, and not give the daemons any more power than it should.'

Over dessert, a laurel in full bloom and a Japanese plant were brought to the table on Goethe's instructions and placed in front of us. I remarked that the two plants gave off a very different aura; the sight of the laurel made one feel cheerful, easy, mellow and calm, whereas there was something savage and melancholy about the Japanese plant.

'You are not wrong,' said Goethe. 'Hence the fact that the vegetation of a country is said to influence the temperament of its inhabitants. And it's true: someone who is surrounded by tall, stern oaks all his life is bound to turn out differently from someone who wanders every day beneath airy birch trees. But you have to remember that the general populace is not made of such sensitive stuff as we are, and that on the whole they just live their lives in their own little world, not realizing how much we are affected by outside influences. But this much is certain: the temperament of a people is shaped not only by the innate characteristics of the race, but also by soil and climate, diet and occupation. And remember, too, that primitive tribes generally settled in a place that appealed to them, so that the territory they occupied was already in harmony with the innate character of the people.

'Turn round,' Goethe went on, 'and take a look at the paper lying on the desk.' 'This blue envelope?' I enquired. 'Yes,' said Goethe. 'Now, what do you think of the handwriting? Wouldn't you say that the man who wrote that address was someone of large and liberal mind? Who do you think it is?'

I studied the envelope eagerly. The handwriting was indeed

1829

very free and full of flourishes. 'Merck could have written this,' I said. 'No,' said Goethe, 'he was not high-minded or positive enough. It's from Zelter! He had the right paper and pen when he wrote this envelope, so the writing perfectly reflects his great character. I shall add the paper to my manuscript collection.'

Friday 3 April 1829

Dined at Goethe's with Chief Planning Officer Coudray. Coudray told us about a staircase in the Grand Duke's palace at Belvedere which has long been thought very awkward and poorly designed. The old Duke had always doubted whether anything could be done about it, but now, under the reign of the young Prince, it was being successfully altered and improved.

Coudray also reported on the progress of various road-building works, telling us that the road over the hills to Blankenhain had had to be rerouted slightly because of a gradient of two feet to the rod, even though in some places the gradient was still eighteen inches to the rod.

I asked Coudray how many inches were considered normal when building roads in hilly terrain. 'Ten inches to the rod,' he replied. 'That feels comfortable.' 'But surely,' I said, 'when you take any road out of Weimar – east, west, north or south – you soon come to places where the gradient must be a lot steeper than ten inches to the rod.' 'Those are just short, insignificant stretches,' replied Coudray, 'and besides, road-builders often route the road that way on purpose, when they are close to a town or village, so as not to deprive the locals of a little income from the hire of draught horses.' We laughed at this harmless little wheeze. 'And in point of fact,' Coudray continued, 'it's not a problem; coaches can easily manage these sections, and the carters are used to coping when the going gets tough. What's more, since draught horses are usually hired from innkeepers, the carters get a chance to wet their whistle; and they wouldn't thank you for depriving them of that.'

'I wonder,' said Goethe, 'whether it might not actually be better, in very flat terrain, to depart from a straight line in places, and make the road rise and fall a little by design; it would not make the road any more difficult to negotiate, and the advantage would be that the improved rainwater run-off would keep the carriageway dry.' 'I dare say that could be done,' replied Coudray, 'and it would more than likely be a very useful thing.'

Coudray then produced a paper, the draft of a set of instructions for a young architect whom the planning department was about to send to Paris for further training. He read the instructions to us, and Goethe indicated his approval. Goethe had persuaded the ministry to provide the necessary financial support, and we were all pleased that it had worked out; we discussed the safeguards to be put in place to ensure that the young man made good use of the money, and that it would last him the whole year. When he returned, the idea was to install him as a teacher in the new trade school that was to be established, thereby giving a talented young man an opportunity to put his talents to good use. It was an excellent arrangement, and I gave the plan my unspoken blessing.

Building plans and a pattern book for carpenters prepared by Schinkel were then produced and studied. Coudray thought the plates very impressive, and eminently suitable for use in the new trade school.

We then talked about buildings in general, about ways of preventing sound transmission, and about the great solidity of the buildings constructed by the Jesuits. 'In Messina,' said Goethe, 'all the buildings were reduced to rubble by the earthquake, but the Jesuit church and cloister remained intact, as if they had been built the day before. There was nothing to indicate that the earthquake had had the slightest effect on them.'

From Jesuits and their wealth, the conversation turned to Catholics and the emancipation of the Irish.[18] 'It looks as if emancipation will be granted,' said Coudray, 'but Parliament will hedge it around with so many conditions that it cannot possibly become a threat to England.'

'It is pointless,' said Goethe, 'to take precautions against Catholics. The Holy See has interests we know nothing of, and the means to protect them behind the scenes such as we could never imagine. If I were sitting in Parliament now, I wouldn't block emancipation either; but I would have it put on record

1829   281

that when the head of the first eminent Protestant falls by the vote of a Catholic, they should remember me.'

The conversation then turned to the latest French literature, and once again Goethe was full of praise for the lectures of Messrs Cousin, Villemain and Guizot. 'Instead of Voltaire's flippant and superficial manner,' he said, 'they display a depth of learning that at one time you only found among Germans. And the power of their intellect, the way they explore every aspect of a subject and wring the last drops from it, as if they were treading grapes – marvellous! They are excellent, all three of them, but if I had to choose, it would be M. Guizot – he's my favourite.'

We then talked about various aspects of world history, and Goethe had this to say on the subject of rulers: 'In order to be popular, a great ruler needs nothing more than his own greatness. If he has striven and laboured to make his realm happy at home and respected abroad, it doesn't matter whether he drives around in his state coach with all his medals, or rattles along in a cart, dressed in a bearskin and smoking a cigar; he has the love of his people and will be respected whatever. But if a prince lacks personal greatness, and fails to win the love of his subjects by good deeds, he must think of other ways of forging a bond; and there is nothing better or more effective for that than religion, and the shared enjoyment and observance of the same customs. The best advice one could give to any young ruler who wants to be popular is to show himself in church every Sunday, look down on the congregation, and let them gaze at him for an hour. Even Napoleon, great as he was, did not disdain to do that.'

The conversation now reverted to the Catholics, and we agreed that the clergy exercised a great deal of influence behind the scenes. We heard the story of a young writer in Hanau who had recently joked about the rosary in the journal that he edited. The journal was soon forced to cease publication, as a result of the influence exerted by priests in their various congregations. 'An Italian translation of my *Werther* appeared very quickly in Milan,' said Goethe. 'But within a short time not a single copy could be found anywhere. The bishop had got wind of it and instructed the priests in their parishes to buy up the entire print run. I wasn't put out – in fact, I rather warmed to this shrewd fellow, who immediately saw that *Werther* was a dangerous book for Catholics, and I had to admire him for taking prompt and effective action to quietly suppress it.'

Sunday 5 April 1829

Goethe told me that he had driven out to Belvedere this morning to take a look at Coudray's new staircase in the palace, which he thought was a great success. He also told me that a large petrified tree stump had just arrived, which he wanted to show me.

'Petrified tree trunks like this,' he said, 'turn up below the 51st parallel all the way round the earth as far as America, like a belt encircling the globe. One never ceases to be amazed! We have no idea how the earth was formed, and I can't blame Herr von Buch for seeking to indoctrinate people in order to give his theories wider currency. He knows nothing, but nobody else knows any more; so in the end it doesn't matter what is taught, so long as it has some semblance of reason.'

Goethe told me that Zelter wished to be remembered to me, which was most pleasing. Then we talked about his travels in Italy, and he told me that in one of his letters from Italy he had found a song that he wanted to show me. He asked me to hand him a bundle of papers lying on the desk across from me. I gave it to him; these were his letters from Italy. He looked out the poem, and read it to me:

'Cupid, such a wanton, self-willed boy!
You asked to lodge with me some hours.
But many days and nights you've stayed,
And lord it here, master now in my own house.

Banished from the comfort of my bed,
I sit upon the ground, tormented night by night.
You cruelly heap the coals upon the flames,
Squandering my winter store to scorch my sorry frame.

> You have turned my household upside down,
> I search in vain, like one who's blind and lost.
> Such clatter you make, my piteous soul flies forth,
> To fly from you, and leave this life behind.'[19]

I greatly enjoyed this poem, which seemed to me entirely new. 'You must know it,' said Goethe, 'because it's in my *Claudine von Villa Bella*, sung by Rugantino. But I've cut it up there, so people just skate over it and nobody really notices or appreciates it. I do think it is rather good, though. It conveys the situation very neatly, and the metaphor is nicely sustained; it's written in the anacreontic style. We really should have included this song, and others like it from my operas, in the reprint of my *Poems*, so that the composer would have all my songs together in one place.' I thought this was a good idea, and made a mental note for future reference.

Goethe had read the poem beautifully. I couldn't get it out of my mind, and it seemed to be going round inside his own head too. Every now and then he would repeat the last lines quietly to himself, as if in a dream:

> 'Such clatter you make, my piteous soul flies forth,
> To fly from you, and leave this life behind.'

He then told me about a recently published book on Napoleon, written by a youthful acquaintance of the great man, which contained the most extraordinary revelations.[20] 'The book,' he said, 'is no hagiography, but a very sober account. When you read it, though, you see how powerful the truth is, when somebody dares to speak it.'

Goethe also told me about a tragedy written by a young poet.[21] 'It's a pathological piece of work,' he said. 'It is overwritten in parts that don't need it, and underwritten in other parts that do. The subject was good, very good; but the scenes I was expecting were not there, and others that I was not expecting were elaborated with much loving care. So I think we can call it "pathological" – or "romantic", if you prefer to think of it in terms of our new theory.'

After that we carried on chatting for a while, and before I left, Goethe regaled me with lots of honey and a few dates, which I took with me.

Monday 6 April 1829

Goethe handed me a letter from Egon Ebert, which I read over dinner with great pleasure. We spoke warmly of Ebert and Bohemia, and also remembered Professor Zauper with affection.

'Bohemia is a curious country,' said Goethe, 'and I've always enjoyed going there. There is something pure about the culture of their literati still, which is already becoming hard to find in northern Germany, where every nobody devoid of moral principles and higher aspirations puts pen to paper.'

Goethe then talked about Egon Ebert's latest epic poem, and also about the rule of women in early Bohemia and the origins of the Amazon myth.

This brought the conversation round to another epic by a different poet, who had gone to great lengths to get his work favourably reviewed in the newspapers. 'Some good reviews were published,' said Goethe. 'But the *Hallische Literaturzeitung* saw through all that and said plainly what it really thought of the poem, thereby cancelling out all the favourable reviews in the other papers. If someone is up to no good, he'll soon be found out; gone are the days when you could fool the public and pull the wool over people's eyes.'

'It amazes me,' I said, 'that people will go to so much trouble just to make a name for themselves, even stooping to deception.'

'My dear fellow,' said Goethe, 'a name is no small thing. After all, Napoleon smashed nearly half the world to pieces for the sake of a great name.'

There was a brief lull in the conversation, before Goethe went on to tell me more about the new book on Napoleon. 'The power of truth is immense,' he said. 'All the mystique, all the illusion, which journalists, historians and poets have woven around Napoleon, are blown away by the shocking reality of

1829

this book; but the hero is not diminished by it – on the contrary, he grows in stature as the truer picture emerges.'

'There must have been some sort of magical power in his personality,' I said, 'to make people fall under his spell, follow him and submit to his will.'

'His personality was certainly of a higher order,' said Goethe. 'But the main thing was that people felt certain of achieving their aims under him. That's why they fell under his spell, as they would with anyone who gave them that certainty. Take actors, for example: they are drawn to any new director who they think will offer them good parts. It's the same old story; that's just how human nature is. No man serves another by choice; but if he knows it will serve his own interests too, he is happy to do it. Napoleon understood men very well, and he knew how to exploit their weaknesses.'

The conversation turned to Zelter. 'As you know,' said Goethe, 'Zelter has been awarded the Prussian Order. But he didn't have a coat of arms yet, though he has a large family, and therefore every hope that the family name will endure. So he needed a coat of arms to give his family social distinction, and I had the bright idea of making one for him. I wrote to him and he agreed; but he insisted on having a horse. "Fine," I said, "a horse you shall have, but one with wings." Take a look behind you, and you'll see a sheet of paper with a pencil sketch I've done.'

I picked up the paper and studied the drawing. The coat of arms looked very impressive, and I admired its inventiveness. The lower field showed the battlements of a city wall, a reference to Zelter's former life as a skilled stonemason. A winged horse was soaring up from behind the wall, reaching for the sky, which represented his genius and lofty aspirations. Above the escutcheon was a lyre, over which shone a star, symbolizing the art by which our excellent friend had won renown under the influence and protection of favourable stars. At the bottom, suspended from the coat of arms, was the Order his monarch had bestowed upon him in just recognition of his great achievements.

'I have had it engraved by Facius,' said Goethe, 'and I'll get a print for you to see. But isn't it nice, for one friend to make a coat of arms for another, and so to confer nobility on him, in a manner of speaking?' We were both much taken with this happy thought, and Goethe sent someone to Facius to fetch a print.

We carried on sitting at the table, finishing our meal with several glasses of old Rhine wine to go with the good biscuits. Goethe was humming something to himself that I couldn't quite make out. Yesterday's poem popped into my head again, and I recited the lines:

> You have turned my household upside down,
> I search in vain, like one who's blind and lost, etc.

'I can't get that poem out of my head,' I said. 'It is very distinctive and expresses so well how love throws our lives into disarray.' 'It evokes a dark state of mind,' said Goethe. 'It reminds me of a painting,' I said, 'by one of the Dutch.' 'There's something of the "Good man and good wife" about it,' said Goethe. 'You've taken the words right out of my mouth,' I said. 'I've been thinking the whole time about that old Scottish ballad, and seeing the picture by Ostade in my mind's eye.' 'But the strange thing is,' said Goethe, 'that neither of these two poems can be painted. They feel very visual and tableau-like, and they create that kind of mood; but they just wouldn't work as paintings.' 'These are good examples,' I said, 'of poetry approximating as closely as possible to painting, without stepping outside its proper domain. Those are the poems I like the best, because they combine observation and emotion. But I struggle to understand how you were able to identify with that sort of situation; the poem feels like something from another age and another world.' 'I won't ever write another one like it,' said Goethe, 'and don't rightly know how I came to write this one – as is so often the way.'

'There's something else that's unusual about the poem,' I said. 'I always think it's written in rhyme, when in fact it isn't. How come?' 'It's all because of the rhythm,' said Goethe. 'The lines begin with a short syllable, followed by a series of trochees, and then the dactyl towards the end, which seems odd, and creates a sombre, plaintive effect.' Goethe took a pencil and divided the line thus:

˘ | ‾˘ | ‾˘ | ‾˘ | ‾˘˘ | ‾˘

Von | meinem | breiten | Lager | bin ich ver | trieben.

We talked about poetic rhythm in general and agreed that such things cannot be analysed. 'The rhythm,' said Goethe, 'flows unconsciously from the poetic state of mind. If we stopped to think about it when writing a poem, we would go mad and produce nothing of any value.'

I waited for the print of the seal to arrive. Goethe began talking about Guizot. 'I am working through his lectures,' he said, 'and they stand up wonderfully well. The ones from this year go as far as the eighth century or thereabouts. He is more profound and perceptive than any other historian I've read. Things we never even think about assume enormous significance in his eyes as the source of major events. What influence, for example, the prevalence of certain religious views has had on history, how the doctrines of original sin, grace and good works have shaped different epochs in different ways – all this we find clearly explained and documented. He is also very good on Roman law as an enduring institution, which disappears from time to time, like a duck diving underwater, but is never entirely lost, always resurfacing at some point, alive and kicking; and the contribution of our own excellent Savigny to this discussion is fully acknowledged.

'Where Guizot talks about the influences that other nations had on the early Gauls, I was particularly struck by what he says about the Germans. "The ancient Germans," he writes, "introduced us to the idea of personal freedom, which was a defining feature of that people." Isn't that good? And isn't he completely correct, in that this idea has continued to inspire us right up to the present day? The Reformation stems from this source, as does the Wartburg Festival – from the sublime to the ridiculous.[22] Similarly, the motley character of our literature, the craving of our poets for originality, each one thinking he has to strike out on his own, as well as the isolation and segregation of our academics, where each man toils away in his own little corner – it all comes from that. The French and the English, on the other hand, stick together much more and take their cues from one another. There is a certain conformity in the way they dress and conduct themselves. They don't want to be different, for fear of calling attention to themselves or inviting ridicule. But the Germans follow their own heads; each one seeks to please himself, without looking to see what others are doing. Because, as Guizot rightly observes, each one has this idea of personal freedom within him – from which, as I say, much that is excellent flows, but also much that is absurd.'

Tuesday 7 April 1829

When I arrived, I found Councillor Meyer, who had been unwell for a time, sitting at table with Goethe, and was pleased to see him looking so much better. They were talking about artworks, specifically Peel and his purchase of a Claude Lorrain for four thousand pounds, which raised Peel very high in Meyer's estimation. The newspapers were brought in; we handed them round and perused them while we waited for the soup.

The subject of Irish emancipation very quickly came up, highly topical as it was. 'What is instructive about it for us,' said Goethe, 'is that things are now coming to light which nobody thought about, and which would never have been aired had it not been for the present crisis. We are never going to get a very clear picture of the Irish situation, because the whole thing is just too complicated. But what we can see is that the country suffers from ills that cannot be remedied by any means – including emancipation, therefore. Hitherto it was Ireland's misfortune to bear its ills alone, and now it is England's misfortune to get drawn in. That's the thing. And the Catholics are not to be trusted. We see how the two million Protestants in Ireland have struggled to hold their own against the superior might of the five million Catholics, and how poor Protestant tenants, for example, living among Catholic neighbours, have been oppressed, harassed and bullied. The Catholics don't get on with each other, but they always stick together when it's a matter of going after a Protestant. They're like a pack of hounds, which bite and fight among themselves, but the moment a stag shows up they act as one and go for it en masse.'

From the Irish the conversation turned to the conflict in Turkey. We expressed surprise that the Russians, as the dominant military power, had not made more progress in their campaign of the previous year. 'The thing is,' said Goethe, 'they did not have enough resources, so too much was expected of individuals, which produced personal acts of heroism and sacrifice without materially advancing the Russian cause.'

'It must be a cursed place,' said Meyer. 'There has always been conflict there from the earliest times, whenever an enemy came down from the Danube and tried to invade through the northern mountains; he always encountered fierce resistance, and hardly ever succeeded in breaking through. If only the Russians can keep their access to the coast open, so that they can be supplied by sea!'

'Let us hope so,' said Goethe. 'I am currently reading about Napoleon's campaign in Egypt, as related by the great man's constant companion, Bourrienne; and his account strips away much of the romantic gloss, leaving the facts revealed in all their naked, sublime truth. It becomes clear that he undertook this expedition simply to fill the time when there was nothing he could do to gain power in France. At first he could not decide what to do; he visited all the French ports on the Atlantic seaboard to inspect the state of the ships and to see whether an invasion of England was possible or not. He found that it was not advisable, and so decided to mount an expedition to Egypt instead.'

I said: 'I have to admire the way Napoleon, at such a young age, was able to toy with the great affairs of the world with such ease and assurance, as if he had had years of practice and experience.'

'My dear fellow,' said Goethe, 'great talents are born with that ability. Napoleon handled the world the way Hummel handles his piano; both seem miraculous to us, both are beyond our comprehension, and yet it is so, and we see it with our own eyes. What is especially great about Napoleon is that he was always the same person; before a battle, during a battle, after a victory or after a defeat, he always had his feet firmly on the ground, and always knew exactly what to do. He was always in his element, equal to every moment and every situation, just as it is all the same to Hummel whether he is playing an adagio or an allegro, or notes in the higher or lower register. This kind of facility is invariably the hallmark of a true talent, whether practising the arts of peace or of war, at the piano or behind the artillery.

'What this book shows us, though,' Goethe went on, 'is the extent to which his Egyptian campaign has been mythologized. Some things turn out to be true, but a lot of it is not true at all – and most of it happened differently anyway. It's true that he had eight hundred Turkish prisoners shot; but this appears to have been the considered decision of a protracted council of war, which concluded, after reviewing all the circumstances, that there was no way of saving them. The story that he climbed down inside the pyramids is pure invention; he stayed safely outside, and got others to tell him what they had seen down there.

'As for the story that he dressed up in Oriental costume, the truth here turns out to be slightly different. He played this party game just the once, at home, parading before his intimates just to see how it looked. But the turban didn't suit him – it never looks right on anyone with an elongated head – and so he never donned Oriental dress again.

'However, he really did visit the victims of the plague, to show that it was possible to conquer the plague by conquering one's own fear. And he is quite right about that. I can recount an incident from my own life, when there was an outbreak of typhus fever and I was unavoidably exposed to infection, and it was only by force of will that I warded off the disease. It is incredible what the moral will can accomplish in such circumstances! It seems to permeate the entire body, activating its defences to fight off all harmful influences. Fear, on the other hand, is a state of inert weakness and susceptibility, in which it is easy for any enemy to take possession of us. Napoleon understood this very well, and he knew he was risking nothing by setting an impressive example to his army.

'But give the man his due,' Goethe continued in a lighter, jesting vein. 'What book do you think he had in his camp library? My *Werther*, that's what!'

'It's clear from his levée at Erfurt,' I said, 'that he had studied the book closely.'

'He had studied it the way a criminal court judge studies his trial documents,' said Goethe, 'and that's how he talked about it when we met.

'M. Bourrienne's work contains a list of the books that Napoleon had with him in Egypt, including *Werther*. The odd thing about this list is the way the books are classified under various headings. Under the rubric "Politique", for example, we find "Le vieux testament", "Le nouveau testament" and "Le coran", which tells you a great deal about Napoleon's perspective on religion.'

Goethe then proceeded to tell us some more interesting facts from the book he was reading, including the story of how Napoleon and his army were crossing the Red Sea at its northern end on the ebb of the tide, and were partway across the dry seabed when the tide turned and caught up with the rearguard; they had to wade through the water up to their armpits, and so this daring exploit nearly ended the same way as Pharaoh's army. This prompted various new reflections from Goethe on the subject of the incoming tide. He compared it to the clouds, which do not travel to us from a great distance, but form simultaneously in multiple places and advance uniformly along a broad front.

Wednesday 8 April 1829

When I entered, Goethe was already sitting at the table laid for dinner. He greeted me very cheerily: 'I have received a letter,' he said. 'Where do you think it's from? From Rome! But from whom? From the King of Bavaria!'[23]

'I share your delight,' I said. 'But here's a strange thing: I've been out walking, and thinking vivid thoughts about the King of Bavaria for the past hour – and now I hear this welcome news.' 'We often get these intimations of things,' said Goethe. 'There's the letter – sit down here next to me and read it.'

I picked up the letter, Goethe picked up the newspaper, and so I was able to read the King's words for myself without interruption. The letter was dated Rome, 26 March 1829, and written in a very clear and imposing hand. The King told Goethe that he had purchased a property in Rome, namely the Villa di Malta and its gardens, close to the Villa Ludovisi at the north-west end of the city; it is situated on a hill, from where he can see the whole of Rome, with a clear view of St Peter's to the north-east. 'It is a prospect,' he writes, 'that one would travel a long way to see, and which I can now enjoy at any hour of the day from the windows of my own house.' He cannot get over his good fortune at having such a wonderful place to live in Rome. 'I had not seen Rome for twelve years,' he writes, 'and I longed to see her as one longs to see a beloved mistress; but from now on I shall return with the settled feelings one has when looking up a dear female friend.' He then writes about the sublime art treasures and buildings with the passion of a connoisseur who cares deeply about true beauty and the need to foster it, and who feels keenly any lapse in good taste. In its sensibility and style the whole letter had a charm and a humanity that one does not expect from such high-placed persons. I told Goethe how pleasing this was. 'There you see a monarch,' said Goethe, 'who has not sacrificed his innate humanity and charm to his royal majesty. It's something you rarely see, and all the more welcome for it.' I went back to the letter, and noted some more fine passages. 'Here in Rome,' the King writes, 'I can put aside the cares of the throne and relax. Art and nature are my daily delights, artists my table companions.' He also writes that he often passes the house where Goethe lived, and always thinks of him then. He quotes some passages from the *Römische Elegien*, which shows that the King remembers them well, and maybe likes to reread them from time to time on their home ground in Rome. 'Yes,' said Goethe, 'he is particularly fond of the *Elegien*; when he was here he kept on at me to tell him how much of it was actually true, because it all seems so delightful in the poems that there really must have been something to it. People seldom stop to think that a poet can generally manage to make something good out of very little.

'I only wish,' Goethe went on, 'that I had the King's book of poems to hand, so that I could say something about them in my reply.[24] Based on what little I have read of his, the poems should be good. In form and treatment he reminds me a lot of Schiller; and if he is now offering us the contents of a lofty mind in a magnificent vessel such as that, then we are in for a real treat.

'Anyway, I am delighted that the King has settled so well in Rome. I know the Villa, the location is quite splendid, and the German artists all live nearby.'

The servant changed the plates, and Goethe asked him to lay out the large engraving of Rome on the floor of the Ceiling Room. 'I'll show you the beautiful spot where the King is living, so that you can get a good idea of the locality.' I felt very beholden to Goethe.

'Yesterday evening,' I said, 'I read *Claudine von Villa Bella*, and found it a delight. It is so tightly constructed and makes for such an audacious, unrestrained and joyous spectacle that I should love to see it performed on the stage.' 'If it is well acted,' said Goethe, 'it works pretty well.' 'I have already cast the play in my mind,' I said, 'and decided who should play what part. Herr Genast would have to play Rugantino – he is made for the part. Herr Franke would be Don Pedro, because he is of similar build, and it is better if two brothers look a little bit alike. Basko would be played by Herr La Roche, who has the skill, with the right make-up, to give the part the touch of wild abandon that it needs.' 'Madame Eberwein,' Goethe continued, 'would make a very good Lucinde, I imagine, and Demoiselle Schmidt would play Claudine.' 'For Alonzo,' I said, 'we need an imposing figure, a good actor rather than a singer, and I should think Herr Oels or Herr Graff would fit the bill. Who composed the music for the opera, and what is it like?' 'Reichardt did the music,' replied Goethe, 'and excellent it is, too. It's just that the instrumentation is a little weak, in keeping with the taste of the times. We would need to do a little work on that now and make the instrumentation a little stronger and fuller. The composer's setting for our song "Cupid, such a wanton, self-willed boy!", etc., turned out particularly well.' 'The curious thing about that song,' I said, 'is the way it puts you into a pleasantly dreamy state of mind when you read it aloud.' 'It was written in just such a state of mind,' said Goethe, 'so it makes sense that it would have that effect.'

We had finished dinner. Friedrich came in to say that he had laid out the engraving of Rome in the Ceiling Room.[25] We went to examine it.

The panorama of the great metropolis lay at our feet; Goethe quickly found the Villa Ludovisi and, close by, the new property purchased by the King, the Villa di Malta. 'Just look at the location!' said Goethe. 'The whole of Rome is spread out before you; the hill is so high that you can see over the city to the south and the east. I have been inside that house and have often enjoyed the view from those windows. Here, where the city extends out in a point to the north-east, on the far side of the Tiber, is St Peter's, and here, close by, is the Vatican. From the windows of his villa, as you see, the King has an uninterrupted view of these buildings across the river. This long road here, entering the city from the north, comes down from Germany; here is the Porta del Popolo; and I lived in one of these streets just inside the gate, in a corner house. Visitors to Rome are now shown another building where I am supposed to have lived, but it's not the right one. Never mind; these things don't really matter, and we must let tradition have its head.'

We returned to the dining room. 'The Chancellor,' I said, 'will be pleased about the letter from the King.' 'I shall show it to him,' said Goethe. 'Whenever I read the speeches and debates in the French Chambers in the Paris newspaper,' he went on, 'I always think of the Chancellor, and that he would be completely at home and in his element there. Because for that kind of job it's not enough to be clever; you also have to feel the need and the desire to speak – both of which are true of our Chancellor. Napoleon also had this need to speak, and if he was not able to speak, he had to write or dictate. Blücher too, we find, liked to speak, and he spoke well and forcefully – a talent he had developed in the masonic lodge. Our own Grand Duke also liked to speak, although he was laconic by nature; and when he couldn't speak, he wrote instead. He drafted many treatises and laws, and for the most part he did it well. It's just that a prince doesn't have the time or leisure to familiarize himself with everything in the necessary detail. Towards the end of his life, for example, he introduced a new system of payment for the restoration of paintings. It's a lovely story. As is the way with princes, he had taken a mathematical approach to the costing of restoration work, based on measurements and numbers. He had decreed that restoration work should be paid for by the square foot. If a restored picture is twelve square feet in area, the work should cost twelve thalers; if four square feet, the cost is four thalers. Decreed like a prince – but not like an artist. A painting of twelve square feet might be in such good condition that it could easily be cleaned in a day, while another work of four square feet might be in such a bad state that a week of hard work would barely suffice to restore it. But with their military background, princes are fond of mathematical calculations, and they like to do things in style with plenty of measurements and numbers.'

I enjoyed this charming anecdote. Then we talked for a while about art and other topics of that nature.

'I have some drawings,' said Goethe, 'done after paintings by Raphael and Domenichino, and Meyer said something very remarkable about them, which I'd like you to hear.

' "The drawings," said Meyer, "betray a certain lack of technical skill, but you can tell that whoever did them had an intuitive rapport with the pictures in front of him, which has carried over into the drawings, so that they give us a very true sense of the originals. If a contemporary artist were to copy those pictures now, he would draw everything far better and possibly more correctly; but we may be sure that he would not have that same true feeling for the original, and that his drawing, while technically superior, would not give us anything like such a clear and perfect idea of Raphael and Domenichino."

'Isn't that good?' said Goethe. 'And the same sort of thing might be true of translations. Voss, for example, has certainly given us an excellent translation of Homer; but it is conceivable that someone else could have had, and conveyed, a more naïve and authentic feeling for the original, without being so accomplished a translator overall as Voss.'

I found all this very compelling and agreed wholeheartedly. As the weather was fine and the sun still high in the sky, we went down into the garden for a while, where Goethe got someone to tie back some branches that were hanging too low across the path.

The yellow crocuses were in full bloom. We gazed at the flowers, then at the path, and found that the images before our eyes appeared violet. 'You recently argued,' said Goethe, 'that green and red each produce the other more readily than yellow and blue, because the former pair are on a higher level and are therefore more perfect, more intense, and more potent than the latter. I cannot agree. Whenever any colour presents itself directly to the eye, it has the same effect of producing the opposite or "required" colour, just as long as our eye is in the right humour, the sunlight is not too glaring, and the conditions for receiving the required image are not unfavourable. With colours, one must take care not to make overly subtle distinctions and determinations, because then one risks being led astray – from the essential to the incidental, from truth to error, and from the simple to the complicated.'

I made a mental note of this as a sound principle for my own studies. By now it was time to leave for the theatre, and I made ready to go. 'Do make sure,' said Goethe with a laugh, as he saw me out, 'that you survive the horrors of *Dreissig Jahre aus dem Leben eines Spielers* this evening!'[26]

Friday 10 April 1829

'While we are waiting for the soup, here is something for you to feast your eyes on.' With this friendly greeting, Goethe placed before me a book of landscapes by Claude Lorrain.

These were the first pictures by this great master that I had seen. They made an extraordinary impression on me, and my astonishment and delight increased as I turned the pages. The brooding power of the shadowy areas on either side, the intense sunlight beaming forth from the background and reflected in the water, which always created a very dramatic and distinctive effect – these recurring motifs I took to be the embodiment of the great master's artistic credo. I also admired the way each picture was a little world in and of itself, in which there was nothing that did not contribute to the overall ambience. Whether it was a harbour with ships at their moorings, fishermen going about their work, and palatial buildings bordering the water; or a barren stretch of isolated hill country, with grazing goats, a little brook and a bridge, a few bushes and a shady tree, beneath which a shepherd is playing on his pipe as he takes his rest; or a low-lying marshy area, with pools of standing water that convey a welcome sense of coolness in the intense summer heat: in each case the picture was a self-contained world entire of itself, with never a trace of anything that did not belong there.

'Now there you have a complete human being,' said Goethe, 'with beautiful thoughts and feelings, in whose mind lay a world the like of which you will not readily find anywhere out there. His paintings are supremely truthful, but not remotely realistic. Claude Lorrain had an intimate and detailed knowledge of the real world, which he used as a means of expressing the world inside his beautiful soul. And that is what true idealism does: it uses the things of the real world to convey a truth that gives the illusion of being "realistic".'

'That sounds like a very good definition,' I said, 'which would surely apply just as much to poetry as to the visual arts.' 'I should say so,' replied Goethe.

'Meanwhile,' he went on, 'it's probably better if you save the rest of the excellent Claude to enjoy as a dessert, because the pictures are really too good to be viewed too many at a single sitting.' 'My feeling exactly,' I said. 'Every time I go to turn the page, I get a certain sense of trepidation. It's a special kind of trepidation, which I feel in the face of such beauty – rather like what happens to us with a very good book, when an accumulation of beautiful passages compels us to pause, and we can only read on with a certain hesitation.'

'I have written back to the King of Bavaria,' said Goethe after a pause, 'and you shall read my letter.' 'That will be very instructive for me,' I said, 'and I look forward to it.' 'Meanwhile,' said Goethe, 'there's a poem here in the *Allgemeine Zeitung* addressed to the King, which the Chancellor read to me yesterday, and you must have a look at it.' Goethe handed me the paper and I read the poem to myself. 'Well, what do you make of that?' said Goethe. 'These are the sentiments of a dilettante,' I said, 'who possesses more goodwill than talent. He writes in a borrowed high literary language that sings and rhymes for him, all the while imagining that he speaks in his own voice.' 'You're absolutely right,' said Goethe, 'and I agree that the poem is very feeble. There's no external observation at all there; it's a purely mental exercise – and not in a good way.'

'In order to write a good poem,' I said, 'you obviously need to know a great deal about your chosen subject, and those who do not, like Claude Lorrain, have a whole world at their command are unlikely to produce anything of value, no matter how good their idealist credentials.'

'And the curious thing is,' said Goethe, 'that only a natural talent actually knows what is important; all the rest of them get it wrong, by and large.'

'As our literary critics demonstrate,' I said. 'Hardly any of them know what should be taught, and they just make our young poets thoroughly confused. Instead of discussing what is real, they talk about the ideal, and instead of showing the young writer what he lacks, they make him doubt what he already has. For example: anyone who is naturally gifted with wit and humour will undoubtedly make best use of those powers if he is scarcely aware that he possesses them. But if someone were to take to heart the much-touted treatises written about those fine qualities, he would be paralysed by self-consciousness and no longer able to exercise those powers spontaneously; and instead of being helped, as he had hoped, he would be mightily hindered.' 'You are absolutely right,' said Goethe, 'and a great deal more could be said on the subject.

'In the meantime,' he continued, 'I have been reading the new epic by Egon Ebert, and you should read it too, so that we can help him out a little from here, perhaps. The man is really very talented, but this new poem lacks the proper poetic foundation, which comes from reality. Landscapes, sunrises and sunsets, passages where the external world was the one he knew – these are all perfectly well done and could not be bettered. But everything else – things that happened in past centuries, things that belong to legend – is not portrayed with proper veracity, and he has failed to capture the real heart of the matter. The Amazons and their life and deeds are portrayed in that generalized way that young people think of as "poetic" and "romantic", and which commonly passes for such in literary circles.'

'This is an error,' I said, 'that infects all our contemporary literature. Writers shy away from truth that is concrete and specific, for fear that it is not "poetic", and they fall back on truisms instead.'

'Egon Ebert,' said Goethe, 'should have kept to the account in his source chronicle, then he might have made something of his poem. When I think how Schiller used to study the historical record, how painstakingly he researched Swiss history when he was writing *Tell*, and how Shakespeare used the *Chronicles*, taking whole passages from them and inserting them into his plays word for word, I can't see why a young poet today should not do the same. I borrowed whole passages from the *Mémoires* of Beaumarchais for my *Clavigo*.' 'But you have transmuted the material in such a way,' I said, 'that nobody notices the borrowing; it's not just undigested content.' 'If I have,' said Goethe, 'then that's good.'

Goethe then told me a little bit about Beaumarchais. 'He was quite a character,' he said, 'and you must read his memoirs. Lawsuits were meat and drink to him – he was in his element there. Some of the speeches of the lawyers at one of his hearings have survived, and they are some of the most remarkable, brilliant and audacious things ever heard in a court of law. The case in question is famous – and Beaumarchais lost. As he was descending the stairs from the courtroom, he met the Chancellor coming up. Beaumarchais should have given way to him, but he refused, and insisted instead that each should yield part-way to the other. The Chancellor, insulted in his dignity, ordered his followers to shove Beaumarchais aside – which they did; whereupon Beaumarchais promptly turned round, went back upstairs to the courtroom and filed a lawsuit against the Chancellor, which he won.'

I enjoyed this amusing story, and we carried on talking about various things over dinner.

'I have taken up my "Zweiter Römischer Aufenthalt" again,' said Goethe, 'so that I can finally get it out of the way and start on something else. As you know, the published text of my *Italienische Reise* was compiled entirely from letters. But the letters I wrote during my second stay in Rome are not very useful in that regard; there are too many references to home and my life in Weimar, and they don't have much to say about my life in Italy. But they do contain quite a few remarks that reveal my inner state of mind at the time. What I am thinking of doing is to extract these passages and insert them as they stand, one after the other, into my account, so that they impart a certain tone and atmosphere to the narrative.' I thought this was a very good idea and encouraged Goethe in his plan.

'Throughout history,' Goethe went on, 'it has been said over and over again that man should try to know himself. This is a strange demand, which nobody has so far succeeded in meeting, and which in fact nobody should try to meet. With all his senses and strivings, man is dependent on externals, on the world around him, and it is as much as he can do to get to know this world well enough to make it serve his ends. It is only when he feels joy or sorrow that he discovers anything about himself, and so it is only through his own experience of joy and sorrow that he learns what he should seek and what he should avoid. Besides, man is a mysterious creature, who knows not whence he comes or whither he goes; he knows little of the world, and less of himself. I don't know myself either, and God forbid that I should. But what I wanted to say was this: in my fortieth year, living in Italy, I was wise enough to know this much about myself: that I had no talent for the visual arts, and that my attempts in this direction were entirely misplaced. As a draughtsman, I had no natural instinct for rendering physical objects; I was scared of making them too overpowering and tended to draw things too faintly instead. If I was drawing a landscape, starting with the faint background and moving forward through the middle distance, I was always too timid to make the foreground stand out properly, so my pictures never really worked. I also found that I made no progress unless I practised, and if I didn't draw for a while I had to start all over again from the beginning. But I was not altogether without talent, especially for landscapes, and Hackert often said to me: "Come and work with me for eighteen months, and you will produce something that gives pleasure to yourself and others."'

I listened with great interest to this. 'But how can you tell,' I asked, 'if somebody has a genuine talent for the visual arts?'

'True talent,' said Goethe, 'has a natural instinct for form, proportion and colour, so that it very soon learns, with a small amount of instruction, how to get these things right. In particular, it has a strong sense of physical form, and knows instinctively how to give objects depth by the use of lighting. Even in the intervals between practising, it does not stop growing and developing. Such a talent is not hard to recognize, but the master sees it best.

'I visited the palace this morning,' Goethe went on brightly. 'The apartments of the Grand Duchess are very tastefully done, and Coudray, with his Italians, has given us fresh proof of his remarkable skill. The decorators were still working on the walls – some fellows from Milan. I spoke to them in Italian and noted that I had not forgotten the language. They told me that their last job was painting the palace of the King of Württemberg, and that they had then been contracted to Gotha, but failed to agree terms there. At the same time, people in Weimar had heard about them, and invited them here to decorate the apartments of the Grand Duchess. I enjoyed hearing and speaking Italian again; the sound of the language does evoke the atmosphere of the country somehow. These good fellows have been away from Italy for three years now, but they told me they plan to go straight home when they have finished here, after they have painted some scenery for our theatre at the request of

Herr von Spiegel – which you probably won't object to. They are highly skilled men; one of them is a pupil of Milan's foremost stage painter, so you can expect to see some fine scenery.'

When Friedrich had cleared the table, a small map of Rome was brought in at Goethe's request and placed in front of him. 'Rome is no place for people like us to live permanently. If you want to stay there and settle, you must marry and become a Catholic – otherwise you won't last, and you'll have a hard time of it. Hackert was quite proud of the fact that he had stuck it out there for so long as a Protestant.'

Goethe then pointed out the most notable buildings and piazzas on the map. 'These,' he said, 'are the Farnese Gardens.' 'Wasn't it here,' I asked, 'that you wrote the witches' scene in *Faust*?' 'No,' he replied, 'that was in the Borghese Gardens.'

I then feasted my eyes again on the landscapes of Claude Lorrain, and we talked some more about this great master. 'Would it not be possible,' I said, 'for a young artist today to model himself on him?'

'Anyone of similar disposition,' replied Goethe, 'would undoubtedly learn a tremendous amount for his own development by studying Claude Lorrain. But someone not blessed by nature with similar gifts of mind and spirit would merely crib the odd motif from this master and use it as a visual cliché.'

Saturday 11 April 1829

Today I found the table laid in the long room, and for several persons. Goethe and Frau von Goethe welcomed me warmly. Others gradually arrived to join us: Madame Schopenhauer; the young Count Reinhard from the French embassy; his brother-in-law, Herr von D., who was passing through on his way to fight with the Russian forces against the Turks; Fräulein Ulrike; and finally, Councillor Vogel.[27]

Goethe was in especially buoyant mood; he entertained the company before dinner with some good Frankfurt stories, particularly about the rivalry between Rothschild and Bethmann, and how each frustrated the other's speculative ventures.

Count Reinhard went off to court, and the rest of us sat down

1829   303

to dinner. The conversation was agreeably lively; we talked about travel, about taking the waters, and Madame Schopenhauer had interesting stories to tell about the furnishing of her new house on the Rhine, close to the island of Nonnenwerth.

Count Reinhard returned as we were eating dessert and was commended for being so quick; not only had he dined at court during his brief absence, but he had also changed his clothes twice.

He brought us the news that the new Pope had been elected – a Castiglione – and Goethe told the assembled company about the formal procedures that are traditionally observed at a papal election.[28]

Count Reinhard, who had spent the winter in Paris, was able to tell us much of interest about famous statesmen, men of letters and poets. We talked about Chateaubriand, Guizot, Salvandy, Béranger, Mérimée and others.

After dinner, when everyone else had left, Goethe took me into his study and showed me two very remarkable manuscripts, much to my delight. These were two letters from Goethe's youth, written from Strasbourg in 1770 to his friend Dr Horn in Frankfurt, one from July of that year, the other from December. Both were the work of a young man who has a presentiment of great things to come in his life. In the later one you can already detect traces of *Werther*; the relationship in Sesenheim had begun by then, and the happy young man seems to be caught up in a whirl of ecstatic emotions, whiling away his days in a dreamlike state.[29] The handwriting in the two letters was composed, clear and elegant, and the characteristic style of Goethe's mature hand was already recognizable. I could not stop reading and rereading these delightful letters, and I left Goethe feeling elated and profoundly grateful.

Sunday 12 April 1829

Goethe read me his reply to the King of Bavaria. He had written it as if he were actually present, walking up the steps of the Villa and speaking directly to the King. 'It must be hard,' I said, 'to know the right tone to adopt in this kind of situation.' 'For someone like me,' replied Goethe, 'who has consorted all his life with persons of high rank, it's not difficult. The only thing is not to be too familiar, but always to observe a certain degree of formality.'

Goethe then talked about his current editing work on his 'Zweiter Römischer Aufenthalt'.

'From the letters I wrote back then,' he said, 'I see very clearly how every time of life has its own advantages and disadvantages compared with earlier or later years. In my fortieth year, for instance, I was as clear and as knowledgeable about certain things as I am now, and in some respects more so. But now, in my eightieth year, I possess advantages that I would not willingly trade for those.'

'As you were speaking,' I said, 'I was reminded of your *Metamorphose der Pflanzen*, and I can understand very well how you would not want to go back in time from the flower to the green leaves, or from the seed and the fruit to the flower head.'

'Your metaphor,' said Goethe, 'expresses my meaning exactly. Imagine a fully formed, serrated leaf,' he went on with a chuckle; 'why would it want to revert from a state of untrammelled development to the stifling confinement of the cotyledon? And how nice it is that we even have a plant that can serve as a symbol of very advanced age, since it continues to grow and thrive beyond the flowering and fruiting stage, without producing anything more.

'The trouble is,' Goethe went on, 'that we are held back so much in life by misguided ambitions, and we never recognize them for what they are until we let go of them.'

'But how can we tell,' I asked, 'if an ambition is misguided?'

'A misguided ambition,' replied Goethe, 'is not productive, or if it is, then what it produces is of no value. It's not very difficult to see this in others, but to see it in oneself – that's a different story, and it takes a very open mind to do so. And it is not always enough just to realize it; we dither and doubt, and can't make up our minds to let go – in the same way that we find it hard to part from a lover who has given us ample proof of her infidelity. I say this because I remember how many years it took me to

1829   305

see that my ambition to become an artist was misguided – and
how many more years after that to give it up.'

'And yet,' I said, 'your pursuit of this ambition has brought
you so many advantages that it can hardly be called misguided.'

'I have learned a great deal,' said Goethe, 'which is some
consolation. And that's the good thing about every misguided
ambition. Someone who takes up music with insufficient talent
will never become a maestro, but he will learn to recognize and
appreciate a maestro's achievements. Despite all my efforts, I
failed to become an artist; but having tried my hand at every
kind of painting and drawing, I learned to appreciate the
draughtsman's technique, and to distinguish the good from
the mediocre. These are valuable lessons, as indeed misguided
ambitions rarely fail to yield something of value. The Crusades,
for example, undertaken to liberate the Holy Sepulchre, were
clearly a case of misguided ambition; but they did some good,
in that the Turks were permanently weakened as a result and
prevented from conquering Europe.'

We talked about various other things, and Goethe then told
me about a book on Peter the Great by Ségur, which he had found
interesting and illuminating. 'The situation of St Petersburg,' he
said, 'is quite inexcusable, especially when you consider that there
is higher ground nearby, so that the Tsar could have spared the
city itself from flooding simply by moving it a little higher up,
and just leaving the port down at sea level. An old mariner tried
to talk him out of it and predicted that the population would
be drowned every seventy years. There was also an ancient tree
standing there, on which the floodwaters had left their mark in
the past. But it was all to no avail. The Tsar would not let go of
his obsession, and he had the tree cut down so that it could not
bear witness against him.

'You must admit that there is something troubling about
such conduct in so great a man. But do you know what I think
is behind it? We human beings can never entirely leave our
youthful impressions behind, so that even the bad things we
grew up with and got used to, at that happy time of life, are
later remembered with such fondness that we are bedazzled, in
effect, and don't see what is wrong with them. So it was that

Peter the Great wanted to recreate the beloved Amsterdam of his youth in a great city at the mouth of the Neva – just as the Dutch have always been tempted to build new Amsterdams in their far-flung possessions.'

Monday 13 April 1829

Today, after Goethe had told me many interesting things over dinner, I feasted my eyes over dessert on some more of Claude Lorrain's landscapes. 'The collection,' said Goethe, 'is entitled *Liber veritatis*, but it could equally well be called *Liber naturae et artis*, because here we have nature and art at their most refined and joined in exquisite alliance.'

I asked Goethe what he knew about Claude Lorrain's background, and in what school he had been trained. 'His immediate teacher was Antonio Tasso, but this man was a pupil of Paul Bril, so it was Bril's school and teachings that formed his real foundation and came into flower, in a manner of speaking, in him; for what seems earnest and austere, still, in the work of these masters evolved, in the hands of Claude Lorrain, into something supremely graceful, charming and free. He had come as far as anyone could ever go.[30]

'The fact is, it is almost impossible to say from whom such a great talent learned, living as he did in such remarkable times and circumstances. He cast around to see what was there, and took whatever he could find to further his development. Claude Lorrain undoubtedly owes just as much to the Carracci school as he does to the renowned masters who taught him directly.

'Similarly, it is generally said that Giulio Romano was a pupil of Raphael; but you could just as well say that he was a pupil of his times. Only Guido Reni had a pupil who so completely assimilated the mind, spirit and art of his master that he virtually became the same person and did the same things; but this was a special case, which has hardly ever been repeated. The Carracci school, by contrast, encouraged each individual talent to develop freely and follow its natural bent, so that it produced masters who were all different from each other. The Carraccis were born art teachers; they lived in an age when painting in general had reached the peak of perfection, so their pupils were able to learn from the very best examples of work in every genre. They were great artists, great teachers, but I wouldn't say they were exactly what you would call "inspired". I'm sticking my neck out when I say that; but that's how it strikes me.'

After I had looked at a few more of Claude Lorrain's landscapes, I opened a lexicon of artists to see what it said about this great master. We found the following observation: 'His main strength lay in his palette.' We looked at each other and laughed. 'It just goes to show how much you can learn,' said Goethe, 'if you rely on books and believe what they tell you.'

Tuesday 14 April 1829

When I came in at lunchtime today, Goethe was already sitting at the table with Councillor Meyer, talking about Italy and works of art. Goethe had a book of Claude Lorrain prints brought in, and Meyer leafed through it until he found the landscape he wanted to show us, the original of which, according to newspaper reports, had been bought by Peel for four thousand pounds. We had to admit that it was a beautiful work, and that Peel had got himself a bargain.

On the right side of the picture you see a group of people, sitting or standing. A shepherd is bending down to talk to a girl; he appears to be instructing her in how to play the pipe. In the centre of the picture is a lake, glistening in the sunlight, and on the left are some cattle grazing in the shade of a grove. The two groups balanced each other perfectly, and the magical lighting was dramatically effective, as with all the master's work. There was some discussion about where the original had been in the meantime, and in whose possession Meyer had seen it in Italy.

The conversation then turned to the King of Bavaria's new property in Rome. 'I know the Villa very well,' said Meyer. 'I have been there often, and have fond memories of the wonderful location. It is a decent-sized mansion, and the King is sure to redecorate it in his own style and make something very charming of it. The Duchess Amalie lived there in my day, and Herder lived next door. It was later occupied by the Duke of Sussex and Count Münster. Upper-class foreigners have always loved the house for its salubrious location and magnificent views.'

I asked Councillor Meyer how far it was from the Villa di Malta to the Vatican. 'From Trinità di Monte, where we artists were living, which is not far from the Villa,' said Meyer, 'it is a good half-hour to the Vatican. We walked it every day, and often more than once.' 'The route via the bridge,' I said, 'seems somewhat roundabout. I should have thought it quicker to cross the Tiber by boat and go across the fields.' 'It isn't any quicker,' said Meyer, 'but we thought the same thing, and often went across by boat. I remember one particular crossing when we were coming back from the Vatican on a beautiful moonlit night. Our friends Bury, Hirt and Lips were with us, and the usual argument had started about who was greater, Raphael or Michelangelo. We climbed into the ferryboat. When we reached the opposite bank, and the argument was still in full swing, some wag – I think it was Bury – proposed that we should stay on the water until the argument was settled and everyone was in agreement. The proposal was accepted, and the ferryman had to push the boat off again and row back to the other side. But now the argument was getting really heated, and every time we reached the bank we had to turn round and go back again, as the matter had not yet been settled. And so we ended up going back and forth for hours, which suited nobody better than the boatman, who was making more and more money with every crossing. He had a twelve-year-old boy with him who was helping out, and who must have wondered what on earth was going on. He finally spoke up: "Father, what's wrong with these men? Why don't they want to go ashore, and why do we have to keep on going back, when we've rowed them to the bank?" "I don't know, my son," replied the boatman, "but I think they are mad." In the end, rather than spend the whole night going back and forth, we reached an agreement of sorts and went ashore.'

We were all highly amused by this charming tale of artistic

obsession. Councillor Meyer was in top form, and went on to tell us more about Rome, while Goethe and I enjoyed listening to him.

'The great Raphael versus Michelangelo debate,' said Meyer, 'was very topical back then, and it went on every day, wherever there were enough artists gathered together for both sides to be represented. The argument generally started in an *osteria*, where they served good cheap wine. Someone would mention certain paintings, or specific parts of them, and if the opposing party disagreed and refused to concede this or that point, it became necessary to go and look at the actual pictures. So then they would all pile out of the hostelry, still arguing, and rush off to the Sistine Chapel, the key to which was kept by a cobbler who charged four pennies to open up. Here, in front of the paintings, there was much waving and pointing and gesticulating, and when they had argued for long enough they all went back to the *osteria* to be friends again over a bottle of wine and forget all their quarrels. It went on like that every day, and the cobbler by the Sistine Chapel collected quite a few fourpenny payments.'

This amusing story called to mind another cobbler, who used to beat out his leather on an antique marble head. 'It was the bust of a Roman emperor,' said Meyer. 'This antiquity stood outside the cobbler's door, and we often saw him engaged in this laudable activity when we walked past.'

Wednesday 15 April 1829

We talked about people who feel compelled to write, even though they have no real talent, and about others who write about things they don't understand.

'What is so beguiling for young people today,' said Goethe, 'is that we live in a time when there is so much culture about that it becomes part of the air a young person breathes, so to speak. Poetic and philosophical thoughts are alive and stirring within him; he has absorbed them from the surrounding atmosphere, but thinks they belong exclusively to him, and so gives them utterance as if they were his own. But when he has given back to the times what he has received from them, he is depleted. He is like a spring that gushes forth for a while, fed by a fresh flow of water, then slows to a trickle and stops as soon as the borrowed supply is exhausted.'

Tuesday 1 September 1829

I told Goethe about a traveller passing through, who had attended a lecture by Hegel on proving the existence of God. Goethe agreed with me that such lectures had had their day.

'The age of doubt is past,' he said, 'and people now no more doubt God than they doubt themselves. Besides, the nature of God, immortality, the essential character of our soul and its relationship with our body – these are eternal problems which the philosophers cannot help us with. One of the latest French philosophers blithely begins his chapter with these words: "It is a known fact that man consists of two parts, body and soul. We shall therefore begin with the body, and then go on to speak about the soul." Fichte went a little further, and extricated himself rather more adroitly from the difficulty by saying: "We shall discuss man in terms of his physical being, and man in terms of his spiritual being." He knew very well that such a tightly knit whole cannot be divided into separate parts. Kant unquestionably helped us the most when he defined the limits beyond which the human intellect cannot go, and left the insoluble problems alone. Just think of all the endless philosophizing about immortality – and how far has *that* got us, exactly? I do not doubt our continuing existence, since nature relies on entelechy.[31] But we are not all immortal in the same way, and anyone who would manifest himself later as a great entelechy has to be one to begin with.

'But while the Germans turn themselves inside out with their attempts to solve philosophical problems, the English, with their very practical minds, laugh at us and gain the world. Everybody knows their declamations against the slave trade; and while they would have us believe this is all driven by humanitarian principles, it now turns out that their real motivation is an entirely practical object, without which the English famously never do anything, and which one might have guessed. They use the negroes themselves in their large plantations on the western coast of Africa, so it is not in their interest to have them shipped out of the country. In America they have established large colonies of negroes, which are very productive and yield large numbers of blacks every year. These are sufficient to supply the needs of North America; and while they carry on this highly profitable trade, the importation of slaves from abroad would be very damaging to their commercial interests. And so, for practical reasons of their own, they preach against this inhuman trade. The English delegate at the Congress of Vienna was still arguing passionately against it, but his Portuguese counterpart was smart enough to reply calmly that he was not aware they had convened in order to sit in judgement on the world or lay down principles of morality. He knew very well what the object of the English really was, and meanwhile he had one of his own, which he knew how to promote and attain.'

Sunday 6 December 1829

After dinner today Goethe read me the first scene from the second act of *Faust*.[32] It made a deep impression on me and filled me with a sense of great inner joy. We are transported back to Faust's study, and Mephistopheles finds everything just where he left it. He takes down Faust's fur-lined gown from its hook; a host of moths and other insects come fluttering out, and as Mephistopheles describes all the different places where they settle, we get a very clear picture of the location. He puts the gown on in order to play the master once more, while Faust lies behind a curtain in a state of paralysis. He pulls on the bell-rope, and the sound of the bell echoing through the ancient, deserted cloister halls is so frightful that the doors fly open and the walls tremble. The student assistant rushes in and finds Mephistopheles sitting in Faust's chair; he doesn't know him, but feels an instinctive respect for him. When questioned, he gives us news of Wagner, who has now become a famous man and is hoping for his master's return. At this very moment, we learn, he is toiling away in his laboratory, trying to produce a homunculus. The assistant is dismissed; the Bachelor now appears, the same man we saw some years ago as a shy young student when Mephistopheles, robed in Faust's gown, made fun of him. He is now a grown man, and so full of self-regard that he is too much even for Mephistopheles, who inches towards the front of the stage in his chair and finally addresses the audience.

Goethe read the scene to the end. His exuberantly youthful productivity and the economy of the writing afforded me great delight.

'As the conception is so old,' said Goethe, 'and I have been thinking about it for fifty years, I have got so much material in my head that the difficult part now is to decide what to cut and discard. The whole of the second part really has been worked out in my mind for that long. But it may be a good thing that I have not written it down until now, when I am so much more familiar with the ways of the world. I am like somebody who has a lot of small silver and copper coins in his youth, which he then exchanges for coins of greater value as he goes through life, until in the end the assets of his youth have been converted into pieces of pure gold.'

We talked about the figure of the Bachelor. 'Isn't he intended to represent a certain school of ideal philosophy?' I asked. 'No,' said Goethe, 'he personifies the pretentiousness that youth is particularly prone to, and which was very much in evidence in the first few years after our War of Liberation. And when we are young, we all think the world only really began with us, and that everything is only there for our sake. There actually was a man in the Far East who gathered his people about him every morning and wouldn't let them start work until he had commanded the sun to rise. But he was canny enough not to give the order until the sun really was on the point of rising all by itself.'

We talked at length about *Faust* and its composition, and other related matters.

Goethe was sunk in silent thought for a while. Then he began again as follows:

'When one is old,' he said, 'one thinks differently about the things of this world than when one was young. I can't help thinking that the demons, in order to taunt and mock mankind, sometimes set up individuals who are so charismatic that everybody strives to emulate them, and so great that nobody can equal them. Hence they set up Raphael, in whom thought and action were equally perfected; a few outstanding painters of later generations have come close, but nobody has equalled him. Hence they set up Mozart, as something unattainable in music. And hence, in poetry, Shakespeare. I know what your objection to him might be, but I'm only talking here about a man's natural bent, the great gifts he was born with. Then there is Napoleon, likewise unattainable. It was quite something when the Russians held back and did not enter Constantinople; but we see the same trait in Napoleon, who also held back and chose not to go to Rome.'

We talked about other matters suggested by this big subject; my private thought, however, was that the demons might have intended something of the kind with Goethe, since he too is a figure too charismatic not to want to emulate, and too great to be equalled.

Wednesday 16 December 1829

After dinner today Goethe read me the second scene from the second act of *Faust*, where Mephistopheles goes to see Wagner, who is busily trying to create a human being in the chemistry laboratory. His efforts are successful; the homunculus appears in the flask as a luminous being, who wants to be up and doing. He brushes aside Wagner's questions about matters beyond our ken; reasoning is not his thing. He is intent on *action*, and his first priority is our hero, Faust, who, in his paralysed state, is in need of help from a higher agency. As a being for whom the present is completely open and transparent, the homunculus sees into the soul of the sleeping Faust, who is enraptured by a beautiful dream about Leda as she is visited by swans while bathing in a lovely spot. The homunculus narrates the dream, and the most delightful scene unfolds before our mind's eye.

But Mephistopheles sees nothing, and the homunculus mocks him for his dour northern sensibility.

'You'll notice,' said Goethe, 'that Mephistopheles generally comes off worse against the homunculus, who is his equal for clarity of mind, and far ahead of him in his affinity for the beautiful and for productive activity. He also calls him "cousin"; spiritual beings like the homunculus, which have not yet become clouded and limited by full incarnation, were classed as demons, so there is a kind of kinship between the two.'

'Certainly,' I said, 'Mephistopheles seems to be the subordinate figure here. But I can't help thinking that he secretly played some part in the creation of the homunculus, given what we already know of him, and given how he always appears in *Helena*, too, as a being who pulls the strings behind the scenes. That evens things up again, so he can well afford to put up with the odd jibe, secure in the knowledge of his own superiority.'

'You understand the relationship very well,' said Goethe. 'That's exactly it, and I did wonder, when Mephistopheles goes to see Wagner and the homunculus is starting to form, whether I shouldn't give him a few lines that would make his involvement plain to the reader.'

'It can't hurt,' I said. 'Then again, it is already hinted at when Mephistopheles ends the scene with the lines:

> When all is said, we all depend
> On creatures of our making.'

'You're right,' said Goethe, 'that might almost be enough for an attentive reader. All the same, I'll see if I can't come up with a line or two.'

'But those closing lines,' I pointed out, 'are so full of meaning that they will keep the reader busy for a very long time.'

'There is certainly food for thought there,' said Goethe. 'A man with six sons is a lost cause, no matter what he does. And kings and ministers who have promoted many persons to important positions may well have their own thoughts on the subject.'

Faust's dream about Leda came back to me again, and in my mind I saw this as a pivotal episode in the overall composition.[33]

'It is wonderful to see,' I said, 'how the different parts of such a work relate and interact with each other, and how one part completes and enhances another. This dream about Leda, here in the second act, provides the real foundation for the later *Helena*. There we hear a lot about swans and the offspring of a swan, but here we see the action played out before our eyes; so when we later come to *Helena*, we already understand the physical reality of that situation, and everything seems to make much more sense.'

Goethe agreed with me, and seemed pleased that I had noticed. 'You will also find,' he said, 'that the classical versus romantic theme comes up for mention repeatedly in these earlier acts, to give a sense of ascending on rising ground towards *Helena*, where the two different kinds of poetry emerge very clearly, and find a kind of accommodation.

'The French,' Goethe went on, 'are also starting to think about these things in the right way now. "Classical and romantic," they say, "are both equally valid; it's just a matter of being able to use these two forms intelligently and achieve excellence in either one. Because it is quite possible to be ridiculous in both, in which case the one is as worthless as the other." That seems to me a sensible way of looking at it, and well said; I think we can safely leave it at that for now.'

Sunday 20 December 1829

Dined with Goethe. We talked about the Chancellor, and I asked Goethe if he had brought him any news of Manzoni on his return from Italy. 'He wrote to me about him,' said Goethe. 'The Chancellor visited Manzoni; he is living on his estate near Milan, and is constantly unwell, I am sorry to say.'

'It's curious,' I said, 'that one so often finds, with persons of exceptional talent, especially poets, that they have a weak constitution.'

'The extraordinary achievements of such people,' said Goethe, 'presuppose a very delicate constitution, which allows them to feel exceptional emotions and hear celestial voices. Such a constitution is easily upset and damaged when it comes into conflict with the world and the elements; and anyone who is not blessed, like Voltaire, with a combination of great sensitivity and extraordinary toughness is apt to feel constantly unwell. Schiller was always ill. When I first met him, I thought he wouldn't live another month. But there was a certain toughness about him, too; he kept going for all those years, and could have lasted even longer if he had lived a healthier life.'

We talked about the theatre, and whether or not a particular performance had been successful.

'I have seen Unzelmann play the part,' said Goethe, 'and one always felt in safe hands with him because his mind was free and at ease – which he communicated to us. Stage acting is like all the other arts; what the artist does, or has done, puts us in the same frame of mind he was in when he did it. A relaxed frame of mind in the artist puts us at our ease, but if he is anxious himself, that makes us feel nervous. This sense of freedom and ease is generally found in artists who know exactly what they are doing – which is why we take so readily to Dutch painting, because those artists were portraying the life they saw around them, which they had mastered completely. Before we can sense that an actor's mind is free and at ease, he must master his role completely through study, imagination and natural disposition; he must have all the physical resources at his command; and he must be sustained by a certain youthful vigour. Study is not enough without imagination; and study and imagination will not suffice without natural disposition. Women accomplish the most through imagination and temperament, which is why Frau Wolff was so good.'

We talked further on this subject, discussing the leading actors of the Weimar stage and recalling many a fine performance.

My own thoughts then turned to *Faust* again, and I wondered how the figure of the homunculus could be put on to the stage. 'Even if we do not see the little man himself,' I said, 'we would need to see the glowing light inside the flask; and what he has to say is of such great import that no child could possibly speak the lines.'

'Wagner,' said Goethe, 'must not let the flask out of his hands, and the voice would have to sound as if it were coming out of the flask. It would be a perfect part for a ventriloquist, of whom I've heard a few, and I'm sure he would do a good job.'

Then we thought about the big carnival scene, and how far it was possible to put that on stage. 'It would be a bit more,' I said, 'than the *Market of Naples*.'[34] 'It would require a very large theatre,' said Goethe, 'and it's almost impossible to imagine.' 'I hope I get to see it one day,' was my reply. 'I'm especially looking forward to seeing the elephant, ridden by Wisdom, with the goddess Victoria borne aloft on its back, and Fear and Hope in chains on either side. It's hard to imagine a finer allegory than that.'

'It wouldn't be the first elephant to be seen on the stage,' said Goethe. 'There's one in Paris who is playing a character in his own right. He belongs to a people's party, and takes the crown from the head of one king and places it on another – which must be quite something to see. And then, at the end of the play, the elephant does his own curtain call; he comes out, unaccompanied, takes his bow and then retires. So you see, we could count on the elephant for our carnival. But the whole thing is much too big, and it needs the kind of director who is very hard to find.'

'But it is such a dazzling extravaganza,' I said, 'that any theatre would jump at the chance to do it. I love the way it builds to a climax, piling on the spectacle! First, we have the beautiful gardeners of both sexes, who decorate the stage and at the same time make up a crowd of onlookers as a backdrop to the ever more spectacular sights that follow. Then, after the elephants, the team of dragons flying through the air from the back of the stage, over the heads of the players. Then the great Pan comes on, and at the end everything appears to be on fire, until wet clouds of mist roll in and damp down the flames and put them out! If all that could be staged just as you imagined it, the audience would sit there in amazement, and be forced to admit that such a lavish spectacle is too much for their intellect and senses to take in properly.'

'Don't talk to me about the audience,' said Goethe, 'I don't want to hear about them. The main thing is that it's written; let the world do with it what it will and put it to whatever use it can.'

We then got talking about the figure of the Boy Charioteer.

'You'll have guessed that the man wearing the mask of Plutus is Faust, and that Mephistopheles is concealed behind the mask of Avarice. But who is the Boy Charioteer?' I hesitated, not knowing how to answer. 'It's Euphorion!'[35] said Goethe. 'But how can he appear here in the carnival,' I asked, 'when he isn't born until the third act?' 'Euphorion is not a human being, just an allegorical one,' replied Goethe. 'He is the personification of poetry, which is not tied to any particular time, place or individual. The same spirit who later chooses to be Euphorion here assumes the guise of the Boy Charioteer, and so he is rather like a spectre, who can be present everywhere and appear at any moment.'

Sunday 27 December 1829

After dinner today Goethe read me the scene about the paper money.

'You'll remember,' he said, 'that the upshot of the imperial assembly is that there is a shortage of money, which Mephistopheles promises to supply. This theme is continued through the masquerade, when Mephistopheles arranges for the Emperor, in the mask of the great Pan, to sign a piece of paper which is thereby invested with monetary value, then printed by the thousand and distributed.

'Now in this scene the matter is brought up in the presence of the Emperor, who doesn't realize what he has done. The treasurer hands over the banknotes and explains what has happened. The Emperor is initially angry, but when the full benefits are made clear to him he is delighted, and showers his entourage with the new paper gifts; as he is leaving, he dispenses a few thousand more crowns, which the fat court jester snatches up before hurrying away to turn his paper into real estate.'

As Goethe was reading this splendid scene, I thought it was a nice touch to trace paper money back to Mephistopheles, thereby slipping in a striking allusion to one of the major concerns of our day.

Scarcely had the scene been read, and various points discussed,

1829   319

when Goethe's son came down and joined us at the table. He told us about Cooper's latest novel, which he had read and which he now described in graphic detail. We said nothing about the scene we had just read, but minutes later he was talking about Prussian treasury bills himself, and saying they were not worth their face value. As young Goethe was speaking, I looked at his father with a little smile, which he reciprocated – a tacit acknowledgement by both of us of the scene's remarkable contemporary resonance.

Wednesday 30 December 1829

After dinner today Goethe read me the next scene.

'Now that they have money at the imperial court,' said Goethe, 'they want to be amused. The Emperor wishes to see Paris and Helen – and he wants to see them in person, brought to him by magic. But as Mephistopheles has nothing to do with Greek antiquity and has no power over such figures, this task is given to Faust, who performs it successfully. I haven't quite finished the section describing what Faust has to do to make the apparition happen; I'll read that to you next time. But the actual appearance of Paris and Helen I can read to you now.'

I could not wait to hear it, and Goethe began to read. I saw the Emperor and his court arrive in the old knights' hall to witness the spectacle. The curtain rises, and I see the theatre, a Greek temple. Mephistopheles is in the prompt box, the astrologer is off to one side of the proscenium, while Faust appears on the other side with his tripod. He recites the magic incantation and Paris appears, emerging out of the incense smoke rising from the bowl of the tripod. The beautiful youth flexes his limbs to the strains of ethereal music, and we hear him described. He sits down, leans back with his arm crooked back over his head, as we see him portrayed in ancient sculptures. He is the delight of the women, who list the finer points of his youthful physique; he is an object of hatred for the men, who are consumed by envy and jealousy and disparage him at every opportunity. Paris falls asleep, and Helen appears. She approaches the sleeping youth, presses a kiss on his lips; she moves away, and turns back to gaze at him. The way she turns is particularly seductive, and she makes the same impression on the men that Paris makes on the women. The men are inflamed with love and praise for her, while the women are full of envy, hatred and spite. Faust himself is completely entranced, and the sight of the beauty he has conjured up makes him forget the time, the place, and what he is doing there, so that Mephistopheles constantly has to remind him to get a grip. Paris and Helen seem to be developing a mutual affection and understanding, and the youth takes her in his arms to carry her off; Faust tries to snatch her from him, but when he points the key at him there is a loud explosion, the apparitions dissolve into vapour, and Faust lies paralysed on the ground.

1830

Sunday 3 January 1830

Goethe showed me the English anthology *The Keepsake* for 1830, with some very fine engravings and a number of extremely interesting letters from Lord Byron, which I read over dessert. Meanwhile he himself had picked up the latest French translation of his *Faust* by Gérard, which he leafed through, occasionally pausing as if to read a passage.[36]

'It is the strangest thing,' he said, 'to think that this book is now being read in a language in which Voltaire reigned supreme fifty years ago. You can't imagine the thoughts that are going through my head, and you have no idea of the significance that Voltaire and his great contemporaries had in my youth, and how they bestrode the entire civilized world. It is not easy to tell from my autobiography how profoundly these men influenced my youth, and what it cost me to resist them and set myself up on my own two feet in a truer relationship to nature.'

We talked further about Voltaire, and Goethe recited his poem 'Les Systèmes' to me, which told me how intently he must have studied and assimilated such things in his youth.

Goethe said that the Gérard translation, though mostly in prose, was very good. 'I don't care to read *Faust* in German any more,' he said, 'but in this French translation it all seems very fresh, new and spirited again. The thing about *Faust*,' he went on, 'is that it's essentially unfathomable, and all attempts to make it accessible to the understanding are a waste of time. You also have to remember that the first part is written from the perspective of an individual struggling in a fairly dark place.

But then, people are drawn to that kind of darkness, and they wrestle with it, as we do with all insoluble problems.'

Sunday 10 January 1830

After dinner today Goethe afforded me great delight by reading the scene where Faust descends to the Mothers. The complete novelty and surprise of the subject matter, as well as the way Goethe read the scene, affected me deeply, so that I identified completely with Faust and felt the same shudder of horror when Mephistopheles told him what was afoot.

I had heard and taken in what had been said, but so much of it remained an enigma to me that I felt compelled to ask Goethe to explain some things. But in his usual fashion he shrouded himself in mystery, looking at me with wide-open eyes and repeating the words:

The Mothers! Mothers! It sounds so strange!

'I can't tell you anything more,' he said, 'except to say that I read in Plutarch that in ancient Greece there were deities referred to as "Mothers". That's the extent of my borrowings from history; the rest is my own invention. I'll give you the manuscript to take home with you. Study it all carefully and see what you make of it.'

I was quite happy to go through this curious scene several times at my leisure, and as a result I formed my own picture of who the Mothers were and what they did, and of the place where they dwelled.

If we imagine this huge planet of ours, the earth, as a hollow sphere, inside which it would be possible to travel hundreds of miles in the same direction without hitting any other physical object, this would be the abode of those unknown goddesses to whom Faust descends. They dwell beyond place, as it were, in that there is nothing solid anywhere near them; they also dwell beyond time, in that they cannot see any celestial bodies, whose rise and fall chart the cycle of day and night.

Abiding thus in eternal twilight and solitude, the Mothers

are creative beings – the creative and sustaining principle behind everything that has life and form on the surface of the earth. Whatever ceases to breathe, returns to them as a spirit, and they preserve it until it finds an opportunity to enter into new existence. All souls and forms of what once was, and will be, float around like clouds in the endless space where the Mothers dwell, enveloping them completely; and so the magician must enter their domain if he wishes to conjure the form of a being through the power of his art, and arouse some former creature to a semblance of life.

The eternal metamorphosis of earthly existence, of birth and growth, destruction and reconstitution, is the never-ending preoccupation of the Mothers. And since, as with all things that receive new life on earth through procreation, the feminine element is principally at work, so these creative deities may rightly be considered feminine, and the august title of 'Mothers' may be conferred upon them with good reason.

Of course, all this is just poetic invention. But we finite humans cannot penetrate much further into these things, and are content to find something that offers some kind of reassurance. Here on earth we see phenomena and feel effects which we do not understand, having no knowledge of where they come from or where they are going. We infer the existence of some primal spiritual source, something divine, which we can neither define nor name, and which we have to draw down to our level and anthropomorphize, in an effort to embody our obscure intimations and make them in some sort comprehensible.

All the myths that have endured in the popular imagination from age to age began life in this way; and so it is with this new one of Goethe's, which at least has some semblance of truth to nature, and probably ranks with the best that have ever been devised.

Sunday 24 January 1830

'I had a letter a few days ago from our celebrated salt miner in Stotternheim,' said Goethe.[37] 'He starts with a remarkable observation, which I must tell you about.

'"I have learned a lesson," he writes, "that will not be lost on me." So what is he talking about here? Nothing less than the loss of a thousand thalers, at least. The shaft that goes down twelve hundred feet to the rock salt passes through softer soil and rock, and he rashly neglected to shore up the sides. The softer soil has fallen in and filled up the pit at the bottom, so that an extremely costly operation is now required to clear it. He will then line the shaft with metal pipes for the full twelve hundred feet, to ensure that such a thing cannot happen again. He should have done this in the first place, and would have done so for sure – except that people like him are prone to a kind of recklessness that we have no notion of, but which is necessary in order to embark on such a risky enterprise. But he is completely unruffled by the accident, and calmly writes: "I have learned a lesson that will not be lost on me." Now there is a man to gladden the heart – a man who gets back on his feet, without complaining, and just gets on with the job. What do you say to that? Isn't it wonderful?'

'It reminds me of Sterne,' I replied, 'who laments the fact that he has not put his bad experiences to good use, like a sensible man.' 'It's a similar sort of thing,' said Goethe.

'It also puts me in mind of Behrisch,' I went on, 'when he tells you what experience is. I've just been rereading that chapter, and enjoying it all over again: "Experience is when you have the experience of experiencing something, the experience of which you would really rather not have experienced."' 'Yes,' said Goethe with a laugh, 'we frittered away a disgraceful amount of time telling those old jokes.' 'Behrisch,' I went on, 'seems to have been a man of great charm and delicacy. I really enjoyed the little joke he played in the wine bar that evening, when he tries to prevent the young man from visiting his sweetheart, which he does in the most amusing fashion by buckling on his sword first this way, and then that, reducing everyone to laughter and causing the young man to miss his rendezvous.' 'Yes,' said Goethe, 'that *was* good; it would make a wonderful scene on the stage, and Behrisch himself was a character made for the theatre.'

We then recollected all those eccentricities of Behrisch that

Goethe relates in his autobiography. His grey clothing, where items of silk, velvet and wool were carefully combined to produce contrasting shades and textures – and the care he took always to add a new shade of grey to his ensemble. And how he would write out the poems in longhand, mimic the antics of the type-setter and celebrate the dignity and decorum of the calligrapher. Also, how his favourite pastime had been to stand at the window, observe the passers-by and imagine them dressed in other clothes that would make them look quite ridiculous. 'And then there was his regular joke about the postman,' said Goethe, 'what about that – wasn't it hilarious?' 'I don't know that one,' I said, 'you don't mention it in your autobiography.'

'That's strange,' said Goethe. 'Then I'll tell you about it now. When we were looking out of the window, and Behrisch saw the postman coming up the street, going from one house to the next, he used to take a penny out of his pocket and put it down beside him on the windowsill. "Do you see the postman?" he would say to me. "He's coming closer, and he'll be up here any minute, I can tell by looking at him. He's got a letter for you, and no ordinary letter at that; it's a letter containing a cheque – a cheque! I won't say how much. Look, he's coming in now. No, he isn't! But he'll be here any moment. There he is again! Now! In here, in here, my friend! He's gone on past. How stupid is that? How can anyone be so stupid, and behave so irresponsibly? It's doubly irresponsible: irresponsible towards you, in that he hasn't deliv-ered your cheque, which he is holding in his hands; and very irresponsible towards himself, in that he has missed out on the penny that I had ready for him, and which I shall now put back in my pocket." Whereupon he returned the penny to his pocket with a dignified flourish, and we burst into laughter.'

I enjoyed the joke, which was very much of a piece with the others. I asked Goethe if he had ever seen Behrisch again in later years.

'I did see him again,' said Goethe, 'not long after my arrival in Weimar, some time around 1776; I accompanied the Duke on a visit to Dessau, where Behrisch had been hired from Leip-zig to tutor the Crown Prince. I found him just the same as ever, a polished courtier, and in the best of spirits.'

'What did he say,' I asked, 'about you having become so famous in the meantime?'

'"Didn't I tell you so," were his first words, "and wasn't it just as well that you didn't publish your poems then, but waited until you had done something really good? Not that your stuff was bad back then, otherwise I wouldn't have written the things out for you. But if we had stayed together, you would have done better not to publish the other things either. I would have written those out for you too, and it would all have turned out just as well." As you can see, he hadn't changed a bit. He was well liked at court, and I always saw him dining at the Prince's table.

'The last time I saw him was in 1801. He was an old man by then, but still in the best of spirits. He had a set of very nice rooms in the palace, one of which he had filled completely with geraniums, which were all the rage at the time. But the botanists had meanwhile identified different varieties of geraniums and reclassified them, giving one particular variety the name "pelargoniums". The old man couldn't be doing with this at all, and he had harsh words for the botanists. "Those idiots!" he said, "I think I've got an entire roomful of geraniums here, and now they come and tell me they are pelargoniums. So where does that leave me, if they are not geraniums? And what do I want with pelargoniums anyway!" He went on like this for half an hour at a time, so, as you can see, he was still the same as ever.'

We then talked about the 'Classical Walpurgis Night', the beginning of which Goethe had read to me a few days before. 'Any number of mythological figures crowd into my mind,' he said, 'but I take care just to use the ones that make the right sort of visual impression. Faust has now met Chiron, and I am hopeful that the scene will work out well. If I stick at it, I can get through the "Walpurgis Night" in a couple of months. And I'm determined not to let anything else distract me now from *Faust*; it would be quite something if I lived to complete it! And it's definitely possible. The fifth act is as good as finished, and after that the fourth will more or less write itself.'

Goethe then spoke about his health, and said how fortunate he was to be keeping so well still. 'The fact that I am in such good shape,' he said, 'is entirely due to Vogel. Without him I would have gone long ago. Vogel is a born doctor, and one of the most brilliant men I have ever met. But we'd better not say how good he is, in case he is snatched away from us.'

Sunday 31 January 1830

Dined with Goethe. We talked about Milton. 'I read his *Samson* recently,' said Goethe, 'which has more of the spirit of the ancients than anything else by a modern poet. He is a very great writer, and his own blindness was an asset to him in portraying Samson's situation so convincingly. Milton was a true poet, and we should stand in awe of him.'

Various newspapers were brought in, and we read about theatre productions in Berlin where sea monsters and whales had been put on the stage.

In the French paper *Le Temps* Goethe read an article on the huge stipends paid to the English clergy, which amount to more than those of the rest of Christendom put together. 'Someone said,' remarked Goethe, 'that the world is ruled by numbers; what I *do* know is that numbers tell us whether the world is ruled well or badly.'

Wednesday 3 February 1830

Dined with Goethe. We talked about Mozart. 'I saw him as a seven-year-old boy,' said Goethe, 'when he was on a concert tour. I must have been about fourteen at the time, and I can still remember the little man very clearly, with his hair all coiffed and a sword at his side.' I was wide-eyed with astonishment to think that Goethe was old enough to have seen Mozart as a child.

Sunday 7 February 1830

Dined with Goethe. We discussed the Prince Primate, and he told me that he had dared to defend him with an adroit turn of phrase while dining at the Empress of Austria's table.[38] There was mention of the Prince's shortcomings in philosophy; his amateur love of painting, devoid of taste; the picture he gave to Miss Gore.[39] His kind-heartedness and tender compassion, giving everything away, so that he was reduced to poverty in the end. Conversation about the definition of 'disobliging'.

After dinner Goethe's son looked in, accompanied by Walter and Wolf, wearing his Klingsor costume for the masked ball, and went off to court.[40]

Wednesday 10 February 1830

Dined with Goethe. He paid warm tribute to Riemer's festive poem, written for the celebrations on 2 February.[41] 'Whatever Riemer does,' Goethe added, 'is good enough to pass muster with master and apprentice.'

We then talked about the 'Classical Walpurgis Night', and he said he was discovering things there that surprised even him. And the subject was taking off in all kinds of unexpected directions.

'I've done a little over half now,' he said, 'but I intend to stick at it, and hope to be finished by Easter. I won't show you any more before then, but as soon as it is finished I shall give it to you to take home and read at your leisure. It would be good if you could put together the thirty-eighth and thirty-ninth volumes, so that we can send off the last batch at Easter – then we'd have the summer free for something substantial. I would carry on with *Faust*, and try to get the fourth act done.' I applauded his plan and promised him my full support.

Goethe then sent his manservant to enquire after the Dowager Grand Duchess. She had been very ill, and her condition gave him cause for concern.

'She should not have gone to watch the carnival parade,' he said, 'but royal personages are used to getting their way, and all the protests of the court and the doctors were in vain. She defies her ailing body just as stubbornly as she defied Napoleon, and I can see how it will end; she will depart this life like the Grand Duke, with all her mental faculties intact, when her body has ceased to obey her.'

1830   329

Goethe seemed very downcast and sat in silence for a while.
But before long we were talking again about happier matters,
and he told me about a book written as an apologia for Hudson Lowe.

'There are some really delightful touches in it,' he said, 'which
can only come from actual eyewitnesses. Napoleon, as you
know, normally wore a dark-green uniform. Over time it had
become very worn and faded, so it was felt necessary to replace
it with another. He wanted the same dark-green colour, but
there was nothing suitable to be had on the island. They did
track down some green cloth, but it was altogether the wrong
shade, a sort of yellowish green. The master of the world would
not have been seen dead in such a colour, and so there was
nothing for it but to have his old uniform turned, and wear it
inside out.

'What do you say to that? Isn't it utterly tragic? How touching, don't you think, to see the conqueror of kings reduced in
the end to wearing a turned uniform? And yet, when one reflects
that the man who ended up like this had trampled the lives and
happiness of millions underfoot, the fate that befell him seems
very mild – a nemesis that cannot help but be a little magnani-
mous, in deference to the great man's standing. The story of
Napoleon shows us how dangerous it is to exalt oneself to the
realm of the absolute, and to sacrifice everything to the pursuit
of an idea.'

We talked more around the subject, and then I went to the
theatre to see *Der Stern von Sevilla*.[42]

Sunday 14 February 1830

At noon today, on my way to dine with Goethe at his invitation, I heard the news that the Dowager Grand Duchess had
just died. My first thought was how this would affect Goethe at
his advanced age, and I entered the house with some apprehension. The servants told me that his daughter-in-law had just
gone to break the sad news to him.

I thought to myself: 'He's been attached to this princess for
more than fifty years, and has enjoyed her special grace and

favour; her death is bound to hit him hard.' I entered his room with these thoughts in my mind – and was not a little astonished to find him in the liveliest of spirits, sitting at table with his daughter-in-law and grandsons and taking his soup as if nothing had happened. We chatted away cheerfully about mundane matters. All the town bells then began to toll; Frau von Goethe shot me a glance and we all started to talk louder, so that the sound of the passing bells would not upset him and cause him distress. We thought he felt things as we did. But he did not feel as we did; he looked at things in a very different light. He sat there before us like a being of a higher order, untouchable by earthly suffering. Councillor Vogel was announced. He sat down with us and related the particular circumstances of Her late Highness's death, which Goethe heard in the same state of complete calm and composure. Vogel then left, and we went on with our lunch and conversation. Among other things, we talked a good deal about the *Chaos*, and Goethe spoke very highly of the 'Reflections on Play' in the latest issue.[43] After Frau von Goethe had gone upstairs with her boys, I remained alone with Goethe. He talked about his 'Classical Walpurgis Night', said he was making progress every day and achieving wonderful things beyond his expectation. Then he showed me a letter from the King of Bavaria which had arrived today, and which I read with great interest. The King's true and noble sentiments spoke from every line, and Goethe seemed especially pleased that the King was still the same towards him as he had always been.

Councillor Soret was now announced, and he joined us at the table. He had come with a message of condolence for Goethe from Her Imperial Highness, which gave an added lift to his mood of cheerful composure. Goethe went on talking, and he mentioned the celebrated Ninon de Lenclos. As a beautiful sixteen-year-old she had lain at death's door; perfectly composed, she had comforted those standing around her bed with the words: 'What is death, after all? I leave only mortals behind me.' As Goethe reminded us, she survived and lived to the age of ninety, having brought joy and despair to hundreds of lovers up until her eightieth year.

1830

Goethe then turned to the subject of Gozzi and his theatre in Venice, where the actors were merely given a theme and expected to improvise. Gozzi took the view that there were only thirty-six tragic situations under the sun. Schiller thought there were more, but had not succeeded in finding even that number.

Then there was some interesting talk about Grimm, his mind and character, and his distrust of paper money.

Wednesday 17 February 1830

We talked about the theatre, and specifically about the colour of the scenery and costumes. We came to the following conclusions:

As a general rule, the scenery should be of a colour that does not overpower any of the colours in the costumes downstage – like Beuther's backdrops, which tend to be brownish in tone, and so make the colours in the costumes stand out bright and fresh. But if the scenery painter is unable to use a neutral colour shade for some reason, perhaps because he has to represent a red or yellow room, a white tent or a green garden, then the actors should have the sense to avoid those colours in their costumes. If an actor wearing a red uniform coat and green trousers enters a red room, his upper body becomes invisible and we see only his legs; if he enters a green garden wearing the same outfit, his legs disappear and his upper body stands out in stark contrast. I once saw an actor in a white uniform coat and dark trousers whose upper body disappeared completely inside a white tent, while his legs became invisible against a dark background.

'And if the scenery painter,' added Goethe, 'does need to create a red or yellow room, or a green garden or forest, he should always tone down these colours to a muted, pastel shade, so that all the costumes downstage will stand out against this background and be seen to advantage.'

We talked about the *Iliad*, and Goethe drew my attention to the clever way Achilles is consigned to idleness for a while, so that the other heroes may be introduced into the narrative and developed.

Regarding his *Wahlverwandtschaften*, he said there is

nothing in it that he has not experienced himself, but none of it is presented in quite the *way* he experienced it. The same is true of the events in Sesenheim.

After dinner we looked through a portfolio of pictures by the Dutch school. A harbour view, where men are taking on fresh water on one side and others are playing dice on a barrel on the other, prompted some interesting reflections on how realism is sometimes sacrificed to artistic effect.[44] The main concentration of light falls on the lid of the barrel; the dice have just been thrown, as we can tell from the gestures of the men; but the dice have not been drawn on the surface of the lid, because they would have broken up the pool of light and spoiled the effect.

We went on to look at Ruysdael's studies for his churchyard painting, which showed what great pains such a master would go to.

Sunday 21 February 1830

Dined with Goethe. He showed me the spider plant, which I studied with great interest. I noted that it seeks to prolong its existence as long as possible before allowing a successor to emerge.

'I have decided,' Goethe then said, 'not to read *Le Temps* or *Le Globe* for the next four weeks. The situation is such that something is bound to happen in that time, and so I shall wait until I hear about it from some outside source.[45] My "Classical Walpurgis Night" will benefit as a result, and anyway, keeping up with these things doesn't get us anywhere – a point that is often overlooked.'

He then handed me a letter from Boisserée in Munich, which had given him pleasure, and which I now read with great enjoyment myself. Boisserée wrote in particular about the 'Zweiter Römischer Aufenthalt', and about a number of points in the latest issue of *Kunst und Altertum*. His judgements in these matters are as generous as they are rigorous, and we had frequent occasion to comment on this remarkable man's great learning and accomplishments.

Goethe then told me about a new painting by Cornelius, which he thought very fine in its conception and execution; and it was remarked that the key to getting the colouration of a picture right lay in the composition.

Later on, as I was taking a walk, the spider plant came into my mind again, and the thought occurred to me that a being prolongs its existence for as long as it can, but then marshals all its energies to produce others of its kind. This law of nature reminds me of that myth where we imagine the deity as being alone at the very beginning of the world, but then creating a son in his own image. In the same way, the most important job that good teachers have to do is to make good students, in whom they see their principles and their work perpetuated. Similarly, every work by an artist or a poet has been made in his own image, and the quality of that work is a direct reflection of the quality of the artist or poet at the time of its creation. A fine piece of work by another should never excite my envy, therefore, because I must suppose it was created by a very fine human being, worthy of producing such a thing.

Wednesday 24 February 1830

Dined with Goethe. We talked about Homer. I remarked on how the gods intervene directly in the midst of real life. 'It is wonderfully tender and human,' said Goethe, 'and I thank God that we are no longer living in the times when the French referred to this intervention of the gods as *machinerie*. But it took a while for them to appreciate the scale of his achievement, because it required a complete transformation of their culture.'

Goethe then told me that he had added a line or two to the passage describing the apparition of Helen, in order to emphasize her beauty more; this was prompted by something I had said, and was a compliment to my sound instincts.

After dinner Goethe showed me the sketch for a picture by Cornelius depicting Orpheus before the throne of Pluto, pleading for the release of Eurydice. A great deal of thought had gone into the composition, we felt, and the detailed execution was excellent; but there was something not quite right about it, something that failed to satisfy. Perhaps, we thought, the whole thing would hang together better when colour had been introduced; and perhaps the following moment would have made for a better picture, when Orpheus has already won Pluto over and Eurydice is being returned to him. Instead of being fraught with tension and expectation, the situation would have felt resolved, and therefore satisfying.

Monday 1 March 1830

Dined at Goethe's with Councillor Voigt from Jena. The conversation was all about natural history, a subject on which Councillor Voigt is singularly well informed. Goethe related how he had received a letter objecting that the cotyledons are not leaves, because they have no buds behind them. However, we satisfied ourselves, by examining various plants, that the cotyledons do indeed have buds behind them, as does every successive leaf. Voigt remarked that the insight into the metamorphosis of plants is one of the most fruitful discoveries of modern times in the field of natural science.

We talked about collections of stuffed birds, and Goethe told us the story of an Englishman who had kept several hundred live birds in large cages. Some of these had died, and he had them stuffed. He liked the stuffed birds so well that he wondered if it would not be better to kill them all and have them stuffed – which he promptly did.

Councillor Voigt told us that he was about to translate the five volumes of Cuvier's *Le Règne animal* and publish it with some additional material of his own.

After dinner, when Voigt had left, Goethe showed me the manuscript of his 'Walpurgis Night', and I was astounded to see how much it had grown in those few weeks.

Wednesday 3 March 1830

Went for a drive with Goethe before dinner. He praised my poem about the King of Bavaria, observing that Lord Byron had had a good effect on me.[46] However, he said I still lacked what they call *convenance*, in which Voltaire so excelled – and he advised me to take him as my model.

1830   335

At table later we talked a great deal about Wieland, and his *Oberon* in particular. Goethe thinks that the work rests on weak foundations, and that the plan was not given enough thought prior to its execution. The use of a spirit to produce the whiskers and back teeth is not a happy contrivance, not least because it leaves the hero with nothing to do. However, Goethe said, this great poet's charming, sensuous and witty writing makes the book so appealing to the reader that he simply skates over the structural weaknesses without noticing.

We carried on talking about all kinds of things, and came round again to the subject of entelechy. 'The persistence of the individual, and the fact that humans cast off anything that doesn't suit them,' said Goethe, 'proves to me that such a thing exists.' I had been thinking the same thing myself for several minutes, and was on the point of saying so – which made Goethe's observation doubly gratifying. 'Leibniz,' he went on, 'had similar thoughts about such autonomous beings, and what we refer to as entelechy he called "monads".'

I resolved to go straight to Leibniz and read up on all this.

Sunday 7 March 1830

Went to see Goethe around noon and found him in very lively form. He told me that he had had to put his 'Classical Walpurgis Night' aside in order to get the last consignment ready for the printer. 'But I had the good sense,' he said, 'to stop at a point where I was still in full flow, with a lot of material already thought out and ready to write. This means it will be much easier to pick up the thread again later on than if I were to carry on now until I get stuck.' This sounded like good advice, and I made a mental note.

We had intended to take a drive before dinner, but we were feeling so settled and comfortable in the room that we cancelled the horses.

Meanwhile Friedrich, the servant, had unpacked a large crate that had arrived from Paris. It was a consignment from the sculptor David, consisting of bas-relief portraits of fifty-seven famous figures, cast in plaster. Friedrich brought the casts in, fitted into a series of drawers, and we had a lot of fun identifying all these celebrities. I was particularly keen to see Mérimée, whose head appeared as big and bold as his talent, and Goethe remarked that there was something humorous about it. Victor Hugo, Alfred de Vigny and Émile Deschamps looked like men at ease and at one with themselves. We also enjoyed the portraits of Mlle Gay, Madame Tastu and other young women writers. The powerful head of Fabvier reminded us of men from earlier centuries, and it was difficult to stop looking at it. And so we moved on from one eminent figure to another, and Goethe kept on saying that David had sent him a precious gift for which he could not thank that fine artist enough. He said he would make a point of showing the collection to visitors passing through, and would ask them to tell him about any of the people he did not recognize.

There were also some books in the crate, which he got his servant to take into the front rooms. We followed on behind and sat down at the table. We were in excellent spirits, and chatted away about work in progress and future projects. 'It is not good for man to be alone,' said Goethe, 'and especially not to work alone. We need the support and stimulation of others, if our work is to prosper. I have Schiller to thank for my *Achilleis* and many of my ballads, which I wrote at his urging; and if I manage to finish the second part of *Faust*, you can claim the credit for that. I have said it many times before, but I must say it again, so that you know.' I was gratified to hear this, and felt that there was probably a good deal of truth in it.

Over dessert, Goethe opened one of the packages. It contained a copy of the poems of Émile Deschamps, with a covering letter, which Goethe handed me to read. I was delighted to see how Goethe is credited with being a great influence on the resurgence of French literature, and how the young generation of French writers love and revere him as their intellectual and spiritual leader. Shakespeare had performed the same function in Goethe's youth. But it cannot be said of Voltaire that he exercised such an influence over the young poets of other countries that they gathered together in his spirit and acknowledged him as their lord and master. The whole tone of the letter from

Émile Deschamps was engagingly warm and open. 'What you see there is the springtime of a beautiful mind,' said Goethe.

Among the other things David had sent was a sheet of paper showing Napoleon's hat drawn in all kinds of different positions. 'This is something for my son,' said Goethe, and sent the sheet straight upstairs. It had the expected effect, and it wasn't long before young Goethe came down full of excitement and declared his hero's hats to be the crowning glory of his collection. Within five minutes the drawings were framed and under glass, and had taken their place among the other emblems and mementoes of his hero.

Tuesday 16 March 1830

Goethe's son came to see me this morning and announced that his long-standing plan to travel to Italy was finally going to happen, that his father had agreed to give him the necessary money, and that he would like me to accompany him. We rejoiced together at the news and discussed our preparations at length.

Later on, as I was passing Goethe's house shortly before midday, Goethe was standing at the window, beckoning me to come in, so I went straight upstairs to him. He was in the set of rooms at the front, and in a very bright and chirpy mood. He immediately started talking about his son's travel plans, saying he approved of them, thought them sensible, and was pleased that I would be going along too. 'It will be good for both of you,' he said, 'and it won't do your culture any harm either.'

He then showed me sketches for a statue of Christ with twelve apostles, and we talked about how little such figures have to offer as subjects for sculpture. 'One apostle,' said Goethe, 'looks much like another, and very few of them have led such an eventful and colourful life that it marks them out clearly as individuals. I have amused myself by making up a cycle of twelve biblical figures where each one is distinctive and different from all the rest, and therefore would make a rewarding subject for the artist.

'First of all we have Adam, the most beautiful of men, as

perfect as we can possibly imagine. He might have one hand resting on a spade, symbolizing that man is called to till the soil. Next comes Noah, marking the beginning of a new creation. He is cultivating the vine, and one might portray him as a sort of Indian Bacchus. Then Moses, as the first lawgiver. Then David, as warrior and king. After him Isaiah, as prince and prophet. Daniel would come next, pointing forward to the *future* Christ. Then Christ Himself, followed by John, who loves the *present* Christ. So Christ would be flanked by two youthful figures, one of whom (Daniel) would be portrayed as a gentle soul with long hair, while the other (John) would be an impassioned character with short, curly hair.

'But after John, who's next? The Centurion of Capernaum, who represents the body of believers, looking for a very present help in time of need. Next comes Mary Magdalene, symbolizing penitent humanity in need of forgiveness and seeking to mend its ways. The essence of Christianity would be embodied in these two figures.

'Then we could have Paul, who did the most to spread the teachings of Christ. After him would come James, who travelled to the most remote peoples, and thus represents missionaries. And the final figure would be Peter. The artist should place him near the door, and make him look as if he is scrutinizing those who come in, to see if they are worthy of entering the sanctuary.

'What do you think of my biblical cycle? I fancy it would be more rewarding than the twelve apostles, where they all look the same. I would show Moses and Mary Magdalene sitting down.'

I heard all this with great delight and urged Goethe to write it down, which he promised to do. 'I will give some more thought to it all,' he said, 'and then let you have it, along with some other recent things, for the thirty-ninth volume.'

Wednesday 17 March 1830

Dined with Goethe. I asked him about a particular passage in his poems, whether it should read: 'As your priest Horace promised in his rapture', as in all the older editions, or: 'As your priest Propertius' etc., which we have in the new edition.[47]

'I made the mistake of changing it on Göttling's advice,' said Goethe. 'And "priest Propertius" sounds awkward, too, and so I prefer the earlier reading.'

'And in the manuscript of your *Helena*,' I said, 'you wrote that Theseus had abducted her as a slender *ten*-year-old fawn. When Göttling quibbled at this, you changed it to a slender *seven*-year-old fawn in the published text – which is too young, both for the beautiful girl herself and for the twin brothers Castor and Pollux who rescue her. The whole episode takes place so far back in a mythical past that nobody can say how old she really was, and besides, all mythology is so adaptable that we can use the material in whatever ways we like.'

'You're quite right,' said Goethe, 'and I, too, favour making her ten years old when Theseus abducts her, which is why I later wrote: "she was no good from her *tenth* year on". So I think you should change the seven-year-old fawn back into a ten-year-old fawn in the forthcoming edition.'

Over dessert, Goethe showed me two notebooks of delightful illustrations to his ballads by Neureuther, and we particularly admired this charming artist's free spirit and sunny mentality.

Sunday 21 March 1830

Dined with Goethe. He talked first about his son's impending travels, and said that we should not expect too much from the experience. 'People generally come back the same as they went,' he said. 'In fact, the danger is that we come back with ideas that have no place in the lives we lead at home. I came back from Italy with my head full of their fine staircases, and have clearly ruined my house in consequence by making all the rooms smaller than they should have been. The main thing is to learn how to rein oneself in. If I were to just let myself go regardless, I could see myself wreaking havoc on myself and everyone around me.'

We then talked about physical ailments, and the interaction between body and mind.

'It's incredible,' said Goethe, 'how much the mind can do to sustain the body. I often suffer from abdominal pain, but will-power and the strength of my upper body keep me going. It's just a case of mind over matter. For example, I find it easier to work when the barometer is high than when it is low; now that I know this, I make more effort when the barometer is low, so as to counteract the negative effect – and it works.

'In poetry, however, certain things can't be forced, and you have to wait until the time is right to do what can't be accomplished by sheer mental willpower. That's why I am taking my time with my "Walpurgis Night", so that all the themes are fully developed and the reader is suitably charmed. I've made good progress and hope to complete it before your departure.

'As for any barbed references in there, I have made them general rather than personal, so that the reader will find plenty of allusions without knowing exactly who is meant. But I have tried to make sure that everything is sharply delineated, in the classical manner, and that there is nothing vague or uncertain in there, which would no doubt suit the romantic way of doing things.

'This whole notion of classical and romantic poetry, which is exercising people all over the world and causing so much strife and division,' Goethe went on, 'goes back to me and Schiller. I espoused the principle of objective treatment in poetry and wouldn't countenance anything else. But Schiller's approach was entirely subjective; he thought his was the right way, and he wrote his essay on naïve and sentimental poetry to defend his views against mine. He showed me that I was a romantic despite myself, and that the prevalence of sentiment in my *Iphigenie* meant that it was by no means as "classical", and written in the spirit of antiquity, as one perhaps liked to think. This idea was picked up by the Schlegels, who took it further, so that it has spread throughout the world; and now everyone is talking about classicism and romanticism, which fifty years ago would not have entered anyone's head.'

I turned the conversation back to the cycle of twelve biblical figures, and Goethe elaborated on his earlier suggestions.

'Adam would have to be represented, as I said, but not

completely naked; I think it would work best to show him after the Fall, clad in a thin deerskin. And at the same time, to convey the idea that he is the father of mankind, it would be good to show him with his eldest son, a truculent lad, looking defiantly about him – a little Hercules, crushing a snake in his fist.

'I've had a further thought about Noah, too, which I think is better. Instead of making him look like an Indian Bacchus, I would show him as a wine grower, so that people could think of him as a kind of redeemer, who, as the first man to cultivate the vine, set humanity free from the torment of care and affliction.'

I was very taken with these happy thoughts and made a mental note to write them down.

Goethe then showed me the engraving by Neureuther illustrating his 'Legende vom Hufeisen'. 'The artist,' I said, 'has given the Saviour only eight disciples.' 'Even those eight were too many for him,' Goethe cut in, 'and he has wisely sought to separate them into two groups, to avoid the monotony of having them standing relentlessly in line.'

Wednesday 24 March 1830

Dined with Goethe and had some very lively conversation. He told me about a French poem entitled 'Le Rire de Mirabeau', the manuscript of which had been included in the consignment sent by David.[48] 'The poem is very witty and audacious,' said Goethe, 'and you must read it. It's as if the poet had written it in ink prepared by Mephistopheles. It's a fine piece of work if he wrote it without having read *Faust* – and equally fine if he had read it.'

Wednesday 21 April 1830

I said goodbye to Goethe this evening, as I am due to leave for Italy tomorrow morning with his son, the Privy Councillor. We discussed many things pertaining to our journey; in particular, he advised me to observe well and to write to him now and then.

I felt quite emotional to be leaving Goethe. But I was re-assured by seeing him in such rude health, and had every expectation of being happily reunited with him again.

As I was leaving he gave me an album, in which he had written these words:

> Behold, he passes by me, and I see him not;
> He moves on, but I do not perceive him.
>
> Book of Job
To the Travellers

Weimar, 21 April 1830   Goethe

Frankfurt, Saturday 24 April 1830

Shortly before eleven, I went for a walk around the city and through the gardens, in the direction of the Taunus Mountains, enjoying the splendours of nature and the abundant vegetation. The day before yesterday, in Weimar, the trees were still in bud; but here I found the young shoots of the chestnut trees a foot long already, and those of the lime trees six or seven inches; the leaves on the birch trees were already dark green, and the oaks were all in leaf. The grass was a foot high, so that I met girls at the gate who were carrying heavy baskets of grass.

I walked through the gardens to get an uninterrupted view of the Taunus range; there was a brisk wind, the clouds were blowing up from the south-west, and casting their shadows on the mountains as they passed over towards the north-east. I watched a few storks landing between the gardens, then lifting off again, which was a lovely sight in the sunshine, in between the scudding white clouds and the blue sky, and added the perfect finishing touch to the scene. When I returned I saw the most beautiful cows coming towards me outside the gate, with brown and white markings and lustrous coats.

The air here is very agreeable and healthy, and the water has a sweetish taste. The beefsteaks are the best I've eaten since Hamburg. I'm also enjoying the excellent white bread.

The fair is now on, and people are out on the streets, singing and making a racket from morning till late into the night. I was particularly struck by a Savoyard boy who was turning a hurdy-gurdy and pulling a dog along behind him with a monkey riding on its back. He was whistling and singing up at us, and kept on entreating us to give him something. We threw down more than he could have expected, and I thought he would have given us a look of gratitude in return. But not a bit of it; he simply pocketed the money and looked around for more people to tap.

Frankfurt, Sunday 25 April 1830

Today we went for a drive around the city in a very elegant carriage owned by our host. The charming parks, the magnificent buildings, the lovely river, the gardens and inviting summerhouses quickened the senses; but I soon perceived that our minds need to formulate thoughts about the objects we see, and that without this it is all just a passing spectacle without meaning.

Over lunch, at the table d'hôte, I saw many faces, but few sufficiently expressive to be at all remarkable. But the head waiter was a most interesting character, and I could not take my eyes off him or his movements. He really was a remarkable man. There were nearly two hundred of us for lunch, seated at long tables, and, incredible as it sounds, this head waiter basically served us all by himself; he served all the dishes and removed the plates afterwards, while the other waiters just handed the dishes to him and took the plates from him. He never spilled anything, never brushed against any of the diners; he darted and flitted like some aerial spirit, propelled by an unseen force. A thousand plates and dishes flew from his hands on to the table, and then from the table into the hands of the waiters following on behind him. Totally absorbed in what he was doing, the man was all eye and hand movements, unsealing his lips only to give a quick answer or instruction. And he was not only serving lunch to the entire table, but also taking individual orders for wine and other things; and he remembered it all, so that when lunch was over he knew exactly what everyone owed and collected the right money. I marvelled at this remarkable young man's all-seeing eye, presence of mind and excellent memory. And he was always perfectly calm and composed, always ready with a joke or a witty riposte, so that a constant smile played about his lips. A French cavalry captain of the old guard commiserated with him towards the end of the meal because the ladies were retiring, whereupon he shot back: 'C'est pour vous autres; nous sommes sans passion.' He spoke perfect French, likewise English, and I was assured that he had three other languages at his command. I got into conversation with him later and found him to be an uncommonly cultivated man in every respect.

In the evening, at a performance of *Don Giovanni*, we had reason to think fondly of Weimar. The players all had good voices and were talented enough, but they nearly all acted and spoke as if they belonged to the naturalist school of drama, owing more to intuition than to tuition. They did not articulate clearly, and carried on as if there were no audience present. The performances of some cast members prompted the thought that ignobleness without character just comes across as crude and obnoxious, whereas, when combined with character, it is elevated to the higher realms of art. The audience was very loud and boisterous, and there were plenty of encores and curtain calls. Zerlina fared well and badly at the same time; half the audience hissed while the other half clapped, so that passions rose on both sides and it ended every time in uproar and tumult.

Milan, 28 May 1830

I've been here nearly three weeks now, and I think it is time I put something down on paper.

We were sorry to find the great La Scala opera house closed; we looked inside, and it was filled with scaffolding. They are doing various repairs and constructing an additional row of boxes, so we are told. The principal singers have taken advantage of this opportunity to travel. Some are now in Vienna, apparently, others in Paris.

I went to the Puppet Theatre as soon as I arrived here, and

was impressed by the remarkably clear diction of the speaking parts. This puppet theatre may well be the best in the world; it is very famous, and you hear people talking about it before you even reach Milan.

The Teatro della Canobbiana, with five rows of boxes one above the other, is the city's largest theatre after La Scala. It holds three thousand people. I like it very much; I have been there often, and always to see the same opera and ballet. For the last three weeks they have been doing *Il Conte Ory*, the opera by Rossini, and the ballet *L'Orfana di Genevra*.[49] The backdrops, painted by San Quirico, or at least under his direction, are very effective, and sufficiently subdued not to compete for attention with the costumes of the players. They say that San Quirico has many skilled men working for him; all the commissions come to him, he delegates them and gives his instructions, so that everything goes under his name, while he does very little himself. I have heard that he pays a handsome fixed salary to many gifted artists, which they get even if they are ill and have nothing to do all year.

At the opera I was glad to see, first, that there was no prompt box. They always block our view of the actors' feet, which is so annoying. Then I liked the way they had positioned the conductor. From where he stood he could look over his entire orchestra and signal and conduct to the right and to the left; they could all see him, standing on a slightly raised, central podium, just in front of the stalls, so that he had a clear view over the orchestra to the stage. In Weimar, on the other hand, the conductor likewise has a clear view of the stage, but he stands with the orchestra behind him, so that he always has to turn round when he wants to indicate to one of the players.

The orchestra itself is very large; I counted sixteen double basses, eight on each wing. The orchestra of nearly a hundred faces inwards on both sides, towards the conductor, with their backs towards the pit boxes that extend into the proscenium, so that they can see the stage with one eye and the stalls with the other, while the conductor is directly in front of them.

As for the voices of the singers, I was entranced by their purity of tone and depth of sound, their ability to hit the right note and project without the slightest effort. I thought of Zelter, and wished I could have had him beside me. I found the voice of Signora Corradi-Pantanelli particularly enchanting; she sang the part of the page. I mentioned this excellent singer to others, and learned that she had been engaged for La Scala for the coming winter. The prima donna, playing the Countess Adèle, was a young novice, Signora Albertini; her voice has a delicacy, a limpid brightness, like the light of the sun. She will delight any visitor from Germany. A young bass also stood out. His voice is immensely powerful but lacking in finesse, just like his acting, which, although not self-conscious, suggests that his art is in its infancy.

The choruses went very well and were in perfect synchrony with the orchestra.

As far as the physical movements of the players were concerned, I noted a certain moderation and restraint, when I had expected to see more signs of the spirited Italian character.

The stage make-up gave the faces a slightly flushed appearance, just enough to look natural and healthy, without making us think of painted cheeks.

It seemed to me remarkable that such a large orchestra never drowned out the voices of the singers, which always remained the dominant sound. I mentioned this at our table d'hôte, and a knowledgeable young man offered his own explanation. 'German orchestras,' he said, 'are self-regarding; it's all about them, and their standing as an orchestra. Italian orchestras, on the other hand, are more discreet. They understand that in an opera the sound of human voices is the main thing, and that the orchestral accompaniment is only there to provide a backing. Italians also believe that the sound of a musical instrument is only beautiful if it is not forced. So it doesn't matter how many violins, clarinets, trumpets and double basses are playing in an Italian orchestra – the overall effect is always restrained and pleasing, whereas a German orchestra, with only a third the number of instruments, soon becomes loud and overbearing.'

I could not argue with any of this, and was glad to have my problem solved so neatly.

'But surely,' I retorted, 'our modern composers are to blame for scoring the orchestral accompaniment to operas with too many instruments?'

'It's true,' replied the stranger, 'that recent composers have made that mistake; but never the really great masters, like Mozart and Rossini. Sometimes these two even introduce different themes into the accompaniment, which are independent of the sung melody line; but they do it so subtly that the voices always remain the dominant element. Our contemporary composers, on the other hand, who struggle to come up with themes for the accompaniment, very often drown out the voices with heavy-handed instrumentation.'

I concurred with our knowledgeable young foreigner. My neighbour at the table told me he was a young baron from Livonia, who had spent a lot of time in Paris and London and had now been here for five years, studying hard.[50]

I must mention something else that I noticed in the opera, and which I was glad to see. When the Italians stage night-time scenes in the theatre, they represent the night symbolically rather than literally. In German theatres I have never liked the way everything goes completely dark when a scene is set at night, so that you can't see the expressions on the actors' faces, or indeed the actors themselves; all you see is an empty blackness. The Italians do these things much better. Night-time in their theatres is never the real thing, but only a figurative representation. They simply dimmed the lights at the back of the stage, while the actors moved towards the front, where they were fully lit, and no detail of facial expression escaped us. I imagine the same approach works well in painting, too; I'd be surprised to find pictures where the night has made the faces so dark that it's impossible to make out their expressions. I would hope that no good artist has ever painted such a picture.

I found the same excellent principle applied in the ballet. They staged a scene at night where a girl is attacked by a robber. The stage lighting is only slightly dimmed, so that you can see all the movements and facial expressions perfectly clearly. When the girl screams, the murderer runs off, and the local peasants come running to the scene from their cottages, carrying lights. But not dim, yellow lights; these were white, like phosphorus, so that it was only the contrast of this intensely bright light that made us realize the previous scene had taken place at night.

What I had been told in Germany about noisy Italian audiences proved to be quite true, and the longer an opera goes on, the more uproarious the audience becomes. Two weeks ago I saw one of the first performances of *Il Conte Ory*. The best singers were applauded when they first appeared; people talked among themselves during uneventful scenes; but at the beginning of a good aria the audience went quiet, and the singers were rewarded at the end with universal applause. The choruses went very well, and I admired the way voices and orchestra always came together with perfect precision. But now that the opera has been performed every evening since then, the audience no longer pays any attention; everybody talks throughout, and the auditorium buzzes with a fearful racket. Hardly anybody can be bothered to clap, and it's hard to see why the singers and musicians would want to sing or play another note. All the passion and precision have gone, and a foreign visitor intent on hearing the performance would be in despair – if it were possible to feel despair in such cheerful company.

Milan, 30 May 1830, on the first day of Pentecost

I am writing down a few other things that I have noted with pleasure in Italy, or that have otherwise interested me.

At the top of the Simplon Pass, in a wilderness of snow and mist, close to a refuge, a boy and his little sister came up the incline towards our carriage. Both were carrying little baskets of wood on their backs, which they had gathered on the lower slopes of the mountain, where there is still some vegetation. The boy handed us some pieces of rock crystal and other minerals, and we gave him a few small coins in return. I shall never forget the look of sheer joy on his face when he glanced furtively at his money as he walked past our carriage. I have never before seen such a beatific expression of bliss. I reflected that God has implanted all the sources of our happiness and all our capacity for happiness within the human heart, and that happiness does not depend at all on where or how a person lives.

1830 349

I was planning to continue these notes, but I was interrupted, and didn't get round to writing again for the rest of my stay in Italy, even though not a day passed without interesting impressions and observations of some kind. It was only after I had taken my leave of Goethe's son and left the Alps behind me that I addressed the following lines to Goethe.

Geneva, Sunday 12 September 1830

I have so much to tell you this time that I hardly know where to begin and where to leave off.

Your Excellency has often remarked in jest that setting out on one's travels is a very fine thing, if only one didn't have to come home again. I now find this to be painfully true, in that I find myself at a crossroads of sorts and don't know which way to go.

My stay in Italy, short though it was, did not fail to make a great impact on me, as you would expect. A bountiful nature spoke to me through her wonders and asked me how far I have come, to be able to understand such a language. Great works of men and great deeds have inspired me and made me look at my own hands to see what I myself can do. All manner of lives have touched my own and asked me what my own life was like. And so I am now conscious of three great needs: to increase my knowledge, to improve my condition in life, and first and foremost, in order to make these two things possible, to *do* something.

As far as this last point is concerned, I am in no doubt at all about what I should be doing. There is a project that has long been close to my heart, and which I have worked on in my spare time for the past few years. It is well on the way to completion, much like a newly built ship that only needs its rigging and sails before putting to sea.

I refer to those conversations about great truths in all branches of science and art, as well as illuminating observations on higher human concerns, works of the mind, and distinguished figures of the age, which have been such a regular feature of the six years that I have been privileged to spend in your company. These conversations have been for me an inexhaustible source of cultural enrichment, and just as I have been supremely blessed to hear them and mark them, so I wanted to share this blessing with other deserving souls by writing them down and preserving them for the better part of humanity.

Your Excellency has seen a few pages of these conversations from time to time, you have indicated your approval, and you have repeatedly encouraged me to persevere with this undertaking. Which I have done, as and when the distractions of my life in Weimar have permitted, with the result that I have now collected sufficient material for maybe two volumes.

Before setting out for Italy, I did not pack these important manuscripts in my luggage along with my other papers, but sealed them up in a separate bundle and entrusted them to our friend Soret for safekeeping, with the request to hand them over to you in the event that some misfortune befell me on my travels and I did not return.

After our visit to Venice, during our second stay in Milan, I went down with a fever and was very ill for several nights; I lay in my sickbed for a whole week in a wretched state, and with no appetite at all. In these lonely, desolate hours I thought a great deal about that manuscript, and it troubled me that it was not in a sufficiently finished state to be of immediate use. I recalled that much of it was written in pencil, that some passages were unclear and not properly expressed, that many things were only hinted at, and that – in a word – it was in need of proper editing and polishing.

In such circumstances, and with these thoughts going through my mind, I felt an urgent need to be reunited with those papers. The joyful prospect of seeing Naples and Rome faded, and I was overcome by a desire to return to Germany, shut myself away in solitary confinement and complete that manuscript.

Without revealing what was at the back of my mind, I spoke to your son about the state of my health; he could see that it was risky to drag me any further in that great heat, and we agreed that I should give Genoa a try first; if my health did not improve there, then I would be free to go back to Germany if I wished.

It was when we had been in Genoa for a while that we received a letter from you, in which you seemed to sense from afar how things stood with us, and in which you said that if I should wish to return to you, I would be very welcome.

We marvelled at your intuition, and were delighted that you had given your blessing, from the other side of the Alps, to an arrangement that we had just agreed between ourselves. I was for leaving immediately, but your son thought it would be nice if I stayed on and left on the same day that he did.

I gladly agreed to this, and so it was on Sunday 25 July, at four o'clock in the morning, that we embraced in the street in Genoa and said our farewells. Two carriages were waiting; your son boarded the one that was headed around the coast to Livorno, while I took my seat with other travellers in the other one, which was going over the mountains to Turin. And so we drove off in opposite directions, both feeling emotional, and with the sincerest good wishes for each other's well-being.

After travelling for three days in the extreme heat and dust, via Novi, Alessandria and Asti, I reached Turin, where I was obliged to spend a few days recovering, seeing the sights, and waiting for a suitable coach to cross the Alps. There was one leaving on Monday 2 August, going over the Mont Cenis pass to Chambéry, where we arrived on the evening of the 6th. On the afternoon of the 7th I found another coach going to Aix, and on the 8th I reached Geneva after dark, in the pouring rain, and found a bed at the Crown Inn.

The place was full of Englishmen who had left Paris in a hurry, and who had much to tell about the extraordinary scenes they had witnessed there.[51] You can imagine the effect on me of learning for the first time of those earth-shattering events, and with what eager interest I read the newspapers, which had been suppressed in Piedmont, and how intently I listened to the stories told by the newcomers who arrived each day, and to the political discussions and arguments across the dinner table. Everyone was in a state of high excitement, and people were trying to predict the possible impact of such violent measures on the rest of Europe. I visited our friend Mme Sylvestre, and Soret's parents and brother; and since everyone had to have an opinion in these tumultuous times, I formed my own: that the French ministers were chiefly to blame for inducing the monarch to take measures that undermined public confidence and damaged the King's reputation.

It had been my intention to write to you at length as soon as I arrived in Geneva. But the excitement and distractions of the first few days were too great for me to be able to settle quietly to writing to you, as I had planned. Then on 15 August I received a letter from our friend Sterling in Genoa containing deeply distressing news, which made it impossible for me to write to Weimar. Our friend reports that on the day we parted your son broke his collarbone when the coach overturned, and is now confined to bed in Spezia. I replied immediately, saying that I was ready to come back over the Alps at a moment's notice, and that I would not leave Geneva and continue my journey to Germany until I had received reassuring news from Genoa. While waiting to hear back, I set myself up in modest private lodgings and used my time to improve my knowledge of French.

Finally, on 28 August, I had cause for double celebration,[52] as I was delighted to receive a second letter from Sterling that day telling me that your son has made a speedy and complete recovery after his accident, and is now safe and sound and in good spirits in Livorno. So all my concerns on his account were instantly banished, and in the stillness of my heart I prayed the lines:

> Give thanks to God in times of pain,
> When respite comes, give thanks again.[53]

I then set about writing to you in earnest with my news. I wanted to tell you broadly what is recorded in the preceding pages. I also wanted to ask you whether I might be permitted to complete that manuscript which is so close to my heart in a place of quiet seclusion, away from Weimar. Because I do not believe that I will feel completely free and easy in my mind until I can lay that long-cherished work before you, in a bound clean copy, for you to approve its publication.

But now I have received letters from Weimar which tell me that I am expected back soon, and that they wish to give me an official position. I must be grateful for this kind offer, but it conflicts with my present plans and creates an awkward dilemma for me.

If I were to return to Weimar now, I would have no chance of completing my current literary projects quickly. I would immediately be distracted again; in a small town like ours, where everyone is living in each other's pockets, I would soon get embroiled again in various trivial affairs that would consume all my time and energy, without doing me or anyone else much good.

There is so much about the place that is good and excellent, and that I have long cherished and will always cherish; but when I look back upon it, it is as if I see an angel with a flaming sword standing at the city gates, denying me entry and driving me away.

I know that I am a bit of an oddity as a person. There are certain things I will not let go of; I stick to my resolutions over the years and see them through doggedly, no matter what it takes; but in the little encounters of everyday life nobody is more dependent, vacillating, impressionable and easily led than me. And so my life swings back and forth between these two poles, forever changing and yet always the same. When I look back over the road I have travelled, the situations and circumstances I have gone through are remarkably varied and different; but when I look more closely I see a certain basic theme running through them all, which is a striving for higher things. And as a result, I have succeeded in cultivating and improving myself by degrees.

But those very qualities of impressionability and amenability have made it necessary for me to adjust my circumstances from time to time; just as a mariner who is blown off course by the vagaries of the winds is constantly trying to get back on track.

To accept a position now would be incompatible with my long-suppressed literary ambitions. I have no desire to go on giving lessons to young Englishmen. I have acquired the language, and that's all I needed – and I'm glad of it now. I am well aware of all the good that has come of my long association with these young foreigners; but everything has its season and its turn.

In fact, teaching and engaging with people via the spoken word is not my thing at all. That is a calling for which I lack both talent and training. I have no gift for eloquence, and whenever I am speaking to someone I am generally so intimidated that I forget myself, get drawn into the other person's character and interests, and feel so defined by this that I rarely manage to think clearly or coherently.

Faced with a sheet of paper, on the other hand, I feel entirely at my ease and completely in control. So developing my thoughts in writing is my true delight and the thing I live for; and any day when I have not written a few pages that I am pleased with is a day wasted, to my mind.

My whole being is now urging me to direct my efforts towards a larger audience, to exert some influence in the world of literature, and – if my luck holds – to make a name for myself at last.

In itself, literary fame is hardly worth bothering about; I have seen for myself that it can be a great nuisance and a distraction. But it has its good side, in that it shows the aspiring writer that his efforts have found an audience; and this is a divine feeling, which lifts the spirits and gives us inspiration and energy that we would not otherwise have.

If, on the other hand, we spend too much time poking around in our own narrow world, our intellect and character both suffer; in the end we become incapable of great things and struggle to rise above our circumstances.

If the Grand Duchess really wants to do something for me, it is easy enough for such high-placed persons to find a way of showing their favour. If she is minded to support and foster my present literary endeavours, she will be doing a good work, the fruits of which will not be wasted.

1830

The Prince, it is true to say, has a special place in my heart. I have high hopes of his intellectual abilities and character, and I shall be happy to place my limited knowledge at his disposal. I shall strive continually to grow in learning as he matures in years, so that he will be able to take in any new knowledge I may have to give.

But for the present, what matters most to me is the completion of the aforementioned manuscript. I should like to devote several months to this, living in quiet seclusion with my beloved and her family near Göttingen, so that by freeing myself of an old burden I shall make myself ready and willing to take up new ones in the future. My life has not really gone anywhere in recent years, and I would love to have a new sense of direction again. Besides, my health is frail and unreliable; I do not know how much time I have left, and I should like to leave something good behind, so that my name lives on for a while in people's memories.

But I can do nothing without you, without your blessing and approval. I don't know what your future plans for me are, nor do I know what good things those in high places might possibly have in mind for me. But that is my situation; and now that I have bared my soul to you, you will easily be able to judge whether more important reasons pertaining to my future happiness demand my immediate return, or whether I can safely pursue my own intellectual plans for the time being.

I shall be leaving here in a few days for Frankfurt, as soon as I can find suitable transport – travelling via Neuchâtel, Colmar and Strasbourg, taking my time and seeing the sights on the way. It would give me enormous pleasure to find a few lines from you waiting for me in Frankfurt – if you could please address them to me there, *poste restante*.

It is a great relief to have got this difficult confession off my chest, and I look forward, in my next letter, to writing to Your Excellency in a lighter vein.

Please convey my regards to Councillor Meyer, Chief Planning Officer Coudray, Professor Riemer, Chancellor von Müller and anyone else there who might be thinking of me.

356 CONVERSATIONS WITH GOETHE

You yourself I embrace warmly, and remain your devoted and affectionate friend, wherever I may be.

Yours ever,
E.

Geneva, 14 September 1830

To my great delight, I gathered from one of your last letters in Genoa that you have successfully filled in the gaps and completed the ending to the 'Classical Walpurgis Night'. So the first three acts are now finished, *Helena* has been worked in with the rest, and therefore the hardest part is done. The ending is already there, as you told me, and so I hope it won't be long before the fourth act falls into place and something great will have been created for the edification and instruction of future centuries. I am really delighted that it is going so well, and I look forward to receiving further news of the onward march of your poetic powers.

On my travels I have had frequent occasion to think of *Faust* and be reminded of certain classic passages. When I was in Italy, seeing all the beautiful people and the healthy vigour of the young children, these lines came to mind:

Here happiness is passed from father on to son,
A bloom on every cheek, a smile on every face.
Strangers to mortality, their days are never done,
Contentment and rude health attend this blessed race.

And so as time goes by, beneath these sunny skies,
The infant grows in strength and imitates the father.
We wonder at the sight – though the question does arise,
Are these gods we gaze upon, or are they humans rather?[54]

On the other hand, whenever I was carried away by the glories of the natural world, feasting my eyes on lakes, mountains and valleys that made my heart swell within me, some unseen little devil, it seemed, would have his sport with me, as he whispered in my ear the lines:

1830   357

> And had I not shaken and heaved from below,
> How could this world be so lovely?[55]

And that was the end of all sensible observation. I was
gradually overcome with a sense of absurdity, I felt a kind of
convulsion within me, and there was nothing for it but to burst
into laughter every time.

These occasions made me very aware of the fact that the
poet really should be positive at all times. People need poets to
say what they themselves cannot express. When we are moved
by some spectacle or feeling, we reach for the right words, but
find our own vocabulary inadequate; and so the poet must
come to our aid, setting us free by satisfying our need.

With this in mind, I have repeatedly blessed those first two
stanzas – and cursed these latter lines daily, albeit with a laugh.
But they work wonderfully well in the context for which they
were written, and we would be the poorer without them.

I didn't keep a diary as such in Italy. There was just too
much for me to take in at the time, confronted as I was by one
spectacular sight after another; and I couldn't have got it all
down on paper even if I had wanted to. But I did keep my eyes
and ears open all the time, and I noted a great deal. I am
planning to group these impressions together under specific
headings and write them up. In particular, I made some
interesting observations regarding the *Farbenlehre*, which I
look forward to relating very soon. It's nothing new, of course,
but it's always good to come across new manifestations of an
old law.

In Genoa, Sterling showed great interest in the theory. What
he had learned of Newton's theory failed to satisfy him, and so
he was very receptive to the outline of your doctrine that I
was able to give him in a series of conversations. If an
opportunity could be found to despatch a copy of the work
to Genoa, I think it safe to say that such a gift would not be
unwelcome.

Here in Geneva I have found an eager disciple for the last
three weeks in the person of our lady friend Sylvestre. Our
time together has shown me that simple things are harder to

grasp than one thinks, and that it takes a lot of practice always to discern the underlying law when the phenomenon manifests itself in so many different ways. But it is good for our mental dexterity; nature is a very delicate thing, and we must always take care not to do her violence by jumping to conclusions.

Incidentally, nobody here in Geneva seems to take the slightest interest in such an important matter. It's not just that they don't have a copy of your *Farbenlehre* in the local library; they don't even know that such a thing exists. It may be that the Germans are more to blame for this than the Genevese, but it annoys me all the same, and I feel driven to make pointed remarks.

It's well known that Lord Byron spent some time here, and since he did not care for society he was out and about day and night, exploring the countryside or out on the lake. They still talk about it here, and he has left us a lovely memorial of those times in his *Childe Harold*. He noted the colour of the Rhône, too, and even though he could not have guessed the cause, he clearly had a sensitive eye. In a note to the Third Canto he says: 'The colour of the Rhône at Geneva is *blue*, to a depth of tint which I have never seen equalled in water, salt or fresh, except in the Mediterranean and Archipelago.'

The Rhône, as it narrows to pass through Geneva, divides into two arms, which are spanned by four bridges; anyone walking across these is ideally placed to observe the colour of the water.

Now the remarkable thing is, the water of one arm is blue, as Byron observed, but that of the other one is green. The arm where the water appears blue is faster-flowing, and the water has scoured out such a deep channel that no light can penetrate to the bottom, where all is total darkness. The very clear water acts as a cloudy medium, and the resulting colour, as our well-known laws would lead us to expect, is a gorgeous shade of blue. The water in the other arm is not so deep, so the light penetrates to the bottom, and we can see the stony river bed; since it is not dark enough down there to appear blue, and the river bed is not sufficiently flat, clean, white and reflective to appear yellow, the colour lies midway between the two, and looks green.

If I were a natural prankster, like Byron, and had the means to indulge my whims, I would conduct the following experiment. In the green arm of the Rhône, near the bridge where thousands of people cross each day, I would secure a large black board or suchlike under the water, sufficiently far down to produce a pure blue colour; and close by I would have a very large sheet of bright metal, positioned at such a depth that under the sunlight it would appear distinctly yellow. When people walked past and saw the yellow and blue patches under the green water, it would be a tantalizing mystery to them, which they would not be able to solve. People get up to all kinds of larks when they are travelling, but this strikes me as one of the better ones; it makes a serious point, and has something useful to tell us.

Some time ago I was in a bookshop, and in the first little duodecimo edition that I picked up my eye fell upon a passage that I have translated thus: 'But tell me this: if one has discovered some truth, is it necessary to tell others about it? If you publicize it, you will be persecuted by a host of people who make their living from the opposite error, who will claim that this very error *is* the truth, and that anything which calls it into question is the greatest error of all.'

This passage seemed to me so relevant to the way your *Farbenlehre* has been received by men of science that it might have been written with that in mind; and I liked it so much that I bought the whole book because of it. The contents included *Paul et Virginie* and *La Chaumière indienne* by Bernardin de Saint-Pierre, so it was money well spent on all counts. I enjoyed reading the book; I found the author's honest, high-minded approach most refreshing, and was impressed by his subtle artistry, particularly his apt use of familiar similes.

I have also discovered Rousseau and Montesquieu for the first time here. But I won't say any more about that now – that, and much else besides – otherwise this letter could easily become a book in its own right.

Having got my long letter of two days ago off my chest, I feel a sense of relief and a lightness of spirit that I haven't felt for years, and I could go on writing and talking for ever. What I need more than anything else is to stay away from Weimar, at least for the time being. I hope you will approve my plan, and I can already see the day when you will say that I did the right thing.

The theatre here opens tomorrow with the *Barber of Seville*, which I want to see; but after that, I'm seriously thinking to leave.[56] The weather seems to be clearing up and looking favourable for my travels. It has been raining here since your birthday, when it began with thunderstorms in the early morning, which came up the Rhône all day from the direction of Lyon and passed over the lake towards Lausanne, so that we had thunder virtually the whole day. I am renting a room for sixteen sous a day, with a beautiful view of the lake and mountains. Yesterday the rain came down; it was cold, and the highest peaks of the Jura appeared white with snow for the first time after the shower had passed, but today the snow has gone again. The foothills of Mont Blanc are already starting to look permanently white; up above the shore of the lake, amid the green of the lush vegetation, some trees have already turned yellow and brown. The nights are getting cold, and you can tell that autumn is just around the corner.

Please give my warm regards to Frau von Goethe, Fräulein Ulrike and Walter, Wolf and Alma. I have a lot to report about Sterling to Frau von Goethe, and am planning to write to her tomorrow.

I look forward to receiving a letter from Your Excellency in Frankfurt, and rejoice in that hope.

With best wishes and sincerest regards,

Yours truly,
E.

I left Geneva on 21 September, and after stopping in Bern for a couple of days I reached Strasbourg on the 27th, where again I stayed for a few days.

Walking past the window of a barber's shop here, I noticed a small bust of Napoleon, which, viewed from the street against the dark background of the shop interior, exhibited every shade of blue, from a pale, pastel blue to a deep violet. I suspected that if the bust were viewed from inside the shop, against the light from the window, it would display every shade of yellow; and I could not resist a sudden urge to step inside, even though I knew nobody there.

I looked immediately towards the bust, and was delighted to see a splendid array of colours from the active side of the spectrum – from the palest yellow to a deep ruby-red. I enquired excitedly whether they would be prepared to let me have this bust of the great hero. The manager of the shop replied that he had only recently brought the bust back from Paris, inspired by a similar attachment to the Emperor; but as my devotion appeared to be a good deal stronger than his own, judging by my joyous enthusiasm, I had the greater claim on ownership, and he was happy to let me have it.

In my eyes this glass effigy was a thing of inestimable value, and so I could not help eyeing the good proprietor with some astonishment as he handed it over for just a few francs.

I sent it to Goethe, along with an equally remarkable medallion that I had bought in Milan, as a small souvenir of my travels, knowing that he would appreciate the true value of the gift.

On arrival in Frankfurt and thereafter, I received the following letters from him.

First Letter

Just a brief note to confirm that your two letters from Geneva arrived safely, although not until 26 September. In haste, therefore, I will just say this: please remain in Frankfurt until we have given proper thought to where you should spend the coming winter.

For now, I enclose a brief note for Privy Councillor von Willemer and his wife, which I would ask you to deliver at the earliest opportunity. You will find in them two friends who are deeply attached to me, who can make your stay in Frankfurt both useful and agreeable.

CONVERSATIONS WITH GOETHE

This must suffice for now. Please write back to me as soon as you receive this letter.

Yours truly,
Goethe

Weimar, 26 September 1830

Second Letter

I send my warmest greetings to you, my dear friend, in my native city, and hope that you will have spent your few days there in the intimate company of my excellent friends.

If you wish to go to Nordheim and spend some time there, I would have no objection. If you intend to work in peace and quiet on the manuscript currently held by Soret, that would suit me very well, since I don't wish to see it rushed into print, but would like to go through it with you and correct it. Its value will be enhanced if people know that it has my personal seal of approval.

I will leave it at that, let you decide and wait to hear back from you. Everyone in my house sends you their best wishes; I have not spoken to any of your other friends and acquaintances since your letter arrived.

All good wishes,

Yours truly,
J. W. v. Goethe

Weimar, 12 October 1830

Third Letter

The vivid impression made on you by the sight of the curious bust in all its different colours; your eagerness to acquire it; the charming little tale of how you obtained it; and the kind thought of giving it to me as a souvenir of your travels: all this shows what an important place this beautiful primary phenomenon, seen here in all its manifestations, occupies in your thinking. This idea, this feeling, and all that flows from it, will accompany you throughout your life, where it will prove productive in many different ways. Error belongs to libraries, truth to the human mind. Books beget

more books, but the study of living primordial laws is pleasing
to the mind that can grasp the simple, disentangle the complex
and bring light into darkness.

If your guiding spirit leads you back to Weimar, you shall
see that effigy set up in the bright, clear sunlight where,
beneath the tranquil blue of the translucent face, the solid
mass of the chest and epaulettes glows in shifting shades of
the most intense ruby red; and as the granite statue of
Memnon comes alive in sound, so here the dull glass figurine
erupts in a riot of colour. So the conquering hero wins
another victory – this time for the *Farbenlehre*. Please accept
my sincere thanks for this unexpected confirmation of the
theory that I hold so dear.

Your medallion, too, is a very welcome addition to my
collection – doubly and trebly so. It has introduced me to
a man by the name of Dupré – an outstanding sculptor,
brassfounder and medallion artist. He was the man who
modelled and cast the likeness of Henri IV on the Pont Neuf.
Prompted by the medallion you sent me, I looked through the
rest of my collection again and found some excellent specimens
by the same man, and others that are attributed to him; so
your gift has been a welcome incentive here, too.

Working on my *Metamorphose*, with Soret's translation
alongside, we have only got as far as the fifth sheet. For a
long time I was unsure whether to bless or curse this
undertaking, but now that I am obliged to reflect on organic
nature once again, I'm finding it enjoyable, and have taken
readily to the work. The approach I adopted more than forty
years ago is still valid: one is led through all the labyrinthine
twists and turns of the comprehensible until one comes up
against the incomprehensible – at which point, having
learned a great deal, one can happily content oneself with
that. None of your philosophers, ancient or modern, has
managed to go any further. More than that one can hardly
presume to say in writing.

J. W. v. Goethe

364 CONVERSATIONS WITH GOETHE

During my time in Nordheim, where I did not arrive until late October, having stayed on a while in Frankfurt and Kassel, everything conspired to make my return to Weimar desirable.

Goethe had not given his approval for the early publication of my *Conversations*, which meant that I had to give up the idea of embarking successfully on a purely literary career.

Furthermore, seeing my dearly beloved of many years again, and being reminded each day of her great virtues, I felt a keen desire to be united with her soon and to put my livelihood on a more secure footing.

Such was my situation when I received a message from Weimar, sent at the behest of the Grand Duchess, which I seized upon with delight, as the following letter to Goethe explains.

Nordheim, 6 November 1830

Man proposes, but God disposes, and in the blink of an eye our circumstances and wishes can take a completely unexpected turn.

A few weeks ago I felt a certain trepidation about returning to Weimar, and now things are such that not only am I looking forward to coming back soon, but I am actually considering setting up house there and making it my permanent home.

A few days ago I received a letter from Soret, with the offer of a regular salary from the Grand Duchess if I was prepared to come back and carry on tutoring the Prince. Soret has more good news for me, which he wants to tell me in person, and so I gather from all this that people there are very well disposed towards me.

I would gladly write back to Soret to accept the offer, but I hear he has gone to Geneva to see his family; so I have no choice but to ask Your Excellency if you would be so kind as to inform Her Imperial Highness of my decision to return soon.

I hope this news also affords you some pleasure, since I know my happiness and peace of mind have long been close to your heart.

My warmest greetings to all your family, and I look forward to seeing you all again soon.

E.

I left Nordheim on the afternoon of 20 November to travel to Göttingen, where I arrived after dark.

That evening, at the table d'hôte, when the landlord heard I was from Weimar and was on my way back there, he calmly remarked that it must have been a grievous blow to the great poet Goethe, at his time of life, to lose his only son, who had died of a stroke in Italy, according to that day's newspapers.

One can imagine how I felt when I heard this. I took a light and went to my room, not wanting the strangers present to see how upset I was.

I spent a sleepless night. The event that affected me so directly was constantly on my mind. The following days and nights on the road, and overnight in Mühlhausen and Gotha, were no better. Alone in the coach during those dull November days, passing barren fields where there was nothing to see and nothing to distract or cheer me, I tried in vain to think about something else; and at the inns, where I was with other people, this tragic event that affected me so deeply was constantly talked about as the big news of the day. My greatest fear was that Goethe might not survive the onslaught of paternal grief at his advanced age. And how will he be affected by your arrival, I said to myself, considering that you left with his son and are now returning alone! It will be like losing his son all over again when he sees you.

Such were my thoughts and feelings as I reached the last toll-house before Weimar, at six o'clock on the evening of Tuesday 23 November. Once again in my life I felt that human existence has its testing times, which one has to get through somehow. My thoughts were with higher beings above me when I caught a glimpse of the moon, which appeared for a few seconds from behind thick clouds, shining brightly, and then was veiled in darkness again, as before. Whether this was coincidence, or whether it was more than that, I took it to be a favourable sign from above, and felt unexpectedly heartened by it.

After looking in briefly at my lodgings, I went straight to Goethe's house. I called first on Frau von Goethe. I found her already in mourning weeds, but calm and composed, and we had much to say to each other.

Then I went down to Goethe. He stood tall and unbowed, and wrapped me in his arms. I found him very cheerful and calm. We sat down and started talking immediately about serious matters, and it was a great joy to be with him again. He showed me two letters that he had started with the intention of writing to me in Nordheim, but had not sent off. We then talked about the Grand Duchess, the Prince and much else besides; but there was no mention at all of his son.

Thursday 25 November 1830

This morning Goethe sent me some books which had arrived from various English and German authors as presents for me. I went to dine with him at midday. I found him looking at a portfolio of engravings and drawings which had been offered to him for sale. He told me he had had the pleasure of a visit from the Grand Duchess that morning, and had informed her of my return.

Frau von Goethe joined us and we sat down at table. I had to report on my travels. I talked about Venice, Milan and Genoa, and he seemed particularly interested in hearing news of the family of the English consul there. I then talked about Geneva, and he made a point of asking after the Soret family and Herr von Bonstetten. He wanted a detailed account of this last gentleman, and I obliged him as best I could.

After dinner, I was pleased when Goethe began talking about my *Conversations*. 'It must be the first thing you do,' he said, 'and we won't let up until it's all finished and in order.'

Incidentally, I thought Goethe seemed unusually quiet today, and often lost in thought. Not a good sign.

Tuesday 30 November 1830

Last Friday Goethe gave us great cause for alarm: in the night he suffered a severe haemorrhage, and was close to death all the following day. With that and the bloodletting, he lost a total of six pounds of blood – which is a lot for a man in his eighties. But the great skill of his doctor, Councillor Vogel, combined

1830 367

with his own incomparable constitution, saved the day once more; he is now recovering fast, already has a healthy appetite again, and is sleeping through the night. Nobody is allowed to see him, and he has been told not to talk; but his ever-active mind cannot rest, and he is already thinking about his work again. This morning I received the following note from him, written in pencil and sent from his bed:

> Please be so good, my dear Doctor, as to go through the enclosed poems again – you will know them already – and insert the new ones at the beginning in the right order, so that the whole thing forms a coherent whole. *Faust* to follow!
>
> I look forward to seeing you again soon!
>
> Goethe

Weimar, 30 November 1830

Following his speedy and complete recovery, Goethe turned his full attention to the fourth act of *Faust* and to the completion of the fourth volume of *Dichtung und Wahrheit*.

He proposed that I should edit his short unpublished papers and look through his diaries and letters, so that we would know how to proceed when the time came to publish them.

I had to give up the idea of editing my *Conversations* with him; I also thought it made more sense, rather than spending time on what I had already written, to go on adding to my stock of material for as long as a benevolent destiny was disposed to permit.

1831

Saturday 1 January 1831

The drafts of Goethe's letters to various correspondents, going back to 1807, have been preserved in a series of bound volumes, some of which I have been studying closely over the last few weeks; and in the paragraphs that follow I shall set down some general observations that may perhaps be useful when and if the letters are edited for publication at a later date.

§1

The first question was whether it is advisable to publish these letters selectively, in excerpted form.

My own view is that it is generally Goethe's nature and practice to approach even the smallest subjects in a very deliberate and purposeful way – something that comes across very clearly in these letters, where the writer always puts himself into it heart and soul. So not only is every page beautifully written from beginning to end, but every line bears the hallmark of a superior and perfectly cultivated mind.

I am therefore in favour of publishing the letters in their entirety, from beginning to end, especially as certain important passages often need to be seen in context for their true brilliance and full meaning to be appreciated.

And when you think about it, looking at these letters in the context of the wider world in all its complexity and diversity, who is to say which passages are important, and therefore worth

1831   369

sharing with readers, and which are not? The grammarian, the
biographer, the philosopher, the ethicist, the natural scientist, the
artist, the poet, the scholar, the actor – the list goes on and on:
they all have their different interests, so that one will just skim
over a passage that another will focus on as highly meaningful
and worthy of note.

For example, in the first volume, for 1807, there is a letter to
a friend whose son wants to go into forestry, and Goethe
sketches out for his friend the career path that the young man
should follow. Now a young literary scholar might well skip
that letter, whereas a forester will surely be pleased to note that
the great poet has also taken an interest in *his* particular area of
expertise and sought to give good advice on these matters, too.

I repeat, therefore, that I am in favour of printing these letters
exactly as they are, without any cuts – especially since they are
already out there in their unabridged form, and we can be sure
that the recipients will one day have them printed exactly as they
were written.

§2

If there are letters, however, whose unabridged publication could
create difficulties, but which nevertheless contain some good
things, these passages should be copied out and either inserted
into the annual volume to which they belong or else published as a
separate collection, at the editor's discretion.

§3

It could happen that the first time we come across a particular
letter in its bound volume it seems of no particular importance,
and so we decide not to publish it. But then we might find in later
volumes that this letter has had certain consequences, so that it
should be regarded as the first link in an extended chain. That
would make it important, and worthy of inclusion among the
letters to be published.

§4

It is open to question whether the letters should be grouped together by correspondent or simply put in chronological order, just as they come.

My own preference is for the latter, firstly because it would make for a pleasing and refreshing variety; not only is the tone of the writing slightly different for each person he is writing to, but the subject matter is always different too, so that the theatre, poetic works, nature studies, family matters, connections with high-placed persons, friendships, etc. are all discussed by turns.

There is another reason why I favour publishing the letters to different correspondents in chronological order: because the letters from any given year touch upon the lives and works of contemporaries, they not only give a general flavour of the year in question, but also tell us about the writer's own circumstances and multiple activities. So these letters from a specific year could serve as a useful supplement to the already published brief biography in the *Tag- und Jahreshefte*, painting a more detailed picture of daily life at particular moments in time.

§5

Letters already published by others, because they contain an acknowledgement of their achievements, perhaps, or some other compliment or curiosity, should be reprinted in this edition, partly because they belong in the chronological sequence, but partly also in order to do such persons a service by proving to the world at large that their letters are genuine.

§6

The question of whether letters of recommendation should be included in the collection or not should be decided on the merits of the person recommended. If that person failed to do anything with his life, the letter should not be included – not unless it contains other things of interest. But if the recommended person has made a name for himself in the world, then the letter should be included.

§7

Letters to persons who are known to us from Goethe's autobiography, such as Lavater, Jung, Behrisch, Kniep, Hackert and others, are of intrinsic interest, and as such should be published, even if they contain nothing else of particular interest.

§8

More generally, we should not be too precious about publishing these letters, because they give us an insight into Goethe's busy life and the sheer variety of his activities and involvements; and because we can learn so much from the way he deals with all kinds of different people in all manner of different situations.

§9

If there are different letters talking about one and the same thing, we should select the best ones; and if a particular point comes up in several different letters, we should omit it from some, but let it stand where it has been best expressed.

§10

In the letters from 1811 and 1812, however, there are perhaps twenty passages asking for the autographs of remarkable individuals. These and similar passages should not be omitted, because they are most delightful and tell us a lot about the man.

The preceding paragraphs were prompted by a study of the letters from 1807, 1808 and 1809. Any further general observations that occur to me as the work progresses will be added later to the present list.

Weimar, 1 January 1831   E.

After dinner today I discussed the above matter with Goethe point by point, and he approved of my suggestions. 'In my will,' he said, 'I shall appoint you as editor of these letters, and I shall indicate that we are in broad agreement about the approach to be adopted.'

Wednesday 9 February 1831

Yesterday I continued with my reading of Voss's *Luise* with the Prince and had several thoughts of my own about the book. I found the portrayal of the setting and the outward circumstances of the characters quite delightful; but it seemed to me that the poem lacks any higher substance, and I was particularly struck by this in the passages where the characters are expressing their innermost thoughts in dialogue. *The Vicar of Wakefield* is another story about a country vicar and his family, but the writer was a more sophisticated man of the world, and this has rubbed off on his characters, who all display a complex inner life.[57] In *Luise* the whole cultural niveau is middlebrow and bourgeois, so there is plenty there to satisfy a certain kind of readership. As far as the versification is concerned, it seemed to me that the hexameter is far too pretentious for such humble circumstances and often feels a bit forced and stilted, while the periods do not always flow naturally enough to make for easy reading.

I mentioned these points to Goethe over dinner today. 'The earlier editions of the poem,' he said, 'are much better in that respect, and I remember reading it aloud with pleasure. But Voss kept on tinkering with it later on, and ended up ruining the natural, easy flow of the verse with his technical whims. Everything is about technicalities these days, and our esteemed critics now whine about whether it's all right for an "s" to rhyme with another "s", or whether it should be a double "s" rhyming with an "s". If I were still young and reckless, I would deliberately fly in the face of all these so-called rules and I would use alliteration, assonance and false rhymes – the whole lot, just as it took my fancy; but I would concentrate on the main thing I

1831 373

wanted to say, and try to say it so well that everyone would feel impelled to read it and learn it off by heart.'

Friday 11 February 1831

At dinner today Goethe told me that he had started the fourth act of *Faust* and was now planning to forge ahead with it – which I was delighted to hear.

He then spoke with admiration of a young literary scholar in Leipzig, Karl Schöne, who had written a study of the costumes in the plays of Euripides, and wore his great learning lightly, not parading it beyond what was necessary for his purposes.

'I like the way he goes straight to the heart of the matter,' said Goethe, 'while other scholars and critics of our day spend far too much time fussing over technicalities and long and short syllables.

'It's always the sign of an unproductive age when it becomes obsessed with technical detail, and likewise it's the sign of an unproductive individual when he frets about such things.

'There are other failings besides that hold a writer back. Count Platen, for instance, possesses nearly all the chief requisites of a good poet: he has imagination, invention, intellect and productivity in abundance, and few others can match him for technical skill, learning and dedication. But he is held back by his unfortunate weakness for polemic.

'The fact that, amid the glories of Naples and Rome, he is unable to forget the sorry state of German literature is unforgivable in a man of such talent. There are indications in *Der romantische Ödipus* that Platen was the man to write the best German tragedy, especially where technique is concerned. But having used tragic motifs in that play for parodic effect, how on earth does he propose to write a serious tragedy now?

'And there's something else that people tend to forget: these squabbles weigh on our minds, and the images of our enemies come between us and any productive work, like unruly spectres, wreaking havoc in an already delicate nature. Lord Byron was ruined by his polemical tendencies, and Platen would be

CONVERSATIONS WITH GOETHE

374

well advised, for the sake of German literature, to abandon such a regrettable path for good.'

Saturday 12 February 1831

I have been reading the New Testament, and was reminded of a picture that Goethe showed me the other day where Christ is walking on the water, and Peter, coming towards Him on the waves, loses heart for a moment and starts to sink.

'This is one of the most beautiful stories,' said Goethe, 'which I love above all others. It teaches us a great lesson: that man, through faith and good courage, can succeed in the most difficult undertaking, but if assailed by the slightest doubt he is immediately lost.'

Sunday 13 February 1831

Dined with Goethe. He told me that he is making progress with the fourth act of *Faust*, and that he has now sorted out the beginning to his satisfaction. 'As you know,' he said, 'I was clear about *what* should happen a long time ago, but I wasn't entirely happy with the *how*. But now I've had some good ideas, I'm happy to say. I shall now think of something to fill the gap between *Helena* and the finished fifth act and note it all down in a detailed outline, so that I can then write it up at my leisure, knowing what I am doing, and make a start on the passages that take my fancy. Again, this act will have a special character all its own; it will be like a separate little world, which doesn't bear on the rest and is only connected to the whole by very loose reference to what has gone before and what comes after.'

'So this follows the same pattern as the rest,' I said. 'Because basically, Auerbach's Cellar, the witches' kitchen, the Blocksberg, the Imperial Diet, the masquerade, the paper money, the laboratory, the Classical Walpurgis Night, *Helena* – they are all separate little worlds, self-contained and entire of themselves, each one loosely related to the others, but in the end having little to do with each other. For the poet, the whole point is to give expression to a world of infinite variety, and he uses the

1831   375

story of a famous hero merely as a kind of thread on which to string what he pleases. It's the same with the *Odyssey* and *Gil Blas*.'[58]

'You are quite right,' said Goethe, 'and the only thing that matters with such a composite work is that the individual sections should all have meaning and coherence in themselves, while the work as a whole always remains unfathomable – and for that very reason, like an unsolved problem, constantly draws people back to study it over and over again.'

I then told him about a letter I had received from a young soldier whom I and other friends had advised to go into foreign service. Having found life abroad not to his liking, he is now blaming everyone who gave him advice.

'Giving advice is a curious thing,' said Goethe, 'and when one has been around long enough to see how the most sensible enterprises fail, and the craziest ones often succeed, one is inclined to think twice before giving advice to anyone. Basically, it's an admission of inadequacy on the part of the one asking for advice, and a mark of presumption on the part of the one giving it. One should only give advice about matters in which one will be personally involved. If somebody asks me for advice, I generally say that I am happy to give it, but only on condition that he promises not to take it.'

The conversation turned to the New Testament, after I mentioned that I had reread the passage where Christ walks on the water, and Peter goes towards Him. 'If one comes back to the Gospels after not having read them for a long time,' I said, 'one is constantly amazed by the moral stature of these people. And in the extreme demands made on our moral strength of will, one also discovers a kind of categorical imperative.' 'In particular,' said Goethe, 'you discover the categorical imperative of faith, which Mohammed then took even further.' 'Incidentally,' I said, 'when you look more closely at the Gospels they are full of discrepancies and contradictions, and many strange twists of fate must have conspired to bring the books together in the form we now know.' 'Once you start looking into the history of all *that*,' said Goethe, 'you might as well give up now; you'll never get to the bottom of it. It's always better just to stick to what is actually there, and to take from it what we can use for our own moral growth and sustenance. By the way, it is nice to be able to visualize the settings, and there's nothing I can recommend more highly than Röhr's splendid book on Palestine. The late Grand Duke liked it so much that he bought two copies, giving the first one to the library when he finished reading it and keeping the other one for himself, so that he always had it to hand.'

I was surprised by the Grand Duke's interest in such things. 'That was one of his great strengths,' said Goethe. 'He was interested in everything of any importance, in whatever area of life. He was always progressive, and sought to adopt any good new inventions or contrivances as they became available. If something didn't work, it was never mentioned again. I often wondered how I was going to explain this or that failure to him, but he just made light of every disappointment and immediately started looking around for the next new thing. This was one of his great defining characteristics, and it was not something he learned, but something he was born with.'

After dinner we looked at some engravings after contemporary masters, mainly landscapes, and were pleased to note that we couldn't find fault with them. 'There has been so much good work in the world for centuries now,' said Goethe, 'that we really shouldn't be surprised if it has a positive effect and inspires more good work in its turn.' 'The only trouble is,' I said, 'that there are so many false doctrines around, and a young man of talent doesn't know which saint to devote himself to.' 'We've seen plenty of examples of that,' said Goethe. 'We've seen whole generations led astray by false precepts, and suffering the consequences – ourselves included. And nowadays the printing press has made it so easy to propagate falsehood to a wide audience. So even if some critic has a change of heart after a few years and publicizes his revised opinions, his false teaching has already done the damage, and will continue to infest the soil like a knotweed alongside the healthy growth. My only consolation is that a really great talent cannot be led astray or blighted.'

We went back to studying the engravings. 'These are really good,' said Goethe. 'What you see here are all very decent talents, who have learned something and acquired a good deal of taste and artistic ability. And yet, all these pictures are lacking something, namely *masculinity*. Make a note of that word and underline it. These pictures lack a certain thrusting urgency, something that found expression everywhere in earlier centuries, but which is missing from our own – and not only in painting, but in all the other arts as well. The present generation is made of feebler stuff – whether by birth, or through education and diet, it's impossible to say.'

'It only goes to show,' I said, 'how much in the arts depends on big personalities, who were certainly more at home in past centuries. Standing before the works of Titian and Paul Veronese in Venice, we feel the mighty intellect of these men, from the first conception of a painting to its final execution. Their powerful emotional energy permeates every element of the composition, and the superior force of the artistic personality enlarges our own being and lifts us out of ourselves when we gaze upon such works. This masculinity that you speak of is a particular feature of the landscapes painted by Rubens. In one sense, what we see before us are just trees, soil, water, rocks and clouds; but all these forms are energized by the force of his personality, so while we still see the natural world as we know it, we also see it imbued with the power of the artist and re-imagined as he would have it be.'

'Indeed,' said Goethe, 'in art and poetry, personality is all. But some of our contemporary critics and pundits have been weak characters who will not admit this, and who would have us believe that a big personality is a kind of minor adjunct to a work of poetry or art.

'But of course, it takes one to know one. Those who said there was nothing sublime about Euripides were either dimwits, incapable of rising to such heights, or else they were shameless charlatans, who thought their pretentiousness would make them look more important than they really were in the eyes of a feeble-minded world – as indeed it did.'

Monday 14 February 1831

Dined with Goethe. He had read the *Mémoires* of General Rapp, which got us talking about Napoleon, and what it must have felt like for Madame Letizia, to be the mother of so many heroes and such a powerful family. 'She had given birth to Napoleon, her second son, when she was only eighteen and her husband only twenty-three, so that the youthful vitality of his parents gave him a physical advantage. Apart from him, she bore three other sons, all very gifted, accomplished and energetic in worldly affairs, and all endowed with some degree of poetic talent. These four sons were followed by three daughters, and finally Jérôme, who seems to have been the least gifted of the siblings.

'Talent is not hereditary, it is true, but it does require a sound physical foundation; so it matters whether a person is the first-born or the last-born, and whether his parents were young and vigorous or old and frail.'

'It's curious,' I said, 'that of all the talents a gift for *music* should be the one that manifests itself earliest. Mozart was only four, Beethoven only seven and Hummel only eight when they astounded their family and friends by their playing and composing abilities.'

'Musical talent,' said Goethe, 'is often the earliest one to manifest itself because music is something entirely innate that comes from within, needing little in the way of external nourishment, and no experience drawn from life. Even so, a phenomenon like Mozart will always remain a miracle that defies explanation. But how would God find opportunities to perform so many miracles if He did not sometimes work His wonders in extraordinary individuals, whom we gaze upon in amazement, not knowing whence they come?'

Tuesday 15 February 1831

Dined with Goethe. I told him about the theatre; he said that yesterday's play, *Henri III* by Dumas, was an excellent piece of work, but he was not surprised that the audience had not really taken to it. 'I wouldn't have risked putting it on when I was in charge,' he said, 'because I remember all too well what trouble we had trying to get the public to watch *The Constant Prince*, which actually has far more human and poetic interest than *Henri III*, and is ultimately much more accessible.'

I mentioned *Der Grosskophta*, which I have just reread. I talked through the scenes one by one and ended by saying that I would love to see it performed one day.

'I am pleased to hear,' said Goethe, 'that you like the play, and are discovering how much I put into it. When all is said and done, it was no small thing to take an episode from real life and turn it first into poetry, and then into drama. And yet you will agree that the whole thing is really made for the stage. Schiller was all for it, and we did put it on once. It went down very well indeed with a more sophisticated audience, but it's not something for the public at large; the crimes it deals with are rather unsettling, and it makes people uncomfortable. Its rather racy character places it firmly in the orbit of *Clara Gazul*, and the French writer might well envy me for pre-empting such a good subject. I say "such a good subject", because in essence it is not just a moral tale, but also has great historical significance; the episode in question immediately preceded the French Revolution, and in a sense laid the foundation for it. The French Queen, so closely implicated in the fateful diamond necklace affair, lost her dignity and her respect, which meant that in the mind of the people she had forfeited the standing that had made her inviolable. People can survive hatred; contempt is what brings them down. Kotzebue was hated for a long time, but that student only took a dagger to him after certain journals had made him look contemptible.'

Thursday 17 February 1831

Dined with Goethe. I brought him his 1807 account of his stay in Karlsbad, which I had finished editing that morning.[59] We talked about some especially thought-provoking passages, where he comments in passing on the events of the day. 'People always think,' said Goethe with a laugh, 'that you have to grow old to become wise, whereas in fact, as you grow older, it's a full-time job staying as wise as you were before. We all change as we go through different stages in life, but none of us can say we become better; and in certain matters we are just as likely to be right at the age of twenty as we are at sixty.

'The world looks different from the lowlands than it does from the top of the foothills, and different again from the glaciers of primeval mountains. From one standpoint you see a little more of the world than from another – but that is all, and you cannot say that you see "better" from one place than from another. So when a writer leaves monuments behind from various stages in his life, what matters chiefly is that he possesses an innate foundation and goodwill; that he has seen and felt things clearly at every stage; and that he has always said exactly what he thinks, with no ulterior motive. That being so, if his writings were right at the time in his life when they were written, they will always be right, no matter how the author develops and changes thereafter.'

I agreed wholeheartedly with all of this. 'A few days ago I came across a piece of scrap paper with some writing on it,' Goethe went on. '"Hm," I said to myself, "what it says there makes a lot of sense; you think along the same lines yourself, and would have put it much the same way." Then I looked more closely, and realized it was a fragment from my own works. I'm always moving on to the next thing, you see, so I forget what I have written previously; and I very quickly find that my own writings seem like the work of somebody else.'

I asked about *Faust*, and how it was progressing. 'It won't leave me alone,' said Goethe, 'and I'm thinking about it and adding to it every day. Today I had the complete manuscript of the second part stitched together, so now I have something I can hold in my hands and see before me. I have put blank sheets of paper where the fourth act will go, and there's no doubt that having so much of it in this finished form is a real incentive to get on with what still needs to be done. There's more to such physical objects than people think, and we need all the help we can get to concentrate our minds.'

Goethe had the freshly bound manuscript of *Faust* brought in, and I was astonished to see the sheer bulk of what he had written; in manuscript form it ran to a good folio volume.

'It's all been done in the six years since I've been here,' I said,

1831   381

'and yet, with all the other things that have happened in the meantime, you haven't been able to put much time to it at all. It just goes to show how a thing can grow, even if you only add to it every now and then.'

'You realize that more and more as you get older,' said Goethe, 'whereas the young think that everything has to be done in a day. But if fortune smiles on me, and I continue to enjoy good health, I hope to make very good progress with the fourth act in the coming spring months. As you know, I've had this act worked out in my head for a long time; but the rest of it has grown so much in the actual writing that I can only use that earlier material as a broad framework now, and I need to bulk out this linking section with new material, so that it is of a piece with the rest.'

'The world we see in this second part,' I said, 'is far more rich and varied than in the first.'

'I rather think so,' said Goethe. 'The first part is almost entirely subjective; it is all the product of a more ingenuous and passionate individual, whose gloomy mentality no doubt appeals to many people. But in the second part there is hardly anything subjective; what we have here is a higher, broader, brighter world, devoid of passion, and anyone who has not been around for a while and seen something of life will not know what to make of it.'

'There are a few mental challenges in there,' I said, 'and I dare say a bit of learning is called for on occasion. I'm just glad that I've read Schelling's little tract on the Cabeiri, and that I now know what you are getting at in that famous passage in the "Classical Walpurgis Night".'[60]

'I've always found,' said Goethe with a laugh, 'that it helps to have a bit of knowledge.'

Friday 18 February 1831

Dined with Goethe. We talked about different forms of government, and remarked on the difficulties that an overly liberal regime creates for itself by encouraging individuals to make their demands known, so that in the end it no longer knows which of all these many wishes it should grant. People will find, we agreed, that exercising power with too much benevolence, leniency and moral delicacy will not work in the long run, because rulers have to deal with a diverse and sometimes wicked world, which needs to respect authority. It was also noted that the business of government is a very demanding job, which requires complete dedication, and that it is therefore not advisable for a ruler to have too many other interests, such as a predilection for the arts – which distracts the prince, and diverts the machinery of government, from other, more important matters. A passion for the arts is better suited to wealthy private persons.

Goethe then told me that his *Metamorphose der Pflanzen*, together with Soret's translation, was making good progress, and that in revisiting this whole subject now, particularly the spiral theory, he had been helped by favourable developments from entirely unexpected quarters. 'As you know,' he said, 'we have been working on this translation for more than a year now; all kinds of obstacles have got in the way, the project has often got horribly bogged down, and I've often cursed the whole thing in private. But now I give thanks for all those obstacles, because these delays have allowed other excellent men abroad to bring their own ideas to fruition, which have been grist to my mill and helped me on tremendously, enabling me to bring my work to a conclusion I could not have imagined a year ago. This sort of thing has happened to me quite often in life, and when it does, one finds oneself believing in a higher power, something daemonic, which one worships without presuming to try and explain it.'

Saturday 19 February 1831

Dined at Goethe's with Councillor Vogel. Goethe had been sent a pamphlet on the island of Heligoland, which he read with great interest, and whose main points he now summarized for us.

After we had talked about this very curious place for a while, we turned to medical matters, and Vogel told us the latest news: there had been another sudden outbreak of natural smallpox in Eisenach, despite a programme of vaccination, and many people had already died within a short time.

'Nature,' said Vogel, 'is always playing tricks on us, and you'll need to check your theory very carefully if you're hoping to outsmart her. Cowpox was considered so safe and reliable that vaccination was made a legal requirement. But now this outbreak in Eisenach, where people who have been inoculated still caught natural smallpox, casts strong doubt on the infallibility of cowpox and undermines people's respect for the law.'

'All the same,' said Goethe, 'I'm in favour of not relaxing the strict requirement for vaccination, since such minor exceptions are as nothing compared with all the good the law does.'

'I'm of the same opinion,' said Vogel, 'and would even argue that in all cases where cowpox has not protected people against natural smallpox the vaccination was not done properly. To be effective, the vaccine needs to be strong enough to produce a fever. A mere inflammation of the skin, without fever, offers no protection. So at today's session I put forward a proposal requiring all medical officers in the country to administer increased doses of the cowpox vaccine.'

'I hope your proposal was carried,' said Goethe. 'I'm always in favour of strict adherence to the law, especially at a time like this, when too much is being conceded out of weakness and misplaced liberalism.'

It was then observed that we are starting to become soft and lax in the matter of criminal responsibility, and that medical testimony and opinion often help the criminal to evade conviction. Vogel took the opportunity to commend a certain young physician who always demonstrated strength of character in such situations, and who only recently, when the court was not sure whether a certain female child murderer was responsible for her actions, had testified that she most certainly was.

Sunday 20 February 1831

Dined with Goethe. He told me that he had tested my observation about the blue shadows on the snow – that they result from the reflection of the blue sky – and acknowledged that I was right. 'But it is possible for the two effects to coexist simultaneously,' he said, 'and the colour requirement produced by the yellowish light may intensify the appearance of the blue.' This I readily conceded, and was delighted that Goethe finally agreed with me.

'It's just annoying,' I said, 'that when I was observing the colours on Monte Rosa and Mont Blanc I did not record my observations in detail at the time. The main result was, however, that at a distance of eighteen to twenty miles, in the bright noonday sun, the snow appeared yellow, or even a reddish yellow, while the dark portions of the mountain, where there was no snow, definitely looked blue from where I was. I was not surprised by the phenomenon; I could have predicted that the reflection of the noonday sun on the white snow, filtered through the intervening layer of cloudiness, would make the snow look a deep yellow. But the phenomenon was especially gratifying because it decisively refuted the erroneous view of some natural scientists who claim that the air has an inherent propensity to make things appear blue. For if the air itself had a bluish tinge, the mass of air between me and Monte Rosa, twenty miles away, would have made the snow appear pale blue, or a bluish white – but not yellow, or a reddish yellow.'

'Your observation,' said Goethe, 'is significant, and completely refutes that error.'

'In itself,' I said, 'the theory of the cloudy medium is so simple that it is easy to think it could be taught to someone else in a few days. The difficulty lies in applying the law, and recognizing the same primary phenomenon at work when it appears in a thousand different guises under countless different conditions.'

'I would compare it to whist,' said Goethe. 'The laws and rules are likewise very easy to teach someone, but you need to have played the game for a very long time before you really master it. In fact, nobody learns anything just by listening, and unless we try our hand at certain things ourselves, we can only know them superficially and by half.'

Goethe then told me about a book by a young physicist which he admired greatly for the clarity of the writing, and whose teleological tendencies he was happy to overlook.

'It is natural for man,' said Goethe, 'to see himself as the ultimate purpose of creation, and to view all other things only in relation to himself, and in so far as they are of use and benefit to him. He makes himself master of the vegetable and animal kingdoms, and because he is able to sustain himself by eating other creatures he acknowledges his God and praises Him for His goodness and fatherly care. He takes milk from the cow, honey from the bee, wool from the sheep; and in ascribing to these things a purpose that is useful to *himself*, he also believes that they were created for that purpose. In fact, he can't imagine that even the meanest plant does not exist expressly for *him*; and even if he has not yet ascertained its use, he firmly believes that it will be revealed to him one day.

'And the way man thinks in general determines the way he thinks in particular. So he projects his view of life in general on to his understanding of science, and wants to know about the purpose and use of the individual parts of an organic being.

'This may do for a while, and he may get by in science for a while with that approach. But soon enough he will encounter phenomena where such a narrow view will not suffice, and where, without some higher point of reference, he will tie himself up in endless contradictions.

'These utilitarians say the ox has horns in order to defend himself. But my question is: "So why doesn't the sheep have any? And when he does have them, why are they twisted around his ears, where they are no good to him at all?"

'But if I say: "The ox defends himself with his horns because he has them", that is a rather different matter.

'To enquire after the purpose and ask the question "*Why?*" is wholly unscientific. But asking the question "*How?*" gets us rather further. If I ask: "*How* does the ox come to have horns?", I find myself studying the animal's physical organism – and also learning why the lion has no horns, and cannot have any.

'We humans have two hollow spaces in our skulls. Asking the question "*Why?*" would not get us very far, but if I ask "*How?*", I discover that these hollow spaces are survivals from the animal skull, which are found in more pronounced form in those lower organisms and are still vestigially present in humans, despite our higher state of evolution.

'The utilitarians would think they had lost their God if they could not worship *Him* who gave horns to the ox so that he could defend himself. But I hope I may be allowed to worship *Him* who, in the abundance of His creation, was so great that after making thousands of different plants He made one more, in which all the others are comprised; and after making thousands of different animals He made one more being who comprises them all, namely man.

'Let people worship *Him* who gives fodder to the cattle and food and drink to man, as much as his heart desires. For my part, I worship *Him* who has put such power of procreation into the world that if only a millionth part of it comes into being the world teems with such an abundance of creatures that neither war, pestilence, fire nor flood can make any impact. Now that is *my* God!'

Monday 21 February 1831

Goethe was full of praise for Schelling's latest speech, which brought an end to the student unrest in Munich. 'His speech,' he said, 'is good from start to finish, and we rejoice once more in that fine talent we have long known and admired. On this occasion he had an excellent subject and a worthy purpose, and the result was a brilliant success. If the same could be said of the subject and purpose of his lecture on the Cabeiri, then we'd have to praise him there, too, because his rhetorical talent and skills are equally in evidence there.'

Mention of Schelling's lecture brought the conversation round to the 'Classical Walpurgis Night', and the difference between this and the scenes on the Brocken in the first part.

'The old Walpurgis Night,' said Goethe, 'is monarchical, in that everyone accepts that the devil is in charge. But the classical version is republican and non-hierarchical; everyone is on the same level, so that each one is as important as the next, and nobody is subordinate or bothered about anyone else.'

'Also,' I said, 'all the characters in the classical version are distinctive, sharply drawn individuals, whereas on the German Blocksberg each figure is lost in the general melee of witches.'

'This is why,' said Goethe, 'Mephistopheles understands the significance when the homunculus talks about "Thessalian" witches to him. To any student of antiquity, the phrase "Thessalian witches" means something, while to the layman it is just a name.'

'The ancient world,' I said, 'must have been very real to you, to bring all those figures so vividly to life again – and to use them as freely as you did.'

'I couldn't have done it,' said Goethe, 'if I hadn't been studying the visual arts all my life. The challenge, in the face of such abundance, was to be selective and reject any figures who were not part of my concept. I haven't used the Minotaur, for example, or the Harpies and a few other monsters besides.'

'But everything you conjure up that night,' I said, 'forms a sequence of coherent, tableau-like groupings, which are easily visualized and readily recollected in our imagination. I'm sure painters will not pass up such promising motifs; I'm particularly looking forward to seeing Mephistopheles among the Phorkyads, where he tries on the famous mask in profile.'[61]

'There are some good jokes in there,' said Goethe, 'which posterity will find various uses for, eventually. Just think what will happen when the French get wind of *Helena*, and see what it could do for their theatre! They'll wreck the thing as it stands; but they will make good use of it for their own purposes, and that's all we can expect or hope for. They are sure to give Phorkyas a chorus of monsters, as already intimated in one passage.'

'What we want,' I said, 'is for a talented poet of the romantic school to adapt the whole thing as an opera, and for Rossini to apply his great talent to writing a brilliant score, and *Helena* could be a great popular success. For it is hard to think of a piece that offers more opportunities for magnificent stage sets, surprising transformations, gorgeous costumes and delightful ballet interludes – not to mention the fact that this entire sensuous extravaganza is underpinned by a clever storyline that could scarcely be improved upon.'

'Let's wait and see,' said Goethe, 'what the gods may bring us. These things move at their own speed. It's a matter of waiting until people see the light, and theatre directors, poets and composers realize what's in it for them.'

Tuesday 22 February 1831

I met Chief Consistorial Councillor Schwabe in the street, and walked with him part of the way while he told me about all the different things he was doing, and I learned more about the busy life of this distinguished man. He said that he was preparing a little edition of his new sermons in his spare time, while one of his school textbooks had recently been translated into Danish; it had sold forty thousand copies, and was now used by the best schools in Prussia. He invited me to visit him, which I gladly promised to do.

At dinner with Goethe later on I mentioned Schwabe, and Goethe joined me in singing his praises. 'The Grand Duchess,' he said, 'also thinks very highly of him, and that lady is a fine judge of character. I shall have a drawing of him done for my portrait collection, and it would be a good idea for you to call on him first and ask his permission. So do go and see him, show an interest in what he is doing and what his plans are. It will be interesting for you to gain an insight into a very different social world, which cannot be properly understood without spending time with a man like him.'

I promised to do so, as the acquaintance of practical men who work for the common good is what I truly desire.

Wednesday 23 February 1831

Before dinner, I was walking along the Erfurt road when I met Goethe in his carriage. He stopped for me, and I climbed in with him. We drove out a good way, up to the top of the hill by the little fir wood, and talked about natural history.

The hills and mountains were covered in snow, and I mentioned the subtle yellow tinge, and the fact that at a distance of a few miles, because of the intervening cloudiness, dark surfaces were more likely to appear blue than white surfaces yellow. Goethe agreed, and we talked about the great significance of primary phenomena, behind which we believe the divinity may be directly discerned.

'I do not ask,' said Goethe, 'whether this supreme Being

possesses understanding and reason, because I feel that He *is* understanding, *is* reason. All creatures are imbued with these faculties, and man has them in such abundance that he can recognize parts of the Almighty.'

At dinner we talked about the attempts of certain naturalists to explore the organic world by starting with mineralogy and working upwards. 'This is a big mistake,' said Goethe. 'In the world of mineralogy things are judged by their simplicity, but in the organic world complexity is king. So the two worlds have completely different dynamics, and there is no natural progression from one to the other.'

I made a mental note of this very important distinction.

Thursday 24 February 1831

I read Goethe's essay on Zahn in the *Wiener Jahrbücher* and was filled with admiration at the thought of all the knowledge needed to write it.[62]

Goethe told me over dinner that Soret had been with him, and that they had made good progress with the translation of the *Metamorphose*.

'The difficulty with nature,' said Goethe, 'is to see the law at work even where it is hidden from us, and not to be led astray by phenomena that defy our senses. For there are many things in nature that defy the senses, and yet they are true. The fact that the sun stands still, that it does not rise or set, but that the earth spins around every day at incredible speed – that goes completely against our senses; yet no informed person doubts that it is so. Similarly, we find phenomena in the plant kingdom that defy our senses, and so we need to be very careful not to be led astray by such things.'

Saturday 26 February 1831

I read a good bit of Goethe's *Farbenlehre* today, and was pleased to note that as a result of my repeated engagement with the phenomena over the last few years I have developed an intuitive understanding of the work that enables me to appreciate its great merits with some clarity. When I think what it took to compile such a work I am filled with admiration, because I see not only the author's conclusions, but also, when I look more closely, everything he had to go through in order to reach those conclusions.

Only a person of great moral strength could accomplish this, and anyone who would emulate him would have to set himself a very high standard. He would need to cleanse his heart of all that is coarse, untrue or egoistic – otherwise nature, pure and true, would spurn him. If people understood this they would happily devote several years of their life to exploring the entire compass of such a science, in a way calculated to test and uplift the senses, mind and character. They would acquire respect for the laws of the universe, and approach as close to the divine as it is possible for a human mind to do.

Instead, people concern themselves far too much with poetry and transcendental mysteries, which are subjective, malleable things that place no further demands on a man, but flatter him, and at best leave him as he is.

In poetry, only what is truly great and pure is good for us, confronting us like a second nature, which either raises us up to her level or spurns us altogether. Inferior poetry, on the other hand, encourages our own failings, in that we take into ourselves the infectious weaknesses of the poet. And we do so without realizing it, because we do not regard as inferior something that appeals to our own nature.

But in order to derive some benefit from the good and the bad alike in poetry, we need to be on a very high level to begin with, and to possess a sufficiently firm foundation to view such things as objects existing outside of us.

This is why I set such store by the study of nature, which does not pander to our weaknesses in any way, and either makes something of us or else has nothing at all to do with us.

Monday 28 February 1831

I spent the whole day reading the manuscript of the fourth volume of Goethe's autobiography, which he sent to me yesterday so that I could see what else might need doing to it. I feel very happy with this work when I think what it already is – and what it could yet become. Some of the books seem quite complete, and nothing more needs to be done. With others, however, we find certain inconsistencies, which are probably due to the fact that they were worked on at very different times in the author's life.

This whole fourth volume is very different from the three earlier ones. All of those move along in a certain given direction, following the author's progress down the years. With this one, however, time almost seems to stand still, and we don't see the protagonist working towards some specific goal. Many things are started, but not finished; some things are planned one way, but turn out another; and so you get the sense of a hidden force at work, a kind of destiny, which is weaving all manner of threads into a fabric that only future years will complete.

So this volume was the right place to talk about that hidden, problematic force that we all feel, which no philosopher can explain, and which the religious gloss over with some pious platitude.

Goethe calls this ineffable mystery of life and the universe the 'daemonic', and when he defines its essence we feel that it is indeed so, and it's as if a curtain is being drawn aside to reveal certain things going on at the back of our lives. We think we can see further, and more clearly, but we soon realize that the subject is too big and complex, and that our eyes can only see so far.

Man is made for the small things in life, and he only understands and enjoys what he knows. A great connoisseur understands a painting; he is able to see its various details in relation to his wider knowledge of art in general, and he is fully alive to both the whole and its parts. He does not prefer one detail over another, is not interested in whether a face is ugly or beautiful, or whether one part of the picture is light or dark; instead, he wants to know if everything is in the right place and as it should be. But if we stand a layman in front of a large painting, we shall see how the composition as a whole either leaves him cold or confuses him; how he is drawn to some parts of the picture and repelled by others; and how, in the end, it is the small things he knows that catch his attention, as he remarks how well the artist has painted this helmet, say, or that plume.

But in essence we are all more or less in the layman's shoes when we stand before the great canvas of world destiny. We are drawn to the highlights, to all that is charming and lovely, and repelled by the dark and forbidding places; the picture as a whole confuses us, and we seek in vain for the idea of a single being who could have created such contradictory images.

Now it is possible for someone to become a great connoisseur in human matters by dint of learning from a master and assimilating all his art and knowledge; but in divine matters this would only be possible for a being who was the equal of the Almighty Himself. And even if the Almighty were to impart such mysteries and reveal them to us, we would not be able to grasp them or make sense of them; so we would be like that layman in front of the painting again, to whom the connoisseur would never be able to explain the premises on which he formed his judgements, no matter how hard he tried.

In which case, it is just as well that religions of all kinds are not given to us directly by God, but are the work of outstanding individuals, calibrated for the needs and the understanding of a large mass of their fellow men.

If they were the work of God, nobody would comprehend them; but as they are the work of man, they do not give utterance to the unfathomable.

The religion of the highly civilized ancient Greeks did not progress beyond the point of physically embodying specific manifestations of the unfathomable in a series of gods. But since these individual gods were finite beings, there was still something missing from the picture, and so the Greeks invented the idea of fate, which they placed above all the gods. However, since fate in its turn remained an unfathomable thing in many respects, the problem was not so much solved as shelved.

In the mind of Christ there was only one God, to whom He ascribed all the qualities that He felt perfected within Himself. This God was the essence of His own beautiful soul, full of goodness and love, like Himself, and eminently calculated to make good people surrender themselves to Him in complete trust and embrace this idea as the sweetest connection with a higher sphere.

But since the great being that we call the godhead manifests itself not just in humans, but also in an abundant and powerful nature and in mighty world events, any conception of it formed by analogy with human characteristics is bound to be inadequate, and the attentive observer will soon stumble across shortcomings and contradictions that will plunge him into doubt, if not despair. Unless, that is, he is either small enough to be satisfied with some specious evasion, or big enough to look at things from a higher perspective.

Goethe found such a perspective early on in Spinoza, and he joyfully acknowledges how closely the views of this great thinker accorded with the needs of his youth. He saw himself reflected in him, and so was able to refine and develop his own thinking by reading him.

And since those views were not subjective in character, being founded on the works and manifestations of God in the world, they were not empty husks that he later cast aside as useless when he came to undertake his own profound study of the world and nature, but were the first germs and roots of a plant that continued to put on healthy growth for many years, until eventually the flower of a bountiful knowledge burst into bloom.

His critics have often accused him of having no belief. But it was just that he did not share theirs, because it was too small a thing for him. If he were to put his own belief into words, they would be astounded; but they would not be capable of understanding it.

Goethe himself, however, does not believe for a moment that he knows the supreme Being as He really is. Everything he has written or said affirms that the Almighty is unfathomable; approximations and intimations are the best that we can hope for.

For the rest, nature and we humans are all so permeated by the divine that it bears us up, that we live and move and have our being within it, that we suffer and rejoice in accordance with eternal laws, that we enforce these and have them enforced upon us, whether we acknowledge them or not.

After all, children eat cake without knowing anything about the baker, and sparrows eat cherries without giving thought to how they are grown.

Wednesday 2 March 1831

At dinner with Goethe today the conversation soon reverted to the subject of the daemonic. He added the following by way of defining the term more closely.

'The daemonic,' he said, 'cannot be explained by reason or understanding. It does not lie within my own nature, but I am subject to it.'

'Napoleon,' I said, 'seems to have been daemonic by nature.' 'He certainly was,' said Goethe, 'and to a degree that is possibly unique. The late Grand Duke was also a daemonic personality, full of boundless energy and restlessness, so that his own realm was too small for him, and even the largest would still have been too small. The Greeks ranked such daemonic beings among the demigods.'

'Don't we see the daemonic manifested in events, too?' I asked. 'Very definitely,' replied Goethe, 'and specifically in those that we cannot explain by reason or understanding. In fact, it manifests itself in all kinds of different ways throughout the natural world, both the visible and the invisible. Many creatures are wholly of the daemonic kind, others partially so.'

'Doesn't Mephistopheles,' I asked, 'exhibit daemonic traits, too?' 'No,' said Goethe, 'Mephistopheles is far too negative a being. The daemonic manifests itself in a wholly positive energy. Among artists,' Goethe went on, 'you find it more in musicians, not so much in painters. You see it to a very marked degree in Paganini, which is why he has such a powerful effect on people.'

I found all these explanations very helpful, and now understood better what Goethe meant by the term 'daemonic'.

We then talked at length about the fourth volume, and Goethe asked me to make a note of whatever still needed to be done.

Thursday 3 March 1831

Saw Goethe at midday. He was looking through some architectural drawings, and said that it took some nerve to build palaces, because you could never be sure how long one stone would be left upon another. 'You are better off living in a tent,' he opined. 'Or doing what certain Englishmen do, travelling from one town and one inn to another, and always finding a good dinner waiting for them.'

Sunday 6 March 1831

Dined with Goethe and talked about all manner of things. We also discussed children and their naughty behaviour, and he compared them to the stem leaves of a plant, which drop off by themselves over time – so there is no need to take such things too seriously.

'Man goes through various stages in life,' he said, 'and each stage brings with it its own peculiar virtues and failings, which are entirely natural in the context of their own time, and to that extent right and proper. At the next stage he is a different person; nothing remains of those earlier virtues and failings, but others have taken their place. And so it goes on, until the final transformation, when we do not yet know what we shall become.'

After dinner, Goethe read me some fragments of his *Hanswursts Hochzeit*, which dated back to 1775. Kilian Brustfleck opens the play with a monologue in which he bemoans the fact that Hanswurst's education, despite his own best efforts, has turned out so badly. This scene, like all the others, is written very much in the style of *Faust*. A wild, almost reckless, productive energy was evident in every line, and I was only sorry that it pushed the boundaries so far that even these fragments cannot be published. Goethe then read me the list of characters, which ran to nearly three pages and must have numbered nigh on a hundred. He had given them all kinds of rude names, some of them so gross and funny that we fell about laughing. Many alluded to physical defects, and painted such a graphic picture that the character came alive before one's eyes; others were suggestive of all sorts of bad behaviour and vices, and presupposed a thorough acquaintance with the seedy underbelly of life. Had the play ever been completed, one would have had to admire the inventive mind that contrived to bring together such a gallery of symbolic figures in a single madcap action.

'I hadn't a hope of finishing the play,' said Goethe, 'because it would have taken a world-class mischief-maker to pull it off. I had my moments, certainly, but at bottom I was too serious by nature for such devilment, and could never have kept it up. Besides, here in Germany we are too narrow and parochial for that kind of thing. It would work well enough in a cosmopolitan place like Paris, where one can be a Béranger and get away with it – something that could never happen in Frankfurt or Weimar.'

Tuesday 8 March 1831

The first thing Goethe said to me at dinner today was that he was reading *Ivanhoe*. 'Walter Scott is a great talent,' he said, 'in a class of his own, and it's not surprising that he has such a powerful effect on readers everywhere. He gives me much food for thought, and I find in him an entirely new art, with laws of its own.'

We then talked about the fourth volume of his biography, and before we knew it we were having another conversation about the daemonic.

'There is always something daemonic about poetry,' said Goethe, 'especially the unconscious kind, which is beyond all understanding and reason, and all the more effective for it.

'It's there in music, too, in the very highest degree, for music stands so high in the order of things that no human mind can comprehend it, and it has an overpowering influence that nobody can explain. That's why religious worship cannot get by without it; it is one of the prime means of working wondrously on hearts and minds.

'The daemonic also likes to take possession of important individuals, particularly if they occupy positions of power, such as Frederick the Great or Peter the Great.

'It was there in the late Grand Duke, so much so that nobody could resist him. People were drawn to him just by his calm presence – he didn't need to show them any special kindness or favour. Everything I undertook on his advice turned out well, so that in instances where my own understanding and reason could not supply the answers, I only had to ask him what should be done; he instinctively knew what was needed, and I could always be sure of a happy outcome.

'I really wish he could have taken up my ideas and higher aspirations; for when the daemonic spirit deserted him and he had to rely on his own human resources, he didn't know what to do with himself and was in a bad way.

'The daemonic element must have been highly active in Byron, too, which is why he had such a powerful magnetism, so that women especially couldn't resist him.'

'That creative force we call the daemonic,' I ventured, 'seems somehow divorced from the idea of the divine.'

'My dear fellow,' said Goethe, 'what do we know of the idea of the divine, and what do our narrow notions of the supreme Being signify? If I were to name it with a hundred names, like a Turk, I would still fall short, and measured against such an infinity of attributes I would have said nothing at all.'

Wednesday 9 March 1831

Today Goethe spoke again about Walter Scott in terms of the highest praise.

'We read far too many trivial things,' he said, 'which just waste time and do nothing for us. We should really read only what we admire, as I did in my youth, and as I am now rediscovering with Walter Scott. I've just started *Rob Roy*, and am planning to read all his best novels back to back. Everything about them is on a grand scale: the subject matter, story, characters, treatment, not to mention the incredible amount of research he has done and the accuracy of detail in the writing! But you realize what English history is, and what can be done with such a legacy in the hands of an accomplished poet. Our *History of the Germans* in five volumes offers thin pickings by comparison, so that even after *Götz von Berlichingen* our writers promptly confined themselves to private life, and gave us things like *Agnes Bernauerin*[63] and *Otto von Wittelsbach*, which are not much to write home about.'[64]

I said that I was reading *Daphnis and Chloe*, in Courier's translation.[65] 'That's another masterpiece,' said Goethe, 'which I have often read and admired. It shows intelligence, art and taste of the highest order, and I have to say it puts dear old Virgil in the shade somewhat. The country setting is very reminiscent of Poussin's style, sketched in behind the characters with a few judicious strokes.

'You know that Courier discovered a new manuscript in the library in Florence, which contained the main section of the poem that previous editions did not have. I have to confess that I have always read and admired the poem in its incomplete state, without ever feeling or noticing that the actual climax was missing. But that's probably a sign of the poem's quality: we were so content with what was there that it never occurred to us that there was something missing.'

After dinner, Goethe showed me a drawing by Coudray of a very tasteful door at Dornburg Castle, bearing a Latin inscription to the effect that he who enters will find a friendly welcome and hospitality, while the passer-by is wished good fortune on his travels.

Goethe had translated this inscription into a German couplet and placed it as a motto at the head of a letter he had written to Colonel von Beulwitz in the summer of 1828, when he was staying at Dornburg following the death of the Grand Duke. I had heard much talk of this letter in public circles at the time, so I was very pleased when Goethe showed it to me today, along with the drawing of the door.

I read the letter with great interest, and admired the way he had used the setting of Dornburg Castle, as well as the valley below, as the starting point for the most elevating reflections, of a kind calculated to give new heart to a man who has suffered a great loss and get him back on his feet again.

I was much taken with this letter, noting that it was not necessary to travel very far to find good material; what matters is that the poet should have sufficient inner resources of his own to make something worthwhile out of virtually nothing.

Goethe placed the letter and the drawing in a special folder, to keep them safe for future reference.

Thursday 10 March 1831

Today I read Goethe's novella about the tiger and the lion with the Prince, which made the Prince very happy, in that he felt the effect of great art; and me no less so, in that it gave me a clear insight into the hidden fabric of a finished composition. I was aware of the writer's thoughts as a kind of all-pervading presence, which may well be due to the fact that he had been mulling over the subject matter in his head for so many years, and had consequently mastered his material to such a degree that he could see both the whole and the parts with absolute clarity, and was able to place each part with great skill where it needed to be – and where, at the same time, it prepared the ground for what was to come. So everything is related to what went before and what comes after, while at the same time being exactly right for where it is placed; it is hard to imagine a more perfectly constructed piece of writing. As we read on, I really wished that Goethe himself could have viewed this gem of a novella from our perspective, as the work of someone else. It also occurred to me that there was just the right amount of material here for the poet to weave it all together very neatly, and for the reader to follow the story as a whole while also taking in all the details of the narrative.

Friday 11 March 1831

Dined with Goethe and talked about all manner of things. 'The funny thing about Walter Scott,' he said, 'is how his great gift for portraying detail often leads him to make mistakes. There's a scene in *Ivanhoe*, for example, where they are sitting at table in the hall of a castle at night, and a stranger comes in. Now it is fine for him to describe the stranger from the head down, what he looks like and how he is dressed; but it was a mistake to describe his feet, shoes and stockings as well. If I am sitting at table in the evening and someone comes in, I only see his upper body. If I then describe his feet, the hall is immediately filled with daylight – and the scene loses its nocturnal character.'

I felt the force of this argument, and made a mental note for future reference.

Goethe then went on to talk about Walter Scott in the most admiring terms. I urged him to put his thoughts down on paper, but he declined, observing that Scott's art is of such a high order that it is difficult to write about it for a public audience.

Monday 14 March 1831

Dined with Goethe and talked of many things with him. I had to tell him all about *La Muette de Portici*, which was performed the day before yesterday, and it was noted that the opera doesn't actually show us any plausible motives for a revolution – which suits audiences very well, since it allows everyone to fill in the gap with whatever he doesn't like about his own city or country.[66] 'The entire opera,' said Goethe, 'is basically a satire on the populace; when they make the love affair of a fisher girl a matter of public interest, and call the prince a tyrant because he marries a princess, they make themselves look utterly absurd and ridiculous.'

After dinner Goethe showed me some drawings based on Berlin sayings, which included some very funny things; we commended the artist's restraint in coming close to caricature, yet ultimately avoiding it.

Tuesday 15 March 1831

I worked all morning on the manuscript of the fourth volume of *Dichtung und Wahrheit*, and composed the following note to Goethe:

> The second, fourth and fifth books can be considered finished, apart from a few minor points that can very easily be dealt with on a final read-through.
>
> Below are a few comments on the first and third books.

First Book

The account of Jung's failed eye operation is of such grave significance that it leads people to reflect deeply, and, if related in company, would assuredly be followed by a pause in the conversation. My advice, therefore, would be to end the first book with this, so that a kind of natural pause ensues.

The charming anecdotes about the fire in the Judengasse and going skating in your mother's red velvet coat, which currently come at the end of the first book, where they don't really belong, would follow on very neatly from the passage where you talk about unconscious and wholly spontaneous poetic production. The point being that those episodes imply a similarly happy state of mind, where we act without agonizing over what should be done, so that the action effectively precedes the thought.

Third Book

As we agreed, any material that might still be dictated on the political situation abroad and in Germany in 1775, the culture of the nobility, etc., would go into this book.

Anything that might be said on the subject of *Hanswursts Hochzeit* and other poetic projects, realized or unrealized, could also go into this third book, unless it would fit more naturally into the – already very long – *fourth* book without disrupting the carefully crafted narrative structure.

To that end, I have put all the outline sketches and fragments together in the third book. I wish you luck, and hope that you will now feel inclined to dictate the missing material with a fresh heart and your customary elegance of style.   E.

Dined with the Prince and M. Soret. We talked at length about Courier, and then about the ending of Goethe's novella, and I observed that the content and art in that work were of far too high an order for people to know what to make of it. They want to go on hearing and seeing what they have already heard and seen before; and since they are used to encountering the flower Poetry in suitably 'poetic' pastures, they are astonished in this instance to see it growing out of soil that is entirely real. In the realm of the poetic, people will accept anything, and there is no wonder so outlandish that they are not willing to believe it. But here, in the bright light of the real day, we are brought up short by the slightest deviation from the normal course of events, and surrounded as we are by a thousand wonders we are used to, we are unsettled by a single one that is new to us. And people don't seem to have any difficulty believing in wonders from a bygone age; but to allow a kind of actuality to a wonder that happens today, and to revere it as a higher reality alongside what is visibly real – that no longer seems to lie within our human capability, or if it does, then it has been driven out by education. So our age is destined to become ever more prosaic, and as we have less and less to do with the transcendental, and our belief in it wanes, all poetry will gradually disappear.

All that is required of us at the end of Goethe's novella is basically just a sense that man has not been entirely forsaken by higher beings, that they are, rather, keeping an eye on him, caring about him, and coming to his aid in time of need.

This belief is such a natural thing that it is an integral part of our humanity, and, as the foundation of all religion, is innate in all peoples. In the early stages of human development it was a very powerful instinct; but it endures even in the most advanced cultures, so that among the ancient Greeks we find it still strong in Plato, and equally compelling later in the author of *Daphnis and Chloe*. In this charming poem the divine is present in the form of Pan and the nymphs, who watch over god-fearing shepherds and lovers whom they protect and preserve by day, and to whom they appear at night in dreams, telling them what they should do. In Goethe's novella this invisible protective power is conceived in the form of the Everlasting and the angels, who once kept the prophet safe in the lions' den, and here stand guard over a gentle child in the presence of a similar wild beast. Instead of tearing the boy to pieces, the lion becomes meek and tame; for the higher beings who are at work throughout all eternity are interceding here as mediators.

But to ensure that this does not appear too far-fetched for an unbelieving nineteenth-century readership, the poet employs a second powerful motif, namely music, whose magical power men have felt since the earliest times, and which still holds sway over us every day, in ways we do not understand.

And just as Orpheus drew all the creatures of the forest to him by such magic, and in the last of the Greek poets a young shepherd leads his goats with his flute, so that they scatter or congregate, run from danger or graze quietly, depending on the melody he plays, so music exerts its power over the lion in Goethe's novella; in thrall to the strains of the sweet-sounding flute, the mighty beast follows wherever the innocence of the boy would lead him.

Having talked to various people about these mysteries, I have observed that man is so enamoured of his own good qualities that he is quite happy to attribute them to the gods, but not so keen on granting the animals a share in them.

Wednesday 16 March 1831

Dined with Goethe, and gave him back the manuscript of the fourth volume of his autobiography, which we discussed at length.

We also talked about the ending to *Tell*, and I said I could not understand how Schiller could have made the mistake of allowing his hero to demean himself by his shabby treatment of the fugitive Duke of Swabia, on whom he passes harsh judgement while boasting of his own deed.

'It is hard to credit,' agreed Goethe, 'but Schiller, like others, was under the influence of women; and if he got it wrong in this instance it was due more to that kind of pressure than to his own good nature.'

Friday 18 March 1831

Dined with Goethe. I brought him *Daphnis and Chloe*, which he wished to reread.

We talked about lofty precepts, and whether it was good, or indeed possible, to impart them to others. 'The capacity for assimilating lofty thoughts,' said Goethe, 'is very rare, so in everyday life it is always better to keep such things to oneself, and only to share as much as is necessary to gain some advantage over others.'

We then touched on the point that many people, especially critics and poets, completely ignore what is truly great, and instead attach extraordinary importance to the mediocre. 'People only acknowledge and praise what they are capable of doing themselves; and since certain people live their lives in mediocrity, their trick is to take a literary work that has its weaknesses, but also its good points, and then to attack it and dismiss it as worthless, so that the mediocre work they praise seems that much better by comparison.'

I made a mental note of this, so that I would know what to think if I came across this sort of practice in future.

We then talked about the *Farbenlehre*, and the fact that certain German professors are still warning their students to disregard it as completely false.

'I'm sorry for all the good students,' said Goethe, 'but it makes no difference to me; my theory of colour is as old as the hills, and in the long run people won't be able to deny or ignore it.'

Goethe then told me that he was making good progress with the new edition of his *Metamorphose der Pflanzen* and with Soret's translation, which was improving all the time. 'It will be a curious book,' he said, 'because all kinds of very different elements have been worked up into a single whole. I'm including some extracts from the writings of a number of important young naturalists, and it is good to see that the better ones in Germany have now developed such a good style that it is difficult to tell them apart. The book has turned out to be more work than I expected, and I was drawn into the project initially almost against my will; but there was something daemonic going on there, so it was no good trying to fight it.'

'You did the right thing by giving in,' I said. 'It seems that the daemonic is so powerful that it is always going to prevail in the end.'

'Except,' replied Goethe, 'that humans in their turn must try to prevail against the daemonic – so in the present case I must aim to work hard and do my job to the best of my abilities, so far as circumstances will permit. It's a bit like that game the French call *codille*, where a lot depends on the throw of the dice, but where it is left to the skill of the players to decide how best to place their pieces on the board.'

I thought this was a wonderful analogy and cherished it as a valuable lesson for life.

Sunday 20 March 1831

Goethe told me at dinner that he has just been reading *Daphnis and Chloe*. 'The poem is so beautiful,' he said, 'that we find it impossible, living in our own wretched circumstances, to retain the impression it makes on us; so every time we read it we are astonished all over again. It is filled with brilliant daylight, and it's like looking at a sequence of paintings from Herculaneum, while those paintings in turn influence our perception of the book and assist our imagination as we read.'

'I've always liked the sense we get of an isolated, self-contained world,' I said. 'There are hardly any extraneous allusions to divert our attention from this happy idyll. The only gods involved are Pan and the nymphs; there's scarcely a mention of any others, and it's clear that these gods are sufficient for the needs of the shepherds.'

'And yet,' said Goethe, 'relatively isolated though it is, the poet has created a complete world here. We see shepherds of all kinds, crop growers, gardeners, winegrowers, seafarers, bandits, warriors and well-to-do townspeople, great lords and serfs.'

'We also get to see,' I said, 'man at every stage of his life, from birth to old age; and all the scenes of home life that the changing seasons bring with them pass before our eyes.'

'And what about the countryside,' said Goethe, 'which is so sharply delineated with just a few brushstrokes that on the higher ground, behind the characters, we see vineyards, fields and orchards; and down below, the pastures and the river, and some patches of woodland, with the sea stretching away in the distance. And not a hint of dull days, mists, clouds or damp, but only the clearest, bluest sky, the balmiest air, and ground that is always dry, so that one would be happy to strip off and lie down anywhere.

'The entire poem,' Goethe went on, 'displays art and culture of the highest order. It has been so carefully constructed that no motif has been left out, and all have been rendered in exquisite detail – like, for example, the scene with the hoard of treasure hidden near the stinking dolphin on the seashore. There is a taste, a perfection and a delicacy of feeling here which are as fine as anything ever written. Anything unpleasant and destructive that enters the happy world of the poem from outside, such as raiders, robbery or war, is always dealt with very quickly, leaving barely a trace behind. Then vice appears, in the entourage of the townspeople, but again not in any of the main characters, but in a minor figure, an underling. It is all beautifully done.'

'And also,' I said, 'I love the way the relationship between masters and servants is presented. The former treat their servants with great kindness, while the latter, for all their naïve liberties, show genuine respect, and seek to win their master's favour by every means. So the young town dweller who has disgusted Daphnis by attempting to have unnatural relations with him tries to win back his favour, when Daphnis has been acknowledged as the master's son, by boldly rescuing the abducted Chloe from the oxherds and bringing her back to Daphnis.'

'All these things show great wisdom and understanding,' said Goethe. 'And the way Chloe, contrary to the will of both lovers, who like nothing more than to lie naked beside each other, retains her virginity right through to the end of the novel, is also wonderful, and so beautifully motivated that the really big things in human life get talked about along the way.

'It would take a whole book to do justice to all the great merits of this poem. We would do well to reread it every year, in order to learn something new from it each time, and to feel the effect of its great beauty all over again.'

Monday 21 March 1831

We talked about politics, the continuing unrest in Paris, and the mania of young people for meddling in the highest affairs of state.

'In England, too,' I said, 'the students tried a few years ago to influence the outcome of the Catholic question by sending in petitions. But they were laughed at, and then ignored.'

'The example of Napoleon,' said Goethe, 'has stirred up a sense of self-importance, particularly among the younger generation in France that grew up under that great man; and now they won't rest until another great despot arises among them, whom they see as the ideal embodiment of what they themselves want to be. It's just a pity that a man like Napoleon is unlikely to come along again any time soon, and I rather fear that several hundred thousand more lives will be lost before the world finds peace again.

'There is no point in publishing works of literature for the next few years. All we can do now is to work away quietly and prepare some good things for more peaceful times to come.'

After this brief digression into politics, we were soon back on the subject of *Daphnis and Chloe*. Goethe praised Courier's translation as quite perfect. 'Courier was wise,' he said, 'to respect the old translation by Amyot and stick closely to it, just improving it in places and tidying it up, so that it is more faithful to the original. The old French has such a naïve quality, and suits the subject matter so well, that I doubt if there will ever be a better translation of this book in any language.'

We then talked about Courier's own works, his little pamphlets, and his defence in the matter of the notorious ink blot on the manuscript in Florence.[67]

'Courier is a great natural talent,' said Goethe, 'who has something of Byron in him, and of Beaumarchais and Diderot. He has Byron's ability to marshal all the facts that support his case, Beaumarchais' gift for advocacy, and Diderot's dialectical skills. And he is such a brilliant wit; there isn't a wittier man alive. But he seems not quite to have salvaged his reputation after the ink blot affair, and his whole tendency is not sufficiently positive to warrant unqualified praise. He picks quarrels with all and sundry, and it is difficult to suppose that he is not partly to blame himself.'

We then talked about the difference between the German word *Geist* and the French *esprit*. 'The French *esprit*,' said

Goethe, 'is very similar to what we call *Witz* in German. Our *Geist* is what the French would perhaps term *esprit* or *âme*. It has connotations of productivity, which the French word *esprit* doesn't have.'

'But Voltaire,' I said, 'had what we call *Geist* in German. If the French term *esprit* doesn't cover it, what do the French say for that?'

'In this exceptional instance,' said Goethe, 'they say *génie*.'

'I'm currently reading one of Diderot's books,' I said, 'and am astonished by the man's extraordinary talent. He knows so much – and writes so powerfully! He shows us a great, bustling world, where people gave each other a hard time, and where the mind and character were so constantly exercised in consequence that they developed a special strength and resilience. But it seems to me quite extraordinary, the calibre of men the French had in their literature in the last century. I am amazed, wherever I look.'

'It was the metamorphosis of a literature that had been gradually growing for a hundred years, ever since Louis XIV,' said Goethe, 'and was now in its full flowering. But it was really Voltaire who spurred on writers and thinkers like Diderot, d'Alembert, Beaumarchais and others; because if you wanted to be anything *at all* next to him, you had to be quite something; so there was no sitting back and taking it easy.'

Goethe then told me about a young professor of Oriental languages and literature in Jena who had lived in Paris for a while, and was a man of such great culture that he would very much like me to meet him.[68] As I was leaving, he gave me an essay by Schrön on the comet that is expected soon, so that I would not be entirely ignorant of such matters.

Tuesday 22 March 1831

After dinner Goethe read me some passages from a letter written by a young friend in Rome. A group of German artists featured in it, with long hair, moustaches, shirt collars turned down over old-fashioned German coats, tobacco pipes – and bulldogs. It seems they hadn't come to Rome to see the great masters and learn something. They don't think much of Raphael, and regard Titian as merely a good colourist.

'Niebuhr was right,' said Goethe, 'when he saw a new age of barbarism coming. It's already here, and we are right in the middle of it; for what else is barbarism, if not a refusal to acknowledge excellence?'

The young correspondent then writes about the carnival, the election of the new Pope, and the revolution that broke out immediately afterwards.[69] We see Horace Vernet setting himself up in baronial splendour, while some German artists stay quietly at home and shave off their beards, which suggests they may not have made themselves very popular with the locals by their behaviour.

We then wondered whether the aberrations we observe in some young German artists originated with certain individuals, and then spread like some sort of intellectual contagion, or whether they are just part of the mood of the age.

'They start with a few individuals,' said Goethe, 'and this has been going on for forty years now. The theory was that what the artist mainly needs in order to emulate the best are piety and genius. It was a very ingratiating theory, and they grabbed it with both hands. Because you don't need to learn anything to be pious – and genius is something we all get from our mothers. One need only say something that flatters men's conceit and indolence to be sure of a great following among the ranks of the mediocre.'

Friday 25 March 1831

Goethe showed me an elegant green armchair that he had recently bought at an auction.

'But I won't be using it much, if at all,' he said, 'because plush living and pampering are really contrary to my nature. You'll notice I have no sofa in my room; I always sit on my old wooden chair, and it was only a few weeks ago that I had a kind of headrest fitted to it. If I am surrounded by comfortable and elegant furniture, it stops me thinking and I fall into a kind of cosy stupor. Unless we have been accustomed to them from

410 CONVERSATIONS WITH GOETHE

our youth, stately rooms and sumptuous furnishings are for people who can't or won't think.'

Sunday 27 March 1831

After a long wait, the loveliest spring weather has finally arrived; the sky is all blue, with just the occasional little white cloud to be seen, and it is warm enough to go out in summer clothes again.

Goethe had the table laid in a pavilion in the garden, and so we were able to dine outside again today. We talked about the Grand Duchess, how she quietly goes about doing good works wherever she can and winning the hearts of all her subjects.

'The Grand Duchess,' said Goethe, 'has a sharp mind and a kind heart to match her goodwill; she's a real blessing for the country. And just as people everywhere are quick to sense where good things come from, worshipping the sun and the other kindly elements, it doesn't surprise me that all hearts turn to her in love, and that she is quickly appreciated as she deserves.'

I said that I had started reading *Minna von Barnhelm* with the Prince, and thought it was an excellent play. 'People have said of Lessing,' I observed, 'that he is a cold rationalist; but for me the play has all the heart and soul, charming artlessness and liberal culture of a genial man of the world that one could possibly wish for.'

'You can imagine,' said Goethe, 'what effect it had on us young people when it appeared in those dark times. It was like seeing a bright meteor. It made us realize that there existed something higher than that paltry literary age could conceive of. The first two acts are a real masterclass in exposition; we learned a lot from them, and we can still learn from them now.

'Nowadays, of course, nobody is interested in exposition; the effect that people used to expect in the third act they now look for in the first scene, and they forget that poetry is like seafaring: you need to push off from the shore and get a certain distance out to sea before you can proceed under full sail.'

Goethe had some excellent Rhine wine brought in, which

1831   411

friends in Frankfurt had sent him for his last birthday. As we drank, he told me some anecdotes about Merck, and how he could not forgive the late Grand Duke for having said, one day in Ruhla near Eisenach, that a mediocre wine was excellent.

'Merck and I,' Goethe went on, 'were always like Faust and Mephistopheles when we were together. He once made fun of a letter I had received from my father in Italy, in which my father complained about the wretched living conditions, the strange food, the heavy wine and the mosquitoes. Merck could not forgive my father, living in that wonderful country and surrounded by magnificent sights, for being bothered by such trivial things as food, drink and flies.

'All Merck's teasing was clearly the product, ultimately, of a highly cultivated mind. But as he was not positively creative himself, but had, on the contrary, a distinctly negative turn of mind, he was always quicker to criticize than to praise, and he couldn't help picking on anything that would gratify that urge.'

We talked about Vogel and his talent for administration, and about *** and his character.[70] '***,' said Goethe, 'is a special kind of man, who can't be compared with anyone else. He was the only one who sided with me against the abuse of press freedom that time; he stands firm, you can rely on him, and he will always be on the side of law and order.'

After dinner we walked up and down in the garden for a while, and enjoyed the white snowdrops and yellow crocuses, which are now in flower. The tulips were also coming out, and we talked about how magnificent and costly Dutch plants of this sort are. 'We won't be seeing any more great painters of flowers,' said Goethe. 'It's all about scientific accuracy these days, and the botanist now counts the stamens to see if the artist has got it right – but he has no eye at all for artistic composition and lighting.'

Monday 28 March 1831

I spent some delightful hours with Goethe again today. 'I'm more or less done with my *Metamorphose der Pflanzen,*' he said, 'and what I wanted to add about the spiral theory and Herr von Martius is also pretty much finished. So this morning I went back to the fourth volume of my autobiography and wrote an outline of what still has to be done. In a sense, I think I am very privileged to be given the chance, at my age, to tell the story of my youth and write about a period that is in many ways so significant.'

We discussed the various sections, which both of us remembered perfectly.

'When you describe your love affair with Lili,'[71] I said, 'we don't get any sense that this is not your younger self – in fact, those scenes have the genuine feel of youth about them.'

'That's because such scenes are poetic,' said Goethe, 'and while I no longer had those feelings of young love, I was probably able to compensate by the power of poetry.'

We then considered the curious passage where Goethe talks about his sister's situation. 'This chapter,' he said, 'will be read with interest by educated women, because there will be many like my sister who possess very fine intellectual and moral qualities, but are not blessed with physical beauty.'

'The fact,' I said, 'that her face usually broke out in a rash before a ball or some other social event is so very strange that one is tempted to see some sort of daemonic influence at work here.'

'She was a curious creature,' said Goethe, 'with very high moral principles, and she didn't have a sensual bone in her body. The thought of giving herself to a man was repellent to her, and one can imagine that this peculiarity led to some unpleasant scenes in her marriage. Women who have a similar aversion or who do not love their husbands will understand what this means. Consequently I could never really think of my sister as a married woman; she would have been much more at home as an abbess in a convent.

'And it was because she was not happy in her own marriage, despite being married to one of the best of men, that she was so vehemently opposed to my marrying Lili.'

Tuesday 29 March 1831

We talked about Merck today, and Goethe told me a little more about him and his ways.

'The late Grand Duke,' he said, 'was very fond of Merck, and he once stood surety for a debt of four thousand thalers. It was not long before Merck, to our astonishment, sent the surety bond back. His circumstances had not improved, and it was a mystery to us what kind of deal he could have struck. The next time I saw him he explained the mystery. "The Duke," he said, "is a fine, generous man, who trusts people and helps them whenever he can. Now I thought to myself: if you cheat this man out of his money, that will have adverse consequences for a lot of other people; his precious trust in others will be forfeited, and many unfortunate good people will suffer because one man behaved badly. So what did I do? I took a gamble and borrowed the money from a rogue. If I don't repay him, it won't matter; but if I had failed to repay the good Duke, it would have been a very poor show."'

We laughed at the magnificent eccentricity of the man. 'Merck had this curious habit,' Goethe went on, 'of muttering "he, he" every now and then in conversation. This habit got worse as he grew older, until in the end it sounded like the barking of a dog. He suffered latterly from a profound hypochondria as the result of his many financial speculations, and in the end he shot himself. He thought he would have to declare himself bankrupt, but it turned out things were nowhere near as bad as he had imagined.'

Wednesday 30 March 1831

We talked about the daemonic again. 'It is drawn to prominent figures,' said Goethe, 'and it also favours rather dark times. In a sunny, prosaic city like Berlin it would find little opportunity to manifest itself.'

Goethe was saying what I myself had thought only a few days earlier – which was gratifying, as it is always good to hear our thoughts confirmed by others.

Yesterday and this morning I read the third volume of his autobiography, and it was like coming back to a book in a foreign language when our language skills have much improved in the meantime; we thought we understood it the first time round, but now we can appreciate the finer details and nuances so much better.

'Your autobiography,' I said, 'is a book that helps us enormously in our own cultural development.'

'It's just what my life has taught me,' said Goethe, 'and the individual incidents I have recorded serve only to confirm a general observation, a higher truth.'

'What you say about Basedow, for example,' I said, 'how he needs people in order to achieve his higher aims, and wants to win their favour, but fails to realize that he will put everybody off by voicing his offensive religious views so thoughtlessly and making people doubt the things they love: these and other human traits of this kind seem to me enormously revealing.'

'I dare say,' said Goethe, 'there are some messages about human life in there. I called the book *Dichtung und Wahrheit* because it has higher ambitions that lift it above the level of mundane reality. Jean Paul then wrote an account he provocatively called *Truth from my Life*! As if the truth from the life of such a man could be anything other than that the author was a philistine. But the Germans don't really know how to take something that's out of the ordinary, and anything more elevated tends to pass them by without their even noticing. An incident from our life is worth recording not because it is true, but because it meant something.'

Thursday 31 March 1831

Dined at the Prince's with Soret and Meyer. We talked about literary matters, and Meyer told us about his first encounter with Schiller.

'I was walking with Goethe,' he said, 'in the park at Jena they call the Paradies, when we met Schiller and I had my first conversation with him. He had not yet finished his *Don Carlos*; he had just got back from Swabia, and was looking very ill and suffering with his nerves. His face reminded me of a painting of the crucified Christ. Goethe thought he would not live another two weeks, but as he became more settled and contented his health improved again, and it was only after that that he wrote all his major works.'

Meyer then told us a few things about Jean Paul and Schlegel, both of whom he had met at an inn in Heidelberg, as well as some tales from his time in Italy, all highly amusing and entertaining.

I always enjoy Meyer's company, probably because he is such a self-reliant, contented soul, who takes little notice of his surroundings and reveals his own relaxed personality at suitable junctures. At the same time he is well informed on all subjects, possesses a vast store of knowledge, and has a memory that can recall the most distant things as if they happened yesterday. He has a formidable intellect, which would be frightening if it were not underpinned by the most refined culture; but as it is, his calm presence is always congenial and invariably instructive.

Friday 1 April 1831

Talked about all manner of things over dinner with Goethe. He showed me a watercolour painting by Herr von Reutern, which depicts a young peasant in the market square of a small town, standing next to a girl selling baskets and blankets. The young man is looking at the baskets laid out in front of him, while two seated women and a coarse-looking girl standing next to them are eyeing the handsome young fellow with approval. The picture is so charmingly composed, and the expressions on the faces are so artlessly true to life, that you never tire of looking at it.

'This is watercolour painting of a very high order,' said Goethe. 'There are some simple souls who say that Herr von Reutern's art owes nothing to anybody else: it all comes from within himself. As if anything ever came from within ourselves except stupidity and clumsiness! Even if this artist did not learn from a famous master as such, he has spent time with accomplished masters, and learned his craft from them and their great predecessors, and from the natural world he sees all around him. Nature has given him a great talent, and art and nature together have honed his skills. He is an excellent painter, and in many ways unique; but you cannot say that it all comes from within himself. It could perhaps be said of an artist who is quite mad and paints badly that it all comes from within himself – but not in the case of an accomplished artist.'

Goethe then showed me an ornate four-sided border painted by the same artist in gold and bright colours, with a space left blank in the middle for an inscription. At the top was a building in the Gothic style; running down both sides were rich arabesques with interwoven landscapes and domestic scenes; forming the bottom edge of the frame was a charming woodland scene, with bright green grass and foliage.

'Herr von Reutern wants me to write something in the empty space,' said Goethe. 'But his border is so magnificent and ornate that I'm afraid I might spoil the picture with my handwriting. I've composed some verses specially, and wondered if it wouldn't be better to get a calligrapher to write them in for me. I would then sign them in my own hand. What do you think? And what would you advise?'

'If I were Herr von Reutern,' I said, 'I would be disappointed if the poem arrived in someone else's handwriting, and pleased to see it written in your own hand. The painter has displayed sufficient artistry in the border, so the writing doesn't need to be a work of art; it just needs to be authentic – written by you. I'd even suggest that you write it in German script rather than Roman, because your handwriting has a more distinctive character in the German script – and besides, it is more in keeping with the Gothic border design.'

'You may well be right,' said Goethe, 'and it will be quicker in the end if I do it like that. Perhaps I'll have a moment in the coming days when I feel brave enough to tackle it. But if I make an ink blot on the lovely painted border,' he added with a laugh, 'it will be your fault.' 'Just pick up a pen and do it,' I said, 'and it will be fine, whatever happens.'

Tuesday 5 April 1831

Saw Goethe at midday. 'In all of art,' he said, 'I don't think I have come across a more satisfying talent than that of Neureuther. Very few artists are content to work within their own capabilities; most of them try to do more than they are able, and are all too apt to stray beyond the natural limits of their talent. But Neureuther could be said to stand *above* his talent. He is at home with objects from every part of the natural world; he can draw different kinds of terrain, rocks and trees just as easily as animals or people. He possesses invention, art and taste in abundance, and while such riches might be thought wasted on slight marginal drawings, he seems to be playing with his capabilities, and the observer shares the special pleasure that is always felt by someone who dispenses his great wealth with a liberal hand.

'Nobody has done more to refine the art of marginal drawings, and even the great talent of Albrecht Dürer was more about inspiration than imitation for him.

'I shall send a copy of these drawings by Neureuther to Mr Carlyle in Scotland,' Goethe added, 'and hope that the gift will be not unwelcome to our friend over there.'

Monday 2 May 1831

Goethe gave me the good news that in the last few days he has more or less finished the beginning of the fifth act of *Faust*, which had previously been missing.

'The idea for these scenes,' he said, 'is more than thirty years old; it was such an important sequence that I've never lost interest in it, but so difficult to write that I was frightened by the thought of it. But now I've contrived by various means to get myself going again, and if fortune smiles on me I shall write the fourth act now straight through.'

Goethe then mentioned the name of a well-known author.[72] 'He is a writer,' he said, 'whose work is driven by party hatred, and who would not have made any impact without it. You find frequent examples in literature where hatred is a substitute for genius, and where minor talents make themselves look important by acting as the mouthpiece for a party. Similarly, you find plenty of people in life who lack the character to stand on their own two feet; so they too attach themselves to a party, which makes them feel stronger and gives them a sense of identity.

'Béranger, by contrast, is utterly self-sufficient as a writer. This is why he has never served any party. He finds so much fulfilment in his own thoughts and feelings that the world can give nothing to him and take nothing from him.'

Sunday 15 May 1831

Dined alone with Goethe in his study. After a good deal of lively talk, he brought the conversation round to his personal affairs, rising to his feet and fetching a paper from his desk.

'When someone like myself is past the age of eighty,' he said, 'he barely has a right to live. He must be ready to be called away at any time, and think about setting his house in order. As I recently told you, I have appointed you my literary executor in my will, and this morning I drew up a little document as a kind of contract, which you and I should sign.'

With these words he placed the document before me. It listed by name the works to be published after his death, some of them finished, some unfinished, and set out the detailed provisions and conditions to be observed. I was broadly in agreement, and so we both signed the document.

The material in question, on which I had already done some editing work from time to time, I estimated at around fifteen volumes. We then discussed a few unresolved matters of detail.

'It could be,' said Goethe, 'that the publisher is reluctant to exceed a certain number of pages, and that various things will therefore have to be omitted. In that case you could leave out the polemical part of my *Farbenlehre*, for example. The substance of my theory is contained in the theoretical section; and the historical section is quite polemical anyway, in so far as the principal errors of the Newtonian theory are discussed there. So it could be argued that the whole thing is polemical enough already. I do not take back any of my rather harsh critique of the Newtonian propositions; it was necessary at the time, and it will remain of value in the future. But the cut and thrust of polemics is not really my style, and I don't enjoy it.'

A second point we discussed in some detail concerned the maxims and reflections that are printed at the end of the second and third parts of the *Wanderjahre*.

When he set about revising and completing this novel, which had earlier been published in a single volume, Goethe had planned to expand it into two volumes, as is stated in the printed announcement of the new edition of his complete works. But in the course of his work on the manuscript it became much longer than he anticipated, and because his secretary's handwriting was somewhat straggly, Goethe misjudged the amount of material, and thought he had enough for three volumes rather than just two; so the manuscript went off to the printer's in three volumes. But when the printing had progressed to a certain point, it became apparent that Goethe had miscalculated, and that the last two volumes especially were going to come out too short. They asked for more manuscript material, but as it was not possible to change the plot line now, or to devise a new novella, write it, and insert it into the narrative in the short time available, Goethe found himself in some difficulties.

In this situation he sent for me, explained what had happened, and told me how he planned to get round the problem. He placed two large manuscript bundles in front of me, which he had asked to be fetched specially.

'In these bundles,' he said, 'you will find various unpublished writings, miscellanea, finished and unfinished pieces, thoughts on natural science, art, literature and life, all mixed up together. Suppose you were to make up six to eight printed sheets of this material, to fill in the gaps in the *Wanderjahre* for the time being? Strictly speaking, they don't belong there, but we could justify it on the grounds that there is talk of an archive in Makaria's house, where miscellanea of this sort are to be found. This would get round the problem for now – and it would also give us a handy vehicle for publishing a collection of very important items.'

I agreed to this proposal, set to work at once, and had soon completed the editing of these miscellanea. Goethe seemed very pleased. I had divided the whole lot into two separate blocks; we gave one of them the title 'Aus Makariens Archiv' ['From Makaria's Archive'], and the other we called 'Im Sinne der Wanderer' ['Reflections for Travellers']. As Goethe had just finished two important poems around this time – 'Bei Betrachtung von Schillers Schädel' ['On Contemplating Schiller's Skull'] and 'Kein Wesen kann zu nichts zerfallen' ['No being can decay to nothing'][73] – he was keen to have them published straightaway as well, and so we included them at the ends of the two sections.

When the *Wanderjahre* was published, nobody knew what to make of it. The flow of the narrative was interrupted by all manner of enigmatic sayings, which made sense only to the initiated, i.e. artists, natural scientists or literary critics, and served only to unsettle all the other readers, especially female readers. And nobody could understand the two poems, or work out how on earth they ended up in such a place.

Goethe laughed at this. 'What is done, is done,' he said today, 'and all you can do, when you edit my papers for publication, is to put these miscellanea back where they belong, so that they are in the right place when a new edition of my works is printed; and then the *Wanderjahre*, minus the miscellanea and the two poems, can be condensed into *two* volumes, as originally planned.'

We agreed that, when the time came, I should put all the aphorisms relating to art in a volume dealing with artistic matters; all the ones relating to nature in a volume devoted to the natural sciences in general; and all the ethical and literary maxims in a separate, dedicated volume.

Wednesday 25 May 1831

We talked about *Wallensteins Lager*.[74] I had often heard it said that Goethe was involved in the writing of this play, and that the Capuchin monk's long speech, in particular, came from him. So I asked him about this at dinner today, and he replied as follows:

'It's basically all Schiller's own work,' he said. 'But we had a very close working relationship, and Schiller not only told me the overall plan of the play and talked it through with me, but he also shared the day-to-day progress of the writing with me, listening to my comments and making use of them. So I dare say I may have contributed something. To help him with the Capuchin monk's speech, I sent him the sermons of Abraham a Sancta Clara, which he then put to brilliant use in composing his own homily.

'I don't really remember if any specific passages came from me, except for the two lines:

> A captain, by another stabbed to death,
> Did me a pair of lucky dice bequeath.

'I wrote the lines into the manuscript with my own hand because I wanted to show how the peasant had come by the loaded dice. That hadn't occurred to Schiller; he'd just gone ahead in his usual fashion and given the peasant the dice, without bothering to ask how he got hold of them. As I've said before, he wasn't one for taking trouble over motivation – which may be why his plays are that much more effective on the stage.'

Sunday 29 May 1831

Goethe told me about a boy who had made some trifling mistake, and just couldn't put it behind him.

'I didn't like to see this,' he said, 'because it points to an overly delicate conscience, which holds its own moral self in such high esteem that it will not forgive the slightest lapse. Such a conscience makes hypochondriacs of men, unless it is balanced by a life of busy activity.'

A few days ago someone brought me a nest containing some young warblers, together with an adult bird caught on a limed twig. I was very struck by the way the bird not only continued to feed its young in my room, but even returned to the young again when it had been let out of the window. Such parental love, defying danger and captivity, moved me deeply, and I told

Goethe today how astounded I was by this. 'Foolish fellow!' he replied with a meaningful smile. 'If you believed in God, you wouldn't be surprised.

> Truly divine is the God immanent,
> Nature in Him, He in nature present.
> So none that in Him do live and have being
> Shall want for His power and His spirit o'erseeing.[75]

'If God did not implant in the bird this all-powerful love for its young, and if the same instinct did not pervade the whole of animate nature, the world could not survive. But as it is, the divine power is everywhere present, and eternal love everywhere at work.'

Goethe said something similar a little while ago, when a young sculptor sent him a replica of Myron's cow with its suckling calf.[76] 'Here,' he said, 'we have a subject of the highest order; the nourishing instinct, which sustains the world and pervades the whole of nature, is presented to us here in the form of a beautiful allegory. I see this and other images like it as the true symbols of God's omnipresence.'

Monday 6 June 1831

Today Goethe showed me the beginning of the fifth act of *Faust*, which had been missing up until now. I read as far as the point where the cottage of Philemon and Baucis is burned down, and Faust, standing out on the balcony of his palace in the night, smells the smoke, blown in his direction by a light wind.[77]

'The names Philemon and Baucis,' I said, 'transport me to the Phrygian coast, and put me in mind of that renowned couple from antiquity; but our scene is set in modern times, and in a Christian landscape.'

'My Philemon and Baucis,' said Goethe, 'have nothing to do with that famous ancient couple or the legend associated with them. I gave my couple those names simply in order to add lustre to the characters. They are similar people in similar circumstances, and so it works well to use the same names.'

We then talked about Faust, who is still plagued in old age by the dissatisfaction that is an ingrained character trait, and who, living in a new realm of his own making, with all the riches of the world at his disposal, is still vexed because a few lime trees, a cottage and a church bell do not belong to him. In this he is not unlike the Israelite King Ahab, who fancied he owned nothing unless he owned Naboth's vineyard as well.[78]

'Faust as he appears in the fifth act,' Goethe added, 'is meant to be exactly a hundred years old, and I wonder if it wouldn't be a good idea to mention this specifically at some point.'

We then discussed the ending, and Goethe drew my attention to the passage that reads:

> Delivered is this valiant spirit
> From the devil's captive bands;
> Those whose striving knows no limit,
> Have earned salvation at our hands.
> And if it be that love divine
> Looks down on him with tender grace,
> The heavenly host will stand in line,
> To bid him welcome in this place.

'These lines,' he went on, 'hold the key to Faust's salvation. In Faust himself we see a higher and purer endeavour that persists to the end, and from above, eternal love coming to his aid. This is all entirely compatible with our own idea of religion, whereby we attain heavenly bliss not just by our own efforts, but with the help of divine grace.

'And I think you'll agree that the ending, where the redeemed soul is taken up to heaven, was very difficult to write, and that it would have been very easy, when dealing with such ineffable, transcendental matters, to lose oneself in vague generalities. But by introducing these sharply delineated figures and ideas from the Christian Church tradition I was able to give my poetic designs a more defined form and substance.'

Goethe went on to complete the missing fourth act in the following weeks, so that by August the whole of the second part was all finished and bound. It gave Goethe great joy to have finally reached the goal he had been working towards for so long. 'Any time remaining to me,' he said, 'I can now regard as a bonus, and what I do now, if I do anything, is really of no consequence.'

Wednesday 21 December 1831

Dined with Goethe. We discussed the reasons why his *Farbenlehre* has not found a wider readership. 'It's very difficult to get people to understand it,' he said, 'because, as you know, it isn't just a matter of reading and studying it; you have to *do* it, and that isn't easy. It's like the laws of poetry and painting: you can teach them to people up to a point, but to be a good poet or painter you need genius, and that can't be taught. To grasp a simple primary phenomenon, recognize its special significance and then work with it, requires a productive mind capable of seeing the bigger picture, and that is a rare gift, only to be found in highly sophisticated individuals.

'And even that is not enough. Just as rules and genius don't, by themselves, make a painter, and ceaseless practice is needed as well, so, with the *Farbenlehre*, it is not enough to know the principal laws and have the right kind of mind; it's a matter of *applying* one's mind constantly to the individual, often very mysterious, phenomena and their origins and connections.

'Thus most people know, for example, that the colour green is produced by mixing yellow and blue. But before anyone can claim to understand the green of the rainbow, or the green of foliage, or the green of seawater, he must make such a thorough study of colour in all its aspects and attain such a level of knowledge in consequence as very few have hitherto managed.'

After dinner we looked at a few landscapes by Poussin. 'Those places where the light in the picture is brightest,' said Goethe, 'cannot be painted in any detail, which is why water, boulders, bare earth and buildings are best suited for this purpose. By the same token, things that need to be drawn in greater detail cannot be placed where the light is most intense.

'A landscape painter,' Goethe went on, 'needs to be knowledgeable about many different things. It's not enough for him

1831 425

to understand perspective, architecture and the anatomy of humans and animals; he also needs to know something about botany and mineralogy. The former, so that he knows how to convey the characteristic features of trees and plants, and the latter, so that he can appropriately render the character of different types of mountains. But he doesn't need to be a professional mineralogist; he is mainly concerned only with limestone, clay schist and sandstone mountains, and all he needs to know are the characteristic rock formations, how the rock is cleft by the elements, and which tree species thrive on it or become stunted.'

Goethe then showed me some landscapes by Herman van Swanevelt and spoke about the art and personality of this distinguished man.

'In him more than anyone else,' he said, 'art and inclination are perfectly attuned. He has a deep love of nature, and a divine inner peace which communicates itself to us when we look at his pictures. He was born in the Netherlands and studied in Rome under Claude Lorrain; under the influence of that master he honed his skills to perfection, and was able to develop his own charmingly individual style with complete freedom.'

We then looked him up in an encyclopaedia of artists, to see what they said about Herman van Swanevelt, and found that he was marked down for being inferior to his master. 'What fools!' said Goethe. 'Swanevelt was different from Claude Lorrain, and Claude cannot claim to be the better of the two. If our lives were nothing more than what our biographers and encyclopaedists say about us, we might as well give it up as a bad job right now.'

At the end of this year and the beginning of the next, Goethe turned his attention to his favourite subject of study again, the natural sciences. Some of his time was spent in investigating further the laws of the rainbow, at the suggestion of Boisserée, but for the most part he was preoccupied with matters relating to the metamorphosis of plants and animals, his interest having been rekindled by the dispute between Cuvier and Saint-Hilaire.[79] He and I also worked together on the editing of the historical section of the *Farbenlehre*, and he took a close interest as well in a chapter on the mixing of colours, which I edited, at his suggestion, for inclusion in the theoretical volume.

During this time we had many interesting conversations and he made many brilliant observations. But, seeing him every day full of energy and zest, I thought things would go on like this for ever, and took less care to record his words than I should have done – until in the end it was too late; and on 22 March 1832 I joined with thousands of noble Germans in mourning our irreparable loss.

What follows was written down shortly afterwards, while the memories were still fresh in my mind.

1832

Early March 1832

Over dinner Goethe talked about the recent visit of Baron Karl von Spiegel, and said that he had taken an enormous liking to him. 'He is a fine young man,' said Goethe. 'There is something in his manner and his bearing that tells you straightaway that he is a nobleman. He could no more deny his high birth than someone else could deny his superior intellect. For both these things, birth and intellect, leave their imprint on the man who possesses them, and no amount of disguise can conceal them. They are elemental forces, like beauty, which we cannot be exposed to without feeling that they are of a higher order.'

A few days later

We talked about the Greek idea of tragic destiny.

'This kind of thing,' said Goethe, 'no longer suits our present way of thinking; it's out of date, and completely at odds with our idea of religion. If a modern poet writes a play based on such notions from an earlier age, it always looks like a kind of affectation. It's like a suit of clothes that went out of fashion a long time ago, which, like the Roman toga, no longer looks right on us.

'We moderns would do better to say, with Napoleon, that *politics* is our destiny now. But we should beware of saying, with the present generation of literary men, that politics is *poetry*, or a fit subject for the poet. The English poet Thomson wrote a very good poem about the seasons, but a very bad one about freedom – not from any lack of poetry in the poet, but from a lack of poetry in the subject matter.

'As soon as a poet decides to be politically active, he must commit to a party; and the moment he does that, he is finished as a poet. He must say goodbye to his free mind and impartial vision, and don the cap of bigotry and blind hatred instead.

'As a human being and a citizen, the poet will love his homeland, but the homeland of his *poetic* powers and his poetic endeavours is the good, the noble and the beautiful, which are not tied to a specific province or country, and are seized upon and cultivated by him wherever he finds them. In this he is like the eagle, who soars high above the lands of the earth, letting his gaze roam free; and when he swoops down on a hare, it doesn't matter to him whether the hare is running in Prussia or Saxony.

'And what does it mean anyway, to love one's country and be a patriot? When a writer has laboured all his life to fight prejudice, overturn hidebound opinion, enlighten the minds of his countrymen, educate their taste and refine their thinking and attitudes: how could he be better employed? And how could he be more "patriotic" than that? To make such inappropriate and thankless demands of a writer would be like expecting the head of a regiment to demonstrate his patriotic credentials by getting involved in political reform, and neglecting his professional duties in consequence. But the homeland of a regimental commander is his regiment, and he will make an excellent patriot by not troubling himself with political matters except in so far as they concern him, and directing all his care and attention instead to the battalions under his command, endeavouring to train and discipline them so well that they will stand fast and do their duty if the country is ever under threat.

'I hate all forms of incompetence like the devil, but especially incompetence in affairs of state, which causes nothing but misery for thousands and millions of people.

'As you know, I pay little attention on the whole to what people write about me, but I get to hear about it all the same, and although I have worked my fingers to the bone all my life, I know perfectly well that all my efforts count for nothing in the eyes of certain people because I have refused to get involved with political factions. To satisfy these people, I would have had to join some Jacobin Club and preach mayhem and murder! But I'd better not say any more; once I start on those hotheads, I'm apt to get hot under the collar myself.'

Similarly, Goethe disapproved of Uhland's political engagement, which others found so commendable. 'You mark my words,' he said, 'the politician will consume the poet. The life of a parliamentarian, exposed to constant friction and excitement, is not for the delicate nature of a poet. There'll be no more poetry coming from him, and in a way that's a pity. Swabia has enough men who are sufficiently educated, well intentioned, capable and eloquent to be members of parliament, but it has only *one* poet like Uhland.'

The last visitor that Goethe received with hospitality was the eldest son of Frau von Arnim; the last words he wrote were some verses inscribed in this young man's album.[80]

The morning after Goethe's death, I was seized with a strong desire to see his earthly remains one last time. His faithful servant Friedrich opened up the room for me where they had laid him out. Lying flat on his back, he seemed to be at rest, as if sleeping; the expression on his noble countenance was one of profound peace and assurance. The mighty brow seemed still to harbour thoughts. I very much wanted a lock of his hair, but respect prevented me from cutting it off. The body lay naked, wrapped in a white sheet, and large blocks of ice had been placed around it to keep it fresh for as long as possible. Friedrich opened up the sheet, and I marvelled at the divine splendour of those limbs. The chest was powerful, broad and arched; the arms and legs full and palpably muscular; the feet dainty and perfectly formed; and not a trace, anywhere on the body, of obesity or emaciation and wasting. A perfect human being lay before me in all his beauty, and in the enchantment I felt, I forgot for a few moments that the imperishable spirit had departed from this mortal shell. I placed my hand upon his heart – a profound stillness lay over everything – and turned away, to let the tears I had held back flow freely.

PART THREE

PREFACE

Now that I see before me this long-promised third part of my conversations with Goethe finished at last, I am filled with the joyous sense of great obstacles overcome.

I was in a very awkward predicament, rather like a mariner who cannot sail with the wind that is blowing today, but must wait with great patience, often for weeks or months at a time, for a favourable wind to blow up as it did years before. When I was fortunate enough to write the first two parts, I was sailing with a fair wind behind me, as it were, because I could still hear the freshly spoken words in my head, and my personal contact with that wonderful man kept me in a constant state of excitement, which made me feel I was being borne towards my destination as if on wings.

But now, so many years after that voice fell silent, when the joy of those personal encounters is a distant memory, I could only rediscover that vital sense of excitement in hours when I was able to retreat within myself in quiet contemplation and revive the past in living colour; whereupon it began to stir again, and I saw great thoughts and great character traits laid out before me like mountain ranges, far off in the distance, but clearly visible, as if bathed in actual sunlight.

And so my delight in these great things rekindled that feeling of excitement; I remembered how he spoke to me, how he developed an argument, as if it were yesterday. The living Goethe was back with me again. I heard again the sweet, distinctive sound of his voice, quite unlike anybody else's. I saw him again in the evening, wearing his black frock coat and star, joking and laughing, and chatting cheerfully with his guests in his brightly lit rooms. Then the next day, when the weather was fine, he was sitting next to me in his carriage, wearing his brown overcoat and blue cloth cap, with the light-grey cloak draped over his knees. His complexion was tanned and healthy, like the fresh air; his conversation brilliant and free-flowing, clearly audible above the sound of the carriage. Or else I saw myself back in his study again, in the still evening candlelight, with him sitting across the table from me in his white flannel dressing gown, in mellow mood, as at the end of a day well spent. We talked about matters great and good, and he showed me the very finest part of his nature; my mind was set on fire by his. There was between us the most intimate harmony; he gave me his hand across the table, and I squeezed it. Then I might take up the full glass I had standing beside me, and raise it to him without a word, as I looked into his eyes over the wine.

And so I was back with him again, in the full flower of life, and heard him talking just like before.

But it is as it is in life: although we may think of a dear departed one, it is often only in passing, as the weeks and months go by and we become absorbed in our busy lives; and such quiet moments of contemplation, when we believe that a deceased loved one is back with us again in the full vigour of life, belong to those rare, magical hours. And so it was with me and Goethe.

Months would often pass when my mind, preoccupied with the pressures of everyday life, was dead to him, and he did not speak to me at all. And then there were other weeks and months when I felt completely unproductive, and nothing would germinate or blossom in my mind. I had to be very patient and let these barren times run their course, because anything written under such circumstances would have been worthless. I had to wait on Fortune to grant me the return of hours when the past came alive for me again, and I felt mentally sharp enough and sufficiently at ease with myself to be a worthy habitation for Goethean thoughts and sentiments. For I was dealing with a heroic figure, and I had a duty not to let him down. I had to show him as he truly was, in all his gentleness of disposition, in the full clarity and power of his intellect, and in the accustomed dignity of an august personage. And that was no small challenge!

PREFACE   435

My relationship with him was of a very special and intimate
kind. It was that of a pupil to his master, of a son to his father,
of one in want of culture to one who had culture in abundance.
He drew me into his own social circles and let me taste the
delights, both intellectual and physical, of a higher way of life.
There were many times when I saw him only once a week, visiting him in the evening; at other times it was every day, when
I had the pleasure of dining with him at midday, either in company or just *à deux*.

His conversation was as varied as his works. He was always
the same – and always different. Sometimes he was absorbed
by some great idea, and his words would come tumbling out in
an unstoppable flow. Often they were like a garden in spring,
where everything is in bloom, and one is so dazzled by the general splendour that one doesn't think to pick oneself a bouquet.
At other times I found him taciturn, monosyllabic, as if some
fog clouded his spirits; there were even days when he seemed to
be filled with an icy froideur, as if a biting wind were sweeping
across fields of hoar frost and snow. And then when one saw
him again, he was like a laughing summer's day, when all the
woodland songbirds are singing their hearts out from every
bush and hedge, the cuckoo is calling through the clear blue
sky, and the babbling brook meanders through meadows of
wild flowers. Then it was a joy to listen to him; to be in his
presence was very bliss, and the heart grew full at his words.

With him, winter and summer, age and youth, seemed to be
engaged in a constant battle for ascendancy; but what was so
wonderful, for a man in his seventies or eighties, was that youth
was constantly gaining the upper hand; and those autumnal
and wintry days I have mentioned were rare exceptions.

He possessed formidable powers of self-restraint – indeed,
this was a salient feature of his character. It was closely related
to that other quality of intense deliberation which enabled him
always to master his material and to give his individual works
that artistic perfection that we so admire in them. That very
characteristic often caused him to be constrained and circumspect in many of his pronouncements, just as he was in many of
his writings. But when, in happy moments, a more powerful

daemon stirred within him and that self-restraint deserted him, his conversation came gushing forth with youthful abandon, like a mountain stream cascading down from the heights. In such moments he expressed all that was greatest and best in his rich personality, and it was easy to understand, at such moments, what his friends in earlier life used to say about him: that his *spoken* words were better than the ones he wrote or published. As Marmontel said of Diderot: those who knew him only from his writings only knew the half of him; but as a talker, once he had warmed to his theme, he was utterly spellbinding.

If, on the one hand, I may venture to hope that I have succeeded in recording in these conversations much that was said in those happy moments, it may, on the other hand, be no less advantageous for this book that at certain points Goethe's personality is seen through *two* pairs of eyes: my own, and those of a young friend.

As a liberal republican living in Geneva, M. Soret was invited to Weimar in 1822 to superintend the education of the heir apparent, and from then until Goethe's death he too enjoyed a very close relationship with him. He was a familiar table companion in Goethe's house, and a frequent and welcome guest at his evening parties. Moreover, his keen interest in the natural sciences afforded many points of contact for a lasting association. As a serious mineralogist, he organized Goethe's collection of crystals, while his knowledge of botany enabled him to translate Goethe's *Metamorphose der Pflanzen* into French, thereby introducing that important text to a wider audience. His position at court likewise brought him into frequent contact with Goethe, sometimes accompanying the Prince to Goethe's house, sometimes visiting Goethe to pass on various requests from His Royal Highness the Grand Duke and Her Imperial Highness the Grand Duchess.

M. Soret frequently recorded these personal encounters in his diary, and a few years ago he was kind enough to give me a short manuscript compiled from these notes, so that I might, if I so wished, insert the best and most interesting parts chronologically into my third volume.

Written in French, these notes were sometimes detailed and

PREFACE 437

at other times cursory and incomplete, depending on how much time the author could find in his busy and often hectic schedule. But as there was nothing in the entire manuscript that Goethe and I had not discussed repeatedly and in detail, my own diaries supplied me with everything I needed to supplement Soret's notes, fill in any gaps, and enlarge upon things that were often only mentioned in passing. All the conversations that are based in whole or in large part on Soret's manuscript, which was particularly the case in the first two years, are marked with an asterisk (*) at the top, after the date, to distinguish them from the pieces that are entirely my own work, which, apart from a few exceptions, make up the years 1824 to 1829, and the bulk of the years 1830, 1831 and 1832.

And now I really have nothing further to add, apart from the wish that this third volume, so long planned and nurtured, might meet with the same kind reception that was so generously accorded to the first two.

Weimar, 21 December 1847

1822

Saturday 21 September 1822 *

Spent the evening at Goethe's with Councillor Meyer. The conversation was mainly about mineralogy, chemistry and physics. He seemed particularly interested in the phenomena associated with the polarization of light. He showed me various pieces of apparatus, largely built to his own design, and said he would very much like to conduct some experiments with me.

In the course of the conversation Goethe became more and more relaxed and communicative. I stayed for more than an hour, and as I was leaving he said many kind things to me.

He still cuts a handsome figure; his forehead and eyes are particularly majestic. He is tall and well built, and looks so hale and hearty that it is hard to understand how he could have been claiming for years that he is too old to attend social gatherings and go to court.

Tuesday 24 September 1822 *

Spent the evening at Goethe's with Meyer, Goethe's son, Frau von Goethe and his doctor, Councillor Rehbein. Goethe was on particularly lively form today. He showed me some magnificent lithographs from Stuttgart, the most perfect examples of their kind I had ever seen. We then talked about scientific matters, especially the advances that have been made in chemistry. Goethe was particularly interested in iodine and chlorine; he spoke about these substances with wonderment, as if the new discoveries in chemistry had come as a complete surprise to him. He

1822   439

had some iodine brought in, and vaporized it before our eyes by holding it to the flame of a wax candle – taking care to draw our attention to the violet haze, as happy confirmation of a law stated in his theory of colour.

Tuesday 1 October 1822*

Attended a soirée at Goethe's. Among the guests were Chancellor von Müller, President Peucer, Dr Stephan Schütze and Councillor Schmidt; the last-named played some Beethoven sonatas with a perfection seldom heard. I also enjoyed greatly the banter between Goethe and his daughter-in-law; young and vivacious, she combines a very quick mind with a most charming disposition.

Thursday 10 October 1822*

At a soirée at Goethe's house I met the celebrated Blumenbach from Göttingen. Blumenbach is elderly, but bright and animated when he speaks; he has somehow managed to retain all the sprightliness of youth. You would never think, from the way he conducts himself, that he is a scholar. He has a natural warmth and sincerity; he doesn't stand on ceremony, and one soon feels completely at ease with him. It was fascinating to meet him – and a great pleasure.

Tuesday 5 November 1822*

A soirée at Goethe's house. Among the guests was the painter Kolbe. We were shown a large, beautifully executed painting by him, a copy of Titian's Venus in the Dresden gallery.

I also saw Herr von Eschwege and the celebrated Hummel at Goethe's this evening. Hummel improvised on the piano for almost an hour, displaying a degree of power and talent which are impossible to imagine if one hasn't heard him. I found his conversation plain and natural, and himself remarkably modest for a virtuoso of such great renown.

Tuesday 3 December 1822 *

Attended a soirée at Goethe's. Riemer, Coudray, Meyer, Goethe's son and Frau von Goethe were among the guests.

The students in Jena are in revolt; they have sent in a company of artillery to pacify them. Riemer read out a collection of songs they had been banned from singing, which had thus become the occasion, or pretext, for the revolt. All the songs he recited were greeted with enthusiastic applause, mainly on account of the talent they displayed; Goethe himself thought they were good, and promised to let me read them for myself later.

After we had spent some time looking at some engravings and rare books, Goethe treated us to a reading of the poem 'Charon'.[1] I admired the clarity, precision and energy of Goethe's delivery. I have never heard such a powerful recitation. Such fire and passion, such expressive eyes – and that voice: thunderous one minute, soft and gentle the next! Perhaps his delivery was a little too forceful in some passages for the size of the room; but really, there was nothing in his performance that one would have wished otherwise.

Goethe then talked about literature and his own works, and about Madame de Staël and related matters. He is currently busy translating and reconstructing fragments of the *Phaethon* of Euripides. He first embarked on this project a year ago and has gone back to it in recent days.

Thursday 5 December 1822 *

At Goethe's this evening I heard the rehearsal of the first act of an opera that is currently being written: Eberwein's *Der Graf von Gleichen*. I was told this was the first time Goethe had seen so many operatic performers in his house since he retired as manager of the Weimar theatre. Herr Eberwein conducted the singers himself. A few ladies of Goethe's acquaintance helped out with the choruses, while the solo parts were sung by members of the opera company. A number of pieces stood out for me, most notably a canon for four voices.

Tuesday 17 December 1822 *

At Goethe's this evening. He was on very good form and talked very wittily about children knowing nothing of the follies of their fathers. The explorations now being undertaken to discover new salt deposits were clearly of great interest to him. He had harsh words for the stupidity of certain operators, who completely ignore the signs on the ground and the disposition and sequence of the strata under which the rock salt lies, and through which the drill has to pass; and who, without knowing the right place to drill or taking the trouble to find out, just drill a single borehole and then doggedly carry on drilling in the same spot, hoping for the best.

1823

Monday 9 February 1823*

At Goethe's this evening, where I found him alone, talking to Meyer. I leafed through an album of past centuries containing a number of very famous manuscripts, including ones by Luther, Erasmus, Mosheim and others. The last-named had written the following curious motto in Latin:

> Fame is a source of toil and sorrow;
> Obscurity a source of happiness.

Monday 23 February 1823*

Goethe has been dangerously ill for a number of days; yesterday he lay without hope. But today there has been a turning point, and he seems to be out of danger. This morning he was still saying that he thought his time was up; later, in the middle of the day, he began to hope that he might recover; and by the evening he was saying that if he did get through this, one would have to admit that, for an old man, he had been pushing his luck.

Tuesday 24 February 1823*

Today we were still very worried for Goethe, because yesterday's improvement in the middle of the day was not repeated. Overcome by weakness, he said to his daughter-in-law: 'I sense the moment has come when the struggle between life and death begins in me.'

1823   443

But by the evening the patient was mentally alert and feeling well enough to be making light of his situation. 'You are too cautious with your remedies,' he said to Rehbein. 'You go too easy on me! You need to take a leaf out of Napoleon's book when dealing with a patient like me: strong-arm tactics work best.' He then drank a cupful of a decoction of arnica, which, administered by Huschke yesterday at the most critical moment, had brought about the turn for the better in his condition. Goethe gave a charming description of this plant and commended its efficacy in glowing terms. He was told that the doctors had not allowed the Grand Duke to see him. 'If I were the Grand Duke,' cried Goethe, 'I would have asked a lot of questions and been very worried for you.'

At one point, when he was feeling better and his chest seemed less congested and he was talking easily and lucidly, Rehbein whispered into the ear of someone next to him: 'An improvement in *re*spiration tends to bring about an improvement in *in*spiration.' Goethe heard him, and piped up brightly: 'I've known that for a long time; but it's not true in your case, you old rascal!'

Goethe sat up in his bed, facing the open door to his study, where his close friends were gathered – unbeknown to him. His face seemed little changed to me; his voice was clear and distinct, though there was a note of solemnity in it, like that of a dying man. 'You seem to think,' he said to his children, 'that I am better; but you're wrong.' We did our best to reassure him by making light of his worries, and he seemed to take the point. By now the room was filling up with visitors, which I thought was not at all good; the presence of so many people was making the air in the room unnecessarily stuffy, and they were getting in the way of the people tending the patient. I couldn't help pointing this out, and went downstairs to the room below, from where I sent my bulletins to Her Imperial Highness.

Wednesday 25 February 1823 *

Goethe asked for an account of the treatment he had received; he also read the lists of names of those who had enquired after his health in large numbers every day. He then received the Grand

Duke, and later seemed none the worse for his visit. I found fewer persons gathered in his study today, and was gratified to think that my comment yesterday had evidently had some effect.

Now, however, when the illness is past, there is some concern about the after-effects. His left hand is swollen up, and there are worrying early symptoms of dropsy. We shall have to wait a few more days until we know the final outcome of his illness. Today was the first time Goethe asked to see one of his friends, namely his oldest friend, Meyer. He wanted to show him a rare medallion that was sent to him from Bohemia, which he is delighted with.

I arrived at twelve o'clock, and when Goethe heard that I was there, he sent for me to come and see him. He gave me his hand, saying: 'You see before you a man risen from the dead.' He then asked me to thank Her Imperial Highness for the concern she had shown for him during his illness. 'My recovery will be very slow,' he added, 'but all credit is due to the doctors nonetheless, for having performed a minor miracle on me.'

I took my leave after a few minutes. He has plenty of colour in his face, but he has lost a lot of weight and his breathing is still somewhat laboured. It seemed to me that talking was more of a struggle for him today than it was yesterday. The swelling on his left arm is very obvious; he keeps his eyes shut, and only opens them when he speaks.

Monday 2 March 1823*

Spent the evening with Goethe, whom I had not seen for several days. He was sitting in his armchair and had his daughter-in-law and Riemer with him. He was looking much better. His voice had regained its natural timbre, he was breathing easily again, his hand was no longer swollen, he looked like his old, healthy self, and his conversation flowed freely. He stood up, went into his bedroom without any difficulty and came back again. We drank tea with him, and as this too was the first time in a while, I jokingly chided Frau von Goethe for having forgotten to put a posy of flowers on the tea tray. Frau von Goethe promptly took a coloured ribbon from her bonnet and tied it around the samovar. This joke seemed to please Goethe greatly.

We then looked at a collection of artificial gemstones that the Grand Duke had had sent from Paris.

Saturday 22 March 1823 *

Today they put on Goethe's *Tasso* in the theatre to celebrate his recovery, with a prologue written by Riemer and read by Frau von Heygendorf. A laurel wreath was placed over his bust, to loud applause from an emotional audience. After the performance, Frau von Heygendorf called on Goethe. Still wearing her costume as Leonore, she handed him Tasso's wreath, which Goethe went and placed on the bust of the Grand Duchess Alexandra.[2]

Wednesday 1 April 1823 *

I brought Goethe an issue of a French fashion journal from Her Imperial Highness, in which a translation of his works was mentioned. This led on to a discussion of *Rameau's Nephew*, the original of which has long since been lost. Some Germans believe the original never actually existed, and that it is all Goethe's own invention. But Goethe claims that he would never have been able to imitate Diderot's witty style and idiom, and that the German *Rameau* is nothing more than a very faithful translation.

Friday 3 April 1823 *

Spent part of the evening at Goethe's, in the company of Chief Planning Officer Coudray. We talked about the theatre, and the improvements that have recently been introduced. 'I notice it, without even being there,' said Goethe with a laugh. 'Only two months ago, my children were still coming home in the evening feeling disgruntled. They were never satisfied with the entertainment on offer. But now it's a very different story; they come home with radiant faces, telling me they've "finally been able to have a jolly good cry". Yesterday they got their "joy of tears" from a play by Kotzebue.'

Monday 13 April 1823 *

Spent the evening alone with Goethe. We talked about literature, Lord Byron, his *Sardanapalus* and *Werner*. We then got on to the subject of *Faust*, which Goethe often likes to talk about. He would like to see it translated into French, preferably in the style of Marot's period. He sees it as the source for the ambience Byron creates in his *Manfred*. Goethe thinks that Byron made significant progress in his last two tragedies, where he comes across as less gloomy and misanthropic. We then talked about the libretto for *Die Zauberflöte*, for which Goethe has written the continuation, but not yet found a composer to do the subject matter justice. He admits that the well-known first part is full of improbabilities and jokes that not everyone can understand and appreciate; but there is no denying that the author knew exactly how to create dramatic theatrical effects by the clever use of contrasts.

Wednesday 15 April 1823 *

At Goethe's this evening, with Countess Karoline Egloffstein. Goethe joked about the German almanacs and other periodicals, saying they were all permeated by a ludicrous sentimentality which appears to be the order of the day. The Countess observed that German novelists had started the rot by corrupting the taste of their many readers, and that the readers in their turn were now corrupting the novelists, who had to pander to the prevailing bad taste of the public in order to find a publisher for their manuscripts.

Sunday 26 April 1823 *

I found Coudray and Meyer with Goethe. We talked of various things. 'The Grand Ducal library,' said Goethe at one point, 'owns a globe that was made by a Spaniard in the reign of Charles V. It bears a number of curious inscriptions, including this: "The Chinese are a people very similar to the Germans." In former times,' Goethe went on, 'the African deserts were indicated on maps with illustrations of wild animals. But they don't do that these days; the geographers prefer to leave us carte blanche instead.'

Wednesday 6 May 1823 *

At Goethe's this evening. He endeavoured to give me an idea of his theory of colour. Light, he said, is not made up of different colours; nor can light produce colours by itself. That always requires a certain modification and blending of light and *shade*.

Tuesday 13 May 1823 *

I found Goethe busy collecting together his short poems and personal dedications and inscriptions. 'In earlier years,' he said, 'when I was not so careful with my things and didn't bother to make copies, I lost track of hundreds of poems like these.'

Monday 2 June 1823 *

The Chancellor, Riemer and Meyer were at Goethe's. The poems of Béranger were discussed, and Goethe commented on and paraphrased some of them with great originality and good humour.

Then the talk turned to physics and mineralogy. Goethe is currently developing a theory of meteorology in which the rise and fall of the barometer are attributed entirely to the influence of our planet as it attracts, and then releases, the atmosphere.

'Our men of science, and especially our mathematicians,' Goethe went on, 'will be sure to find my ideas utterly ridiculous – or else they'll go one better and loftily ignore them completely. And do you know why? Because they say I am not a professional scientist.'

'But you can understand the cliquishness of academics,' I ventured. 'If some errors have crept into their theories and then been perpetuated down the years, the reason is surely that these things were handed down to them as dogma when they themselves were still sitting in the school classroom.'

'That's exactly the point!' cried Goethe. 'Your academics are

448　　　　　　　　　　　　　　CONVERSATIONS WITH GOETHE

just like our Weimar bookbinders. The masterpiece they have to produce to be admitted to the guild is not some fancy binding in the latest modern style. Not a bit of it! They are still required to produce a hefty folio Bible, of the sort that was in fashion two or three centuries ago, bound in heavy boards and thick leather. It's an absurd task to set them. But it wouldn't end well for the poor artisan if he were to say that his examiners are fools.'

Friday 24 October 1823 *

At Goethe's this evening. Madame Szymanowska, whom he had met this summer in Marienbad, was improvising on the piano. Goethe listened intently, and seemed at times much affected by her playing.

Tuesday 11 November 1823 *

A small soirée hosted by Goethe, who has been unwell again for quite some time. He had wrapped his feet in a woollen blanket, which has gone with him everywhere since the campaign in France. This blanket put him in mind of an anecdote from 1806, when the French had occupied Jena and the chaplain of a French regiment was requisitioning hangings for his altar. 'He'd been given a length of shiny crimson cloth,' said Goethe, 'but it wasn't good enough for him. He complained to me about it, so I said: "Send the cloth over to me, and I'll see if I can find you something better." In the meantime we were preparing to put on a new play in our theatre, and I used this gorgeous red material to deck out my actors. As for my chaplain, he got nothing more from me; he was forgotten, and had to fend for himself.'

Sunday 16 November 1823 *

Goethe is still not better. This evening I brought him some very fine medallions from the Grand Duchess, which she sent in the hope that the sight of them might take his mind off things and cheer him up. Goethe took obvious pleasure in Her Highness's thoughtful gesture. He then complained to me that he felt the same pain on his left side that had preceded his serious illness of last winter. 'I can't work,' he said, 'I can't read, and even thinking is difficult, apart from odd moments of relief when the pain eases.'

Monday 17 November 1823 *

Humboldt is here.[3] I called in briefly to see Goethe today, and it seemed to me that Humboldt's presence and conversation had done him good. His malady appears not to be purely physical in origin. It seems more likely that the passionate affection he conceived for a young lady in Marienbad this summer, which he is now struggling to overcome, is the main cause of his current illness.[4]

Friday 28 November 1823 *

The first part of Meyer's *History of Art*, which has just been published, seems to be giving Goethe great enjoyment. He spoke about it today in terms of the highest praise.

Friday 5 December 1823 *

I brought Goethe some mineral samples today, in particular a piece of argillaceous ochre, which Deschamps had found in Cormayan and which is much prized by M. Massot.[5] But how astonished was Goethe when he recognized the colour as the very same one that Angelika Kauffmann used for the flesh tones in her paintings! 'She thought the little bit she had was worth its weight in gold,' he said. 'But she didn't know where it came from, or where it can be found.' Goethe said to his daughter-in-law that I treated him like a sultan who is brought new gifts each day. 'He treats you more like a child!' replied Frau von Goethe, at which he could not help smiling.

Sunday 7 December 1823 *

I asked Goethe how he was feeling today. 'Not quite as bad as Napoleon on his island,' was the reply, uttered with a sigh. His

450 CONVERSATIONS WITH GOETHE

sickly state of health, which has been going on for so long now, does seem to be gradually affecting his spirits.

Sunday 21 December 1823 *

Goethe was in excellent form again today. We have reached the shortest day, and the anticipation of the days getting longer again with every week that passes seems to be having a wonderful effect on his mood. 'Today we celebrate the sun's rebirth!' he exclaimed cheerily, when I called in to see him this morning. I am told that during the weeks leading up to the shortest day he is always in a depressed state of mind, and is constantly sighing to himself.

Frau von Goethe came in to tell her father-in-law that she was about to leave for Berlin, where she had arranged to meet up with her mother, who was returning there imminently.

After Frau von Goethe had left, Goethe joked with me about the lively imagination that is typical of the young. 'I'm too old,' he said, 'to argue with her and make her understand that the pleasure of seeing her mother again for the first time would be exactly the same here as it is there. Undertaking such a journey in the winter is a lot of trouble for nothing; but that kind of nothing often means a very great deal to a young person. And when all is said and done, what does it matter? One has to do something crazy from time to time, just to keep on going in life. I was just the same when I was young, and I don't think it did me a great deal of harm.'

Tuesday 30 December 1823 *

Spent the evening with Goethe, talking about all manner of things. He told me he planned to include his 'Reise in die Schweiz vom Jahre 1797' in his collected works. We then talked about *Werther*, which he had not reread more than once, about ten years after it first came out. It had been the same with all his other works. Then we moved on to the subject of translations, and he said to me that he found it very difficult to translate English poems into German verse. 'If you try to render the stressed monosyllables of the English,' he said, 'with polysyllabic or compound German words, the whole force and effect is lost.' He said that his translation of *Rameau* had taken him four weeks, doing it all by dictation.

We then talked about the natural sciences, and in particular the petty-minded rivalry between certain academics. 'I have learned more about human nature through my scientific endeavours,' said Goethe, 'than through anything else. It has cost me a great deal and caused me a lot of trouble along the way; but I'm glad all the same to have learned what I have.'

'There is something about the sciences,' I remarked, 'that seems to excite people's egoism; and once that is in play, all their character weaknesses very soon emerge.'

'Matters of science,' replied Goethe, 'are very often matters of livelihood. A single discovery can make a man famous and set him up for life. This is why you have this great rigour in the sciences, and this refusal to let go, and this jealousy of others when they have a new insight. In the realm of aesthetics, on the other hand, things are much more casual; the ideas as such are more or less common property, innate to all men, so it all comes down to the treatment and execution, and envy, quite rightly, hardly comes into it. A single idea can form the basis for a hundred epigrams, and the only question is which poet was able to embody this idea in the most effective and beautiful manner.

'With science, however, the treatment is irrelevant, and the whole point is the insight itself. And there's not much that is general or subjective about it; the individual manifestations of nature's laws are all out there in the world, fixed, immovable and silent, like so many sphinxes. Each new phenomenon observed is a discovery, and every discovery is somebody's property. So if someone else lays a finger on that property, all the basic human passions are immediately aroused.

'But the other thing about the sciences,' Goethe went on, 'is that people have a personal stake in what they were taught at university. So if somebody comes along with something new, which conflicts with, and even threatens to overturn, the credo we have been parroting for years and passing on to others, we stir up passions against him and do our very best to put him down. We resist change in every way we can; we act as if we hadn't heard, as if we don't understand; we speak of it with disdain, as if it were not worth even considering; and so a new truth can wait a long time before it gains any ground. A Frenchman once said to one of my friends, apropos of my *Farbenlehre*: "We have worked for fifty years to establish and consolidate Newton's dominion; it will take another fifty years to topple it."

'The mathematical brotherhood has sought to make my name so suspect in the scientific world that people are afraid even to speak it. A little while ago a pamphlet came into my hands which discussed various aspects of colour theory; the author seemed to have assimilated my theory completely, and had based his entire argument on the same foundations. I read the text with great excitement; but to my no small astonishment I found that the writer did not even mention my name. The mystery was later solved. A mutual friend came to visit me, and confessed that the talented young author had set out to establish his reputation with that pamphlet, and had rightly been worried that his prospects in the academic world would have been damaged if he had dared to mention my name in support of his argument.[6] The pamphlet was well received, and the bright young author later came to see me in person and apologized.'

'That seems all the more strange to me,' I replied, 'in that people have good reason to invoke your authority with pride in all other matters, and anyone would think himself fortunate to be facing the world under the powerful protection of your endorsement. The problem with your *Farbenlehre*, it seems to me, is that you are not just dealing with the famous and universally esteemed Newton, but also with his followers all over the world, who are devoted to their master and whose number is legion. So even if you are proved right in the end, you will still be on your own with your new theory for a long time to come.'

'I'm used to it, and resigned to it,' said Goethe. 'But tell me,' he went on, 'have I not reason to be proud, that for the past twenty years I have had to conclude that the great Newton, and all the mathematicians and illustrious scientists along with him, were completely wrong about colour theory, and that I am the only one among millions who knows the truth about this important natural phenomenon? Safe in the knowledge of my own superiority, I was able to endure the stupid arrogance of my opponents. They tried everything possible to attack me and my theory and ridicule my ideas; but despite all that, the completion of my work afforded me great joy. All the attacks of my enemies only served to show me how weak and fallible humans can be.'

While Goethe was speaking thus, with a force and a fluency that I cannot possibly do justice to, his eyes shone with an extraordinary fire. It was a look of triumph – while an ironic smile played about his lips. The features of his handsome face were more imposing than ever.

Wednesday 31 December 1823

Dined with Goethe, and talked about all manner of things. He showed me a portfolio of drawings, among which the early attempts of Henry Fuseli were of special note.

We then talked about religious matters and the abuse of the divine name. 'People bandy it about,' said Goethe, 'as if the unfathomable and ineffable supreme Being were more or less one of them. Otherwise they wouldn't be saying the *Lord* God, the *dear* God, or the *good* God. For them, and especially the clergy, who talk about the Deity all the time, the name becomes just a verbal reflex, a word they say without even thinking about it. If they had a proper sense of His greatness they would be silent, not wishing to name Him out of reverence.'

1824

Friday 2 January 1824

Dined at Goethe's, with much lively conversation. The talk turned to a young beauty of Weimar society, and one of the guests remarked that he was almost in love with her, even though she wasn't what you would call a brilliant intellect.

Goethe gave a snort of derision. 'As if love had anything to do with intellect! We love a young woman for very different reasons. We love her beauty, her youth, her coquettishness, her childlike trust, her character, her faults, her caprices, and who knows what other ineffable qualities besides; but we don't love her for her intellect. We *respect* her intellect, if she has a brilliant mind, and it can infinitely enhance a girl's worth in our eyes. A good mind may also serve to cement our attachment, once we have fallen in love. But the intellect as such is not the thing that lights our fire and arouses our passion in the first place.'

We felt that Goethe's words made a lot of sense, and agreed readily with his point of view.

After dinner, when the others had left, I stayed behind and sat with Goethe, conversing further on various subjects.

We talked about English literature, Shakespeare's greatness, and how difficult it was for all those other English dramatists who had to follow in the footsteps of that poetic colossus.

'A dramatic talent of any significance,' Goethe went on, 'could not help but be aware of Shakespeare – indeed, he could not avoid studying him. But when he did study him he must have realized that Shakespeare had already exhausted the entire gamut of human nature, in all its heights and depths, and that in essence there was nothing left for him to do, as a latecomer to the party. And how could anyone with a just appreciation of excellence possibly find the courage even to put pen to paper, knowing that those unfathomable and incomparable master-pieces already existed?

'I was in a much better position fifty years ago, here in dear old Germany. I very quickly got the measure of what had already been written; there wasn't much there to impress me or detain me for long. I very soon left German literature, and the study of it, behind me and turned my attention to life and productive work. I made steady progress, developing my own natural potential and learning my craft in preparation for the works I have produced during successive periods of my life. And my notion of excellence at each stage of my life and development was never very far ahead of what I could actually *do* at that stage. Had I been born an Englishman, however, and exposed from earliest youth to the full force of all those masterpieces, it would have been too much for me, and I wouldn't have known what to do. I would not have been able to go forward with a light heart and good courage, but would for certain have had to think long and hard, and look around for some new outlet.'

I brought the conversation back to Shakespeare. 'If one were to uproot him, so to speak, from English literature,' I said, 'and transplant him to Germany in isolation, his giant presence would appear nothing less than miraculous. But if we look for him on his home ground and imagine ourselves treading the soil of his native land and breathing the air of the age in which he lived; and if, furthermore, we study his contemporaries and immediate successors and feel the power that speaks to us from the works of Ben Jonson, Massinger, Marlowe, Beaumont and Fletcher, Shakespeare will still be a towering presence; but we come to realize that many aspects of his genius are in some sort accessible, and that much of what he wrote was in the air at the time – the richly productive air of that age.'

'You are absolutely right,' replied Goethe. 'It's the same with Shakespeare as it is with the Swiss Alps. If you were to trans-plant Mont Blanc to the great flat expanse of the Lüneburg

Heath, its towering magnitude would leave you speechless with amazement. But if you go and see it in its monumental natural setting, and approach it via its giant neighbours – the Jungfrau, the Finsteraarhorn, the Eiger, the Wetterhorn, the Gotthard and Monte Rosa – Mont Blanc will still be a giant, but it will not excite the same degree of amazement.

'And those who find it hard to believe,' Goethe went on, 'that much of Shakespeare's greatness belongs to the great productive age in which he lived, only have to ask themselves this: do you really think such an astonishing phenomenon would be possible in the England of 1824, in these wretched times of carping and hair-splitting journals?

'That trance-like state of undisturbed, innocent creativity, from which alone something great can emerge, is just not possible any more. Our present generation of talents live their lives in the full glare of publicity. With critical journals appearing every day in fifty different places, feeding the public appetite for gossip, there's no place for anything of genuine worth. These days, unless you turn your back on all this and cut yourself off completely, you won't survive. A kind of half-baked culture is spreading among the masses, based on the largely negative criticism of the arts in our wretched press; but it affects the productive talent like a cloud of poison gas or a toxic rain, which destroys the tree of his creative power, from its crown of green leaves to its innermost pith and fibre.

'And how tame and feeble life itself has become, these last two shoddy centuries! When was the last time you met a true original, who didn't care what others think? And who can find the strength these days to be his own man and show himself in his true colours? This affects the poet, too, who now has to find everything within himself, because the outside world is a constant disappointment.'

The conversation turned to *Werther*. 'That's another creature,' said Goethe, 'that I've nourished, like the pelican, with my own heart's blood. There's so much of my own heart and soul in there, such a welter of thoughts and emotions – enough, probably, for a novel running to ten such volumes. As I've often said: I've only reread the book once since it came out, and have taken good care not to repeat the experience. It's incendiary stuff! I find it quite unsettling to read, and the thought of revisiting the pathological state of mind that gave birth to it frightens me.'

I reminded him of his conversation with Napoleon, which I know about from the sketch among his unpublished papers, which I have repeatedly urged him to write up properly. 'Napoleon,' I said, 'mentions a passage in *Werther* which he feels does not bear close scrutiny – and you concede the point. I'd really love to know which passage he meant.' 'Guess!' said Goethe, with an enigmatic smile. 'Well,' I said, 'I rather think it might be the one where Lotte sends the pistols to Werther without saying a word to Albert, and without sharing her fears and misgivings with him. You did go to a lot of trouble to motivate this silence, but considering the urgency of the situation, when the life of their friend is at stake, it still doesn't feel very plausible.' 'You make a fair point,' Goethe conceded. 'But whether Napoleon was referring to this passage or a different one, I'd rather not say. But as I said, your observation is just as valid as his.'

I said I wondered if the great impact *Werther* had when it came out was really a reflection of the zeitgeist. 'I know this is the commonly held view,' I said, 'but I am not convinced. *Werther* was a sensation because the book was published – not because it was published at a certain time. In every age there is so much unspoken suffering, so much hidden dissatisfaction and ennui, and so many individuals who feel at odds with the world and in conflict with society, that *Werther* would still be a sensation if it were published for the first time today.'

'I'm sure you are right,' said Goethe, 'which is why the book still has the same effect on young people of a certain age today as it did back then. And I hardly needed to look to the general influences of my time, or my reading of certain English authors, to explain my feelings of youthful dejection. It was more a case of my own immediate, personal circumstances preying on my mind and getting me down, until I ended up in the emotional state that resulted in *Werther*. I had lived, loved, and suffered a lot – that's where it all came from.

'When you look at it more closely, the much-discussed "*Werther* period" is not some historical phase in the world's cultural evolution, but rather an episode in the life of every individual who is born a free spirit, but must then learn to accept and conform to the restrictions imposed by an outmoded world. Frustrated happiness, thwarted activity and unfulfilled wishes are not problems specific to a particular period in history, but are part of every person's experience; and it would be a poor thing if everyone didn't have *one* time in his life when *Werther* seemed to have been written specially for him.'

Sunday 4 January 1824

After dinner today Goethe went through the portfolio of Raphael drawings with me. He returns to Raphael frequently in order to commune continually with the very best work and school his mind continually on the thoughts of a great man. It also gives him pleasure to introduce me to such things.

Afterwards we talked about the *Divan*, and in particular the 'Book of Discontent', in which he gave vent to much of the resentment he was feeling about his enemies.

'I was very restrained,' he added. 'If I had wanted to say everything that was rankling with me and getting me down, those few pages might have turned into a whole book.

'The fact of the matter is, people were never satisfied with me, and always wanted me to be different from the way it had pleased God to make me. And they were rarely satisfied with what I produced. Having slaved away for a year and a day to write a new work that would give people pleasure, I was then expected to thank them for finding it merely passable. If someone praised me, I was not supposed to feel pleased with myself and take it as my well-deserved due; instead, I was expected to respond with some faux-modest disclaimer in which I humbly declared the complete worthlessness of my person and my work. But that was not in my nature, and I would have had to be a miserable wretch to lie and dissemble like that. But since I was confident enough to be myself and not pretend otherwise, I was considered "proud", and am considered so to this day.

'In matters of religion, science and politics, I was always

1824   459

getting myself into trouble because I didn't hide my feelings, and had the courage to say what I thought.

'I believed in God, and in nature, and in the triumph of good over evil; but that wasn't enough for our pious souls. They also wanted me to believe that three is one and one is three; but that went against my own feeling for the truth. And anyway, I couldn't see that such beliefs would help me in the slightest.

'It didn't help me either that I realized Newton's theory of light and colour was wrong, and that I had the courage to contradict the generally held belief. I saw light for what it was, in all its purity and truth, and I considered it my duty to take up the fight. But the opposing party did everything they could to obscure the light, claiming that *shade is a part of light*. Put like that, it sounds absurd; but that's how it was. They said that *colours*, which are shadowy and translucent things, *are light itself*, or – which amounts to the same thing – they *are the light's rays refracted in various different ways.*'

Goethe paused, while an ironic smile played over his imposing features. He went on:

'And as for politics, don't get me started! I can't tell you the trouble I've had, and what I've had to put up with. Do you know my play *Die Aufgeregten*?'

'I read it for the first time yesterday,' I replied, 'in connection with the new edition of your works, and am heartily sorry that it remains unfinished. But even in its present form every right-thinking person will agree with your views.'

'I wrote it at the time of the French Revolution,' Goethe went on, 'and in a way it could be seen as my political credo for that time. The countess character was there to represent the aristocracy, and the words I put into her mouth were meant to show how the aristocracy should think. The countess has just come back from Paris, where she witnessed the revolutionary events and learned a valuable lesson for herself. She has concluded that the people can be pushed down, but they cannot be *kept* down, and that the revolutionary uprising of the lower classes is a consequence of the injustices of the ruling class. In future, she says, I shall take great care to avoid any action that seems to me unjust, and I will speak up, in society and at court, if I see others acting in that way. I will no longer remain silent about any form of injustice, even if I am decried as a democrat.

'I would have thought,' Goethe went on, 'that these sentiments are perfectly respectable. They were mine at the time, and they still are. But my reward was to be called all kinds of names that I do not care to repeat.'

'People only need to read *Egmont*,' I said, 'to find out what you think. I know of no German play that champions the cause of popular freedom more passionately than that one.'

'People choose not to see me as I am,' replied Goethe, 'and to avert their gaze from anything that might show me in my true light. Schiller, on the other hand – who, between you and me, was far more of an aristocrat than I am, but also far more circumspect about what he said – had the strange good fortune to be regarded as a special friend of the people. I am delighted for his sake, and I console myself with the thought that others before me fared no better.

'It is true that I could not support the French Revolution. Its atrocities were all too real to me, and I was constantly shocked by what was going on, while its beneficial consequences were not yet apparent. Nor could I watch with indifference while attempts were made to engineer similar scenes in Germany, which in France were the consequence of grave necessity.

'But nor was I a supporter of autocratic rule. I was also entirely persuaded that great revolutions are never the fault of the people, but of the government. Revolutions cannot happen as long as governments act justly and remain vigilant, so that they can anticipate trouble by introducing reforms in good time, instead of resisting change until it is forced upon them from below.

'But because I hated revolutions, I was called *a friend of the status quo*. Now that's a very ambivalent label, which I do not accept. If the status quo were all sweetness and light and justice, I would have nothing against it. But since, alongside all the good things, there is also much that is bad, unjust and imperfect, a *friend of the status quo* is often enough a friend of the outmoded and bad, in effect.

'But time never stands still, and human affairs look very

1824   461

different after the passage of fifty years; so an institution that was perfect in 1800 may become a liability by 1850.

'Furthermore, whatever is good for a nation has to come from its own core and its own general need, without imitating other nations. What may be healthy nourishment for one people at a certain stage of development may turn out to be poison for another. So all attempts to introduce some foreign innovation, the need for which is not rooted deep within one's own nation, are foolish, and all revolutions engineered in this fashion are doomed to failure. *For they are undertaken without God, who has no truck with such incompetence.* If, on the other hand, there is a real need for major reform within a people, then God is on their side, and the reform will be successful. He was manifestly with Christ and His early disciples, because the revelation of the new doctrine of love was something that the nations needed; He was likewise manifestly with Luther, because the cleansing of that doctrine, corrupted by the priesthood, was no less necessary. But neither of those towering figures was a friend of the status quo. On the contrary: both had a lively conviction that the old leaven must be cleared out, and that things could not be left to go on in the same old untrue, unjust and imperfect way.'

Wednesday 5 May 1824

I have been very busy for the last few days with the papers containing the studies that Goethe did with the actors Wolff and Grüner, and I have managed to knock these highly fragmented notes into some sort of shape. The result is something that could probably form the basis of a practical handbook for actors.

I discussed this work with Goethe today, and we went through the individual points. We both felt that the references to pronunciation, and the shedding of provincialisms, were especially important.

'In my long experience,' said Goethe, 'I have got to know beginners from every region of Germany. The pronunciation of North Germans left little to be desired on the whole. It is very pure, and in many ways may be regarded as the standard. On the other hand I've often had a lot of trouble with native Swabians, Austrians and Saxons. Natives of our very own Weimar have also made my life difficult at times. These tend to make the most ridiculous mistakes, owing to the fact that the schools here don't make them distinguish clearly between B and P, or between D and T, in their pronunciation. You would scarcely think they regarded B, P, D and T as *four* different letters, because they only ever talk about a soft B and a hard B, or a soft D and a hard D – as if to imply that P and T don't exist at all. So with them, *Pein* sounds like *Bein*, *Pass* sounds like *Bass*, and *Teckel* sounds like *Deckel*.'

'One of the actors here,' I remarked, 'who also failed to distinguish properly between T and D, recently made a similar mistake, with most unfortunate consequences. He was playing a lover who had committed some minor infidelity, and the angry young woman was giving him a real dressing-down. When he'd had enough, he was supposed to say: "*O ende!*" ["Do stop!"]. But because he failed to distinguish between T and D, what he actually said was: "*O Ente!*" ["O duck!"] – which got a huge laugh.'

'That's a good one,' said Goethe, 'and probably worth including in our theatre handbook.'

'A young female singer here,' I went on, 'who also couldn't distinguish between a T and a D, recently had to say: "I will hand you over to the initiates [*Eingeweihten*]." But because she pronounced her T like a D, it sounded as if she was saying: "I will hand you over to the entrails [*Eingeweiden*]."'

'And recently,' I went on, 'an actor here who was playing the part of a servant had to say to a caller: "My master is not at home, he is sitting in council [*im Rate*]." But because he pronounced his T and D the same, it sounded like: "My master is not at home, he is sitting in the wheel [*im Rade*]."'

'Those are not bad either,' said Goethe, 'and we must make a note of them. You get similar absurdities when an actor can't differentiate between a P and a B; so when he is meant to say: "*Packe ihn an!*" ["Seize him!"], it comes out as: "*Backe ihn an!*" ["Bake him lightly!"] instead.

1824 463

'In the same way,' Goethe went on, 'the *Ü* is often pronounced like an *I* here, which can also lead to the most unfortunate misunderstandings. For example, I've often heard people say *Kistenbewohner* [box-dweller] when they mean *Küstenbewohner* [coastal dweller]; *Tierstück* [animal motif] when they mean *Türstück* [door decoration]; *grindlich* [scurfy] instead of *gründlich* [thorough]; *Triebe* [urges] instead of *Trübe* [cloudiness]; and *Ihr misst* [you miss] instead of *Ihr müsst* [you must]. And it always makes me laugh.'

'I recently witnessed a very funny example of this at the theatre,' I added, 'when a lady in a difficult predicament has to follow a man she has never seen before. She had to speak the line: "I don't know you, but I have every confidence in the nobility of your countenance [*Züge*]." But she pronounced the *Ü* like an *I*, so it came out as: "I don't know you, but I have every confidence in the nobility of your goat [*Ziege*]." That got a big laugh.'

'That's another good one,' replied Goethe, 'and another one for our handbook. Similarly,' he went on, 'people here often get *G* and *K* mixed up, saying one when they mean the other – probably, again, because they are not sure if the letter is pronounced hard or soft, which comes from the way they are taught here. I expect you've often heard them say in our theatre – or you will do – *Kartenhaus* [house of cards] when they mean *Gartenhaus* [summerhouse], *Kasse* [ticket office] when they mean *Gasse* [alley], *klauben* [pick] instead of *glauben* [believe], *bekränzen* [crown with a wreath] instead of *begrenzen* [limit], and *Kunst* [art] instead of *Gunst* [favour].'

'I've heard something similar,' I replied. 'An actor here had to say: "Your sorrow [*Gram*] touches my heart." But he pronounced the *G* like a *K*, and was heard to say, very distinctly: "Your stuff [*Kram*] touches my heart."'

'And it's not just actors,' said Goethe, 'who get their *G*s and *K*s mixed up like that. I've heard very learned theologians do it, too. I'll tell you a story about what happened to me once.

'Some years ago, when I was staying in Jena for a while and lodging at the Fir Tree Inn, a theology student called on me one morning. We'd had a very nice chat, and as he was leaving he

464   CONVERSATIONS WITH GOETHE

came out with a very peculiar request. He asked me if I would allow him *to preach in my stead* the following Sunday. I saw at once which way the wind was blowing, and realized this hopeful young man was one of those who get their *G*s and *K*s mixed up. So I cordially informed him that I could not assist him personally in this matter, but that he would undoubtedly fare better if he would be so good as to apply to Archdeacon *Koethe*.'

Tuesday 18 May 1824

Spent the evening at Goethe's, with Riemer also present. Goethe told us about an English poem on the theme of geology.[7] He went through it from start to finish, doing his own impromptu translation with such wit, imagination and good humour that every detail came to life before our eyes, as if he were thinking the whole thing up there and then. We saw the hero of the piece, King *Coal*, seated on his throne in a magnificent audience chamber, with his consort *Pyrites* at his side, awaiting the nobles of his realm. Entering one by one in order of rank, to be presented to the King, there now appeared: Duke *Granite*, Marquis *Slate*, Countess *Porphyry* and the rest, all of them characterized with a few choice epithets and jokes. They are followed by Sir Laurence *Limestone*, a great landowner and a popular figure at court. He brings apologies from his mother, Lady *Marble*, who excuses herself on the grounds that she lives too far away; she is also said to be a cultivated and highly polished lady. We are given to understand that her absence from court today is probably due in part to her dalliance with *Canova*, who likes to flirt with her. *Lias*, sporting a headpiece of lizards and fish, seems somewhat tipsy. *Marl* and Jack *Clay* appear towards the end; the latter is a special favourite of the Queen, because he has promised her a collection of shells. And so it went on for quite a while in this amusing vein; but there was too much detail for me to be able to remember the rest of the story.

'A poem like this,' said Goethe, 'is designed to amuse sophisticates, while at the same time disseminating useful information that everyone really ought to know. It encourages the upper classes to take an interest in science, and you never know what good may come of such an entertaining, tongue-in-cheek piece. Many a thinking man will perhaps be inspired to make a study of his own particular patch. And personal observations of this kind, drawn from the natural world we see around us, are often all the more valuable because the observer is not himself a professional scientist.'

'You seem to be suggesting,' I ventured, 'that the more a man knows, the less well he observes things.'

'When people imbibe errors along with the knowledge they are taught,' replied Goethe, 'then certainly. Once a professional scientist aligns himself with a specific narrow doctrine, all just and unbiased perception goes out of the window. The committed Vulcanist will always look at things through a Vulcanist's spectacles, just as the Neptunist, and adherents of the latest elevation crater theory, will see things through theirs. The world view of all such theorists, locked into a single, exclusive ideology as they are, has lost its innocence, and objects no longer appear to them in their natural purity. When these men of science account for their observations, what we get, notwithstanding their fierce personal love of the truth as individuals, is not the objective truth about the objects in question, but a view of them that is highly coloured by their own subjectivity.

'But I am not saying that unbiased, *sound* knowledge gets in the way of observation – not at all. On the contrary, the old truth still holds good: we only have eyes and ears for what we *know*. When a professional musician listens to an orchestral performance, he hears each instrument and each individual note, whereas the layman hears only a monolithic wall of sound. Someone just out to enjoy the countryside sees a grassy or flower-strewn meadow as nothing more than a nice view, whereas the eye of a botanist sees an infinite variety of individual plants and grasses.

'But everything has its limits, and as it says in my *Götz* that the son is so full of book-learning that he no longer recognizes his own father, so we find professional men of science who are so full of book-learning and theories that they have forgotten how to look and listen. These people quickly become bound up in themselves; they are so preoccupied with their own thoughts that they are like someone in love, who hurries past his closest friends in the street without even seeing them. The observation of nature requires a degree of mental focus and inner calm, with nothing to disturb or distract. When a child spies a beetle on a flower, all his senses are concentrated on the one thing that interests him, and it doesn't occur to him to look up at the sky in case there might be something interesting going on at the same time with the cloud formations.'

'That suggests,' I said, 'that children and their like might make quite good field workers in science.'

'Would to God,' Goethe rejoined, 'we were all nothing more than good field workers. It's because we want to be more, and insist on carting around a load of philosophical and theoretical baggage, that we ruin everything.'

There was a pause in the conversation, which Riemer ended by bringing up the subject of Lord Byron and his death. This prompted Goethe to give a brilliant account of his writings, and he paid tribute to him in the most glowing terms. 'Incidentally,' he went on, 'although Byron died so young, literature has not lost much by his failure to develop further. In a sense, Byron had gone as far as he could. He had reached the pinnacle of his creative powers, and whatever he might have done thereafter, he would not have been able to push beyond the limits set to his talent. With his incomprehensible poem *The Vision of Judgement* he achieved the utmost of which he was capable.'

The conversation then turned to the Italian poet Torquato Tasso, and how he compared with Lord Byron. Goethe made no bones about the great superiority of the Englishman in intellect, worldly polish and productive power. 'You can't compare the two poets,' he added, 'without killing off one with the other. Byron is the burning thorn bush that reduces the holy cedar of Lebanon to ashes. The great epic poem of the Italian has maintained its reputation for centuries; but the whole of *Jerusalem Delivered* could be poisoned by a single line from *Don Juan*.'

1824

Wednesday 26 May 1824

I said goodbye to Goethe today, before leaving to visit my loved ones in Hanover and then go on to the Rhine, as had long been my intention. Goethe embraced me affectionately. 'If you should chance to meet Charlotte Kestner, an old friend of mine from my youth, at the Rehbergs' house in Hanover, please give her my kind regards. I shall write on your behalf to my friends in Frankfurt – the Willemers, Count Reinhard and the Schlossers.[8] You'll also find devoted friends of mine in Heidelberg and Bonn, who will give you a warm welcome. I had planned to spend some time in Marienbad again this summer, but I won't leave until you get back.'

I found it hard to say goodbye to Goethe. But I left with every confidence that I should see him again, fit and well, when I returned two months later.

Next day I was glad to be sitting in the carriage taking me home to my beloved Hanover, where, in my heart of hearts, I always long to be.

1825

Tuesday 22 March 1825

Last night, shortly after midnight, we were woken by the fire alarm, and heard people shouting: 'The theatre's on fire!' I threw on my clothes and hurried to the scene. Everyone was in a state of shock. Only a few hours before, we had been savouring a wonderful performance by La Roche in Cumberland's *Jew*, and Seidel had excited general laughter by his good humour and jokes. And now, in the same place where we had only just been enjoying such intellectual pleasures, the most terrifying element of destruction was raging.

The fire had apparently broken out in the stalls, started by the heating system, and quickly spread to the stage and the dry lathwork of the sets. Fuelled by an abundance of combustible materials, it was soon raging out of control; and it was not long before the flames were leaping through the roof and the rafters collapsed.

Everything possible was done to extinguish the blaze. The building was soon surrounded by a growing number of fire pumps, which directed a vast quantity of water into the inferno. But it was all to no avail. The flames leaped upwards as before, throwing up a continuous stream of glowing sparks and burning fragments of lightweight materials into the dark night sky which then drifted sideways over the town on a light breeze. The noise was tremendous, what with the shouts and cries of all the people manning the fire ladders and pumps. Everyone was working flat out, as if determined to conquer the blaze by sheer force of effort. Standing a little off to the side, as close as the heat of the fire permitted, was a man in a coat and military cap, smoking a cigar with the utmost composure. At first glance he appeared to be an idle bystander; but not so. People came up to him, he spoke briefly to give them their orders, and off they went to carry them out. It was the Grand Duke, Karl August. He had soon seen that the building itself could not be saved, and therefore ordered that it should be left to collapse, while any pumps that could be spared were to be turned on the neighbouring houses, which were much at risk from the nearby flames. I fancied him thinking, in royal resignation:

> Let it burn down! –
> It will rise again, more beautiful than before.[9]

He was not wrong. The theatre was old, not beautiful by any reckoning, and had long been too small to accommodate audiences that grew bigger by the year. All the same, it was sad to see this building irreparably destroyed, when it was associated with so many memories of Weimar's illustrious and cherished past.

I witnessed beautiful eyes shedding many a tear for its destruction. I was no less touched to see a member of the orchestra crying over his violin, which had been lost to the flames.

As day broke, I saw many pallid faces. I noticed various girls and women of the higher classes who had been watching the blaze all night and were now shivering slightly in the cold morning air. I went home to get a little rest, and then called on Goethe later in the morning.

The manservant told me he was unwell, and in bed. But Goethe asked to see me, and I went to his bedside. He stretched out his hand to me. 'We have all suffered a loss,' he said, 'but what can be done? Little Wölfchen came to my bed early this morning. He took hold of my hand, looked at me with big eyes, and said: "*These things happen!*" What more is there to say, apart from the wise words of my darling Wolf, as he sought to console me? The place where I laboured with love for nearly thirty years has been reduced to rubble and ashes. But as Wolf says: these things happen! I hardly slept all night; from my front windows I could see the flames constantly leaping up into the sky. As you can imagine, all kinds of thoughts about the old days were going through my mind, about my many years of collaboration with Schiller, and about the blossoming and growth of many a favourite pupil – and of course it was all quite upsetting. So I think it would be wise for me to keep to my bed today.'

I commended him for his caution. But he didn't seem at all weak or exhausted to me, but rather quite relaxed and cheerful. I had the feeling that this lying in bed was an old ruse of his, which he employs whenever some extraordinary event has occurred, and he can't face crowds of visitors.

Goethe asked me to sit down on a chair next to his bed and stay a little while. 'I've thought about you a lot, and felt sorry for you,' he said. 'What will you do with your evenings now?'

'You know,' I replied, 'how passionately fond I am of the theatre. When I arrived here two years ago I knew virtually nothing, apart from three or four plays I had seen in Hanover. It was all new to me, the actors and the plays; and since I did as you suggested, and surrendered myself completely to first impressions, without trying to analyse it or think too much about it, I can honestly say that the hours I have spent in the theatre these last two winters have given me more harmless enjoyment than anything else I have known. I was so mad about the theatre that I not only went to every single performance, but also secured admission to the rehearsals; even that wasn't enough for me, though, and if I happened to be passing during the day and saw the doors open, I would sometimes go in and sit for half an hour at a time on the empty benches in the stalls, picturing imaginary scenes being played out on the stage at that moment.'

'Well, you're just crazy,' returned Goethe with a laugh, 'but there's nothing wrong with that. Would to God the entire audience were made up of similar folk! And when all is said and done, you are right: it *is* quite something. Anyone who is not utterly spoiled and still sufficiently young will not easily find anywhere to pass the time more agreeably than in the theatre. Nobody expects anything of you, you don't have to open your mouth if you don't want to; you sit there completely at your ease, like a king, and just let it all happen in front of you, feasting your mind and your senses to your heart's content. You've got poetry, you've got painting, you've got singing and music, you've got professional acting, and I don't know what else besides! When all these arts and the charms of youth and beauty come together on a grand scale on a single evening, it creates a sense of occasion that nothing else can match. Even if it is bad in parts, and only good in some parts, it's still better than staring out of the window, or playing a hand of whist at some private party in a room full of cigar smoke. The Weimar theatre is not at all to be despised, as you yourself know; there is still a hard core left over from our glory days, to which fresh young talents have been added over time, and we can still produce something that charms and pleases, and at least offers the semblance of something complete.'

'I'd love to have seen it twenty or thirty years ago!' I replied.

'That certainly was a time,' agreed Goethe, 'when we did enjoy some big advantages. You have to remember that the tedious period of French taste had only just ended, and theatre audiences were not yet overstimulated; that people were being exposed to Shakespeare for the very first time; that the operas of Mozart were still relatively new; and lastly, that these were the years when Schiller's plays were being written and performed for the first time, in all their glory, on the Weimar stage, under his personal direction. So you can imagine what a feast this was for young and old alike, and how we were always playing to grateful audiences.'

'Older persons,' I remarked, 'who were around during those years, never tire of telling me how highly regarded the Weimar theatre was back then.'

'I won't deny,' said Goethe, 'that it was quite something. But the main thing was that the Grand Duke gave me a completely free hand, and I could do whatever I wanted. I wasn't interested in magnificent scenery and gorgeous costumes; I was interested in getting good plays. From tragedy to farce, any genre was fine by me; but a play had to be special enough to make the grade. It had to be bold and well constructed, amusing and graceful, but more especially it had to be wholesome, and have some solid substance at its heart. Anything morbid, feeble, maudlin or sentimental, and anything horrific or gruesome or morally offensive, was ruled out from the start; the risk of corrupting both actors and audiences with such stuff was too great.

'But by choosing good plays I also raised the standard of acting. For the study of excellence, and the constant practice of excellence, was bound to make something of a man who was not without natural talent to start with. And I was in constant personal contact with the actors. I conducted the reading rehearsals and explained everyone's part to them; I attended the dress rehearsals and discussed any possible improvements with the cast; I always went to the performances, and pointed out next day anything I felt was not quite right.

'In this way I helped them to improve their skills. But I also sought to raise the social standing of actors as a professional class, by inviting the best and most promising ones into my own social circle, thereby showing the world that I considered them good enough to associate with me. The effect of this was to make the rest of Weimar high society follow suit, and actors and actresses were soon being welcomed into the best social circles as honoured guests – which of course meant that they became more cultivated in mind and more polished in manner. My pupil Wolff in Berlin and our own Durand are men of the finest social sensibility. Herr Oels and Graff are sufficiently cultured to do credit to the best society.

'Schiller adopted the same approach as me. He spent a lot of time with actors and actresses. Like me, he attended all the rehearsals, and after every successful performance of one of his plays he would invite them to his house and have a good time with them. They shared their pleasure in what had gone well, and discussed anything that might be done better next time. But actors and audiences were already highly cultivated by the time Schiller joined us, and there is no doubt that this contributed to the rapid success of his plays.'

It was a joy to hear Goethe talking at length on a subject that was always of great interest to me, and which was uppermost in my mind after the terrible events of the previous night.

1825 473

'It's as if the burning down of the theatre last night,' I said, 'where you and Schiller did so much good work over so many years, marks the end of an era, the like of which Weimar will probably not see again any time soon. It must have given you a lot of pleasure back then, when you were running the theatre and it was having such extraordinary success.'

'Not to mention quite a bit of toil and trouble!' replied Goethe with a sigh.

'It must have been difficult,' I said, 'to keep such a many-headed hydra under control.'

'You can achieve a lot with strict discipline,' replied Goethe, 'and even more with love; but the most important things are intelligent understanding and impartial justice that is no respecter of persons.

'I had to beware of two enemies that might have got me into trouble. One was my passionate love of talent, which might easily have made me partial. The other – well, I won't say it, but you can guess. Our theatre had no lack of good-looking young women with charming personalities. I felt passionately attracted to many of them; and some were more than ready to oblige. But I restrained myself and said: *No further!* I was fully aware of my position and my responsibilities. I was not there as a private individual, but as the head of an institution, whose success was more important to me than my own momentary gratification. If I had embarked upon some love affair I would have been like a compass that cannot possibly point in the right direction when a magnet is placed next to it.

'But because I remained completely chaste and always in control of myself, I also remained in control of the theatre, and I never forfeited the respect without which no authority can last for long.'

This confession of Goethe's impressed me deeply. I had already heard similar stories about him from others, and was glad to have confirmation now from his own lips. I loved him more than ever, and we parted with a hearty handshake.

I returned to the scene of the fire, where flames and columns of smoke were still rising from the great heap of ruins. People were still working to douse the flames and beat out the embers.

Close by, I found some scorched fragments of an actor's script. They were passages from Goethe's *Tasso*.

Thursday 24 March 1825

Dined with Goethe. The loss of the theatre was almost the only subject of conversation. Frau von Goethe and Fräulein Ulrike were recalling the happy hours they had spent in the old building. They had recovered a few relics from the rubble which they considered priceless; it was nothing more than a few bricks and scorched fragments of wallpaper. But they claimed they had come from the exact same spot in the balcony where they used to sit!

'The main thing,' said Goethe, 'is to move on and sort out alternative arrangements as soon as possible. If it was me, I'd be putting on performances again next week, either in the palace or in the main room of the public hall – whichever. But we mustn't leave it too long, in case our audiences start looking for something else to while away their evenings.'

'But we've lost pretty much all our scenery,' said someone.

'We don't need much in the way of scenery,' replied Goethe. 'And we don't need epic dramas. It's not even necessary to perform a whole play, and certainly not a major work. The main thing is to choose something without any major scene changes: a one-act comedy, say, or a one-act farce or operetta. Then an aria of some sort, a duet, or the finale from a popular opera – and you'll have a passable evening's entertainment. We just have to get through April somehow; in May you'll have the woodland songbirds.

'Meanwhile,' Goethe went on, 'you will be able to watch the spectacle of a new house going up during the summer months. It's a very strange thing about this fire. This much I can tell you, that I sat down with Coudray during the long winter evenings to draw up plans for a very handsome new theatre that would be right for Weimar. We had sent away for the ground plans and sections of some of the finest German theatres, and by using what was best in these and avoiding anything we didn't like, we have come up with a design that we think works well.

As soon as the Grand Duke approves it, construction can begin; and the fact that this disaster finds us so remarkably well prepared is no small consideration.'

We were delighted to hear this exciting news from Goethe.

'In the old house,' Goethe went on, 'there was adequate provision for the nobility in the balcony, and for the serving class and young artisans in the gallery. But the many theatregoers from the well-to-do, respectable middle class were often hard done by, because when certain plays were being performed the orchestra would be taken over by students, and middle-class patrons had nowhere to go. The handful of small boxes behind the orchestra, and the few benches in the stalls, were not enough. But now we have made better provision. We plan to have a whole tier of boxes running right round the orchestra, and we're putting in another tier of upper-circle boxes between the balcony and the gallery. This gives us a lot more seating, without making the building itself significantly larger.'

We very much liked the sound of this, and applauded Goethe for having the best interests of theatre audiences at heart.

Determined to do something myself for our fine future theatre, I went off after dinner with my friend Robert Doolan to Upper Weimar, where we ordered a cup of coffee in the tavern there and started to write an opera libretto based on Metastasio's *Issipile*. The first thing we did was to draft a playbill, and to cast the work with the most popular singers from the Weimar theatre. We had a lot of fun with this. It was almost as if we were back in our seats in front of the orchestra pit again. Then we started work in earnest and completed a substantial portion of the first act.

Sunday 27 March 1825

Dined at Goethe's with a large party. He showed us the design for the new theatre. It was as he had said a few days before: the new house promised to be a very beautiful building, both inside and out.

It was pointed out that such a fine theatre called for new scenery and better costumes than we had had before. We also

476 CONVERSATIONS WITH GOETHE

agreed that the company was starting to look a little thin, and that it was time to engage some talented young members, both for the theatre and for the opera. At the same time, we were well aware that all this would involve significant costs, which the exchequer would probably be unable to meet from its existing resources.

'I know very well what will happen,' said Goethe. 'They'll hire a few nobodies who don't cost much, on the grounds that it will save the exchequer money. But don't go thinking that will help the exchequer. Nothing costs more money than trying to save on the important things. What you really need is a full house every evening; and a young singer of either sex, plus a dashing hero and a doughty young heroine, if they are very talented and reasonably good-looking, will make a big difference there. And if I were still in charge, I would now go one step further to ease the pressure on the exchequer, and you'd find that the money we needed would soon be raised.'

When asked what he had in mind, Goethe replied: 'It's very simple, really. I would stage performances on Sundays, too. That would give us the extra takings from at least forty more evenings, and it would be a poor job if the exchequer didn't get an extra ten to fifteen thousand thalers a year from that.'

We thought this a very practical solution. Someone pointed out that the large working-class population, which is usually working until the late evening on weekdays, has Sunday as its only day off, and would surely prefer the more sophisticated pleasures of the theatre to dancing and drinking in some village tavern. It was also felt that all the farmers and landowners, as well as the officials and well-to-do residents of the other small towns in the area, would view Sunday as a good day to come in to Weimar for the theatre. Also, Sunday evenings in Weimar have always been very dull and boring for those who don't go to court, have no immediate family around them or don't belong to a private club; anyone on his own just doesn't know what to do with himself. And yet people feel there should be somewhere on a Sunday night where they can relax and forget about the weekly grind.

So Goethe's suggestion for putting on Sunday performances,

as is already customary in other German towns and cities, met with complete agreement, and was welcomed as a great idea. The only slight doubt was whether the court would approve it.

'The Weimar court,' said Goethe, 'is too well-meaning and wise to block any measure that will be good for the town and one of its leading institutions. I am sure the court will not mind making the small sacrifice of switching its Sunday soirées to another night. But if this were not acceptable, we could find enough plays for the Sundays that the court would not want to see anyway, but which are just the thing for the common people, and would fill the coffers nicely.'

The conversation turned to the actors, and there was a lot of discussion about the use and abuse of their resources.

'The main thing I've learned in the course of my long experience,' said Goethe, 'is never to put a play, let alone an opera, into rehearsal unless you can be reasonably certain that it will be a success for years to come. Nobody gives sufficient thought to the resources needed to rehearse a five-act play or indeed an opera of similar length. I can tell you, my friends, that it takes a lot of work before a singer knows his part inside out, in every scene and every act, and even more work before the choruses go the way they should. I shudder sometimes when I hear how casually people often give the order to rehearse an opera, when they don't have the faintest idea whether it will be a success, having only heard about it from very unreliable newspaper reports. Since we have a pretty decent mail coach service in Germany, and are even starting to get express mail coaches now, what I would do, if I heard about some new opera being performed somewhere to positive reviews, is to send the director or some other reliable member of the company to the town in question, so that he could attend an actual performance and judge for himself whether the new opera was any good, and whether or not we had sufficient resources to stage it. The cost of sending someone is as nothing compared with the enormous advantages we would gain by sending him, and the disastrous mistakes we would avoid by doing so.

'And then, once a good play or opera has been fully rehearsed, it should be performed at short intervals and allowed to run for as long as it continues to pull in audiences and fill the house. The same applies to a good older play or opera, which may not have been performed for ages, and which also needs quite a bit of rehearsal work now to make a success of it. These performances should likewise be repeated at short intervals for as long as the public shows any interest. This mania for having something new all the time, and performing a good play or opera just the once, or maybe twice, when so much work has gone into rehearsing it – or else letting long periods of six to eight weeks elapse between performances, so that fresh rehearsals are needed every time: it's very detrimental to the theatre, and an unforgivable waste of the performers' time and energy.'

Goethe seemed to regard this matter as so important, and he seemed to take it so much to heart, that he got quite worked up about it – which is unusual for him, who is normally so composed.

'In Italy,' Goethe went on, 'they perform the same opera every night for four to six weeks, and the Italians, big children that they are, are not looking for anything different. Cultured Parisians see the classical plays of their great writers so often that they know them off by heart and have a well-tuned ear for the accentuation of every syllable. Here in Weimar, they did do me the honour of performing my *Iphigenie* and *Tasso*; but how often was that? Once every three or four years at most. Audiences find them boring. And understandably so: the actors are not used to performing the plays, and audiences are not used to hearing them. If the actors were to play their parts more often, so that they really made them their own, and their performances took on a life that made it all seem to come from the heart, rather than being learned and rehearsed, then audiences would surely not be uninterested or unmoved.

'There was a time when I really fancied it possible to create a German theatre. I even fancied I could contribute something myself and lay a few foundation stones for such an edifice. I wrote my *Iphigenie* and *Tasso* in the childish hope that this was the way forward. But there was no reaction, and nothing changed. If I had made an impact and been applauded for my efforts, I would have written a dozen plays like *Iphigenie* and

Tasso; there was no shortage of material. But as I say, we didn't have the actors to perform that kind of thing with verve and intelligence, and we didn't have receptive or responsive audiences.'

Wednesday 30 March 1825

Big tea party at Goethe's this evening, where I met a young American, as well as the young Englishmen living here.[10] I also had the pleasure of seeing the Countess Julie von Egloffstein and having an interesting conversation with her on all kinds of subjects.

Wednesday 6 April 1825

They followed Goethe's advice, and the first performance took place this evening in the main room of the public hall. The programme consisted of shorter pieces and fragments, as dictated by the limited space and lack of props and scenery. The short opera *Das Hausgesinde* was just as effective here as in the theatre.[11] Then a popular quartet from Eberwein's opera *Der Graf von Gleichen* was received with enthusiastic applause. Our first tenor, Herr Moltke, then sang a well-known song from *Die Zauberflöte*, followed, after an interval, by the rousing grand finale of the first act of *Don Giovanni*, bringing today's first alternative theatre evening to a stirring climax.

Sunday 10 April 1825

Dined with Goethe. 'I have some good news to report,' he said. 'The Grand Duke has approved our plan for the new theatre, and we are going to start laying the foundations without delay.'

I was delighted to hear this.

'We had to contend with all kinds of obstacles,' Goethe went on, 'but we won through in the end. We owe a great debt to Privy Councillor Schweitzer, who staunchly backed our side, as one would expect from him. The plan now carries the Grand Duke's personal signature, and as such cannot be altered. Be glad, therefore: you're going to get a very fine theatre!'

Thursday 14 April 1825

Spent the evening at Goethe's. As our conversations about the theatre and theatre management were so topical now, I asked him what principles he had adopted when selecting a new member of the company.

'It's hard to say,' replied Goethe. 'I adopted very different approaches. If the new actor came with an impressive reputation, I would get him to perform, and see how he fitted in with the others – whether his style and manner would unsettle our ensemble, and whether he actually filled a gap that needed filling. But if he was a young fellow who had not been on the stage before, then I would focus on his personality, and see whether there was something engaging and attractive about him, and above all whether he was in full possession of himself. An actor who lacks self-possession, and who cannot present himself to a stranger in the way he wants to be seen, has very little talent to speak of. His whole job, after all, requires him to deny himself at all times and to inhabit an alien persona!

'If I liked his appearance and demeanour, I would get him to read a speech, in order to gauge the power and range of his voice as well as his emotional range. I would give him some sublime passage from a great poet, to see whether he was capable of feeling and expressing something truly great; then something passionate and tempestuous, to test his power. Then I would switch to something discursive, witty, ironic or amusing, to see how he handled that kind of thing, and whether he possessed the necessary mental agility. Then I would give him something that showed the pain of a wounded heart or the suffering of a great soul, to find out whether he was capable of expressing pathos.

'If he passed muster in all these areas, I could reasonably hope to make a very good actor out of him. If he was clearly better in some areas than in others, I made a mental note of the type of role for which he was best suited. I also knew by now where his weak points lay, and tried to get him to work on these and improve them. If I noticed him lapsing into dialect and so-called provincialisms, I would urge him to drop the habit, and recommend that he spend some time practising informally with a member of the theatre company whose speech was entirely free from such things. Then I asked him if he could dance and fence, and if not, I would hand him over to the dancing and fencing master for a while.

'When he was ready to go on stage, I would start by giving him parts that suited his personality, and all I asked to begin with was that he should play himself. Then, if he seemed to me a little too fiery by nature, I gave him stolid characters to play; if too placid and slow, I gave him fiery, mercurial roles, so that he would learn to step outside himself and take on the personality of someone else.'

The conversation turned to the casting of plays, and at one point Goethe said the following, which I thought worthy of note:

'It's a great mistake,' he said, 'to think that you can cast a mediocre play with mediocre actors. A second- or third-rate play can be incredibly improved by casting first-rate actors, and made into something really good. But if I cast a second- or third-rate play with second- or third-rate actors, you shouldn't be surprised if it falls completely flat.

'Second-rate actors are a real asset in great plays. They are like the shadowy figures in paintings, who perform a very useful function by making the fully lit figures appear even more imposing.'

Saturday 16 April 1825

Dined at Goethe's with D'Alton, whom I met last summer in Bonn and was delighted to see again. D'Alton is a man after Goethe's own heart, and the two of them have a lovely rapport. He is seen as an important figure in his own field of science, so Goethe values his observations and takes careful note of everything he says. At the same time D'Alton is very personable, witty, and so eloquent and bursting with ideas that he can have few equals, and one never tires of listening to him.

Goethe, who, in his quest to fathom the natural world, would gladly encompass the entire universe, is nevertheless at a disadvantage vis-à-vis any natural scientist of note who has devoted a whole lifetime to one specific field of study. The latter has mastered an infinite wealth of detail, whereas Goethe is more at home contemplating great universal laws. This is why Goethe – who is constantly looking for some great synthesis, but is unable to confirm his intuitions because he lacks sufficient knowledge of the individual facts – grasps so eagerly at every opportunity to connect with leading natural scientists. For he finds in them what he himself lacks; they can fill in the gaps in his own knowledge. He will be eighty in a few years' time, but he never tires of experimentation and discovery. He has not yet finished with any of his lines of investigation; he always wants to push on further, to keep on learning more and more – all of which marks him out as a man of eternal, irrepressible youth.

These thoughts were prompted by his lively conversation with D'Alton at lunch today. D'Alton talked about rodents and the formation and adaptations of their skeletons, and Goethe could not get enough of the new facts he was learning.

Wednesday 27 April 1825

Called on Goethe towards evening, having received an invitation to take a drive with him to the lower garden. 'Before we go,' he said, 'let me give you a letter from Zelter which arrived yesterday, in which he touches on our theatre project.'

'I would never have put you down,' writes Zelter at one point, 'as the man to build a theatre for the people in Weimar. Give them an inch, and they'll take a mile. Other persons in authority who would cork the wine during fermentation would do well to remember that. Friends, we've seen it before, and we're seeing it still.'

Goethe looked at me and we laughed. 'Zelter is a great character,' he said, 'but sometimes he doesn't quite understand me, and takes my words the wrong way.

'I have devoted my entire life to the people and their cultural improvement, so why shouldn't I build a theatre for them, too? But here in Weimar, this small royal seat, which, so the joke goes, has ten thousand poets and a few residents, there isn't much of a people to speak of – and not much call for a

1825   483

"people's theatre", therefore. Weimar will undoubtedly become a great city one day; but we could be waiting centuries before the population of Weimar has grown sufficiently to be able to fill a theatre and justify the building and upkeep of a theatre.'

By now the horses had been hitched up, and we drove down to the lower garden. The evening was still and mild, verging on the sultry, and large cloud masses were gathering, threatening a storm. We walked up and down the dry, sandy path, Goethe at my side, silent and seemingly lost in thought. I listened to the sounds of the blackbird and thrush, perched on the topmost branches of the bare ash trees on the far side of the Ilm and singing in anticipation of the gathering storm.

Goethe gazed about him, looking up at the clouds, then at the green shoots and leaves bursting forth everywhere – on both sides of the path, on the meadow, on the shrubs and hedgerows. 'A warm thunder shower, which looks likely this evening,' he said, 'and spring will be here again in all her glory and abundance.'

By now the clouds were looking more threatening, we heard a low rumble of thunder, a few raindrops fell, and Goethe thought it wise to drive back to town. 'If you don't have other plans,' he said as we alighted outside his house, 'then come upstairs and stay with me a while.' Which I very gladly did.

Zelter's letter was still lying on the table. 'It's a very strange thing,' said Goethe, 'how easy it is to be misunderstood by public opinion! As far as I know, I have never done anything to offend the people, yet now it has been decreed that I am no friend of the people. I am certainly no friend of the revolutionary mob, which is intent on robbery, murder and arson, and, under the false pretence of serving the public good, pursues only the meanest and most self-serving ends. I am no friend of such people, as I am no friend of any Louis XV. I hate all violent revolution, which destroys as much good as it accomplishes. I hate those who carry it out, and those who give them cause to do so. But does that mean I am no friend of the people? Does any right-minded man think differently?

'You know how much I rejoice at every improvement that the future holds in prospect. But as I said, sudden, violent change is anathema to me, because it is *not nature's way*.

484 CONVERSATIONS WITH GOETHE

'I love plants, and I love the rose as the most perfect flower brought forth by nature here in Germany; but I'm not such a fool that I expect my garden to bring forth roses this early, in late April. I am content when I see the first green leaves at this time of year, content when I see the stem growing one leaf at a time, week by week; I am pleased when I see the buds in May, and happy when June finally gives me the rose itself, in all its glory and all its fragrance. But anyone who cannot wait must resort to the hothouses instead.

'They also say that I am a servant of princes, a lackey – as if that meant anything! Do I serve a tyrant? A despot? Do I serve a prince who simply gratifies his own appetites at the expense of the people? Such princes, and such times, are long gone, I'm glad to say. I have been intimately associated with the Grand Duke for half a century, and have striven and worked with him for half a century; but I would be lying if I said that a single day had gone by when the Grand Duke did not think about doing something that would benefit the country and also improve the lot of every individual. As for himself personally, what has his royal rank brought him other than toil and trouble? Are his residence, his wardrobe or his table any better furnished than those of a wealthy private citizen? You need only go to our maritime cities to find respected merchants with kitchens and cellars better furnished than his.

'This autumn,' Goethe went on, 'we shall be celebrating fifty years of the Grand Duke's reign and rule. But when I stop to think about it, what has his rule been, other than continual service? What has it been, other than service in the pursuit of great ends, service for the benefit of his people? If I am forced to be a servant of princes, I can at least console myself with the thought that I am only the servant of one who is himself a servant of the common good.'

Friday 29 April 1825

The construction of the new theatre had been proceeding apace; the foundation walls were going up on all sides, with every prospect of a very beautiful building to come.

1825   485

But today, when I visited the building site, I saw to my dismay that the work had stopped. I also heard a rumour that another party had finally won out over the Goethe–Coudray plan, that Coudray was stepping down as director of the project, and that another architect would now be building the theatre to a new design, altering the already-laid foundations to suit.

It grieved me deeply to see and hear this, because I and many others had been looking forward to seeing a new theatre being built in Weimar which incorporated Goethe's practical recommendations regarding the internal layout, and whose aesthetic design reflected his own highly cultivated taste.

But I was also aggrieved on behalf of Goethe and Coudray, who must have felt quite offended by this local turn of events.

Sunday 1 May 1825

Dined with Goethe. Not surprisingly, the change of plan for the new theatre was the first thing we talked about. As I said, I had feared that this highly unexpected development would offend Goethe deeply. But not a bit of it. I found him in very mellow and cheerful mood, not at all disposed to nurse a petty grudge.

'They sought to win over the Grand Duke,' he said, 'on the grounds of cost, claiming that the revised design would save a lot of money – and they got their way. It's all the same to me. In the end, a new theatre is just another bonfire waiting to happen, and sooner or later there'll be some accident and it will go up in flames again. I console myself with that thought. And besides, a bit more or a bit less – it's not worth talking about. You'll still get a very decent building, even if it's not quite what I wanted and planned. You will go there, and so will I, and it will turn out all right in the end.

'The Grand Duke,' Goethe went on, 'once stated it as his opinion that a theatre doesn't need to be an architectural showpiece. And really, you can't argue with that. Then he said that it's basically just a building for making money. Put like that, it sounds a little materialistic; but when you think about it there is an important truth behind it. If a theatre doesn't just want to cover its costs, but also to make money and operate at a profit, then everything about it has to be excellent. It must be run by the best managers, the actors must be among the best available, and every play on the programme must be so good that the crowd appeal necessary to fill the house every night never falters. Now that's quite a lot to ask, and almost impossible to achieve.'

'The Grand Duke's view,' I said, 'that the theatre is there to make money, seems a thoroughly practical one, because implicit in it is the need to maintain oneself continually at the peak of excellence.'

'Shakespeare and Molière,' replied Goethe, 'were of the same mind. Both of them wanted above all to make money with their theatres. But in order to achieve this, their principal aim, they had to try and maintain the highest standards of excellence all the time by introducing some decent new work every now and then alongside the best of the old in a bid to tempt and attract audiences. The ban on *Tartuffe* was a hammer blow for Molière – not just for Molière the playwright, but also for Molière the theatre manager, who was responsible for the welfare of a major theatre company and had to put food on the table for himself and his actors.[12]

'Nothing,' Goethe went on, 'is more dangerous for the well-being of a theatre than when the theatre management has no personal stake in the size of the box-office takings, and can carry on in the blithe assurance that any shortfall in ticket receipts over the year will be made up from some other source of funding at the year's end. It is human nature to sit back and take it easy when not constrained by personal advantage or disadvantage. Now it would be unreasonable to expect a theatre in a small town like Weimar to be entirely self-supporting, so that no annual subsidy from the royal exchequer was needed. But everything has its limits, and a few thousand thalers more or less each year is no trifling matter, especially as diminishing receipts go hand in hand with declining standards, entailing a loss not just of money, but of reputation as well.

'If I were the Grand Duke, I would in future, in the event of a change of theatre management, set aside a fixed sum every

1825 487

year as a regular subsidy; I would take the average of the subsidies from the previous ten years, say, and use that to work out a figure that should be sufficient to provide a decent level of support. They'd have to make the money last, of course. But then I would go a step further: if, by clever and diligent management, the theatre manager and his stage directors finished the year with a budget surplus, the manager, stage directors and leading members of the company would be paid a bonus out of this surplus. You mark my words: that would soon stir things up, and rouse the place from the torpor into which it is bound to fall over time.

'Our theatre statutes,' Goethe went on, 'list plenty of sanctions, but not a single provision for encouraging and rewarding excellent work. This is a serious omission. If I can expect a deduction from my salary for every mistake I make, I should also expect to be offered an incentive for doing more than can reasonably be asked of me. And that's how a theatre really thrives – when everybody does more than is expected or asked of them.'

Frau von Goethe and Fräulein Ulrike now came in, both charmingly dressed in summer clothing on account of the fine weather. The conversation at table was lively and jolly. We talked about various outings that had taken place the previous week, and about the prospects for similar pleasures in the week to come.

'If these fine evenings continue,' said Frau von Goethe, 'I'd love to have a tea party in the park in the next few days, when the nightingales are singing. What do you think, father dear?' 'That sounds lovely!' replied Goethe. 'And what about you, Eckermann?' said Frau von Goethe. 'Would you like to come?' 'But Ottilie,' interjected Fräulein Ulrike, 'how can you think of inviting the doctor? He won't come, and even if he does he'll be like a cat on hot bricks, with his mind clearly elsewhere, and wishing he could leave – the sooner, the better.' 'If I'm honest,' I rejoined, 'I'd really rather be rambling through the fields with Doolan. Tea and tea parties and tea-party conversation are so contrary to my nature that it makes me uncomfortable even to think about it.' 'But Eckermann,' said Frau von Goethe, 'when you're having tea in the park, you're in the open air and completely in your element.' 'On the contrary!' I said. 'If I am so close to nature that I can smell all the aromas, and yet can't actually immerse myself in it all, then I feel as twitchy as a duck that's placed next to the water, but prevented from diving in.' 'Or you could say,' added Goethe with a laugh, 'that you feel like a horse that pokes its head out of the stable, and sees other horses galloping around in a big field outside. He can smell the joys and freedom of the great outdoors, but he can't get outside himself. Leave Eckermann alone; he is the way he is, and you won't change him. But tell me, my friend, what is it that you and your Doolan get up to on these long, sunny afternoons, out there in the fields?' 'We seek out some deserted valley,' I said, 'and shoot with bows and arrows.' 'Hm,' said Goethe, 'I dare say that's good fun.' 'It's a great way,' I said, 'to get rid of winter ailments.' 'But how on earth,' said Goethe, 'did you get hold of bows and arrows here in Weimar?' 'As far as the arrows are concerned,' I said, 'I brought one back from Brabant in the campaign of 1814. Archery is a popular pastime there. Even the smallest town has its own archery clubs. They have a shooting range set up in some tavern, similar to our skittle alleys, and generally meet in the late afternoon, when I've often enjoyed watching them. The men were great strapping fellows, and when they stood there and pulled back the bowstring they looked like figures from some classical painting: they had such a well-developed physique, and their aim was so accurate. They generally shot from a distance of sixty to eighty paces at a paper target fixed to a damp cob wall; they would shoot one after another in quick succession, and leave their arrows sticking in the wall. It was not unusual for them to put five arrows out of fifteen into the bull's eye, no bigger than a coin, with the rest of them grouped close in around. When they'd all taken their turn, they would go and retrieve their arrows from the soft wall, and then play another round. At the time, I was so mad about this archery business that I thought it would be a great thing to introduce it to Germany, and I was stupid enough to think it could be done. I tried hard to get a good deal on a bow, but there were none to be had for less than twenty francs; and as a poor rifleman I couldn't possibly come up with that kind of money. So I made do with an arrow – which is the more critical part, requiring more skill in the making – which I bought for a franc from a workshop in Brussels and brought home with me, together with a drawing, as my only spoils of war.'

'That's just like you,' said Goethe. 'But don't run away with the idea that something natural and beautiful can be made popular. At the very least it takes time and requires a desperate amount of effort. But I can well believe this Brabant archery is a beautiful thing to see. The pleasures of our German skittle alleys seem coarse and vulgar by comparison, and there's something quite philistine about them.'

'The great thing about archery,' I said, 'is that it develops the whole body and exercises every part of it. You've got the left arm holding the bow out, taut, firm and rigid; you've got the right arm which pulls back the bowstring with the arrow, and needs to be just as strong. At the same time you've got both feet and legs firmly planted on the ground, to support and steady the upper body. The eye is focused on the target, the muscles of the shoulders and neck are all tensed and working. And then that pleasurable sensation when the arrow hisses away and embeds itself in the target. I know of no physical exercise that remotely compares with it.'

'Our public gymnasia could offer archery training,' replied Goethe. 'And I shouldn't wonder if we had thousands of competent archers in Germany in twenty years' time. You can't do much with an adult generation – physically, mentally, or in matters of taste or character. But if you are smart, and start in the schools, then you will get somewhere.'

'But our German gym teachers,' I said, 'don't know how to handle a bow and arrow.'

'Well, in that case,' replied Goethe, 'a group of gymnasia should get together and arrange for an experienced bowman from Flanders or Brabant to come and teach them. Or else they could send a few fine strapping young gymnasts to Brabant to train as bowmen there, and also to learn how to carve a bow and make the arrows. They could then go into the public gymnasia in Germany as teachers, itinerant teachers, who stay in one gymnasium for a while, then move on to another.

'Personally,' Goethe went on, 'I have nothing against the German gymnastic movement.[13] So I found it doubly regrettable when gymnastics became a political issue, so that the authorities felt it necessary to restrict them or even ban them altogether. As a result, they've thrown out the baby with the bath water. But I hope they will reinstate the public gymnasia, because our young people in Germany really need them, especially the students, who spend so much time using their brains and studying that they lack the balance of physical exercise and the much-needed energy this gives them. But tell me more about your bow and arrow. You say you brought an arrow back from Brabant: I'd like to see it.'

'It got lost a long time ago,' I replied. 'But I remembered it so well that I managed to reproduce it – and not just the one, but a whole dozen. But it was not as easy as I thought. I tried and failed many times, and made lots of mistakes, but at least I learned a lot in the process. The first thing was the shaft, which had to be straight and not liable to warp over time; it also had to be light, and at the same time strong enough not to shatter when it hit a hard object. I tried using poplar, then spruce, then birch; but all of them proved unsatisfactory in one way or another, and none of them gave me what I needed. Then I experimented with wood from the lime tree, taken from a slender, straight-grained trunk section; and this turned out to be exactly what I was looking for. An arrow shaft made from this wood was light, straight and strong, thanks to its very fine fibres. The next thing was to tip the arrow with horn; but I soon found that not every type of horn is suitable, and that it has to be cut from the heart of the horn, so that it doesn't shatter when shooting at a hard object. The most difficult and exacting task had still to be done, however – and that was fletching the arrow. What a mess I made of that! It took me ages to get it right and to develop a reasonable degree of skill.'

'I think I'm right in saying,' ventured Goethe, 'that the fletchings are not let into the shaft, but glued on?'

'They're glued on,' I replied, 'but the joint has to be so strong, tight, and neatly done that it looks as if they are an integral part of the shaft itself – as if they had just sprouted from the wood. It's also important to use the right glue. I found that isinglass was the best, softened in water for a few hours, and then dissolved with a little added alcohol over a low charcoal fire to produce a kind of jelly. And you can't just use any old feathers. The vanes of the flight feathers from any large bird are good, but I have found that the best ones are the red wing feathers of the peacock, the large feathers of the turkey, and especially the strong and magnificent feathers of the eagle and bustard.'

'This is all most fascinating,' said Goethe. 'Anyone who doesn't know you would hardly believe you had such exciting hobbies. But tell me how you got hold of a bow.'

'I have made a few for myself,' I replied, 'but again, I made the most awful hash of it to begin with. Then I talked to joiners and cartwrights, tried out all the different species of wood from around here, and finally managed to produce something quite good. I needed to find a timber that would bend easily when the bow was drawn, spring back quickly and powerfully, and retain its elasticity permanently. I made my first attempts using ash, cut from the knot-free trunk of a tree about ten years old and roughly the thickness of a human arm. But as I was working it, I got down to the heartwood, which was coarse-grained and generally of inferior quality. I was then advised to pick a trunk that was large enough to rive into four quarters.'

'Rive?' asked Goethe. 'What's that?'

'It's a special term used by cartwrights,' I explained, 'and it basically just means "split". You drive a wedge along the length of the trunk, from one end to the other. If it is a straight-grown trunk – meaning one where the fibres extend upwards in a straight line – then the riven sections will also be straight, and ideal for making bows. But if the trunk is twisted, then the riven sections will also be winding and twisted, because the wedge follows the direction of the fibres; and these will be no good for making bows.'

'What about,' said Goethe, 'if you were to *saw* such a trunk into four sections? You'd get straight pieces that way, for certain.'

I replied: 'If the trunk was a bit twisted, you would end up cutting through the fibres with the saw; and that would make the sections useless for a bow.'

'I can see that,' said Goethe. 'A bow where you'd cut through the fibres would simply break. But tell me more; this is all most interesting.'

'So I made my second bow,' I went on, 'from a piece of *riven* ash. None of the fibres on the back face had been cut through, the bow was strong and sturdy, but it had one defect: it did not bend easily when drawn. "You must have used a piece of seedling ash," said the cartwright, "which is always a very stiff timber; but if you go for the tough variety that grows around Hopfgarten and Zimmern, you'll get on better." This was when I discovered that not all varieties of ash are the same, and that a lot depends, with all timber species, on the location and the soil where the trees are grown. I learned that the timber from the heights of the Ettersberg is of little commercial value, whereas timber grown in the area around Nohra is noted for its strength – which is why the carters of Weimar swear by Nohra as the place to get their wagons repaired. In the course of my further efforts I also learned that timber grown on a north-facing slope is stronger and more straight-grained than timber grown on a south-facing one. Which makes perfect sense, because a young stem growing on a shady, northern slope can only get light and sun from above, which means it is constantly straining upwards, seeking the sun, and drawing the fibres up with it in a straight line. A shady location also encourages the formation of finer fibres, which is very noticeable in free-standing trees whose south side has been exposed to the sunlight throughout the life of the tree, while their north side has always been in the shade. If we examine the trunk of such a tree when it has been sawn into sections, we find that the core or heart of the tree is not in the centre at all, but visibly displaced to one side. The reason for this is that constant exposure to the sun has caused the annual rings on the south side to grow thicker and wider than the annual rings on the shady north side. So when joiners and cartwrights need a strong, close-grained timber they choose the more finely developed north side of a tree trunk, which they call the winter side, and which they know they can rely on.'

'As you can imagine,' said Goethe, 'your observations are of particular interest to me, having spent half my life studying the growth of plants and trees. But do go on! I assume you went on to make a bow from the tough variety of ash.'

'I did,' I replied, 'and I used a well-riven piece from the winter side, which was quite close-grained. The bow was easy to draw, and sprang back strongly. But after a few months of use it took on a permanent curvature, and it was clear that the bow was losing its elasticity. I then tried again with the trunk of a young oak, which was also a very good timber, but after a while I found the same problem with this; then I tried the trunk of a walnut tree, which was better; and finally I used the trunk of a small-leafed maple, the so-called field or hedge maple, which was the best of all and fitted the bill perfectly.'

'I know the wood,' rejoined Goethe, 'you often see it growing in hedges. I can well imagine that it is good for this. But I have seldom seen a young trunk that didn't have side branches, and to make a bow, surely you need a wood that's completely knot-free?'

'A young trunk,' I said, 'does have side branches; but if it is allowed to grow on into a full-size tree, these are removed, or else they drop off by themselves in time, if the tree is growing in a thicket. If a trunk is about three to four inches in diameter when the side branches are taken off, and if it is left to grow on and put on new wood on the outside every year, then after a period of fifty to eighty years the knotty core will be encased in more than six inches of sound, knot-free timber. The outside of such a trunk will be perfectly smooth; but you have no way of knowing what it's like on the inside. So the safest thing, when working with a plank sawn from such a trunk, is to keep to the outside, and cut off a few inches from the part that was immediately under the bark – the sapwood, in other words, and the wood closest to it. This is always the youngest and toughest wood, and the most suitable for making bows.'

'But I thought,' said Goethe, 'that the wood for a bow shouldn't be sawn, but had to be split – or riven, as you call it.'

'When it can be riven,' I rejoined, 'then yes. Ash, oak and even walnut can be riven, because the wood is coarse-grained. But not maple. The wood has such a fine and interlocked grain that it doesn't split cleanly along the grain; instead of following the natural direction of growth, along the line of the fibres, it just tears out randomly. So maple has to be cut with the saw, which in this case does not compromise the strength of the bow.'

'Hm,' said Goethe. 'I must say that your interest in bows has given you a lot of specialized knowledge. And it's the kind of real knowledge that is only acquired through practical experience. But that's always the advantage when we pursue an interest with real passion – that it takes us right to the heart of the matter. Trying different things, and failing, is also good, because it's through trial and error that we learn. And we learn not just about the thing itself, but about the wider context. What would I know about plants and colours, if my two theories had just been handed to me on a plate and I had learned them by heart? The fact that I had to find out everything for myself, and sometimes made mistakes, means that I can now say I know something about both these subjects – and rather more than I have put down on paper. But tell me something else about your bow. I have seen Scottish ones which were straight all the way out to the tips, and others whose tips were bent forward. Which are best, do you think?'

I replied: 'I think you get a much stronger springback with a recurve bow. To begin with I made them straight, because I didn't know how to bend the tips. But now that I have learned how to do it, I always put a bend on the tips, and I find that the bow not only looks better, but also delivers more power.'

'You bend the wood by applying heat, don't you?' asked Goethe.

'Moisture and heat combined,' I replied. 'When the bow is finished in so far as the tension is evenly distributed and not greater or less than it should be at any point, I place one end in boiling water, about six to eight inches deep, and boil it for an hour. I then clamp the softened end, while it is still very hot, between two little blocks of wood, whose mating surfaces are shaped to the curvature I wish to give to the bow. I leave it clamped like this for at least a day and a night, so that it dries out completely, and then I do the same thing with the other end. The resulting shape is permanent, as if the ends had grown with a natural curvature.'

'You know what?' said Goethe with a mysterious smile. 'I think I have something for you that you might quite like. What would you say if we went downstairs together and I put a genuine Bashkir bow in your hands?'

'A Bashkir bow?' I exclaimed, full of excitement. 'You mean a genuine one?'

'Yes, you daft thing, a genuine one!' said Goethe. 'Come and see.'

We went down into the garden. Goethe opened up the downstairs room of a small outbuilding, which appeared to be crammed with all kinds of curios and strange objects, placed on tables or up against the walls. I gave these treasures a cursory glance only; my eyes were seeking the bow. 'Here it is,' said Goethe, pulling it out from a heap of strange tools and implements in the corner. 'I see it is still in the same condition as it was when a Bashkir chieftain presented it to me in 1814. Well, what do you say to that?'

I was thrilled to be holding the precious weapon in my hands. It seemed to be quite undamaged, and even the string was still perfectly serviceable. I tried it in my hands and found that it was still reasonably springy. 'It's a good bow,' I said. 'I especially like the shape, which I shall copy for my own bows in future.'

'What wood is it made of, do you think?' asked Goethe.

'As you see,' I replied, 'it is covered with a fine birch bark that leaves little of the wood visible; only the curved ends remain exposed. And these have darkened over time anyway, so it is difficult to tell what it is. At first glance it looks like young oak, or possibly walnut. I think it is walnut, or some similar wood. It's definitely not maple. It's a more coarse-grained wood, and I can see signs that it has been riven.'

'How about trying it out?' said Goethe. 'I've got an arrow here as well. But be careful with the iron tip; it may be poisoned.'

We went out into the garden again and I drew back the bow. 'Now,' said Goethe, 'where do you want to shoot it?' 'Up into the air to start with, I thought,' I replied. 'Off you go, then!' said Goethe. I shot up towards the sunlit clouds in the blue sky. The arrow climbed straight and true, turned over at the top of its travel, came whizzing down again and stuck in the ground. 'Let me have a go,' said Goethe. I was delighted that he wanted to try the bow as well. I handed it to him and fetched the arrow. Goethe placed the notch of the arrow on the string, and he was holding the bow correctly; but it took him a little while to get comfortable with it. Then he aimed up into the sky and drew back the bowstring. He stood there like Apollo, old in body, but irrepressibly youthful in spirit. The arrow did not reach any great height before falling back to earth. I ran and fetched the arrow. 'Another go!' said Goethe. This time he aimed the arrow flat, along the sandy garden path. The arrow went quite well for about thirty paces, then lost height and skittered along the ground. It was such a delight to see Goethe shooting with the bow and arrow like this. I thought of the lines:

> Has old age let me down?
> Am I a child again?[14]

I retrieved the arrow for him. He asked me to take a low shot myself, and suggested I aim for a spot on the window shutter of his study. I shot my arrow, which landed not far off target, but was so deeply embedded in the soft wood that I couldn't pull it out again. 'Leave it there,' said Goethe; 'it will be a reminder to me for the next few days of the fun we've had.'

We walked up and down the garden, enjoying the fine weather. Then we sat on a bench, with our backs against the young foliage of a thick hedge. We talked about the bow of Odysseus, Homer's heroes, the Greek tragedians, and finally about the popular view that Euripides was responsible for the decline of Greek theatre. Goethe did not share this view at all.

'I don't believe,' he said, 'that an art form can go into decline because of any one man. It takes a lot of different factors working together, though it's hard to say what these are. The decline of Greek tragedy was not the fault of Euripides, any more than the decline of sculpture was the fault of some great sculptor who was the contemporary of Phidias, but also his inferior. If the age itself is great, it takes its lead from what is superior, while the inferior remains a dead end.

'And what a great age it was, when Euripides was alive! It was an age of progressive, not regressive, taste. Sculpture had not yet attained its peak of perfection, and painting was still in its infancy.

'If the plays of Euripides had serious faults compared with those of Sophocles, that did not mean that later writers were doomed to imitate these faults and be fatally corrupted by them. But if they had great virtues, so that some were even thought better than the plays of Sophocles, why didn't later writers strive to emulate those virtues, and why didn't they become at least as great as Euripides himself?

'But if the three great Greek tragedians were not followed by an equally great fourth, fifth and sixth, it is not so easy to say why – though we can speculate, and we may not be very wide of the mark.

'Man is a simple creature. And as rich, and complex, and unfathomable as he may be, there are only so many situations he finds himself in.

'If their circumstances had resembled those of us poor Germans, where Lessing wrote two or three passable plays, I myself three or four, and Schiller five or six, then doubtless there would have been room for a fourth, fifth and sixth tragic poet.

'But with the Greeks, and the sheer volume of their output, where each of the three great dramatists wrote nigh on a hundred, or more than a hundred, plays, and the tragic themes of Homer and Greek myth were sometimes covered three or four times – with so much work already in existence, one can well imagine that the stock of available material was gradually exhausted, and that any writer following in the footsteps of those three titans would not really know where to begin.

'And when you think about it, why bother anyway? Surely they already had enough to be going on with? And surely the work produced by Aeschylus, Sophocles and Euripides was of sufficient quality and depth that it could be heard over and over again, without being trivialized or done to death? These few sublime remains that have come down to us are so substantial and important in themselves that we poor Europeans have been studying them for centuries, and will be feeding on them and working on them for centuries to come.'

1826

Monday 5 June 1826

Goethe told me that Preller had called on him to say goodbye before leaving to spend some years in Italy.

'My parting piece of advice to him,' said Goethe, 'was not to let himself be distracted, to pay particular attention to Poussin and Claude Lorrain, and to study the works of these two great painters above all others, in order to understand how they viewed nature and how they used it to express their artistic ideas and sentiments.

'Preller is a significant talent, and I have no fears for his future. He also seems to me a very serious man, and I am almost certain he will take to Poussin rather than Claude Lorrain. But I have recommended the latter to him for his especial study, and for a particular reason. Training an artist is much like training anyone else. Our strengths can more or less be left to develop by themselves, whereas those proclivities and aptitudes that are not in constant use and therefore not so powerful need to be specially nurtured, so that they too become strengths.

'A young singer, as I have often said, may be born with the ability to sing certain notes so well that they are simply perfect. Other notes produced by his voice may sound less strong, pure and full. But these are the very ones he needs to practise regularly, to bring them up to the same standard as the others.

'I am sure that Preller will one day master the art of the solemn, the sublime, and perhaps also the savage. Whether he will also develop a lighter touch, and paint scenes that charm and delight, is another question, and that's why I have particularly recommended Claude Lorrain to him, so that he may acquire through study what does not perhaps come easily to him by nature.

'There was something else I pointed out to him. I have seen many of his studies of nature. They were excellent, and full of energy and animation; but they were all just isolated objects, which won't be much use to him later when he comes to devise his own compositions. So now I have advised him not to single out individual objects from nature to draw by themselves, such as a tree, or a heap of stones, or a cottage, but always to show them in some sort of setting, and with a bit of background.

'My reasons were as follows. In nature we never see anything in isolation, but always in relation to other things – in front of it, beside it, behind it, beneath it and above it. An individual object may strike us as particularly beautiful and picturesque; but it is not the object by itself that produces this impression, but the object in relation to what is beside it, behind it and above it – all of which contributes to that impression.

'On a walk I might come across an oak tree whose picturesque appearance takes me by surprise. But if I were to draw the oak tree by itself, it might not strike me the same way any more, because I have left out the things that contributed to and enhanced the picturesque effect it had in its natural setting. Similarly, a patch of woodland might appear beautiful because it is seen under a particular sky, in a particular light, and with the sun in a particular position. But if my drawing omits all these things, it may well end up looking lifeless and dull, because the magic ingredient is missing.

'And there's something else as well. Nothing in nature is beautiful unless it can be shown to be *true* – that is, created in accordance with the laws of nature. But for something that is true to nature to *appear* true in a picture, you need to show the things that have shaped and influenced it.

'Suppose I come across some rounded stones by a stream, whose surfaces exposed to the air have a picturesque covering of green moss. But it is not just the moisture from the water that has caused the moss to form; its formation at this particular point in the stream is also influenced by the north-facing aspect, perhaps, or by the shade afforded by trees and shrubs. If I fail to show these environmental influences in my picture, it will lack truth and fail to convince.

'Similarly, the location of a tree, the type of soil beneath it, the other trees growing behind and alongside it, have a significant influence on its development. An oak tree standing on the windswept western summit of a rocky hill will take on a totally different shape from another one growing down in the soft soil of a sheltered valley. Both may be beautiful in their own way, but they will be very different in character; and in a landscape imagined by the artist, each type can only be used in the same sort of location it occupies in nature. This is why it is so important for the artist to draw the tree in its natural surroundings, to show the kind of location in which it is found.

'Then again, it would be foolish to try and include in the picture all kinds of mundane incidentals that had no influence on the shape and development of the main motif, or on its present picturesque appearance.

'I passed on the main points from all these little suggestions to Preller, and I am quite sure that it will take root and bear fruit, given the man's natural talent.'

1827

Wednesday 21 February 1827

Dined with Goethe. He talked at length in admiring terms about Alexander von Humboldt, whose book about Cuba and Colombia he has just started to read, and whose views on the project to cut through the Isthmus of Panama seemed to hold a special interest for him. 'Humboldt,' said Goethe, 'is an expert on the subject, and has identified other points where one might do better to make use of existing rivers that flow into the Gulf of Mexico, rather than cutting through at Panama. But all this is for the future, and for some great enterprising spirit. What is certain, however, is that if they succeed in cutting a canal such that ships of every size, laden with every kind of cargo, can pass through from the Gulf of Mexico to the Pacific Ocean, the resulting benefits for the entire human race, civilized and un-civilized, would be incalculable. I'd be surprised, though, if the United States were to let slip a chance to get their hands on such a project. We can expect that in thirty or forty years' time this young nation, which is constantly looking to the West, will have occupied and populated the large tracts of territory that lie beyond the Rocky Mountains. We can also expect that along this whole Pacific coast, where nature has already formed the most commodious and secure harbours, a series of major trad-ing cities will gradually be established to handle a large volume of trade flowing between China and the East Indies and the United States. In which case it would not only be desirable, but virtually essential, for merchant vessels and warships to be able to travel more quickly between the west and east coasts of

1827

North America than has hitherto been possible on the long, dangerous and costly route round Cape Horn. So I repeat: it is imperative for the United States to create a passage from the Gulf of Mexico to the Pacific Ocean; and I am sure they will find a way.

'I'd love to live to see it; but I won't. The second thing I'd love to see is a canal linking the Danube and the Rhine. But this, too, is such a massive undertaking that I doubt if it can be done, especially when you consider the resources available to us Germans. And thirdly and lastly, I'd like to see the British in possession of a canal at Suez. I should love to live long enough to see these three great projects completed, and it would probably be worth the effort of hanging on for another fifty years just to be able to do so.'

Thursday 1 March 1827

Dined with Goethe. He told me he had received a package from Count Sternberg and Zauper, which had given him much pleasure. We then talked at length about the *Farbenlehre*, the subjective prismatic experiments, and the laws governing the formation of rainbows. He was pleased by my continuing and growing interest in these difficult subjects.

Wednesday 21 March 1827

Goethe showed me a little book by Hinrichs on the nature of classical tragedy. 'I've read it with great interest,' he said. 'Hinrichs bases much of his argument on the *Oedipus* and *Antigone* of Sophocles. It is very remarkable, and I'll give it to you to read, so that we can talk about it afterwards. I don't agree with him at all; but it is highly instructive to see how a man so thoroughly schooled in philosophy approaches a poetic work of art from the specific standpoint of his philosophical beliefs. I shall say nothing more today, because I want you to make up your own mind. Just read it; I guarantee you'll find it thought-provoking.'

Wednesday 28 March 1827

I returned the book by Hinrichs to Goethe, having read it with keen interest. I had also gone through all the plays of Sophocles again, to make sure I was completely au fait with the subject matter.

'Well,' said Goethe, 'how did you find him? He really tackles things head-on, doesn't he?'

'It's a strange thing about this book,' I said. 'I found it more thought-provoking than anything I have read, and yet I found myself disagreeing with just about everything he says.'

'That's just it!' said Goethe. 'What we agree with leaves us unmoved; dissent is what makes us productive.'

'His intentions,' I went on, 'struck me as highly laudable, and he certainly looks beyond the surface of things. But he often loses himself to such a degree in subtleties and hidden motivations, and in such a subjective way, that he loses sight of the actual subject, both in detail and in terms of a general overview; so one ends up having to do violence to oneself, and to the subject matter, in order to think as he does. I often had the feeling that my faculties are too crude to grasp the peculiar subtlety of his distinctions.'

'If you had his philosophical training,' said Goethe, 'you would find it easier. But if I'm honest, it saddens me that a man from the German North Sea coast like Hinrichs, who was undoubtedly born with a healthy, wholesome mind, should have been so damaged by Hegelian philosophy that all objective, natural observation and thought have been drummed out of him, and he has gradually picked up an artificial, ponderous way of thinking and expressing himself, so that we come across passages in his book where our understanding grinds to a halt, and we no longer know what we are reading.'

'I got on no better myself,' I said. 'But I was glad to come across other passages that seemed to me very human and accessible, such as his account of the story of Oedipus.'

'In that instance,' said Goethe, 'he was obliged to stick closely to the matter in hand. But there are plenty of places in his book where the thought itself does not develop and progress, and the obscure language simply goes round in circles in the same place, exactly like the witch's times table in my *Faust*.[15] Here, give me the book. He talks about the chorus in his sixth lecture, and I barely understood a single word. What do you make of this, for example, which comes near the end:

'"This reality (i.e. of the life of the people), as the true meaning of the plot, is therefore also its only true reality, which at the same time constitutes, as itself, truth and certainty, and therefore the universally spiritual certainty, the which certainty is at the same time the reconciling certainty of the chorus, so that only in this certainty, which has proved to be the result of the entire movement of the tragic plot, does the chorus first truly conduct itself in accordance with the universal consciousness of the people, and as such no longer merely represents the people, but rather is itself the people in and of itself, according to its certainty."

'Well, I think we've heard quite enough of *that*! But what must the English and French think of the language of our philosophers, when we Germans can't understand it ourselves?'

'All the same,' I said, 'we both agree that the book is driven by a noble aspiration, and that it does have a way of stimulating our thinking.'

'His conception of the relationship between family and state,' said Goethe, 'and the tragic conflicts that may arise from this, is certainly good and useful; but I cannot agree that it is the best, or indeed the only, basis for tragic art. We all live in families and in the state, yes; and any tragic fate that befalls us is likely to affect us as members of both. But we can perfectly well be tragic figures as members only of a family, or only of the state. Because in the end it is all about a conflict that cannot be resolved, and this can arise out of the clash between any two things you like, as long as it is genuinely tragic and genuinely founded in nature. So Ajax falls victim to the demon of injured honour, and Hercules to the demon of jealousy. In neither case is there any conflict whatsoever between family loyalty and civic virtue – which, according to Hinrichs, is supposed to be the essence of Greek tragedy.'

'It is obvious,' I said, 'that he was thinking only of *Antigone* when he put forward this theory. He also seems to have had only this heroine's character and actions in mind when he made the claim that family loyalty appears in its purest form in women, and at its absolute purest in a sister; and that a sister can love only a *brother* in a completely chaste and sexless way.'

'I would have thought,' countered Goethe, 'that the love between two sisters is even more chaste and sexless! We can't pretend we don't know about the countless instances where a strong sexual attraction has developed between sister and brother, whether knowingly or not.

'More generally,' Goethe went on, 'you'll have noticed that Hinrichs approaches Greek tragedy from the starting point of the *idea*, and that he sees Sophocles as a man who likewise devised and constructed his plays on the basis of an idea, which then determined his characters, their family provenance and social status. But Sophocles did not start from an idea when he wrote his plays; instead, he took up some long-established popular myth or legend, which already contained a good idea, and simply sought to adapt it for the theatre in the best and most effective way possible. The Atreides don't want Ajax to be buried; but as in *Antigone* the sister fights for the brother, so in *Ajax* the brother fights for the brother.[16] The fact that the sister looks after the unburied Polyneices, and the brother looks after the fallen Ajax, is coincidental, and not something invented by the poet; it is part of the traditional narrative that the poet inherited, and which he had to follow.'

'What he has to say about Creon's behaviour,' I said, 'seems equally unconvincing. He tries to argue that by prohibiting the burial of Polyneices, Creon is acting purely out of civic virtue; and since Creon is not just a man, but also a prince, the author puts forward the proposition that, since the tragic power of the state is represented by a man, this can be none other than the one who is the *personification of the state itself*, namely the *prince*; and that of all persons the man *as prince* is the person who practises the most moral civic virtue.'

'These are arguments,' replied Goethe with a little smile, 'that are unlikely to persuade anyone. Creon doesn't act out of civic virtue at all; he is motivated by hatred of the dead man.

When Polyneices tried to take back his patrimony from which he had been forcibly expelled, this did not amount to such a monstrous crime against the state that his death alone was not sufficient, and that the innocent corpse needed to be punished as well.

'In fact, it is wrong to describe any form of action as a civic virtue if it offends against virtue as such. When Creon forbids the burial of Polyneices, and not only taints the air with the decaying corpse but is also responsible for dogs and birds of prey dragging around pieces torn from the dead body and even defiling the altars with them, such behaviour, offensive to men and gods alike, is not by any reckoning a civic *virtue*, but a crime against the state. Apart from that, everyone in the play is against him. He has the elders of the state, who make up the chorus, against him; he has the people in general against him; he has Teiresias against him; he has his own family against him. But he doesn't listen. He obstinately persists in his sacrilegious behaviour, until he has destroyed his entire family and ends up a broken man, a shadow of himself.'

'And yet,' I said, 'when you hear him speak, you can't help thinking that he's right in some ways.'

'That's the very thing,' replied Goethe, 'in which Sophocles excels, and which is at the heart of all drama. All his characters are so eloquent, and know how to explain the reasons for their actions so persuasively, that the audience is nearly always on the side of the last speaker.

'You can tell that he received a very good education in rhetoric in his youth, which trained him to look for all the reasons, real or professed, behind people's actions. However, his great skill in this area could also lead him astray, and sometimes he went too far.

'In *Antigone*, for example, there is a passage that always jars with me, and I would give a great deal for some eminent scholar to come along and prove that it is not original, but a later interpolation by somebody else.

'The heroine, you see, has acted throughout the play from the finest of motives, and shown herself to be noble-minded and pure in heart; but as she is going to her death at the end, she suddenly comes out with a motive so implausible that it verges on the comical.

'If she had been a *mother*, she says, she would not have done for her dead *children*, or her dead *husband*, what she has done for her *brother*. If my husband had died, she explains, I would have married someone else; and if my children had died, I would have had more children by my new husband. But it is different with my brother. I cannot have another brother, because my mother and father are dead, and so there is nobody left to beget one.

'This is the gist of the passage anyway, and, put into the mouth of a heroine going to her death, it seems to me to clash with the tragic tone, and to be altogether too contrived and too much like an exercise in logical argument. As I say, I would very much like a good literary scholar to prove that the passage is not authentic.'

We then talked more about Sophocles, and agreed that he was less interested in pursuing a moral line in his plays than in doing full justice to the subject he happened to be dealing with, especially in terms of its theatrical impact.

'I have nothing against a dramatic poet wanting to exert a moral influence,' said Goethe. 'But when it's a matter of presenting his chosen theme clearly and effectively to an audience, his high moral purpose is not going to help him very much. What he needs are great powers of exposition and description and a sound knowledge of the stage, so that he knows what to put in and what to leave out. If the story has a moral message, this will come across anyway, even if the writer is only interested in telling his story in an effective and artistic way. If a poet has the lofty soul of a Sophocles, he will always be a moral influence, no matter what he does. And of course Sophocles really knew his stuff when it came to writing for the stage.'

'How well he knew the theatre,' I replied, 'and how he had an eye for a theatrical effect, can be seen from his *Philoctetes*, and the great similarity in structure and plot between this play and *Oedipus at Colonus*. In both plays we see the hero in a helpless state, old and physically frail. Oedipus has his daughter at his side to guide and support him; Philoctetes leans on his bow. The similarity extends beyond that. Both have been cast out in their affliction; but after the oracle has said of both that victory can only be attained with their help, efforts are made to get them back again. Odysseus comes to Philoctetes, Creon to Oedipus. Both begin their speeches with cunning and honeyed words; but when these don't work they resort to violence, and we see Philoctetes robbed of his bow and Oedipus of his daughter.'

'Such brutal acts,' said Goethe, 'gave rise to some terrific dialogue, and the helplessness of the characters excited the emotions of the spectators and listeners, which is why the dramatist liked to contrive such situations – because he wanted to produce an effect on his audience. To amplify this effect in the case of Oedipus, Sophocles has him appear as a feeble old man, when in fact, based on all that we know, he must have been a man still in the prime of life. But the dramatist could not have used him in this play at such a vigorous age; the audience would have been unmoved, and so he made him into a weak and helpless old man.'

'The similarity with Philoctetes,' I went on, 'goes further. The hero in both plays is not an active agent, but a passive victim. Yet each of these passive heroes is up against two active agents: Oedipus has to contend with Creon and Polyneices, Philoctetes with Neoptolemus and Odysseus. It was necessary to have *two* such antagonists in order to articulate multiple points of view, and also to give the play itself the requisite depth and body.'

'You could also argue,' added Goethe, 'that both plays are similar in another respect, in that we see in both the highly effective situation of a joyous reversal of fortune, where one hero is reunited in his despair with his beloved daughter, and the other with his equally beloved bow.

'The two plays also end on a similarly conciliatory note, as both heroes are delivered from their sufferings. Oedipus finds a blissful release from this life, while Philoctetes, as foretold by the oracle, will be healed before Troy by Asclepius.

'Of course,' Goethe went on, 'if we want to learn about stagecraft for our modern purposes, then Molière is the man for that. Do you know his *Malade imaginaire*? There's a scene in there that always strikes me, every time I read the play, as a textbook example of how to write for the theatre. I'm talking about the scene where the imaginary invalid asks his little daughter Louison if her elder sister has not had a young man in her room.

'Another dramatist who had not mastered his craft like Molière would have got Louison to tell the tale straight off, and that would have been that. But Molière enlivens the scene to great effect by introducing all kinds of delaying tactics into the inquisition. He starts by making Louison pretend that she doesn't understand her father; then she denies all knowledge of the matter; then, threatened with the rod, she collapses as if in a faint; then, as her father vents his despair, she jumps up again from her feigned swoon with impish glee and finally, little by little, confesses all.

'That summary gives you only a feeble idea of the drama in that scene. But go and read it for yourself, see how well it works as a piece of theatre; and I think you'll agree that it has more to teach us than all the treatises on drama ever written.

'I have known and loved Molière all my life,' Goethe went on, 'and have never stopped learning from him. I make a point of rereading some of his plays every year, to remind myself what great writing means. It's not just the perfect artistic technique that so delights me in him; it's also this writer's likeable personality and highly cultivated sensibility. There is such a grace about him, a feeling for what is appropriate, a tone of social refinement, which his innately beautiful nature could only attain to through daily association with the most distinguished persons of his time. I know only a few fragments of Menander; but he, too, has risen so high in my estimation on the strength of these that I regard this great Greek as the only man who could have been compared to Molière.'

'I'm delighted,' I replied, 'to hear you speak so highly of Molière. Herr von Schlegel tells a rather different story.[17] I was reading his *Lectures on Dramatic Poetry* the other day and found his remarks on Molière very hard to stomach. He is very patronizing about him, as you know, and views him as a vulgar buffoon, who only gazed upon polite society from a distance,

1827

511

and whose job it was to devise all manner of farces for the amusement of his master. These low, riotous farces were his natural milieu, according to Schlegel, who claims that the best of them were stolen from other writers anyway, and that when he moved on to comedies of a more sophisticated kind he really struggled, and never made a success of it.'

'A writer of Molière's stature,' said Goethe, 'is a real thorn in the side of a man like Schlegel. He realizes that he can't hold a candle to him, and so he cannot abide him. He loathes *Le Misanthrope*, which I reread constantly, and which is one of my favourite plays in the world; he has a few grudging words of praise for *Tartuffe*, but then proceeds to tear it apart. Schlegel can't forgive Molière for ridiculing the affectations of bluestockings; he probably feels, as one of my friends remarked, that he himself would have been the target of Molière's ridicule if they had been contemporaries.

'There is no denying,' Goethe went on, 'that Schlegel knows a very great deal, and the extent of his knowledge and reading is almost frightening. But that only gets you so far. All the learning in the world does not amount to judgement. His theatre criticism is totally one-sided, being concerned in most cases only with the structure of the plot and composition, and only pointing up minor similarities with great predecessors, without being in the least bit interested in what the author has to show us of life's rich tapestry and the culture of a refined mind. But what use are all the technical skills in the world if a play does not engage us through the author's charming or noble personality – the only thing that crosses over into popular culture?

'The way Schlegel writes about French drama exemplifies everything about a bad critic, who is completely incapable of recognizing and admiring excellence and who dismisses proficiency and strength of character as though these things were mere chaff and stubble.'

'On the other hand,' I countered, 'he does treat Shakespeare and Calderón fairly, and he clearly likes them, too.'

'Both of them,' replied Goethe, 'are certainly of such a calibre that one can never say enough good things about them, although it wouldn't surprise me if Schlegel had brazenly disparaged them, too. He is also fair in his treatment of Aeschylus and Sophocles; but this seems to be driven not so much by a lively personal sense of their extraordinary merit as by the consensus view of literary scholars, who rate both writers very highly. The fact of the matter is that Schlegel is not man enough himself to understand and appreciate such lofty figures. If he were, he would have to be fair to Euripides as well, and he would have approached him in a very different way. As it is, he knows that scholars do not esteem this poet very highly, and so he takes no small pleasure in the licence that their example gives him to attack this great ancient in an utterly shameful manner and teach him the error of his ways.

'I don't deny that Euripides has his faults; but he was still a worthy competitor for Sophocles and Aeschylus. If he lacked the high seriousness and artistic refinement of his two predecessors, and as a dramatist took a slightly more tolerant and humane view of things, he probably knew his Athenians well enough to know that the tone he struck was the right one for contemporary audiences. But a poet whom Socrates called his friend, whom Aristotle rated highly and Menander admired, and for whom Sophocles and the city of Athens put on mourning when they heard of his death, must surely have been quite something. And if a man of the modern age like Schlegel wants to pick holes in such a great ancient, he should get down on his knees to do it.'

Sunday 1 April 1827

Spent the evening with Goethe. I talked to him about yesterday's performance of his *Iphigenie*, in which Herr Krüger from the Theatre Royal in Berlin played the part of Orestes – to great applause.

'The piece,' said Goethe, 'has its difficulties. There is a lot going on inside the characters, but not a lot of external action. So it's all about revealing this inner life on the stage. The play is full of the most effective devices, which grow out of the catalogue of horrors on which it is based. The words on the page give only a faint notion of what was going on inside me as I was writing it. The job of the actor is to transport us back to

1827   513

this fervour which first inspired the poet in the presence of his
material. We want to see mighty Greeks and heroes, who feel
the fresh sea breeze on their faces, who are beset by all manner
of evils and perils, and speak out boldly as their hearts direct
them. What we don't want are actors of limited emotional
range, who have just learned their parts quickly by rote – or
even worse, actors who don't even know their lines.

'I must confess that I have yet to see a perfect performance of
my *Iphigenie*. That's also the reason why I didn't go last night.
It pains me terribly when I have to fret over these spectres who
do not manifest themselves in the manner intended.'

'I think you would have been pleased with the Orestes that
Herr Krüger gave us,' I said. 'It was a performance of such
clarity and precision that it made his character completely
intelligible and accessible. It was all there, and I shall never forget his words and gestures.

'The fevered, visionary aspect of the character found such
vivid outward expression in his physical gestures and in the
modulations of his voice that you felt you could actually see it
there before you. If Schiller had seen *this* Orestes, he would
surely not have complained about the missing Furies; they were
there all around him, hunting him down.

'The important scene where Orestes awakes from his unconscious state and thinks himself transported to the underworld
was a brilliant *coup de théâtre*. We saw his ancestors parading
through and talking together, then we saw Orestes fall in with
them, question them, and join their ranks. We felt as if we ourselves had been transported into the midst of these departed
souls, so pure and profound was the artist's sensibility, so great
his ability to conjure up the most unfathomable mysteries.'

'My word, you *are* an impressionable audience!' said Goethe
with a laugh. 'But do go on and tell me more. I gather he was
really good, then, and a very physical actor?'

'His voice,' I said, 'was clear and mellifluous, well trained,
and therefore capable of extraordinary flexibility and range.
And he had the physical strength and agility to cope with every
acting challenge. It looked as though he had spent a lifetime
training and exercising his body in every kind of way.'

'Every actor,' said Goethe, 'should also take lessons from a sculptor and painter. Before he can play the part of a Greek hero, he needs to study the human images that have come down to us from antiquity, taking careful note of the natural grace with which they sit, stand and walk.

'But it's not enough just to train the body. He also needs to school his mind through intensive study of the best ancient and modern authors. This will not only help him to understand his part better, but also give his whole being, and his whole bearing, a touch of class. But tell me more. What else was good about him?'

'It seemed to me,' I said, 'that he had a great love of his subject. He had mastered every detail by diligent study, so that he inhabited the character of his hero with complete freedom, and there was nothing about that character that he had not made his own. This meant that he was able to give the right expression and emphasis to every word, and to speak his lines so confidently that he had no need of the prompter.'

'I'm glad to hear it,' said Goethe, 'and that's as it should be. There's nothing worse than when actors don't know their parts and have to listen for the prompt at every new sentence; it ruins their performance, which becomes limp and lifeless. In a play like my *Iphigenie* the actors need to know their parts inside out – otherwise it's better not to put it on at all. For the play to succeed, the performances need to be assured, brisk and lively.

'Still, I'm delighted that it all went so well with Krüger. He was recommended to me by Zelter, and I would have been vexed if he had not turned out as well as he has. I think this calls for a little gesture on my part, and I shall send him a handsomely bound copy of *Iphigenie* as a memento, with a little inscription commending his performance.'

The conversation turned to the *Antigone* of Sophocles, to the high moral tone that prevails throughout, and thence to the question of where our moral sense comes from.

'From God Himself,' replied Goethe, 'like every good thing. It is not a product of human reflection, but a beautiful natural endowment, inherent and innate. It is more or less inherent in all men, but some outstandingly gifted minds possess it to an exceptionally high degree. Through great deeds or teachings these persons manifested their divine nature, which was so beautiful to behold that it won men's love and excited them to devotion and emulation.

'People learned to value the morally beautiful and the good through experience and wisdom. The bad was revealed for what it was by its consequences, destroying the happiness of the individual and of the collective; what was right and noble, on the other hand, was seen to conduce both to the particular and to the general happiness. And so moral beauty became a doctrine to live by, which spread throughout the nations as a thing expressly stated.'

'I read somewhere recently,' I said, 'the view that Greek tragedy was all about showing the beauty of morality.'

'Not so much morality,' said Goethe, 'as pure humanity in all its forms, but especially in situations where it came into conflict with raw power and harsh laws, with the potential for tragic consequences. Morality was never very far away, of course, being a principal component of human nature.

'Sophocles did not invent the moral element in *Antigone*, by the way. It was already there in the subject matter. But what particularly drew him to the story may well have been its peculiar combination of moral beauty and great dramatic potential.'

Goethe then talked about the characters of Creon and Ismene, and about the vital importance of these two figures for the development of the heroine's beautiful soul.

'The quality of nobility,' he said, 'is essentially placid and seemingly in a state of slumber, until it is roused and challenged by some kind of antagonist. Creon is such an antagonist; he is there partly as a foil to Antigone, so that she can display her noble nature and argue her righteous cause, and partly as a character in his own right, so that his calamitous mistake will appear hateful to us.

'But Sophocles also wanted to show us the lofty soul of his heroine *before* the deed, and for that he needed a different antagonist to bring out and develop her character: her sister Ismene. Furthermore, in this figure the dramatist has given us a handy yardstick of the commonplace, measured against which the exceeding superiority of Antigone is all the more strikingly apparent.'

The conversation then turned to dramatists in general, and the powerful influence that they can and do exert on the masses. 'A great dramatic poet,' said Goethe, 'who is also productive and imbued with a strong, noble spirit which informs all his works, may be so successful that the soul of his plays becomes the soul of the people. Now that, it seems to me, is something worth working for. Corneille's plays were a school for heroes – which was just the thing for Napoleon, who needed a nation of heroes. Hence his remark that if Corneille had still been alive, he would have made him a prince. A dramatist who is sure of his calling should therefore work ceaselessly to refine his talent, so that his influence on the people is a noble and beneficent one.

'My advice is not to study contemporary writers, but rather the great figures of antiquity, whose works have retained their value and their reputation over the centuries. A truly gifted man will feel the need to do this for himself anyway, and it is precisely this need to spend time in the company of great predecessors that is the hallmark of a superior talent. Let us study Molière, Shakespeare, and above all the ancient Greeks – always the Greeks.'

'I dare say,' I observed, 'that the study of ancient literature is invaluable for highly talented natures; but in general it seems to have little effect on personal character. If it did, then all literary scholars and theologians would be the best of men. But this is not at all the case, and students of ancient Greek and Latin literature may be very able men or pitiful creatures, depending on the good or bad qualities that God has given them, or that they have inherited from their parents.'

'That is true enough,' said Goethe, 'but it doesn't mean that the study of ancient literature has no effect on the formation of character. A nobody will always be a nobody, and a small-minded person will not expand his horizons one jot by spending time with the great minds of antiquity, even if he reads them every day. But a noble spirit, in whose soul God has implanted the capacity for future greatness of character and intellectual

1827   517

distinction, will thrive wonderfully through a knowledge of, and intimate association with, the sublime minds of Greek and Roman antiquity, and will grow visibly in stature each day to become like them.'

Wednesday 18 April 1827

Went for a drive with Goethe before dinner, a little way along the road to Erfurt. We met all kinds of wagons carrying goods for the Leipzig Fair. And a few teams of horses, some of them very fine animals.

'The critics make me laugh,' said Goethe, 'when they turn themselves inside out trying to define the ineffable thing we call "beauty" in a few abstract words. Beauty is a primary phenomenon, which is never seen in itself but is reflected in a myriad different expressions of the creative spirit, and is as diverse and varied as nature herself.'

'I have often heard it said,' I ventured, 'that nature is always beautiful; but she is the despair of artists, because they are seldom capable of capturing her completely.'

'I agree,' replied Goethe, 'that nature can often be impossibly enchanting; but I certainly don't believe that she is beautiful in all her manifestations. Her intentions are always good, but not so the conditions that are required for them to be fully realized all the time.

'The oak, for example, can be a very beautiful tree. But how many favourable circumstances must conspire before nature succeeds in producing a truly beautiful specimen! If the oak is growing in the depths of a wood, surrounded by other substantial trees, its natural tendency will always be to grow straight upwards, seeking the open air and light. It will only put out a few thin side shoots, and over the course of a century these few will wither and drop off. When the topmost branches finally emerge into the open air above, the oak will relax and start to spread sideways and form a crown. But at this stage the tree is already past middle age; its long years of pushing steadily upwards have consumed its best energies, and its efforts now to put on significant lateral growth will not be very successful.

The fully grown tree will be tall, strong and slender-stemmed, but the trunk and crown will not be in the right proportion to be considered beautiful.

'Then again, if the oak is growing in damp, boggy ground and the soil is too rich, it will, given enough room, prematurely put out many branches and twigs in all directions. But the opposing and retarding influences will be lacking; the oak's natural character – gnarled, stubborn, jagged – will not develop, and, seen from a little distance, the tree will look plain and undistinguished, more like a lime, and it will not be beautiful – not as an oak tree, at any rate.

'And if, finally, it is growing on mountainous slopes, in thin, stony soil, it will grow exceedingly gnarled and jagged, but it will not be able to develop freely; its growth will be prematurely stunted, and it will never get to the point where we say of it: "There's something about that tree that has the power to astonish us."'

I thought this said it all very well. 'I saw some very beautiful oaks a few years back,' I said, 'when I was making occasional short excursions from Göttingen into the Weser valley. The biggest ones I saw were in the Solling hills around Höxter.'

'Oaks seem to do best in sandy soils, or soils mixed with sand,' Goethe went on, 'where they can put out strong roots in all directions. They also like to grow out in the open, where they are exposed on all sides to the light and sun, the rain and wind. If they grow in a very sheltered spot, where they are shielded from the wind and weather, they won't amount to anything; but a century of battling against the elements makes them strong and sturdy, so that fully grown specimens have a presence that fills us with astonishment and admiration.'

'Could one not draw from your remarks the general conclusion,' I said, 'that a living organism is beautiful when it has attained the peak of its natural development?'

'Indeed,' replied Goethe, 'but first you have to define what you mean by "the peak of natural development".'

'I take it to mean,' I said, 'that phase of growth where the distinguishing characteristics of this or that organism appear fully formed.'

1827

'In that sense,' said Goethe, 'there's nothing wrong with your definition, especially if one adds the proviso that one of these fully formed characteristics is that the build of an organism's various members should be commensurate with its natural purpose.

'So a girl of marriageable age, for example, whose natural purpose is to bear and suckle children, would not be beautiful without a suitably broad pelvis and suitably full breasts. Too much, on the other hand, would also not be beautiful, because it would go beyond what is actually required.

'Why was it that we described some of the saddle horses we met earlier as "beautiful", if not because they are built for their intended purpose? It was not just the elegance, grace and effortlessness of their movements, but something else besides, which only a good horseman or a good judge of horseflesh could put into words, and which remains just a general impression for the rest of us.'

'Could one not also,' I enquired, 'call a carthorse beautiful, like those powerful beasts we saw earlier, pulling the wagons of the Brabant carters?'

'Certainly,' replied Goethe, 'and why not? A painter would probably find more of beauty in the rugged character and expressive power of bone, sinew and muscle in such an animal than in the softer and smoother character of a dainty saddle horse.

'The main thing always,' Goethe went on, 'is that the race is kept pure, and that man has not applied his mutilating hand. A horse whose mane and tail have been shorn, a dog with cropped ears, a tree whose heaviest branches have been lopped and the rest trimmed into a neat ball, and, worst of all, a young woman whose youthful figure has been spoiled and deformed by stays: all these are things that good taste rejects, and which only belong in the philistine's lexicon of beauty.'

By the time we had talked of these and similar matters we were back at the house again. We took a few turns round the garden before dinner. The weather was very fine; the spring sun was now getting quite intense, causing shrubs and hedges of every kind to burst into leaf and blossom. Goethe was filled with thoughts and hopes of an enjoyable summer.

At dinner we were a very jolly company. Young Goethe had read his father's *Helena*, and spoke about it with much perception and good sense. He was very enthusiastic about the section written in the classical style, but we could tell that the operatic, romantic half had left him rather cold.

'You are basically right,' said Goethe, 'and it is a curious thing. One cannot say that the rational is always beautiful, but the beautiful is always rational, or at least it should be. You like the classical section because it is comprehensible, because you can see the overall structure and can follow my thinking with your own powers of reason. A great deal of understanding and reason has gone into the second half, too, but it is difficult, and requires some study before one can follow what is going on and think one's way into the author's mind again.'

Goethe then spoke in admiring terms about the poems of Madame Tastu, which he has been reading in recent days.

When the others left and I was making ready to leave myself, he asked me to stay a while longer. He asked for a portfolio to be brought in, containing engravings and etchings by Dutch masters.

'I want to treat you to something special by way of dessert,' he said. With these words he placed an engraving in front of me, a landscape by Rubens. 'You have seen this picture here before,' he said. 'But something really fine can't be studied often enough, and in this case there is something very special about it, too. Would you care to tell me what you see?'

'Well,' I said, 'starting from the back and moving forward, we have a very bright sky in the background, as when the sun has just set. Then, also a long way off, we see a village and a town bathed in the bright evening light. In the middle ground of the picture we see a path, on which a flock of sheep is hurrying towards the village. On the right of the picture are a series of haystacks, and a wagon that's just been loaded with hay. A few unharnessed horses are grazing nearby. Further back, scattered off to the side among thickets, are several mares grazing with their foals, who look like they will be spending the night outdoors. Then, closer to the foreground, there is a group of tall trees, and finally, right in the foreground on the left, various labourers making their way home.'

'Good,' said Goethe, 'that's probably everything. But you're missing the main point. All these things that we see represented here – the flock of sheep, the hay wagon, the horses, the farm labourers making their way home: from which side are they lit?'

'The light falls on the side facing us,' I said, 'so their shadows are cast back into the picture. The farm labourers on their way home in the foreground are particularly highlighted, and the effect is quite dramatic.'

'And how has Rubens produced this striking effect?'

'By placing these brightly lit figures against a dark background,' I answered.

'But this dark background,' said Goethe, 'where does that come from?'

'It's the dense shadow cast over the figures by the group of trees,' I said. 'But just a minute,' I went on, suddenly brought up short. 'The figures are casting their shadow back into the picture, but the group of trees casts its shadow forward, towards the observer. So the light is coming from two opposite directions at once – which is completely contrary to nature!'

'That's just the point,' replied Goethe with a little smile. 'That is the genius of Rubens: he is a free spirit who stands *above* nature and makes her subservient to his higher purposes. The double light source certainly breaks all the rules, and you can say it is contrary to nature if you like. But if it *is* contrary to nature, my answer to that is that it is higher than nature: it is the bold stroke of the master, whereby he brilliantly demonstrates that art is not necessarily subject to the laws of nature, but obeys laws of its own.

'The artist,' Goethe went on, 'must be faithful and true to nature in matters of detail; he cannot arbitrarily alter an animal's bone structure, or the position of its sinews and muscles, so that its distinctive character is violated. That would be to destroy nature altogether. But at a more advanced level of the artistic process, where an image is fashioned into a finished picture, he has a freer hand, and may even resort to *fictions*, as Rubens has done in this landscape, with the double light source.

'The artist has a twofold relationship with nature: he is at once her master and her slave. He is her slave in so far as he must work with the things of this earth in order to be understood; but he is her master in so far as he makes these earthly things subservient to his own higher purposes.

'The artist seeks to speak to the world through a complete whole. But he does not find such a whole in nature; it is the fruit of his own mind, or of divine inspiration, if you will.

'If we merely glance at this Rubens landscape in passing, it all appears so natural, as if it had just been copied from nature. But this is not the case. Nowhere in nature has so beautiful a picture ever been seen, any more than a landscape by Poussin or Claude Lorrain, which also looks very natural to us, but which we will never find anywhere in the real world.'

'I wonder,' I said, 'if there are any examples in *literature* of bold artistic licence like this double light source of Rubens?'

'We don't need to look very far to find them,' replied Goethe, after some reflection. 'I could show you dozens in Shakespeare. Take *Macbeth*, for example. When Lady Macbeth is inciting her husband to do the deed, she says: "I have given suck", etc. Whether this is true or not is neither here nor there; but the Lady says it, and she has to say it in order to lend emphasis to her speech. Later on in the play, however, when Macduff hears that his family has been slaughtered, he cries out in savage fury: "He has no children!" etc. These words of Macduff's contradict what Lady Macbeth said earlier, but that doesn't bother Shakespeare. He is only interested in making each speech as powerful as possible, and just as the Lady has to say: "I have given suck" to lend weight to her words, so Macduff, for the same reason, has to say: "He has no children!"

'As a general point,' Goethe went on, 'we should not be overly pedantic about the painter's every brushstroke, or the poet's every word. Where a work of art is the product of a bold and unfettered mind, we should try if possible to view it and enjoy it in the same spirit ourselves.

'It would be stupid, for example, to draw from Macbeth's words "Bring forth men-children only", etc. the conclusion that Lady Macbeth is a young thing who has not yet given birth. And it would be just as stupid to go a step further and insist that the Lady must be portrayed on the stage as a very young woman.

'Shakespeare doesn't put these words into Macbeth's mouth in order to demonstrate his wife's youthfulness. These words, like those of Lady Macbeth and Macduff I quoted just now, are there for rhetorical purposes only, and they prove nothing, apart from the fact that the poet always makes his characters say what is appropriate, effective, and right for *that particular moment*, without worrying too much, or bothering to check, whether these words might appear to contradict something said elsewhere.

'In fact, when Shakespeare wrote his plays it's unlikely that he thought of them appearing in print, to be picked over and analysed word by word. Instead he wrote for the stage, and saw his plays as moving, living things, which, in stage performance, would quickly pass before the eyes and ears of the audience – not something that could be pinned down and picked apart in detail; and all that mattered was to make an impact in the passing moment.'

Tuesday 24 April 1827

August Wilhelm von Schlegel is here. Goethe took a drive with him before dinner, around the Webicht, and this evening gave a big tea party in his honour, which was also attended by Schlegel's travelling companion, Dr Lassen. All the leading lights of Weimar society had been invited, and Goethe's rooms were packed with people. Herr von Schlegel was surrounded by ladies, to whom he was showing some narrow scrolls with images of Indian gods, as well as the complete texts of two great Indian poems, which probably meant nothing to anybody apart from himself and Dr Lassen. Schlegel was dressed extremely neatly, and looked exceedingly youthful and blooming, prompting some of those present to suggest that he was no stranger to the use of cosmetics.

Goethe drew me over to the window. 'Well, what do you make of him?' 'Still the same as ever,' I replied. 'In many ways, certainly, he is not a proper man,' Goethe went on, 'but I think we can make allowances for him, given his great learning and accomplishments.'

Wednesday 25 April 1827

Dined with Goethe and Dr Lassen. Schlegel was dining at court again today. Herr Lassen talked very knowledgeably about Indian poetry, and Goethe appeared to listen with great interest, welcoming the chance to fill in the large gaps in his own knowledge of these things.

I called on Goethe again for a few moments in the evening. He told me that Schlegel had been with him as the daylight was fading, and that they had had a very interesting conversation about literary and historical matters, which he had found most instructive. 'As long as you don't expect to get grapes from thornbushes or figs from thistles,' he added. 'Otherwise it's all absolutely fine.'

Thursday 3 May 1827

The excellent translation of Goethe's dramatic works by Stapfer was given an equally good review by Monsieur J. J. Ampère in last year's Parisian *Globe*, and Goethe was so impressed that he made frequent reference to it and said how much he appreciated it.

'M. Ampère,' he said, 'judges from a very high standpoint. German critics, in a similar situation, tend to start from philosophy, and when reviewing literary works they go about it in such a manner that what they offer by way of enlightenment is only intelligible to philosophers of their own school, while for other people it is far more obscure than the actual work they are trying to explain. But M. Ampère takes a very practical and down-to-earth approach. As someone who really understands his craft, he explores the relationship between the work and the writer, and judges the different poetic creations as different products from different periods in the writer's life.

'He has made a detailed study of the changing course of my

1827

earthly career and my emotional states, and has even been able to see things that I have not talked about, and which could only be read between the lines, as it were. He rightly observes that I produced next to nothing during my first ten years of service at court here in Weimar; that despair drove me to Italy; and that while I was there, feeling a new surge of creativity, I took up the story of Tasso, so that by writing about such a personally charged subject I might free myself from the painful and troubling impressions and recollections of my life in Weimar. So when he calls *Tasso* a heightened *Werther*, he makes a very shrewd point.[18]

'He has some equally perceptive things to say about *Faust*, pointing out that the scorn and bitter irony of Mephistopheles are just as much a part of myself as the gloomy, discontented striving of the main character.'

Goethe often spoke of M. Ampère in these and similarly admiring terms. We developed a keen interest in the man, and tried to imagine what he was like as a person; and even though this was obviously not possible, we agreed that he must be a man in his middle years, to have such a thorough understanding of the interaction between life and writing.

So we were very surprised when M. Ampère arrived in Weimar a few days ago and turned out to be a sprightly youth in his early twenties; and we were equally surprised when he revealed to us, during our subsequent time together, that all the contributors to *Le Globe*, which we had frequently admired for its wisdom, moderation and cultural sophistication, were young people like him.

'I can understand,' I said, 'how it is possible to *produce* something of significance at a young age, and be like Mérimée, who wrote excellent plays at the age of twenty. But the idea that someone of such tender years could have the breadth of vision and depth of insight required for the maturity of *judgement* shown by the writers at the *Globe* – that is something entirely new to me.'

'It has not been so easy for you, of course, up there on your heath,' replied Goethe, 'and those of us here in central Germany have also had to work hard for our little bit of wisdom.

The truth is that we all lead such isolated and impoverished lives. We get very little culture from the common people as such, and all our talented artists and intellectuals are scattered across the whole of Germany. One is in Vienna, another in Berlin, another in Königsberg, and another in Bonn or Düsseldorf – all of them living fifty or a hundred miles apart, so that personal contacts and personal exchanges of ideas are rare events. But I realize what I am missing when men like Alexander von Humboldt come through here and help me on further, in a single day, in my search for knowledge than I would have got in years of solitary plodding.

'Now imagine a city like Paris, where the leading minds of a great realm are all gathered together in one place, learning from each other and spurring each other on through daily contact, conflict and rivalry; where the very best of art and nature from all over the world can be seen every day. Imagine this great metropolis, where you can't cross a bridge or a square without being reminded of a great past, and where history has been made on every street corner. And then imagine, not the Paris of a benighted, brutish age, but the Paris of the nineteenth century, where for three generations men such as Molière, Voltaire, Diderot and their ilk contributed to a flowering of intellectual life, the like of which has not been seen again in any other city on earth: then you will understand how it is possible for a clever man like Ampère, growing up surrounded by such riches, to amount to something at the age of twenty-four.

'You said just now,' Goethe went on, 'that you could well understand how a man of twenty could write plays as good as those of Mérimée. I would not argue with that, and on the whole I agree with you that good original work comes more easily to a young man than sound critical judgement. However, in Germany it is probably better for someone of Mérimée's age not to try and produce something as mature as the plays in his *Théâtre de Clara Gazul*. It's true that Schiller was very young when he wrote *Die Räuber*, *Kabale und Liebe* and *Fiesko*. But if we are honest, all these plays are more expressions of an extraordinary talent than testimony to the author's cultural sophistication. The fault lies not with Schiller, however, but with the state of his nation's culture, and the great difficulty we all have in making our way on our own.

'Take Béranger, on the other hand: he is the son of poor parents, the descendant of a poor tailor; he was a poor printer's apprentice, then employed as some kind of clerk on a meagre salary; he never went to a traditional school or university. And yet his songs are so full of sophisticated culture, so full of grace, so full of wit and subtle irony, and they display such artistic refinement and mastery of language, that he is the admiration not just of France, but of all civilized Europe.

'But imagine this selfsame Béranger, instead of being born in Paris and brought up in this great cosmopolitan city, as the son of a poor tailor in Jena or Weimar. Imagine him living a life of obscurity in these provincial little towns. Then ask yourself this: what fruit would this same tree have borne, if it had been grown in such soil, and in such a climate?

'So, my friend, I say again: in order to thrive and flourish, a man of talent needs to be nurtured by a public life of intellectual and cultural distinction.

'We admire the tragedies of the ancient Greeks; but properly speaking we should be admiring the age and the nation that made them possible, rather than the individual men who wrote them. Because by and large, even though those plays differ a little from each other, and even though one dramatist seems a little less great and accomplished than another, they all share a kind of common identity, whose defining characteristics are the sublime, the sound and the wholesome, perfected humanity, great worldly wisdom, nobility of mind, pure, robust intuition – and whatever other qualities one could list. Now if all these qualities are to be found not just in the dramas that have come down to us, but also in the lyrical and epic works; if, furthermore, we find the same qualities in the philosophers, rhetoricians and historians, and to an equal degree in the works of visual art that have come down to us; then we probably have to conclude that such qualities were not simply confined to certain individuals, but were common to the nation and to that whole period of history.

'Take Burns, for example. What made him great was the fact

that the old songs of his forefathers lived on in the mouths of the people, that they were sung to him in the cradle, so to speak; that he grew up with them as a boy, and became so deeply imbued with the excellence of these poetic models that they were for him a living foundation on which he could build. And again, what made him great was the fact that his own songs instantly found receptive ears among his compatriots; that he heard them sung in the fields by reapers and binders, and was regaled with them in the tavern by riotous drinking companions. So it's not surprising that he made a name for himself.

'We Germans are in a parlous state by comparison. We had old songs just as good when I was young, but when did you hear them being sung by the people? It was left to Herder and his successors to start collecting them and rescuing them from oblivion; then at least we had printed copies in our libraries. And later on, Bürger and Voss wrote masses of songs! Who is to say that they are any less good, or less rooted in the people, than those of the excellent Burns? But how much of that became a living legacy, heard from the mouths of the people? They were written down and printed, and now they are languishing in libraries – the usual fate of German poets. And what has happened to my own songs? One or two may be sung from time to time by a pretty girl sitting at the piano, but you don't hear anything from the common people. And to think there was a time when Italian boatmen would sing passages from *Tasso* to me!

'We Germans are stuck in the past. Yes, we have worked hard for a century now to cultivate ourselves; but it will take a few more centuries yet before the intellectual and cultural life of our compatriots has advanced to the point where they worship beauty like the Greeks, take a beautiful song to their hearts, and where people can say of them: "The days when they were barbarians are long gone."'

Friday 4 May 1827

A grand dinner at Goethe's in honour of Ampère and his friend Stapfer. The conversation was loud, jolly and wide-ranging.

Ampère told Goethe stories about Mérimée, Alfred de Vigny and other important writers. There was also much talk of Béranger, whose incomparable songs are daily in Goethe's thoughts. Someone asked whether Béranger's merry songs about love were better than his political ones; whereupon Goethe opined that, in general, a purely poetic subject is superior to a political one, in the same way that a pure, eternal truth of nature is superior to a partisan view.

'Of course,' Goethe went on, 'in his political poems Béranger showed himself to be the benefactor of his nation. After the invasion of the Allies the French found in him the best outlet for their feelings of despondency. He put new heart into them by his frequent reminders of the glory of French arms under the Emperor, whose memory lives on in every shack and cottage, and whose great qualities the poet loves, without wishing to see a continuation of his despotic rule. He doesn't seem very comfortable now, under the Bourbons. They are a degenerate lot, certainly! And today's Frenchman looks for great qualities on the throne, even though he likes to be involved in the business of government himself and likes to have his say.'

After dinner the company spilled out into the garden, and Goethe beckoned me to accompany him on a drive around the wood on the road to Tiefurt.

In the carriage he was in a very genial and affable mood. He was pleased that he and Ampère had hit it off, and thought this augured well for the reception and dissemination of German literature in France.

'Ampère,' he added, 'is so refined in his culture that he has left the national prejudices, dislikes and parochialism of many of his countrymen far behind. In his own thinking he is much more a citizen of the world than a citizen of Paris. But I see a time coming when there will be thousands in France who think like him.'

Sunday 6 May 1827

Another dinner party at Goethe's, attended by the same people who came the day before yesterday. There was much talk of

Helena and *Tasso*. Goethe then told us about the plan he had conceived in 1797 to write an epic poem in hexameters, recounting the legend of William Tell.

'I was revisiting the four small cantons around Lake Lucerne that year,' he said, 'and the beauty and grandeur of the magnificent natural setting made such an impression on me again that I felt inspired to capture the richness and variety of that incomparable landscape in a poem. But in order to inject more charm, interest and life into my portrayal, I thought it would be a good idea to populate this highly dramatic landscape with equally striking human figures – and the legend of Tell seemed to me just what I needed.

'I pictured Tell as a heroic type, immensely strong, at ease with himself, with a childlike innocence about him. He travels the cantons, working as a bearer, known and liked by all, always helpful, quietly going about his business, providing for his wife and children, and treating all men just the same, regardless of rank.

'Gessler, on the other hand, I pictured as a tyrant, but a tyrant of the easy-going kind, who sometimes does good, because it amuses him, and sometimes does evil, because it amuses him; other than that, the people and their welfare or suffering are matters of supreme indifference to him, as if they didn't exist.

'But the higher and better aspects of human nature – love of one's native soil, the feeling of freedom and security under the protection of the laws of the land, the feeling, too, of humiliation at being subjugated, and sometimes ill-treated, by some foreign brute, and finally the strength of will, hardening to a firm resolve, to cast off this hated yoke – all these higher, benign human qualities I had attributed to those renowned men of noble character, Walther Fürst, Stauffacher, Winkelried and others. These were my true heroes, my men of action, conscious of a higher purpose, whereas Tell and Gessler, while occasionally seen in action, were basically passive figures.

'I was completely absorbed in this beautiful subject matter, and already murmuring my hexameters to myself. I saw the lake in the peaceful moonlight, which picked out the low-lying mists in the mountain defiles. I saw it bathed in the bright light of a lovely sunny morning, when the woods and meadows were alive with joyous sounds. Then I pictured a storm, a thunderstorm, rolling out over the lake from the mountain gorges. Not to mention scenes set at dead of night, with shadowy figures crossing bridges and landing stages to attend secret meetings.

'I told Schiller about all this, and in his mind my landscapes and my characters took on the shape of a drama. Since I had other things to do, and kept on deferring the execution of my plan, I let Schiller have the subject himself in the end; and the rest is history, of course.'

We listened with delight and fascination as Goethe told the tale. I remarked that the magnificent description of the sunrise in the first scene of the second part of *Faust*, written in tercets, sounded to me as though it might have been based on his memories of the landscape around Lake Lucerne.

'I won't deny,' said Goethe, 'that they were the inspiration for those lines. And without the fresh impressions of that marvellous setting, I could not even have imagined what I wrote in those tercets. But that's all I coined from the gold of my exploration of Tell country. Everything else I left to Schiller, who made the most marvellous use of it, as we all know.'

The conversation turned to *Tasso*, and the *idea* Goethe had been trying to bring out in the play.

'*Idea*?' said Goethe. 'How on earth should I know? I had the *life* of Tasso and I had my own life, and by combining two such curious figures, with all their oddities, I found an image of Tasso emerging in my mind, whom I then contrasted with the prosaic figure of Antonio, for whom I also had no shortage of role models. Otherwise, court life, human relationships and love affairs were much the same in Weimar as they were in Ferrara, so I can truly say of my portrayal that it is *bone of my bones, and flesh of my flesh*.

'The Germans are a strange lot, though! Searching for deep thoughts and ideas in everything, and reading them into everything, they make their own lives harder than they need be. Just have the courage for once to *trust your impressions*; allow yourself to be delighted, moved, uplifted, enlightened, and even inspired and emboldened to some great enterprise; but don't imagine that anything which is not an abstract thought or idea is therefore worthless!

'People keep on asking me what idea I was trying to embody in my *Faust*. As if I knew the answer myself and could put it into words! *From heaven, through the world, to hell* – that might do, at a pinch; but that's not an idea, that's a plot summary. Then again, the fact that the devil loses the wager, and that a man who has gone badly astray and is continually striving to do better can be *redeemed* – that is a good and powerful thought, which explains a great deal; but it is not an *idea* that runs through the whole thing and lies at the heart of every single scene. It would have been a fine thing indeed if I had tried to thread the rich abundance and variety of life that I portrayed in *Faust* on to the thin string of a single idea running through the entire work!

'In general,' Goethe went on, 'it was not my style as a poet to try and represent something *abstract*. I received *impressions* in my mind – sensuous, vivid, delightful, colourful impressions of a hundred different kinds, just as a lively imagination presented them to me; and as a poet, all I had to do was to give artistic shape to these visions and impressions that I had inside me, and then to put them down on paper in such a way, by the power of my portrayal, that others would receive the same impressions when hearing or reading what I had written.

'If I did ever want to portray some idea as a poet, then I did so in *short* poems, which had a natural unity and were easier to grasp as a whole – like, for example, "Die Metamorphose der Tiere", "Die Metamorphose der Pflanzen", the poem "Vermächtnis", and many others. The only *longer* work where I consciously set out to construct the whole thing around a specific idea was my *Wahlverwandtschaften*. That has made the novel easier to understand, but I wouldn't claim that it has made it any *better*. In fact, I tend to think that *the more unfathomable and difficult to understand a poetic work is, the better it is for it.*'

Tuesday 15 May 1827

Herr von Holtei arrived here from Paris some days ago, and his winning personality and talents have made him a welcome guest everywhere. He has also become very friendly with Goethe and his family.

Goethe has been living in his garden house for the past few days, where he has been very happy working away quietly by himself. I visited him there today with Herr von Holtei and Count Schulenburg; the former had come to say goodbye, as he was leaving for Berlin with Ampère.

Wednesday 25 July 1827

Goethe recently received a letter from Walter Scott which has given him great pleasure. He showed it to me today, and since he had great difficulty reading the English handwriting he asked me to translate the contents. It appears that Goethe wrote to the celebrated English author first, and that this letter is a reply to that.

> I feel very honoured [writes Walter Scott] that any of my productions have been fortunate enough to attract the attention of Goethe, among whose admirers I have numbered myself since 1798, when, notwithstanding my limited knowledge of the German language, I was bold enough to translate *Götz von Berlichingen* into English. In embarking on this youthful undertaking, I had entirely forgotten that it is not enough to feel the beauty of a work of genius; one must also be thoroughly acquainted with the language in which it is written, before attempting to communicate its beauty to others. I still set some value on that youthful attempt, however, because it does at least show that I knew how to select a subject worthy of admiration.
>
> I have heard much about you from my son-in-law Lockhart, a young man of some literary standing, who had the honour, some years ago, before his connection with my family, to be introduced to the father of German literature. It is

impossible that you should remember every single one of the large number of persons who feel compelled to pay you their respects; but I believe you have no more devoted admirer than this young member of my family.

My friend Sir John Hope of Pinkie had the honour of seeing you recently, and I was hoping to write to you – indeed, I took the liberty of doing so – through two of his relatives, who were planning to tour Germany. But they were prevented by illness from proceeding with their plans, so that my letter was returned to me two or three months later. So I did presume to seek Goethe's acquaintance some time ago – and *before* the flattering notice which he has been kind enough to take of me.

It gives all admirers of genius much gratification to know that one of the greatest European models is enjoying a happy and honourable retirement at an age when he is so universally honoured and respected. Fate destined no such happy lot for poor Lord Byron, who was taken from us in the flower of his years, when so much had been hoped and expected of him. He esteemed himself fortunate in the honour which you did him, and was conscious of the debt he owed to a poet to whom all the authors of this present generation are so indebted that they feel bound to look up to him with filial reverence.

I have taken the liberty of asking Messrs Treuttel and Würtz to send you my attempt at a biography of that remarkable man who had for so many years such a terrible influence on the world that he bestrode. I am not sure, however, that I do not owe him some obligations, since I spent twelve years under arms because of him, during which time I served in a corps of our yeomanry, and notwithstanding an early lameness, became a good horseman, hunter and shooter. These good qualities have somewhat deserted me of late, when rheumatism, that sorry torment of our northern climate, has affected my limbs. But I do not complain, as I now see my sons pursuing the sport I have been obliged to give up.

My eldest son has a troop of hussars, which is quite an honour for a young man of twenty-five. My youngest son has just been made Bachelor of Arts at Oxford, and is now planning to spend some months at home before venturing out into the world. As it has pleased God to take their mother from me, my youngest daughter manages my household. My eldest is married, and has a family of her own.

Such are the domestic circumstances of the man whom you were kind enough to enquire after. For the rest, I have sufficient to live on in the way I like, notwithstanding some very heavy losses. I live in a stately old chateau, where any friend of Goethe's will be a welcome guest at any time. The entrance hall is filled with armour that would have done justice to Jaxthausen, and a huge bloodhound guards the entrance.

I have, however, forgotten one who saw to it that he was not forgotten in his lifetime. I hope you will forgive the faults of the work, in consideration of the author's wish to treat the memory of that extraordinary man as fairly as his own insular prejudices would permit.

As this opportunity of writing to you has suddenly presented itself through a chance traveller, and must be instantly embraced, I have no time to say anything more, other than to wish you continuing good health and tranquillity, and to subscribe myself with the most sincere and profound respect,

Edinburgh, 9 July 1827 Walter Scott

This letter, as I said, afforded Goethe great pleasure. He did think, however, that it was so flattering to him that much of it should be put down to the habitual courtesy of a man of rank and cosmopolitan refinement.

He then referred to the open and warm way in which Walter Scott talked about his family circumstances, which gratified him immensely as a mark of the close trust between them.

'I can't wait now,' he said, 'to see his *Life of Napoleon* that he mentions there. I have heard so many conflicting and passionately held views about the book that I am quite sure it will be a very important publication, in any event.'

536 CONVERSATIONS WITH GOETHE

I enquired about Lockhart, and whether Goethe still remembered him.

'I remember him very well,' replied Goethe. 'His personality makes a strong impression, so you don't forget him again in a hurry. From what English travellers and my daughter-in-law tell me, he is a young man of whom great things are expected in literature.

'I am rather surprised, by the way, that Walter Scott doesn't mention Carlyle, who is such a keen student of German culture that he must know of him. The great thing about Carlyle is that he judges our German writers by what is most important, namely the intellectual and moral core of their work. Carlyle is a moral force of great significance. He has great potential, and who can say what he will achieve or what influence he will have?'

Wednesday 26 September 1827

Goethe had invited me to take a drive with him this morning to the Hottelstedter Ecke, the most westerly eminence on the Ettersberg, going on from there to the Ettersburg hunting lodge. It was a beautiful day, and we drove out in good time through the Jakobstor gate. Beyond Lützendorf, where the road climbs steeply and we had to slow to a walking pace, we had plenty of opportunity to take in our surroundings. In the hedgerow on the right, beyond the royal demesne, Goethe noticed a cluster of birds, and asked me if they were larks. 'Bless you,' I thought to myself, 'for someone who knows a lot more about the natural world than most people, you seem to be a complete beginner when it comes to ornithology!'

'Those are buntings and sparrows,' I replied, 'and perhaps a few late warblers, which have emerged from the covert of the Ettersberg after moulting, come down to the gardens and fields, and are now getting ready to migrate; but they are not larks. Larks don't normally settle on bushes. The field lark or skylark flies straight up in the air, and then drops back down to the ground again; in the autumn they fly around in flocks, and then go to ground in some stubble field, but they don't perch on hedges or bushes. The woodlark, on the other hand, likes to sit at the very top of tall trees; it flies up into the air from here, singing its song, and then drops back down to its treetop perch. There is also another species of lark, which you find in remote areas on the southern edge of forest clearings, and which has a very soft, flute-like, but rather melancholy song. You don't see them on the Ettersberg, which is too busy for them, and too close to human habitation; but they don't settle on bushes, either.'

'Hm,' said Goethe, 'it sounds as if you are not a complete beginner in these things.'

'I've had a passion for the subject since I was a boy,' I replied, 'and have always kept my eyes and ears open for birds. There are very few places in the whole of the wood on the Ettersberg that I have not explored many times. Now, when I hear a single note of birdsong, I can say with confidence which bird it comes from. And if somebody brings me a bird that has lost its feathers because it was mistreated in captivity, I will undertake to restore it to health and full plumage very quickly.'

'That certainly shows,' said Goethe, 'that you have a lot of experience in these matters. I would advise you to persist with your study of birds; you are obviously cut out for it, so it is bound to lead to something very worthwhile. But tell me more about this moulting business. You said something about late warblers coming down to the fields from the covert of the Ettersberg after moulting. Does that mean that moulting happens at a certain time, and do all birds moult at the same time?'

'With most birds,' I replied, 'moulting takes place as soon as the breeding season is over; in other words, as soon as the young from the last brood are far enough on to fend for themselves. The question is, whether the bird has sufficient time to moult between the last brood and its migration. If it has, it moults here, and migrates with new plumage. If not, it migrates with its old plumage and moults later, in the warm south. Birds don't all arrive here at the same time in the spring, nor do they migrate at the same time in the autumn. This is because some species are less affected by colder temperatures and rough weather and can tolerate them better than others. But a bird that arrives here early migrates late, while a bird that arrives late migrates early.

'Even among the warblers, which all belong to the same species, you see big differences. The lesser whitethroat can be heard here by late March; two weeks later the blackcap arrives; then, a week or so after that, the nightingale; and not until the very end of April or the beginning of May do we see the grey warbler. All these birds moult here in August, including the young from the first brood, which is why one can catch young blackcaps at the end of August that already have black heads. The young from the last brood, however, migrate with their first plumage, and moult later in southern climes; hence the fact that one can catch young blackcaps in early September, young male birds, that still have red heads like their mother.'

'So is the grey warbler the last bird to arrive here,' asked Goethe, 'or are there others that arrive even later?'

'The so-called icterine warbler and the magnificent golden oriole,' I replied, 'do not arrive until shortly before Whitsun. Both migrate towards the middle of August, at the end of the breeding season, and moult with their young in the south. If they are kept in cages they moult here in the winter, which is why these birds are very difficult to rear. They need a lot of warmth. But if we hang the cage too close to the stove, they waste away through lack of fresh air; if we place them too close to the window, on the other hand, they waste away in the cold of the long nights.'

'They do say,' said Goethe, 'that moulting is a disease, or at least makes the bird physically weak.'

'I wouldn't say that,' I replied. 'It is a state of heightened productivity, which creates no problems at all for the bird when it takes place in the open air; and in the case of reasonably robust specimens it works perfectly well indoors as well. I have kept warblers that continued to sing while they were moulting – a sure sign that they felt fine. But if a bird that is kept indoors appears unwell while it is moulting, this indicates that it has not been properly fed or given enough fresh air and water. If an indoor bird, deprived of air and liberty, has become so weak over time that it doesn't have the energy to moult, it's just a

1827   539

matter of taking it out into the healthy fresh air, where the
moult will then go ahead without difficulty. With a bird in the
wild, however, the process is so gentle and gradual that the bird
hardly notices.'

'Yet you seemed to suggest earlier,' said Goethe, 'that warblers retreat into the covert of the woods while moulting.'

'They do need some protection during this time,' I replied.
'It's true that nature, as ever, proceeds with such wisdom and
moderation that a bird never loses so many feathers all at once
during moulting that it becomes unable to fly far enough to
find its food. But it can happen that it loses the fourth, fifth and
sixth flight feathers from its left wing, and the fourth, fifth and
sixth flight feathers from its right wing, all at the same time; it
can still fly quite well, but not well enough to escape pursuing
birds of prey, particularly the very fast and agile hobby. So a
thick covert comes in very handy then.'

'That makes sense,' replied Goethe. 'But do both wings moult
at the same rate, and symmetrically, so to speak?'

'As far as I have been able to observe, yes,' I replied. 'And that
is a very good thing. If, for example, a bird were to lose three
flight feathers from its left wing without at the same time losing
the corresponding feathers from its right wing, its wings would
be completely unbalanced, and the bird would no longer have
proper control of its flight movements. It would be like a ship
whose sails are too heavy on one side and too light on the
other.'

'It only goes to show,' said Goethe, 'that wherever you choose
to delve into nature, you always discover some new wisdom.'

We had been climbing steadily while we talked, and had just
about reached the summit, on the edge of a spruce wood. We
passed a place where they had been breaking stones, which
were piled up in a heap. Goethe told the coachman to stop and
asked me to get out and take a look, to see if I could find any
fossils. I picked up a few seashells and some broken ammon-
ites, which I handed to him as I climbed back in. We drove on.

'The same old story!' said Goethe. 'The old seabed keeps
coming back to haunt us! When you look down on Weimar
from this height, and on all the villages round about, it seems

unbelievable to think there was a time when whales were swimming about in the broad valley down there. And yet it is true – or highly likely, at least. But the seagull flying over the sea that covered these heights back then certainly never imagined that you and I would be taking a drive here today. And who knows whether, thousands of years from now, the seagull will not be flying over these heights again?'

We were now at the top, and travelled on at speed. On our right were oaks, beeches and other deciduous trees. Weimar lay behind us, lost to sight by now. We had reached the westernmost height, and the broad valley of the Unstrut lay beneath us in the glorious morning sun, dotted with villages and small towns.

'This is a good place,' said Goethe, telling the coachman to stop. 'I think a little breakfast would go down very well here in the fresh air.'

We alighted from the carriage and walked up and down for a few minutes on dry ground, at the foot of some semi-mature oak trees that had been battered and stunted by many storms. Meanwhile Friedrich unpacked the breakfast we had brought with us and laid it out on a grassy knoll. The view from this spot, in the clear morning light of the autumn sun, was truly magnificent. To the south and south-west you could see the whole sweep of the Thüringer Wald mountain range; to the west, beyond Erfurt, the summit of the Inselsberg and the great Friedenstein Palace complex above Gotha; further to the north, the mountains behind Langensalza and Mühlhausen, until the view was bounded to the north by the blue Harz Mountains. I called to mind the lines:

> Far, wide, glorious the vista,
> Of life all round about!
> From mountain top to mountain top
> The eternal spirit soars,
> Eternal life foreshadowing.[19]

We sat down with our backs to the oak trees, so that we could enjoy the panoramic view over half of Thuringia while we breakfasted. We ate a couple of roasted partridges with freshly

1827

541

baked white bread, washed down with a bottle of very good wine, which we drank from a bowl of fine, flexible gold that Goethe always takes with him on these outings, packed in a yellow leather case.

'I've sat here many times before,' he said, 'and in recent years have often thought it would be the last time that I surveyed the kingdoms of the earth and their splendours from this spot. But I seem to keep going somehow, and I hope that today will not be the last time you and I have a good day out here, either. We should come here more often in future. You close in on yourself if you're stuck in the house all the time. But here you feel larger, freer, like the great natural world you see before you – which is how it should always be, really.

'I can see so many places from up here,' Goethe went on, 'that are associated with wonderful memories of a long life. What times I had in my youth over there in the hills of Ilmenau! And what adventures I had down there in my beloved Erfurt! When I was very young I spent a lot of happy times in Gotha, too; but for many years now I've hardly been there at all.'

'I don't remember you ever going there,' I remarked, 'since I've been in Weimar.'

'Well, there's a reason for that,' replied Goethe with a laugh. 'I'm somewhat *persona non grata* there – and I'll tell you the story. When the mother of the previous ruler was still a pretty young woman, I spent a lot of time there. I was sitting alone with her at the tea table one evening when the two princes, fine young lads of about ten and twelve with blond hair, came bounding in and rushed up to the table. Rather cheekily, as was sometimes my way, I ran my hands through the hair of the two boys and said: "Now then, what are you pair of Goldilocks up to?" The two lads looked at me aghast, quite taken aback by my temerity, and in later years they never quite forgot the incident.

'It's not something I'd boast about, exactly, but that's how I was, and I just couldn't help it: I never had much respect for princely rank as such, not unless the man behind the title was a thoroughly decent human being. The fact is, I was so comfortable in my own skin, and felt so distinguished in myself, that if they had made me a prince I would not have found it particularly strange. When they gave me my patent of nobility, many people thought it would make me feel different, elevated to a higher status. But between ourselves, it meant nothing to me, nothing at all! We Frankfurt patricians always considered ourselves the equals of the nobility, and to my mind, when they gave me the patent, they were only giving me what I had possessed for a long time already.'

We took another good draught from the golden bowl and drove around the northern side of the Ettersberg, to the Ettersburg hunting lodge. Goethe had all the rooms opened up; their walls were covered with cheerful wallpapers and pictures. In the west corner room on the first floor he told me that Schiller had lived there for a while. 'We spent many a happy day here back in the beginning,' he went on, 'and frittered away many a happy day, too. We were all young and full of high spirits; in the summer we went in for all kinds of impromptu theatricals, and in the winter it was all dancing and sleigh rides by torchlight.'

We went outside again, and Goethe led me along a footpath into the wood, heading in a westerly direction.

'I must show you the beech tree,' he said, 'where we carved our names fifty years ago. But how different it all looks, and how everything has grown up tall! That must be the tree over there. As you see, it's still in its prime! And you can just make out our names still, although the letters are now so distorted and grown together that they are hard to decipher. Back then this tree was standing on its own, in an open, dry spot. It was lovely and sunny all around it, and this is where we acted out our impromptu farces on fine summer days. Now it is damp and uninviting here. What were then only low shrubs have now grown into shady trees, so that it is hard to find the splendid beech of our youth among all these other trees.'

We returned to the lodge, and after looking over the sizeable collection of arms we drove back to Weimar.

Thursday 27 September 1827

Called in briefly on Goethe this afternoon, where I met Privy Councillor Streckfuss from Berlin, who had gone for a drive

1827 543

with him this morning and then stayed to dinner. When Streck-fuss left I accompanied him, and then went for a walk through the park. As I was returning across the market square I met the Chancellor and Raupach, and we called in at the Elephant. I returned to Goethe's in the evening, and we discussed a new issue of *Kunst und Altertum*, along with twelve pencil sketches by the Riepenhausen brothers, in which they had endeavoured to reconstruct the frescoes painted by Polygnotus in the *Lesche*, or meeting house, at Delphi, based on the account given by Pausanias. Goethe was full of praise for their efforts.

Monday 1 October 1827

Houwald's *Das Bild* performed at the theatre. I watched two acts, and then went to see Goethe, who read me the second scene of his new *Faust*.

'I have tried to show in the Emperor,' he said, 'a ruler who has all the necessary qualifications for losing his country, which in the end he manages to do.

'He is not interested in the welfare of his realm and his subjects; he thinks only about himself, and how he can amuse himself each day with something new. The country is without law or justice; the judiciary itself is partly to blame, and sides with the criminals, while the most appalling crimes go unchecked and unpunished. The army is unpaid, and discipline has broken down; the soldiers roam at large, looting and stealing to get their pay wherever they can. The exchequer is empty, with no prospect of future receipts. The state of the Emperor's own household is no better; food and drink are running out. The marshal of the household is getting more and more desperate by the day, and is already in the hands of Jewish moneylenders, to whom everything has been pawned, so that the bread on the Emperor's table is eaten before it is paid for.

'The privy council wishes to make representations to His Majesty about all these evils and discuss possible remedies; but the gracious sovereign is disinclined to lend his noble ear to such disagreeable matters; he would much rather amuse himself. Here Mephistopheles is in his element, having swiftly got

544 CONVERSATIONS WITH GOETHE

rid of the previous court fool and taken his place at the Emperor's side as his new fool and adviser.'

Goethe then gave a wonderful reading of the scene, including the interspersed murmurings of the crowd, and I had a very good evening.

Sunday 7 October 1827

The weather was beautiful this morning, and before eight o'clock I was sitting in the carriage with Goethe, on the road to Jena, where he planned to stay until tomorrow evening.

Arriving there in good time, we went first to the Botanical Gardens, where Goethe inspected all the shrubs and plants and found everything thriving and in excellent order. We also looked round the Mineralogical Collection and a few other scientific collections before driving on to Herr Knebel's house, where we were expected for dinner.

Knebel, now very advanced in years, rushed forward at the door to embrace Goethe, almost stumbling in his haste. The mood at table was very friendly and jolly, but we talked about nothing of any great significance. The two old friends were content just to enjoy each other's company.

After dinner we took a drive, heading south, following the Saale upstream. I knew this charming region from earlier times, but it all looked so fresh to me, as if I had never seen it before.

When we were back in the streets of Jena, Goethe told the coachman to turn up beside a stream and to stop at a certain house, which looked nothing special from the outside.

'This is where Voss lived,' he said, 'so this is hallowed classical ground, which I wanted you to see.' We went through the house and stepped out into the garden. There was not much in the way of flowers or ornamental planting; it was just grass, with an abundance of fruit trees. 'This was for Ernestine,' said Goethe. 'Even when she was living here, she could never forget the wonderful apples she had had in Eutin; she used to tell me there was nothing else like them. They were the apples from her childhood – that's why. I spent many a happy day here with Voss and his delightful Ernestine, and I remember those times with great fondness. We shall not see the like of Voss again any time soon. Few men have had as much influence on German high culture as he did. Everything about him was wholesome and down-to-earth, which is why his relationship to the Greeks was not something artificial but a totally natural thing, which has yielded the most magnificent fruits for the rest of us. Anyone who really appreciates what he achieved, as I do, is hard put to think of a way to pay his memory sufficient honour.'

By now it was getting close to six o'clock, and Goethe thought it was time to retire to our rooms for the night, which he had booked at the Bear Inn.

They gave us a large room, with an alcove containing two beds. The sun had set not long before, and the windows of our room were still bathed in the evening afterglow. We were content to sit there for a while without a light.

Goethe brought the conversation back to Voss. 'He was very dear to me,' he said, 'and I should love to have kept him here, for the Academy and for myself. But the offer he received from Heidelberg was too good for us to match, given our limited resources. It pained me to let him go, but I had no choice.

'It was lucky for me, then,' Goethe went on, 'that I had Schiller. As different as our characters were, we were both working towards the same end; it made our relationship so intimate that neither one of us, basically, could live without the other.'

Goethe then told me a few anecdotes about his friend, which seemed to me to capture the man very well.

'As one can easily imagine from his noble character, Schiller hated all the hollow tributes and the empty lionizing that people went in for – or tried to. When Kotzebue proposed staging a public celebration in his honour, he found the whole idea so abhorrent that it nearly made him sick with disgust. He also loathed it when visiting strangers were announced at his house. If he was too busy to see the man there and then, and put him off until four in the afternoon, say, you could be fairly sure that at the appointed hour he would feel sick with apprehension. And in such situations he could sometimes be very impatient, or even downright rude. I once witnessed his angry outburst when a foreign surgeon called in unannounced to pay him a visit; the poor man, completely wrong-footed, could not get out of there fast enough.

'We were, as I said, and as we all know,' Goethe went on, 'very different kinds of personalities, even though we were interested in the same things – and different not only in intellectual matters, but also in our physical make-up. An air that Schiller found salutary affected me like poison. I called on him one day, and, finding he was not at home, I was told by his wife that he would be coming back soon. So I sat down at his desk to make a few notes. I had not been sitting there for long before I began to feel strangely nauseous; the feeling got gradually worse, until in the end I was close to fainting. At first I didn't know what could possibly be the cause of this wretched, and for me very unusual, state, until I finally became aware of an awful smell coming from a drawer next to me. When I opened it, I found to my astonishment that it was full of rotten apples. I went straight to the window, breathed in the fresh air, and instantly felt restored. In the meantime his wife had come in, and she told me that the drawer had to be kept filled with rotten apples because the smell did Schiller good, and he could not live or work without it.

'Tomorrow morning,' Goethe went on, 'I will show you where Schiller lived here in Jena.'

By now they had brought in lights; we ate a little supper, and then sat talking and reminiscing for a while.

I told Goethe about a strange dream from my boyhood, which literally came true the following morning.

'I had raised three young linnets,' I said, 'and was terribly fond of them, and loved them more than anything else. They flew around quite freely in my room and would fly towards me and land on my hand when I entered the room. One day, as I entered the room at lunchtime, I had a bit of bad luck, and one of the birds flew over me and out through the door. I had no idea where it had gone. I spent the whole afternoon looking for it on all the roofs, and was inconsolable when evening came and I had found no trace of it. I went to sleep, my mind full of sorrow and regret, and towards dawn I had the following dream. I saw myself going around the neighbouring houses, looking for my lost bird. All at once I heard him singing, and saw him perched on the roof of a neighbour's house at the end of our garden. I saw myself calling to it, and it came down closer, flapping its wings towards me as if wanting to be fed; but it was not quite bold enough to fly down on to my hand. Then I saw myself running through our little garden into my room and fetching the cup of soaked rapeseed; I saw myself offering it its favourite food, and it came down and perched on my hand, and I took it back, full of joy, to join the other two in my room.

'At this point I woke up. As it was already broad daylight, I threw on my clothes and rushed out through the garden towards the house where I had seen the bird. Imagine my amazement when the bird was really there! And now it all happened exactly as I had seen it in my dream. I called to it, it came closer, but hesitated to come and perch on my hand. I ran back and fetched the food, it flew on to my hand, and I took it back inside to the others.'

'This event from your boyhood,' said Goethe, 'is certainly very curious. But things of this kind do happen in nature, even if we don't yet have the right key to them. We walk with mysteries all the time. We are enveloped by an aura, but have no idea what is going on inside it, or how it is connected to our own minds. But this much is sure: there are certain states in which the antennae of our souls are able to sense things beyond the confines of our body, so that we are given a presentiment, or even an actual insight into the immediate future.'

'I experienced something like that only recently,' I replied, 'when I was coming back from a walk along the Erfurt road. I was about ten minutes away from Weimar when I had a mental impression of running into someone at the corner of the theatre whom I had not seen or thought about for ages. It unsettled me to think that I might meet this person, and so I was not a little astonished when, just as I was about to turn the corner, there he was, coming towards me at the exact same spot where I had pictured it happening ten minutes previously.'

'That is also very remarkable, and more than coincidence,' said Goethe. 'As I said, we wander blindly in mysteries and wonders. One mind can also influence another by its mere presence, with nothing said. I could give you several examples. It has often happened to me that I've been walking with someone I know well, and thinking vivid thoughts about something, when that person has promptly started talking about the very thing that was on my mind. I knew a man once who could suddenly silence lively conversation at a party without saying a word, just by the power of his mind. He could even turn the mood sour, so that everyone felt uncomfortable.

'We all have some sort of electrical and magnetic forces inside us, and, just like a magnet, we exert a force of attraction or repulsion, depending on whether we come into contact with like or unlike. It is possible, indeed probable, that if a girl were to find herself in a dark room with a man she didn't know was there, who was planning to murder her, she would have an eerie premonition of his unseen presence, and would be overcome by a terror that would drive her from the room and back to her housemates.'

'I know a scene from an opera,' I rejoined, 'where a pair of lovers who have been living far apart for a long time find themselves together in a dark room without knowing it. But they haven't been together for very long before the magnetic force starts to work: each senses the proximity of the other, they are drawn towards each other involuntarily, and in no time at all the young girl is in the arms of her lover.'

'Between lovers,' said Goethe, 'this magnetic force is especially strong, and is even effective over long distances. In my younger years I experienced plenty of instances where I was walking alone and was suddenly overcome with a strong desire to see the girl I was in love with; I kept on thinking about her until she was actually there, coming to meet me. "I felt restless, stuck at home," she would say, "and I couldn't help myself, I just had to come."

'I recall one instance from the early years of my time here, when I had very quickly fallen in love again. I had been away on a journey and had come back a few days earlier, but court duties which kept me occupied until late into the night had so far prevented me from visiting my beloved. Our attachment

had already attracted attention, and so I was reluctant to visit
her during the day, so as not to encourage more gossip. But by
the fourth or fifth day I could not wait any longer, and I was on
my way to her and standing outside her house before I knew it.
I tiptoed up the stairs and was about to enter her room when I
heard voices – plural – and realized she was not alone. I crept
back down again without being seen and was soon out in the
dark streets again, which were still unlit in those days. In an
angry and frustrated mood I wandered back and forth through
the town for an hour or so, passing repeatedly by her house,
full of longing to see my beloved. In the end I was on the point
of going home to my lonely room, when I walked past her
house one more time and noticed that the lights were out. "She
must have gone out," I said to myself, "but where can she have
gone, in the dark, at night? And how am I to find her?" I
retraced my steps through several streets, met many people,
and often fancied I saw her, only to find, when I got closer, that
it was someone else of similar build and height. Even back then
I believed firmly in a kind of mutual magnetism, and was convinced I could draw her to me just by the force of my desire.
I also believed I was surrounded by invisible higher beings,
whom I implored to guide her steps to me, or mine to her. But
then I said to myself: "What a fool you are! You were not prepared to try one more time and go to her house, yet here you
are, demanding signs and portents!"

'By now I had gone down the Esplanade, as far as the little
house where Schiller lived in later years, when I suddenly felt
compelled to turn round, go back towards the palace, and then
turn right into a little side street. I had gone barely a hundred
yards in this direction, when I saw coming towards me a female
figure who looked exactly like my beloved girl. The street was
only dimly lit by the faint light coming from the odd window,
and as I had been fooled several times already this evening by a
seeming resemblance, I didn't have the courage to speak to her
on the off chance. We passed very close to each other, so that
our arms brushed together; I stopped and looked round, and
she did the same. "Is it you?" she said, and I recognized her
dear voice. "At last!" I said, and was so happy that I cried. Our

hands clasped each other. "So," I said, "my hopes have not deceived me. I have been looking for you, longing to see you; my instinct told me that I would surely find you, and now I am happy, and thank God it has come true." "But why didn't you come, you wicked man?" she said. "I found out by chance today that you've been back for three days, and I cried all afternoon because I thought you had forgotten me. And then, an hour ago, I suddenly felt a great desire to see you, and I couldn't settle – I can't explain. A couple of girlfriends had come round, and I thought they would never leave! When they finally went, I found myself reaching for my hat and coat; I just had to get out of the house, out into the dark – I had no idea where I was going. I was thinking about you all the time, and felt sure we would run into each other." While she spoke thus from her heart, our hands were still clasped, and we gave each other a squeeze and let each other know that absence had not cooled our ardour. I walked with her back to her door and into the house. She went up the dark stairs ahead of me, holding on to my hand and pulling me along behind her. My joy was indescribable, both because we were reunited at last, and because my faith had not been misplaced and my sense of an invisible force at work had turned out to be right.'

Goethe was in the mellowest of moods, and I could have listened to him for hours. But he seemed to be gradually tiring, and so we very soon went to bed in our alcove.

Jena, Monday 8 October 1827

We got up early. As we were dressing, Goethe told me a dream he'd had in the night, in which he found himself in Göttingen, where he had all kinds of interesting conversations with the professors he knew there.

We drank a few cups of coffee, and then drove to the building that houses the scientific collections. We looked at the Anatomical Collection, various skeletons of animals, extant and prehistoric, as well as human skeletons from earlier centuries, which prompted Goethe to remark that their teeth suggested they were a very moral race.

He then got the driver to take us to the observatory, where Dr Schrön showed us the most important instruments and explained their function. We also studied the adjoining Meteorological Collection with great interest, and Goethe congratulated Dr Schrön on the excellent good order in which he kept all these things.

We then went down to the garden, where Goethe had organized a little breakfast for us, all laid out on a stone table in an arbour. 'I don't suppose you know,' he said, 'what a special place this is. This is where Schiller lived. We often used to sit here in this arbour, at this old stone table, on these very benches which are now falling apart, and talk about all kinds of interesting things. He was still in his thirties at the time, and I was in my forties, both of us at the height of our aspirations. It was quite something. But all things pass; I am no longer the man I was, but the old earth is still going strong, and air and water and soil are just the same as ever.

'You must go upstairs with Schrön afterwards and get him to show you the room in the attic where Schiller lived.'

In the meantime we thoroughly enjoyed our breakfast *al fresco* in this charming little corner. Schiller was there, too, at least in our thoughts; and Goethe spoke about him several times with fond remembrance.

I then went up to the attic with Schrön and enjoyed the magnificent view from Schiller's windows. The room faced due south, so you could see for miles up the lovely river, occasionally hidden from view by thickets or bends. You also had an uninterrupted view of the broad horizon – which made this an ideal vantage point for observing the rising and setting of the planets. So this must have been the perfect place for Schiller to write the astronomical and astrological passages in *Wallenstein*.

I went down to join Goethe again, and we drove next to see Councillor Döbereiner, of whom he thinks very highly, and who showed him some new chemical experiments.

By now it was midday, and we were sitting back in the carriage again. 'I thought,' said Goethe, 'we wouldn't go back to the Bear to eat, but make the most of the splendid weather and spend the day in the open air. I thought we would go to Burgau.

552 CONVERSATIONS WITH GOETHE

We've got our own wine, and we are sure to find some good fish there, which we can have either boiled or fried.'

So that's what we did – and we had a splendid time. We drove upriver, along the banks of the Saale, past the thickets and bends, following the lovely route I had observed earlier from Schiller's attic window. We were soon in Burgau. We alighted at the little inn by the river, close to the bridge, where the road goes on to Lobeda, a small town we could see on the other side, beyond some meadows.

At the little inn it was just as Goethe had said. The landlady apologized for having nothing prepared, but said she could make us some soup and a nice piece of fish.

While we waited we strolled up and down the bridge in the sunshine and enjoyed the river, watching the comings and goings of the raftsmen who glided under the bridge from time to time on rafts made of spruce planks lashed together, and went about their wet and laborious business in high spirits and loud voice.

We ate our fish out in the open air, and then sat for a while over a bottle of wine, talking of this and that. A small falcon flew past, looking very similar to a cuckoo in its shape and flight pattern.

'There was a time,' said Goethe, 'when the study of natural history was so backward that it was commonly thought the cuckoo was a cuckoo only in summer, and in winter became a bird of prey.'

'This view,' I replied, 'is still prevalent among the common people. Some even claim that the bird devours its own parents as soon as it is fully grown. So it is used as a metaphor for the most shameful ingratitude. I know people now who cannot be persuaded to abandon these absurd beliefs, and who cling on to them as tenaciously as they would to any article of their Christian faith.'

'As far as I know,' said Goethe, 'the cuckoo is classed as a member of the woodpecker family.'

'It sometimes is,' I replied, 'probably because its weak feet have two toes pointing backwards. But I wouldn't class it as a woodpecker myself. It doesn't have the woodpecker's powerful beak, capable of breaking through the dead bark of a tree, or the woodpecker's stiff and very strong tail feathers, designed to support the bird during this operation. Nor do its toes have the sharp claws necessary for clinging on, so while its small feet may look like climbing feet, I don't think they really are.'

'I expect it gives the ornithologists great pleasure,' Goethe replied, 'to put some strange bird into a neat little category. But nature does as she pleases, and cares little about the classification systems devised by puny humans.'

'Then there's the nightingale,' I went on, 'which is classified as a warbler, when in fact it is much more like the thrushes in its energetic temperament, its movements and its habit. But I wouldn't exactly classify it with the thrushes, either. It's a bird that falls between the two, a bird apart, just as the cuckoo is a bird apart too, with a quite distinctive individuality of its own.'

'Everything I've heard about the cuckoo,' said Goethe, 'makes me very interested in this curious bird. It is a highly problematic creature, a manifest mystery, but one that is no less difficult to solve for being so manifest. And how often in life do we find *that* to be the case! We are surrounded by mysteries, and the ultimate truth of things is inaccessible to us. Take the bees, for example. We see them fly for miles in search of honey, and every time in a different direction. Now they fly for weeks in a westerly direction, to a field of rapeseed in blossom. Then they fly north for just as long, to find some heath full of wild flowers. Then they are off in another direction, in search of buckwheat flowers. Then somewhere else, to a field of clover blossom. And finally, off they go again, in a different direction, seeking out lime blossom. Who told them: "Fly over here, here is something for you. And then over there, there's something new!"? And who leads them back to their village and their hive? They travel this way and that, as if on the end of some invisible string; but what it actually is, we just don't know. It's the same with the lark. It climbs high above a cornfield, singing its heart out, and hovers in the air above a sea of corn that the wind blows this way and that, where one ripple looks exactly like another; then it drops back down again to its chicks, and lands unfailingly on the tiny spot where it has made its nest. We see all these outward things, plain as day; but their inner spiritual connection is a closed book to us.'

'It's the same with the cuckoo,' I said. 'We know that it doesn't hatch its own young, but lays its egg in the nest of some other bird. We also know that it chooses to lay in the nest of the warbler, the yellow wagtail, the blackcap, and also in the nest of the dunnock, the robin and the wren. This much we know. We also know that these are all insect-eating birds, which they have to be, since the cuckoo is itself an insect-eating bird, and so cuckoo chicks could not be reared by a seed-eating bird. But how can the cuckoo tell that these are all insect-eating birds, when all the birds I mentioned look wildly different from each other, both in their shape and in their colouring – not to mention the enormous differences in their song and in their call notes? Furthermore, how is it that the cuckoo can entrust its egg and its tender young to nests that could not be more different in terms of their structure, temperature, dryness and moisture? The nest of the warbler is built from dry grass and horse hairs, and is so flimsy that the cold easily penetrates inside, and every draught blows right through it; it is also open at the top, with nowhere to shelter. Yet the young cuckoo chick positively thrives in it. The wren's nest, on the other hand, is a strong, densely woven structure, made of moss, stalks and leaves on the outside, and carefully lined on the inside with all sorts of wool and feathers, so that not a breath of air can get through. It is also covered at the top, where the walls curve inwards, leaving just a small opening for the very small bird to slip in and out. You would think that on hot June days, inside such an enclosed space, the heat would be suffocating. And yet the young cuckoo does very well in there. And how different again is the nest of the yellow wagtail! The bird lives by the water, on the banks of streams, in all kinds of wet conditions. It builds its nest on damp meadows, in a clump of rushes. It digs a hole in the damp earth, and lines it with a few token blades of grass, so that the baby cuckoo is hatched and reared in the damp and cold. Yet here, too, it thrives. So what kind of bird is this, which, at the tenderest age, can happily tolerate damp and dry conditions, heat and cold – extremes that would be fatal to any other bird? And how does the adult cuckoo know that these differences don't matter, when it is so susceptible itself to wet and cold when it is fully grown?'

'It is indeed a mystery,' said Goethe. 'But tell me, if this is something you have observed: how does the cuckoo place its egg inside the wren's nest, when the opening is so small that it cannot get inside itself and sit on it?'

'It lays the egg in some dry spot,' I replied, 'and places it inside with its beak. I believe this is what it does with all the other nests – not just the wren's. The thing is, the nests of the other insect-eating birds, even if they are open at the top, are so small, or so hemmed in by twigs, that the large cuckoo, with its long tail, could not sit on them. This one can understand. But how it comes about that the cuckoo lays such an extraordinarily *small* egg, small enough to be the egg of a small insect-eating bird: that is another mystery, which we marvel at but cannot solve. The cuckoo's egg is only slightly larger than the egg of the warbler, and it cannot really afford to be any larger than that if it is to be hatched by these small insect-eating birds. Which again makes perfectly good sense. But the fact that nature, in its wisdom, has deviated in this particular instance from a great and otherwise universal law, whereby there is a correlation between the size of the egg and the size of the bird, from the hummingbird all the way up to the ostrich – this random departure must surely surprise and astonish us.'

'It is indeed astonishing,' observed Goethe, 'because our point of view is too narrow for us to see the bigger picture. If more were revealed to us, we should probably find that these apparent deviations are actually within the scope of the law. But do go on, and tell me more. Do we know how many eggs the cuckoo lays?'

'Anyone who claimed to answer that question for certain,' I replied, 'would be a big fool. The bird is hard to spot – it is here, there and everywhere, and we only ever find one egg in any one nest. It must lay several eggs, but who knows where they all are? It's impossible to track the bird. But if we suppose it lays five eggs, and all five are successfully hatched and reared by loving foster parents, that only presents us with another conundrum:

how can nature consent to sacrifice at least *fifty* chicks of our finest songbirds for the sake of five baby cuckoos?'

'In such matters,' said Goethe, 'nature is not overly scrupulous, as we see from other instances. She has massive resources of life to squander, and sometimes she does it without much thought. But how is it that so many songbird chicks are lost for a single baby cuckoo?'

'First of all,' I replied, 'the first brood doesn't survive. If the songbird's eggs are hatched at the same time as the cuckoo's egg, which is what generally happens, the parents take such delight in the larger bird they have bred, and have such tender affection for it, that it is the only one they think about and feed – with the result that their own smaller chicks die and get pushed out of the nest. Also, the young cuckoo is always hungry, and needs all the food that the little insect-eating birds can possibly bring back to the nest. It is a long time before it has grown to its full size and acquired its full plumage, and before it is able to leave the nest and fly up to the top of a tree. And long after it has flown the nest it still needs to be fed constantly, so that the loving foster parents spend the entire summer running around after their big offspring, and don't think about a *second* brood. This is how so many other young birds come to be sacrificed for a single baby cuckoo.'

'That all makes sense,' said Goethe. 'But tell me, when the young cuckoo has flown the nest, does it get fed by other birds, who have not hatched it? It seems to me I have heard something of the sort.'

'This is true,' I replied. 'As soon as the cuckoo leaves its nest down below and perches somewhere like the top of a tall oak tree, it lets out a loud cry, which tells other birds that it is there. All the small birds in the neighbourhood that have heard it now turn up to welcome the newcomer. The warbler arrives, and the blackcap; the yellow wagtail flies up; and even the wren, which by habit likes to hide away in low hedges and dense shrubbery, defies its natural instincts and flies up to the top of the tall oak to greet the beloved newcomer. But the pair that have reared it are more dedicated when it comes to regular feeding, whereas the other birds just drop in from time to time with some choice morsel.'

'So it seems,' said Goethe, 'that there is a great deal of affection between the young cuckoo and the smaller insect-eating birds.'

'The affection felt by the smaller insect-eating birds for the young cuckoo,' I replied, 'is so great that when one approaches a nest where a young cuckoo is being nurtured, the little foster parents get beside themselves with panic, fear and alarm. The blackcap in particular seems overcome by despair, fluttering about on the ground as if seized with convulsions.'

'How very curious,' said Goethe, 'but I can well imagine. What puzzles me, though, is why a pair of warblers, say, which are about to sit on their own eggs, would allow the adult cuckoo to approach their nest and place its egg inside.'

'That is certainly puzzling,' I replied, 'but perhaps not altogether. The very fact that all the small insect-eating birds bring food to the cuckoo once it has flown the nest, including, therefore, birds that have had nothing to do with hatching it, means that a kind of affinity develops between the two, so that they know each other from now on and regard themselves as members of one big family. You even find cases where the same cuckoo that was hatched and reared by a pair of warblers last year brings its egg to them this year.'

'I hear what you are saying,' said Goethe, 'though I don't pretend to understand it. But I still marvel at the fact that the young cuckoo gets fed by birds that have not hatched and reared it.'

'It is a marvel, certainly,' I replied, 'and yet there are parallels. I do wonder, in fact, if this is not a manifestation of some great law that runs throughout the whole of nature.

'I once caught a young linnet that was already too big to be fed by humans, but still too young to feed itself. I struggled with it for half a day, but it would not take anything from me. So I put it in with an adult linnet, a fine songster, which I had had for ages, and kept in a cage that was hanging outside my window. I thought to myself: if the young bird sees how the old one feeds, it will perhaps go to the food itself and mimic him. But it didn't. Instead, it opened its beak towards the older bird and fluttered its wings with a beseeching cry; whereupon the old linnet immediately took pity on it, adopted it as a chick, and fed it as if it were its own.

'And then there was the time someone brought me a grey warbler and three chicks, which I put all together in a large cage, and the adult bird fed the young. Next day, someone brought me two young nightingales that had already flown the nest, which I put in with the warbler, and which were likewise adopted and fed by her. A few days later I put in a nest with young, nearly fledged lesser whitethroats, as well as a nest with five young blackcaps. The adult grey warbler adopted them all, and fed them and nurtured them like a devoted mother. Her beak was constantly full of ant's eggs, and she was bobbing around from one corner of the roomy cage to another; wherever a hungry mouth opened wide, there she was. And that's not all. One of the grey warbler's own chicks, grown to adolescence in the meantime, now began to feed some of the younger chicks – in a playful, childlike sort of way, but still, clearly driven by an instinct to copy the actions of its admirable mother.'

'Now here,' said Goethe, 'we are in the presence of something truly divine, which fills me with joyous wonder. If it were true that this feeding of a stranger is a kind of universal law of nature, it would solve many a riddle, and one could say with confidence that God does indeed take pity on the orphaned young ravens which cry unto Him.'

'It does seem to be a kind of universal law,' I replied. 'Even in the wild, I have observed birds feeding those that can't help themselves and taking pity on the abandoned.

'Last summer, near Tiefurt, I caught two young wrens who had probably only just left their nest. They and seven of their brethren were sitting in a row, on a twig, in a bush, while their parents fed them. I wrapped the two young birds in my silk handkerchief and walked back towards Weimar, as far as the Shooting Gallery, then turned right, down towards the meadow by the Ilm, past the bathing place, then left again into the little wood. Here, I thought to myself, you can take a moment to check on your wrens in peace. But as I unwrapped the handkerchief they both escaped and disappeared into the grass and undergrowth. I searched for them, but without success. Three days later I happened to be in this spot again, and as I could hear the call of a robin, I guessed there must be a nest nearby, which I found after looking around for a bit. Imagine my astonishment, however, when I found the nest contained not only some nearly fledged young robins, but also my two baby wrens, who had made themselves at home here and were getting themselves fed by the adult robins. I was thrilled by this remarkable discovery. "Since you are so clever," I thought to myself, "and have managed to fend for yourselves so successfully, and since the good robins have been so helpful and accommodating, far be it from me to interfere in these hospitable arrangements. On the contrary: I wish you every good fortune."'

'That is one of the best bird stories I have ever heard,' said Goethe, raising his glass. 'A toast: your very good health, and long may your observations continue! Anyone who hears that, and does not believe in God, will not be helped by Moses and all the prophets. Now that's what I call the omnipresence of God, who has spread and implanted a portion of His infinite love everywhere and shows us, in the animal kingdom, the bud that flowers gloriously in noble mankind. You should continue your studies and observations; you seem to have a special facility for them, and you may make some invaluable discoveries in the future.'

While we talked thus of the mysteries and joys of life at our table in the open air, the sun was dropping down towards the crest of the hills in the west, and Goethe thought it was time for us to go home. We drove speedily through Jena, and after we had settled our account at the Bear and paid a brief visit to the Frommanns, we headed back to Weimar at a smart trot.

Thursday 18 October 1827

Hegel is here. Goethe esteems him very highly on a personal level, even if some of the fruits of his philosophy are not particularly to his taste. This evening Goethe gave a tea party in his honour, which Zelter also attended, though he was planning to leave Weimar again later tonight.

We talked a great deal about Hamann, and Hegel rather

monopolized the conversation, speaking about that extraordinary mind with the authority that can only come from serious and painstaking study.

The conversation then turned to the nature of dialectics. 'In essence,' said Hegel, 'it is nothing more than the formalized, systematically trained spirit of contradiction that we all have inside us – a gift that proves its worth in distinguishing between truth and falsehood.'

'If only,' interjected Goethe, 'such intellectual arts and skills were not frequently misused and employed to make the false true and the true false!'

'That kind of thing does happen,' replied Hegel, 'but only with people who are mentally ill.'

'Which is why,' said Goethe, 'I am a great believer in the study of nature: it keeps you sane. Because what we are dealing with here is infinite and eternal truth, which has no time for anyone who is not entirely pure and honest in the observation and treatment of his subject. And I am certain that many of those made ill by dialectics would find healing in the study of nature.'

The conversation was still in full flow, and the mood highly convivial, when Zelter stood up and left the room without a word. We knew how hard it was for him to say goodbye to Goethe, and that he preferred to slip away quietly like this, to avoid the painful moment of parting.

1828

Tuesday 11 March 1828

I've been feeling rather unwell for several weeks now. I am sleeping badly and having fitful dreams throughout the night, in which I see myself in all kinds of different situations, having conversations with persons known and unknown, getting into arguments and quarrels – and all of it so vividly real that I can remember every detail next morning. But this dream existence saps my mental energies, so that I feel limp and weary the next day, with no desire or thought for any intellectual activity.

I had frequently complained of my condition to Goethe, and he had repeatedly urged me to consult my doctor. 'Whatever the problem is,' he said, 'I'm sure it's nothing serious, just some minor blockage, which can be cleared with a few glasses of mineral water or some salts. But don't just let it drag on – do something about it!'

Goethe was probably quite right, and I told myself that he was right. But my indecision and reluctance took over once more, and I let more restless nights and wretched days go by without making any effort to seek relief.

After dinner today, when he saw me looking rather preoccupied and down in the mouth again, Goethe finally lost patience, and could not help giving me an ironic smile and making fun of me a little.

'You are just like old Shandy,' he said, 'the father of the famous Tristram, who was annoyed half his life by a creaking door, and could not get round to ending his daily irritation with a few drops of oil.[20]

'But we're all the same! *Benighted and inspired are the ways of men!* We need to be taken in hand each day by our daemon, who would tell us what to do and make us do it. But the good spirit deserts us, and we grope about in the dark, no use to anyone.

'Napoleon, though – he was something else! Always inspired, always clear-sighted and decisive, and blessed at every moment with sufficient energy to take whatever action he deemed advantageous and necessary. He lived life as a demigod who strode from battle to battle and from victory to victory. It could be said of him that he was in a constant state of inspiration, which is why his destiny shone so brightly; the world had not seen his like before and may not see his like again.

'Oh yes, my friend, he was something else altogether, and in a class of his own!'

Goethe was pacing up and down the room. I had sat down at the table, which had already been cleared, but there was a little wine left, and some biscuits and fruit. Goethe poured me some wine and made me eat a little of both. 'You spurned our dinner table today,' he said, 'but I fancy a glass of this – a present from dear friends – will go down well.'

I savoured these delicacies while Goethe went on pacing up and down the room, his mind racing, murmuring to himself and occasionally saying something that I couldn't quite make out.

I was reflecting on what he had just said about Napoleon, and endeavoured to bring the conversation back to that subject. 'It does seem to me, though,' I began, 'that Napoleon was in that constant state of inspiration principally when he was still young and growing in strength, when we see him protected by the hand of God and attended by unbroken good fortune. In later years that inspiration seems to have deserted him, along with his good fortune and his lucky star.'

'What do you expect?' replied Goethe. 'I never wrote my love poems or my *Werther* again, either. That divine inspiration, the source of all that is extraordinary, will always be found in league with youth and *productivity* – and Napoleon was one of the most productive human beings that ever lived.

'Oh yes, my friend, one doesn't have to write poems and plays

1828   563

to be productive; there is also such a thing as a *productivity of deeds*, which in many cases amounts to a good deal more. Even a doctor has to be productive, if he really wants to heal his patients; if he is not, he will only succeed in curing the odd patient by chance, but on the whole he will remain a charlatan.'

'You seem to be using the word "productivity" here,' I said, 'to describe what is generally termed "genius".'

'The two things are very closely related,' replied Goethe. 'For what is genius, if not the productive power that brings forth deeds good enough to pass muster in the sight of God and nature, and which consequently make a difference and endure. All Mozart's works are of this kind; there is a procreative power in them that goes on from generation to generation and is unlikely to be exhausted any time soon. The same is true of other great composers and artists. Think of the influence Phidias and Raphael have had on succeeding centuries, likewise Dürer and Holbein! The man who first devised the forms and proportions of Gothic architecture, which in due course made it possible to build Strasbourg Minster and Cologne Cathedral, was also a genius, because his thoughts have retained their productive power and continue to influence us today. Luther was a genius of a very special kind; his influence has persisted for many a long day, and we cannot tell how many days will pass before he ceases to be productive in some distant future. Lessing spurned the lofty title of genius, but his enduring influence argues otherwise. Then again, in literature we have other names, eminent names, who were thought to be great geniuses during their lifetime, but whose influence ended with their death, so that they were less than they and others thought. As I said, genius is not genius without the enduring power to inspire productivity in others. And furthermore, it makes no difference what business, art or profession one pursues: it's all the same. Whether one proves to be a genius in science, like Oken and Humboldt; or in war and public administration, like Frederick, Peter the Great and Napoleon; or whether one writes a song, like Béranger: it is all one, and the only thing that matters is whether the thought, the insight, the deed, is alive and has the capacity to live on.

'And the other thing I would say is this: a productive person is not defined by the *quantity* of works and deeds he has to his name. In literature we have poets who are held to be very productive because they have published volume after volume of poetry. To my way of thinking, however, these people should be considered wholly unproductive, because what they wrote is lifeless and transient. Goldsmith, on the other hand, wrote so few poems that in terms of quantity they are almost negligible; but I consider him highly productive as a poet, because the little that he did write has an inherent life that has endured.'

A pause ensued, during which Goethe continued to pace up and down the room. I was keen to hear more on this important point, and sought to get Goethe's attention again.

'So this productivity that defines a genius,' I said, 'does it reside just in the mind of an eminent man, or does it also reside in his body?'

'The body,' replied Goethe, 'has the greatest *influence* on it, at any rate. There was a time when the popular image of a genius in Germany was someone short, weak, and very likely hunchbacked as well. But my kind of genius is one who is fit in mind *and* body.

'When people said of Napoleon that he was a man of granite, this is particularly true of his physical constitution. Think of the demands he made on himself – just because he could! From the burning sands of the Syrian desert to the snowfields of Moscow: think of all the marches, battles and overnight bivouacs that lay in between! And all the ordeals and physical privations he had to endure on the way! Not much sleep, not much food, and always in the highest state of mental activity! When it got to midnight after the appalling strain and excitement of the 18th Brumaire, he had eaten nothing all day; and yet, ignoring the needs of his body, he summoned enough strength to work far into the night, drafting his famous proclamation to the French people.[21] When you consider all that he had been through and endured, you would think that in his fortieth year the man would be a physical wreck. And yet at that age he was still in his prime, every inch the hero.

'But you are right, of course: the real high point of his

achievement was in the years of his youth. And it was quite something for a man of obscure origins, in an age that mobilized everyone of talent, to so distinguish himself that he became the idol of a nation of thirty million in his twenty-seventh year! Yes indeed, my friend, you have to be young to do great things. And Napoleon is not the only one!'

'His brother, Lucien,' I remarked, 'also accomplished a great deal at an early age. We find him as President of the Council of Five Hundred, and then as Minister of the Interior, when he was still in his twenty-fifth year.'

'Never mind Lucien!' Goethe interjected. 'History shows us hundreds of highly competent men who made their name by conducting affairs of the greatest importance, in the cabinet and in the field, at a very young age.

'If I were a prince,' he went on, warming to his theme, 'I would never give the top jobs to people who have been promoted steadily on the basis of birth and seniority, and who now, in their mature years, go on at a leisurely pace in their own settled ways; they're not exactly going to set the world on fire. Give me young men every time! But they would have to be highly capable, clear-thinking and energetic, and at the same time men of goodwill, and of the noblest character. Then it would be a joy to rule, and improve the lives of one's people. But where is there a prince so fortunate, and so well served?

'I have great hopes of the present Crown Prince of Prussia.[22] From all that I know and hear of him, he is a very impressive man. And that's a necessary qualification for recognizing and choosing clever and talented people. Say what you like, but it takes one to know one; and only a prince who possesses great abilities himself will be able to recognize and appreciate great abilities in his subjects and servants. "Let the path be open to talent," as Napoleon famously said, and of course he had a very special instinct when it came to choosing his people, always knowing where to place each major figure so that he would be in his element – which meant that he was served in all the great enterprises of his life as few others have been.'

I thought Goethe was in particularly good form this evening. He seemed animated by all that was best in him; his voice was strong and firm, and his eyes were aglow, as if the fires of his youth had flared up again and burned brightly within him. I found it remarkable that a man of his age, who continued to hold an important position even at his time of life, should argue the case for youth with such conviction, insisting that the highest offices of state should go, if not to youths, then at least to men who were still young. I could not resist mentioning the names of a few German men in senior positions who, even at their advanced age, seemed to have no shortage of energy and youthful agility to conduct all manner of important business.

'Such men and their like,' replied Goethe, 'are natural geniuses, and they are a special case; they go through a *second puberty*, whereas other people are only young once.

'Every soul is a piece of eternity, and the few years when it is tied to the mortal body do not age it. If this soul is of a lesser order, it will not exercise much sway while it is eclipsed by the body; instead, it is the body that dominates, and as the body ages, the soul will not retard or block that process. But if the soul is naturally powerful, as is the case with all men of genius, then, as it permeates and stimulates the body, it will not only have a strengthening and improving effect on the physical organism, but will also, given its spiritual supremacy, seek constantly to assert its right to eternal youth. This is why we see highly gifted persons still experiencing new periods of extraordinary productivity during their old age; they seem to go through recurrent phases of temporary rejuvenation – and that's what I mean by "second puberty".

'But youth has its day, and however powerful a soul might be, it will never exercise complete control over the physical body. It also makes a huge difference whether the body co-operates or resists.

'There was a time in my life when I was capable of producing a whole printer's sheet of text in a day, and I had no difficulty in doing so. I wrote my *Geschwister* in three days, my *Clavigo* in eight, as you know. I probably don't need to be doing that kind of thing now; but still, I can't complain about lack of productivity, even at my advanced age. But the things I was able to do daily in my younger years, regardless of circumstances, I can now manage only periodically, and under certain favourable conditions. When I was completely taken up with the poems of the *Divan* in that happy time, ten or twelve years ago, after the War of Liberation, I was often productive enough to write two or three in a single day; and I could be out in the open air, riding in a carriage or sitting in an inn – it was all the same to me. But now I can only work on the second part of my *Faust* in the early part of the day, when I feel refreshed and invigorated by sleep, and the distractions of daily life have not yet started to crowd in on me. And yet, how much do I really get done? If I'm very lucky, I can produce a page of writing, but normally it's only as much as would fit under your hand – and even less if I'm in an unproductive mood.'

'More generally,' I said, 'is there some way to conjure up a productive mood, or to enhance it if it is not intense enough?'

'That's a very interesting point,' replied Goethe, 'and there is a great deal to be thought and said on the subject.

'All productivity of the highest order, all important insights, all fictional creations, all great thoughts which lead to something worthwhile, are outside anyone's control and beyond the command of any earthly power. Such things must be viewed as unexpected gifts from above, as pure children of God, to be received and revered by man with joyful thanks. They are akin to the daemonic, which does with man what it will, and to which he unwittingly submits in the mistaken belief that he is acting on his own impulse. In many such instances man may be viewed as the instrument of a higher world governance, as a vessel deemed worthy to receive a divine influence. I say this, mindful of how often a single thought has changed the course of entire centuries, and of how individual men have, by their influence, set a stamp on their epoch which was still discernible, and still having a positive effect, in succeeding generations.

'But there is also another kind of productivity, which is subject to influences of a rather more earthly kind, and over which man has more control – although here, too, he still finds cause to bow down before something divine. In this category I would place everything required for the execution of a plan; all the successive links in a chain of thought whose final conclusions are already abundantly clear; and everything that makes up the visible form and body of a work of art.

'So when Shakespeare had the initial idea for his *Hamlet*, and a sense of the whole presented itself to his mind's eye as an unexpected vision; and when, in an exalted state of mind, he saw the individual situations, characters, and the play's ending, this was a pure gift from above, over which he had no direct influence – although the possibility of having such an inspiration in the first place always presupposed a mind of his calibre. But when he later came to write the individual scenes and dialogue, he was in full command of what he was doing, so he could work away at it by the day, by the hour, for weeks on end, just as it suited him. So the same productive energy is evident in everything he wrote, and we never encounter a passage in any of his plays of which it could be said that it was not written in the right frame of mind or with supreme mastery. When we read him, we get the impression of a man who was always thoroughly healthy and robust, in mind and in body.

'But if a dramatist's physical constitution were not so strong and sound, and he were prone to frequent illness and weakliness, the creative energy he needs to work on his scenes every day would surely flag very often, and quite possibly desert him completely for days at a time. Were he to drink spirits, say, in an effort to summon up the creative energy he lacks or to augment what energy he has, that might well work up to a point, but it would be obvious which scenes had been artificially induced, so to speak – to their great detriment.

'My advice is therefore never to force anything artificially. When you are feeling unproductive it is better just to idle away the time, or stay in bed, than to try and produce something on such days that gives you no pleasure later.'

'What you say,' I replied, 'is something I have often felt and experienced myself, and I'm sure we should respect it as a true fact of life. All the same, it does seem to me that it should be possible to enhance one's productive mood by natural means, without exactly forcing it. There have been many times in my life when I found myself in a difficult dilemma, and unable to come to any proper decision. But if I drank a few glasses of

1828   569

wine in such situations it immediately became clear to me what
I should do, and my mind was made up there and then. The
business of reaching a decision is a kind of productivity, after
all, and if a few glasses of wine can bring about this happy outcome, then surely we should not dismiss such an expedient
altogether.'

'I'm not going to say you are wrong,' said Goethe, 'but what
I said just now is also right. Which only goes to show that truth
is like a diamond, which sends out rays of light not just in one
direction, but in many. And as you know my *Divan* so well,
you'll know that I myself wrote:

> When a man has had a drink,
> He knows the right way forward . . .[23]

and that I therefore agree with you entirely. Wine has very
special powers to make us productive; but it all depends on the
circumstances and the timing, and what is helpful to one person is harmful to another. There are powers in rest and sleep
which make us productive – likewise in exercise. Such powers
are to be found in water, and especially in the atmosphere. The
fresh air of the countryside is the place where we really belong,
as though the spirit of God breathed directly on man there, and
a divine power exercised its influence. Lord Byron spent several
hours each day in the open air, sometimes riding along the seashore on a horse, sometimes sailing or rowing in a boat, or
bathing in the sea and building up his strength by swimming.
And he was one of the most productive men that ever lived.'

Goethe had sat down opposite me, and we talked more about
all kinds of other things. Then we came back to Lord Byron
and touched on the many misfortunes that overshadowed his
later years until in the end a noble aspiration, but a fateful destiny, led him to Greece and destroyed him utterly.

'You will find in general,' Goethe went on, 'that a change
often takes place in a man's middle years, and that as fortune
smiled on him in his youth and he succeeded in all his endeavours, so now everything suddenly changes, and one misfortune
and one mishap follows hard upon the heels of another.

'But do you know what I think it is? *We humans have to be brought low again.* Every extraordinary man has a certain mission that he is called upon to fulfil. Once he has accomplished it, he is no longer needed on this earth in that particular guise, and so providence uses him for something else. But since everything here on earth happens in a natural way, the demons keep on tripping him up until he finally succumbs. This is what happened to Napoleon and many others: Mozart died in his thirty-sixth year, Raphael at almost the same age, and Byron when he was not much older. But all of them had fulfilled their mission to perfection, and it was probably time for them to go, so that there would be something left for other people to do in this world of ours, which was made to last for a long time.'

It was late in the evening by now. Goethe gave me his dear hand, and I left.

Wednesday 12 March 1828

After I left Goethe last night I could not get our remarkable conversation out of my mind. We had also touched upon the beneficial effects of the sea and the sea air, and Goethe said that he regarded all islanders and coastal dwellers in the temperate climate zone as far more productive and active than the peoples living in the interior of large continents.

Whether it was because I fell asleep with these thoughts, and with a certain yearning for the invigorating powers of the sea, I don't know; but in the night I had the following charming, and to me very curious, dream.

I saw myself in an unfamiliar place, among strangers, but feeling altogether cheerful and happy. It was a beautiful summer's day, in a delightful natural setting, as you might find on the Mediterranean coast, in southern Spain or France, or in the area around Genoa. We had been carousing merrily around the lunchtime table, and I was now going off with another group of somewhat younger people to enjoy ourselves on an afternoon outing. We had been wandering through some pleasant bushy hollows when we suddenly found ourselves in the sea, on a tiny island, a rocky outcrop barely big enough for five or six

1828   571

people, where one dare not move for fear of falling off into the water. Behind us, in the direction we had come from, there was nothing to be seen but sea; in front of us lay the shore, a quarter of a mile distant, stretched out before us and looking most inviting. The shoreline was flat in some places, in other places rocky and slightly elevated; and we could see, in between leafy arbours and white tents, a crowd of people in light-coloured clothes making merry to the sound of lovely music, which drifted across to us from the tents. 'There's nothing for it,' one of us said to another, 'we'll have to strip off and swim across.' 'That's all very well for you,' I said, 'but you are young and good-looking, and good swimmers, too. But I'm a poor swimmer, and I don't have the good looks to feel happy or comfortable displaying myself to those strangers on the shore.' 'You're a fool,' said one of the most handsome. 'Just take off your clothes, and give me your body, and you shall have mine.' At these words I undressed quickly, went into the water and promptly discovered, in the body of the other man, that I was a strong swimmer. I soon reached the shore and mingled with the crowd of people, naked and dripping, but perfectly happy in my own skin. I took pleasure in the sensation of my finely formed limbs, I felt relaxed and uninhibited, and immediately made friends with the strangers sitting at a table outside an arbour, where everyone was having a jolly time. My companions had also come ashore one by one and had joined us at the table; the only one missing was the young man with my body, in whose own limbs I felt so good. Eventually he also approached the shore, and people asked me if I would like to see my former self. I felt uneasy at these words, partly because I thought I would not much enjoy looking at myself, and partly because I was afraid my young friend might now ask for his body back. I turned towards the water nevertheless, and saw my other self swim up close to me; turning his head a little to one side, he looked up at me with a laugh. 'There's no strength in those limbs of yours for swimming,' he called out to me. 'I had to battle hard against the waves and surf, so it's not surprising that it has taken me so long, and I am the last to arrive.' I recognized the face immedi-ately: it was my own, but younger, and somewhat fuller and broader, and with the freshest complexion. He now stepped ashore, and as he straightened up and took his first steps across the sand I had a good view of his back and legs and took pleasure in the perfection of his physique. He came up the rocky shore to join the rest of us, and as he came up to me he was exactly my new size. How is it, I thought to myself, that your little body has grown so big and handsome! Have the elemental powers of the sea worked wonders with it, or is it because the youthful spirit of your friend has spread throughout those limbs? As we sat together for quite a while, having a good time, I was secretly surprised that my friend showed no sign of wanting his own body back again. He really does look very fine as he is, I thought, and maybe it doesn't matter to him one way or the other; but it does matter to me, because I'm not sure I wouldn't shrink again inside that body and become as small as I was before. In order to put my mind at rest, I took my friend aside and asked him how he felt in my limbs. 'Absolutely fine,' he said. 'I feel the same on the inside and with the same strength as before. I don't know what you have against your limbs; they suit me perfectly well, and it's just a matter of making something of oneself, you see. Stay in my body as long as you like, because I'm perfectly happy to stay in yours indefinitely.' I was very pleased to hear this, and since I, too, felt I was still the same person in all my sensations, thoughts and memories, I had the impression in my dream that our soul is completely independent, and that it is possible for us to have a future existence in a different body.

'That's a very nice dream,' said Goethe, when I related the gist of it to him after dinner today. 'I can see,' he went on, 'that the muses visit you even in your sleep, and that they come bearing special gifts; because you must admit that it would be hard for you to make up something so strange and intriguing in your waking state.'

'I hardly know how it came about,' I replied. 'I had been feeling really depressed prior to that, so the idea of such a fresh new life was very far from my mind.'

'There are wondrous powers in human nature,' said Goethe, 'and it has something good in store for us when we least expect it. There were times in my life when I went to sleep in tears, but the most delightful creatures visited me in my dreams to comfort and cheer me, and the next morning I got out of bed feeling bright and fresh again.

'On the whole, things are not looking at all good for us old Europeans; our social situation is far too artificial and complicated, our food and way of life have lost touch with nature, and our social relationships are lacking in real love and goodwill. Everyone is very polished and courteous, but nobody has the courage to be warm and genuine, so that an honest man with natural inclinations and sentiments has a really hard time of it. It's often tempting to wish one had been born a so-called savage on one of the South Sea Islands, just to enjoy human existence in its pure, unadulterated form.

'If one is depressed, and dwells on the wretched state of the world today, it often seems as if the Last Judgement must be just around the corner. And things are getting worse from one generation to the next. It's not enough that we have to suffer for the sins of our fathers; we pass on these inherited afflictions to our descendants, and throw in some of our own as well.'

'I often have similar thoughts myself,' I said, 'but when I then see some regiment of German dragoons riding past, and think how handsome and strong these young people look, I feel encouraged again, and tell myself that the prospects for the future of the human race are not that bad after all.'

'Our rural population,' replied Goethe, 'has certainly managed to remain vigorous, and hopefully will long continue not only to supply us with fine horsemen, but also to save us from total degeneracy and corruption. It serves as a kind of reservoir, from which the powers of a declining human race are constantly replenished and refreshed. But if you go into our big cities you will get a very different impression. Just go on your rounds with a latter-day *Diable boiteux*,[24] or with a doctor who has a large practice, and he will whisper stories in your ear that will leave you horrified at the misery and shocked at the afflictions visited upon human nature, which are the scourge of our society.

'But enough of such melancholy thoughts. How are you?

What are you up to? What else have you been doing today? Tell me, and let me hear some positive thoughts.'

'I've been reading the passage in Sterne,' I replied, 'where Yorick is wandering about the streets of Paris and observes that every tenth person is a dwarf.[25] I thought of that just now, when you mentioned the afflictions of the big cities. I also remember seeing a battalion of French infantry in Napoleon's day that consisted entirely of Parisians, and they were all so small and slight of build that it was hard to see what use they could be in wartime.'

'The Duke of Wellington's Scottish Highlanders,' said Goethe, 'were no doubt fighting men of a very different stamp!'

'I saw them in Brussels, a year before the Battle of Waterloo,' I said. 'They were indeed handsome fellows! All strong, alert and light on their feet, as if they had come straight from the hand of God. They held their heads so proud and high, striding along so easily with their strong, bare legs, as if there was no such thing for them as original sin or the sins of the fathers.'

'It's a curious thing,' replied Goethe, 'and I don't know whether it's in the blood, or whether it comes from the soil, their liberal constitution, or their healthy upbringing: but the English in general seem to have an advantage over many other peoples. Here in Weimar, of course, we see only a handful of them, and probably not the pick of the crop; but they are all fine, handsome fellows, just the same! And even when they arrive here at the tender age of seventeen, they don't feel in the least awkward or out of place in these foreign German parts; on the contrary, their whole demeanour in society is as confident and easy-going as if they were lords of all they survey, and as if the entire world belonged to them. This is what our women find so attractive, and why they wreak havoc in the hearts of our young ladies. As a German *paterfamilias*, who cares about his family's peace of mind, I often feel a certain dread when my daughter-in-law tells me some new young islander is expected to arrive soon. In my mind's eye I can already see the tears that will be shed for him when he leaves. These are dangerous young men; but then, that is what makes them attractive in the first place.'

1828 575

'Still,' I replied, 'I wouldn't say that the young Englishmen we get in Weimar are cleverer, more intelligent, better informed and altogether more worthy than other people.'

'That's not the point, my friend,' returned Goethe. 'It's not a matter of birth or wealth, either. Their secret is having the self-confidence to be what nature intended them to be. There is nothing over-sophisticated or corrupt about them, nothing half-hearted or mealy-mouthed; such as they are, they are always complete persons. And sometimes complete fools, I'll gladly admit; but that's still something, and it still tips the scales when weighed in nature's balance.

'The joy of personal freedom, the awareness of the English name and the weight that this carries with other nations – all this gives their children a good start in life; they are treated with far more respect within the family and in their schools and they enjoy a far happier and freer upbringing than here in Germany.

'I only need look out of the window here in our very own Weimar to see how things are with us. When there was snow on the ground recently, and the neighbourhood children wanted to try out their little sledges in the street, a policeman was soon on the scene, and I saw the little mites scamper off as fast as they could go. And now, when the spring sunshine entices them out-doors and they want to play in the street with their friends, I can tell that they are nervous, as if they don't feel quite safe and are afraid that some figure of authority from the police might come round the corner. The moment a boy cracks a whip, or sings or shouts, the police are right there to stop him. Every-thing with us is designed to tame sweet youth prematurely and drive out every vestige of nature, originality and wildness, so that nothing is left in the end but the philistine.

'As you know, hardly a day goes by when I do not receive a visit from some stranger who is passing through. But if I were to say, thinking particularly of young German academics who hail from a certain north-eastern quarter, that I found their personal appearance especially pleasing, I would be lying. Short-sighted, pale and pigeon-chested, young, but old before their time: that's the image that most of them present to me.

And when I engage them in conversation, I notice straightaway that the things which interest the likes of you and me seem vacuous and trivial to them; they are obsessed with ideas, and only the ultimate questions of speculative philosophy are deemed worthy of their interest. They do not appear to have functioning senses at all, and take no delight in sensual things; all the emotions and joys of youth have been drummed out of them, once and for all; for if a man is not young at the age of twenty, how can he be young at forty?'

Goethe sighed and fell silent.

I thought about the happy time in the last century when Goethe was young; I imagined the summer air of Sesenheim, and I reminded him of the lines:

> In the afternoons we sat,
> Youngsters together, in the cool.[26]

'Ah yes,' sighed Goethe, 'those were the days! But we won't dwell on them, in case they make the grey, misty days of the present seem utterly unbearable.'

'What we need,' I said, 'is a second Redeemer to come and deliver us from the seriousness, the malaise, and the oppressive burden of our present situation.'

'If he did come,' replied Goethe, 'they would crucify him again. But we don't need anything so dramatic. If only one could teach the Germans to follow the example of the English, and have less philosophy and more action, less theory and more practice, we would be well on the way to redemption by ourselves, without having to wait for a second Christ to come in majesty and in person. A lot could be done at the grassroots level, by the people, through our schools and family upbringing; and a lot could be done from the top, by our rulers and those around them.

'I think, for example, that far too much emphasis is placed on theoretical and academic knowledge when young people are studying for the civil service; this exhausts them before their time, both mentally and physically. If they subsequently undertake some practical form of service, they possess a vast store of knowledge about philosophy and other learned matters, but they cannot apply it within the narrow compass of their normal working lives, and so it gets forgotten again as a pointless irrelevance. But in the meantime they have missed out on what they needed most: they lack the mental and physical energy that is essential if they are going to play an effective role in practical affairs.

'And surely love and kindness also have an important place in the life of a public servant, who is dealing with people all the time? But how can anyone possibly feel and show kindness towards others if he is not at ease with himself?

'But these people are all really struggling. A third of all the academics and public servants chained to their desks are in ailing health, and have succumbed to the demon hypochondria.[27] Something needs to be done by those in authority to safeguard future generations, at least, against a similar fate.

'In the meantime,' added Goethe with a smile, 'we can only hope, and wait to see how things turn out for us Germans in a hundred years from now, and whether we shall have learned by then to be human beings rather than academics and philosophers who deal in abstractions.'

Friday 16 May 1828*

Went for a drive with Goethe. He recollected with amusement his quarrels with Kotzebue and Co., and recited a few satirical epigrams aimed at the former which were actually more comical than hurtful. I asked him why he had not included them in the edition of his works. 'I've got a whole collection of these little poems,' replied Goethe, 'which I keep secret and only show occasionally to my closest friends. This was the only harmless weapon I had to defend myself against the attacks of my enemies. It was my way of venting my feelings in private – which was very liberating; it purged me of the awful feelings of bitterness that I would otherwise have harboured about the public and often malicious digs of my enemies. So I did myself a big favour by writing those little poems. But I have no wish to burden the public with my private squabbles, or to offend any persons still living. I see no reason why selected pieces should not be published at a later date, however.'

Friday 6 June 1828 *

Some time ago the King of Bavaria sent his court painter Stieler to Weimar, in order to paint Goethe's portrait. As a kind of letter of introduction, and a testimonial to his skill, Stieler brought with him the finished life-size portrait of a very attractive young woman, namely the Munich actress Fräulein von Hagn. Goethe duly agreed to all the sittings Herr Stieler requested, and his portrait was finished a few days ago.

Today I dined with him alone. During dessert he got up and led me into the small room adjoining the dining room and showed me Stieler's newly completed work. Then, with an air of great mystery, he led me on further into the so-called Majolica Room, where the portrait of the beautiful young actress was kept. After we had studied it for a while, he said: 'Now that was time well spent, wasn't it? Stieler is no fool. He used this tasty morsel as bait, and having persuaded me by this ploy to sit for him, he flattered my hopes that another angel would take shape under his brush, even though he was only painting the head of an old man.'

Friday 26 September 1828 *

Today Goethe showed me his extensive collection of fossils, which is kept in the detached pavilion by his garden. He established the collection himself, and his son has added greatly to it; especially remarkable is the extended series of fossilized bones, all of which were found in the area around Weimar.

Monday 6 October 1828 *

Dined with Goethe, together with Herr von Martius, who arrived here several days ago to discuss botanical matters with Goethe. Herr von Martius talked mainly about the spiral tendency of plants, an area in which he has made important discoveries.

This has opened up a whole new field of inquiry for Goethe, who seemed to take up his friend's idea with a kind of youthful ardour. 'It adds greatly to our understanding of the physiology of plants,' he said. 'This new insight into the spiral tendency is entirely consistent with my own theory of metamorphosis; it was discovered in the same way, but takes us a huge step forwards.'

Friday 17 October 1828*

For some time now Goethe has been a keen reader of *Le Globe*, and he often finds occasion to talk about this journal. He believes the work that Cousin and his followers are doing is very important.

'These men,' he said, 'are well on the way to effecting a rapprochement between France and Germany by developing a discourse eminently calculated to facilitate the exchange of ideas between our two nations.'

The *Globe* is also of special interest to Goethe because the latest works of French literature are reviewed there, and the liberties of the romantic school, or rather the liberation from the shackles of meaningless rules, are often defended very vigorously in its pages.

'Why should we lumber ourselves with specific rules that belong to a rigid bygone age,' he said today, 'and why all this fuss about "classical" versus "romantic"? What matters is that a work should be good and sound through and through – then it is sure to be classical.'

Thursday 23 October 1828

Goethe had warm words of praise today for a little essay that the Chancellor has written about the Grand Duke Karl August, in which he gives a concise account of the eventful life of this remarkable prince.

'This little piece has really come out very well,' said Goethe. 'He has assembled the material with great diligence and sensitivity, the whole thing is animated by the breath of a heartfelt love, and at the same time he has kept his account so concise and brief that it feels packed with action and incident, and the spectacle of such a busy life lived to the full almost makes our heads spin. The Chancellor sent his essay to Berlin, too, and a little while ago he received a most remarkable letter from Alexander von Humboldt in reply, which I could not read without deep emotion. Humboldt was a very close friend of the Grand Duke throughout his long life, which is not surprising, since the Duke's deep and well-stocked mind was always hungry for new knowledge, and Humboldt, with his extraordinary breadth of learning, was just the man to supply the best and most complete answer to every question.

'So it was a great blessing that the Grand Duke was able to spend the last few days before his death in Berlin with Humboldt almost constantly at his side, and that his friend was able to shed light on many important questions that weighed on his mind. And it was surely thanks to some higher, benevolent agency that one of the greatest princes Germany has ever known had a man like Humboldt to witness his final days and hours. I've had a copy made of the letter, and I will read some of it to you now.'

Goethe got up and went over to his desk, where he picked up the letter and then sat down again at the table with me. He read for a while in silence. I saw tears welling up in his eyes. 'Here, read it for yourself,' he said then, and handed me the letter. He stood up and paced up and down the room while I read.

Nobody could have been more shocked than myself at the sudden departure of the deceased [writes Humboldt]. For thirty years he had treated me with such kindly attention, and I venture to say, such sincere fondness. Even here, he wished to have me with him nearly the whole time; and it was as if this lucidity, like the evening light on the snow-capped peaks of the mighty Alps, were the harbinger of approaching darkness: never have I seen our great, compassionate prince more animated, more brilliant, more mellow and more deeply engaged with all aspects of his people's future than during those last few days when we had him here.

Full of anxious foreboding, I said more than once to my friends that this animation, this strange mental clarity, combined with such physical frailty, was to me a very alarming sign. He himself oscillated visibly between hopes of recovery and the expectation of the final hour.

When I saw him for the last time at breakfast, twenty-four hours before the end, ill and with no appetite for food, he was still questioning me earnestly – about the granite boulders from the Baltic countries that had come across from Sweden; about the possible clouding of our atmosphere by comet tails; about the cause of the severe winter cold on all east-facing coasts.

When I saw him for the last time he squeezed my hand as I was leaving and said brightly: 'Do you think, Humboldt, that Töplitz and all the other warm springs are like water that has been artificially heated? That doesn't come from any kitchen range! We'll argue about it in Töplitz, when you come with the King. You'll see – your old kitchen range will do the trick again and keep me going.' Strange! For with a man like him, nothing is insignificant.

In Potsdam I sat for several hours alone with him on the sofa; he drank and slept by turns, drank some more, got up to write to his consort, then slept again. He was cheerful, but completely drained. In the intervals he bombarded me with very difficult questions about physics, astronomy, meteorology and geognosy; about the transparency of a comet's nucleus, the moon's atmosphere, and coloured binary stars; about the influence of sunspots on temperature, the emergence of organic forms in the prehistoric world, and the internal heat of the earth. He fell asleep while either he or I was talking, often became restless, and then said, apologizing for his seeming inattention in the most gentle and kindly manner: 'As you see, Humboldt, it's all over with me!'

He suddenly began talking in a disjointed way about religious matters. He deplored the spread of pietism, and the links between this type of religious fanaticism and the political drift towards absolutism and the suppression of all free thought. 'They are devious fellows, too,' he exclaimed, 'who think they can ingratiate themselves with princes in this manner, in order to get positions and honours for themselves! They wormed their way in on the back of the poetic fashion for the Middle Ages.'

His anger soon abated, and he went on to say that he now found a great deal of solace in Christianity. 'It is a humane, compassionate doctrine,' he said, 'but it has been perverted from the outset. The first Christians were the freethinkers among the extremists.'

I intimated to Goethe how much pleasure this wonderful letter had given me. 'You can see,' said Goethe, 'what a special person he was. But how good it is of Humboldt to have recorded these last few vignettes, which really capture the essence of that most excellent prince's character! That's exactly what he was like – and I am in the best position to say, because nobody, ultimately, knew him as intimately as I did. But isn't it a great shame that death makes no distinctions, and that such a man must depart this life so soon, like the rest of us? Just one paltry century longer, and think how far, in his position of power, he would have advanced his age! But you know what? The world is not going to reach its goal as soon as we think or wish. The demons that slow us down are always there, interfering everywhere and getting in our way, so that while we are ultimately moving in the right direction, progress is very slow. As you get older, you'll find that I'm right.'

'The evolution of mankind,' I said, 'seems to be something that's measured in thousands of years.'

'Who knows,' replied Goethe, 'maybe millions! But however long the human race lasts, it will never lack for obstacles to make life difficult, or for trials of every kind to build up its strength. Men will become cleverer and wiser, but not better, happier, or more enterprising – or only at certain epochs in history. I can foresee a time when God no longer delights in man and has to destroy everything again to make a new creation. I am certain that everything is planned for this, and that the day and the hour have already been appointed in the distant future when this period of renewal will begin. But that time is a long way off, and we may have thousands and thousands of years yet to amuse ourselves on this dear old planet of ours.'

Goethe was in a particularly sunny and elated mood. He called for a bottle of wine to be brought in, and poured a glass for himself and me. We reverted to the subject of the Grand Duke Karl August.

'You can see,' said Goethe, 'how his extraordinary mind ranged over the whole realm of nature. Physics, astronomy, geognosy, meteorology, prehistoric plant and animal morphology, and everything else – he had a mind that was interested in all of it. He was eighteen when I first came to Weimar, but even then you could tell from the seeds and buds what the full-grown tree would look like. He soon became very attached to me and took a close interest in everything I did. It was good for our relationship that I was nearly ten years older than him. He used to sit with me for whole evenings, while we had deep discussions about art and nature, and all sorts of other interesting things. We often sat together far into the night, and there were quite a few times when we fell asleep next to each other on my sofa. We worked together for fifty years, so it wouldn't be surprising if in the end we managed to achieve something.'

'It must be a rare thing,' I said, 'for a prince to be as well educated as the Grand Duke seems to have been.'

'Very rare,' replied Goethe. 'Many of them can hold their own very well on any subject, but it doesn't come from any inner conviction, and they just scratch around on the surface. And it's not surprising, when you think about the dreadful distractions and diversions that come with life at court, and to which a young prince is exposed. He is expected to take notice of everything. He's expected to know a little bit of this, and a little bit of that, and then a little bit of something else besides. But none of it can really stick or take root, and it requires a powerful personality not to be crushed by such demands. But the Grand Duke was a natural – born for greatness: and that says it all.'

'For all his sophisticated scientific and intellectual interests,' I said, 'he seems to have understood the art of government as well.'

'He was all of a piece,' replied Goethe, 'and everything with him sprang from a single great source. And just as the whole was good, so were the individual parts – regardless of what he turned his hand to. Three things in particular proved helpful to him as a head of government. He was an excellent judge of intellect and character and knew where each man would be best placed. That was a great asset. But then he had something else, which was just as important, if not more so: he was animated by the noblest benevolence, the purest philanthropy, and he passionately desired only the best for others. He always thought about the good of the country first, and only then did he take a little thought for himself. He was always ready with open hand to help noble men and support good causes. There was more than a little of the divine in him. He would have liked to make the whole of mankind happy. But love begets love, and when a man is loved, he can govern others with ease.

'And thirdly: he was a greater man than those around him. If he heard ten people's opinions on a given matter, he heard an eleventh, and wiser, voice inside his own head. He paid no attention to malicious gossip, and he rarely demeaned himself by favouring some worthless nobody who'd been recommended to him over some deserving soul who'd been maligned. He saw for himself and judged for himself – and his own instincts were always the most reliable. He was a man of few words, but his words were always followed by actions.'

'It is such a regret to me,' I said, 'that I knew little more of him than the man you saw on the outside; but what I did see made a profound impression on me. I can still see him, in his old carriage, wearing his shabby grey coat and army cap, smoking a cigar, going off to hunt, with his favourite dogs trotting alongside. I've never seen him travelling in anything else but that unsightly old carriage, and never with more than two horses. A fancy turnout with six horses, and dress coats with gold stars and medals, seem not to have been his style.'

'That kind of thing,' replied Goethe, 'has rather gone out of fashion with princes in general. What matters now is what a man weighs in the scales of humanity; all the rest is empty show. A coat with a gold star and a carriage with six horses now impress nobody apart from the vulgar masses, if indeed it still impresses them. That old carriage of the Grand Duke's had almost parted company with its springs. If you took a drive with him, you had to put up with the most frightful bumps and jolts. But he didn't care. He liked things rough and uncomfortable, and he hated any form of cosseting.'

'You can see traces of that,' I said, 'in your poem "Ilmenau", where you seem to have portrayed him to the life.'

'He was very young at the time,' replied Goethe, 'but we certainly went a bit wild. He was like a fine wine, but still fermenting furiously. He didn't know what to do with all his energy, and we were often lucky not to break our necks. We wore ourselves out riding our hunters all day long, jumping hedges and ditches, fording rivers, up hill and down dale; then at night we would camp out under the stars, sometimes lighting a fire in the woods: that was just his kind of thing. Inheriting a dukedom meant nothing to him, but if he'd been able to get hold of one by hunting it down and taking it by storm – that would have been a different matter.

'The Ilmenau poem,' Goethe went on, 'revisits an episode from a time several years before I wrote it in 1783, so that I was able to portray myself in the poem as a historical figure, and conduct a dialogue with my own self from former years. There is a night-time scene in it, as you know, that might very well have followed such a day of reckless riding and hunting in the mountains. We had built some little shelters for ourselves at the foot of a rock and covered them with fir branches, so that we could sleep inside on the dry ground. In front of the shelters we had several fires burning, and we were cooking and roasting the game we had caught. Knebel, who even then smoked his pipe constantly, was sitting next to the fire and entertaining the company with all sorts of dry jokes, while the bottle of wine was passed from hand to hand. The slender Seckendorff, with his long, delicate limbs, was sprawled at the foot of a tree, humming all kinds of poetic stuff to himself. Off to one side, in a small shelter like the others, the Duke was sound asleep. I myself was sitting outside, watching the glowing embers, lost in sombre thoughts, and feeling pangs of regret about the harm

586   CONVERSATIONS WITH GOETHE

my writings had done. I still think I captured Knebel and Seckendorff pretty well, and likewise the young prince, in the sullen
impetuosity of his twentieth year:

> Adventure calls, enticing him to stray,
> No crag too steep, no plank too narrow seems;
> Mishap lies in wait, one false step away
> To cast him into torment's waiting arms.
> Unruly, restless, the impulse of his heart
> Drives him forth, to roam he knows not where;
> Moodily he wanders, discontent his part,
> Rest brings no relief, but only more despair.
> Sullen and morose, on days of sunny cheer,
> His wild and headstrong ways delight him not;
> In body bruised and broken, in spirits low and drear,
> He lays him down to sleep on a hard, unyielding cot.

And that's exactly how he was. I haven't exaggerated a single
detail. But the Duke soon worked through this *Sturm und
Drang* phase, and found a benevolent clarity of purpose; so I
felt it was all right to remind him of his earlier self on the occasion of his birthday in 1783.

'I won't deny that in the beginning he gave me a good deal of
trouble and a lot of worry. But his innate goodness soon got
him back on the straight and narrow, and he became a very fine
young man indeed, so that it was a joy to spend time with him
and work with him.'

'In those early days,' I remarked, 'you did a tour of Switzerland together, just the two of you.'

'He loved to travel,' replied Goethe, 'but it was not so much
about enjoyment and distraction, more about keeping his eyes
and ears open and noting anything good or useful that he could
introduce into his own country. Our agriculture, livestock
farming and industry owe him an enormous debt in consequence. His inclinations in general were not personal or selfish,
but purely productive – and productive for the general good.
As a result, he has acquired a reputation that extends far
beyond the borders of this small country.'

'His simple, carefree exterior,' I observed, 'seemed to suggest that he didn't seek fame, and didn't attach much importance to it, either. It seems that he became famous without any conscious effort on his part, simply because of his quiet good work.'

'It's a curious thing,' replied Goethe. 'A log burns because it already contains what is needful; and a man becomes famous because he already has what is needful inside him. Fame cannot be sought, and chasing after it is a futile exercise. A person may, by clever manoeuvring and all manner of artifice, make a name for himself of sorts. But if he lacks natural charisma it will all be a waste of effort, because his fame won't last beyond the first day.

'It's just the same with the affection of the people. He did not seek it, and he certainly didn't butter people up. But the people loved him, because they felt that he really cared about them.'

Goethe then went on to talk about the other members of the Grand Duke's family, and how they were all distinguished by their nobility of character. He spoke about the kind-heartedness of the present Regent, about the great hopes that people had of the young Prince; and he dwelled with evident affection on the rare qualities of the reigning Grand Duchess, who was investing large amounts of resources in her well-intentioned efforts to alleviate suffering and foster good works. 'She has always been a guardian angel to the country,' he said, 'and she is becoming more and more so, the longer her connection with it lasts. I have known the Grand Duchess since 1805, and have had plenty of occasions to admire her mind and character. She is one of the best and most distinguished women of our time, and would still be so if she were not a sovereign. And that's what counts: that even when the purple has been laid aside, much that is great – the very best, in fact – still remains.'

We then talked about German unification, and in what sense it was possible or desirable.

'I have no fears,' said Goethe, 'for the future unity of Germany; our good roads, and in due course the railways, will help to bring that about. But above all, may it be united in love between Germans, and united always against foreign enemies. May it be united in the sense that the German coinage has the same value throughout the empire; united in the sense that my travelling trunk can pass through all thirty-six states without being opened. May it be united in the sense that the municipal passport of a Weimar citizen will not be rejected by the border official of a large neighbouring state on the grounds that it is a *foreigner's* passport. May we cease to distinguish between "domestic" and "foreign" within the union of German states. May Germany be unified in its weights and measures, its trade and commerce, and in a host of other things too numerous to mention.

'But it would be a mistake to think that the unity of Germany depends on this great empire having a single great capital city, and that this one great city would be good both for the development of talented individuals and for the welfare of the population at large.

'A state has been compared to a living body with many limbs, and so the capital city of a state could be compared to the heart, from which life and well-being flow out into the individual limbs, near and far. But where the limbs are a long way from the heart, the life that flows out to them feels increasingly weak with distance. An ingenious Frenchman – I think it was Dupin – drew a map of France's cultural condition, using lighter or darker colours to indicate the varying degrees of enlightenment in the different *départements*. Now there are some *départements*, especially in parts of the south, a long way removed from the capital, which are coloured in black, to show how utterly benighted they are down there. But would that be the case, I wonder, if *la belle France*, instead of *one* great national centre, had *ten* regional centres from which light and life emanated?

'What has made Germany great is its admirable popular culture, which has spread throughout every part of the land. But where does it come from, if not from the regional royal courts, which promote and nurture it? Supposing, for centuries past, Germany had had only the two royal seats, Vienna and Berlin, or indeed only one: I'd like to see where our German culture would be then, not to mention our economy and general prosperity, which go hand in hand with culture.

'Germany has over twenty universities spread across the whole land, and over a hundred public libraries similarly dispersed; likewise a large number of art collections and scientific collections. This is because every prince has taken care to surround himself with beautiful and useful objects of this kind. We have an abundance of grammar schools and schools of technology and industry; there is hardly a village in Germany that doesn't have its own school – which is a lot more than can be said of France!

'And then there is the quantity of German theatres, more than seventy of them, which have played no small part in raising cultural standards among the general population. In no other country is the love of music and singing and music-making so widespread as it is in Germany – and that is also quite something!

'Think, too, of cities like Dresden, Munich, Stuttgart, Kassel, Braunschweig, Hanover and the like; think of the seminal cultural and social influences coming out of these cities, and the impact they have on the surrounding region; and ask yourself if this would be the case if they had not been, historically, places of royal residence.

'Frankfurt, Bremen, Hamburg and Lübeck are great and magnificent cities, and their effect on Germany's prosperity is incalculable. But would they still be what they are today if they were to lose their sovereign status, and be incorporated into some great German empire as provincial cities? I am inclined to doubt it.'

Wednesday 3 December 1828*

Today Goethe and I had some fun of a rather unusual kind. Madame Duval, from Cartigny in the canton of Geneva, who is a very skilled jam-maker, had sent me a few candied citrons for the Grand Duchess and Goethe as samples of her art, quite convinced that *her* jams are as superior to all others as Goethe's poems are to those of most of his German contemporaries.

Since the eldest daughter of this lady had long desired to obtain Goethe's autograph, I now hit upon the ingenious idea of enticing Goethe to write a poem for my young friend by using the sweet citrons as bait.

Adopting the air of a diplomat charged with some important mission, I went to him and negotiated with him as one power with another, stipulating that the proffered citrons would be handed over in return for an original poem in his own hand. Goethe laughed at this joke, which he took in very good part, and immediately asked for the citrons, which he found to be excellent. A few hours later, I was very surprised to see the following verses arrive as a Christmas present for my young friend:

> O happy land, where citrons grow,
> To perfect ripeness, as we know!
> Where clever women them do sweeten,
> For our pleasure to be eaten! etc.

When I next saw him, he joked about the new-found perks of his poetic calling, when as a young man he couldn't even find a publisher for his *Götz*. 'I'm fully signed up to your trade treaty,' he said. 'When my citrons have all been eaten, don't forget to order some more; I shall pay promptly with my poetic currency.'

Sunday 21 December 1828

Last night I had a curious dream, which I told to Goethe this evening, and he was very taken with it. I saw myself in a strange city, on a broad street looking towards the south-east, where I was standing with a crowd of people and gazing up at the sky, which seemed to be shrouded in a light mist and bathed in a bright yellow light. Everyone was waiting expectantly to see what would happen next, when two fiery dots appeared, which smashed into the ground like meteorites, not far from where we were standing. We all rushed over to see what had come down, and lo and behold, there were Faust and Mephistopheles, coming towards me. I was at once delighted and astonished, and joined them as if they were old friends; we walked along together, conversing cheerily, and turned the corner at the next street. I don't remember what we were talking about; but the impression of their physical presence and appearance was so vivid that it is still perfectly clear in my mind, and not easily forgotten. Both of them were younger than we normally think of them; Mephistopheles might have been about twenty-one, while Faust could have been twenty-seven. The former looked very distinguished, serene and relaxed; he tripped along with a light step, like some latter-day Mercury. His face was handsome, devoid of malice, and it would have been hard to tell that he was the devil, were it not for the two dainty horns that sprouted from his youthful brow and curved away to the sides, rather as a fine head of hair grows upwards and sweeps back in a wave on either side. When Faust turned his face towards me as we walked and talked, I was astonished by his distinctive expression. The finest moral sensibility and kind-heartedness spoke from every feature as the defining quality, the essence, of his personality. It seemed as though all human joys, sorrows and thoughts had already passed through his soul, despite his youth – so careworn was his face. He looked a little pale, and so attractive that I couldn't take my eyes off him. I tried to memorize his features so that I could draw them. Faust was walking on the right, Mephistopheles was between us, and the abiding impression I have is of Faust turning his handsome and striking face to speak to Mephistopheles or myself. We walked on through the streets, and the crowd dispersed without taking any further notice of us.

1830

Monday 18 January 1830*

Goethe talked about Lavater, and had much good to say about his character. He also told me things about their early, very close friendship, and how in those days they often slept in the same bed, like a pair of brothers. 'It's a pity,' he added, 'that the wings of his genius were clipped so early on by a half-baked mysticism!'

Friday 22 January 1830*

We discussed Walter Scott's *Life of Napoleon.*

'It is true,' said Goethe, 'that one can accuse the author of serious inaccuracies and blatant partiality; but in my eyes these very shortcomings give his work its special value. The book was a sensational success in England, so one can see that it was Walter Scott's hatred of Napoleon and the French that made him the true spokesman and representative of English popular opinion and English national sentiment. His book tells us more about the history of England than it does about the history of France. At all events, his is a voice that needed to be heard in this important historical debate.

'I like to hear conflicting opinions about Napoleon. I'm currently reading Bignon's *Histoire*, which seems to me very good indeed.'

Monday 25 January 1830 *

I brought Goethe the lists of the late Dumont's writings, which I had catalogued in preparation for a published edition of his works. Goethe read them with close attention, and seemed astonished by the vast quantity of knowledge, interests and ideas that must have been required to produce such substantial manuscripts on so many different subjects.

'Dumont,' he said, 'must have been a man of very broad intellect. Among the subjects he discusses there is not a single one that is not interesting and important in itself; and the subjects a man chooses to write about always show what kind of man he is. You can't expect the human mind to be so universal that it can treat every subject with equal talent and success; but even if the author hasn't succeeded equally well with all of them, the very fact that he wanted to write about them gives me a very high opinion of him. I am particularly impressed by his practical, helpful and sympathetic attitude.'

I had also brought the first chapter of the *Travels to Paris*, which I had planned to read to him, but he preferred to look at it by himself.

He then joked about the difficulty of reading, and about the arrogance of the many people who think they can just pick up any work of philosophy or science and read it like a novel, without any kind of previous knowledge or study.

'These poor souls,' he went on, 'have no idea how much time and effort it takes to *learn how to read*. I've been working at it for eighty years, and I'm still learning.'

Wednesday 27 January 1830

Dined most enjoyably with Goethe today. He spoke with great approval of Herr von Martius. 'His discovery of the spiral tendency,' he said, 'is of the utmost importance. I do wish he would have the courage of his convictions, though: having discovered this primary phenomenon, he should not hold back, but boldly proclaim an observed fact as a law, instead of casting around everywhere for confirmation.'

He then showed me the proceedings of the meeting of natural scientists in Heidelberg, with facsimiles of their handwriting printed at the end. We studied these and tried to work out what they told us about the character of the writer.

'I know very well,' said Goethe, 'that these meetings don't do as much as one might suppose to advance the cause of science; but what *is* very good about them is that people get to know each other, and quite possibly learn to like each other – which means that one will accept some new theory from a distinguished colleague, while he in turn will be inclined to acknowledge and encourage us in our own endeavours in some other field. At all events, we get to see what is happening in science – and who knows what might come of it?'

Goethe then showed me a letter from an English author, addressed to 'His Serene Highness, Prince Goethe'. 'I dare say I've got German journalists to thank for this title,' said Goethe with a laugh. 'In their overenthusiasm they probably called me "the prince of German poets", and so the innocent German mistake led the Englishman to make an equally innocent mistake.'

Goethe then returned to Herr von Martius, and praised him as a man of imagination. 'In the end,' he said, 'you can't be a really great natural scientist without this special gift. And I don't just mean the kind of imagination that goes off on flights of fancy and imagines things that don't exist; I'm talking about the sort that stays firmly planted on the ground, and uses the yardstick of the real and the known to explore things that are merely sensed and surmised. In this way it can tell whether the thing sensed is also possible, and whether or not it conflicts with other known laws. Of course, such an imagination does presuppose an expansive and calm mind, capable of taking a broad overview of the living world and its laws.'

As we were talking, a package arrived with a Czech translation of *Die Geschwister*, which seemed to give Goethe a great deal of pleasure.

1830   595

Sunday 31 January 1830 *

Called on Goethe, accompanied by the Prince. He received us in his study.

We talked about the various editions of his works, and I was surprised to hear him say that he himself did not possess copies of most of them. He didn't even have the first edition of his *Roman Carnival*, with engravings after his own original drawings. He said he had bid six thalers for it at an auction, but had failed to win it.

He then showed us the first manuscript of his *Götz von Berlichingen*, in its completely original form, as written down in a few weeks, more than fifty years ago, at the urging of his sister. The fine strokes of his handwriting already had that free, clear quality that always characterized his German script in later years, as it still does. The manuscript was very clean, and there were whole pages without a single correction, so that it looked more like a later copy than a first rough draft.

Goethe's earliest works, as he now told us, were all written in his own hand, including his *Werther*, the manuscript of which has gone missing. In later years, however, he dictated almost everything, and the only things he wrote out himself were poems and hastily sketched outlines. In many cases he didn't think to get a copy made of some new work; instead, he often took a risk with his most precious texts, more than once sending the only copy he possessed to the printer's in Stuttgart.

When we had finished studying the *Berlichingen* manuscript, Goethe showed us the original of his *Italienische Reise*. The handwriting in these observations and notes, recorded on a daily basis, exhibits the same fine qualities as in his *Götz* manuscript. Every stroke is bold, firm and confident; there are no corrections, and one can tell that the writer was making these notes when the details were still fresh and clear in his mind. The only thing that changes is the paper, which varies in colour and format with each town where the traveller happened to be staying.

Towards the end of this manuscript there was a jaunty little pen-and-ink drawing dashed off by Goethe, which showed an

Italian lawyer addressing the court in his full judicial robes. He was the most exotic creature imaginable, and his attire was so striking that one might well suppose he had donned fancy dress to go to a masquerade. And yet the whole scene was an accurate representation of real life. With his index finger resting on the tip of his thumb and the rest of his fingers outstretched, the portly orator was clearly in his element, and this dainty gesture accorded well with the large periwig that graced his pate.

Wednesday 3 February 1830*

We talked about *Le Globe* and *Le Temps*, and this led us on to the subject of French literature and writers.

'Guizot,' said Goethe at one point, 'is a man after my own heart – sound and rock-solid. He has a great depth of knowledge, combined with an enlightened liberalism that is completely non-partisan and knows its own mind. I look forward to seeing what role he will play in the Chambers, to which he has just been elected.'

'People who appear to have just a passing acquaintance with him,' I replied, 'have told me he is rather pedantic.'

'It all depends,' countered Goethe, 'what sort of pedantry these people are talking about. All eminent men who live a life of regular routine according to fixed principles, who have reflected deeply and treat life as a serious business, can very easily be taken for pedants by superficial observers. Unlike his mercurial compatriots, Guizot is a far-sighted, calm and dependable man, who cannot be too highly regarded on that account and who is just the kind of man the French need.

'Villemain,' Goethe went on, 'is perhaps the more brilliant speaker; he has a knack for developing a subject clearly, starting from the basics; he is never at a loss for telling turns of phrase that hold the attention of his listeners and rouse them to loud applause; but he is far more superficial than Guizot, and far less practical.

'As for Cousin, he does not have a great deal to say to us Germans, in that the philosophy which he is introducing to his countrymen for the first time is something we have been familiar with for many years. But for the French he is a very important figure, who will point them in an entirely new direction.

'Cuvier, the great naturalist, is to be admired for his powers of exposition and his style. Nobody is better at explaining something than him. But he has almost no philosophy. He will turn out students who are very well informed, but there will be few deep thinkers among them.'

It was especially interesting to me to hear all this, as it coincided very closely with Dumont's views on the men in question. I promised Goethe that I would copy out the relevant passages from Dumont's manuscripts, so that he could compare them at some point with his own views.

The mention of Dumont brought us on to the subject of his relationship with Bentham, prompting the following observation from Goethe:

'It's a real mystery to me,' he said, 'how a rational, reasonable and practical man like Dumont could have become the disciple and loyal devotee of a fool like Bentham.'

'In a manner of speaking,' I replied, 'Bentham was really two persons in one. I would distinguish between Bentham the genius, who devised the principles that Dumont rescued from oblivion by developing and elaborating them; and Bentham the passionate enthusiast, who, in his obsession with utility, overstepped the limits of his own theory and became a radical in both politics and religion.'

'But that's something else I find mystifying,' replied Goethe, 'the idea that an old man can end the career of a long lifetime by becoming a radical in his last days.'

I tried to resolve this contradiction by arguing that Bentham, convinced of the merits of his theory and his principles of legislation, and given the impossibility of introducing them without a complete change in England's system of government, was more apt to let himself be carried away by his passionate zeal because he had little contact with the outside world and was not in a position to judge the danger of a violent revolution.

'Dumont, on the other hand,' I went on, 'who is less passionate and more clear-sighted, never approved of Bentham's extremism, and was never going to make the same mistake himself. He also had the advantage of applying Bentham's principles in a country that could almost be regarded as *new* at that time, following recent political events – namely, Geneva; and there the experiment was very successful and showed the value of those principles.'

'Dumont,' replied Goethe, 'is just a moderate liberal, as all sensible people are and should be, and as I am myself. I have tried to act in that spirit throughout the course of a long life.

'The true liberal,' he went on, 'seeks to do as much good as he can with the means at his disposal; but he knows better than to try and eradicate the often unavoidable ills by immediate recourse to fire and sword. He endeavours to eliminate failings in public life gradually, through careful, considered action, without taking forcible measures that often do more harm than good. This is an imperfect world, and he contents himself with the good until time and circumstances enable him to achieve something better.'

Saturday 6 February 1830

Dined with Frau von Goethe. Goethe's son regaled us with some nice stories about his grandmother, Frau Goethe, who lived in Frankfurt. He had visited her as a student, twenty years earlier, and one day they had been invited to dine with the Prince Primate.

Apparently the Prince had come out to greet Frau Goethe on the steps as a special courtesy; but as he was wearing his normal ecclesiastical robes she had taken him for some abbé and paid him little regard. And, seated next to him at table, she did her best to ignore him at first. But in the course of the conversation it had gradually dawned on her, from the way the other guests were behaving, that he was the Prince Primate.

The Prince then proposed a toast to Frau Goethe and her son, whereupon she rose to her feet and drank to the health of His Highness.

Wednesday 10 February 1830*

After dinner today I stayed behind a moment with Goethe. He was looking forward to the approaching spring, and the days getting longer again. We then talked about his theory of colour. He seemed doubtful about the possibility of making any headway with his simple theory. 'The errors of my opponents,' he said, 'have gained too much currency for a century now, for me to have any hope of finding the odd travelling companion on my solitary path. I shall always be a lone figure. I often feel like a shipwrecked man, who grabs hold of a plank that can only carry one person. This man survives, while all the other poor wretches are drowned.'

Sunday 14 February 1830*

Today was a day of mourning for Weimar: the Grand Duchess Luise died at half past one this afternoon. The reigning Grand Duchess instructed me to pay a visit of condolence on her behalf to Fräulein von Waldner and Goethe.

I went first to Fräulein von Waldner. I found her in tears, quite overcome by grief and the sense of her loss. 'I was in the service of the late Princess for more than fifty years,' she said. 'I was her own personal choice to be her lady-in-waiting – and that has been my pride and my joy ever since. I left my native land to devote my life to her service. I wish she had taken me with her now, so that I would not have so long to pine for a reunion with her!'

I then called on Goethe. How different things were with him! He felt the loss he had suffered no less keenly, for sure, but he seemed determined at all costs to master his own feelings. I found him still sitting at table with a good friend, drinking a bottle of wine. He was talking animatedly and seemed to be altogether in a very cheerful mood. 'Now then,' he said when he saw me, 'come and join us, take a seat! The blow that we have long been dreading has finally fallen, and at least we no longer have to contend with cruel uncertainty. Now it's a matter of getting back to the business of living again.'

'Those are your comforters,' I said, pointing to his papers. 'Work is a wonderful way to pick ourselves up again in times of trouble.'

'As long as it is still day,' returned Goethe, 'we will keep our chin up, and as long as we can still produce something, we will not weary.'

He then talked about individuals who had reached a ripe old age, and mentioned the celebrated Ninon. 'In her ninetieth year,' he said, 'she was still young; but she also understood how to maintain her composure, and didn't set too much store by the things of this earth. Even death she refused to take very seriously. When she was recovering from a serious illness in her eighteenth year, and those at her bedside were describing the danger she had been in, she said quite calmly: "What is death, after all? I would have left only mortals behind me." She lived for another seventy years or more, a charming and much-loved woman who enjoyed life to the full while always keeping herself aloof, with that characteristic equanimity of hers, from every consuming passion. Ninon had the right idea! There aren't many who can say the same.'

He then handed me a letter from the King of Bavaria which arrived today, and which had doubtless contributed in no small measure to his cheery mood. 'Read it,' he said. 'You must admit that the kindness which the King continues to show me, and the lively interest he takes in the progress of literature and the advancement of human civilization, are exceedingly gratifying. And to think that the letter arrived today, of all days! I thank heaven for this special blessing.'

We then talked about the theatre and dramatic poetry. 'Gozzi claimed,' said Goethe, 'that there are only thirty-six tragic situations in the world. Schiller did his best to find more, but never managed to find even as many as Gozzi.'

This led us on to an article in *Le Globe*, a critical review of Arnault's *Gustave-Adolphe*. Goethe very much liked the reviewer's approach and was full of praise for the piece. The writer had contented himself with identifying all the author's antecedents, without otherwise attacking the author himself or his poetic principles. 'The critic for *Le Temps*,' Goethe added, 'was not so well advised. He presumes to tell the writer how he should have done things differently. This is a big mistake; you don't make anybody a better writer that way. In fact, there is nothing more stupid than telling a writer: "You should have done this bit like this, and that bit like that." I speak from long experience. You'll never make a writer anything other than what nature intended. If you try to force him to be someone else, you'll destroy him.

'As I said, my friends, the gentlemen at the *Globe* have taken a very shrewd line. They print a long list of all the commonplaces that M. Arnault has borrowed from here, there and everywhere. And by doing this they have neatly contrived to indicate the trap that the author will need to avoid in future. It is almost impossible to find a situation today that is wholly new. Only the writer's perspective on it, and the way it is treated and portrayed, can be new. And here one has to be especially careful to avoid imitation.'

Goethe then told us how Gozzi had set up his Teatro dell'Arte in Venice, and how his company of improvisers had been so popular. He said: 'I saw two actresses from that company in Venice, in particular the one playing Brighella, and I attended performances of several such improvised pieces. The effect produced by these people was extraordinary.'

Goethe then talked about the Neapolitan figure of Pulcinella. 'One of the favourite gags of this character from low comedy,' he said, 'was sometimes to pretend that he had completely forgotten he was on stage, playing a part. He made as if he had just got home from the theatre, talking intimately with his family and telling them about the play he had just been performing in, and another one he was about to do; and he was quite relaxed about letting small bodily needs vent themselves freely. "But, dear husband," his wife would then exclaim, "you seem to forget yourself entirely; think of the esteemed company before whom you stand!" "*E vero! E vero!*" replied Pulcinella, recollecting himself; and then he would slip back into his former role, to rousing applause from the audience. The theatre of Pulcinella has such a reputation that no person of quality would ever boast of having been there. Women, as you can imagine, never go there at all; it is only frequented by men.

'Pulcinella generally functions as a kind of walking newspaper. Anything remarkable that has happened in Naples during the day will be reported by him at the evening performance. His focus on matters of local interest, coupled with his use of vulgar dialect, means that it is virtually impossible for a foreigner to understand him.'

Goethe led the conversation round to other memories from his earlier years. He spoke about his distrust of paper money, and what sort of experiences he had had in that regard. To underline the point he related an anecdote of Grimm's from the time of the French Revolution, when the latter, no longer believing that Paris was safe, moved back to Germany and made his home in Gotha.

'We were dining with Grimm one day,' said Goethe. 'I don't recall how the subject came up, but Grimm suddenly exclaimed: "I wager that no monarch in Europe possesses a finer pair of ruffles than mine, and that none of them has paid such a high price for them as I did." As you can imagine, we all voiced our incredulous astonishment at this, especially the ladies, and were very curious to see such a prodigious pair of ruffles. So Grimm rose to his feet and fetched a pair of lace ruffles of such magnificence from his cabinet that we all burst into cries of amazement. We tried to guess how much they had cost, but thought it couldn't be more than a hundred to two hundred louis d'or. Grimm laughed, and exclaimed: "You are way off the mark! I paid *twice a hundred and fifty thousand francs* for them, and was lucky to have invested my *assignats* so well.[28] The next day they were worthless."'

Monday 15 February 1830 *

I called in briefly on Goethe this morning to enquire after his health on behalf of the Grand Duchess. I found him in sombre and thoughtful mood, with no hint of yesterday's slightly manic excitement. Today he seemed to feel deeply the void that death had left in his life, after a friendship that had lasted fifty years. 'I must work furiously,' he said, 'to keep my spirits up and resign myself to this sudden separation. Death is something so strange that, contrary to all experience, we think it cannot happen to someone near and dear to us, and so it always comes as something unbelievable and unexpected. If you like, it's an impossibility that suddenly becomes a reality. And this transition, from an existence we know to another of which we know nothing, is something so violent that it is bound to come as a profound shock to those left behind.'

Friday 5 March 1830*

Fräulein von Türckheim, a close relative of Goethe's youthful amour, had been in Weimar for a while. Today I said to Goethe that I was sorry she had left. 'She is so young,' I said, 'and shows a high-mindedness and a mental maturity that one seldom finds in someone of her age. She made a big impression when she arrived here in Weimar. If she had stayed longer, she might well have broken a few hearts.'

'I very much regret,' replied Goethe, 'that I didn't see more of her, and kept on putting off inviting her to begin with, so that I could talk to her quietly on my own and rediscover in her the beloved features of her relative.

'The fourth volume of *Dichtung und Wahrheit*,' he went on, 'where you'll find related the tale of happiness and woe of my love for Lili, has been finished for some time now. I would have written it and published it much earlier, had I not been held back by certain delicate considerations – not for myself, but for my beloved, who was still living at the time. I would have been proud to tell the whole world how much I loved her, and I fancy she would not have blushed to admit that my feelings were reciprocated. But did I have the right to publish the story without her consent? I always intended to ask her; but I kept on delaying, until in the end it was no longer necessary.

'Hearing you talk so warmly,' Goethe went on, 'about the charming girl who has just left us has reawakened all my old memories. I see the delightful Lili before me again, full of life and fun, and it's as if I could feel the aura of her enchanting presence once more. She really was my first true love. I can also say that she was the last; all the little attachments that have come my way later in life were just frivolous and superficial compared with that first one.

'I have never,' Goethe went on, 'been closer to true happiness than in the time of my love for Lili. The obstacles that kept us apart were not ultimately insurmountable – and yet I lost her anyway!

'There was something so delicate and special about my affection for her that it influenced my style when I came to write about that painfully happy time in my life. When you read the fourth volume of *Dichtung und Wahrheit* at some point, you will find that this love is quite different from the love described in novels.'

'The same thing,' I replied, 'could be said of your love for Gretchen and Friederike. The portrayal of both is likewise so fresh and original, unlike anything the novelists invent or imagine. This would seem to derive from the great truthfulness of the writer, who has not tried to hide what happened in order to cast himself in a better light, and who has steered clear of all sentimental rhetoric when a straightforward account of events sufficed.

'And love itself,' I added, 'is never the same. It is always original and always different, depending on the character and personality of the one we love.'

'You are absolutely right,' said Goethe, 'because love is not just about *us*, but also about the loved one to whom we are attracted. And then there's a powerful third factor we must not forget, namely the daemonic, which generally accompanies any strong passion and finds its true element in love. It was very much at work in my relationship with Lili, and gave a whole new direction to my life. It is no exaggeration to say that my move to Weimar, and my life here now, were a direct consequence of that.'

Saturday 6 March 1830*

For some time now Goethe has been reading the *Mémoires* of Saint-Simon.

'I have stopped at the death of Louis XIV,' he told me a few days ago. 'Up until that point I had found the dozen volumes really fascinating for the way they show the contrast between the intentions of the ruler and the aristocratic virtue of the servant. But from the moment when that monarch departs this life, and another personage comes on the scene who is too awful for Saint-Simon to appear to advantage alongside him, I didn't want to go on reading. I felt a kind of distaste, and I left the book at the point where the "tyrant" left me.'

Goethe also stopped reading *Le Globe* and *Le Temps* about two weeks ago, having read them with great enthusiasm for several months. As the new issues arrive from the publisher in their paper wrappers, he lays them aside unopened. Meanwhile he is asking his friends to tell him what is happening in the world. He has been very productive for some time now, completely immersed in the second part of his *Faust*. The 'Classical Walpurgis Night' in particular has occupied all his attention for the last few weeks and has expanded rapidly in consequence. In these periods of intensive productivity Goethe doesn't like to read at all, unless it is light reading, which serves as welcome relaxation, or else something related to the work he is doing, which could be useful to him. He avoids at all costs anything weighty and stimulating, which might divert his attention and distract him from getting on with his own work. And at the moment, *Le Globe* and *Le Temps* would appear to fall into this category. 'I see,' he said, 'that significant events are brewing in Paris, and we are on the eve of a great explosion. But as I am powerless to influence these things, I shall quietly await the outcome, and not get unnecessarily agitated by following the drama as it unfolds day by day. So I am not reading *Le Globe* or *Le Temps* at the moment, and my "Walpurgis Night" is making good progress as a result.'

He then talked about the current state of French literature, which is something that interests him greatly. 'What the French think is new,' he said, 'about the present literary trend in France is really nothing more than the reflection of what German literature has been successfully trying to do for the last fifty years. The germ of these historical dramas that are now a novelty for them can be found in my *Götz*, written half a century ago. Not that German authors,' he added, 'have ever deliberately set out to influence the French. I myself have always written only for a German audience, and it has only lately occurred to me to direct my gaze westwards, to see what our neighbours beyond the Rhine make of me. Even so, they have no influence on my work. And even Wieland, who imitated French forms and styles, was always a German at heart and wouldn't come across well in a translation.'

Sunday 14 March 1830

Spent the evening at Goethe's. He showed me all the treasures from the crate sent by David, which I had found him unpacking a few days earlier and which had now been properly sorted. The plaster medallions with profiles of France's best young writers had been carefully arranged in order on tables. He talked again about David's extraordinary talent, which excelled equally in conception and in execution. He also showed me a quantity of books – the latest works from the foremost writers of the romantic school, sent by their authors as gifts through the intermediary of David. I noted works by Sainte-Beuve, Ballanche, Victor Hugo, Balzac, Alfred de Vigny, Jules Janin and others.

'This consignment of David's,' he said, 'has given me days of enjoyment. I have spent the whole week reading these young writers, and they have given me a new lease of life through all the fresh impressions I get from them. I shall make a separate catalogue of these precious portraits and books and give them both a special place in my art collection and library.' It was obvious that Goethe was deeply gratified by this homage from the young poets of France.

He then read some passages from the *Études* of Émile Deschamps. He praised the translation of 'Die Braut von Korinth' for its accuracy and felicity. 'I possess the manuscript,' he said, 'of an Italian translation of this poem, which reproduces the original right down to the verse metre.'

Mention of 'Die Braut von Korinth' prompted Goethe to talk about his other ballads, too. 'I owe most of them to Schiller,' he said, 'who encouraged me to write them because he always needed something new for his *Horen*. I'd had them all in my head for many years, running through my mind as charming images, delightful dreams, which came and went; and I really enjoyed playing with these things in my imagination. So it was hard to say goodbye to these shining apparitions, my friends for so long, by embodying them in words – poor, inadequate words. When I saw them set down on paper I contemplated them with mixed feelings of sadness; it was as if I were parting for ever from a very dear friend.

'At other times,' Goethe went on, 'my poems came about in very different ways. I would have no ideas beforehand and no intimation; they just came over me, all of a sudden, and had to be written straightaway, so that I felt driven to set them down there and then, following my instinct, as if in a dream. In this trance-like state it often happened that the piece of paper in front of me was lying on the skew, and I only noticed this when I had finished writing, or when I ran out of space to write anything more. I used to have several such sheets, where the writing ran diagonally across the page; but they have gradually gone missing over time, so I'm afraid I can't show you any examples of my complete absorption in poetic composition.'

The conversation then reverted to French literature, and to the very latest ultra-romantic tendency of certain quite prominent writers. Goethe took the view that this emerging poetic revolution was very good for literature as such, but damaging for the individual writers who were working to bring it about.

'In any revolution,' he said, 'you can't avoid the extremes. Most political revolutions start from a simple desire to abolish abuses of one sort or another; but before you know it you are knee-deep in bloodshed and atrocities. Similarly, when the French embarked on their present literary revolution, all they wanted was greater freedom of form; but now they are not stopping at that, and along with the form they are rejecting the old content as well. They are starting to dismiss the representation of noble sentiments and deeds as boring, and are experimenting with the portrayal of all sorts of abominations. Instead of the beautiful subject matter of Greek mythology we have devils, witches and vampires, and the sublime heroes of antiquity must give way to crooks and galley slaves. This is racy stuff, and it goes down well. But once the public has sampled this highly seasoned dish and acquired a taste for it, it will always want more, and stronger fare at that. A young man of talent who wants to make a name for himself, but is not original enough to plough his own furrow, must follow the contemporary literary fashion, and indeed must seek to outdo his predecessors in shock and horror. But in chasing after superficial effects, any deeper study, and any gradual and painstaking development of the talent and the man from within, are completely neglected. And that is the worst thing that can happen to a talent – even though literature in general will benefit from this present trend.'

'But how,' I asked, 'can an endeavour that ruins individual talents be good for literature in general?'

'The extremes and abuses I have described,' replied Goethe, 'will gradually disappear, but one very great advantage will remain: alongside a greater freedom of form, we will also have achieved a greater richness and diversity of content, and no longer will any subject in the whole wide world, and in all of human life, be ruled out as unpoetic. The present literary epoch is like a state of high fever, which is not good or desirable in itself, but is the precursor to happier, healthier times. The really unsavoury stuff, which now often constitutes the entire content of a poetic work, will in future just be one useful element in the mix; and the pure and the noble, which are currently banished, will be sought out again with renewed appetite.'

'I can't help noticing,' I remarked, 'that even Mérimée, who is one of your favourites, has also gone down that ultra-romantic route with his *Guzla* collection and its barbarous subject matter.'[29]

'Mérimée,' replied Goethe, 'treated these things quite differently from his contemporaries. These poems have their fair share of nightmarish motifs, certainly: graveyards, crossroads at dead of night, ghosts and vampires. But none of these horrors touches the innate character of the poet; instead, he treats them with a certain objective distance, or even irony, if you like. He goes about it like an artist who just fancies trying his hand at this kind of stuff for once. As I say: he acted completely out of character, and even denied his character as a Frenchman – so successfully, in fact, that people initially thought these *Guzla*

1830

poems were genuine Illyrian folk ballads. So he very nearly pulled off the intended literary hoax.

'Mérimée,' Goethe went on, 'is a force to be reckoned with. And it takes more strength and genius to treat a subject objectively than people think. Byron, too, despite his very dominant personality, sometimes found the strength to deny himself completely, as we can see from some of his dramatic pieces, and especially his *Marino Faliero*. In that play you completely forget that it was written by Byron, or indeed by an Englishman at all; we become Venetians, living in Venice at the time when the action takes place. The characters speak entirely from their own point of view and their own situation; nothing about them reflects the subjective feelings, thoughts and opinions of the writer. Now that's the way to do it! You can't say the same for our young French romantics of the extreme variety. Everything I've read of theirs – poems, novels, dramatic works – has been coloured by the author's personality, and none of it ever made me forget that it was written by a Parisian and a Frenchman. Even when their work is set in some foreign land, you are still in France, in Paris, completely embroiled in the desires, needs, conflicts and turmoils of the present day.'

'Even Béranger,' I ventured, 'has only ever written about life in the great capital, and about his own innermost thoughts.'

'Well, he's the man for it,' replied Goethe, 'because his powers of description and his innermost thoughts are worth something. He has all the substance of an important personality. Béranger is a man blessed with many gifts; secure in his own identity, his own man in every way, and completely comfortable in his own skin. He has never asked: "What is fashionable?", "What is popular?", "What will please the public?", or "What are others doing?", so that he can copy them. He has always written only what was in his own heart and mind, without worrying about what the public, or this or that faction, expects. There have indeed been critical times when he has listened to the mood, the wishes and the needs of the people; but that has only confirmed his own instincts by showing him that his thinking was in tune with popular sentiment. It has never misled him into saying anything other than what was already in his own heart.

'As you know, I don't normally have much time for so-called "political" poems; but I don't mind the sort that Béranger wrote. With him, nothing is simply plucked out of the air, and he doesn't deal in imagined or imaginary interests; he never shoots blindly, but always has very specific, and important, subjects in his sights. His affectionate admiration for Napoleon and his reminiscences of the great feats of arms that were accomplished under him, at a time when such memories were a comfort to the rather despondent French; and then his hatred of clerical rule, and of the darkness that threatened to return with the Jesuits: these are things of which we must surely approve wholeheartedly. And how masterly is his treatment of every subject! How he turns it over in his mind and works it into shape before he puts it into words! And then, when everything has sufficiently matured, what wit, intellect, irony and satire, and what warmth of feeling, naïveté and grace he displays at every step! Year after year, his songs have given joy to millions of people; they are eminently singable, even for the working classes, and yet they are so far above the commonplace that the common people, by consorting with these blithe spirits, are gradually conditioned and compelled to think nobler and better thoughts themselves. What more do you want? And what higher praise could possibly be bestowed on a poet?'

'He is first-rate, no question,' I replied. 'You know yourself how much I have loved him for many years, and you can imagine how gratifying it is for me to hear you talk about him in these terms. But if I had to say which of his songs I prefer, then I like his love poems better than his political ones, where I don't always understand the specific references and allusions anyway.'

'That's your personal preference,' said Goethe, 'and besides, the political ones were not written for you. But if you ask the *French*, they will tell you what is good about them. At its best, a political poem is only ever the mouthpiece of a single nation, and in most cases only the mouthpiece of one particular party; but if it is good, it will be taken up with enthusiasm by that nation and that party. Furthermore, a political poem always has to be seen as the product of its time and circumstances; when history moves on, the poem loses any value it derived

1830

from its subject matter. But Béranger had everything in his favour. Paris *is* France. All the important interests of his great country are concentrated in the capital; this is where they properly live; this is where they fully resonate. Nor is he to be seen, in most of his political songs, as the mere mouthpiece of a single party; rather, the things he is opposed to are for the most part of such general, national interest that the poet is nearly always heard as the great voice of the people. Here in Germany such a thing is not possible. We have no city – in fact, we don't even have a country – where we could definitely say: "This is Germany!" If we ask in Vienna, they will say: "This is Austria!" If we ask in Berlin, they will say: "This is Prussia!" The only time it was all one Germany was sixteen years ago, when we were desperate to get rid of the French. A political poet could have spoken for the generality then – but of course he wasn't needed. The universal distress, and the universal sense of humiliation, haunted the popular imagination like a daemonic force; the fire of inspiration the poet might have lit was already burning by itself throughout the land. I won't deny, though, that Arndt, Körner and Rückert did make some impact at the time.'

'You have been criticized,' I remarked somewhat rashly, 'for not having taken up arms yourself during those momentous times, or at least not playing your part as a poet.'

'Let's not get into that, my friend!' replied Goethe. 'We live in a crazy world, which doesn't know what it wants, so we must just step back and let it have its way. How could I have taken up arms, without hatred in my heart? And how could I have felt hatred at my age? If I'd been affected by those events as a twenty-year-old, then I'm sure I wouldn't have been the last in line. But I was already in my mid-sixties when they occurred.

'And besides, we can't all serve our country in the same way. We all do our best, according to the gifts that God has given us. I have done more than my fair share for half a century now. I can honestly say that in the things that nature has given me to do I have laboured day and night, with no respite; I have always pushed myself hard in my work and in my research, and done as much as I could, to the best of my ability. If everyone could say the same, the world would be a better place.'

'When you think about it,' I said brightly, 'you should not be annoyed by that accusation, but should rather take it as a compliment. After all, the implication is that the world has such a high opinion of you that people think the man who has done more for the culture of his nation than anyone else should ultimately have done *everything*.'

'I won't say what I really think,' Goethe rejoined. 'There is more ill will towards me behind that sort of talk than you realize. I suspect it's just a new form of the old hatred that has driven people to pursue me for years, and try to get at me on the quiet. I know very well I am a thorn in the side of many people, who would all love to get rid of me; and since they can't attack my talent, they attack my character instead. I have variously been called proud, selfish, jealous of young talent, a debauched sensualist, a non-Christian – and now, apparently, I have no love for my country or my own fellow Germans. You've known me well enough for years, and can judge for yourself what there is to all the gossip. But if you really want to know what I've had to put up with, you should read my *Xenien*, and you'll see from my ripostes what people have done at various times to make life unpleasant for me.

'A German author is a German martyr by another name. Oh yes, my friend – you'll find it's true! And I myself have relatively little to complain about; none of the others have fared any better, and most of them have fared a good deal worse. And it's no different in England or France. Think what Molière had to put up with, and Rousseau, and Voltaire! Byron was driven out of England by malicious tongues and would have fled eventually to the ends of the earth, if an early death had not delivered him from the philistines and their hatred.

'And if only it was the ignorant masses who persecuted eminent men! But no: it's a case of one talented man persecuting another! Platen provokes Heine, and Heine Platen, and each tries to make the other look bad, when the world is big enough for everyone to live and let live, and go about their own business in peace; and we all have enough trouble anyway, doing battle with our own talent.

'To write songs of war while sitting in my room: that would

have been my style! To write them in a bivouac, where you can hear the horses of the enemy pickets whinnying at night: I could have coped with that. But that wasn't *my* life, and that wasn't *my* thing; but it was Theodor Körner's thing. So his songs of war suit him perfectly. But with me, not being warlike by nature and having no martial inclinations, songs of war would have been a mask that I put on, which would have looked completely wrong on me.

'I have never feigned anything in my poetry. If I hadn't experienced it, if it wasn't preying on my mind and troubling me, then I didn't write about it. I only wrote love poems when I was in love. So how could I have written songs of hate without actually hating someone? And between you and me, I didn't hate the French, although I thanked God when we were rid of them. How could I, for whom culture and barbarism are the only things that matter, ever have hated a nation that is one of the most cultivated on earth, and to which I owe so much of my own culture?

'Hatred of another nation,' Goethe went on, 'is a very peculiar thing. You'll always find it strongest and most virulent among the least cultivated classes. But at a certain stage of cultural development it vanishes altogether, and one stands *above* nationhood, as it were, and feels the weal or woe of a neighbouring nation as keenly as if it were one's own. I felt very much at home when I reached this stage, and had firmly adopted such a view long before I reached my sixties.'

Monday 15 March 1830

Spent an hour or so at Goethe's this evening. He talked a lot about Jena, and about the changes and improvements he had introduced into the various departments of the university. He told me how he had established separate chairs for chemistry, botany and mineralogy, which had previously been studied only as adjuncts to pharmacy. Above all, he had done a great deal to improve the facilities at the natural history museum and the library.

He took the opportunity to repeat the story, with much

self-satisfaction and good humour, of his forcible seizure of a room adjoining the library which had been occupied by the medical faculty, who were not prepared to give it up.

'The library,' he said, 'was in a very bad state. The place was damp and cramped, and ill suited to housing its treasures in the proper manner, especially since the acquisition of Büttner's library by the Grand Duke had added another 13,000 volumes to the collection, which now lay around in great piles on the floor, because, as I said, there was not enough space to store them properly. This placed me in a difficult position. The obvious answer would have been to build a new extension, but the funds were not available; also, the need for a new extension could easily be avoided, as there was a large room immediately adjoining the library premises which was standing empty, and which was the perfect answer to all our needs. But it did not belong to the library; it was used by the faculty of medicine, who sometimes held meetings there. So I applied to these gentlemen, and asked them very politely if they would let me have this room for the library. But they were not prepared to do so. They would only consent to my request if I agreed to build them a new conference chamber immediately. I told them I was quite happy to arrange alternative premises for them, but could not promise them a new building straightaway. But my answer did not satisfy these gentlemen apparently, because when I sent someone for the key the following morning he was told it could not be found.

'So there was nothing for it but to take matters into my own hands. I sent for a mason, took him into the library and showed him the wall that divided the library from the adjoining room in question. "This wall, my friend," I said, "must be very thick, because it separates two different parts of the building. Have a go, and see how thick it is." The mason set to work, and after five or six hearty blows, bricks and mortar came tumbling down, and through the resulting opening we could just make out some portraits of venerable, bewigged dignitaries which adorned the walls of the room. "Carry on, my friend," I said, "I can't quite see clearly enough yet. Don't hold back – just do as you would in your own house." This friendly encouragement

1830   615

spurred the mason on to such efforts that the opening was soon
large enough to serve as a doorway; whereupon my library
assistants went through into the room, each with an armful of
books which they tossed on to the floor to signify that they had
taken possession. Benches, chairs and desks vanished in an
instant, and my assistants worked so fast and furiously that
after a few days all the books were arranged in good order
around the walls in their bookcases.

'The medical men, who not long afterwards entered the
room in a body through their usual door, were dumbfounded
to find such a great and unexpected change. They didn't know
what to say, and quietly withdrew; but they all nursed a secret
resentment against me. Yet whenever I see one of them on his
own, and especially when I have one or other of them to dine
with me, they are all quite charming, and my very dear friends.
When I told the Grand Duke the tale of this exploit, which of
course had been undertaken with his consent and full approval,
he was royally amused, and we often laughed about it later.'

Goethe was in very fine form, and enjoying these happy
memories. 'Yes, my friend,' he went on, 'it was often a struggle
to get things done. Later on, when I wanted to pull down and
clear away a section of the old city wall that now served no
useful purpose and was causing a serious damp problem in the
library, I fared no better. My various requests, sensible arguments and reasonable representations fell on deaf ears, and
here too I was forced in the end to take matters into my own
hands.

'When the municipal authorities saw my workmen demol-
ishing their old wall, they sent a deputation to the Grand Duke,
who was staying in Dornburg at the time, with the humble
request that it might please His Highness to issue an order
commanding me to cease tearing down their ancient and his-
toric city wall. But the Grand Duke, who had secretly authorized
me to proceed in this matter too, gave them a clever answer: "I
don't interfere in Goethe's affairs. He knows what he is doing,
and must act as he thinks fit. Go and tell him yourself – if
you've got the nerve!"

'But nobody showed up,' added Goethe with a laugh. 'I went

ahead, pulled down as much of the old wall as I needed to, and had the pleasure of seeing my library dry at last.'

Wednesday 17 March 1830 *

Spent a couple of hours at Goethe's this evening. I brought with me the copy of *Gemma von Art* which the Grand Duchess had asked me to return, and told him all the things I liked about the play.[30] 'I'm always glad,' he replied, 'when something new comes out that shows genuine originality and talent.' Then, picking up the book in both hands and looking at it a little askance, he added: 'But it always bothers me when I see dramatists writing plays that are far too long to be performed as written. This is a mistake, and it takes away half the pleasure I would otherwise feel. See what a great tome this *Gemma von Art* is!'

'Schiller,' I ventured, 'didn't do much better, and yet he is a very great dramatist.'

'Yes, he was sometimes guilty of that,' replied Goethe. 'His early plays especially, written in the full bloom of youth, seem to go on for ever. He had too much on his mind, and too much that he wanted to say: it was more than he could cope with. Later on, when he became aware of this failing, he took endless trouble, and tried to overcome it by study and hard work; but he never really succeeded. To truly master one's subject matter, and keep it at arm's length, and focus only on what is absolutely necessary, requires the strength of a poetic giant, and is harder than people think.'

Councillor Riemer was announced and entered the room. I made as if to leave, knowing that this was the evening when Goethe generally did some work with Riemer. But Goethe asked me to stay, which I was very glad to do; and as a result I sat in on a conversation full of high spirits, irony and Mephistophelian caprice on Goethe's part.

'I hear Sömmerring has died,' Goethe began, 'and scarcely a paltry seventy-five years old, too. How feckless people are, that they don't have the heart to hold out longer than that! My friend Bentham, that ultra-radical fool, has the right idea; he's still going strong, and yet he's a few weeks older than I am.'

1830

'One could add,' I remarked, 'that he is like you in another respect, too, because he is still working with all the energy of youth.'

'That's as may be,' replied Goethe, 'but we are at opposite ends of the chain. He wants to tear things down, and I want to preserve them and build them up. To be so radical at his time of life is the height of folly.'

'I think one must distinguish,' I countered, 'between two kinds of radicalism. The one kind wants to tear everything down and clear the ground in order to rebuild in the future, whereas the other confines itself to pointing out the weaknesses and mistakes of a government in the hope of bringing about reform without recourse to violence. Had you been born in England, you would certainly have belonged to the second category.'

'What do you take me for?' rejoined Goethe, who now adopted the mien and tone of his Mephistopheles. 'So you're saying it would have been my job to seek out abuses, and then name and shame the guilty, when in fact, as an Englishman, I would have been living off abuses myself? Had I been born in England, I would have been a wealthy duke, or rather a bishop, with an income of £30,000 a year.'

'Very nice,' I said, 'but what if, by some chance, you hadn't won the big money, but had drawn a blank instead? The world is full of losers.'

'Not everyone, my good friend,' replied Goethe, 'is cut out to be a winner. Do you really think I would have been foolish enough to draw a blank? First and foremost, I would have supported the Thirty-Nine Articles, and championed them against all comers, especially the Ninth Article, which for me would have been an object of special attention and tender devotion.[31] I would have dissembled and lied, so much and for so long, in verse and in prose, that my £30,000 a year would have been assured. And then, having once attained this eminence, I would have spared no effort to stay on top. In particular, I would have done my utmost to make the dark night of ignorance even darker, if that were possible. Oh, how I would have sought to cajole the good, gullible masses and browbeat the darling schoolchildren, to stop anyone noticing, or even having the courage to remark, that my brilliant situation rested on a foundation of the most shameful abuses!'

'In your case,' I replied, 'people would at least have been able to comfort themselves with the thought that you had attained such eminence by sheer talent. In England it is often the most stupid and incompetent people who are in possession of the greatest worldly wealth, which they owe not to their own merits, but to patronage, chance, and above all to an accident of birth.'

'In the end,' said Goethe, 'it is all the same whether great worldly possessions are acquired by seizure or by inheritance. The first usurpers were certainly men of genius, who exploited the ignorance and weakness of others. The world is so full of fools and idiots that one doesn't need to go to a madhouse to find them. Which reminds me that the late Grand Duke, who knew that I had an aversion to madhouses, once tried to trick me by arranging a surprise visit to one of these places. But I smelled a rat in good time, and told him I felt no need to see the fools who were locked up inside, when there were quite enough of them running around on the outside. "I am perfectly willing," I said, "to follow Your Highness to hell if need be, but not into a madhouse."

'What fun it would be to rework the Thirty-Nine Articles in my own way, and astonish the gullible masses!'

'You could give yourself the pleasure,' I said, 'even without being a bishop.'

'No,' replied Goethe, 'I shall keep quiet; you need to be very well paid to lie like that. Without the prospect of a bishop's mitre and my £30,000 a year, I couldn't agree to take it on. Though as it happens, I have already tried my hand at this kind of thing. At the age of sixteen I wrote a dithyrambic poem about Christ's descent into hell, which was actually published, but never became well known; I came across it again only the other day. The poem is full of orthodox bigotry, and will do me very well as my passport to heaven. You know it, Riemer, don't you?'

'No, Your Excellency,' replied Riemer, 'I don't know it. But I do remember that you fell seriously ill in the first year after my

1830 619

arrival, and while you were delirious you suddenly recited some beautiful verses on that very subject. These were no doubt recollections from that poem of your early youth.'

'That is very likely,' said Goethe. 'I know of a case where an old man of humble condition, lying at death's door, suddenly began reciting the most beautiful Greek aphorisms. People were quite certain that the man didn't understand a word of Greek, and were utterly amazed by this, therefore; some cunning individuals were already looking to capitalize on the credulity of these fools, when it was unfortunately discovered that the old man had been forced in his early youth to learn all kinds of Greek sayings by heart, in the presence of a boy of noble family, who, they hoped, would be inspired by his example. He had learned Greek – proper, classical Greek – purely by rote, without understanding a word, and had not given it another thought for fifty years, until finally, in his last illness, that jumble of words suddenly began to stir and come alive again.'

Goethe then returned, with the same malice and irony, to the enormous salaries paid to senior members of the English clergy, and related the story of his encounter with Lord Bristol, the Bishop of Derby.

'Lord Bristol,' said Goethe, 'came through Jena, wished to make my acquaintance, and sent word to me to come and visit him one evening. He liked to be brutally direct on occasion, but if one responded with equal directness he was affability itself. In the course of our conversation he proceeded to lecture me about *Werther*, trying to make me feel guilty for encouraging people to commit suicide. "*Werther*," he said, "is a thoroughly immoral, execrable book!" "Stop right there!" I cried. "If you are going to talk about poor *Werther* in that manner, what do you have to say about the great rulers of this earth, who, with a single stroke of the pen, send a hundred thousand men into battle, eighty thousand of whom will kill each other and incite each other to murder, arson and pillage? You give thanks to God after such atrocities and sing a Te Deum! And what about when your sermons on the horrors of the torments of hell so terrify the frail brethren in your congregations that they lose their minds and end their wretched days in a madhouse! Or when you sow the pernicious seed of doubt in the minds of your Christian parishioners with many of your orthodox, rationally untenable dogmas, so that these souls, strong and weak in equal measure, lose themselves in a labyrinth from which their only escape is death! What do you say to yourselves then, and what hellfire sermons do you preach to yourselves? And now you want to call a writer to account and condemn a work which, misunderstood by a handful of halfwits, has freed the world from maybe a dozen idiots and good-for-nothings, who couldn't do anything better than blow out what little light was left to them! I would have thought I had done mankind a real service and deserved your thanks; instead of which, here you are, trying to make out that this little good deed of mine is a crime, while you lot, the priests and the princes, get away with murder!"

'This outburst had an excellent effect on my bishop. He became as meek as a lamb, and from then on, throughout the rest of our conversation, he conducted himself with the utmost courtesy and the most delicate tact. I subsequently spent a very good evening with him. Offensive as he could sometimes be, Lord Bristol was an intelligent man of the world, perfectly well able to converse on all manner of subjects. When I left, he accompanied me so far in person, and then asked his abbé to do the honours from that point. When I emerged on to the street with the latter, he exclaimed: "You said just the right thing there, Herr von Goethe, and it went down very well with my Lord Bishop. You understood exactly how to find your way to his heart. If you hadn't been quite so direct and blunt, I'm sure you wouldn't be going home as pleased as you are now."'

'You've had to put up with quite a lot on account of your *Werther*,' I observed. 'Your brush with Lord Bristol reminds me of your discussion with Napoleon on the subject. Wasn't Talleyrand there, too?'

'He was there, yes,' replied Goethe. 'But I had no reason to complain about Napoleon. He was most gracious towards me, and treated the subject in a manner befitting such a brilliant mind.'

From *Werther* the conversation turned to novels and plays in general, and their moral or immoral effect on the public. 'Things would have to be pretty bad,' said Goethe, 'for a book to be more immoral than real life, where every day we see, or at least hear about, one scandal after another. Even with children, we don't need to worry too much about the effect a book or play might have on them. As I say, everyday life teaches us more than the most instructive book.'

'And yet,' I remarked, 'we try to be careful around children, not to say things in their presence which we think they should not hear.'

'That is very laudable,' said Goethe, 'and I do the same myself. But I think such precautions are pointless. Children are like dogs: they have such an acute and delicate sense of smell that they detect and sniff out everything – especially the bad things. They also know exactly how things are between any given friend of the family and their parents, and since they don't generally hide their feelings they serve as an excellent barometer of where we stand in the favour – or disfavour – of their family.

'Someone had once spoken ill of me in society, and I felt the matter was so serious that I needed to find out where this attack had come from. People here were generally very well disposed towards me; I racked my brains, but couldn't work out who might be the source of this malicious gossip. Then it suddenly dawned on me. One day, in the street, I encountered a group of small boys of my acquaintance who didn't say hello to me, as they normally did. That was all I needed, and I soon discovered, by following this trail, that it was their parents who had been wagging their tongues at my expense in such a nasty way.'

Monday 29 March 1830*

Called in briefly on Goethe this evening. He seemed very calm and cheerful, and in the most mellow of moods. I found him with his grandson Wolf and Countess Karoline Egloffstein, an intimate friend of his. Wolf was giving his dear grandfather quite a hard time. He was clambering all over him, sitting now on one shoulder, now on the other. Goethe tolerated it all with great fondness, though the weight of the ten-year-old boy must have been quite trying for a man of his age. 'Wolf, my dear,' said the Countess, 'don't pester your dear grandfather so! You are heavy, and he must be quite exhausted.' 'That doesn't matter,' replied Wolf, 'we are going to bed soon, so Grandpa will have plenty of time to recover completely from his fatigue.' 'You see,' Goethe chipped in, 'there's always something slightly impertinent about love.'

The conversation turned to Campe, and his writings for children. 'I've only met Campe twice in my life,' said Goethe. 'I last saw him in Karlsbad, after an interval of forty years. I found him very old, withered, stiff and formal. He had written only for children all his life, whereas I had written nothing for children, not even for big children of twenty. And he couldn't stand me. I was a thorn in his side, a stumbling block, and he did his utmost to avoid me. But one day fate unexpectedly threw us together, so that he was forced to speak to me. "I have every regard," he said, "for your intellectual capabilities. You have attained extraordinary eminence in a number of fields. But you see, these are all things that don't interest me, and I cannot attach the same importance to them that others do." I was not at all offended by this rather discourteous candour, and I said all kinds of obliging things in return. And the fact is, I have a lot of time for Campe. He has done children an incredible service; he is their delight – their gospel, you might say. Though I would like to see him taken to task a little for two or three quite horrible stories, which he was unwise enough not only to write, but also to include in his collection for children. Why should anyone – for no reason at all – cloud the bright, fresh, innocent imagination of children with such horrid images?'

Monday 5 April 1830

It is well known that Goethe is not a great fan of spectacles.

'Call me eccentric, if you like,' he said to me on numerous occasions, 'but I just can't help it. Whenever a stranger wearing spectacles comes to see me, it immediately puts me in a bad mood, and I simply can't get past it. It bothers me so much that a large part of my goodwill evaporates the moment the man enters the room, and I find myself so distracted that I am completely unable to develop my own thoughts freely and naturally. It always comes across as faintly hostile, as if a complete stranger were going to say something offensive to me on our first encounter. I feel this even more keenly, having stated publicly for years how disagreeable spectacles are to me. If a stranger turns up now wearing spectacles, I immediately think: he hasn't read your latest poems – which is already a bit of a black mark against him. Or else I think: he has read them, knows the kind of thing you write, and thinks it beneath his notice – which is even worse. The only person whose spectacles don't bother me is Zelter; on anyone else, they make me feel uncomfortable. I always get the feeling that I'm going to be the object of close scrutiny by the stranger, as if they are going to use their enhanced vision to penetrate my innermost secrets and study every wrinkle on my aged face. But while they seek to make *my* acquaintance in this way, they give themselves an unfair advantage by preventing me from making *theirs* in return. What can I possibly know of a man if I can't look into his eyes when he is talking, and if the mirror of his soul is hidden away behind two discs of glass that reflect the light and dazzle me?'

'Someone once suggested,' I said, 'that wearing spectacles makes people conceited, because the spectacles endow them with a degree of sensory perfection far beyond their own natural capabilities, which eventually deludes them into thinking that this artificial acuity is in fact their own natural power.'

'That's a very nice idea,' replied Goethe, 'which sounds as if it came from a natural scientist. But when you examine it more closely, it doesn't really hold up. If it were true, then all blind people would be exceedingly modest, while all those with good eyesight would be conceited. But this is definitely not the case. Indeed, what we generally find is that all those who are well endowed by nature, mentally or physically, are the most modest, while those who are defective, especially in the mental department, are far more likely to think highly of themselves. It appears that bountiful nature has given to all those who are lacking in the higher endowments the gift of conceit and self-regard, as a kind of compensation and consolation prize.

'Anyway, modesty and conceit are moral and mental things, which have very little to do with the body. Conceit is common among the narrow-minded and the dim-witted; but people who are mentally bright and highly gifted are never conceited. At most, they have a happy sense of their own power; but as this power is real enough, their sense of it is anything but conceit.'

We talked about various other matters, and finally got on to the subject of *Chaos*, the Weimar journal put out by Frau von Goethe, which publishes contributions not only by local German ladies and gentlemen, but also by the young Englishmen and Frenchmen and other foreigners staying here. Consequently, nearly every issue contains a mix of nearly all the major European languages.

'It was a nice idea of my daughter's,' said Goethe, 'and she deserves our praise and thanks for starting this highly original journal, and for getting individual members of our society so involved that it has now been going for nearly a year. It's only a bit of dilettante fun, of course, and I know very well that nothing great or lasting is going to come out of it. But still, it is a lovely idea, and serves as a kind of mirror of the intellectual distinction of our present Weimar society. And the main thing is, it gives our young ladies and gentlemen, who are often at a loose end, something to do; it also provides an intellectual focus for them, which affords them subjects for discussion and conversation, and so stops them wasting their time in idle gossip. I read every issue, straight off the press, and I can say that on the whole I have not yet come across anything badly done, and indeed have found some very nice things in there on occasion. For example, how could anyone take exception to the elegy by Frau von Bechtolsheim on the death of the Dowager Grand Duchess? Is it not a very charming poem? The only criticism that might be made, of this and most of the other things contributed by our young ladies and gentlemen, is that they are rather like trees with too much sap, which throw out a lot of parasitic shoots: they suffer from an excess of thoughts and feelings, which they cannot keep under control, so that they seldom know how to restrain themselves or where to stop. Frau von Bechtolsheim is a case in point. In order to sustain a rhyme, she had added an extra line, which detracted considerably from the poem, and in a way spoiled it. I noted this mistake in the manuscript and was able to delete it in time.

'You have to be an old hand,' he said with a laugh, 'to know how to cut a text. Schiller was a past master at it. Once, when he was editing his *Musenalmanach*, I saw him cut an over-blown poem of twenty-two stanzas down to just seven, and the piece lost nothing by this drastic surgery; on the contrary, those seven stanzas still contained all the good ideas from the original twenty-two.'

Monday 19 April 1830 *

Goethe told me about a visit he had today from two Russians. 'They were nice enough, on the whole,' he said, 'but one of them behaved somewhat disagreeably, in that he didn't utter a single word from start to finish. He bowed silently when he came in, did not open his mouth the whole time he was here, and took his leave after half an hour or so with another silent bow. He seemed to have come for the sole purpose of looking at me and studying me. We sat facing each other, and he never once took his eyes off me. This annoyed me, and so I started to spout all kinds of nonsense – whatever came into my head. I believe my chosen theme was the United States of North America, which I wittered on about in the most flippant way, saying things I knew and things I didn't know, without stopping to think. But it seemed to go down well enough with my two foreign friends, who left not at all dissatisfied, as far as I could tell.'

Thursday 22 April 1830 *

Dined with Goethe. Frau von Goethe was present, and the conversation was agreeably lively. But I remember little or nothing of what was said.

During dinner, a foreigner on his way through Weimar was announced, with the message that he had no time to stop and would be leaving the next morning. Goethe said to tell him that he was very sorry he could not see anyone today, but perhaps tomorrow lunchtime? 'I think,' he added with a smile, 'that should do it.' At the same time, however, he promised his daughter that he would receive young Henning after dinner, on her recommendation, and in consideration of his brown eyes, which were said to resemble his mother's.

Wednesday 12 May 1830*

Standing in Goethe's window was a small bronze figure of Moses, a miniature replica of the famous Michelangelo original. I thought the arms looked too long and too thick in relation to the rest of the body, and I said as much to Goethe.

'But what about the two heavy tablets with the Ten Commandments?' he cried. 'Do you think it was a small matter to carry those? And furthermore, do you think that Moses could have managed with perfectly normal arms when he had to command an army of Jews and keep them under control?'

Goethe laughed as he said this, so that I couldn't tell if I was mistaken, or if his defence of the artist was only meant as a joke.

Monday 2 August 1830*

News of the outbreak of the July Revolution reached Weimar today and caused a general commotion. I went to see Goethe in the course of the afternoon. 'Well now,' he greeted me, 'what do you make of this great event? The volcano has erupted; everything is ablaze, and there's no more negotiating behind closed doors!'

'A frightful business,' I replied. 'But under the circumstances, and under such a ministry, what else could be expected? It was bound to end in the expulsion of the royal family.'

'We seem to be at cross-purposes, my dear fellow,' replied Goethe. 'I'm not talking about those people, but about something quite different. I'm talking about the dispute between Cuvier and Geoffroy de Saint-Hilaire, which has now broken out openly in the French Academy and has huge implications for science!'

This remark of Goethe's was so totally unexpected that I didn't know what to say, and for the next few minutes my thought processes were completely paralysed.

'The matter is of the utmost importance,' Goethe went on, 'and you cannot imagine what I felt when I heard about the meeting of 19 July. We now have a powerful ally for the future in Geoffroy de Saint-Hilaire. But I also see from this how interested the French scientific world must be in this matter, given that the meeting of 19 July attracted a full house, despite the terrible political turmoil. But the best part is that the synthesizing approach to nature pioneered in France by Geoffroy is now here to stay. The matter has now become public, through the open debates conducted in the Academy before a large audience; it can no longer be referred to secret committees and made to go away behind closed doors. So from now on, mind will rule over matter in the work of French naturalists. They will see into the great laws of creation, into the hidden workshop of God! What is the point, really, of studying nature, if we simply spend our time analysing its individual, material parts, and do not feel the breath of the spirit that gives to every part its appointed direction, and curbs or sanctions any deviation by the operation of an inherent law?

'I have been working away at this great endeavour for fifty years, alone to begin with, and then supported by, and finally, to my great joy, surpassed by, kindred spirits. When I sent my initial discovery of the intermaxillary bone to Peter Camper, I was completely ignored, to my great sorrow.[32] I had no more luck with Blumenbach, although he came round to my view after we had got to know each other personally. But then I gained the support of like-minded men such as Sömmerring, Oken, D'Alton, Carus and others of similar distinction. And now Geoffroy de Saint-Hilaire is firmly on our side, too – and with him all his eminent disciples and adherents in France. This is an event of incredible significance for me, and I rightly rejoice that I have finally witnessed the triumph of a cause to which I have devoted my life, and which I have made very much my own.'

Saturday 21 August 1830*

I recommended a promising young man of my acquaintance to Goethe. He undertook to do something for him, but didn't seem very hopeful.

'Anyone like me,' he said, 'who has wasted valuable time and money all his life sponsoring young persons of talent who initially aroused high hopes, but in the end came to nothing, must gradually lose all enthusiasm for doing this kind of thing. Now it's up to you young people to play the patron and take over my role.'

Hearing Goethe's comment, I likened the false promises of youth to trees that bear double blossoms, but no fruit.

Wednesday 13 October 1830*

Goethe showed me some tables in which he had written the names of many plants in Latin and German with a view to learning them by heart. He told me he had once had a whole room wallpapered with such tables, and he used to go in there and pace around the walls, studying and learning the names. 'I am sorry to say,' he added, 'that the walls were later whitewashed. I had another room, where the walls were covered with notes on my work over many years, in chronological order, to which I always added anything new I had written. That room was also whitewashed, unfortunately, which was a great shame, because it would have been really useful to me now.'

Wednesday 20 October 1830*

Called in on Goethe for an hour or so, to consult with him on behalf of the Grand Duchess about a silver shield that the Prince is to present to the local crossbow archery club, of which he is now a member.

Our conversation soon turned to other matters, and Goethe asked me what I thought about the Saint-Simonians.[33]

'The main thrust of their teaching,' I replied, 'seems to be that each individual should work for the happiness of society as a whole, as the necessary condition of his own happiness.'

'I rather think,' said Goethe, 'that the individual should start with himself, and seek his own happiness first; from this, the happiness of society must then necessarily follow. And anyway, their teaching strikes me as completely impractical and unrealistic. It flies in the face of nature, experience, and thousands of years of history. If each individual just does his duty, and does his own job to the best of his ability, then society as a whole will prosper. In my work as a writer I have never asked: "What do the masses want, and how can I benefit society?" Instead, I have always sought to make myself a wiser and better writer, to enrich my own personality, and then only to say what I have found to be good and true. I won't deny that my work has reached a wider audience and has been of use to them; but this was not my aim, but rather a necessary *consequence*, just as any natural force produces an inevitable effect. If, as a writer, I had attended to the wishes of the general multitude and sought to satisfy these, I would have had to tell them little stories and play games with them, like the late Kotzebue.'

'There's nothing wrong with any of that,' I said. 'But it's not just about the happiness I enjoy as a solitary individual, but also the happiness I enjoy as a citizen, and a member of the wider community. If we don't work on the principle of attaining the greatest possible happiness for the whole people, where else is our legislation going to start from?'

'If that's where this is going,' replied Goethe, 'then of course I have no objection to make. But in such a case only a very select few would be in a position to apply your principle. It would be a recipe for rulers and lawmakers only; but even there, it seems to me, the purpose of laws should be to diminish the amount of evil in the world, rather than presume to add to the sum of human happiness.'

'They both pretty much amount to the same thing,' I replied. 'Bad roads, for example, are a great evil, it seems to me. If a prince builds good roads throughout his state, serving even the smallest hamlet, he has not only eradicated a great evil, but also made his people very happy. Slow justice is another great evil.

But if the prince establishes a system of public oral proceedings, and thus gives his people speedy justice, then once again he has not only abolished a great evil, but also conferred a great good.'

'I could tell you some very different stories along those lines,' Goethe rejoined. 'But let's leave some evils unmentioned, so that there is something left for mankind to practise its powers on. But for now my philosophy of life is this: let the father take care of his household, let the tradesman take care of his customers, let the priest take care of brotherly love, and let the police not be killjoys and busybodies.'

1831

Tuesday 4 January 1831*

Goethe and I leafed through some books of drawings by my friend Töpffer in Geneva, who writes as well as he draws; but so far he seems to prefer expressing his lively imaginings in visible shapes rather than ephemeral words. The book containing the *Voyages et aventures du Docteur Festus* in delicate pen-and-ink drawings was just like a comic novel, and Goethe was delighted by it. 'This is wild stuff!' he cried from time to time, as he turned the pages; 'the whole thing fizzes with talent and wit! Some of these drawings are quite superb. If he were to choose a less risqué subject in future and rein himself in a bit more, he could accomplish incredible things.'

'He has been compared to Rabelais,' I said, 'and accused of imitating him and stealing ideas from him.'

'People don't know what they want,' replied Goethe. 'I see nothing of the sort. On the contrary: Töpffer seems to me to be entirely his own man, and as wholly original as any talent I have come across.'

Wednesday 17 January 1831.*

I found Coudray with Goethe, studying some architectural drawings. I had a five-franc piece from 1830 on me, with the head of Charles X, and took it out to show them. Goethe joked about the pointed head. 'The organ of religiosity seems to be very highly developed in him,' he observed. 'No doubt he was too pious to deem it necessary to pay his debts; we, on the other hand, are deeply indebted to him, since it is thanks to his masterstroke that Europe will not be at rest again for the foreseeable future.'

We then talked about *Le Rouge et le noir*, which Goethe regards as Stendhal's best work. 'Though I can't deny,' he added, 'that some of his female characters are a bit *too* romantic. But they all bear witness to his great powers of observation and psychological insight, so that one is happy to forgive the author the occasional implausible detail.'

Tuesday 23 January 1831*

At Goethe's, together with the Prince. His grandsons were amusing themselves with conjuring tricks, which Walter is particularly good at. 'I've nothing against the boys filling their idle hours with such nonsense,' said Goethe. 'Especially if you've got a small audience, it's a wonderful way to practise the art of ad-libbing and improve your mental and physical dexterity – something with which we Germans are not exactly over-endowed. The disadvantage – that it might make them a little vain – is completely outweighed by these benefits.'

'And anyway, the spectators see to it that such feelings are kept in check,' I observed, 'as they generally keep a very sharp eye on the young performer and are mean enough to laugh at his mistakes and reveal his little secrets to all and sundry, much to his chagrin.'

'They get the same treatment as actors,' said Goethe, 'who are clapped one day and booed the next, which keeps everything on an even keel.'

Wednesday 10 March 1831*

Spent half an hour or so with Goethe at lunchtime. I had been asked to bring him the news that the Grand Duchess has decided to give our theatre management a gift of one thousand thalers, to be used for the training of promising young actors. The news gave Goethe obvious pleasure, as one who cares deeply about the future of the theatre.

I then had a commission of a different kind to discuss with him. It is the intention of the Grand Duchess to invite the best German writer of the day to Weimar, on condition that he has no official position or fortune of his own and has to support himself entirely by his talent; and to give him a suitable sinecure, so that he might find the time to allow each of his works to develop and ripen to full perfection, and not be forced by necessity to work in a slapdash and rushed fashion, to the detriment of his own talent and of literature.

'The Grand Duchess's proposal,' replied Goethe, 'is a most regal one, and I bow to her noble sentiments; but it will be very difficult to choose a suitable candidate. The best of our present crop of talents are already well provided for by state employment, pensions or private means. Besides, not everyone would fit in here, and not everyone would really benefit from the opportunity. But I shall bear this noble scheme in mind, and see if the next few years bring us anything good.'

Wednesday 31 March 1831*

Goethe has been very unwell again for some time, able to receive only his most intimate friends. A few weeks ago he had to be bled by the doctor, after which he complained of pain in his right leg. In the end his internal malady was relieved by a cut in his foot, and he recovered very quickly after that. This cut had also healed a few days ago, and now he is as bright and lively as ever.

The Grand Duchess called to see him today and came away very pleased. She had enquired after his health, to which he had very gallantly replied that he had not been sensible of his recovery until today, but that her presence had made him feel again the blessing of restored health.

Wednesday 14 April 1831*

Attended a soirée at the Prince's. One of the older gentlemen present, who remembered a good deal from the early years of Goethe's time here, related the following very characteristic story:

'I was present,' he said, 'when Goethe made his famous speech at the official opening of the Ilmenau mine in 1784, to which all the officials and other interested parties from the town and surrounding area had been invited. He appeared to have memorized his speech well, because he spoke for a while quite fluently and without any hesitation. But then it was as if his guardian spirit suddenly deserted him, and he lost the thread of his thoughts; he seemed quite unable to remember what it was he wanted to say next. This would have been utterly mortifying for anyone else – but not for him. He surveyed his numerous audience with a calm and steady gaze for at least ten minutes; spellbound by the force of his personality, everyone remained perfectly still throughout this very long, and slightly ridiculous, pause. Eventually he seemed to get a grip on his theme again, and went on to the end without hesitation, speaking as freely and easily as if nothing had happened.'

Sunday 20 June 1831

Spent half an hour or so with Goethe this afternoon, having found him still at table.

We talked about various scientific questions, including the imperfection and inadequacy of language, whereby errors and misconceptions are spread abroad and cannot easily be corrected later on.

'The point is simply this,' said Goethe. 'All languages arose out of immediate human needs, human occupations, and the general feelings and thoughts common to all men. But when a more sophisticated man comes to understand a little of the secret workings of nature, the language he has inherited is not adequate to express something so entirely remote from human affairs. He would need to have the language of spirits at his command to do justice to perceptions that are peculiarly his own. But as it is, he has to rely on everyday human language when describing unusual natural phenomena; and in so doing he nearly always falls short of what his theme requires, even to the extent of undermining his own case.'

'Coming from you,' I replied, 'given that you always tackle

your subject head-on, eschew empty rhetoric, and always find the most telling turn of phrase to express your visionary ideas, that is really saying something! I should have thought, though, that we Germans can be quite satisfied on the whole. Our language is so extraordinarily rich, well developed and susceptible of further refinement that even if we occasionally have to resort to figures of speech, we still get pretty close to a direct expression of our meaning. Compared with us, the French are at a great disadvantage. When called upon to give an account of a complex natural phenomenon they have observed, they generally rely on some image or metaphor borrowed from technology, which reduces everything to the level of the material and commonplace, and entirely fails to do justice to these visionary conceptions.'

'You are so right,' said Goethe, 'as I was reminded recently by the quarrel between Cuvier and Geoffroy de Saint-Hilaire. Geoffroy de Saint-Hilaire is a man who really has a high degree of insight into the spiritual workings of nature; but the French language lets him down, to the extent that he is forced to make use of conventional expressions. And not only when writing about unseen, spiritual things, but also in the case of visible, purely physical objects and phenomena. If he wants to describe the individual parts of an organic being, he has no other word except "materials". So for example the bones that constitute a homogeneous group of parts making up the organic whole of an arm are referred to in exactly the same terms as the bricks, beams and boards used to build a house.

'Equally inappropriate,' Goethe went on, 'is the French use of the term "composition" to refer to objects produced by nature.[34] I can construct a machine, say, by putting together its individual parts piece by piece, and call this a "composition"; but not when I am talking about the individual, living and growing parts of an organic whole that is imbued with a common soul.'

'It almost seems to me,' I ventured, 'that the term "composition" is inappropriate and demeaning even when applied to genuine works of art and poetry.'

'It is a thoroughly despicable word,' replied Goethe, 'which we have the French to thank for, and which we should try to get rid of as soon as possible. How can it be said that Mozart "composed" his *Don Giovanni*? "Composition" – as if it were a piece of cake or a biscuit, made by mixing together eggs, flour and sugar! It is a creation of the human mind, the parts and the whole bearing the stamp of *one* mind, suffused with the breath of *one* life; its creator was not trying things out and cobbling them together just as the fancy took him, but rather was driven by the daemonic spirit of his genius, so that he had to do as it commanded.'

Sunday 27 June 1831 *

We discussed Victor Hugo. 'He is a fine talent,' said Goethe, 'but completely caught up in the unholy romantic tendency of his age, which leads him to portray things that are utterly hideous and quite unbearable alongside what is beautiful. I've just been reading his *Notre-Dame de Paris*, and it took a fair amount of patience to endure the torment of getting through to the end. It is the most abominable book that's ever been written! And it's not as if one is compensated for the agonies one has to endure by the pleasure of seeing human nature and human character truthfully represented. On the contrary: his book is completely unnatural and devoid of truth. His so-called *dramatis personae* are not living people of flesh and blood, but miserable wooden puppets whom he manipulates at will, making them contort themselves and pull faces, just to suit the effects he wishes to create. But what kind of an age is it that not only enables and invites the writing of such a book, but actually finds it quite acceptable and entertaining!'

Wednesday 14 July 1831 *

Together with the Prince, I accompanied His Majesty the King of Württemberg to call on Goethe. On our way back the King seemed very pleased, and asked me to convey his thanks to Goethe for the pleasure that this visit had given him.

1831 637

Thursday 15 July 1831 *

Called in briefly to see Goethe, and delivered yesterday's message from the King. I found him engrossed in studies relating to the spiral tendency in plants, a recent discovery that he believes will open up new horizons and have a great influence on science. 'There is nothing to compare,' he added, 'with the joy that we get from studying nature. Her secrets are unfathomable, but we humans are permitted and enabled to learn more and more about them. And the very fact that she remains, in the end, unfathomable is a constant incentive to us to go back to her time and again in search of fresh insights and new discoveries.'

Tuesday 20 July 1831 *

Spent half an hour or so with Goethe after dinner and found him in very cheerful and mellow mood. We talked about all kinds of things, including Karlsbad, and he joked about the various love affairs he had experienced there. 'A little *amour*,' he said, 'is the only thing that makes a stay in a spa bearable – you would die of boredom otherwise. And nearly every time, I was fortunate enough to find some little "elective affinity" there that kept me amused for those few weeks. I particularly recall one instance that still gives me pleasure now.

'I was visiting Frau von Reck one day. After we had chatted for a while about nothing in particular and I had taken my leave, I met a lady on the way out, accompanied by two very pretty girls. "Who was the gentleman we just saw leaving?" asked the lady. "That was Goethe," replied Frau von Reck. "Oh, what a pity he didn't stay longer," said the lady, "and that I missed the chance to meet him!" "You haven't missed anything, my dear," said *la Reck*. "He's very boring in female company, except when they are pretty enough to excite his interest. Women of our age shouldn't expect to get him talking or find him attentive."

'As the two girls were making their way home again with their mother, they recalled what Frau von Reck had said. "We are young, we are pretty," they said, "let's see if we can't ensnare and tame the famous savage beast!" The next morning, on the promenade by the hot spring, they kept on bowing to me in passing, in the most graceful and delightful way, so that I couldn't help approaching them and speaking to them from time to time. They were utterly charming! I spoke to them again and again, they took me to see their mother, and that was it: I was captivated. From then on we saw each other every day, and indeed spent whole days together. To throw us even closer together, it so happened that the fiancé of one of the girls turned up, which meant that I was able to give the other one my undivided attention. I also made myself very agreeable to the mother, as you can imagine. In short, we all got along famously with each other, and I spent such a happy time with this family that the memory of it still gives me pleasure today. The two girls told me, very soon after we met, about the conversation between their mother and Frau von Reck, and about the plot they had successfully hatched for my conquest.'

This reminds me of another anecdote that Goethe told me earlier, which might usefully be included here.

'I was walking,' he told me, 'with a good friend early one evening in some palace garden, when we suddenly noticed two other persons from our circle at the far end of the avenue, who were walking along side by side and conversing quietly. I can't tell you the name of the gentleman, or of the lady, but that's neither here nor there. So they were chatting away, seemingly oblivious, when all of a sudden their heads came together and they exchanged a passionate kiss. Then they carried on walking in the same direction and continued their earnest conversation as if nothing had happened. "Did you see that," exclaimed my friend in amazement, "or did my eyes deceive me?" "I saw it," I replied calmly, "but I don't believe it."'

Monday 2 August 1831 *

We talked about the metamorphosis of plants, and in particular about de Candolle's theory of symmetry, which Goethe regards as quite mistaken.

'Nature,' he added, 'does not yield up her secrets to everyone.

To many she is like a coquettish girl, who beguiles us by a thousand charms, only to slip from our arms just when we think we will seize and possess her.'

Wednesday 19 October 1831*

Today the Society for the Promotion of Agriculture held its meeting at Belvedere, which also hosted the first exhibition of agricultural produce and industrial artefacts. There was more to see than we had expected. This was followed by a formal dinner for the numerous members present. Goethe joined them, to the surprise and delight of all those present. He stayed for a while and examined the items on display with evident interest. His appearance at the event made a most favourable impression, especially on those who had not seen him before.

Thursday 1 December 1831

Spent an hour or so with Goethe, talking about all kinds of things. Then the conversation turned to Soret.

'I have recently read a very nice poem by him,' said Goethe, 'a trilogy, in fact, whose first two parts are jauntily rustic in mood, while the last part, entitled "Midnight", is rather dark and scary.[35] This "Midnight" has turned out very well. You really catch a whiff of the night when you read it, almost like you do in the paintings of Rembrandt, where you feel you are actually breathing the night air. Victor Hugo has written about similar subjects, but not so successfully. He's a very great talent, no question, but in his nocturnal scenes it never gets properly dark; he wants us to think it is night-time, but things are as clear and as visible as if it were still really day. Soret has unquestionably outdone the famous Victor Hugo in his "Midnight".'

I was gratified to hear Soret praised in these terms, and resolved to read his trilogy as soon as possible. 'We don't have very many trilogies in our literature,' I observed.

'This particular form,' replied Goethe, 'is very rare among the moderns generally. It all depends on finding a subject that lends itself naturally to being treated in three parts, starting with some sort of exposition in the first part, followed by some sort of catastrophe in the second, and then a reconciliation or accommodation in the third. My own series of poems about the bachelor and the miller's daughter meets these requirements, even though at the time I wrote them I had no thoughts of composing a trilogy.[36] My "Paria" cycle is another classic trilogy, and in this case I planned it as a trilogy from the outset, and wrote it accordingly. My so-called *Trilogie der Leidenschaft*, on the other hand, was not originally conceived as a trilogy, but gradually turned into one as I was writing it – by accident, as it were. To begin with, as you know, I just had "Elegie" as a poem by itself. Then Madame Szymanowska visited me, after being with me at Marienbad that summer, and her delightful melodies awakened in me an echo of those blissful days of new-found youth. The verses I dedicated to this friend are consequently written in the very same metre and tone as "Elegie", so that they form a kind of satisfying coda to it. Then Weygand wanted to publish a new edition of my *Werther*, and asked me to write a preface for it, which came as a very welcome prompt for me to write my poem "An Werther". But as I still harboured traces of that old passion in my heart, the poem worked really well as a natural introduction to the original "Elegie". That's how it happened that all three poems which now stand together were inspired by the same lovesick feelings, and the *Trilogie der Leidenschaft* came about almost by chance.

'I have advised Soret to write more trilogies, and told him he should go about it in the way I have just described. He should not bother looking for suitable new material to write a trilogy from scratch, but should instead pick out something of substance from his ample stock of unpublished poems and then, when the occasion presents itself, write a kind of introduction and a satisfying conclusion to it, but in such a way that each of the three pieces is separated by a palpable break. This is a much easier way of doing it, and it saves a lot of thinking – which, as Meyer says, is notoriously hard work.'

We then talked about Victor Hugo, and agreed that his excessively prolific output was very bad for his talent.

'How can a writer not go downhill and ruin the finest of

talents,' asked Goethe, 'if he has the temerity to write two tragedies and a novel in a single year, and if he appears to work for
the sole purpose of making vast sums of money? I'm not blaming him at all for wanting to get rich, or for wanting to become
a celebrity in his day; but if he wants his fame to live on for
posterity, he needs to start writing less and working more.'

Goethe then went through the text of *Marie Delorme*, and
endeavoured to show me that the subject only contained
enough material for one good and very tragic act, but that the
author had been induced by purely secondary considerations to
spin his subject out to five long acts.[37] 'The only advantage,'
Goethe added, 'is that we get to see that the writer is also very
good at portraying details – which is no small thing in itself,
and certainly not to be despised.'

1832

Thursday 5 January 1832 *

Some new books of pen-and-ink drawings and watercolours had arrived from my friend Töpffer in Geneva, mostly views of landscapes in Switzerland and Italy, which he had gradually put together during his various walking tours. Goethe was so struck by the beauty of these drawings, particularly the water-colours, that he said it was like looking at the works of the famous Lory. I observed that these were by no means Töpffer's best pictures, and that he had better things than these he could send. 'I don't know what it is you want!' replied Goethe. 'What could be better than these? And even if it were a little bit better, what of it? Once an artist reaches a certain level of excellence, it hardly matters whether one of his works is slightly more suc-cessful than another. The connoisseur discerns the hand of the master in all of them, and sees the full extent of his talent and resources.'

Friday 17 February 1832 *

I had sent Goethe a portrait of Dumont which had been engraved in England, and which he seemed to find very interesting.

'I have been studying the portrait of this eminent man a great deal,' he said, when I called on him today towards evening. 'There was something repellent about it for me at first, which I am inclined to attribute to the artist's technique; the features are rather too hard-edged and deeply incised. But the longer I looked at this most remarkable head, the more all the hardness

1832

disappeared, and what emerged from the dark background was a lovely expression of repose, kindliness and acutely perceptive humanity – the defining characteristics of this clever, benevolent and public-spirited man, which so gladden the heart of the beholder.'

We went on to discuss Dumont further, particularly his *Souvenirs de Mirabeau*, in which he reveals the many different resources that Mirabeau was able to tap, and names the many persons of talent whom he mobilized for his purposes and whose abilities he harnessed. 'I know of no more instructive book,' said Goethe, 'than these memoirs, which afford us a deep insight into the most hidden recesses of those times and make the astonishing Mirabeau phenomenon appear natural without in any way diminishing his heroic stature. But the writers of the most recent reviews in the French journals take a rather different view. These good folk believe the author of these memoirs is intent on discrediting their Mirabeau by revealing the secret of his superhuman activity and allowing others a share of the glory that has hitherto been monopolized by the Mirabeau name.

'The French view Mirabeau as their Hercules, and quite rightly so. But they forget that even the Colossus is made up of separate parts, and that even the Hercules of antiquity is a collective being, a great champion of his own deeds and the deeds of others.

'But in the end we are all collective beings, no matter what we tell ourselves. So little of what we have and what we are can truly be called our own. We all have to receive and learn, both from our predecessors and from our contemporaries. Even the greatest genius would not get very far by relying entirely on his own inner resources. But many very good men fail to grasp this, and they spend half their lives stumbling around in the dark while they pursue their dreams of originality. I have known artists who boasted that they had followed no master, and owed everything to their own genius. The fools! As if that were ever possible! And as if the world did not press in upon them at every turn, and make something of them in spite of their own stupidity. I maintain that if such an artist were just to walk round this room and cast a passing glance at the drawings by great masters that I have hung on the walls he would, if he had any genius at all, leave this room a different and a better man.

'And indeed, what is there good about us, if not the strength and the desire to appropriate the resources of the outside world and make them serve our own higher purposes? If I may speak for myself and say in all modesty what I feel: it is true that I have done and accomplished many things in the course of my long life that I could boast about if I wanted to. But if we are honest, what did I have that was really mine, other than the ability and the desire to see and to hear, to discriminate and to select, to bring to life what I had seen and heard with a degree of thought and imagination, and to render it with a degree of skill? I owe my works not to my own wisdom alone – far from it – but to thousands of things and persons all around me who provided me with the material. I met with fools and wise men, bright sparks and dimwits, children, young people and those of mature years; they all told me how they felt, what they were thinking, how they lived and worked, what lessons life had taught them; and all I had to do was to help myself and reap what others had sown for me.

'And in the end, it is foolishness to ask whether what a person has comes from himself or from others, or whether he gets things done by himself or through others: the main thing is *to want something very badly and then to have the skill and the perseverance to see it through*; nothing else matters. So Mirabeau was quite right to make what use he could of other people and their capabilities. He had the gift of recognizing talent, and persons of talent felt drawn by the daemon of his powerful personality, so that they willingly surrendered themselves to him and his guidance. Consequently he was surrounded by large numbers of outstanding people, whom he fired up and set to work for his own higher purposes. And therein lay his genius, his originality and his greatness: that he understood how to get things done *with* others and *through* others.'

Sunday 11 March 1832

Spent an hour or so with Goethe this evening, talking about all kinds of interesting things. I had bought an English Bible, and was very disappointed to find that it did not contain the apocryphal books. They had been left out on the grounds that they were not considered genuine or of divine origin. I missed the noble Tobit, that paragon of pious living, as well as the Wisdom of Solomon and Ecclesiasticus – all writings of such high intellectual and moral calibre that few others can equal them. I told Goethe that I deplored this very narrow-minded approach, whereby some Old Testament texts were deemed to have been directly inspired by God while others, equally fine, were not – as if there could be anything noble and great that did not come from God and was not the result of His influence.

'I entirely agree,' replied Goethe. 'But there are two ways of looking at the Bible. We can look at it from the standpoint of a kind of primitive religion, of pure nature and reason, which is divine in origin. This will always remain unchanged, and will endure and prevail as long as there are divinely inspired beings on this earth. But it is for the select few only, being far too sublime and noble to become universal. Then there is the standpoint of the Church, which is an essentially human one. This is flawed, mutable, and constantly evolving; but it too will endure, in that state of perpetual change, as long as frail human beings walk the earth. The light of unclouded divine revelation is far too pure and dazzling to be borne by poor weak mortals. But the Church steps in here as a benevolent mediator, to temper and moderate, to the benefit of all and the comfort of many. Because the Christian Church believes, as the heir of Christ, that it can free mankind from the burden of sin, it is a very powerful force. And the primary concern of the Christian clergy is to maintain itself in this power and standing, and thus to secure the edifice of the Church.

'So it is not the role of the clergy to ask whether this or that book of the Bible enlightens the mind or instructs us in high moral principles and the best of human nature. Their job, rather, is to highlight the story of the fall of man in the Pentateuch, and the origin of our need for the Redeemer; to point out the repeated references to Him, the Expected One, in the prophets; and to focus on His actual appearance on earth in the Gospels and His death upon the cross in atonement for our sins. So you can see that for such purposes, and weighed in such a balance, neither the noble Tobit, nor the Wisdom of Solomon, nor the sayings of Ecclesiasticus, carry much weight.

'And anyway, whether things in the Bible are "genuine" or "spurious" is a strange question to ask. What is genuine, other than what is truly excellent, in harmony with purest nature and reason, and still conducive today to the perfecting of our being? And what is spurious, other than what is absurd, empty, stupid, and bears no fruit, or at any rate no good fruit? If the authenticity of a biblical text is to be judged by whether or not its contents are entirely true, then one could even doubt the authenticity of the Gospels on some points, about which Mark and Luke did not write from direct personal knowledge and experience, but only long after the event, based on oral tradition; while the last Gospel was written by the disciple John at a very advanced age. Nonetheless I believe all four Gospels to be entirely genuine, because you see in them the reflection of a glory that emanated from the person of Christ, which was as divine as any manifestation of divinity ever seen on earth. If you ask me if it is in my nature to pay Him devout reverence, then I say: Absolutely! I bow down before Him as the divine revelation of the highest principle of morality. If you ask me if it is in my nature to revere the sun, then I say again: Absolutely! For it, too, is a manifestation of the supreme Being, the most powerful that it is granted to us mortals to behold. I worship it for its light, and for the procreating power of God through which alone we live, move and have our being – we and all the plants and animals too. But if you ask me if I am minded to bow down before a bone from the thumb of the apostle Peter or Paul, then I say: Leave me alone, and spare me your absurdities!

'"Quench not the spirit," says the apostle. There is so much nonsense in the articles of the Church. But it seeks to rule, and therefore must have a blinkered multitude that bends the knee and is willing to be ruled. The worst nightmare of the well-remunerated senior clergy is the education of the lower orders. They kept the Bible away from them for a long time, too – for as long as they possibly could. After all, what *was* a poor Christian parishioner supposed to make of the princely pomp of a highly paid bishop, when he sees in the Gospels the poverty and indigence of Christ, travelling humbly on foot with His disciples, while the princely bishop bowls along in a coach and six?

'We have no idea,' Goethe went on, 'how much we owe to Luther and to the Reformation in general. We have been freed from the fetters of spiritual bigotry, and as we have progressed in our cultural development we have been able to go back to the source and appreciate Christianity in its pure form. We have found the courage again to plant our feet firmly on God's earth and to feel at home in our own God-given human nature. However sophisticated our intellectual culture becomes, however much the natural sciences continue to grow in scope and depth, and however much the human mind continues to expand: it will never surpass the majesty and moral culture of Christianity as it shines forth in the Gospels.

'But the greater the strides we Protestants make in our noble development, the sooner the Catholics will follow. Once they become caught up in the great enlightenment of the age, which is gathering momentum everywhere, they will *have* to follow, kick and struggle as they may; and eventually the time will come when all are one.

'All this wretched Protestant sectarianism will also cease, and with it the hatred and hostility between father and son, brother and sister. Because once people have understood the pure teaching and love of Christ for what it is, and have fully internalized it and made it their own, they will feel enlarged and liberated as human beings, and will no longer care much about minor differences in forms of worship.

'Meanwhile all of us will gradually progress from a Christianity of words and faith to a Christianity of conviction and action.'

The conversation turned to great men who had lived before Christ among the Chinese, Indians, Persians and Greeks; and we agreed that the power of God had been at work in them just as much as in some great Jews of the Old Testament. We also got on to the question of how far God was at work in the great figures of our contemporary world.

'To hear people talk,' said Goethe, 'you'd almost think that God had gone into retirement since those ancient times, leaving man to his own devices; and now man must manage as best he can without God, and without being touched each day by His unseen breath. People allow that God has a hand in religious and moral matters, but when it comes to science and the arts, they think that these are things of this world, the product of purely human powers, and nothing more.

'But just you try producing something that can stand alongside the works of a Mozart, a Raphael or a Shakespeare by relying on human will and human powers alone. I am well aware that those three titans are not the only ones, by any means, and that countless brilliant minds have laboured in every field of art to produce things just as good as they did. But if they were as great as those three, then they towered just as high above the human norm and were just as divinely gifted as they were.

'And in the end, what does it all matter anyway? God did not retire to rest after the famous imagined six days of creation, but indeed remains as active as He was on the first day. It would surely have given Him little pleasure to construct this physical world of ours from simple elements and then let it roll on, year after year, in the light of the sun, if He were not planning to establish a nursery for a world of spirits upon this material foundation. So now He is constantly at work in higher individuals in order to bring on our weaker brethren.'

Goethe fell silent. But I treasured up his wise and wondrous words in my heart.[38]

Notes

INTRODUCTION

1. 'Bemerkungen über Goethes Wahlverwandtschaften', in J. P. Eckermann, *Beyträge zur Poesie mit besonderer Hinweisung auf Goethe* (Stuttgart, 1824), pp. 150–89 (p. 153).

2. Eckermann, 'Über den Ausgang tragischer Charactere', in *Beyträge*, pp. 80–88 (p. 83). See 'Über Egmont, Trauerspiel von Goethe' (1788), in Friedrich Schiller, *Sämtliche Werke*, ed. Gerhard Fricke and Herbert G. Göpfert, 5 vols (Munich, 1958), vol. 5, pp. 932–42 (p. 942).

3. Quoted in H. H. Houben, *J. P. Eckermann: Sein Leben für Goethe* (Leipzig, 1925), pp. 256–7.

4. Letter to Thomas Carlyle, in Johann Wolfgang Goethe, *Sämtliche Werke: Briefe, Tagebücher und Gespräche*, ed. Friedmar Apel and others, Deutsche Klassiker–Ausgabe, 40 vols (Frankfurt a.M., 1986–2000), vol. 38, p. 399. This edition is henceforth cited as FA.

5. See the text in FA, vol. 39, p. 924.

6. *Briefe an Goethe*, ed. Karl Robert Mandelkow, 2 vols, 2nd edn (Munich, 1982), p. 555. My translation.

7. FA, vol. 39, pp. 918–19. My translation.

8. Ernst Beutler, 'Einführung', in Eckermann, *Gespräche mit Goethe* (Munich, 1976), p. 813. This was originally published in vol. 24 of the *Gedenkausgabe der Werke, Briefe und Gespräche Johann Wolfgang Goethes* (Zurich, 1948). Beutler gives many more examples.

9. These and many other errors are noted in the still indispensable study by Julius Petersen, *Die Entstehung der Eckermannschen Gespräche und ihre Glaubwürdigkeit*, 2nd edn (Frankfurt a.M., 1925).

10. See the passage from Soret in FA, vol. 38, p. 295.

11. See Petersen, *Die Entstehung*, p. 122.

650 NOTES

12. Quoted in Petersen, *Die Entstehung*, p. 110.

13. Müller, 8 June 1830, in FA, vol. 38, pp. 278–9.

14. Soret, 6 June 1828, in FA, vol. 37, pp. 615–16.

15. FA, vol. 39, p. 919.

16. Heinrich Heine, 'Die deutsche Literatur von W. Menzel', in *Sämtliche Schriften*, ed. Klaus Briegleb, 6 vols (Munich, 1968–76), vol. 1, p. 455.

17. Ludwig Börne, *Briefe aus Paris*, 20 Nov. 1830, in *Sämtliche Schriften*, ed. Inge and Peter Rippmann, 5 vols (Dreieich, 1977), vol. 3, p. 71.

18. FA, vol. 5, pp. 486–7; cf. also Alba's words on p. 525. Translation from *Five German Tragedies*, tr. F. J. Lamport (Harmondsworth, 1969), p. 131.

19. See Adam Sisman, *Boswell's Presumptuous Task* (London, 2000).

20. See Eduard Goldstücker, 'Kafkas Eckermann? Zu Gustav Janouchs *Gespräche mit Kafka*', in Claude David (ed.), *Franz Kafka: Themen und Probleme* (Göttingen, 1980), pp. 238–55.

21. FA, vol. 13, p. 239.

22. The beautifully illustrated guide issued by the Klassik Stiftung Weimar, *Goethes Wohnhaus*, ed. Wolfgang Holler and Kristin Knebel (n.p., n.d.), has been of great value to me in annotating the *Conversations*.

23. FA, vol. 37, p. 527.

24. See Friedrich Sengle, *Das Genie und sein Fürst. Die Geschichte der Lebensgemeinschaft Goethes mit dem Herzog Carl August* (Stuttgart, 1993), pp. 514–15.

25. FA, vol. 38, p. 37 (15 August 1828).

26. See Leslie O'Bell, 'Chinese novels, scholarly errors and Goethe's concept of world literature', *Publications of the English Goethe Society*, 87 (2018), pp. 64–80. Goethe's word '*Roman*', translated as 'novel', can also mean a verse narrative.

27. See Ben Hutchinson, *Comparative Literature: A Very Short Introduction* (Oxford, 2018).

28. See D. Pieter Strauss, 'Why did Goethe hate glasses? Two puzzling passages in the *Wahlverwandtschaften* and the *Wanderjahre*', *Journal of English and Germanic Philology*, 80 (1981), pp. 176–87.

29. For introductions to Goethe's science, written from differing points of view, see H. B. Nisbet, *Goethe and the Scientific Tradition* (London, 1972), and Astrida Orle Tantillo, *The Will to Create: Goethe's Philosophy of Nature* (Pittsburgh, 2002).

30. As has been shown brilliantly by Albrecht Schöne in *Goethes Farbentheologie* (Munich, 1987).

NOTES   651

31. See his review of J. C. Lavater's *Aussichten in die Ewigkeit* in the *Frankfurter gelehrte Anzeigen*, 1773, in FA, vol. 18, pp. 80–83.
32. Letter to Johann Caspar Lavater, 29 July 1782, in FA, vol. 29, p. 436.
33. FA, vol. 38, p. 381.
34. Friedrich Nietzsche, *Menschliches, Allzumenschliches*, Part II (1880): *Der Wanderer und sein Schatten*, §109.

PART ONE

1. In December 1810 Eckermann's home region was thus incorporated into the French Empire.
2. Not identified.
3. These belonged to the then fashionable genre of 'fate-tragedies', in which the protagonist's doom results from a series of apparent coincidences which are explained as due to a hereditary curse.
4. Johanna Bertram (1801–34), to whom Eckermann had been engaged since summer 1819.
5. 'Ottilie' is Goethe's daughter-in-law, later referred to as Frau von Goethe, and the boy is probably her eldest child Walter; see List of Persons Mentioned.
6. Iphigenia was the subject of many plays, including Euripides' *Iphigenia at Aulis* and *Iphigenia at Tauris*, Racine's *Iphigénie* (1674) and Goethe's *Iphigenie auf Tauris* (1787).
7. 'his star' was the insignia of the Order of the White Falcon, bestowed on Goethe by Grand Duke Karl August on 30 January 1816; Goethe's favourite among the many decorations he had received.
8. The Ceiling Room was Goethe's picture gallery. It was not here, but in the nearby Juno Room, that the *Aldobrandini Wedding* was displayed; this was a copy by Goethe's friend Johann Heinrich Meyer of the Roman fresco depicting ritual preparations for a wedding, discovered in 1606 and named after its owner, Cardinal Pietro Aldobrandini; now in the Vatican Museums.
9. Goethe's son, August von Goethe; see List of Persons Mentioned.
10. Goethe and Beethoven met at Teplitz in Bohemia in July 1812; Goethe admired Beethoven's character and his works, but also found both disturbing. He described him to his musical friend Zelter: 'His talent astonished me, but unfortunately he is a completely uncontrolled personality' (letter, 2 September 1812).

11. The 'witty lady' is Marie Kunigunde von Savigny (1780–1863), wife of the famous legal academic Friedrich Karl von Savigny (1779–1861); we know from another source that both Savignys were present, with their daughter Bettina (1805–35), but Eckermann suppresses their names, presumably out of discretion.

12. Goethe followed closely the Greek War of Independence against Turkish rule.

13. George Gordon, Lord Byron, whose poems, especially *Childe Harold's Pilgrimage*, enjoyed a huge vogue throughout Europe. In 1823 he went to Greece to support the independence struggle and died of fever at Missolonghi on 19 April 1824.

14. The pianist Maria Szymanowska; see List of Persons Mentioned.

15. *Die Schachmaschine* (*The Chess Machine*), a comedy adapted by Heinrich Beck (1760–1803) from an English original.

16. Known as the 'Marienbader Elegie', this poem was written very soon after Ulrike von Levetzow (1804–99) had rejected a proposal of marriage from Goethe, who was fifty-five years her senior, and who had first met her in 1821 in Marienbad. Goethe spent time with the Levetzows in Karlsbad in August and September 1823, made his unsuccessful proposal, and wrote the poem immediately after leaving Karlsbad. The poem, one of his greatest, expresses desolation at his loss. Goethe showed the poem to only a very few friends, besides Eckermann, before publishing it as the second part of his *Trilogie der Leidenschaft* (*Trilogy of Passion*) in 1827.

17. Tiefurt was a mansion and park near Weimar.

18. The poem was 'Paria', first published in *Kunst und Altertum*, January 1824; a poem in three parts, centring on the adaptation of an Indian legend about how the Untouchables ('pariahs') acquired a tutelary divinity.

19. *Die Schwestern von Prag* (*The Sisters of Prague*, 1794) was a comic opera by Wenzel Müller (1767–1835).

20. 'elderly gentleman': Christoph Erhard Sutor (1754–1838), servant to Goethe from 1776 to 1795.

21. The three-part 'Paria'.

22. *Ghaselen*: a collection of poems using a Persian verse form, the ghazal, in which the same rhyme recurs in alternate lines throughout the poem.

23. *Nibelungen*: the medieval epic poem known as the *Nibelungenlied* (*c.*1200) was the subject of scholarly controversy: Goethe's critic Schubarth maintained that it had not been composed as a unit but compiled from numerous shorter heroic lays. F. A. Wolf,

NOTES 653

just mentioned, had argued a similar case about the Homeric epics.

24. In August 1814 Goethe and Zelter attended the consecration of the chapel of St Roch at Bingen on the Rhine; Goethe described the event in the essay *Sankt-Rochus-Fest zu Bingen* (published 1817).

25. 'continuation of his memoirs': the fourth part of Goethe's autobiography, *Aus meinem Leben. Dichtung und Wahrheit*, mainly dealing with the events of 1775 down to his departure for Weimar. The first three parts had appeared in 1811–14.

26. 'my colossal Juno': a plaster cast of the enormous head of a goddess, dating from the first century CE and known as the Juno Ludovisi, which Goethe received as a present from State Councillor Schultz on 7 October 1823. In 1787 Goethe had seen the original at Rome in the collection formed by Cardinal Ludovico Ludovisi.

27. At the request of the town council of Goethe's native Frankfurt, Rauch made four models for a statue of Goethe, but did not complete any of them; his work later served as inspiration for the sculptor Pompeo Marchesi, who made a statue of Goethe which in 1840 was displayed in the vestibule of the Frankfurt City Library.

28. *Der Paria* (*The Pariah*, 1826), play by Michael Beer (1800–1833); Goethe thought highly of it, and introduced it into the repertoire of the Weimar Court Theatre.

29. Probably one of the *Römische Elegien*, which Goethe wrote after returning from Italy in 1788; he initially withheld them from publication as too sexually frank, but Schiller insisted on publishing most of them in his journal *Die Horen* in 1795, apart from a few which he judged too outspoken. Another may be *Das Tagebuch* (*The Diary*, 1810), a narrative poem commending marital faithfulness in remarkably sexually explicit terms, which was first published privately in a limited edition in 1861 and included in an official edition of Goethe's works only in 1914. See Goethe, *Roman Elegies; The Diary*, tr. David Luke, with an introduction by Hans R. Vaget (London, 1988), reprinted as Goethe, *Erotic Poems* (Oxford, 1997).

30. The expurgated edition by Thomas Bowdler, entitled *The family Shakespeare, in which nothing is added to the original text, but those words and expressions are omitted which cannot with propriety be read aloud in a family* (1807; often reprinted).

31. France, now under the Bourbon monarchy, had intervened in Spain to restore the absolute regime of Ferdinand VII.

654 NOTES

32. Charles André Vanloo (1705–65); the engraving is based on his *Conversation espagnole* (*Spanish Conversation*).

33. Goethe, *Faust I*, lines 3851–2.

34. Painted by Johann Heinrich Meyer around 1796, it now hangs in the Small Dining Room in Goethe's house.

35. The opening of an eight-line poem which Goethe wrote in 1782, referring to Charlotte von Stein, his close friend during his first period in Weimar (1775–86), and published first in 1789.

36. Staberle was a humorous figure in Viennese popular comedy, created by Adolf Bäuerle (1786–1859).

37. *Das neue Sonntagskind* (*The New Sunday Child*) is a comic opera by Wenzel Müller.

38. Franz Volkmar Reinhard; see List of Persons Mentioned.

39. By the Greek poet Nonnus (fourth or fifth century CE).

40. *Zahme Xenien*: short verse epigrams, mostly composed from 1815 on; called 'tame' in contrast to the polemical *Xenien*, aimed at contemporaries, which Goethe and Schiller wrote in the 1790s.

41. Also called the Bridge Room, where Goethe kept his large collection of sculptures.

42. 'Lili' Schönemann, briefly engaged to Goethe in 1775; see List of Persons Mentioned.

43. 'continuation of *Faust*': these plans were not included in Goethe's final text.

44. *Morgenblatt* (*Morning Paper*), prestigious journal published by Cotta in Stuttgart; *Abendzeitung* (*Evening News*), newspaper in Dresden.

45. *Die Horen* (*The Hours*) and *Musenalmanach* (*The Muses' Almanac*), literary periodicals edited by Schiller in the 1790s.

46. Goethe's opinion of Dante has evidently risen since he recalled in his *Italian Journey* (written 1813–17): 'I had never been able to understand how people could take the trouble to read these poems. I thought the *Inferno* absolutely horrible, the *Purgatorio* ambiguous, and the *Paradiso* a bore' (*Italian Journey*, tr. W. H. Auden and Elizabeth Mayer (Harmondsworth, 1970), p. 371).

47. Rousseau: this comes from 'Lettre de J.-J. Rousseau à M. de Voltaire', in Jean-Jacques Rousseau, *Œuvres complètes*, ed. Bernard Gagnebin and Marcel Raymond, 5 vols (Paris, 1959–95), vol. 4, pp. 1059–75 (p. 1061).

48. 'Mr H.' is identified in Goethe's diary as 'Captain Hutton'.

49. Conjectured to be Agnes Franz (1794–1843), author of *Die Heimkehr* (*The Homecoming*).

NOTES   655

50. *Cellini*: Goethe's translation (1803) of the autobiography of the
     Italian artist Benvenuto Cellini (1500–1571).

51. Therese von Jakob (1797–1870), married to the American cler-
     gyman Edward Robinson; she translated Serbian folk songs
     from the collection made by Vuk Stefanović Karadžić.

52. *The Taming of the Shrew*, Act IV, scene 5.

53. Thomas Medwin reports Byron as saying: 'As to originality, Goe-
     the has too much sense to pretend that he is not under obligations
     to authors, ancient and modern; – who is not? You tell me the
     plot is almost entirely Calderon's. The fête, the scholar, the
     argument about the *Logos*, the selling himself to the fiend, and
     afterwards denying his power; his disguise of the plumed cava-
     lier; the enchanted mirror, – are all from Cyprian. That *magico
     prodigioso* must be worth reading, and nobody seems to know
     any thing of it but you and Shelley. Then the vision is not unlike
     that of Marlow's, in his "Faustus". The bed-scene is from "Cym-
     beline"; the song or serenade, a translation of Ophelia's, in
     "Hamlet"; and, more than all, the prologue is from Job, which
     is the first drama in the world, and perhaps the oldest poem.'
     Thomas Medwin, *Conversations of Lord Byron, noted during a
     residence with his Lordship at Pisa, in the years 1821 and 1822*
     (London, 1824), pp. 141–2. Goethe encountered Calderón's *El
     mágico prodigioso*, with its magician-hero Cipriano, only in
     1794, after publishing the first version of *Faust* as *Faust: Ein
     Fragment* in 1790.

54. Walter Scott: in Goethe's *Egmont*, the hero's girlfriend Klärchen
     admires her lover's gala costume; Amy Robsart, secretly married
     to Robert Dudley, Earl of Leicester, does the same in Scott's
     Kenilworth (1821), ch. 7. The mysterious deaf-mute Fenella,
     described in ch. 16 of *Peveril of the Peak* (1823), is modelled on
     Mignon in Goethe's *Wilhelm Meisters Lehrjahre*.

55. 'transformed devil': in Byron's play *The Deformed Transformed*
     (1821).

56. 'manuscript': the autobiographical notes which Goethe kept
     under the title *Tag- und Jahreshefte*.

57. 'a journalist': probably Friedrich Nicolai (1733–1811), an import-
     ant writer of the Berlin Enlightenment.

58. Schiller's drama *Wilhelm Tell* (1804), in which the tyrannical
     Swiss governor Gessler orders Tell to prove his marksmanship by
     shooting an apple off his son's head.

59. *Eugenie*: Goethe's play *Die natürliche Tochter* (*The Natural
     Daughter*, 1803), whose heroine is called Eugenie.

656   NOTES

60. *Die Räuber* (*The Robbers*, 1781), Schiller's first play.
61. *Rameau's Nephew*: the novel by Denis Diderot (1713–84), which Goethe translated into German.
62. Byron's play *Marino Faliero, Doge of Venice* (1821).
63. See *Henry IV, Part I*, Act II, scene 4.
64. 'The Burial of Sir John Moore at Corunna' by Charles Wolfe (1791–1823); finding it praised by Medwin, Goethe and Eckermann assumed it was by Byron.
65. 'young student': not identified.
66. Cologne Cathedral had been left unfinished in 1473. Goethe's friend the architect Sulpiz Boisserée drew up plans for its completion around 1811. After a fundraising campaign, work was begun in the 1840s and completed in 1880.
67. *Wilhelm Meister*: see the *Lehrjahre*, Book VIII, ch. 5.
68. *Wanderjahre*: see Book I, ch. 4.
69. William Parry (1773–1859), an artillery officer who was with Byron in Greece, published *The Last Days of Lord Byron* (1825).
70. Lucretia: ancient Roman noblewoman who committed suicide after being raped by Sextus Tarquinius (*c*.510 BCE). Mucius Scaevola: ancient Roman who proved his courage by holding his right hand in the fire (*c*.508 BCE).
71. On 28 August 1824 Goethe had his seventy-fifth birthday, which was formally celebrated on 3 September.
72. 'golden apples': a self-quotation from *Wilhelm Meisters Lehrjahre*, Book V, ch. 4; also used on 22 October 1828.
73. Platen: see List of Persons Mentioned.
74. 'improviser': there was at this time a vogue for improvisers who, on being given a theme, would compose and recite a poem about it on the spot. See Angela Esterhammer, *Romanticism and Improvisation, 1750–1850* (Cambridge, 2008).
75. Wellington was on his way to St Petersburg to attend the coronation of Tsar Nicholas I.
76. 'Poetische Gedancken über die Höllenfahrt Jesu Christi' ('Poetic Thoughts on Jesus Christ's Descent into Hell'), a poem of 160 lines written by Goethe in his early teens, in 1764 or 1765, and published without his consent, and to his annoyance, in the journal *Die Sichtbaren* (*The Visible Ones*).
77. Philipp Friedrich Seidel (1755–1820), Goethe's servant from 1775 to 1788.
78. 'A Song over the Unconfidence towards my Self', included by Goethe in a letter to his sister Cornelia, 11 May 1766.

NOTES   657

79. Arminius: early Germanic leader (?18 BCE–19 CE) who defeated the Romans at the Battle of the Teutoburg Forest in 9 CE; celebrated from the sixteenth century onwards under the name Hermann as a German national hero, and the subject of plays by Klopstock (see List of Persons Mentioned).

80. Byron's dedication in the second edition of *Sardanapalus* (1823) runs in part: 'To the illustrious Goëthe a Stranger presumes to offer the homage of a literary vassal to his liege lord, the first of existing writers – who has created the literature of his own country [. . .]'.

81. An invitation from Byron's friend John Cam Hobhouse to join the committee planning a monument to Byron.

82. Literary journal in Paris; Goethe received it regularly from September 1824 onwards, often spoke of it with enthusiasm, and learned much from it about contemporary French literature.

83. A spa town near Halle, some thirty-seven miles from Weimar, with a small theatre which put on plays from the repertoire of the Weimar theatre.

84. Illustrations to Albert Stapfer's French translation of *Faust I* by Eugène Delacroix (1798–1863). Delacroix eventually provided seventeen illustrations.

85. Mozart: this letter to 'Baron v. T.' was published in the *Allgemeine Wiener Theaterzeitung*, no. 138 (1824).

86. Goethe is quoting from Leonardo's *Trattato della pittura* (*Treatise on Painting*).

87. Phidias: Greek sculptor whose reliefs on the Parthenon had been taken to London by Lord Elgin and were now reproduced in the book *The Elgin Marbles from the Temple of Minerva at Athens*, which Goethe saw in the possession of the Grand Duke.

88. Probably H.-S. Leprince, author of *Nouvelle Chroagénésie, ou Réfutation du traité d'optique de Newton*, Part 1 (Paris, 1819).

89. On 12 December 1826 George Canning, the British Foreign Secretary, persuaded the House of Commons to intervene in Portugal in order to preserve its constitutional government, installed with British support in 1825, against an invasion from Spain.

90. The young composer is Felix Mendelssohn (1809–47).

91. Quotes from two love poems in the section of the *Divan* entitled '*Suleika Nameh* / Buch Suleika' ('The Book of Zuleika'). 'Jussufs Reize möcht' ich borgen' ('I'd like to borrow Joseph's charms') is from the untitled poem no. 120, beginning 'Lieb' um Liebe, Stund' um Stunde' ('Love upon love, hour upon hour'). The other quotation is from poem no. 138, beginning 'Ach! um deine

658   NOTES

feuchten Schwingen, / West, wie sehr ich dich beneide' ('Ah, how much I envy you, West Wind, for your moist wings'). The translations are taken from the parallel-text edition: Johann Wolfgang von Goethe, *West-Eastern Divan*, translated by Eric Ormsby (London, 2019).

92. The third Act of *Faust II*, published separately in 1827.

93. The novel *Wilhelm Meisters Wanderjahre* had appeared in 1821; Goethe was now preparing a revised and enlarged edition (not strictly a 'continuation'), which was published in 1829.

94. 'novella': published separately in 1828 under the title *Novelle*. Originally conceived in 1797 as a narrative poem entitled *Die Jagd* (*The Hunt*). Although *Wilhelm Meisters Wanderjahre* includes several self-contained stories, Goethe does not seem ever to have intended this to be one of them.

95. 'Classical Walpurgis Night': the second Act of *Faust II*.

96. 'hereditary Grand Duke': Eckermann has confused the Grand Duke Karl August, who visited Goethe on 11 January 1827, with his heir.

97. 'Faust's speech to Proserpine': this speech was never written.

98. Urbino Room: one of the rooms Goethe used for entertaining guests; it was dominated by a portrait of the Duke of Urbino. The room next to it is not the Ceiling Room but the Juno Room.

99. *Fiesko*: play by Schiller, *Die Verschwörung des Fiesco zu Genua* (*The Conspiracy of Fiesco at Genoa*, 1783). The first edition used the spelling '*Fiesko*'. Schiller's other early plays are *Die Räuber* (1781) and *Kabale und Liebe* (*Intrigue and Love*, 1784).

100. Quatrain from Goethe's *Zahme Xenien* (see List of Works by Goethe).

101. *Clara Gazul*: a collection of plays (1825, 1830) by Prosper Mérimée, set in Spain or South America and presented as translations from Spanish.

102. 'a foreigner': probably Charles Des Voeux (1802–33), a member of an Irish noble family, who, with help from Ottilie von Goethe, translated Goethe's *Tasso* into English; Ottilie wrote a preface for the second edition, *Torquato Tasso, a Dramatic Poem, from the German of Goethe* (Weimar, 1833).

103. 'Horace and Hafiz': did this inspire Conan Doyle to make Sherlock Holmes say: 'there is as much sense in Hafiz as in Horace, and as much knowledge of the world' ('A Case of Identity', 1891)?

104. 'Chinese novel': apparently an English translation, entitled *Chinese Courtship in Verse*, of a novel belonging to the seventeenth-century genre of romances involving a scholar and a beautiful girl;

NOTES   659

but either Goethe or Eckermann seems to have confused it with another novel, published in English in 1761 under the title *Hau Kiou Choaan, or The Pleasing History*, and with a third, called *Yü-kiau-li*, of which Goethe had recently seen the French translation reviewed, and which he obtained and read a few months later.

105. *The Peasants' Return from the Fields* (c.1640), now in the Galleria Palatina in Florence. Goethe showed Eckermann an engraving of this painting by the Dutch engraver Schelte a Bolswert (1586–1659) which is now in the Fitzwilliam Museum in Cambridge. See *Goethe on Art*, ed. John Gage (Berkeley, 1980), pp. 203–6.

106. Lessing said this in *Eine Duplik* (*A Rejoinder*, 1778): see Lessing, *Philosophical and Theological Writings*, ed. H. B. Nisbet (Cambridge, 2005), p. 9.

107. 'monument': in *Helena*, which became Act III of *Faust II*, the son of Faust and Helen, Euphorion, tries to fly too high and crashes to earth; the stage direction says: 'we seem to recognize his face as that of a well-known figure'. As Euphorion represents 'the modern poetic age', the 'figure' is generally understood to be Byron.

108. Quatrain from Goethe's collection of poetic maxims, published under the heading *Sprichwörtliches* (*Proverbial Pieces*) in 1815.

109. 'Englishman': Goethe and Eckermann, like most continental Europeans at this time, rarely distinguished between Scotland and England; but cf. the conversation on 11 October 1828.

110. Manzoni, *I promessi sposi* (*The Betrothed*, 1827).

111. *Sieben Mädchen in Uniform* (*Seven Girls in Uniform*), a popular comedy by the Berlin playwright and restaurant-owner Louis Angely (1788–1835).

112. *Galeerensklaven*: *Die beiden Galeerensklaven* (*The Two Galley-Slaves*), a popular melodrama.

113. Romantic opera composed by Carl Maria von Weber (1821).

114. Wilhelm Müller (1794–1827), whose collections *Die Winterreise* and *Die schöne Müllerin* were set to music by Schubert. Goethe disliked both him and his poems.

PART TWO

1. Opera by Carl Maria von Weber, composed in 1826.

2. Poem by Goethe entitled 'Jägers Abendlied' ('Huntsman's Serenade', 1776), set to music by many composers, including Schubert and Zelter.

660   NOTES

3.   *Le Porteur d'eau*: *The Water-Carrier*, opera by Luigi Cherubini (1760–1842).

4.   Carlyle, 'Goethe', *Foreign Review*, no. 3 (1828).

5.   A mountainous locality in the Peloponnese, site of a temple of Apollo.

6.   'State of German Literature' by Carlyle, published anonymously in the *Edinburgh Review*, no. 92 (October 1827), pp. 304–51.

7.   'couplets': satirical poems from the collection *Xenien*: see List of Works by Goethe.

8.   Loosely quoted from *Faust I*, lines 1990–96.

9.   The 'ballad about the children and the old man' is 'Ballade' (1820); in 'Die glücklichen Gatten' ('The Happy Couple', 1804), an elderly couple look back over their happy married life.

10. 'I loved you, princess, and I dared to tell you so; in waking me, the gods have not deprived me of everything; I have lost nothing but my empire.'

11. 'Good man and good wife': a Scottish ballad which Goethe translated as 'Gutmann und Gutweib'.

12. 'Vermächtnis' ('Legacy').

13. Henry Colebrooke (1765–1837), Sanskrit scholar, who wrote extensively on Indian philosophy and law.

14. Artaria: a publishing house in Mannheim.

15. Not the political writer Niccolò Machiavelli (1469–1527), but a character, based on a historical original, who appears in *Egmont* and gives sensible but unheeded advice to the Regent of the Spanish-ruled Netherlands.

16. 'Nadowessiers Totenlied' (1798), a poem mourning the death of a Native American warrior.

17. 'daemons', 'daemonic': nothing to do with devils or evil spirits, but an expression of Goethe's sense of irrational powers active in history and embodied in certain outstanding persons.

18. British opposition to equal rights for Catholics in Ireland, though reinforced by King George IV, was now dwindling sufficiently to allow the passage of the Roman Catholic Relief Act in 1829.

19. The poem beginning 'Cupido, loser, eigensinniger Knabe!', which Goethe wrote in Italy and included in the revised version of his *Singspiel* (musical drama) *Claudine von Villa Bella* (1788).

20. Louis Antoine Fauvelet de Bourrienne, *Mémoires sur Napoléon, le directoire, le consulat, l'empire et la restauration*, 10 vols (Paris, 1828–30).

21. Not identified.

NOTES

661

22. Wartburg Festival: a gathering of some 500 German students on 18 October 1817 at the Wartburg, the fortress where Martin Luther had stayed in hiding in 1521–2, to celebrate a Protestant conception of German national identity. Goethe had a low opinion of such nationalism.

23. Ludwig I (1786–1868), patron of the arts, responsible for many neoclassical buildings in and near Munich; he visited Goethe in Weimar in 1827.

24. Ludwig I published altogether four volumes of poems; they were ridiculed by Heinrich Heine.

25. Friedrich: the servant Gottlieb Friedrich Krause; see List of Persons Mentioned.

26. *Dreissig Jahre aus dem Leben eines Spielers* (*Thirty Years from the Life of a Gambler*, 1830), comedy by Theodor Hell (1775–1856).

27. 'Herr von D.': Georg Freiherr von Diemar, a relative of Count Reinhard.

28. Pius VIII (reigned from March 1829 to his death in November 1830).

29. Sesenheim: village in Alsace where Goethe in 1770–71 conducted a love affair with the clergyman's daughter Friederike Brion, as recounted with poetic licence in Books 10 and 11 of *Dichtung und Wahrheit*.

30. Antonio Tasso: a mistake for Agostino Tassi; see List of Persons Mentioned.

31. Entelechy was an important concept for Goethe: every being contains a dynamic core which strives to realize its potential. The term was coined by Aristotle, but Goethe associates it with Leibniz's conception of the monad or irreducible core of a being: see also 3 March 1830.

32. That is, of *Faust II*, on which Goethe worked from now till shortly before his death in 1832. 'Wagner' is the assistant to the scholar Faust. The Bachelor ('Baccalaureus') is often taken to be a satire on idealist philosophy; he affirms in line 6795 that he is responsible for the sun rising. The homunculus is an intelligent but disembodied being whom Wagner has created in a test tube. To understand the many further allusions to *Faust II*, the reader is advised to read a translation.

33. 'Faust's dream about Leda': see *Faust II*, lines 6903–20.

34. *Market of Naples*: evidently a play, about which nothing is known.

35. Euphorion: cf. note 107 to Part One.

662   NOTES

36. The French poet Gérard Labrunie (1808–55), who translated *Faust I* into French (1828); in 1841 he assumed the name Gérard de Nerval.

37. Karl Glenck (1779–1845). Stotternheim is now a suburb of Erfurt, some thirteen miles from Weimar. A salt mine was opened there in 1828.

38. Prince Primate: Karl von Dalberg; see List of Persons Mentioned.

39. Either Eliza Gore (1753–1802) or her sister Emily (1755–1832), daughters of Charles Gore (1729–1807), an Englishman who lived in Weimar from 1791, became friendly with Goethe and was present with him at the Siege of Mainz in 1793. Probably Eliza is meant, since Goethe mentions her artistic talents in the brief biographical remarks on Charles Gore in his memoir of the artist Philipp Hackert, from whom both Gore and Goethe took lessons in drawing.

40. 'Klingsor costume': may allude to the magician Klingsor in Wolfram von Eschenbach's narrative poem *Parzival* (*c.*1210) or to his namesake the poet in Novalis's novel *Heinrich von Ofterdingen* (1802).

41. 'Der Sänger-Wettstreit auf der Wartburg' ('The Singers' Competition at the Wartburg'), written to celebrate the Grand Duke's birthday.

42. *Der Stern von Sevilla* (*The Star of Seville*), tragedy by the then popular Joseph Christian von Zedlitz (1790–1862).

43. *Chaos*: a magazine edited by Ottilie von Goethe.

44. 'harbour view': perhaps a copy of a painting by Johannes Lingelbach (1622–74).

45. 'situation': increasing tensions between the French parliament and the Bourbon King Charles X, which would lead on 18 March to Charles's dissolution of Parliament, on 25 July to his suspension of press freedom, and on 27–9 July to the July Revolution which ended the Bourbon monarchy.

46. 'Goethes Porträt. Auf Befehl Seiner Majestät des Königs von Bayern gemalt von Stieler 1829' ('Goethe's Portrait, painted by Stieler in 1829 on the orders of His Majesty the King of Bavaria'). Stieler's well-known portrait shows Goethe seated at his desk and holding a sheet of paper on which can be made out part of a poem by Ludwig I of Bavaria.

47. 'passage': in no. 15 of the *Roman Elegies*.

48. 'Le Rire de Mirabeau' ('Mirabeau's Laugh'), poem by A. Cordellier-Delaroue (d. 1854).

49. *L'Orfana di Genevra* (correctly *Ginevra*; *The Orphan of Geneva*), ballet choreographed by Giovanni Galzerani (*c.*1789–1853).

NOTES   663

50. Livonia: province of the Russian Empire, largely coextensive with present-day Latvia, with a German-speaking upper class.

51. 'left Paris in a hurry': to escape the July Revolution.

52. 28 August was Goethe's birthday.

53. From the poem 'Talismane' in Goethe's *West-östlicher Divan*.

54. *Faust II*, lines 9550–57.

55. *Faust II*, lines 7552–3.

56. *The Barber of Seville*: *Il barbiere di Siviglia*, comic opera (1816) by Rossini.

57. *The Vicar of Wakefield*: novel (1766) by Oliver Goldsmith (1728–74), hugely popular in German translation; Goethe used it in *Dichtung und Wahrheit* to shape his account of his visits to Friederike Brion, daughter of the vicar of Sesenheim.

58. *Gil Blas*: picaresque novel (1715–35) by Alain-René Lesage (1668–1747).

59. Goethe never completed this work.

60. 'Cabeiri': gods worshipped in a mystery cult on the Greek island of Samothrace; alluded to in *Faust II*, lines 8070–77, 8178.

61. Phorkyads: Greek mythological beings, imagined as aged hags; Mephistopheles assumes the guise of one in *Faust II*, lines 8697–9126.

62. 'essay on Zahn': the archaeologist Wilhelm Zahn published in 1830 a study of the wall paintings found at Pompeii, which Goethe reviewed at considerable length in the Vienna *Jahrbücher für Literatur*, 51 (1830), pp. 1–12.

63. *Agnes Bernauerin* (1780), historical drama by Joseph August, Graf von Törring (1753–1826), about the mistress (c.1410–35) of the Duke of Bavaria, unjustly condemned to death for political motives. The best-known play about her is Friedrich Hebbel's *Agnes Bernauer* (1855).

64. *Otto von Wittelsbach*: play (1782) by Joseph Marius von Babo (1756–1822), likewise taken from Bavarian history, dealing with Duke Otto II (1206–53).

65. *Daphnis and Chloe*: ancient Greek pastoral novel by Longus (second century CE).

66. *La Muette de Portici* (*The Dumb Girl of Portici*), opera by Daniel Auber (1782–1871), dealing with Masaniello's unsuccessful uprising in Naples in 1647, and first performed in Paris in 1828. Its heroine, Masaniello's sister Fenella, named after the deaf mute in Scott's *Peveril of the Peak*, has been seduced and abandoned by the son of the Viceroy of Naples. The premiere prompted riots which led to the separation of Belgium from the Netherlands.

664   NOTES

67. The librarians of the Laurentian Library accused Courier (see List of Persons Mentioned) of leaving an ink blot on the manuscript of *Daphnis and Chloe* which he discovered there.

68. Johann Gustav Stickel (1805–96), who visited Goethe on 11 March 1831.

69. Gregory XVI (reigned 1831–46).

70. ***: Johann Friedrich Christoph Gille (1780–1836), a Weimar administrator, who asked Eckermann not to mention his name.

71. Lili: Lili Schönemann (see note 42 to Part One, and List of Persons Mentioned).

72. Probably Ludwig Börne (1786–1837), radical journalist, who moved to Paris after the July Revolution of 1830.

73. 'No being can decay to nothing': opening line of the poem 'Vermächtnis' (1829).

74. The first part of Schiller's *Wallenstein* trilogy, *Wallensteins Lager*, includes a comical homily by a Capuchin monk, modelled on the style of the popular Viennese preacher Abraham a Sancta Clara (1644–1709).

75. Close of the poem beginning 'Was wär ein Gott', expressing Goethe's version of pantheism (first published 1815).

76. Myron, a Greek sculptor of the fifth century BCE, made a bronze image of a cow which has not survived but is described by many ancient authors. Goethe published an essay on it in the journal *Kunst und Altertum* (1818).

77. Philemon and Baucis: an elderly couple in Greek mythology who gave hospitality to the gods Zeus and Hermes without recognizing them and were duly rewarded; Ovid (43 BCE–18 CE) tells the story in his *Metamorphoses*.

78. See 1 Kings:21.

79. 'dispute': see below, 2 August 1830.

80. Siegmund von Arnim (1813–90), second son of Bettina von Arnim (1785–1859). Bettina corresponded with Goethe between 1807 and 1811, and published their correspondence after his death, with much fictional elaboration, as *Goethes Briefwechsel mit einem Kinde* (1835).

PART THREE

1. A poem which Goethe, with some help from Riemer, had translated on the previous day (2 December 1822) from modern Greek; first published in *Kunst und Altertum* in 1823.

NOTES   665

2. In the first Act of Goethe's *Torquato Tasso*, the protagonist is
    crowned with laurel by his admirers, the Princess of Ferrara and
    her friend Leonore Sanvitale.

3. Wilhelm von Humboldt, not his brother Alexander (whom Goe-
    the also knew well); see List of Persons Mentioned.

4. In summer 1823, Goethe proposed marriage to the nineteen-
    year-old Ulrike von Levetzow, whom he had first got to know in
    Marienbad two years earlier. She considered his proposal seri-
    ously, but refused him. His grief found searing expression in the
    'Marienbader Elegie'. See note 16 to Part One.

5. Deschamps: a mineralogist, known to Goethe's friend Soret (not
    the poet Émile Deschamps, for whom see List of Persons
    Mentioned).

6. pamphlet: by Jan Evangelista Purkinje (1787–1869), a noted
    Czech physiologist.

7. *King Coal's Levee, or, Geological Etiquette* (1820), by John
    Scafe (1776–1843).

8. The Schlossers were relatives of Goethe through his sister Cor-
    nelia (1750–77), who had married the lawyer Johann Georg
    Schlosser (1739–99).

9. From Goethe's verse play *Pandora* (1807).

10. 'young American': George Henry Calvert (1803–89), Harvard
    graduate, writer and later professor of moral philosophy at the
    University of Baltimore.

11. *Das Hausgesinde* (*The Domestic Staff*, 1808), a highly successful
    opera by Anton Fischer (1778–1808).

12. *Tartuffe*: Molière's comedy (1664) about a religious hypocrite
    provoked the Archbishop of Paris to threaten to excommunicate
    anyone who watched or even read it.

13. 'gymnastic movement': in 1811 Friedrich Ludwig Jahn (1778–
    1852) founded the first of many gymnastic societies, intended
    not only to promote physical health and clean living, but to
    encourage resistance to the French occupation of Prussia. The
    gymnastic movement led to the foundation of nationalist stu-
    dent societies (*Burschenschaften*), seeking a united Germany;
    the first was formed at Jena in 1815. The *Burschenschaften*
    held the Wartburg Festival in October 1817. One of their mem-
    bers, Karl Sand, assassinated the German dramatist and Russian
    diplomat August von Kotzebue in 1819. Thereupon Metter-
    nich, the dominant statesman in post-Napoleonic Europe,
    instigated the Karlsbad Decrees, which banned the *Burschen-
    schaften*, placed universities throughout Germany under close

666   NOTES

supervision, required professors with politically liberal views to be dismissed, and strengthened censorship.

14. From Goethe's *Zahme Xenien*.

15. See *Faust I*, lines 2540–52, in the scene 'Witch's Kitchen'.

16. In Sophocles' play, the titular heroine is obliged to bury the corpse of her brother Polyneices, though Creon, King of Thebes, has forbidden this on pain of death. For Hegel, with whom Hinrichs had studied, this was the cardinal example of an insoluble tragic conflict between the claims of the individual conscience and those of the state.

17. August Wilhelm Schlegel, not his brother Friedrich; see List of Persons Mentioned.

18. This judgement is Goethe's; Ampère wrote 'dans cette poésie si harmonieuse, si délicate, il y a du *Verther*' ('in such harmonious and delicate poetry there is something of *Werther*'). See Elizabeth M. Wilkinson and L. A. Willoughby, *Goethe: Poet and Thinker* (London, 1962), p. 187.

19. From Goethe's early poem 'An Schwager Kronos' (1774).

20. 'Shandy': in Sterne's *Tristram Shandy* (1759–67).

21. 18th Brumaire: bloodless *coup d'état* which brought Napoleon to power as First Consul on 9 November 1799 (18 Brumaire, Year VIII, in the French revolutionary calendar).

22. The future Frederick William IV (1795–1861), who ascended the throne in 1840.

23. From the 'Schenkenbuch' ('Book of the Cupbearer') in the *West-östlicher Divan*.

24. Alludes to a novel by Alain-René Lesage (1668–1747), *Le Diable boiteux* (*The Lame Devil*, 1707), in which the devil Asmodeus lifts the roofs of the houses of Madrid to reveal to his human companion what is going on in secret.

25. In *A Sentimental Journey* Sterne writes: 'every third man a pigmy!' (Oxford, 1968, p. 59).

26. Opening of the poem 'Stirbt der Fuchs, so gilt der Balg', written around 1775. The title, 'If the Fox Dies, We'll Use His Skin', is part of a nonsense poem to be recited during a game of forfeits.

27. 'hypochondria': used in the eighteenth century to mean melancholy or depression.

28. *assignats*: paper money issued in France, 1789–96, to avert state bankruptcy, but leading to inflation.

29. A collection of poems (1827) by Mérimée, presented as ballads translated from Serbian.

NOTES 667

30. *Gemma von Art*: tragedy (1829) by the Swiss dramatist Thomas Bornhauser (1799–1856).

31. 'Thirty-Nine Articles': the Church of England's official statement of doctrine. The Ninth Article, headed 'Of Original or Birth-Sin', begins: 'Original sin standeth not in the following of Adam, (as the Pelagians do vainly talk;) but it is the fault and corruption of the Nature of every man, that naturally is engendered of the off-spring of Adam; whereby man is very far gone from original righteousness, and is of his own nature inclined to evil'. This was wholly antithetical to Goethe's own convictions.

32. Goethe's one actual scientific discovery. Most mammals have an upper jaw consisting of two bones on either side, together form-ing the maxilla or jawbone, and separated by the frontal intermaxillary bone, in which the incisor teeth are set. The inter-maxillary bone is marked by three sutures. Humans were thought to lack this bone, because in adult humans the intermaxillary bone is fused with the jaw, but in embryos and sometimes in children's skulls the two outer sutures can still be detected by a keen observer, and Goethe perceived them in 1784. Goethe's dis-covery (which had already been made by the French physiologist Félix Vicq d'Azyr) was received sceptically by his fellow scien-tists. He did not publish it until 1820.

33. (Claude) Henri de Rouvroy, comte de Saint-Simon (1760–1825).

34. 'composition': *Komposition*, an obvious borrowing from French. Despite Goethe's objections, *komponieren* is the standard word for 'composing' a piece of music.

35. Soret (see List of Persons Mentioned) had sent Goethe three linked poems ('L'invocation du Berger', 'Le Volcan', 'L'étoile filante'); his poem 'Minuit' was printed in Ottilie von Goethe's journal *Chaos*.

36. Published in 1798 in Schiller's *Musenalmanach für das Jahr 1799*.

37. *Marie Delorme*: correctly *Marion Delorme*, tragedy (1829) by Victor Hugo.

38. Cf. Luke 2:19: 'But Mary kept all these things, and pondered them in her heart.'

Index

Goethe's works are indexed under the German title. Page references for notes are given in the form 649n1.

Abeken, Bernhard Rudolf vii, 231
absolutism li, 581–2
academics 447–8, 451–2, 575–6
Académie Française (French
    Academy) 626–7
Achilleis xxxiii, 336
actors and acting 50, 157, 316, 344,
    453, 472, 476
  casting 293–4, 480–1
  guidance for 94–5, 461–4,
    513–14
adaptations 38, 258, 267–8
Aeschylus 498, 512
  Philoctetes 190–1
age/ageing 100, 304, 305–6, 566,
    569, 600
  see also youth
agriculture 12, 586, 639
Alberti, Agnes née Tieck xxvii, 239,
    243, 379–80
Albertini, Signora (singer) 346
alcohol 68, 179, 410–11, 568–9
'Alexis und Dora' xxxii, 135–6
Allgemeine Zeitung (newspaper)
    298
ambiguity 203–4, 310, 374
ambition 304–5, 354–5
Ampère, Jean Jacques vii, 524–6,
    528–9, 533

Angely, Louis, *Sieben Mädchen in
    Uniform* 218
animals
  bees 262, 553
  elephants 317
  horses 247–8, 279, 516–17, 519
  lions 166, 167, 174–5, 191, 212
  monkeys 212–13
  psychology of 11, 77–8
  representation of 77–8, 166,
    174–5, 191, 247–8, 403
  sheep 77
Anna Amalia (Amalie) of Brunswick-
    Wolfenbüttel, Grand Duchess of
    Saxe-Weimar-Eisenach l, 260,
    308
Anschauung (intelligent absorption) liv
appropriation, literary 113–14,
    191–2, 299
archery xlvi, 488–96, 628
architecture 43–4, 259–61, 275,
    280, 394, 563
  see also Coudray, Clemens
arguments 246–7, 308–9, 560
Ariosto, Ludovico vii, 72
Aristotle 218, 232–3
Arminius (Hermann) 144–5
Arnault, Émile-Lucien vii
  Gustave-Adolphe 600–1

INDEX

Arndt, Ernst Moritz 611
Arnim, Bettina von 429
Arnim, Siegmund von 429
art 11–14
  antiquarian 163
  appreciation of 71, 76–7, 408–9
  collection of 267
  composition of 333–4
  context in 500–1
  conventions of 247–8
  drawings 209, 337, 631, 642
  education in 152–3, 306–7
  evaluation of 76–7
  flowers in 411
  French 69
  frescos 543
  German 153–4
  illustrations 151–2, 339, 341
  lack of talent for 300–1, 304–5
  lithographs 438
  mannerism 80
  marginal drawings 417
  masculinity, lack of 377
  nature studies in 500
  painting 68, 125, 126
  and poetry 286
  portraits 143, 642–3
  prices of 288
  realism in 71–2, 163, 202, 297,
    332, 520–2
  religion, relation to 93–4
  restoration of 295
  stage painting 301–2
  technique vs. feeling in 295–6
  watercolours 68, 415–16
  see also engravings; landscape art;
    sculpture
Artaria (publisher) 267
Auber, Daniel, La muette de Portici
  400
Aufgeregten, Die xxxii, 459
Ausgabe letzter Hand xxxviii, 81,
  229–30
authenticity xlv, xlviii, lvi, 5, 416,
  507–8, 646

Babo, Joseph Marius von, Otto von
  Wittelsbach 398
'Ballade' xxxiv, 251–2
Ballanche, Pierre-Simon vii
ballet 345, 347
Balzac, Honoré de vii, liii
barometers 83–4, 200–1
Basedow, Johann Bernhard vii
Bäuerle, Adolf 86
Beaumarchais, Pierre-Augustin
  Caron de vii, 299–300
  Mémoires 299
beauty 297–8, 500–1, 517–19, 520
Bechtolsheim, Julie von vii, 624–5
Beck, Heinrich, Die Schachmaschine
  46, 48
Becker, Heinrich vii, 76
Beer, Michael, Der Paria 69–70, 106
Beethoven, Ludwig van 42
Behrisch, Ernst Wolfgang vii, 324–6
'Bei Betrachtung von Schillers
  Schädel' xxxiv, 420
beiden Galeerensklaven, Die (play)
  218
Bentham, Jeremy viii, 597–8,
  616–17
Béranger, Pierre-Jean de viii, 163,
  180, 183, 188, 418, 447
  background of 527
  imprisonment of 277–8
  interiority of 609–10
  political poems of 529, 610–11
Berka 221, 222
Berlin xlii–xliii, 62, 65, 90, 156–7, 327
Berliner Jahrbücher (journal) 266
Bernardin de Saint-Pierre, Henri viii
Bertram, Johanna xl, xli, xliii, 23, 355
Bethmann, Simon Moritz von viii, 302
Beulwitz, Friedrich August von viii,
  398–9
Beuther, Friedrich viii
Bignon, Baron Louis Pierre
  Édouard viii
  Histoire de France sous Napoleon
  592

INDEX 671

Bingen 64
biography xlviii, 131–2, 215, 216,
579–87
see also Dichtung und Wahrheit
birds 84–5, 315, 334, 421–2, 536–9,
546–7, 552–9
black people 310–11
Blücher, Gebhard Leberecht von
294–5
Blumenbach, Johann Friedrich viii,
439, 627
bodies 570–1, 574–6
Bohemia 284
Karlsbad (Karlovy Vary)
379, 637
Marienbad (Mariánské Lázne) l,
47, 56, 58–9, 81–2
Boisserée, Sulpiz viii, lvi, 332, 425
Bonaparte, Jérôme 378
Bonaparte, Letizia 378
Bonaparte, Lucien, Prince of Canino
viii, 565
Bonaparte, Napoleon *see* Napoleon
Bonaparte
Bonstetten, Victor von viii, 366
Börne, Ludwig xlviii, 417
Bornhauser, Thomas, *Gemma von
Art* 616
botany 195–6, 205, 227–8, 262,
326, 334, 628
spiral theory 412, 578–9, 593–4,
637–8
Böttiger, Karl August viii, 134
Bourrienne, Louis Antoine Fauvelet
de viii
Mémoires sur Napoléon 283,
284–5, 289, 291
Bowdler, Thomas, *Family
Shakespeare* 72
Brandt, Heinrich Franz 71
'Die Braut von Korinth' xxxii, 606
Bremen 259
'Brief des Pastors' xxxi, 81
Bril, Paul viii, 306
Brion, Friederike 303

Bristol, Frederick Augustus Hervey,
4th Earl of (Bishop of Derry)
ix, 619–20
Brockhaus (publisher) xliv
Buch, Leopold von ix, 262–3
Buff, Charlotte, later Kestner xvii, 467
Burgau 551–2
Bürger, Gottfried August ix, 528
'Frau Schnips' 130
Bürgergeneral, Der xxxii, 252–3,
258
Burns, Robert ix, 527–8
Bury, Friedrich ix, 308
Büttner, Christian Wilhelm 614
Byron, George Gordon, Lord
ix, liii, 42, 118–23, 177–8,
210–11
biography of 131–2
criticism of 138, 612
'daemonic' force in 397
death of 569–70
Faust I, views on 113–14
Faust II, represented in lii
in Geneva 358
Goethe, correspondence with
145–6
letters of 321
as literary role model 334
polemical tendencies of 373–4
productivity of 569
Scott on 534
and Shakespeare 137
talent of 79, 254–5
—, works
Beppo 149, 150
Cain 70, 207
Childe Harold 358
Deformed Transformed 149,
150–1
Don Juan 73, 210, 466
*English Bards and Scotch
Reviewers* 120
Manfred 446
Marino Faliero, Doge of Venice
118, 609

672 INDEX

Byron, George Gordon, – *con'd*
   Sardanapalus 145
   Two Foscari 146–7, 210–11
   The Vision of Judgement 466

Cagliostro, Count (Giuseppe
   Balsamo) ix, 265
Calderón de la Barca, Pedro ix, liii,
   87, 129, 137, 147, 511
   The Constant Prince 379
Calvert, George Henry 479
Campe, Johann Heinrich ix, 622
Camper, Pieter (Peter) ix, 627
canals 502–3
Candolle, Augustin Pyrame de
   xi, 638
Canning, George ix, 161, 214
Carlyle, Thomas ix, xxxix, 417, 536
   German Romance 215–17
   'Goethe' 243–4
Carracci, Agostino ix, 306–7
Carracci, Annibale ix, 306–7
Carracci, Lodovico ix, 306–7
Carus, Carl Gustav ix, 196
celebrity xxxv, 67, 586–7
censorship 213–14, 281–2, 440, 486
certainty 203, 310, 374
change 73–4, 193–4, 483–4
Chaos (journal) 330, 624–5
character 78–80, 92–3, 132–3, 278,
   376, 418
   see also genius; talent
characterization 50, 181, 182,
   189–90, 235, 259, 636
Charles X, King of France 631–2
'Charon' 440
Chateaubriand, François-René,
   vicomte de x, 162
Cherubini, Luigi, *Le Porteur
   d'eau* 240
children 395, 441, 575, 621, 622
Chinese Courtship (novel) liii,
   187–8
Chodowiecki, Daniel Nikolaus
   x, 45

Christianity lv–lvi, 256, 582, 645–7
   Bible lvi, 236–8, 374, 375–6, 645–7
   Catholicism lvi, 206–7, 219,
     280–1, 288–9, 302, 647
   clergy 327, 619–20
   Protestantism lvi, 206–7, 288–9,
     302, 617–18, 647
   Reformation 287, 647
Cicero, Marcus Tullius 21, 108
classical culture
   education in 19
   Greek literature 189, 190
   Greek theatre 496–8, 503–9, 527
   history 101–2, 195
   literary 190–1
   mythology 387–8, 392
   scholarship of 68, 161–2, 516–17
   tragedy 503–9
classicism xlvii–xlviii, 211, 277,
   315, 340, 520, 579
Claudine von Villa Bella xxxii, 283,
   293–4
Clavigo xxxi, 148, 242, 299, 566
clothing 329, 602
coats of arms 285–6
Colebrooke, Henry 265
Cologne (Köln) Cathedral 123
colonialism 311
colour theory 192–5, 222, 250,
   268–70, 331, 357–9, 425, 599
   Eckermann's theory of 268–74,
     383–4
   of Goethe xxxvi, liii, liv, 42, 94
   and light 154–6, 157–60, 268–70,
     384, 447
   Newtonian 194, 250–1, 357, 452–3
   'required' colours in 193–4,
     269–72, 296
   and snow 268–74, 383–4, 388
comedy 86, 395–6, 601–2
   see also humour
comfort 409–10
commedia dell'arte 601–2
comparative literature liii, 113,
   188–9, 216–17

INDEX

composition 49, 333–4, 635–6
  of music 63, 345–6
Congress of Vienna (1815) l, 311
context 454–6, 500–1, 525–8
Cooper, James Fenimore x, 319
Cordellier-Delaroue, A., 'Le Rire de
  Mirabeau' 341
Corneille, Pierre x, 87, 516
Cornelius, Peter x, 332–3
Corradi-Pantanelli, Clorinda 346
Correggio, Antonio da x, 153–4
correspondence 96, 135, 181–2,
  303, 368–72
corruption 81, 183, 446, 461, 497,
  573
Cotta, Johann Friedrich von x,
  xxxviii, 26, 28, 32, 33, 183
Coudray, Clemens Wenzeslaus x,
  106, 208–9, 260–1, 279–81, 398
  Schloss Weimar (Stadtschloss) 301
  Weimar Court Theatre 474–5, 485
Courier, Paul Louis x, 398, 401, 407
court culture 100, 259
Cousin, Victor x, 265, 277, 281,
  596–7
creativity 123, 212, 323, 456, 594
  and beauty 517
  'daemonic' force in 397
  freedom and 275
  and productivity 563
criticism 131–3, 138, 404, 456
  English 243–4, 249
  French 524–6
  limitations of 298, 511, 600–1
  literary 132, 215–17, 243–4,
    249–50, 379
  of natural sciences 262–3
  negative 197, 411
Cumberland, Duchess of (Friederike
  Karoline, Princess of
  Mecklenburg-Strelitz) x, 90–1
Cumberland, Richard x
  The Jew 468
'Cupido, loser, eigensinniger Knabe!'
  282–3, 286–7, 294

Cuvier, Georges-Frédéric de xi, lv,
  425, 597, 626–7, 635
  Le Règne Animal 334

'daemonic' force 394, 396–7,
  404–5, 413, 604
Dalberg, Karl von, Prince Primate of
  Confederation of the Rhine xi,
  327–8, 598
D'Alembert, Jean Le Rond xi
D'Alton, Eduard Joseph Wilhelm xi,
  196, 481–2
dance 345, 347
Dante Alighieri 103, 105
Danube (river) 503
darkness xlix–l, 347–8
David d'Angers, Pierre xi, 335–6, 606
Dawe, George xi
death 94, 227–9, 323, 600, 602–3
  reactions to 329–30, 365–6, 599
  suicide 413, 620
debt 413, 543
Delacroix, Eugène xi, 151–2
Delavigne, Casimir xi, 161
Delille, Jacques xi, 183
'Der Erlkönig' xxxi, 164
Des Voeux, Charles 182–3
Deschamps, Émile xi, 336–7
  Études 606
detail 234, 399–400, 641
dialectics 560
dialogue
  dramatic 168, 193, 252
  in fiction 180, 372
  Platonic 180
Dichtung und Wahrheit xxxiii,
  xxxvi, 66–7, 412
  Behrisch in 324–5
  completion of 603
  composition of xxxix, 274
  Eckermann's contribution to li,
    97–9, 390–2, 400–2
  Eckermann's reading of 18, 414
Diderot, Denis xi, 162, 408
  Rameau's Nephew 118, 445, 451

674INDEX

'Die glücklichen Gatten' xxxiii,
251–2
Diemar, Georg Freiherr von 302–3
dilettantism 95, 126–7, 182–3
disease/illness 15–16, 53, 221,
442–4, 561–2
body-mind interaction 339–40
depression 573, 576, 577
fever 350–1
haemorrhage 366
rheumatism 534
romanticism as 277
smallpox 382–3
talent, linked to 315–16
will, defeated by 290–1
Dissen, Ludolf xi
distractions 127, 605
diversity 18, 124–9
divinity 323, 333, 392–4, 647–8
and 'daemonic' force 397
of the human mind 390
of nature 264
and primary phenomena 388–9
see also God
divorce 87
Döbereiner, Johann Wolfgang xi, 551
doctors 15, 366, 443–4, 561, 563,
573, 633
see also Rehbein, Wilhelm; Vogel,
Karl
Domenichino (Domenico Zampieri)
xi, 295
Doolan, Robert xi, 475, 488
Dornburg l, 228–9, 398
doubt 203, 310, 374
drama see plays
dreams xlvi, 313–15, 546–7, 550,
561, 570–3, 590–1
Du Châtelet, Émilie xii, 254
Dumas, Alexandre, père xii
Henri III 378–9
Dumont, Pierre-Étienne-Louis xii,
593, 597–8, 642–3
Recollections of Mirabeau 643
Travels to Paris 593

Dupin, Charles xii, 588
Dupré, Guillaume xii, 363
Dürer, Albrecht 417, 563
Duval, Marie xii, 589

earthquakes 55–6, 280
Ebert, Karl Egon xii, 233–4, 284,
299
Eberwein, Karl xii, 164
Der Graf von Gleichen 440, 479
Eberwein, Max 164
Eberwein, Regina Henriette xii, 91,
164–5, 293
Eckermann, Johann Peter xxxv,
9–26, 353
artistic talent of 11–12, 13–15
Beiträge zur Poesie
xxxvii–xxxviii, 25–6, 28, 63
Bertram, Johanna, engagement to
xl, xli
Bertram, Johanna, marriage to
xliii
childhood and family 9–10
education of 10–12, 14–16, 19–24
English language, learning of 42
in Frankfurt 342–4, 361
in Geneva 351–2, 357–9
'Goethes Porträt' 334
health of 355
illnesses of 15–16, 20–1, 350–1,
561–2
introversion of 92–3
in Italy xli–xlii, 337, 344–52, 357
libretti 475
literary ambitions of 354–5
Molière, translations of 141
in Napoleonic Wars 13–14, 17
Paria (Beer), review of 69–70
picnics, dislike of 487–8
plays of 21–2
poetry of 17–18, 21, 22–3
reading of 16–19
theatre, love of 469–70
—, career of xxxvi, xxxix–xli,
xlii–xliii, l, 364

INDEX

administration 12–13, 15–16
literary 103–4, 353–4
—, *Conversations with Goethe* xli,
 xlii–xliii
authenticity of xlv, xlviii, 5
composition of xliv–xlv, 3–4,
 349–50, 352–3
publication of xliv
reception of lvi
—, Goethe, works of
contribution to xxxviii–xxxix,
 li–lii, 336, 367
editing of xxxviii, 95–6, 97–9,
 372, 418–20, 461
—, Goethe, relationship with
xxxix–xlii, 4–5, 433–5
correspondence with xxxvi–
 xxxvii, 26, 34–5, 349–60,
 361–3, 364
first meeting with xxxviii, 28–9
first reading of 18
literary executor 418
Edinburgh Review (journal) liii, 249
education 10–12, 14–16, 19–24, 70,
 79–80, 354
in architecture 280
artistic 123–6, 202, 306–7
auto-didacticism 152–3
classical 19, 68, 161–2, 516–17
German 576–7, 588–9
of women 260
see also universities
Egloffstein, Julie von 479
Egloffstein, Karoline von xii, 91,
 446, 621–2
Egmont xxxii, xxxv, xxxvii–xxxviii,
 109, 114, 137, 267–8, 460
writing of 110, 117, 190
egoism 451, 623–4
Elective Affinities, see
 Wahlverwandtschaften, Die
'Elegie' 640
elitism 244–6, 262
emotions
anger xlvi–xlvii

anxiety 229–31
elation 240
fear 218, 290–1, 297–8
grief 227–8, 330, 365–6, 599
happiness 348, 629–30
hatred 417–18, 613
jealousy 135–6
representation of 58–9
empiricism liii–liv, 149, 150, 158–9,
 205, 482, 494
Enghien, Louis Antoine, duc d' xii, 208
England 107–8, 202, 310–11, 327,
 397–8
English language xl, 42–3, 89, 105,
 144, 344, 354, 450–1
English literature 209–11
Englishness 121, 574–5
engravings 43–4, 64, 69, 76–7, 137,
 169, 257
entelechy lv, 310, 335
environment *see* context
equality 178–9, 254
Erfurt 540, 541
errors 128, 323–4, 399–400, 421, 494
Eschwege, Wilhelm Ludwig von
 xii, 439
esprit, concept of 407–8
Ettersberg 492, 536–42
Eugène Napoleon (Eugène de
 Beauharnais, Duke of
 Leuchtenberg) xix, 81–2
Euripides 373, 377, 496–7, 498, 512
 Phaethon 119, 190, 440
 Philoctetes 190–1
European Review (journal) xl,
 103–5
Eurydice 333–4
exceptionality 142–4, 154, 313,
 377, 424, 516–17
 see also genius
experience 263, 324, 331–2
exposition 98, 182
in drama 119, 147, 410
in fiction 176, 182, 185, 191
eyes 271–2

676 INDEX

Fabvier, Baron Charles-Nicolas
   xii, 336
Facius, Friedrich Wilhelm xii, 285–6
Falk, Johannes Daniel xxxvii
fame xxxv, 67, 586–7
families l, 9–10, 505–7, 534–5
Farbenlehre xxxiii
Farbenlehre, Zur xxxvi, 154–5,
   192–6, 264, 266
   criticism of 404, 459
   Eckermann's reading of 389–90
   editing of 418–19, 425–6
   on rainbows 503
   reception of 358–9, 423, 452
   responses to 268–70, 273–4
farming 12, 586, 639
Faust (character) 590–1
Faust I xxxii, xxxv, lii, 18, 79, 109,
   145, 275, 532
   Brocken scene 386
   Byron's views on 113–14
   criticism of 525
   illustrations to 151–2
   Mephistopheles in 149, 150–1, 394
   translations of 321, 446
   unfathomableness of 321–2
   Witches' Kitchen 505
   writing of 260, 302
Faust II xxxii, xxxix, xlv, xlvii, lii,
   lv, 98, 123, 165, 166, 356–7
   completion of 417, 422–4
   drafts of 167–8
   Emperor in 543–4
   Faust's character in 423
   Goethe, read aloud by 311–20
   Leda 314–15
   Mephistopheles in 311–12,
   313–14, 394
   Mothers, realm of 322–3
   music for 184–5
   Philemon and Baucis 422
   publication of 183–4
   staging of 184–5, 316–18, 387
   writing of 311–20, 373, 374–5,
   380–1, 567, 605

see also Helena
—, Walpurgis Night 167–8, 356, 605
   writing of 326, 328, 330, 334,
   386–7
femininity 323
Ferdinand VII of Spain 73
Fichte, Johann Gottlieb xii, 310
fiction
   characterization in 636
   dialogue in 180, 372
   exposition in 176, 182, 185, 191
   historiography in 219–20
   interiority in 217, 372
   novel form 234–5, 240–1
   novella form 185
   social class in 372
fictionality xliv–xlv
Finckenstein, Countess Henriette
   von xii, 238, 239
'Der Fischer' xxxi, 51
Fischer, Anton, *Das Hausgesinde* 479
Fischerin, Die xxxi, 164–5
Fleming, Paul xiii, 163–4
flooding 106, 305
focus, vs. diversity 124–9
food 42, 116, 246, 343–4, 589
   picnics 222–3, 487–8, 540–1
Foreign Review (journal) 243
forgiveness 89, 101, 122, 259, 338,
   411, 421
fossils 539–41, 578
Fouqué, Friedrich Heinrich Karl,
   Freiherr de la Motte xiii, 215–16
   Sängerkrieg auf der Wartburg
   233, 234
   Undine 233
France 73, 81, 213–14, 588
   18th Brumaire 564
   1789 Revolution 162, 253, 379,
   459–60, 602
   1830 (July) Revolution lv, 351–2,
   626, 632
   culture of 526
   French Academy (Académie
   Française) 626–7

INDEX

Paris 526, 574
political situation in 332, 405–6
Strasbourg 360–1
theatre in 478
Franke, Heinrich xiii, 293
Frankfurt 69, 342–4, 351
Frankfurter gelehrte Anzeigen
(journal) xxxviii, 29–30, 31
Franklin, Benjamin xiii, 196
Franz, Agnes, *Die Heimkehr*
110–11
Fraser, William 243
Frauenplan house (Goethe's house,
Weimar) 205
Ceiling Room 40, 293
Juno Room 169, 205, 651n8
Majolica Room 578
Room of Busts (Bridge Room)
96, 220
Urbino Room 168–9
Frederick II, Holy Roman Emperor
133
Frederick the Great (Frederick II of
Prussia) 73, 108
Frederick William IV of Prussia
192, 565
free will 134
freedom xlviii, 178–9, 287–8
French Academy (Académie
Française) 626–7
French language 41, 183, 344, 635–6
German literature, translated into
102–3
French literature 87, 102, 146,
161–3, 180, 408, 596–8
drama 119
German influence on 605–6
gifts of, to Goethe 606
revolution in 607–8
and writing style 89
French Revolution *see* France
Frommann, Carl Friedrich Ernst
xiii, 31, 32, 559
Froriep, Emma von xiii, 91
Fürnstein, Anton xiii, 37

Fuseli, Henry (Füßli, Johann
Heinrich) xiii, 453

gardens 82–6, 296, 484, 533
Gay, Delphine xiii, 180, 336
Geist, concept of 407–8
gemstones 71–2, 445
Genast, Caroline xiii, 257–8
Genast, Eduard xiii, 257–8, 293
gender 111, 141, 377
genius 323, 454–6, 563–4, 569–70,
648
Genlis, Stéphanie Félicité (Madame)
de xiii, 134
Geoffroy de Saint-Hilaire, Étienne
xiii, lv, 425, 626–7
Gérard, François xiii, 169
Gerhard, Wilhelm xiii, 185–6
'Dance for us, Theodor!' 186
'The Key to the Dungeon' 185
German culture 115–16, 309–10,
525–6, 528, 573, 575–7
German history 133, 144–5, 287–8
German language 107–9, 450–1,
461–4, 635
German literature 89–90, 102–3,
105, 115–16, 233, 287–8,
605–6
German unification 587–9, 611
Geschwister, Die 566, 594
Gille, Johann Friedrich Christoph 411
Glenck, Karl 323–4
Globe, Le (journal) liii, 146, 161,
235–6, 524–5, 579, 600–1
Goethe ceases reading 332, 605
God 385–6, 392–4, 647–8
belief in 402–3, 559
existence of 310
immanent 422
and morality 514–15
naming of 453
omniscient 134
and political change 461
and primary phenomena 388–9
and productivity 567

678 INDEX

gods
  Greek 387–8, 392
  Indian 523
  intervention of 333
Goethe, Alma von xiii, l
Goethe, August von xiii, xxxv,
  xli–xlii, xlix, 40–1, 169, 206,
  438
  breaks collarbone 352
  in court uniform 63
  death of 365
  and death of Grand Duke 227
  fossils, collection of 578
  on *Helena* 520
  Italy, visit to 337, 339, 350–1,
  352
  on Katharina Goethe 598
  in masked ball costume 328
  on Napoleon 337
  reading of 319
  as student 68
Goethe, Cornelia von (later
  Schlosser) 412
Goethe, Johann Caspar 259–60
GOETHE, JOHANN
  WOLFGANG VON
  appearance 28–9, 429, 434, 438
  death 426, 429
  drawings 595–6
  fame of xxxv
  health of 326–7
  homes 542 *see also* Frauenplan
  house
  illnesses of 53, 56, 59–60, 168–9,
  366–7, 442–4, 448–50, 469,
  633
  influence of 39–40
  Italy, 'flight' to xxxv, 259–60,
  282–3
  languages spoken by xl, 41, 42,
  144, 183, 301
  love affairs xxxix, l, 47, 58–9,
  473, 548–50, 603–4, 637–8
  miscellanea 419–20
  portraits of 4, 84, 578, 662n46

  productivity of 566–7
  religious beliefs 75–6, 310,
  393–4, 459, 646–7
  spectacles, aversion to liii–liv,
  622–4
  youth 303, 576
—career
  awards and celebrations li, 40,
  135, 542, 651n7
  collected works xxxviii, 81,
  229–30
  correspondence, publication of
  368–72
  court responsibilities 259–60
  critical reception of lii, 131,
  134–6, 243–4, 458–9
  criticism of 89–90, 101, 484–5,
  611–13
  libretti 446
  literary methods of 165–6, 335
  religious beliefs lv–lvi
  reputation xxxv–xxxvi,
  xlvii–xlviii
  reviews by xxxviii, 29–30, 31, 70
  scientific work liii–lv, 160, 204–5,
  425–6, 438–9, 481–2, 627 *see
  also* colour theory
  speeches 634
  theatre management 95, 146–9,
  236–7, 470–3, 480–1
  translation of works 182–3, 363,
  382, 404, 524–5, 533, 594
  translations by 111, 115, 118,
  440, 445, 451
  Weimar court, appointed to xxxv,
  259–60
  William Tell, proposed epic poem
  on 530–1
—character
  charm 107, 110
  confidence of 634
  conversational style xlvi, 435–6
  diligence 54–6
  emotion xlvi–xlvii
  expressiveness 88

INDEX 679

self-restraint 435-6
shortest day, depression caused
by 450
—political views li, 213-14, 428-9,
459-61
criticism of xlvii-xlviii, 484-5
on liberalism 73-4, 598
on radicalism 597-8, 616-17
on revolution lv, 607-8
on royalism 74
Goethe, Katharina Elisabeth Textor
xiii, 260, 598
Goethe, Ottilie von xiii, xlix, 27, 42,
58, 63, 206, 302-3, 438
Berlin, visits to 90
Chaos, editing of 330, 624
character of 439, 444
Goethe, relationship with 40
humour of 449, 487-8
on reading 235
on shopping 169
singing of 64, 91
Weimar Court Theatre, relics
of 474
Goethe, Walter Wolfgang von xiv,
xlix-l, 27, 42, 63, 207, 328, 632
Goethe, Wolfgang Maximilian von
xiv, l, 207, 219, 328, 469, 621-2
Goldsmith, Oliver xiv
The Vicar of Wakefield 372
Gore, Eliza 328
Gotha 540, 541-2
Gothic style 170-1
'Der Gott und die Bajadere'
xxxii, 218
Götter, Helden und Wieland xxxi, 81
Göttingen 23-5, 355, 365
Göttling, Karl Wilhelm xiv, 239,
240, 274, 339
Götz von Berlichingen xxxi, xxxv,
67, 101, 137, 398, 465
dramatic limitations of 147
dramatic unities in 120
manuscript of 595
realism of 78

Scott's translation of 533
subject matter of 145
governmental systems 381-2,
583-4
Gozzi, Carlo xiv, 331, 600, 601
Graff, Johann Jacob xiv, 293, 472
greatness 244-5, 254-5, 262, 281,
403-4
Greece 101-2, 247-8, 276-7,
496-8, 503-9, 527
Greek language 19
Greek literature 189, 190
Greek War of Independence
(1821-9) 42
Gregory XVI, Pope 409
Grillparzer, Franz xiv
Ahnfrau 22
Grimm, Baron Friedrich Melchior
xiv, 602
Grosskophta, Der xxxii, 265, 379
Grüner, Karl Franz xiv, 95, 461
Guizot, François xiv, 265, 277, 281,
287, 596

Hackert, Philipp xiv, 301, 302
Hafiz (Muhammad Shemseddin)
xiv, 183
Hagen, August xiv
Olfried und Lisena 36
Hagn, Charlotte von xiv, 578
Hallische Literaturzeitung (journal)
284
Hamann, Johann Georg xiv, 199,
266, 559-60
Hamburg 140
Handel, George Frideric, *Messiah*
90-1
handwriting 118, 278-9, 303, 416,
594, 595-6, 607
Hanover 14-15, 16
Hanswursts Hochzeit xxxi,
395-6, 401
Harz Mountains 540
*Hau Kiou Choaan or the Pleasing
History* (novel) 658n104

680 INDEX

Haugwitz, Count Christian August Heinrich Kurt xiv
health 326–7, 355, 569–70
Heavyside, John xli
Heeren, Arnold Hermann Ludwig xiv, 70
Hegel, Georg Wilhelm Friedrich xv, 256, 266, 310, 504, 559–60, 666n16
Heidelberg 68
Heine, Heinrich xlvii, 612
Heinrichshofen (publisher) xliv
Helen of Troy lii, 184, 319–20, 333, 339
Helena xxxiv, 165, 183–4, 211–12, 314–15, 339, 387, 520
Heligoland 382
Hell, Theodor, *Dreissig Jahre aus dem Leben eines Spielers* 296
Herder, Johann Gottfried xv, 63, 100, 116, 199–200, 528
Ideen zur Geschichte der Menschheit 101
Hermann und Dorothea xxxii, 57, 115, 160, 166, 187, 258, 276
heroes/heroism 235, 262, 516, 530
Herschel, Sir William xv, 195
Hetschburg 222
Heygendorf, Karoline, née Jagemann xv, 95, 445
Hinrichs, Hermann Friedrich Wilhelm xv, xxxvii, 503–6
Hirt, Aloys xv, 308
historiography 194–5, 216, 219–20, 290, 592
history
  art 198
  classical 101–2, 195
  in drama 189–90
  German 133, 144–5, 170–1
  as literary subject 132, 299, 397–8
Hobhouse, John Cam 146
Hoffmann, Ernst Theodor Amadeus xv

Holbein, Hans 563
Holtei, Karl von xv, 533
Homer 19, 197, 277, 296, 333, 497
  Iliad 137, 331
  Odyssey 375
Hope, Sir John 534
Horace (Quintus Horatius Flaccus) xvi, 183
  Odes 21
Horen (journal) 104, 115, 606–7
Horn, Franz xvi
Horn, Johann Adam xvi, 303
Houwald, Christoph Ernst von xvi
  Das Bild 41, 118, 543
  Die Feinde 120
Hugo, Victor xvi, 161–2, 336, 640–1
  Marion Delorme 641
  Notre-Dame de Paris liii, 636
Humboldt, Alexander von xvi, lv, 130, 152, 502, 580–1
Humboldt, Wilhelm von xvi, 54, 56, 130, 449, 526
Hummel, Johann Nepomuk xvi, 289–90, 439
humour 91, 324–5, 387, 444, 449, 464–5, 590
  see also comedy
Huschke, Wilhelm Ernst xvi, 443

idealism 102, 297
ideas 44, 48, 263–4, 465–6, 531–2, 576–7
Iffland, August Wilhelm xvi, 102, 141
  Die Hagestolzen 86–7
illness *see* disease/illness
Ilm (river) 82, 208, 222
'Ilmenau' xxxi, 585
imagery xlv, 144, 175, 283, 304, 635
imagination 37, 136, 186, 212, 316, 405, 594
immediacy 58–9
Immermann, Karl Leberecht xvi
  Gedichte 63
immorality xxxvi, 72–3

INDEX

681

immortality lv, 75–6, 256–7, 310
imperialism 311
improvisation 80, 139–40
'In this quiet place ...' ('Erwählter
    Fels') xxxi, 85
individualism 199, 236, 287–8, 335,
    629–30
influence 232, 250, 277–8, 403,
    547–8, 563, 564–5
    literary 129, 130–1, 336–7
inns 68, 351, 545, 552
inspiration 37, 562–3
intellect 134, 263, 310, 454
interiority 217, 372, 609–10
Iphigenie auf Tauris xxxii, xxxv,
    257, 340, 478–9, 512–14
Ireland 280, 288–9
irony 608
Italian language 301
Italienische Reise xxxii,
    xxxiii, xli, 153–4, 274, 300,
    595–6
    'Zweiter Römischer Aufenthalt'
    300, 304, 332
Italy xli–xlii, 281–2, 344–50, 411
    Borromean Islands 68
    Genoa 351
    Lago Maggiore 68
    Lake Como 219
    Messina 56, 280
    Milan 344–6
    Naples 601–2
    La Scala (Milan) 344
    Simplon Pass 348
    theatre of 478, 601–2
    Turin 351
    Venice 601
    see also Rome

Jacobi, Friedrich Heinrich xvi,
    198–9, 259
'Jägers Abendlied' xxxi, 239
Jahn, Friedrich Ludwig 665n13
Jakob, Therese von 111–13
Janin, Jules xvi, 606

Janouch, Gustav, *Conversations with
    Kafka* xlviii
Jean Paul (Johann Paul Friedrich
    Richter) xvii, 414, 415
Jena 30, 32, 33–4, 440, 448, 544–5,
    613–14
Jérôme Bonaparte 378
Jesus Christ 144, 154–5, 337–8,
    374, 375, 646–7
Johnson, Samuel xvii, xlviii
    Rasselas 209
judgement 86, 101, 121
Julius Caesar, *Commentaries* 21
Jung, Johann Heinrich (Jung-Stilling)
    xvii
Juno Ludovisi (sculpture) 68
jurisprudence 23–5, 287, 629–30

Kant, Immanuel xvii, 130, 204–5,
    310
    Critique of Judgement 204
    Critique of Pure Reason 266
Kapo d'Istrias (Kapodistrias), Count
    Ioannis xvii, 208, 276–7
Karl (Charles) of Prussia, Prince 192
Karl Alexander, Grand Duke of
    Saxe-Weimar-Eisenach (Crown
    Prince) xliii, l, 355, 364, 414,
    587, 595
Karl August, Grand Duke of
    Saxe-Weimar-Eisenach xvii,
    xxxv, xxxvi, xxxix, 168, 413, 485
    biography of 579–87
    in *Conversations with Goethe* l
    'daemonic' force in 394, 397
    death of xlix, 227–8, 580–2
    Goethe, relationship with li, 192,
    443–4, 614
    Marienbad, visits to 56
    progressiveness of 376
    and Schiller 179
    as speaker 295
    and Weimar theatre 468–9, 479
    and Wolf, Friedrich August 91
    youth of 585–6

682 INDEX

Karl Friedrich, Grand Duke of Saxe-Weimar-Eisenach l, 229
Karlsbad (Karlovy Vary) 379, 637
Kauffmann, Angelika xvii, 449
Keepsake, The (anthology) 321
Kestner, Charlotte, née Buff xvii, 467
Kind, Friedrich xvii
kings *see* rulers
Kladzig, Auguste xliii
Klettenberg, Susanne Katharina von xvii, 144
Klopstock, Friedrich Gottlieb xvii, 18, 100–1, 144–5
  Messias 100
  Oden 100
Knebel, Karl Ludwig xvii, 28, 32, 544, 585
Kniep, Christoph Heinrich xviii
knowledge 78–80, 201, 465–6
Kolbe, Heinrich Christoph xviii, 439
Köln (Cologne) Cathedral 123
Körner, Theodor xviii, 611, 613
  Lyre and Sword 16–17
Kotzebue, August von xviii, 44–5, 86, 102, 141, 445
  Die beiden Klingsberg 45
  Goethe's satirical epigrams on 577–8
  murder of 379, 665n13
  and Schiller 179–80, 545
  Die Versöhnung 44
  Verwandtschaften 44
Krause, Gottlieb Friedrich xviii, 294, 302, 335–6
Kräuter, Friedrich Theodor xviii, xxxvii, 29, 51, 63
'Kriegsglück' xxxiii, 64
Krüger, Wilhelm xviii, 512, 513
Kunst und Altertum see Über Kunst und Altertum

La Fontaine, Jean de 87
La Motte-Fouqué, Friedrich *see* Fouqué, Friedrich

La Roche, Carl August xviii, 258, 293, 468
Lagrange, Joseph Louis xviii, 260–1
Lamartine, Alphonse de xviii, 161
landscape 177, 222, 228, 356, 541, 570
  mountains 68–9, 342, 360, 540–1
landscape art 64, 68, 296–8, 301, 307, 376, 424–5, 500–1, 642
languages 107–9, 301, 450–1, 461–4, 634, 635
  see also English language; French language
Lassen, Christian xviii, 523, 524
Latin language 19, 21
Lauchstädt 148
Lavater, Johann Caspar xviii, 265, 592
  Physiognomische Fragmente 265
law 23–5, 287, 629–30
Le Prince, H. S. 156
Leben des Benvenuto Cellini xxxiii, 111, 115, 655n.50
'Legende vom Hufeisen' xxxiii, 341
Légion d'Honneur li
Leibniz, Gottfried Wilhelm von xviii, 335
Leiden des jungen Werthers, Die xxxi, xxxv, 67, 456–8, 525, 640
  Napoleon, read by 291, 457
  origins of 303
  reception of 131, 619–20
  suppression of, in Italy 281–2
  writing of 145, 260
Lenclos, Ninon de (Anne de L'Enclos) xviii, 330, 600
Leo, Heinrich xix, 216
Leonardo da Vinci 153, 250
Lesage, Alain-René, *Gil Blas* 375
Lessing, Gotthold Ephraim xix, 116, 130, 134, 199, 203–4, 497
  Eine Duplik 204
  Emilia Galotti 197
  Laocoon 203–4
  Minna von Barnhelm 147, 197, 410
  Nathan der Weise 197

INDEX

Leuchtenberg, Duke of (Eugène Napoleon de Beauharnais) xix, 81–2

Levetzow, Ulrike von l, 47, 58–9, 449

libraries 362, 407, 446, 588, 614–16

light liv, 307, 332, 521
and colour theory 154–6, 157–60, 268–70, 384, 447

Lips, Johann Heinrich xix, 308

Livy 195

Lockhart, John Gibson xix, 533–4, 536

Longus, *Daphnis and Chloe* 398, 402, 403, 405–6, 407

Lope de Vega ('Lopez') xix, 127

Lorrain, Claude (Claude Gellée) xix, 288, 296–8, 302, 306–7, 425, 499, 500

Lory, Gabriel xix, 642

Louisa Ulrika of Prussia, Queen of Sweden 254

Louise of Mecklenburg-Strelitz, Queen of Prussia 244

love l, 412, 421–2, 506, 603–4
Goethe, affairs of xxxix, 47, 58–9, 473, 548–50, 637–8

Lowe, Sir Hudson xix, 329

Lucien Bonaparte, Prince of Canino viii, 565

Luden, Heinrich xix
History of the Germans 170, 397–8

Ludwig I, King of Bavaria 291–4, 303–4, 307–8, 330, 334, 600

Luise of Hesse-Darmstadt (Dowager Grand Duchess of Saxe-Weimar-Eisenach) xii, l, 168, 228, 230, 328, 448, 587
death of 329–30, 599–600, 624

Lüneburg 13

Luther, Martin 461, 563, 647

magic (conjuring) 632

mail 477

Malkolmi, Carl Friedrich (Malcolmi) xix, 252

mannerism 80, 141, 163

Manzoni, Alessandro xix, 161, 189–90, 315–16
Il cinque maggio [ode on the death of Napoleon] 215
I promessi sposi liii, 215, 217–20

maps and globes 446–7

Maria Pavlovna of Russia, Grand Duchess of Saxe-Weimar-Eisenach l, 354, 364, 388, 410, 602, 632–3

Marie Antoinette, Queen of France 379

Marienbad (Mariánské Lázne) l, 47, 56, 58–9, 81–2

Market of Naples (play) 317

Marmontel, Jean-François xix

Marot, Clément xix

marriage 87, 257, 412

Martius, Karl Friedrich Philipp von xix, 236–8, 578–9, 593–4

Masaniello (Tommaso Aniello) 663n65

masculinity 377

Massot, Firmin xix, 449

Matthisson, Friedrich von 188–9

Medem, Count Christoph Johann von xix, 241–2

Medem, Countess Maria 241

medicine *see* doctors

Medwin, Thomas, *Conversations with Lord Byron* xli, 118

memory 114–15, 433–4

Menander xx, 129, 510, 512

Mendelssohn, Felix 164

Mengs, Johann Anton ('Raphael') xx, 16

Mephistopheles (character) 149–51, 311–14, 394, 590–1

Merck, Johann Heinrich xx, 101, 259, 266–7, 411, 413

INDEX

Mérimée, Prosper xx, 180, 336, 525
   Clara Gazul 379, 526
   Guzla 608–9
Metamorphose der Pflanzen xxxii,
   195–6, 204–5, 304, 363, 382,
   404, 411–12
'Die Metamorphose der Pflanzen'
   (poem) 532
'Metamorphose der Tiere' xxxiv
'Die Metamorphose der Tiere' 532
metaphor 283, 304, 635
Metastasio, Issipile xx
   Issiplile 475
Meyer, Ernst xx, 196
Meyer, Friedrich Adolf Carl xx,
   67–8, 72
Meyer, Johann Heinrich xx, 40–1,
   127–8, 288, 414–15, 438–9, 444
   Aldobrandini Wedding 651n8
   Goethe, portrait of 84
   History of Art 198, 449
   on Old Master copies 295
   on Rome 307–9
Meyerbeer, Giacomo xx, 261
Michelangelo 308, 309
   Moses 626
military service 13–14, 17, 64,
   534, 574
Milton, John xx
   Samson Agonistes 327
mines 323–4, 441
Mirabeau, Honoré Gabriel Riqueti
   xx, 643, 644
modesty 623–4
Molière (Jean-Baptiste Poquelin) xx,
   liii, 129–30, 141–2, 509–11, 612
   L'Avare 129–30, 141
   Le Malade imaginaire 509–10
   Le Médecin malgré lui 141
   Le Misanthrope 511
   Tartuffe 147, 486, 511
money 413, 486–7
   paper 318–19, 602
Montesquieu (Charles-Louis de
   Seconda) 359

monuments 208
moon 200
Moore, Thomas xx
morality xxxvi, 72–3, 141, 260–1,
   508, 514–16, 620–1
Morgenblatt (newspaper) 111
mortality *see* death
Moses 236–7, 626
Mosheim, Johann Lorenz von
   xx, 442
Mozart, Wolfgang Amadeus xx,
   153, 313, 327, 471, 563, 570
   Don Giovanni 261, 344,
   479, 636
   Die Zauberflöte 91, 446, 479
Müller, Friedrich von xx, xxxix,
   xlvi–xlvii, xlix, 52, 169, 207,
   212–15
   Dante, discussion of 105
   Karl August, memoir of 579–80
   Manzoni, visits to 315
   reads aloud 56
   as speaker 294
Müller, Wenzel
   Das neue Sonntagskind 86
   Die Schwestern von Prag 54
Müller, Wilhelm 221
Müllner, Adolf xx
   Schuld 22
Murray, John xli
Musäus, Johann Karl August xx, 215
Musenalmanach (journal) 104, 625
museums 544, 550–1
music 52, 227, 402–3
   architecture as 275
   composition of 63, 345–6
   conductors 345
   'daemonic' force in 396
   for *Faust* 184–5, 261
   German 589
   orchestras 345–7
   piano 42, 45, 48, 164,
   439, 448
   street musicians 343
   talent for 378

INDEX 685

for the theatre 137
see also opera; songs
Myron 422
mythology 187, 322–3, 339, 387–8, 392

names and naming 395–6
Napoleon Bonaparte li, 87, 143, 161–2, 169–70, 208, 337
  biographies of 283, 284–5, 534, 535, 592
  charisma of 285
  'daemonic' force in 394
  downfall of 570
  Egypt campaign 289–91
  exceptionality of 313, 564–5
  glass bust of 361, 362–3
  physical strength of 564–5
  political legacy of 407
  productivity of 562
  Red Sea, crossing of 291
  as speaker 294
  talent of 289–90
  uniform of, turned 329
  Werther, read by 291, 457, 620
narrative form 119, 133, 175–6, 240, 391, 399
nationalism 287, 665n13
nationality 278, 446–7, 574–6
natural sciences liii–liv, 232–3, 384–6, 560
  anatomy 550
  astronomy 408, 551
  chemistry 438–9
  criticism of 262–3
  earth, origins of 237–8
  earth science liv–lv, 198, 200, 322
  geology liv–lv, 464–5
  mathematics 123, 155–6, 295, 452
  meteorology 83–4, 200–1, 264, 291, 447, 551
  methodological disputes in 626–7
  mineralogy 196, 205, 232, 247, 264, 388–9, 449
  museums of 544, 550–1

optics liii–liv, 154–6, 157–60, 268–70, 384, 447
ornithology xlvi, 552–3
palaeontology 539–40, 550, 578
physics liii–liv
physiogomy 265, 336
as profession 451–2, 465–6
psychology, of animals 11, 77–8
and religion 237–8
Vulcanism 232–3
see also botany
nature
  beauty in 517–19
  observation of 177
  in poetry 37, 48–9
  representation of 187–8
  understanding of 263–4
  unfathomableness of 637
  violence of 106
natürliche Tochter, Die xxxiii, 117
Nees von Esenbeck, Christian xxi, 106
Nerval, Gérard de (Gérard Labrunie) 321
Neureuther, Eugen Napoleon xxi, 339, 341, 417
newspapers 42, 351
Newton, Isaac xxxvi, liii, liv, 128, 155–6, 194, 418–19
  colour theory of 194, 250–1, 357, 452–3
Nibelungenlied (epic poem) 64, 277
Nicolai, Friedrich 116
Niebuhr, Barthold Georg xxi, 409
Nietzsche, Friedrich lvi
Nohra 492
Nordheim 364
novel form 234–5, 240–1
novella form 185
Novelle xxxiv, li, 166–7, 171, 173–7, 180, 399
  choice of title for 185
  Eckermann's comments on 182, 183
  reception of 401–2
  revisions to 191

686 INDEX

objectivity 140–1, 192, 204–5,
    268–70
observation 177, 465–6, 504
Oels, Karl Ludwig xxi, 293, 472
Offenbach 98
Oken, Lorenz xxi
opera 106, 293–4, 344–6, 400, 440
Order of the White Falcon 40,
    651n7
Orfana di Genevra, L' (ballet)
    345, 347
originality 130
Orpheus 333–4
Ostade, Adriaen van xxi, 257, 286
Ovid, *Metamorphoses* 21

Paganini, Niccolò xxi, 394
Panama Canal, idea for 502–3
Panckoucke, Ernestine xxi
Pandora xxxiii, 42–3
'Paria' xxxiv, 53–4, 56
Parry, William, *The Last Days of
    Lord Byron* 131–2
parties 40–2, 45–6, 48, 164–5
patent of nobility 542
patriotism 428, 611–12
patronage 21, 23, 628, 633
Pausanius 543
pedantry 161–2, 522–3
Peel, Sir Robert xxi, 288
Peter I of Russia (the Great) xxi,
    305–6
Peucer, Heinrich Karl
    Friedrich xxi
Phidias 153–4, 563
Philoctetes 190–1
philosophy 57, 203–5
    German 266, 504–5
    idealist 312
    Indian 265–6
    and religion 256–7
    utilitarianism 597–8
    writing style, effect on 89
phrenology 631–2
Pius VIII, Pope 303

plants 84–5, 195–6, 278, 296, 326,
    332, 334, 411
    see also botany; trees
Platen, Count August xxi, 87,
    373–4, 612
    Ghazalen 61–2
    Der romantische Oedipus 373
Plato 250
plays
    characterization in 189–90
    choruses in 185, 193, 211
    construction of 410, 508–11
    dialogue in 168, 193, 252
    and gender 141
    historical 189–90
    inconsistency in 522–3
    length of 616
    morality in 141, 508, 515–16
    prose 45
    selection of, for Weimar theatre
    471–2, 477–8
    symbolic construction of 146–8
    tone of 193
    unities of 119–20
    verse forms 45
    writing of 126–7
plot 234–5, 240–1
Plutarch 101, 322
'Poetische Gedancken über die
    Höllenfahrt Jesu Christi'
    xxi, 144
poetry 16–17, 35–9, 48–9
    appreciation of 53–4, 390, 401–2
    ballads 18, 606–7
    commentaries on 54
    'daemonic' force in 396
    doggerel 259
    editing of 624–5
    elegies 135–6, 211, 624
    epic 64, 284, 652n23
    exercises in 48–9, 52–3
    folk 233
    ghazals 61–2
    hexameters 43, 166–7, 176–7, 372
    historical 132

INDEX

immoral 72–3
improvised 139–40
Indian 523, 524
individual representation in 48–9
love 111–13
morality in 72–3
motifs in 111–13
on nature 37, 48–9
ottava rima 176–7
vs. philosophy 57
political 427–8, 529, 610–11
realism in 210
religion in 144–5
reviews of 284
rhyme 176–7, 372–3
rhythm 286–7
short 532
'sickbay' 221
skills in 125–7
subjective vs. objective 140–1
subjects for 36–8, 132
translation of 185
trilogy form 639–40
truth in 299
unfathomableness of 532
uses of 357
verse forms 43, 45, 72–3, 176–7, 372–3
as world literature 188–9
writing of 606–7
Pogwisch, Ulrike von xxi, 42, 63, 91, 474, 487–8
politics 310–11, 381–2, 628
autocracy 74, 460, 575
democracy 216, 459–60
liberalism 74, 213–14, 598
radicalism 597–8, 616–17
revolutionary 102, 607–8
speeches on 294–5
see also French Revolution
Polygnotus 543
Pope, Alexander 122
popularity 244–6, 262
Portugal 161
post 477

Poussin, Nicolas xxi, 69, 398, 424, 499
poverty 9–10, 328
Preller, Friedrich xxi, 499–501
premonitions 546–8
present moment 35–6, 52, 59
press 42, 351, 446
'primary phenomena' (Urphänomene) liv, 251, 263–4, 266, 362–3, 388–9, 424
princes 212–13
productivity 561–4, 566–9
prose 165–6, 187, 212
see also fiction; historiography
Pulcinella (character) 601–2
puppets 344–5
Purkinje, Jan Evangelista 452
Pustkuchen, Johann li–lii
Putyatin, Prince Nikolay Abramovich xxi, 172

quality 124, 333, 563

Racine, Jean 87
Ramberg, Johann Heinrich xxi, 14–15, 80
Rameaus Neffe xxxiii, 118, 445, 451
Raphael 163, 295, 306, 308–9, 313, 458, 563, 570
Rapp, Count Jean (General) xxii, 378
rationality 134, 212, 262, 264, 520
Rauch, Christian Daniel xxii, 69
Raupach, Ernst Benjamin Salomo xxii, 543
Erdennacht 44
reading 593, 605
reading aloud 64, 88, 111, 114–15, 118, 186, 242
realism 135–6, 141–2, 166, 210, 297, 332
in art 71–2, 163, 202, 247–8, 297, 332, 520–2
Recke, Elise von der (Reck) xxii, 637, 638

Rehbein, Wilhelm xxii, 56, 91,
110–11, 112, 438, 443
Rehberg, August Wilhelm xxii
Reichardt, Johann Friedrich xxii,
293–4
Reinhard, Count Karl Friedrich
xxii, 39, 302–3, 467
Reinhard, Franz Volkmar xxii, 87
Reise in die Schweiz xxxiii, 45,
51–2, 450
religion xxxvi, lv–lvi, 392–4
and art 93–4
and censorship 281–2
devil 149, 150–1
divisions in 206–7
doubt in 310
in England 202, 617–18
faith 374, 375
immortality 75–6
influence of 287
Islam 202–3
negative criticism and 197
and philosophy 256–7
pietism 581–2
in poetry 144–5
second coming 576
sin 617–18
see also Christianity; God; gods
Reni, Guido xxii, 306
Reutern, Gerhardt Wilhelm von
xxii, 260, 415–16
revolution 102, 607–8
Rhine (river) 68, 96, 503
Rhône (river) 358
Richardson, Samuel 187
Riemer, Friedrich Wilhelm xxii,
xxxviii, 41, 96, 112–15, 440
'Der Sänger-Wettstreit auf der
Wartburg' 328
Riepenhausen, Franz xxii, 543
Riepenhausen, Johannes xxii, 543
road-building 279–80
Röhr, Johann Friedrich xxii, 91,
164, 376
Romano, Giulio xxii, 306

romanticism xlvii–xlviii, 211, 277,
315, 340, 520, 579, 608–9
Rome 101–2, 239–40, 292–4, 302,
408–9
Villa di Malta 292, 293, 294,
307–8
Römische Elegien xxxii, 72–3,
292–3, 338–9, 653n29
Römische Karneval, Das xxxii, 595
Roos, Johann Heinrich xxiii,
77–8, 80
Rossini, Gioachino xxiii
The Barber of Seville 360
Il Conte Ory 344–5, 347, 348
Moses 236–7, 239–40
Rothschild, Amschel Mayer von
xxiii, 302
Rousseau, Jean-Jacques 359
royalism 74
Rubens, Peter Paul xxiii, 377
*The Peasants' Return from the
Fields* 201–2, 520–2
Rückert, Friedrich xxiii, 611
Östliche Rosen 54
rulers 281, 284, 292, 303–4, 543–4,
565, 583–5
Russia, St Petersburg 106, 305–6
Russo-Turkish War (1828–1829)
289
Ruysdael, Jacob van xxiii, 93, 332

Saale (river) 552
Sainte-Beuve,Charles-Augustin xxiii
Saint-Hilaire, Étienne Geoffroy de
see Geoffroy de Saint-Hilaire,
Étienne
Saint-Pierre, Bernardin de 359
Saint-Simon, Louis de Rouvroy,
duc de xxiii, 604–5
Saint-Simonianism 628
Salvandy, Narcisse-Achille, comte de
xxiii
San Quirico, Allesandro 345
Sankt-Rochus-Fest zu Bingen xxxiii,
653n24

INDEX 689

Saussure, Horace-Bénédicte de xxiii, 269

Savigny, Friedrich Karl von xxiii, 287, 652n11

Savigny, Marie Kunigunde von 42

Scafe, John, *King Coal's Levee* 464–5

Schellhorn, Franz Wilhelm xxiii, 105

Schelling, Friedrich Wilhelm Joseph von xxiii, xxxix, 381, 386

Schiller, Johann Christoph Friedrich von xxiv, xxxviii, xlvii, 115–18, 177–9, 414–15, 471, 497

  actors, work with 472

  Carlyle on 216

  character of 545–6

  death of 118, 179

  Eckermann's reading of 18

  on freedom 178–9

  history, study of 299

  homes of 542, 551

  illnesses of 316

  on Kant 205

  letters from 117–18

  mementos of 231–2

  style of 89

  subjectivity of 340

  talents of 129, 178

  and the theatre 57, 86, 87, 116–17, 148

  on tragedy 331

  Zelter on 63

—and Goethe

  collaboration with 249–50

  influence on 130, 176, 275, 336, 606–7

  relationship with 90, 199, 276

  Römische Elegien, publication of 653n29

—works

  Egmont, adaptation of 267–8

  Fiesko 171–2, 526

  Horen, Die (journal) 104, 606–7

  Kabale und Liebe 526

  Musenalmanach 104, 625

  "Nadowessische Totenklage" 275–6

  plays, length of 616

  Die Räuber 117, 172, 526

  Der Tierkreis 116

  Wallenstein 57–8, 76, 147, 176, 220, 420–1

  Wilhelm Tell 117, 177, 299, 403, 531

  Xenien 116

Schinkel, Karl Friedrich xxiv, 280

Schlegel, August Wilhelm xxiv, 88, 130, 340, 510–12, 523–4

Schlegel, Friedrich xxiv, 88, 130, 340

Schlosser, Cornelia, née Goethe 412

Schlosser, Friedrich Christoph xxiv, 216, 467

Schmidt, Christian Friedrich xxiv, 42, 439

Schmidt, Maria xxiv, 293

Schöne, Karl 373

Schönemann, Anna Elisabeth ('Lili') xxiv, xxxix, 98, 99, 412, 603–4

schools 19–21, 260

Schopenhauer, Johanna xxv, 302–3

Schrön, Ludwig xxv, 408, 551

Schubarth, Karl Ernst xxv, 43, 62, 256, 652n23

Schubert, Franz 659n2

Schulenburg, Friedrich Albrecht, Graf von der xxv, 533

Schultz, Christoph Ludwig Friedrich xxv, 39–40, 653n26

Schütze, Stephan xxv, 223

  Heitere Stunden 146

Schwabe, Johann Friedrich Heinrich xxv, 388

'An Schwager Kronos' xxxi, 540

Schweitzer, Christian Wilhelm xxv, 479

sciences *see* natural sciences

690 INDEX

Scott, Sir Walter xxv, 114, 191–2, 399–400, 533–6
   Fair Maid of Perth 234–5, 238–9, 240–1
   Ivanhoe 396, 399
   Life of Napoleon Buonaparte 534, 592
   Rob Roy 397
   Waverley 217, 241, 243
sculpture 212, 247–8, 626
   biblical figure cycle 337–8, 340–1
   of Dante 103, 105
   by David d'Angers 335–6, 606
   Greek 247–8
   Juno Ludovisi 68, 205
   medallions 363, 444, 448
   Napoleon, glass bust of 361, 362
Seckendorff, Karl Sigmund von xxv, 585
Ségur, Philippe, comte de xxv, 305
Seidel, Dorothea xxv, 258
Seidel, Max Johann xxv, 227–8, 468
Seidel, Philipp Friedrich 144, 227–8, 468
selfhood 18, 123–5, 285, 300, 570–1
sensuality 257–8, 266
sentimentality 57, 140, 209, 217, 340, 446
Sesenheim 303, 332
sex and sexuality l, 47, 72–3, 110–11, 473, 506, 519, 638
shadows 155, 157–60
Shakespeare, William liii, 19, 121–2, 336, 471, 486, 511
   exceptionality of 313, 454–6
   stagecraft of 147–8
—works
   characterization in 190
   expurgated editions of 72
   Hamlet 568
   Henry IV Part I 118
   Macbeth 137–8, 149–50, 522–3
   Romeo and Juliet 270–1
   sources of 299
   Troilus and Cressida 137

Sichtbaren, Die (journal) 144
slave trade 310–11
Smollett, Tobias xxv
   Roderick Random 209
sociability 92–3, 136, 487–8
social class 122, 131–2, 136, 183, 213–14, 216
   aristocracy 541–2
   in fiction 372
   and freedom 178–9
   injustices of 459–60
   and theatre attendance 475, 476–7, 601
Society for the Promotion of Agriculture 639
Socrates 512
Solger, Karl Wilhelm Ferdinand xxv, 180–2, 216
Sömmerring, Samuel Thomas von xxv, 616
'A Song over the Unconfidence towards my Self' xxxi, 144
songs 17, 63, 140, 164–5, 345–6, 440, 528
   'Ach, um deine feuchten Schwingen' 165
   'Ich hab's gesagt der guten Mutter' 164–5
   'Im Felde schleich ich still und wild' 239
   'Jussufs Reize möcht ich borgen' 165
   Tyrolese 227
   'Um Mitternacht' 164, 165
Sophocles xxv, 19, 129, 497–8, 503–9, 512
   Ajax 506
   Antigone 503, 505–8, 514, 515–16
   Oedipus 503, 504
   Oedipus at Colonus 508–9
   Philoctetes at Troy 190–1, 508–9
   translations of 180, 181, 216
Soret, Frédéric Jakob xxvi, xliii, xlix, 58, 183, 330, 364

INDEX

Conversations with Goethe,
  contributions to xlv, l, 436–7
Conversations with Goethe,
  safekeeping of xlii, 350
Metamorphose der Pflanzen,
  translation of 363, 382, 404
  poetry of 639–40
souls 256–7, 310, 323, 423,
  547, 566
Spain 73
spectacles, Goethe's aversion to
  liii–liv, 622–4
Spiegel, Karl Emil Freiherr von
  xxvi, 427
Spiegel, Wilhelmine Emilie von xxvi,
  74–5
Spinoza, Baruch xxvi, lvi, 393
sports xlvi, 488–96, 628
Stadelmann, Karl Wilhelm xxvi, 46,
  59, 60, 76
Staël, Germaine de xxvi, 440
Stapfer, Albert xxvi, 524, 528
Stendhal (Marie-Henri Beyle) xxvi
  Le Rouge et le noir liii, 632
Sterling, Charles xxvi, 352, 357
Sternberg, Count Kaspar Maria von
  xxvi, 205–6, 207, 503
  Flora Subterranea 205
Sterne, Laurence xxvi
  A Sentimental Journey 574
  Tristram Shandy 561
Stickel, Johann Gustav 408
Stieler, Joseph Karl xxvi, 578,
  662n46
'Stirbt der Fuchs, so gilt der Balg'
  575–6
Stolberg, Christian xxvi, 99
Stolberg, Friedrich Leopold xxvi, 99
storytelling 119, 133, 175–6, 240,
  391, 399
Stosch, Baron Philipp von xxvi, 212
Streckfuss, Karl xxvii, 542–3
strength, physical 564–5, 568, 569,
  574
students 194–5, 440, 665n13

Sturm und Drang period 259
style 88–90, 114–15
subjectivity 139–41, 192, 204–5,
  268–70, 608–9
subjects
  (im)morality of 183, 188, 253–4
  in art 51
  choice of 35–7, 102, 111–12
  correct form for 176–7
  expansion of 607–8
  history as 132
  knowledge of 298
  lack of 144–5, 197
  and novelty 601
  for opera 236–7
  personal nature of 176
  religious 337–8, 340–1
  and success of artworks 45
  'unpoetic' 210–11
Sutor, Christoph Erhard 54–6
Swabia 429
Swanevelt, Hermann van xxvii, 425
Switzerland 69, 586
  Geneva 351–2, 357–60, 366
  Lake Lucerne 531
Sylvestre, Espérance xxvii
symbolism 147
Szymanowska, Maria xxvii, 45, 48,
  50–1, 56, 448, 640

Tag- und Jahreshefte 114–15
Tagebuch, Das xxxiii, 72–3
talent
  artistic 77–81
  exceptional 142–3, 154, 313
  and experience 263
  forced 45
  harm to 640–1
  innate 121–2, 258, 298–9, 300–1
  lack of 300–1, 304–5
  limits of 417
  misdirection of 376
  and morality 260–1
  for music 378
  physicality of 315–16, 378

692 INDEX

'Talismane' 352
Talleyrand (Charles Maurice de Talleyrand-Périgord) xxvii, 620
Tassi, Agostino xxvii, 306
Tasso, Torquato xxvii
Jerusalem Delivered 466
taste 76–7, 86, 172–3, 446
Tastu, Amable xxvii, 336, 520
Taunus Mountains 342
Teatro dell'Arte (Venice) 601
Teatro della Canobbiana (Milan) 345
Temps, Le (newspaper) 327, 332, 600, 605
Teniers, David, the Younger xxvii
Teutsche Merkur (journal) 259
theatre xlix, 39–40, 44–5, 108–9, 141–3, 344–5, 468–73
audiences 142, 317, 344, 348, 601
in Berlin 156–7, 327
characterization in 50
colour in 331
commedia dell'arte 601–2
costume 331
design of 474–7
elephants in 317
in France 478
Frankfurt 344
in Geneva 360
genre in 86–7
German 478–9, 497–8, 589
Greek 496–8, 503–9, 527
Italian 344–5, 478, 601–2
management of 95, 146–9, 236–7, 470–3, 480–1
music in 137
profitability of 485–7
realism in 141–2
rehearsals 477, 514
repertory 477–9
scenery 301–2, 331, 345
writing for 146–8, 258
see also Weimar Court Theatre
theory 263–4, 465–6, 576–7
Thomson, James xxvii, 427–8
thought 121, 409–10

Thüringer Wald 540
Tieck, Dorothea xxvii, 243
Tieck, Ludwig xxvii, 88, 180, 238–9, 241–3
Tiedge, Christoph August xxvii, 74–5
Urania 75–6
Tiefurt l, 48–9, 52–3
Titian 377, 439
titles of works, selection of 185–6
Töpfer, Carl xxvii, 258
Töpffer, Rudolf (Rodolphe) xxvii, 642
Voyages et aventures du Docteur Festus 631
Torquato Tasso xxxii, xxxv, 109, 257, 474, 525, 531
performance of 445, 478–9
Törring, Joseph August Graf von, *Agnes Bernauerin* 398
tragedy 43, 86, 129–30, 218, 283, 373, 427–8, 503–9
situations for 331, 600
travel 186–7, 339, 351, 586
trees 85, 93, 282, 342, 492–4, 517–18, 542
Trilogie der Leidenschaft 640
'Marienbader Elegie' xxxiv, l, 46–7, 56, 58–9
'An Werther' xxxiv, 640
truth 5, 197, 259, 299, 359, 636
and beauty 500–1
in literary criticism 132–3
vs. opinion 194–5
Turkey 289

Über Kunst und Altertum (journal) xxxvii, 26, 53, 69–70, 111–12, 186, 332, 543
Eckermann's work on 31, 32–3, 61–2
Uhland, Ludwig xxvii, 43, 429
'Um Mitternacht' xxxiii
understanding 78–80, 263–4, 391–2, 532
United Kingdom of Great Britain & Ireland 81, 202, 617–18

England 107–8, 202, 310–11, 327, 397–8
Ireland 280, 288–9
United States of America 311, 502–3
unities, dramatic 119–20
universities 21, 22–5, 70, 194, 588, 613–16
Unzelmann, Karl xxviii, 316
utilitarianism 385–6

vaccination 382–3
vanity 134
Vanloo, Charles André, *Conversation espagnole* 77
variety/variation, necessity of 193–4
'Vermächtnis' xxxiv, xlv, 260, 420, 532
Vernet, Horace xxviii, 409
Veronese, Paolo (Paul) 377
verse *see* poetry
Versuch, die Metamorphose der Pflanzen zu erklären, see Metamorphose der Pflanzen
Vigny, Alfred de xxviii, 336
Villemain, Abel-François xxviii, 265, 266, 277, 281, 596
Virgil 398
Eclogues 21
Vogel, Karl xxviii, 164, 302–3, 327, 330, 366–7, 382–3, 411
Voigt, Friedrich Sigismund xxviii, 334
Voltaire (François-Marie Arouet) xxviii, 134, 233–4, 253–4, 266, 281, 336
genius of 408
influence of 321
as literary role model 334
La Mort de César 254
'Les Systèmes' 321
Voss, Johann Heinrich xxviii, 296, 528, 544–5
Luise 372–3
vulgarity xlvi, 183, 188, 510–11
Vulpius, Christiane xxxv

Wahlverwandtschaften, Die xxxiii, xxxvi, xxxvii, 87–8, 180–2, 218, 259, 331–2, 532
Waldner, Luise Adelaide von xxviii, 599
Walker, Alexander xl
Walpurgis Night lii, 167–8
War of Liberation (War of the Sixth Coalition (1813–1814)) 13–14, 17, 312, 611–13
wars 133
Napoleonic 13–14, 17, 102
Peninsular War 73
Seven Years' War 73
Wartburg Festival 287, 665n13
water, 'affirmation/negation' of 83–4, 200–1
weakness
physical 261
of writers 373
weather
snow 14, 268–74, 348, 360, 383–4, 388
spring 519
sun 268–9
thunderstorms 106, 360, 482–3
see also natural sciences: meteorology
Weber, Carl Maria von xxviii
Euryanthe 127
Der Freischütz 218, 240
Oberon 227
Weimar xlii–xliii, 34–5, 63, 99, 353
Frauenplan xlix–l
Goethe's garden 82–6, 533
landscape of 93
Schloss Belvedere 279, 282
Schloss Weimar (Stadtschloss) 261, 301
Webicht 94
see also Frauenplan house
Weimar Court Theatre xlix, 148, 445, 476–7, 632
fire in 468–75
reconstruction of 474–6, 479, 482–7

694 INDEX

Weissenthurn, Johanna Franul von
xxviii
Johann von Finnland 50
Wellington, Arthur Wellesley, 1st
Duke of xxviii, 143–4, 208
Werner, Abraham Gottlob xxviii,
liv–lv, 196
West–östlicher Divan xxxiii–xxxiv,
165, 352, 458, 567, 569
Weygand, Christian Friedrich
xxviii, 640
Wieland, Christoph Martin xxix, 63,
116, 199–200, 208, 259, 606
Oberon 335
Wiener Jahrbücher für Literatur
(journal) 389
Wilhelm I, Emperor of Germany 192
Wilhelm Meisters Lehrjahre xxxii,
li–lii, 18, 115, 125, 128–9,
136–7, 244, 275
Wilhelm Meisters Wanderjahre
xxxiv, li–lii, 68, 125
composition of 167, 177, 419–20
Eckermann's editing of 264
publication of 274
responses to 420
revision of 165–6, 230–1
will 290–1, 340, 375
Willemer, Jakob xxix, 351, 467
William I, King of Württemberg
636, 637
Winckelmann, Johann Joachim
xxix, 16, 130, 198, 212
Winsen an der Luhe 9, 13, 14
Winterberger, Georg xxix, 258
wisdom 262, 525–6
Wolf, Friedrich August xxix, 64, 91,
197, 652n23
Wolfe, Charles, 'The Burial of Sir
John Moore at Corunna' 122
Wolff, Amalie, née Malcolmi xxix, 316
Wolff, Oskar Ludwig Bernhard
xxix, 139–40
Wolff, Pius Alexander xxix, 95,
246–7, 461, 472

women 169–70, 248–9, 260, 403,
412, 454
actors 453
attractiveness of 453, 473
as musicians 50–1
reading of 235, 244
representation of 64, 210, 276,
506–8, 632
as rulers 284
sisters 506
as theatregoers 142, 601
writers 89, 110–13
wonder 266, 401–2
work 37–8, 80, 186–7, 256–7, 599,
602–3
world literature liii, 113, 188–9,
216–17

Xenien xxxii, 115, 116

youth 172–3, 309–12, 450, 525–6,
563–7, 585–6, 628
Yü-kiau-li (novel) 658n104

Zahme Xenien xxxiii,
173, 496
Zahn, Wilhelm xxix, 389
Zauper, Joseph Stanislaus xxx, 60,
503
Studien 48
Zedlitz, Joseph Christian von, *Der
Stern von Sevilla* 329
Zelter, Karl Friedrich xxx, 62–5,
282, 482, 514, 559, 560,
659n2
coat of arms designed by Goethe
285–6
handwriting of 278–9
letters of 207–8
on *Macbeth* 137
on *Messiah* 261
Prussian Order, awarded 285
spectacles of 623
Zweiter Römischer Aufenthalt
xxxiii

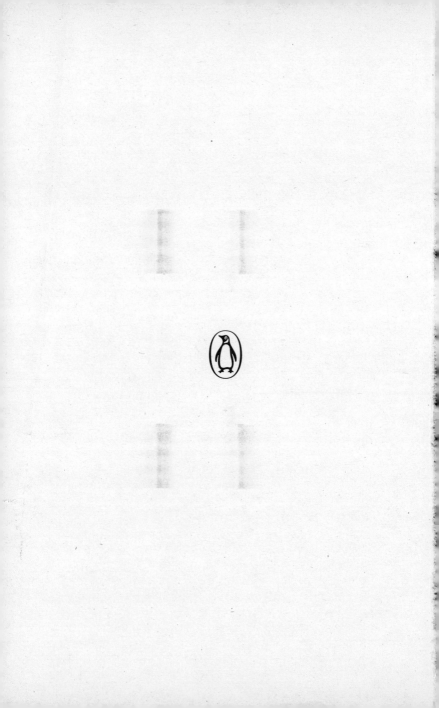